Handbook for Creative and Innovative Managers

Robert Lawrence Kuhn

Editor in Chief

McGraw-Hill Book Company

New York   St. Louis   San Francisco   Auckland   Bogotá
Hamburg   London   Madrid   Mexico   Milan
Montreal   New Delhi   Panama   Paris   São Paulo
Singapore   Sydney   Tokyo   Toronto

Library of Congress Cataloging-in-Publication Data

Handbook for creative and innovative managers.

Includes index.
1. Creative ability in business.   I. Kuhn,
Robert Lawrence.
HD53.H356   1988   658.4'094   87-3189
ISBN 0-07-035607-6

1234567890   DOC/DOC   89210987

ISBN 0-07-035607-6

The editors for this book were William A. Sabin and Nancy Young,
the designer was Naomi Auerbach, and the production
supervisor was Richard A. Ausburn. It was set in
Baskerville. It was composed by the McGraw-Hill
Book Company Professional & Reference
Division composition unit.

Printed and bound by R. R. Donnelley & Sons Company.

Contents

Part 7 Creative Culture for Knowledge Organizations

Editor in Chief

Robert Lawrence Kuhn is an investment banker specializing in mergers and acquisitions, leveraged buyouts, new business formation, venture capital, and the structuring of innovative financial transactions. He is a scientist, strategist, author, and scholar who is at home in the complementary worlds of business, academia, and government. Dr. Kuhn is a senior research fellow in Creative and Innovative Management, IC^2 Institute, University of Texas at Austin; and adjunct professor (corporate strategy and policy), Department of Management and Organizational Behavior, Graduate School of Business Administration, New York University. He has advised several governments on financing and commercializing technology. He speaks and lectures at numerous symposia and is quoted and published widely. Recent books include: *The Deal Maker: All the Negotiating Secrets and Skills You Need, To Flourish Among Giants: Creative Management for Mid-Sized Firms, The Firm Bond: Linking Meaning and Mission in Business and Religion, Micromanaging: Transforming Business Leaders with Personal Computers* (book and disk), *Frontiers in Creative and Innovative Management, Commercializing Defense-Related Technology, Corporate Creativity: Robust Companies and the Entrepreneurial Spirit, Managing Take-Off in Fast-Growth Companies, Technology Venturing: American Innovation and Risk Taking,* and *Regulatory Reform: New Vision or Old Curse.* He is editor in chief of the forthcoming *Handbook of Investment Banking.* He is senior editor of *Texas Business* magazine, and a contributing editor of the *Journal of Business Strategy.* Dr. Kuhn has a B.A. in human biology (Phi Beta Kappa), from The Johns Hopkins University; a Ph.D. in neurophysiology from the Department of Anatomy and Brain Research Institute, University of California at Los Angeles; an M.S. in management from the Sloan School of Management, Massachusetts Institute of Technology, where he was a Sloan fellow and a research affiliate in psychology.

Contributors

Joshua C. Abend is president of Innovation America Group, Inc., in Syracuse, New York. (CHAPTER 16)

Russell L. Ackoff is the Anheuser-Busch Professor of Management Science at the Wharton School, University of Pennsylvania, in Philadelphia, Pennsylvania. (CHAPTER 10)

Teresa M. Amabile is associate professor of psychology at Brandeis University in Waltham, Massachusetts; she is also research associate at the Center for Creative Leadership in Greensboro, North Carolina. (CHAPTER 56)

Ariane Berthoin Antal is a research associate at the Wissenschaftszentrum Berlin für Sozialforchung in Berlin, West Germany. (CHAPTER 66)

David L. Antion is a clinical psychologist and marriage and family counselor in Pasadena, California. (CHAPTER 60)

Marvin Blumenfeld is president of Eagle Clothes, and April-Marcus. (CHAPTER 38)

Bertram Brown is senior vice president of Healthcare, Inc., and former president of Hahnemann University in Philadelphia, Pennsylvania. He is also a psychiatrist and former executive director of the National Institutes of Mental Health. (CHAPTER 53)

Colby H. Chandler is chairman and chief executive officer of Eastman Kodak Corporation in Rochester, New York. (CHAPTER 43)

H. Stephen Cranston is president of Knapp Communications (publishers of *Architectural Digest, Bon Appetit, Home,* and other magazines) in Los Angeles, California. (CHAPTER 26)

Philip B. Crosby is founder and president of Philip Crosby & Associates in Miami, Florida. He has authored several books on quality. (CHAPTER 44)

John A. Cunningham is president of Competitive Technologies, Inc., in Easton, Connecticut; he is a former senior manager on the Corporate Information Systems Staff of General Electric Corporation. (CHAPTER 51)

Richard M. Cyert is president of Carnegie-Mellon University in Pittsburgh, Pennsylvania. He has authored numerous works on organizational theory. (CHAPTER 19)

Gunter David is a journalist and writer in Philadelphia, Pennsylvania. (CHAPTER 53)

Martin S. Davis is chairman and chief executive officer of Gulf + Western, Inc., in New York. (CHAPTER 29)

Meinolf Dierkes is president of the Wissenschaftszentrum Berlin für Sozialforchung in Berlin, West Germany. (CHAPTER 66)

William Ebeling is senior partner in the strategy practice of Braxton Associates, a Touche Ross company in Boston, Massachusetts. (CHAPTER 34)

David G. Eller is president of Granada Corporation in Houston Texas and chairman of the board of trustees of Texas A&M University in College Station, Texas. (CHAPTER 65)

Edward M. Esber, Jr., is president and chief executive officer of Ashton-Tate, Inc., in Los Angeles, California. (CHAPTER 52)

Eric G. Flamholtz is president of Management Systems Consulting Corporation and professor of management at the Graduate School of Management, University of California at Los Angeles. (CHAPTERS 26, 55)

J. B. Fuqua is chairman and chief executive officer of J. B. Fuqua Industries, Inc., in Atlanta, Georgia. He is also chairman of the board of Triton Group Ltd. (CHAPTER 41)

Caren Calish Gagliano is president of the Services Division of Innotech Corporation, a creativity development company in Trumbull, Connecticut. (CHAPTER 12)

R. Don Gamache is chairman and chief executive officer of Innotech Corporation, a creativity development company in Trumbull, Connecticut. (CHAPTER 12)

George T. Geis is research coordinator at the Center for Human Resource Management, Institute of Industrial Relations, University of California at Los Angeles. He teaches accounting and computing in UCLA's Graduate School of Management. He coauthored *Micromanaging: Transforming Business Leaders with Personal Computers.* (CHAPTERS 3, 6, 17, 52)

Michael D. Gill, Jr., is a research fellow of the IC^2 Institute of the University of Texas at Austin and is an associate of United Capital Ventures in Austin, Texas. (CHAPTER 68)

Frederick Gluck is a director and partner of McKinsey & Company in New York, where he heads the strategic management practice. (CHAPTER 32)

W. L. Gore is founder and former chairman of the board of W. L. Gore and Associates in Newark, Delaware. (CHAPTER 27)

Harry J. Gray is chairman of the board, and former president and chief executive officer, of United Technologies Corporation in Hartford, Connecticut. (CHAPTER 30)

Stanley S. Gryskiewicz is the director of creative development programs at the Center for Creative Leadership in Greensboro, North Carolina. (CHAPTER 56)

Peter Hannaford is president of The Hannaford Company, a public relations firm, in Washington, D.C. (CHAPTER 46)

Richard A. Harriman is president of Synectics, Inc., a creativity development company in Cambridge, Massachusetts. (CHAPTER 14)

Philip R. Harris is an organizational psychologist, management consultant, and author in La Jolla, California. (CHAPTER 61)

Ned Herrmann is president, Applied Creative Services, and chairman, the Whole Brain Corporation, in Lake Lure, South Carolina. (CHAPTER 7)

David Bendel Hertz is distinguished professor of artificial intelligence and director of the Intelligent Computer Systems Research Institute at the University of Miami. He is a former partner of McKinsey & Company (CHAPTER 51)

Charles W. Hucker is division vice president for public affairs and communications of Hallmark Cards Incorporated in Kansas City, Missouri. (CHAPTER 28)

Charles Hurwitz is chairman of the board and chief executive officer of MCO Holdings in Los Angeles, California; Maxxam Group in New York; the Pacific Lumber Company in Scotia, California; United Financial Group in Houston, Texas; Federated Development Company in Houston, Texas. (CHAPTER 31)

Scott B. Isaksen is director of the Center for Studies in Creativity at the State University College at Buffalo. (CHAPTER 15)

F. Kenneth Iverson is president and chief executive officer of Nucor Corporation in Charlotte, South Carolina. (CHAPTER 58)

Rosabeth Moss Kanter is Class of 1960 Professor of Business Administration at the Harvard Business School in Cambridge, Massachusetts; she is president of Goodmeasure, Inc., also in Cambridge. (CHAPTERS 11, 20, 21)

Robert S. Kay is senior partner of Touche Ross & Co. in New York. He is the editor of *Handbook of Accounting and Auditing*. (CHAPTER 50)

David T. Kearns is chairman, president, and chief executive officer of Xerox Corporation in Stamford, Connecticut. (CHAPTER 25)

Brian Knowles is a professional artist and writer. He is also editor of *Propane-Butane News* in Arcadia, California. (CHAPTER 8)

George Kozmetsky is director of the IC^2 Institute of the University of Texas at Austin. He is executive associate for economic affairs of the University of Texas System, the Marion West Chair Professor of Constructive Capitalism, the former dean of the School and Graduate School of Business of the University of Texas at Austin in Austin, Texas. He is chairman of the RGK Foundation in Austin and was the cofounder of Teledyne, Inc. (CHAPTER 67)

Louis Kuhn is founder and past president of Chief Apparel in New York. (CHAPTER 42)

Robert Boynton Lamb is founder and editor in chief of *The Journal of Business Strategy* and associate professor of management, Graduate School of Business Administration, New York University. (CHAPTER 33)

Lewis W. Lehr is former chairman and chief executive officer of 3M in Minneapolis, Minnesota. (CHAPTER 22)

Arthur Lipper III is chairman and publisher of *Venture Magazine* and chairman of New York & Foreign Securities Corporation in New York. (CHAPTER 49)

William C. Miller is senior management consultant for managing innovation and change at SRI International in Menlo Park, California. (CHAPTER 13)

William F. Miller is president and chief executive officer of SRI International in Menlo Park, California. He is also professor of public and private management and of computer science at Stanford University in Palo Alto, California. (CHAPTER 63)

George P. Mitchell is chairman, president, and chief executive officer of Mitchell Energy & Development Corp., The Woodlands, Texas. (CHAPTER 68)

Barry Munitz is president of Federated Development Company in Houston, Texas, and vice chairman of the board of MCO Holdings in Los Angeles, California. He is former chancellor of the University of Houston. (CHAPTERS 54, 62)

Robert C. Ochsner is senior vice president and practice director of the total compensation practice for Hay Management Consultants in Philadelphia, Pennsylvania. (CHAPTER 57)

W. Arthur Porter is president and chief executive officer of the Houston Area Research Center in the Woodlands, Texas. (CHAPTER 68)

Simon Ramo is cofounder and director emeritus of the board of TRW Corporation. (CHAPTER 1)

Eugene Raudsepp is president of Princeton Creative Research, Inc., in Princeton, New Jersey. (CHAPTER 18)

Al Ries is vice president of Trout & Ries Advertising, Inc. in New York. (CHAPTER 45)

Gerald Rosenthal is a professor in the Department of Humanities and Social Sciences and coordinator of international activities at Hahnemann University in Philadelphia, Pennsylvania. (CHAPTER 53)

Jack Rutherford is president, International Consulting Management, Chicago, Illinois. He is former vice chairman of the board of International Harvester Corp. (CHAPTER 36).

Brian Saffer is vice president, Swergold Chefitz & Sinsabaugh in New York; he was formerly national director of mergers and acquisition for the Hay Group. (CHAPTER 40)

Sanford C. Sigoloff is chairman, president, and chief executive officer of Wickes Companies in Santa Monica, California. (CHAPTER 37)

Herbert A. Simon is Richard King Mellon University Professor of Computer Science and Psychology in the Graduate School of Industrial Administration, Carnegie-Mellon University, Pittsburgh, Pennsylvania. He was the 1978 Nobel Laureate in Economics. (CHAPTER 2)

Raymond W. Smilor is executive director of the IC^2 Institute of the University of Texas at Austin; he is editor of *The Journal for High Tech Marketing*. (CHAPTER 68)

Francis X. Stankard is chairman and chief executive officer of Chase Investment Bank, Chase Manhattan Bank, in New York. (CHAPTER 48)

John P. Thompson is chairman of the board of the Southland Corporation (7-Eleven Stores) in Dallas, Texas. (CHAPTER 39)

Jack Trout is president of Trout & Ries Advertising, Inc. in New York. (CHAPTER 45)

Elsa Vergara has been assistant administrator for planning at the Phoebe Putney Hospital in Albany, Georgia. (CHAPTER 10)

Karl H. Vesper is professor of entrepreneurship in the Graduate School of Business at the University of Washington in Seattle, Washington. (CHAPTER 24)

Sandra Gerson Weis is program manager, Telecommunications Strategy, Trintex (A CBS/IBM/Sears Company) in White Plains, New York. She is a former manager of business development strategy for GTE Corporation. (CHAPTER 23)

Elmer L. Winter is cofounder and past president of Manpower, Inc., in Milwaukee, Wisconsin. He is president of the Committee for the Economic Growth of Israel. (CHAPTER 59)

Abraham Zaleznick is the Konosuke Matsushita Professor of Leadership at the Harvard Business School in Cambridge, Massachusetts. He has authored numerous books on organizations. (CHAPTER 4)

Foreword

The Need for Creative and Innovative Managers

Creative and innovative managers think differently about business. They use a new framework to integrate resource allocation, economic wealth generation, competitive positioning, and product and personnel development. The framework requires creative management, innovative management, and creative and innovative management.

Creative management consists of devising new concepts, new ideas, new methods, new directions, and new modes of operation. The operative word is "new." *Innovative* management consists of implementing creative ideas and/or moving successfully in such new directions. The operative words are "implementing" and "moving successfully." *Creative and innovative* management focuses on coupling or linking creative and innovative managements. The operative notion here is an "act of management" rather than an act of an individual.

Creative management is what R&D managers and entrepreneurs deal with—new things. Innovative management is what entrepreneurs must do in the start-up phase, particularly in new product development, and what professional managers must do in the take-off phase, particularly in marketing, distribution, manufacturing, and finance. Creative and innovative management is the province of the leadership of organizations.

Creative and innovative management implies dynamic managerial practices on the one hand and visionary commitment to implement them on the other. Traditional management decision making centered on efficiency and effectiveness. Creative and innovative management targets flexibility and adaptability to deal with the process of managing change. It is grounded in the belief that leadership makes a significant difference in the way organizations respond to and cope with shift and shock. It is involved with generating real economic value and with adapting personal aspirations to the evolving objectives of the firm. Creative and innovative management covers a spectrum of activities, such as organizational design for improving creativity and innovation, organizational strategy for R&D and competitive positioning, fresh initiatives for joint public/private ventures, and implications for public policy. Creative and innovative management is more than important. It is essential.

GEORGE KOZMETSKY
Director, IC² Institute, University of Texas at Austin,
and Cofounder, Teledyne, Inc.

How to Use
This Handbook

Creative and innovative management is surprise, breakthrough, leaps of logic and sudden jumps. It propels companies and catapults careers. It is the way of dynamic change, potent growth, competitive advantage. This is the frontier, the cutting edge of contemporary business. It is intense, gutsy, spirited, strange. It is also fun. Even heroic. Creative and innovative management, in short, builds strong and successful companies. It wins.

The *Handbook* is for reading and browsing, instruction and entertainment, stimulation and inspiration. Ideas and examples intermix, the former giving general application, the latter specific relevance. We present tangible tools to build better businesses, stronger strategies, higher profits. The principles of managerial novelty are practical, meaningful, useful. Enjoy, but also apply.

Handbook contributors are pioneers and practitioners of creative and innovative management—the best of the breed—those who have developed the ideas and those who have tested the techniques. There is a rich mixture of chief executives and renowned authorities. Chapter authors are founders, chairmen, and presidents of major corporations; creativity enhancing specialists; innovation experts in diverse areas; and leading thinkers, researchers, and teachers. All focus on creative and innovative management—what it means to them, how it applies to you. The personal emphasis is deliberate. We talk about things most meaningful, real-world stuff that can be used daily by managers and executives.

Creative and innovative management is both content and process. It is, on the one hand, understanding the essence of creativity (Part 1), how to stimulate it (Part 2), and how to structure it (Part 3). It is, on the other hand, the mechanism for energizing all business functions: devising new strategies, companies and industries (Part 4); making dramatic advances in R&D, quality, finance, information (Part 5); improving human resource management (Part 6); and building creative culture for diverse organizations (Part 7). Creativity is a vital part of contemporary companies. Finding new and better products to sell, services to offer, and ways to work is essential for survival in highly competitive environments. With increasingly rapid obsolescence, the need to anticipate change is critical. What drives the best companies? An almost "paranoic need" to innovate, to stay ahead of voracious competitors. Successful innovators are rolling dynamos; they may have to be stifled or stopped but never pushed or shoved. They make things happen.

Is being a creative manager the same as being a manager of creativity? No, and the distinction is important. The crux of the difference lies in the locus of creative action and hits the heart of managerial process. A creative manager is himself or herself creative, producing creative content personally in the conduct of managerial tasks. A manager of creativity, on the other hand, is a facilitator of the creative process, working to generate creative content in others. The skill sets for each are not the same—indeed there is little overlap—although either one can also be the other. Furthermore, those who generate ideas are often not the best ones to implement them. Again, skill sets are different. Organizations grow only when personnel increase opportunities for current products and services or produce new ones. All managers should therefore aspire to be creative, and if they cannot personally parent innovation, they should assist subordinates in its gestation. Managers must be sensitive to change and ready to accept new ideas, irrespective of direction or source. This means, by necessity, that existing strategies, structures, systems, and services are not permanent. To think that everything in the organization is replaceable can be unnerving and risky, but those who must maintain the status quo run the higher risk of being overthrown by committed individuals who are not bound by conventional wisdom.

Donald Treffinger and Scott Isaksen believe that everyone has the capacity to be creative, but misunderstandings get in the way. They define creativity as the process of making and communicating meaningful new connections, and they describe four common *myths* about it ("Straighten Out That Mess with Creativity," *Gifted Children Monthly*): (1) Creativity can be reduced to workbook activities (*fact:* long-term energy and motivation are needed to generate original ideas and solve problems in novel ways), (2) creativity is all arts and crafts (*fact:* any area of human endeavor can be fertile soil for creativity to flourish), (3) creativity is a rare form of genius (*fact:* this myth tragically puts creativity out of reach—in fact all can learn to be more imaginative), (4) creativity is not "real" work (*fact:* some mistakenly assume that divergent thinking is little more than comic relief from the "serious" work of using convergent thinking to determine a single correct answer). Remember what Abraham Maslow said: "Creativity might as much be found in a first-rate chicken soup as in a third-rate painting."

Creative and innovative acitivities must have two basic ingredients according to Carnegie-Mellon's Yuji Ijiri, "being different" and "being better." They must be different in means or better in ends relative to an "established way of doing things." To recognize creative and innovative activities, therefore, there must be an accepted method for getting things done against which such activities can be judged novel. This is the benchmark, and a creative approach often begins by questioning these preconceived ways. Creativity is distinguished from productivity, believes Ijiri, in that productivity means moving along the learning curve while creativity shifts the curve. Experts and innovators are not the same: Experts follow an established way but do it more efficiently through practice; innovators avoid the established way and search for means to do things differently and better. Activities may seem creative up front based on intent but uncreative with hindsight based on results. Those who engage in creative activities have the burden of proof that their unestablished way is better than the established way.

How to approach problems when seeking creative solution? I define the following steps: (1) *problem recognition* (finding or sensing an unstable situation or disturbance), (2) *"naive" incubation/gestation* (personal immersion—time of reflection and quiet contemplation allowing subconscious manipulation, restructuring, and new pattern making), (3) *information/ knowledge search and detailed preparation* (learning everything about the problem—factual information and expert opinion, each from diverse viewpoints), (4) *"knowledgeable" incubation/gestation* (personal consideration of unusual approaches and ideas, now melding naive notions of step 2 with factual information and expert opinion of step 3), (5) *alternative solution formulation* (group intuitive phase—generating numerous possibilities, using creativity-enhancing techniques discussed in Part 2), (6) *alternative solution evaluation* (group analytical phase—rigorous testing of possibilities by tough-minded methodologies), (7) *chosen solution implementation* (putting ideas into action), (8) *feedback and reassessment* (judging by results, improving the original idea).

A problem-solving procedure can be transformed into a creative one only by breaking constraints, especially subtle ones. For example, it is often a mistake to get too smart too quickly. "Expert opinion" fouls up the creative engine. You are led, however unwittingly, into preformed channels of thinking, boxed by received tradition, and strait-jacketed by vaunted authorities. "Conventional wisdom" is creative death. The easiest way to escape is not to get caught. Develop your own ideas initially *without* external information. Your naivete will be more ally than enemy on the creativity battlefield, more asset than liability on the innovation balance sheet. Then, only after formulating your own ideas, can you with confidence confront the experts. Now you will not be so intimidated. That is why I recommend putting a gestation/incubation step *both* before and after the information-gathering step, whereas normal problem-solving procedures put it only after. You must think through the problem yourself, alone, in solitude, before accessing others. Brood. Cogitate. Meditate. Agonize. Experience tension, frustration, stress. Creativity breeds suffering. Exhilarating free fall is not what it's all about. Uncertainty, ambiguity, and doubt are all friends of the creative process.

Creative and innovative management is more than general techniques for fostering novelty; it is also specific applications in diverse functions and fields of business and industry. Note that some chapters are about creative management per se, understanding it and stimulating it, while other chapters describe things that creative managers do, can do, or should do. The latter chapters, largely in Parts 4 (business strategy), 5 (functional areas), 6 (human resources), and 7 (knowledge organizations), are designed to spark ideas in managerial readers. Learn what new or novel things business leaders employ in their situations; then apply the principles in your situation. Chapter 60, for example, shows how counseling and psychotherapy are new tools for optimizing employee productivity and fulfillment. Managers who so stretch we call creative and innovative.

Though the book proceeds linearly, the reader should not. Take charge! Enter and exit at any point. Select by personal interest not numerical order. Each chapter stands alone, the best its author offers. Contributors present their favorite topics—so expect redundancy; yet similar concepts are viewed from different angles and cut from different companies—so seek insight. If there is overlap among chapters, look for panorama and perspective, greater dimension and deeper grain. It is important to see subjects from various viewpoints. Watch for twists in the path, curves in the road. Sweeping essays, case histories, and personal confessions mingle with focused expositions, orderly instructions, and logical steps. Chapters are not meticulously manicured; nor do they fit together neatly as pieces in a puzzle. Creativity means pieces too few or pieces too many. Successful creativity is not often manicured or neat; nor is productive innovation normally tucked or trimmed.

The *Handbook* is *not* a textbook. There is no artificial smoothness, no cosmetic harmony. Fret not. Remember our quest—creativity. To exclude the spontaneous would be criminal, leaving too much good stuff a permanent prisoner of floppy disks. Ignore linearity, regularity, continuity. Seek ideas, insight, inspiration. You get raw material here, nothing less than what some really smart heads think about creative and innovative management. Fancy theory is not our bag. (Provocation, insolence, petulance—maybe.) New ideas are the *Handbook's* hallmark. Allow freshness and novelty to wash over you. Read and learn, sure, but also imbibe and experience. Feed your subconscious. Build inner understanding. The outcome is action. What's here is what works. What's here is what counts.

Robert Lawrence Kuhn
*IC² Institute of the University of Texas at Austin
and Graduate School of Business Administration
New York University*

Acknowledgments

Creative and innovative management is, in a real sense, the personification of Dr. George Kozmetsky, director of the IC^2 Institute of the University of Texas at Austin. It was his vision that catalyzed the concept, and it is his intensity that carries it forward. My profound appreciation to George for energizing me with the fire of the new field.

This handbook has as antecedents two pioneering symposia on creative and innovative management, both sponsored by the IC^2 Institute. The first, cochaired by Abraham Charnes and W. W. Cooper, reviewed theory and practice in private and public sectors. The second, which I chaired, focused on intellectual institutions and brought together presidents and directors who run organizations that generate new knowledge (think tanks, research institutes, universities, national laboratories, and consulting companies). Symposia proceedings were published by the Ballinger Publishing Company (*Creative and Innovative Management: Essays in Honor of George Kozmetsky*, edited by A. Charnes and W. W. Cooper, Cambridge, 1984; *Frontiers in Creative and Innovative Management*, edited by Robert Lawrence Kuhn, Cambridge, 1986). Several papers we commissioned for these conferences reflect cutting-edge thinking and have direct relevance for executives and managers. Elements and ideas from several chapters in this handbook (2, 4, 5, 6, 12, 17, 43, 70) are derived in part from these original papers (especially from the *Frontiers* conference).

My thanks to the IC^2 staff—Linda Teague, Becky Jessee—for typing and handling the manuscript. Special thanks go to Elaine Chamberlain who organized, coordinated, and monitored the multifaceted logistics. I would also like to express personal appreciation to William A. Sabin, editor in chief of McGraw-Hill's business book program. Bill's confidence and sensitivity were invaluable throughout the complex process; his insights, understanding, and editorial rigor were prime sources of support.

PART 1:

Understanding the Creative Process

What Is Creativity and How Does It Work?

What are creativity and innovation, and how does each affect business? What causes creativity: what's going on in your head, and what's happening in your company? Can the process be controlled and focused for business benefit? Though words flow easy, definitions come hard. "Creativity" is the process by which novel ideas are generated, and "innovation" is the process by which those novel ideas are transformed into things tangible and useful. Creativity forms something from nothing, and innovation shapes that something into practical products and services. Ideas and implementation go together. Creativity without innovation is aimless while innovation without creativity is sterile. Peter Drucker believes that innovation is not mysterious, nor does it require genius (*Innovation and Entrepreneurship*). **He talks about "purposeful innovation" and suggests seven sources:**

1. The unexpected (success, failures, events of all kinds)

2. The incongruous (differences between the way things are and the way they ought to be)

3. The need to perform tasks better (new processes)

4. Unforeseen shifts in market demands or industry structure

5. Changes in population (demographics)

6. Changes in collective personality (new perceptions, moods, meanings)

7. Novel information and fresh knowledge

Successful innovators—both individuals and companies—have a virtual compulsion to create. In Part 1 we examine the nature of creativity and explore the differences between creativity and innovation. We see why they are important for managers and how they work in business. We view the creative process from various perspectives. We check your brain and probe your mind. We examine personality factors and psychological fundamentals: What can we learn, for example, from risk takers and artists that can enhance creativity for managers?

1

Creativity in Business Management

Simon Ramo

Cofounder and Director Emeritus, TRW Corporation

Occasionally an individual, perhaps a sculptor or composer, may judge pure creativity to be the central goal in life. But it is not conceivable that a successful business would ever be founded or managed with the single end objective of merely being creative. Creativity in thought and action often may be a route to or a necessary ingredient for the flourishing of a business enterprise; however, such innovative effort would constitute only a means to attain the real end. That goal would be described better by such phrases as maximizing return on investment, increasing market share, or attaining steady growth. Thus, creativity in business management should not be worshipped for itself. Indeed, creativity may yield both positive and negative consequences. An exaggerated emphasis on innovation may be translated in practice into a misdirected drive simply to do things differently, to change policies and strategies for the sake of change, to develop an unthinking preference for the new over the old, to assume that anything untried is automatically worth trying. The trick is to be creative on the right things in the right areas at the right time, to mix the proven and the novel so as to attain an optimum, harmonious ensemble.

Creativity in management is not a stand-alone concept. The role of creativity must be tailored to fit with other key intellectual disciplines for managing the business. Creativity must be combined with wisdom stemming from experience, and, for new ideas to yield maximum gains, efforts must be carefully planned. Still, innovation will not flow if its channels are overly constrained or if it is perceived as suitable only for narrow, isolated functions. Original and stimulating thought processes should be regarded as potentially valuable and eligible for application in every dimension of a business—financing, marketing, product development, manufacturing, public relations, employee communications, and the rest. It is a beneficial bias to believe that no matter how well a business is being directed in any area or function, it can be managed more productively. Superior ideas continually await birth and implementation. It is hard to imagine any business, however certain and deep its past record of success, that cannot gain greatly from well-chosen and well-led creative effort.

Older and Larger Companies

It is more difficult to spur and integrate high creativity in an old or large organization than in a new or small one. A long-established unit almost certainly will have developed a substantial bureaucracy, and bureaucracy is the natural enemy of creativity. A degree of creativity arises naturally with almost all people who conscientiously apply themselves to their jobs, but it can be easily stifled if too many steps and hurdles are involved in obtaining approvals and support for altering existing approaches or introducing radically new ones. A business entity is not likely to become big and venerable unless it has enjoyed considerable success, and the record of that very success can cause everyone concerned to be too impressed with it and rather reluctant to tinker with a seemingly permanent, winning formula. The more outstanding has been an activity's performance, the more difficult it will be to invent and inject change. If an organization's prosperity goes back many years, numerous approaches already will have been incorporated or else rejected for good reasons. The challenge is thus all the greater to identify those additional concepts whose introduction will offer the potential of sufficient improvement to justify the trouble.

A large and mature company usually will have an established base of products that enjoy high customer favor. It will have substantial inventories in those products. It will have invested heavily in their development, in manufacturing facilities, and in gaining a strong market position. Everything from acceptance by government regulatory agencies to detailed contracts with labor unions will have been worked out around existing products and the entrenched procedural base of the company. Numerous constituencies, from employees to customers, may become upset by major departures from long-set existing patterns. Thus, a large oil or chemical company cannot suddenly and cheaply alter a hugely expensive processing installation. Again, when any system for mass production of complex apparatus has gone through the debugging phase, it cannot easily, quickly, and economically be modified to incorporate still another good idea, even one that promises to cut costs and increase quality.

Newer and Smaller Companies

Any new company that is enjoying rapid growth, is not fully established, and has yet to reach the limits of its products' potential can almost certainly be categorized as creative. It would not be wrong, in fact, to say it was an act of creativity to start the company. It is unlikely that it would have been financed and launched had there been nothing innovative about its plans and prospects. If a venture is not based on a new product or a new way to manufacture an existing one or a new concept in marketing and distribution, it is likely to be a new company that is not needed. If that point was missed by the original founders and backers, the reality of the competitive marketplace will soon force it to their attention. The firm will then have to become creative quickly or pass out of existence. When a business is far from maturity, a host of ideas can more easily be conceived that are worth considering. After all, a new company will not have had time to think up and install more than a small fraction of all worthwhile innovations.

Troubled Companies

Whether old or new, large or small, most companies can find themselves in serious trouble on occasion. What they have been doing may be disclosed as having severe, perhaps fatal, shortcomings. Something must be changed and creativity becomes essential. The more severe the company's ills and the more critical its condition, the easier it will be for management to take considerable risk in order to attempt averting some final catastrophe. Imminent collapse can be a powerful stimulant for the mounting of creative effort. Moreover, the probability is high that creativity will pay off in such circumstances. If a business has been badly conceived or is being horribly mismanaged, something different must be tried. At least, there is little to lose in making that assumption.

High-Tech Companies

Creativity obviously has a special role to play in the management of high-technology corporations. In assessing the value of creativity and in seeking the best ways to encourage it, a company may deserve being classified as "high technology" not only because its products may embody recent advances in science. It may be that the manufacturing process has unusual ingenuity in the application of current technology. Such novel improvements may cut costs, increase reliability and quality, and offer quicker response to customer needs and requests. High tech may even be resident in the distribution and marketing of the product where sophisticated techniques are paying off (for example, in the application of computer communications systems that reduce inventories while improving customer support).

Technology-based firms must give special emphasis to facilitating steady utilization of creativity because of the rapid advance of science-based fields. Dramatic step-function changes can take place in the nature of the product, its application, the overall system in which the product is a component, and in the technologies of production and distribution. A technology company is in constant danger that a scientific advance or technological breakthrough occurring outside the company may destroy a market position, threaten revenues and earnings, and require the write-off of inventory and facilities. For defensive reasons alone a technology company must maintain adequate creative strength. It must be in a position to adjust quickly to the shifting technological environment on which it depends. Equally important is the opportunistic side of science-based advances. A successful technology company must produce such advances internally to enhance and broaden its product line and improve its production and marketing. If it is to enjoy a good return on investment and high growth, a competent high-tech firm must constantly seek to capture or maintain an edge over competitors.

Pushing creativity as a way of life is fundamental in the management of technological companies, but it is also basic to avoid exaggerations and misconceptions about creativity in such companies. Much creativity originates with scientists and engineers, and some of them will be inclined to make innovation in technology a god to be worshipped, with novel approaches assumed to be right until proven wrong. Young engineers in particular often come to their first jobs with the impression that the trite adage "design a better mousetrap and the world will beat a path to your door" is always true. In reality, the better mousetrap may not be needed (rats or snakes being the problem), or the better mousetrap may be too expensive, or it may really be an old idea unknown to the inexperienced but enthusiastic inventor (and one long since rejected by potential users because the bait was too expensive or hard to procure). New companies are regularly formed based on new technological ideas, but, unfortunately, many of those companies are all too often mismanaged by founder-inventors who have little business experience combined with naive notions about economics, production, and marketing.

Creative people tend to be more creative when they are constantly made aware of new ideas coming from others. Management should seek out information about future scientific and engineering gatherings with agendas that focus on new discoveries and developments. Creative members of the staff should be encouraged to attend and participate. The more isolated a research and development unit within an industrial organization, the less likely that its results will be highly successful, and the more likely that its staff will pursue, in ever increasing detail, year after year, those areas chosen early and will drift from current concerns. Such an R&D lab will suffer from inadequate connection to the outside world's progress and even to the rest of the company. They will miss useful criteria for judging where to allocate resources and efforts.

Ensuring Healthy Creativity

In today's rapidly changing society, most managers of industry readily claim that they appreciate creativity's importance. Few principal policy-makers in a typical company, however, deliberate much on how to encourage and use creativity to enhance their company's fortunes. This is regrettable because the practical consequence is that the creative efforts of such a company will proceed in a hodgepodge, hit-or-miss fashion. Those personnel who happen to be innately creative will, to some extent, creatively attack their responsibilities no matter how modestly the overall company encourages imagination or how meager the managerial effort is to promote creativity. Other employees, those who happen not to be particularly imbued with the creative spirit, will settle down to a largely dull and mundane approach to their work. Whatever potential they may have for innovating will remain undeveloped and may even decay. If management desires to exploit the basic concept that creativity can be nurtured and utilized to great advantage, they must address the issue productively.

How does a company ensure a healthy, creative dimension in management? A beginning is to hire creative people in the first place. Whether the individual being hired is a new graduate or a seasoned veteran, whether trained and experienced in engineering design or in business administration, the decision makers in the personnel selection process need to exert special efforts, perhaps fresh ones, to seek signs of creativity. They need to give such talents adequate weight as they choose and place additions to the staff. People who are discovered to be especially talented in devising imaginative and sound ideas should be encouraged by management to meet the challenge of specifically described problems or potential opportunities for invention. Such problems and opportunities should themselves be discovered early and communicated to employees who might have a reasonable probability of generating useful innovation in response. Innovation efforts require continual nurturing.

Top management must be willing to consider unusual organizational structures to make maximum use of personnel creativity. If a team of creative individuals is needed to solve a problem or develop an opportunity, management should be flexible in arranging for that team to get its job done with the least handicap from administrative constraints. The structural organization for that team should be designed to maximize its creative performance.

In many operations of a company, technological or nontechnological, creative potential often depends on tolerating a patient, long-time schedule for the initiation and implementation of new ideas. Of course, if a company happens to be in a critical situation, management may give highest priority to solving immediate problems. It may be necessary for management to put aside temporarily the sponsoring of creative effort that relates to longer-range objectives. For companies that are reasonably stable, however, and for which management effort and investment can be allocated sensibly in a practical division between immediate and far-out objectives, creativity should be seen as having both a long- and a short-term role.

Guidelines for Creativity

Innovation may be enhanced or handicapped by the specific company culture—and companies vary greatly, particularly when the whole international arena is considered. To most effectively utilize creativity, management should observe other companies. No limitation should be set, not by industry, not by geography. Analyzing the techniques of others everywhere in the world can be helpful, even granted the enormous variations among companies and countries. Not every superior idea of others can be copied and incorporated. But some can. Most approaches to creativity can be studied with benefit. The study effort itself can give rise to valuable ideas if those carrying out the studies are themselves innovative.

General rules can help. Some of the following may seem simple and obvious. Yet failure by management to have them in mind will handicap a company as it seeks to generate useful creativity. Here are my recommended guidelines for managers to enhance creativity:

1. If overall operating results over a substantial period are poorer than expected or desired, try something different.

2. If at first you don't succeed with an idea, do not try it again and again. Change it.

3. If things are working out well, don't alter anything unless you have first asked why the success is occurring. Plan to achieve future success through creative effort based upon understanding how present success was achieved.

4. The best way to be confident about anyone's creative strength is to observe a steady record of proven good-idea generation by that individual. This means care must be taken to uncover creative effort that has worked out well, trace its origins to the people responsible for it, and support those employees in their future proposals.

5. Good communication is needed between a management interested in creativity and the originators of creative ideas if there is to be useful assessment and employment of creativity.

6. The development of a concept from seed to full utilization usually will involve multiple joint actions by many. A group of creative people who communicate their rough ideas to one another will bring forth finished and beneficial innovation far more certainly and rapidly than will a collection of lone contributors.

7. Steady mass touting and urging of novel proposals should not be confused with generating true creativity because too many of the submitted ideas will be harebrained.

8. A highly creative individual will make 10 times as many contributions as one who is only marginally creative.

9. Whether a company is large or small, innovation is most likely to be successful if proposal ideas are discussed with all entities who will be critical to success, from research lab to factory plant, from inventor to potential customer.

10. Don't overplan and overformalize in the early stages of the creative process. Nothing can be more discouraging to someone pregnant with an idea than being pressed to prove what the embryo will turn into when fully developed, especially if the seed idea is then no more than a gleam in the inventor's eye.

11. Do not think of creativity as always connoting breakthroughs, radical inventions, or major reorganizations. Ingeniously conceived, well-implemented, small deviations from existing products or practices can yield spectacular results.

12. The right organization to turn small deviations into high payoffs may differ greatly from one geared to seeking the big, super-valuable discontinuity. Most companies will find that some sponsoring of each kind of creative effort is appropriate.

13. Don't generalize too much about how to encourage and use creative effort. Doing it right depends on the detailed area of endeavor and current circumstances. If the problems and opportunities are understood and a healthy respect exists for the potential of creative effort in handling them, the best way to employ creativity will virtually suggest itself.

14. Creative people need not be put on special pedestals, and extreme prima donnas need not be tolerated. But the company must be prepared to act promptly on ideas coming from those individuals with proven creativity. If the new idea should not be carried further, the decision should be made quickly. A truly creative person will usually shift attention to something else.

15. To encourage creativity, it must be rewarded. Cash bonuses are excellent but constitute only one dimension of the remuneration process. Award dinners can be helpful. The innovative accomplishments of individuals should be well publicized both inside and outside the company.

16. A management that is reluctant to engage in special effort to put creativity to work is unlikely to realize productive yields. Investment in creativity, however, will generate substantial corporate benefit.

2

Understanding Creativity and Creative Management

Herbert A. Simon

Professor of Psychology and Computer Science,
Carnegie-Mellon University

The fact that a person does creative things does not mean that he or she understands the creative process. To imagine that a scientist can give a full scientific account of his or her own thought processes is no more reasonable than putting a Geiger counter on the podium and expecting it to deliver a lecture on the theory of radiation. Much of what goes on when we are thinking is inaccessible to our conscious awareness. We use such terms as "judgment," "intuition," and "creative insight" to name and label those phenomena that occur without awareness. But labels are not explanations.

Many scientists and philosophers have doubted whether a scientific explanation of discovery is possible or whether there is even something describable as a method of discovery. Einstein himself is quoted as saying, "There is no logical path leading to [scientific] laws. They can only be reached by intuition, based upon something like an intellectual love of the objects of experience." If Einstein meant by "logical path" a deductive route to discovery, he was surely right. If he meant to say that there is no method in the madness of discovery, we might question whether his pessimism was justified.

The fact that many books and articles have been written on the subjects of invention, discovery, and creativity suggests that we believe that at least some significant aspects of these processes are amenable to investigation and description. Until recent times, most of our knowledge about them has derived from the experience and observations of thoughtful practitioners. In this case, the Geiger counter does indeed have something to say about the theory of radiation. But creative processes are also now the objects of direct scientific investigation. In the past two decades, some psychologists have sought to build and test theories about the processes, both conscious and unconscious, that go on in the human brain when discovery and invention are taking place.

Much can be said about the differences in process at the two ends of the continuum from basic discoveries to development and application. In particular, the development of products from basic discoveries takes place in a complex social and economic environment in which both motivations and definitions of the problem differ very much from those in the environments in which basic discoveries typically occur. I stress, however, the commonality of process—that while discovery and development usually address different substantive problems, the psychological processes of problem solution are quite similar.

Research on creativity has been carried out most often in the natural sciences, to a lesser extent in the arts and humanities, and to a very slight extent in professional domains such as management or law. Here again, there is great commonality among creative processes, wherever they appear. If this is so, a general review of creative processes will be of interest and value to all concerned with creative management.

Creativity

About 40 years ago, the federal courts required that, for an invention to be patentable, there must be proof that a "spark of genius" had occurred. The language was Mr. Justice Hand's, and it left a generation of patent attorneys with the desperate problem of making such flashes visible. The trouble with sparks of genius and similar evidences of creativity is that they are not photographable, hence are difficult to introduce as courtroom evidence. As long as we emphasize the unfathomability of creativity, we are unlikely to achieve an understanding of their mechanisms. And without such understanding, we are unlikely to encourage and enhance them.

Fortunately, it is not necessary to surround creativity with mystery and obfuscation. No sparks of genius need be postulated to account for human invention, discovery, or creation. These acts are acts of the human brain, the same brain that helps us dress in the morning, arrive at our office, and go through our daily chores—however uncreative most of these activities may be. The same processes that people use to think and to solve problems can explain the thinking and problem solving that is called creative.

Defining and Distinguishing Creativity

My basic claim is that creativity is "thinking writ large." Evidence supports two central hypotheses: (1) Thinking is information processing that involves reading symbols, writing symbols, assembling symbols in relational symbol structures, storing symbols, comparing symbols for identity or difference, and branching on the outcome of the comparison. Intelligence calls for these, and only these, processes. (2) The processes required for creative acts are the same as those required for all intelligent acts. Before we can test this claim, we must define creativity. The simplest way to find such a definition is to observe when people apply the term "creative" to some human act. What is the basis for such attribution?

From time to time, human beings arrive at ideas that are judged by their fellows to be both novel and valuable or interesting. The values discerned in these new ideas may be intellectual, esthetic, practical, or what not. It does not matter. A psychological theory of creativity (or discovery or invention) would account for the processes that are involved in bringing about such novel and valuable or interesting products. Interesting or valuable novelty, then, is the touchstone of the creative. Acquaintance with a creative act, one's own or another's, is often accompanied by surprise. "How did he (or she) manage to do that?" This quality of unobviousness partly accounts for the sense of mystery and awe that creativity often evokes.

Novelty can have either of two meanings: It can mean wholly new in the world or it can mean new to the discoverer. Usually, the medal of creativity goes only to the first discoverer. Second discoveries, however independent, win no awards from the U.S. Patent Office. There are exceptions. We celebrate the birthday of Columbus although his discovery was rather thoroughly anticipated by native Americans.

Histories of science can also be kind to independent discoverers. They remember Leibnitz as an inventor of the calculus although the historical record shows that Newton had 10 years' headstart. But Newton failed to publish promptly, and it was Leibnitz's version that was diffused and developed. Independent discovery may also be used as evidence of the discoverer's abilities, for the processes must be the same as those employed in first discovery. When the young Gauss immediately found the formula for the sum of the first n integers, his teacher correctly predicted that he would be a creative mathematician—even though the formula was old hat to trained mathematicians. Thus, we differentiate creativity in the weaker, or individual, sense, from creativity in the stronger, or social, sense—but rightly regard the former as a harbinger of the latter.

The literature on creativity draws partly on historical, biographical, and autobiographical accounts of discovery, on systematic surveys of creative (and uncreative) persons, on a limited number of laboratory studies aimed at eliciting creative behavior or comparing creative with noncreative styles of problem solving, and a number of recent attempts to simulate creative behavior with computer programs. At the level of observable events, there is great consistency among all the findings of this research, whatever its methods. I can sum up these findings in a few generalizations.

What chiefly distinguishes creative thinking from more mundane forms are (1) willingness to accept vaguely defined problem statements and gradually to structure them, (2) continuing preoccupation with problems over considerable periods of time, and (3) extensive background knowledge in relevant and potentially relevant areas. Not all of these conditions—tolerance of ambiguity, persistence, and knowledge—are satisfied in all cases of discovery, but their presence has been observed and commented on too many times to suppose that their association with success in discovery is accidental. None of these conditions is very surprising; they all have a strong motivational component, and they satisfy our sense of justice—the virtues of patience, persistence, and diligence are likely to be rewarded even though there may be, as in gold mining, a large chance element in who wins the reward. The virtues only allow you to buy a ticket in the lottery, and some tickets, as in all lotteries, pay off and some do not.

Of other uses of the term "creativity"—"creative advertising" or "creative writing"—I have little to say. One has the impression that such language is loose or at least generous to the products to which it is applied. But in the last analysis, each field must make its own judgments of creativity; each must decide what is novel and what products are interesting or valuable. There are no reasons to suppose that the basic processes underlying the humbler forms of creativity are different in kind from those that account for the great leaps (which are not really leaps, but successions of tiny steps) of a Newton or a Leibnitz. I think that applies even to singing commercials. What we wish to understand, then, are the sequences of processes that enable a man or a woman or a child to bring into being something that is novel and interesting or valuable.

The Prepared Mind

Chance, in the words of Pasteur, favors the prepared mind. "Accidental" discoveries are exceedingly common in the history of science. Take Becquerel's discovery of radioactivity or Fleming's of penicillin. Those discoveries could have been made by other scientists than Becquerel or Fleming, but they could not have been made by just anyone. Assigning the accidents to randomly chosen members of the population would not have done the trick. To exploit an accident—the image that appears on Becquerel's photographic plate or the destruction of bacteria in proximity to the penicillium molds—one must observe the phenomenon and understand that something surprising has happened. No one who did not know what a dish of bacteria was supposed to look like could have noticed the pathology of the dish that was infected by the mold, nor would he or she have been surprised if it had been called to his or her attention. It is the surprise, the departure from the expected, that creates the fruitful accident; and there are no surprises without expectations, nor expectations without knowledge.

The ability to achieve sudden insights into situations by recognizing familiar features in them depends on having stored a great deal of knowledge—knowledge about the familiar patterns that can be recognized and knowledge of the cues for recognition. We know a good deal about the amount of knowledge that a world-class expert must have and about the length of time it takes to acquire it. A study by John R. Hayes of world-class experts in a number of different domains, including chess playing, painting, and musical composition, shows that no one reaches world-class level before he or she has devoted a decade or more of intensive, single-minded effort to acquiring knowledge and skill. (Bobby Fisher, who became a grand master only 9 years and some months after learning the game of chess is a near-exception, but the only one.) Child prodigies are not exempt from this rule. Mozart was composing music (but not especially creative music) by age 4, but his first world-class compositions were written no earlier than his late teens or early twenties (depending on one's standard). Picasso, whose father was a professional painter, painted from early childhood, but his productions were not world-class until after his move to Paris in early adulthood.

Expertness, in turn, is the prerequisite to creativity. One need only visit a regional art exhibit and then an international one to realize that amateurs are not a major source of the world's important innovations. In making this claim, we must be careful: The vital point is the possession of relevant skill and knowledge, and at certain key periods in the history of science and of other domains, the relevant knowledge comes from a field other than the one to which it is applied. That is why many of the major discoveries of modern molecular biology were made by biochemists or even physicists rather than by traditionally trained biologists. The 10 years of dues that the world-class expert must pay must be paid in the right field, and choosing that field may itself involve accident and gambler's luck.

How much knowledge does the world-class expert need and how is it organized in his or her mind or brain? A college graduate is likely to have a vocabulary of 50,000 words (or even twice or 4 times that) in his or her native language. Each word is immediately recognizable when it is heard or seen in print and upon recognition, evokes from long-term memory a more or less rich set of meanings and associations. A psychologist would say that each person has 50,000 familiar "chunks" of knowledge, each accessing sets of stored information.

Estimates have been made of the number of chunks held by chess grand masters—patterns of pieces that recur on the chessboard and that they will recognize and assess immediately. These estimates again range around 50,000 familiar "friends." Fifty thousand is not a surprising number, given the 10 years of effort during which the grand master is acquiring these chunks. Until we have better numbers, 10 years and 50,000 chunks will indicate the effort and knowledge that are prerequisite to expertness and hence to creativity. If these are necessary conditions, they are not sufficient conditions. Yet they suggest that hard work and persistence represent vital components of creativity. We should not be surprised that many (most?) highly creative people are workaholics.

Do we deny the more romantic view of discovery that speaks of "insight" and "intuition" and the "creative moment?" There is no doubt that the final step of discovery is often a sudden event and sometimes an unexpected and surprising one to the inventor, who can give little account of the process that arrived at it. Often, the final step was preceded by a period of "incubation" during which the discoverer was ostensibly preoccupied with other matters.

Methods for Creative Solution

To construct an adequate theory of discovery, one must attend to conditions under which novelty is likely to emerge. Problems that call for creativity are precisely problems that have not already been well worked over and for which sophisticated, systematic algorithms for solution do not exist. For such ill-structured problems, problem-solving methods cannot be closely attuned to the characteristics of the problem environment—such tuning requires that a great deal be known about that environment. If we are given a linear algebraic equation in one variable to solve, we simply apply a well-worn algorithm to solve it. Ingenuity is required only when such an algorithm is not known to us. Hence, we may predict that persons tackling problems whose solution will have marks of novelty and require creativity will use very general methods that do not rely on specific knowledge about the problem area. Such methods, on the other hand, are likely to be highly inefficient; all that commends them is that no better ones are available.

Research using computer programming languages to design problem solvers has uncovered a number of such methods, which are usually called "weak methods." An example of a weak method is "generate and test," which consists simply in devising possible solutions and then testing each one to see whether it satisfies the solution conditions of the problem—essentially trial-and-error search. A somewhat more powerful weak method, which requires for its application only a little more knowledge about the problem area, is "means-ends analysis." In this method, a present situation is compared with a goal situation and one or more differences between them are detected. When a difference is noted, it may (by recognition) call forth from memory an approach that can reduce differences of this kind. The approach is then applied, a new situation is created, and the whole cycle is repeated as often as desired. Most weak methods require larger or smaller amounts of search before problem solutions are found, but the search need not be blind trial-and-error—in fact, usually it cannot be, for the search spaces are generally far too vast for unselective trial and error to be effective. Weak methods generally incorporate "heuristics"—rules of thumb that allow searchgenerators to be highly selective instead of searching the entire space.

Regarding differences in creative processes between basic discovery and practical development, I would hypothesize that the major shift, as we move from discovery to development, is in the formulation of the criteria that define problem solutions. From a central concern with understanding phenomena in depth and a strategy of abstracting a few variables from many, we move to a concern for the whole technical and

social context in which a principle is to be applied, including unanticipated consequences and side effects, as well as questions of efficacy and
economy. Many of the difficulties in communication among the groups
at different points along the research and development continuum are
associated with these issues of problem formulation. I doubt whether
they imply any differences in the basic psychological processes that are
required for problem solution.

Taking Risks

Creativity is a sport for gamblers. In science, for example, highly
creative research almost always requires calculated gambles, although
journeyman work can be done without much risk taking. By its very
nature, scientific discovery derives from exploring previously unex-
plored areas. If it were already known which path to take, there would
be no major discovery—and the path would most likely have previously
been tried by others.

   In this respect, successful scientific research has much in common
with successful stock market investment. Information is only valuable if
others don't have it or don't act on it. The investor is pitting his or her
knowledge, beliefs, and guesses against those of other investors. In
neither domain—science or the stock market—is the professional
looking for a "fair bet." On the contrary, he or she is looking for a
situation in which superior knowledge can be made to pay off. Sometimes that superior knowledge comes from persistence in acquiring
more "chunks" than most others have. Sometimes it comes from
accidents. But whatever the source, it seldom eliminates the element of
risk. Investors and scientists require a "contrarian" streak that gives
them the self-confidence to pit their own knowledge and judgment
against the common wisdom and belief of their colleagues.

Creativity in Management

To talk about creativity in management, we must use the same definition of creativity that we use to talk about scientific discovery. We
attribute creativity to behavior when it produces interesting or useful
novelty. What evidence can we use to detect or identify *managerial*
creativity? Its peculiar characteristic is that we must assess it not by
personal accomplishments of managers but by achievements of organizations for which they are responsible. Thus we may expect that the

motivation for managerial creativity may be rather different from the motivation for individual creativity of other sorts. We may also wonder whether there are fundamental differences in the creative processes as well.

Motivations

There is no reason to believe that the basic motivations of managers are different from those of other people, although the mix may not be exactly the same. People receive satisfaction from accomplishment (solving the problem), material rewards, the esteem of others, and power. Undoubtedly there are other motives, but these are prominent and potent ones, and they suffice for our purposes. What would seem to distinguish management most sharply from other kinds of work is the nature of the sense of accomplishment it provides. In most other endeavors, accomplishment is a highly personal matter—the direct product of working with one's own head and hands. An author writes books, a doctor treats patients, a lawyer represents clients. The sense of accomplishment of managers, on the other hand, arises out of what they see *others* doing. For this to provide satisfaction, managers must see or imagine a causal connection between the works of their organizations and their own efforts in structuring, leading, and controlling them.

In all human affairs, the assignment of credit and blame is a difficult matter. The role of accident, hence of luck, in scientific discovery is strong. Management inserts another step of indirectness in the causal chain linking personal behavior with outcomes, thus making assessment even more difficult. Moreover, hands-on, direct accomplishment generates, for many people, a qualitatively different effect from at-a-distance, indirect accomplishment. Even the intervention of a power tool may alter radically the feelings associated with handicraft activities. True, there has been more speculation about these matters than hard evidence, but we have only to consult our own feelings to know that there are differences, and often important ones.

Inability to delegate effectively is a common managerial failing. It is usually attributed to feelings of responsibility for results and an unwillingness to depend on others to discharge that responsibility. But it may also be caused by the diminished satisfactions some managers feel when delegation deprives them of participating directly in the problem-solving process. They may get greater satisfactions from exercising their problem-solving skills than from exercising their people-influencing skills.

Creative managers, then, are people who, by their own propensities or through learning, can receive great satisfaction from creative outcomes even when their role in producing those outcomes has been an indirect one—specifically a managerial one. Management is the discipline *par excellence* that depends for its achievement satisfactions on influencing the accomplishments of others. No one is likely to succeed in management or to be creative in it for whom this particular kind of achievement is not congenial.

Cognitive Aspects of Managerial Creativity

Since my thesis is that creativity consists of good problem solving, in considering the creative process in management I need to point out the principal kinds of managerial problems for which creativity is called for. First, however, I should comment on the nature of managerial expertness. In what are managers expert, and how does that expertness reveal itself in their behavior?

We have seen that a major component of expertise is the ability to recognize a very large number of specific relevant cues when they are present in any situation and then to retrieve from memory information about what to do when those particular cues are noticed. Because of this knowledge and recognition capability, experts can respond to new situations rapidly—and usually with considerable accuracy. Of course, on further thought, the initial reaction may not be the correct one, but it is correct in a substantial number of cases and is rarely irrelevant. Chess grand masters, looking at a chessboard, will generally form a hypothesis about the best move within less than 5 seconds, and in four out of five cases, this initial hypothesis will be the move they ultimately prefer. Moreover, it can be shown that this ability accounts for a large proportion of their chess skill. For, if required to play moves fast ("blitz"), the grand master may not maintain a grand master level of play but will almost always maintain a master level. In rapid play, there is only time to react to the first cues noticed on the board.

We usually use the word "intuition"—also "judgment" or even "creativity"—to refer to this ability of experts to respond to situations in their areas of expertise almost instantaneously and with relative accuracy. The streetwise slum resident has good intuitions about how to react to situations often encountered in a slum environment. The business manager has good intuitions about how to react to situations often encountered in business organizations. Both skills have the same basis in knowledge and recognition capability. Present a capable and experienced executive with the financial statements of a company, and he or she, within a matter of minutes, will make some shrewd conjectures about the firm's strengths and weaknesses. Present the same manager with a case describing a personnel problem, and a diagnosis of the difficulty and comments on possible courses of action will be forthcoming almost at once.

The point is not that managers either do or should act on impulse. Rather, it is that the expert ones have learned their 50,000 chunks, and with them, the ability to respond "intuitively" to business situations as they present themselves. It follows from this that schools of business, even the best, do not produce expert managers. They do not charge the 10 years' dues that expertness would demand, nor can they provide the full environment of organizational situations in which the perceptual cues can be learned and practiced. But this conclusion will surprise none of us. As a surrogate for some of this experience and as an alternative means for developing the perceptual recognition skills that underlie expertness, business schools often use the case method and the business game as instructional aids. These techniques could probably be used more effectively if they were recognized for what they are: methods for giving students opportunities to practice searching for relevant and important cues in business situations and associating potentially useful responses to these cues. By these methods, the business school can at least start its students on the way toward accumulating those 50,000 chunks they will need as managers.

A more difficult question addresses the content of the chunks. What does a streetwise—or more accurately, companywise—manager know? The requisite inventory has never been taken, but we can conjecture that managerial knowledge falls into two main categories: on the one hand, knowledge about human behavior in organizations and about how organizations operate and, on the other, knowledge about the content of an organization's work, knowledge that may be largely specific to an industry or even to a particular company or plant.

It has been argued that managerial expertise is a general skill that can be transferred from any organizational environment to any other. I do not think the evidence bears out this claim. The Peter Principle is a refutation as it applies to vertical transfer, and we can see as many instances of failure as of success in horizontal transfer between organizations. The hypothesis of transferability probably approaches truth most closely toward the top levels of large corporations or governmental organizations. In the former, responsibilities at the top, in addition to the selection of key personnel, are most likely to resemble those of an investment banker. In the latter, responsibilities for mediation between political and administrative levels are likely to bulk large.

It would seem that knowledge of an organization's technical content can be harmful to managers only if it tempts them to resist delegation of responsibility. Nevertheless, it is characteristic of managerial jobs that managers are continually in the position of directing operations whose technical content they cannot master fully. To cope with this difficulty, they develop a number of strategies. One strategy is to encourage multiple channels of communication from below so that they will not be captives of any one set of experts. Another strategy is to develop skills of cross-examination—skills for inducing experts to reveal the hidden assumptions on which their conclusions and recommendations are based. A third strategy is to strengthen the identifications of associates and subordinates with top-level goals of the collective organization, weakening their attachments to personal subgoals.

One way to probe the content of knowledge that underlies organizational success is to enumerate the various ways in which an organization can enjoy an advantage over competitors and then to assess the historical role these different forms of competitive advantage have played in the growth of especially successful organizations. Even in the absence of such systematic data, we can point to many different dimensions in which organizations have behaved creatively and prospered as a consequence. Consider innovation in manufacturing methods (interchangeable parts and the assembly line) and even a few instances of innovation in organizational form (divisionalization by product groups). Technical innovation, the creation of new products, is the major factor underlying the rise of whole new industries. But within individual industries, the forms of creativity that provide particular firms with competitive advantage are more difficult to specify.

Managerial Risk Taking

Is every expert manager creative? What are the additional ingredients, beyond the intuitive skills based upon the 50,000 chunks of knowledge, that are required for creativity? We return to understanding scientific creativity for part of the answer. There are, in science as in business, competent journeymen and especially creative masters. At least three stigmata seem to characterize scientists who are unusually creative: first, sensitivity to accidents and readiness to respond to them, even abandoning an ongoing program (as the Curies did in their search for radium); second, care and thoughtfulness in defining and selecting research goals and research problems; third, a propensity for risk taking. (Of course, we must interpret this last characteristic with care, for the creative-scientists we know about are the ones whose bets paid off.)

Translated into terms of business and management, these traits sound rather familiar. The first is sensitivity to opportunity and the ability to marshal multiple resources to initiate new programs of activity. The second is attention to strategic planning, to understanding relevant future trends and developments, and to the setting of long-term goals. The third is a willingness to adventure, even with risks of failure. I am not recommending any particular level of risk preference but simply claiming that the opportunity to be creative can seldom be fully separated from the opportunity to fail.

The common romantic scenario for the creative hero postulates an underdog who is willing to risk all to achieve his or her visionary goals and who finally reaches those goals after surviving many perils and overcoming many obstacles. We have seen that a more realistic scenario pictures the creative person as a professional gambler who prefers odds that are stacked in his or her favor and who secures those odds by acquiring superior knowledge about the area in which the gamble is taking place. I put the matter this way not to discount the genuine element of risk associated with most creative accomplishment but rather to emphasize the skill and knowledge (the 50,000 chunks) that form the foundation for most successful risk taking.

Creative processes are problem-solving processes—we need not postulate any special kind of "genius" to explain the creative act. The evidence shows, further, that effective problem solving rests on knowledge, including the kind of knowledge that permits the expert to grasp situations intuitively and rapidly. But intuition is no mysterious talent. It is the direct by-product of training and experience that have been stored as knowledge. Creative performance also involves taking calculated risks, where the accuracy of the calculations rests, again, on the foundation of superior knowledge. What appears to be the reckless gamble of the successful creator is more likely much less a gamble than it appears—if only because the risk taker understood the situation better than competitors did.

Science does not demean phenomena by explaining them. Creativity is no less challenging or exciting when the mystery is stripped from the creative process. The most beautiful flowers grow under careful cultivation from common soil. The most admirable products of human effort flourish when ordinary knowledge is nurtured by the solid processes of problem solving. Creativity is understandable, but no less admirable for that.

Bibliography

Mayes, J. R.: *Cognitive Psychology*, Dorsey, Homewood, IL, 1978. (See pp. 215–244 for a general survey of psychological research on creativity.)

Simon, H. A.: *Models of Discovery*, D. Reidel, Dordrecht, Netherlands, 1977. (See Sec. 5, pp. 265–338.)

Simon, H. A.: "Discovery, Invention and Development: Human Creative Thinking," *Proc. Natl. Acad. Sci.*, vol. 80, July 1983, pp. 4569–4571.

3

Making Companies Creative: An Organizational Psychology of Creativity

George T. Geis

Research Coordinator, UCLA Center for Human Resource Management

"I guess we need those creative oddballs in advertising, but how do we keep them away from the rest of the company—and from our customers?" "We need to document how we developed and marketed our most innovative product. That's how to repeat creative successes, isn't it?" Although questions like these were commonly asked in the past, executives today have different interests. No longer is creativity seen as emanating from the fringe of corporate society. Generating new ideas and bringing them to market is now seen as a (if not *the*) central task of corporate management.

Contemporary executives are asking: "How can I be more inventive and imaginative in my job? How do I inspire my subordinates? " The players in the game of innovation are *all* the human resources in an organization, not only a few "creative types." Innovation is more than a technical process to be studied clinically. Creativity is more than an abstract routine in the R&D lab. A company culture must cherish creative endeavor for innovation to flourish, and innovation cannot be understood apart from the people and groups responsible for it.

The time is right to develop a psychological framework for explaining how creativity works in organizations. We begin by defining creativity and innovation. Next, we summarize what experts know about individual creativity and its social influences. Then, we list the central components necessary for company creativity and innovation. Finally, we suggest what executives can do to encourage inventiveness and imagination in the achievement of organizational goals.

Definition of Creativity

For our purposes, a response is creative if (1) it is a novel and potentially useful response to a task at hand and (2) the task cannot be solved by following a clear and straightforward path. Tasks that can be solved by following a path that is clear and straightforward are called "algorithmic," whereas tasks that cannot are called "heuristic" (Hilgard and Bower). So to qualify as creative, a response to a task must be novel. The element of newness must be present. The response must also be potentially useful, even if the use may not be immediately evident. Finally, the response must be heuristic, that is, it must contain an element of discovery. The response cannot be the result of following a routine cookbook solution. For example, if a computer programmer follows a well-known, step-by-step procedure for writing code to convert dollar amounts (such as $12.52) into words (such as TWELVE DOLLARS AND FIFTY-TWO CENTS) for check writing, the program would not be considered creative. If, on the other hand, the programmer had to discover how to write a program to do the conversion, we might consider the response creative.

There is one other distinction in characterizing a creative act. In the above example, if our programmer was simply not aware of the conversion procedure and therefore had to develop it, should the act be considered creative? Is creativity to be judged in comparison to what has already been generally discovered by society (on a *normative* basis) or specifically by the individual in question (on an *ipsative* basis)?

We will assume that organizational creativity is primarily to be judged on a normative basis (Amabile). In an efficient marketplace in which information about products and services flows swiftly and strong competition exists, it is important to judge creative responses in terms of what is already known. This is not to imply that organizational innovation must meet our definition of creativity. Responding to changes in industry, markets, technology, or population (or to other opportunities) by replicating the business plans, practices, products, or services of others has been the basis of many successful enterprises. Such company response to customer needs is innovation that is not based on creativity. Although some innovation is linked directly to creativity, not all is (Drucker). Similarly, not all creativity leads to economic innovation. We will focus here on how organizational leaders can promote the type of creativity that can lead to innovation.

Areas of Creativity Research

Investigators studying the psychology of creativity tend to center on one of three areas: (1) the personality characteristics of highly creative people (often scientists or artists), (2) the special cognitive skills of creative thinking, and (3) the social environment conducive to (or destructive of) creativity (Amabile). We will summarize the research findings relevant to organizational creativity.

Personality Characteristics of Creative People

Creative people typically have a strong sense of independent judgment (Chambers, 1969). This link between autonomy and creativity has been established for a wide range of professionals, including architects (MacKinnon, 1962), research chemists (Stein), and female mathematicians (Helson). Other key personality characteristics commonly found in creative people are a willingness to take risks (McClelland; Glover and Sautter), personal flexibility and a tolerance for ambiguous circumstances (Chambers, 1969), a high degree of self-discipline and commitment to their work (Chambers, 1964; Roe), and a personal need to view oneself as imaginative and original (MacKinnon, 1963).

Cognitive Skills of Creative People

A uniformly low level of creativity is found in people with low intelligence, whereas all levels of creativity are present in people with high intelligence (Getzels and Jackson; Wallach). This implies that a threshold effect appears to operate, so that below a certain level of intelligence, high creativity is rarely found, whereas above that level, creativity is simply not related to intelligence.

Specific mental abilities that allow for mastery of facts, concepts, and methods of a particular field are also required for creativity (Chapter 2). An example of such required abilities would be the quantitative skill needed to master information or concept "chunks" in finance or computer science. However, as implied above, creativity requires more than either general or field-specific intelligence. Cognitive skills, such as the ability to deal with complexity and subtlety, to shatter structure and see problems from new perspectives, and to sustain almost unbearable tension in keeping open possible alternative solutions, have been associated with creative thinking (T. Kuhn).

Social Environments Conducive to Creativity

As mentioned earlier, creative people have high levels of commitment to their work. Furthermore, creativity flourishes when an individual is motivated by intrinsic aspects of the task and not by external factors. Introspective accounts written by highly creative people stress the importance of intellectual playfulness and freedom from outside control in the creative process (cf. Einstein).

Of considerable interest to companies is that under some circumstances an individual's intrinsic motivation for a task can be *diminished* if external reward (such as payment) or external constraint should become too prominent in the mind of an employee (Amabile). Problems discovered by employees themselves are more likely to be solved in a creative manner than are problems presented by superiors (Getzels). (Ideas about how executives can promote employee intrinsic motivation follow later.)

Andrews conducted a study of scientists working in research organizations and found the following factors to be important for creativity to flourish: (1) high responsibility for initiating new activities or projects, (2) power to hire research assistants (i.e., the opportunity to provide for and select key support staff), (3) no interference from administrative superiors, and (4) high security of employment. The presence of a major challenge (from others within an organization, from competition, or from within oneself) that leads to a burning desire for achievement has also been linked to creativity (Pelz and Andrews).

The opportunity to work as an apprentice with a highly creative master in the field helps develop creativity (Wallach; Zuckerman). Creative thought has been described as resulting from "quasi-spiritual" activities that are tied to ways of life acquired from contact with associates (Cattell and Butcher). Apprenticeships are especially important at the highest levels of creativity.

Components of Organizational Creativity

Teresa Amabile, in *The Social Psychology of Creativity*, presents a working model of creative performance that integrates these three areas of creativity research. Amabile's model includes three major components of creativity: domain-relevant skills, creativity-relevant skills, and task motivation. We will discuss each of these components and then suggest a fourth that is especially important for stimulating creative performance in organizations.

Domain-Relevant Skills

Creative performance involves mastery of the domain in question and includes understanding the facts and methods necessary to solve problems in the domain. Highly creative scientists are more likely than their less creative peers to actively seek information in their discipline as well as to cultivate exposure to other disciplines (Kasperson). Creative chemists and psychololgists read more professional journals than do control groups (Chambers, 1964).

Talent, where an individual has natural aptitude, is an important domain-relevant skill. Thus at high levels of creativity there appears to be a "match" between individuals and domains (Feldman). An extraordinary sense of visual, auditory, or kinesthetic mental imagery is often related to talent in an area or domain. Thus Einstein saw himself as traveling alongside a beam of light; Mozart reported hearing in his imagination (with his "mind ear") all the musical parts at once; and to use a contemporary example, Wayne Gretsky attributes his enormous success in hockey to picturing and then skating to where the puck *will be* and not where it now is. (Consider how Gretsky would perform as an executive if he had the same sense of imagery in the business domain.)

Creativity-Relevant Skills

In order for creative achievement to occur, it is not enough for an individual to have highly developed domain-relevant skills. Creative performance requires something extra. As noted, uniformly low creativity exists in people of low IQ, whereas all ranges of creativity are found in people of high IQ. Creativity requires more than intelligence, and part of this additional something is described by creativity-relevant skills. These skills include a style of thinking that is characterized by an ability to deal with complexities and subleties, to shatter structure and see problems from new perspectives, to abandon old "performance scripts" (or rules for solving programs in a given domain), and to endure extraordinary tension as one avoids foreclosing on alternative solutions (T. Kuhn).

Regarding sustaining tension in problem solving, a number of highly creative people have stressed the need for a period of incubation during which conscious work on a problem ceases and after which an apparent flash of illumination occurs (Poincare). In a well-known description of the creative process, Wallas listed the following sequence of steps: preparation, incubation, illumination, and verification (checking the validity of the creative solution).

Another important creativity-relevant skill is knowing how to use devices or techniques that generate novel solutions to problems. These techniques are known as "creativity heuristics" and include using the counterintuitive, analyzing case studies and analogies that account for exceptions, and structuring the familiar so that it becomes strange (see Part 2).

The personality variables linked to creative behavior (discussed earlier) are also important contributors to creativity-relevant skills. Recall that these personality characteristics include high self-discipline and commitment to work, strong independence of judgment, willingness to take risks, and high level of tolerance for ambiguous circumstances. Note that some creativity-relevant skills may depend on innate personality characteristics, whereas others (such as creativity heuristics) may be acquired through training.

Task Motivation

Task motivation is seen as largely explaining the difference between what a creative individual *can* do (as a result of domain-relevant and creativity-relevant skills) and what he or she *will* do. Amabile suggests that creativity is best served when an individual's motivation to achieve is—and remains—intrinsic or inherent to the task at hand. When external rewards or directives become too prominent in the mind of an employee, there is danger of contaminating his or her intrinsic motivation.

Organizational Commitment

Assume that you have a highly creative employee who has the necessary domain-relevant and creativity-relevant skills. Assume further that the employee is intrinsically interested in the project to which he or she is assigned. What else is necessary for this creative employee to fulfill the goals of your particular company? What else must be present so that creative energy is directed for organizational purposes and not just individual interests?

Personal *commitment* to one's company is vital for creative discovery to be beneficial to that company (Holtzman). Commitment is the psychic knot that ties individual meaning and institutional mission (Kuhn and Geis). It is a primal force that drives employees to exert creative effort in achieving organizational goals. Chapter 17 examines this commitment-creativity connection.

Implications for Creative Executives

How can we apply creativity research and the components of organizational creativity? How can senior managers increase inventiveness and imagination in themselves as well as in subordinates? The following are some ideas:

1. Given the high degree of autonomy and independence of judgment associated with creativity, it is not surprising that the systems found in for-profit organizations can run counter to the personalities of creative people (Argyris, 1957, 1970). If creativity is to flourish in an organization, much responsibility and power must be given to those selected to run projects. A secure environment with minimal administrative or financial interference is desirable.

2. The culture of the organization must make it attractive and easy for people to discover and solve problems independently. The identification of problems must not be seen as a sign of failure. Creativity must be encouraged with a light touch; it cannot be jammed down anyone's throat (Kanter). Formal and informal information channels should flow freely, with requests for needed data requiring minimal justification.

Control systems should be based upon mechanisms such as peer discussion and debate rather than top-down authority.

3. Rewards for employee performance must be structured to minimize the chances that intrinsic motivation will be contaminated. If external rewards (or constraints) become too prominent as motivational factors, creativity can be harmed. Desirable work environments include those in which financial reward for success is viewed as less important than the opportunity to work on another challenging project. A compensation strategy in which bonuses are paid to everyone—not only a select few—has been used by successful companies to make payment less salient. This strategy helps establish a "we-we" organizational environment for employees and diminishes the "we-they" feeling that can result when only a senior elite are given special financial reward. Don't misunderstand. Employee remuneration is crucial for organizational creativity. Indeed, without competitive compensation the chances of recruiting and retaining necessary talent is reduced dramatically. Once competitive salary structures have been established, however, human resource policy and practice should be designed and implemented to reduce the chances that compensation is the predominant motivating factor.

4. An executive must be willing to take risks in the targeted areas of creativity and innovation. Drucker stresses the importance of systematically defining and confining risks. Risks do need to be analyzed and contained. In fact, risk analysis often provides the psychological and strategic basis for confident and bold risk taking. Risk taking is vitally linked to innovation. Ready, aim, aim, aim . . . will not do; the trigger must be pulled after aim is taken, even if the target may be missed. (See Chapter 6.)

5. Recruit people with creative potential and provide them with formal and informal training to enhance creativity. Both the domain-relevant and creativity-relevant components of creative performance can serve as a basis for establishing employee selection criteria. Use the "spiritual" power of a highly creative mentor in informal training to develop an apprentice's creativity. Formal training in the general rules that guide invention or discovery (creativity heuristics) can also be considered.

6. Employ strategies to build employee commitment to organizational mission and goals (Kuhn and Geis). Strong commitment is the force that will impel an employee to allocate a significant share of creative energy to fulfill company purposes. (See Chapter 17.)

In order to stimulate creativity and innovation, executives are becoming actively involved in human resource policies and practices. No longer does the contemporary executive merely review and approve company personnel policy. A fundamental change has occurred and human resource management is now a center-stage performance. (See Part 6.) To encourage a culture in which creativity can thrive is worthy of focused and sustained effort.

Bibliography

Amabile, T. M.: *The Social Psychology of Creativity*, Springer-Verlag, New York, 1983.

Andrews, F. M.: "Social and Psychological Factors which Influence the Creative Process," In I. Taylor and J. Getzels (eds.), *Perspectives in Creativity*, Aldine, Chicago, 1975.

Argyris, C.: *Personality and Organization: The Conflict between System and the Individual*, Harper & Row, New York, 1957.

_____: *Integrating the Individual and the Organization*, John Wiley, New York, 1964.

Cattell, R. B. and H. J. Butcher: *The Prediction of Achievement and Creativity*, Bobbs-Merrill, New York, 1968.

Chambers, J. A.: "Relating Personality and Biographical Factors to Scientific Creativity," *Psychological Monographs*, vol. 78, 1964 (7, Whole no. 584).

_____: "Beginning a Multidimensional Theory of Creativity," *Psychological Reports*, vol. 25, 1969, pp. 779–799.

Drucker, P. F.: *Innovation and Entrepreneurship*, Harper & Row, New York, 1985.

Einstein, A.: "Autobiography," in P. Schlipp, *Albert Einstein: Philosopher-Scientist*, Library of Living Philosophers Inc., Evanston, 1949.

Feldman, D.: *Beyond Universals in Cognitive Development*, Ablex, Norwood, NJ, 1980.

Getzels, J.: "Problem-Finding and the Inventiveness of Solutions," *Journal of Creative Behavior*, vol. 9, 1975, pp. 12–18.

Getzels, J. and P. Jackson: *Creativity and Intelligence: Explorations with Gifted Students*, John Wiley, New York, 1962.

Glover, J. and F. Sautter: "Relation of Four Components of Creativity to Risk-Taking Preferences," *Psychological Reports*, vol. 41, 1977, pp. 227–230.

Helson, R.: "Women Mathematicians and the Creative Personality," *Journal of Consulting and Clinical Psychology*, vol. 36, 1971, pp. 210–220.

Hilgard, E. and G. Bower: *Theories of Learning*, Prentice-Hall, Englewood Cliffs, NJ, 1975.

Holtzman, W.: "Psychology and Managerial Creativity," in A. Charnes and W. Cooper (eds.), *Creative and Innovative Management: Essays in Honor of George Kozmetsky*, Ballinger, Cambridge, MA, 1984.

Kasperson, C.: "An Analysis of the Relationship between Information Source and Creativity in Scientists and Engineers," *Human Communication Research*, vol. 4, 1978, pp. 113–119.

Kanter, R.: *The Change Masters*, Simon & Schuster, New York, 1983.

Kuhn, R. and G. Geis: *The Firm Bond: Linking Meaning and Mission in Business and Religion*, Praeger, New York, 1984.

Kuhn, T.: "The Essential Tension: Tradition and Innovation in Scientific Research," in F. Barron and C. Taylor (eds.), *Scientific Creativity: Its Recognition and Development*, John Wiley, New York, 1963.

MacKinnon, D.: "The Nature and Nurture of Creative Talent," *American Psychologist*, vol. 17, 1962, pp. 484–495.

_____: "Creativity and Images of the Self," in R. White (ed.), *The Study of Lives*, Atherton, New York, 1963.

McClelland, D.: "The Calculated Risk: An Aspect of Scientific Performance," in C. Taylor (ed.), *Scientific Creativity: Its Recognition and Development*, John Wiley, New York, 1963.

Manafield, R. and T. Busse: *The Psychology of Creativity and Discovery*, Nelson-Hall, Chicago, 1981.

Pelz, D. and F. Andrews: *Scientists in Organizations: Productive Climates for Research and Development*, John Wiley, New York, 1966.

Poincare, H.: *The Foundations of Science*, Science Press, New York, 1924.

Roe, A.: "A Psychologist Examines Sixty-Four Eminent Scientists," *Scientific American*, vol. 187, 1952, pp. 21–25.

Stein, M.: "Creativity and the Scientist," in B. Barber and W. Hirsch (eds.), *The Sociology of Science*, Free Press, New York, 1962.

Wallach, M.: *The Creativity-Intelligence Distinction*, General Learning Press, New York, 1971.

Wallas, G.: *The Art of Thought*, Harcourt, Brace, New York, 1926.

Zuckerman, H.: *Scientific Elite: Nobel Laureates in the U.S.*, The Free Press, New York, 1977.

4

Making Managers Creative: The Psychodynamics of Creativity and Innovation

Abraham Zaleznick

Konosoke Matsushita Professor of Leadership,
Harvard Business School

Creative and innovative management links two concepts: the essence of creativity and innovation as mental processes and the setting of such processes within organizational environments. We explore the fundamental nature of creativity and innovation, including differences between them, and then suggest how they might be supported in organizations.

Nature of Creativity

Creativity reflects a major shift both in the definition of problems and the approach to solutions. The creative act breaks out of traditional modes of thinking and sees the world in new ways. It destroys habitual modes of perceiving and knowing to arrive at fresh syntheses. In Arthur Koestler's terms, creativity is "an act of liberation—the defeat of habit by originality." The process might be likened to taking two pictures, overlaying them, and seeing a third picture emerge that destroys the two originals. The mental process requires escape from routine and draws on unconscious activity. The ability to see things in new ways obliges flirtation with absurdity and humiliation. Most mortals defend against such painful exposure. For the creative individual, however, the exposure is essential. Indeed, it goes beyond tolerance and envelops active use of mental anguish. If one asks a potentially absurd and humiliating question, the risk is isolation, being considered a fool, and, worse, not being taken seriously. Why do people accept such insult?

Compensation comes from the mental state that accompanies discovery. It has been described, variously, as an oceanic feeling or union with a loved object once lost. Most of us experience this feeling in connection with humor. For example Koestler borrowed the following story from Freud's essay on the comic:

> A marquis enters his wife's boudoir and finds her in the arms of a bishop. The marquis walks calmly to the window and goes through the motions of blessing people in the street below. When his distraught wife cries out, "What are you doing," he answers, "Monseigneur is performing my functions, so I am performing his."

The humor derives from the juxtaposition of conventions that are rendered absurd. Authority figures are dropped from their lofty positions. The release of laughter comes from the momentary unity one achieves when a wish to debase authority is freed from taboo. In art and science, the comparable experience is when, after having labored diligently, there comes the moment of awe when one feels he or she has received a gift. The gift is so special that it heals, at least for the moment, whatever breach exists between self and world.

Howard Gardner highlights the risks creative people face:

> Despite the pleasures that individuals obtain from their world, they are typically embarked on a solitary voyage, where the chances of failure are high. To pursue this risky tack, they must be courageous and willing to deviate from the pack, to go off on their own, to face shame or even outright rejection. It requires a strong constitution to go it alone in creative matters.

Creative people "experience a strong need for personal, communal, or religious support." Gardner also describes the emotional attachment of a creative person to his or her work that is sensual in its attraction.

> The individual experiences a strong, almost primordial tie to the subjects of his curiosity. Einstein, Darwin, Piaget—all felt a special intimacy with the natural world. In each case, a loving dialogue with nature, dating back to childhood, was transformed into a scientific journey. The creative individual comes to love his work—indeed, cannot thrive without it. And, the kind of pleasure he derives from making scientific discoveries, from solving a puzzle of nature, or from completing an artistic work can be compared in a nonfacetious way with the kind of pleasure most individuals gain from sexual involvement with someone they love.

The idea of creativity began with religion, moved into art, and then, in the modern period, found a home in science before moving into commerce. In its evolution, the idea of creativity maintained a striking continuity in people's efforts to understand and control their environment. Michael Walzer explains Calvin's doctrine of predestination as being a response to the disorder and threat of the world in which he lived. Science became for its practitioners during the seventeenth century a means for imposing order on chaotic and seemingly irrational events. The artist's work, from prehistoric times to the present, has expressed a yearning to master the unknown as represented by one's separateness and estrangement from nature and from other people.

Creativity in recent years has become an ideal of democratic living and institutions. Fueled by the writings of Maslow, Rogers, and other humanistic psychologists, this desire to stimulate creativity at all levels of society, including the work force, has taken form in encounter groups, T-groups, and other activities that fall somewhere between education and psychotherapy. The assumption behind these movements is that all people have creative potential. The problem for society is to develop methods for tapping and releasing this potential, which usually include some means for converting authority from repressive to benevolent. This egalitarian thrust overlooks an important idea: that creativity depends in large measure on the presence of individual talent. While authority may stifle the expression of talent in creative work, it cannot inject talent where it does not exist. Talent is mysterious. Even Freud was awestruck: "Before the problem of the creative artist, analysis must, alas, lay down its arms."

Differences between Creativity and Innovation

Creativity has precise qualities that distinguish it from innovation. The most obvious distinction is that creativity is scarce while innovation is, or should be, plentiful. Innovation is making changes or introducing novelty, such as new customs, manners, and things. As this definition suggests, innovations are related to membership—advances that occur when individuals, steeped in the traditions of a craft, activity, or organization, apply collective knowledge to make things better. The French call this kind of work *bricolage*, or tinkering. The person who does this kind of work is a *bricoleur*, or handyman. Lest one think that innovation is debased by being linked to *bricolage*, let me assert that the art and craft of the handyman enjoys a special position in the social sciences, thanks to the work of Claude Levi Strauss. In his theory of myth, this extraordinary anthropologist likens the construction of myth to efforts of a society to solve a problem by adapting local materials. *Bricolage* done well is important whether applied to major causes of anxiety in primitive cultures, to normal anxieties connected with keeping plumbing in working order, or, in the case close at hand, performing work in organizations.

Bricolage, or innovation, is largely traditional and grows out of accumulated knowledge existing within a social system. The key to understanding innovation, or more important, its absence, is to discover circumstances in which knowledge of the *briocoleur* becomes either forgotten or suppressed. The same analysis cannot be applied to creativity, because society's lore, wisdom, and understanding do not apply to the creative act. Writers with widely differing backgrounds — scientists and humorists—believe that creativity requires a mental act, or state of mind, that frees the individual from the boundaries of common knowledge. To think today what was unthinkable yesterday requires a revision in the elements of consciousness constituting "conventional wisdom." Whereas the knowledge required for innovation is contained *within* the social structure, the work of the creative individual has to be *divorced* from such ties.

There is a marked difference between creative and innovative work. Creative work disrupts habitual ways of thinking. Innovative work utilizes habit, tradition, and culture to arrive at new ways of doing things. The steps in innovation are incremental and do not involve breakthroughs and quantum jumps. Innovation is needed to deal with problems that interfere with the achievement of collective objectives. Innovators are usually an integral part of the social structure and rely on common ideas and materials to evolve solutions. In many cases, innovations are the result of memory: Someone remembers a solution that had once worked. This memory, perhaps with variations, is brought forth to meet current needs. Innovation then, unlike creativity, is a highly socialized activity. Handymen as innovators work at the point at which problems are perceived. Their identification with their craft and organization motivates them to find efficient solutions: the best solution provided by the least effort. Because solutions are often both elegant and practical, innovators take pride in their accomplishments and receive peer or public recognition.

Bricolage, the traditional means of innovating in business, has fallen to a very low level. This craft of solving problems can be applied at all levels of an organization, but the value assigned to *bricolage* depends upon the example of leaders at the top. Modern organizations have failed to build and maintain an environment in which problem solvers can perform. Organizations lack the cohesiveness that enables people to maintain their identity in and with an organization. People forget or suppress their ability to solve problems because they do not maintain the state of mind that equates what they do in an organization with any personal fulfillment. Innovation grows out of membership and the sense of responsibility people feel for their work and the organizations that employ them. Creativity, on the other hand, depends upon the presence of gifted people who are capable of escaping from the channels of thought that are intrinsic to the culture of organizations. Creative people tend to be disruptive, while innovators support the social structure upon which they depend.

Creativity and innovation involve different modes of thinking. The movement in thought processes is *vertical* in creativity, from highly structured and disciplined to loose, associative, and symbolic. The vertical movement is from secondary process thinking, which is sequential as well as logical, to primary process thinking, which is characteristic of the unconscious. The innovator applies *horizontal* modes of thinking. While horizontal thinking uses analogies and past experience, it depends on a limited number of styles of thinking, the most predominant being linear reasoning and successive trials. Innovation therefore involves lower levels of emotion and less anxiety.

Organizational Support for Creativity

Examination of the needs of gifted people can help organizations facilitate creativity. Failure to provide proper support causes a shortfall between goals and outcomes for creative productivity. Gifted individuals often embark on a course of work that simultaneously attempts to resolve personal conflict while solving objective problems in a unique way. Carrying out this complicated psychological effort requires considerable emotional support, resembling the support necessary to undertake an investigation of unconscious motivation. In psychoanalysis and some forms of psychotherapy, this support is sometimes called the "therapeutic alliance," but for organizational creativity a more apt description is the "holding environment." Within the holding environment, gifted people can venture into vertical thinking being assured they will not become engulfed in psychological conflict. While it is true that not all vertical thinking is creative, all creative work may require vertical thinking. In some cases, gifted people provide their own holding environments by maintaining an inner connection with benevolent figures from their past through the psychology of identification. When the benevolent inner world cannot exist (e.g., such figures in the past are absent), it becomes crucial for the individual to find a support matrix that can erect this holding environment. The mentor relationship is a classic example. If such an intense personal relationship is successfully established, the structure of the organization may make little difference. The holding environment is relatively insulated from the strains of the larger organization in which it is embedded.

Such relationships are more easily established in organizations in which authority can be made personal and human rather than abstract and institutional. Companies often segregate gifted people into separate structures that encourage the formation of holding environments and personal relationships. Bell Laboratories, for example, was developed apart from the institutional structures of AT&T. Evidently, companies like AT&T that use this approach can transfer creativity from the laboratories to the institution, with its requirements for standardization, routine, and habitual practices in the work force.

Innovation can be augmented by involving an abstract principle and using an interactive method. The abstract principle is to secure a just environment that meets the standards of equity and due process. This encourages a belief in the organization's rationality and a willingness to exchange one's best efforts for the mix of compensation that an organization promises. The interactive method is to make it easy for participants to meet and exchange ideas in solving problems. Individuals and groups have only partial access to information and ideas, and by bringing participants together, limitations of partial knowledge can be more readily overcome.

Innovation inertia in institutions is an endemic problem, sometimes called "the bureaucratic malaise." Bureaucracy tends to produce power struggles, displacement of goals, and "trained incompetency," along with equity, due process, and practical rationality. These bureaucratic problems cause the skills and energy of the *bricoleur* to become repressed and suppressed, when just the opposite should be occurring to stimulate innovation in organizations. Often, bureaucratic deficiencies are recognized, but solutions to problems exacerbate rather than remedy the "illness."

Innovation calls for the rediscovery of intuition, judgment, and fruitful trial and error. Yet, paradoxically, the formalization of these activities often frustrates instincts that are the foundation for innovation. The work of innovation is extracting from memory and habit those techniques that solve problems gracefully as well as efficiently. There are certain rituals connected with innovation. The rituals bring the individual closer to the organization. In contrast, bureaucratic systems tend to alienate and, ultimately, to suppress intuition, judgment, and trial and error.

Organizations are characterized by leaders, and creative organizations require creative leaders. Leadership can be based on either charisma or consensus and the style affects output. Two qualities, innovation and flexibility, interact to generate creativity in organizations: Innovation must have flexibility to broaden horizons; flexibility must have innovation to focus intensity. Charismatic leaders, by nature, are not flexible. They are committed deeply to their own internal standards; their strength of conviction and sense of command inhibit adaptation to new conditions, and high self-esteem leaves little room for ideas of others. Consensus leaders, by contrast, are malleable and fit easily into fluid situations; they have shallow personal beliefs and adapt readily to sources of power; they lack independence, have weak inner lives, and do not innovate. The paradox is that organizations take risks if they follow charismatic leaders toward their uncompromising, private goals, but they immobilize themselves if they become entangled by the meandering looseness of consensus leaders. The trick for companies seeking to be creative and innovative is to meld charismatic innovation with consensus flexibility.

Bibliography

Gardner, Howard: *Art, Mind, and Brain: A Cognitive Approach to Creativity*, Basic Books, New York, 1982.

Koestler, Arthur: *The Act of Creation*, The Macmillan Co., New York, 1964.

Levi-Strauss, Claude: *The Savage Mind*, U. of Chicago Press, Chicago, 1966.

Prigogine, Ilya and Isabelle Stengers: *Order Out of Chaos*, Bantam Books, New York, 1984.

Rothenberg, Albert and Carl Hausman (eds.): *The Creativity Question*, Duke University Press, Durham, NC., 1976

Walzer, Michael: "Puritanism as a Revolutionary Ideology," in S. N. Eisenstadt, *The Protestant Ethic and Modernization*, Basic Books, New York, 1968.

Zaleznick, Abraham and Manfred F. R. Kets de Vries: *Power and the Corporate Mind*, Houghton Mifflin, Boston, 1975.

5

What Makes Creative Personality in Business?

Robert Lawrence Kuhn

Investment Banker; Senior Research Fellow,
IC² Institute, University of Texas at Austin; and
Adjunct Professor, Graduate School of Business
Administration, New York University

How do creative types think and act? What makes managers imaginative, executives innovative, entrepreneurs inventive? Much, we read, depends on organizational structure. Yet the most critical part of the process is often overlooked—the *personality* of the individual manager, executive, entrepreneur. Personalities, like fingerprints, are unique. Though composed of similar elements, endless combinations make each pattern special. Every human being is an aggregate sum of numerous traits, a complex amalgam of inner attitudes and outer actions. When creative managers pioneer original products, when innovative executives design novel strategies, when dynamic entrepreneurs build new businesses, individual personality is an underlying factor.

Creativity, like lightning, seems spasmodic. Yet there is reason and cause, and, with careful study, both can become known. Creative types

43

often did not have normal, predictable childhoods. Both diversity and adversity seem to engender creative development. A wider variety of experience (cultural and intellectual) combined with greater opportunity to make decisions (not necessarily good ones) gives an ability to view issues from different angles. Early problems, such as family conflict, are common.

Creativity research on artists reveals two modes of thinking: "opposition thinking," the ability to conceptualize and integrate opposite ideas simultaneously (this has been called "janusian" thinking, after the Roman god Janus who had two bearded faces, back-to-back, looking in opposite directions); and "homospatial thinking," the ability to actively conceive more than one entity as occupying the same place (this generates effective metaphors). In a study of art students, works rated highest in originality were produced by those who had explored more intensely and who had taken the most time, both before they began work and before the final form became recognizable.

Mental Characteristics

There is a distinction between creative *capacity* and creative *performance*; the former suggests general ability; the latter, specific results. Is creative capacity applicable to various fields and diverse areas or is it limited to defined fields and tight areas? Is it likely, for example, that a wonderfully creative physicist would be equally as creative in literature or law, assuming equivalent aptitude and training? The answer seems more positive than negative. Creativity is more a general ability than a specific talent, and the qualities of mind that set creative types apart from their less creative peers transcend bounded areas of expression or endeavor. Studies of especially creative architects show that not only do they approach architecture from different perspectives, but they also perform a host of other, unrelated tasks in ways and manners distinct from their less creative colleagues. How creative personalities tackle problems—all kinds of problems—is just plain different. Creativity, to overly simplify its essence, can be likened to musical ability. You can learn theory and techniques, you can practice as much as you like, you can improve your skills significantly—but current mental aptitude, whether derived from nature or nurture, does set some limits. This is not to say, of course, that people cannot learn to be more creative. Sure they can. Proof is abundant—including chapters in this book.

Personality characteristics that emerge from research on creative people show a high correlation irrespective of the field of creative expression. Thus creative chemists and creative writers may have more traits in common than do creative and uncreative chemists or creative and uncreative writers. Gary Steiner summarizes numerous assessments of creative people. Although measures of general intelligence do not correlate well with creativity, "highs" (high creative performers) out-score "lows" in the following categories. *Conceptual fluency:* Highs have more ability to generate large numbers of ideas rapidly for random requests (e.g., novel uses of a brick; categories into which the names of a thousand great men can be sorted). *Conceptual flexibility:* Highs can more easily shift gears, change approach, discard one paradigm for another. *Originality:* Highs have the ability and/or tendency to give more unpredictable answers to questions, more unexpected responses to situations, more unusual interpretations of events (e.g., rare, surprising uses of bricks, as well as a larger number of uses). *Preference for complexity:* Highs desire to see beyond the simple and obvious (e.g., whole interpretations of inkblots, however abstruse, rather than simple descriptions of detailed parts that more clearly resemble certain things). *Independence of judgment:* Highs are more opinionated and stubborn in their beliefs, especially when confronted by disagreement. *Deviance:* Highs envision themselves as different in trivial as well as significant life factors; they feel more isolated and lonely. *Attitude toward authority:* Highs consider authority as more temporary than permanent, more contingent on current performance than confirmed by absolute command; personal allegiance is more a matter of present expediency than moral obligation; information is judged on its own merits irrespective of source. *Impulse acceptance:* Highs enjoy flights of fancy, expressing and entertaining wild and whimsical ideas; they listen to their inner voices; they are "free spirits." To be called "a bit bizarre" would be taken as a compliment not a criticism by highs.

Creative types are more comfortable without clear structure; they are tolerant of unresolved situations and are content to entertain fuzzy, abstract suggestions even when they seek focused, literal solutions. Creative types identify more with their task than with their department, more with their profession than with their company. Long-term loyalty to organization and structure is less meaningful than short-term commitment to idea and concept. Creatives approach problems differently. They are not as concerned about ambiguous issues, uncertain progress, suspended judgments, unclear analysis; they are not bothered by long corridors and blind alleys. They relish undisciplined exploration, sudden starts and stops, flashes of insights, and changing ideas. Constantly shifting shades of gray, not perfectly consistent blacks or whites, are their favorite colors.

David Ogilvy, founder of the international advertising agency, asserts that creative talent is most likely to be found among "nonconformists, dissenters, and rebels." Yet few nonconformists, dissenters, and rebels are really creative, and a creative organization requires more than a collection of anarchists. Ogilvy states, "I have observed that no creative organization, whether it is a research laboratory, a magazine, a Paris kitchen, or an advertising agency, will produce a great body of work *unless it is led by a formidable individual.*" Ogilvy, like his early mentor the head chef at the Hotel Majestic in Paris (who inspired "white-hot morale"), is such a leader. At an annual meeting of his employees, held at the Museum of Modern Art, he said, "I admire people who work with gusto. If you don't enjoy what you are doing, I beg you to find another job. Remember the Scottish proverb, 'Be happy while you're living, for you're a long time dead.' "

Personality Dipoles

The personality characteristics arrayed below describe the creative process in behavorial terms. Traits are organized as linear spectrums, with each word of the pair defining an extreme. Most people fall in the middle, some more to the right, some more to the left. It's the combination, the exquisite weaving of strands, that makes us unique. The trait-spectrums are introduced with a question. What is the essence of the personality element, and how might it affect the creative process? That's what we highlight. There is, of course, no right or wrong answer, just reflections on the way people feel. Creative types, remember, are rich with variety, and personality assessment should enhance not limit such expression.

Convergent ↔ *Divergent.* When working on a business problem, what do you do first: zero in on the best possible solution from among known alternatives, or seek to expand those alternatives however silly your suggestions? When are you happiest, when choices are narrowing and an answer is clearly in sight or when choices are expanding and an answer is nowhere to be found? Creatives spend more time in the initial stages of problem formulation, in the broad generation of alternatives. Those who seek optimal solutions by focusing on and evaluating progressively fewer options are convergent in thinking style. Those who desire greater variety of potential solutions, even if mutually contradictory, think divergently. Convergent types do not tolerate uncertainty and ambiguity very well; divergent types thrive on unstructured and amorphous problems. Convergent thinking reflects the logical rigor of the rational analyst. Divergent thinking is a classic descriptor of the creative mind.

Conforming ↔ *Iconoclastic.* When given a work assignment, is your natural inclination to do it in an accepted manner or different from the norm? Iconoclastic types do things in unusual ways even when those ways are less effective and more risky. They go out of their way to be off center; they are idiosyncratic and deem it a compliment to be considered peculiar. Iconoclastics are more likely to be creative than conformists—indeed habit is an arch enemy of novelty. Creatives may be disruptive in organizations; they can be contemptuous of authority and disobey orders when they do not agree; they can upset routine and be bothersome to others.

Logical ↔ *Emotional.* When making business decisions, which carries greater weight, rigorous analysis or intuitive insight? Creative types follow their hunches; they are great skeptics and show disdain for orderly consideration of problems. Indeed they seek unstructured situations that cannot be reduced to simple, straightforward statements. Complex, asymmetrical issues are their forte. Disorder is their friend, order their foe. The greater the confusion the better they feel.

Objective ↔ *Subjective.* In selecting an administrative assistant, on what would you put more weight, his or her scores on intelligence tests and psychological profiles or your personnel director's first impressions after a 15-minute interview? In an age of accelerating data collection and computer analysis, instincts and insights are under heavy siege. Others, however, speak of articulating rational analysis with nonrational (not *ir*rational) perception. Creatives come down clearly on the subjective side; an objective personality is often inhibited from seeing spontaneous sparks and sudden flashes, from finding the novel among the known.

Rigid ↔ *Flexible.* In tackling a complex problem do you like shifting from one approach to another? Creativity is said to result from the interaction of diverse disciplines of knowledge (content) and opposing modes of thinking (process). Do not misunderstand: Those who use traditional information and accepted methods ("rigids") will usually solve most kinds of business problems more efficiently than those who seek diversity in data and approach ("flexibles"). Yet rigids cannot be as creative and will have no chance at all to solve the problem if innovative solution is required. (Flexibility is an important modality of creativity.)

Consistent ↔ *Capricious.* How predictable are you? Does your boss have confidence that you will do the job as he or she expects? In trying to win back old customers, for example, would you give everyone the same pitch? Do you enjoy job jumping or company switching? It is rare when consistency is not a virtue, and reliable employees are considered golden. On the other hand, firms operating in rapidly changing industries need a few capricious sorts, creative tigers who growl with new ideas. (They must, of course, operate under control—which poses problems when the capricious one is the entrepreneurial boss.) While creativity and capriciousness are not synonymous, regularity and repetition stifles originality.

Inward ↔ Outward.   In what forum are you most effective, directing spreadsheet analysts or hosting business luncheons? Those choosing the former are more "inward" (or "introverted" in Jung's terminology); those choosing the latter more "outward" (or "extroverted"). Whether one is inward or outward might affect the creative process in different situations; for example, working in an "open office" environment with no private enclosures favors outward employees. Inward people might have more time for private contemplation, though outward people might have a better sense of practical application. Being a loner is no creative asset. Scientists who communicate more with peers are more likely to produce more innovation (patents, papers, etc.).

Active ↔ Passive.   As sales manager, which task would you prefer (assuming equal salary and status), opening up new accounts or servicing current accounts? Actives are generally more creative, taking interest in affecting their environment not just finding a comfortable place in it. (Passives can be "sleepers." Don't ignore ideas from timid sorts.) A company must have balance; too many actives will cause chaos; too many passives will produce stagnation.

Independent ↔ Dependent.   In taking responsibility for introducing a major new product—with promotion promised for success and dismissal likely for failure—would you rather report to your superior frequently (e.g., daily) or infrequently (e.g., monthly)? Independent people are usually more creative; they care less about custom and more about content. Though independent people have more status in society, companies would fall apart if overendowed with them. Furthermore, a person dependent in one mode, say as an office manager, might be quite independent in another mode, say as an officer in the Naval Reserve.

Dominant ↔ Recessive.   When serving on interdepartmental committees, are you ever selected as chairman? Dominants in business, like dominants in genetics, express their traits and get their way—but too many dominants, of course, clash and cause conflict. The revolving-door exodus of "heirs apparent" in corporations run by aging though strong founders are classic cases of colliding dominants. Dominants can be creative, but the correlation may not be cause and effect. Recessive personalities, relatively unencumbered with people control, can allocate more effort and attention to fresh ideas.

Competitive ↔ *Cooperative.* Assume you work on the sales staff of a company selling office equipment to corporate clients. Which method of compensation do you prefer: (1) Each salesperson is free to approach any potential customer and is paid a commission, say 6 percent, based on his or her personal sales only? Or (2), each salesperson is assigned to cover an equal number of potential customers and is paid a commission based on the sales of the entire sales staff, say 4 percent, as well as on his or her personal sales, say 2 percent? The balance between competition and cooperation is a difficult one to keep, as when three senior vice-presidents—VPs of administration, marketing, and finance—are all candidates for president. Creative types are often competitive, though their arena of competition may be more achievement and recognition than remuneration and promotion.

Intense ↔ *Lethargic.* Would you ever work on Thanksgiving to test a critical new product that you have been developing? If so, you're probably intense. Do you often have to be told what to do? If so, you're probably lethargic. Intensity correlates highly with creativity; the creative process demands high energy and persistent effort. Intensity is an important trait for entrepreneurs who must build from nothing, but it can be disrupting for middle managers who must maintain steady work output.

Acquisitive ↔ *Quiescent.* Do you need to build and accumulate in order to feel accomplished? Are you constantly seeking new things to buy and use? The founders of companies are more often concerned with augmenting their firms' power than with boosting their personal finances. Acquisitives, of course, are high-risk personalities, often operating at the brink of disaster. Creative managers are found on both sides of this spectrum, each with a different cast. Acquisitives are dynamos; quiescents pull the surprises.

Conceited ↔ *Modest.* Can we expect to hear all your fabled exploits every time we see you? Assuming your subordinates would never know the truth, would you rather overplay or underplay your personal relationship with the president? Society, if we believe convention, considers modesty a virtue and conceit a vice. Yet to be successful business people, we are told, one must flip those pairings around. The truth in business, of course, is both and neither. Few creative types hold

their long suit in modesty; they feel their ideas are supremely important
and demand immediate recognition and instant action.

How to find creative personnel? There are tests that purport to
discern creative ability, and some are rather interesting. But beware:
Both natural creative ability and actual creative productivity are extraordinarily hard to assess much less predict. The problem of creativity
is knotty and labyrinthian and mocks up-front quantification. Motivation, for example, exerts significant influence on capacity—and motivation, like interest, changes constantly. Commercial creativity just
cannot be judged by aptitude or achievement tests. Predicting creativity
in employees, at best, is an art not a science. It is wiser for managers to
enhance creative *output* through stimulating the creative process (Part
2) and structuring a creative organization (Part 3) rather than by
attempting to choose especially creative people.

Bibliography

Ogilvy, David: *Confessions of an Advertising Man*, Atheneum Publishers, New York,
    1963.
Steiner, Gary A.: *The Creative Organization*, The University of Chicago Press, Chicago,
    1965.

6

How Risk Takers
Take Risks

George T. Geis

*Research Coordinator, UCLA Center for Human
Resource Management*

It's been quipped that there are three types of people found within organizations: risk takers, caretakers, and undertakers. The truth, of course, is that most of us play each of these roles from time to time, even though there may be a dominant mode in which we usually operate. In this chapter we ignore the undertakers, people involved with burying programs or projects. We briefly discuss the caretakers, employees working to preserve existing resources. Our focus is on the risk takers, for it is this group that has a special link to creativity in organizations.

Creativity involves the act of producing a new or novel response to a task that cannot be solved in a clear and straightforward manner. Since creativity is connected with the new, the unknown, or the untried, it almost always involves risk, especially in the commercial world. Risk takers are organizational innovators.

How do we encourage individuals within organizations to take risks? Should we try to turn everyone into an experimenter, stimulating all employees to search out the new and novel? How can we encourage a risk-taking pattern that will be in a company's best interests? In order to promote organizational innovation we must understand why people choose and refuse to take risks. We must also understand how to design an organizational environment that fosters the risk-taking behavior top management desires.

Caretakers

Caretakers play an important role in companies. Their mission is to preserve existing programs, products, and resources. They tend to see environmental changes as threats not opportunities. Caretakers respond predictably to change by advocating strategies that guard current product-market share. Caretakers are shepherds of the organizational flocks, and for them the environment consists of wild-eyed wolves behind every bush.

Of course, there are times when even caretakers realize that the usual defensive means of preserving company assets will not hold. Sometimes the threats are so ominous that the riskiest strategy would be to stay in a maintenance mode. Not wanting to turn into a risk taker, the caretaker in these inverted circumstances supports innovation and change. However, the caretaker's statement of company mission remains basically the same: "This outside threat forces us to take aggressive action in order that our overall organizational resources can be maintained."

Risk Takers

Risk takers see the world from a different perspective. Changes or challenges in the environment are viewed as opportunities not threats. Furthermore, risk takers do not see the environment as something to which they should passively respond but as something they should actively shape. The organizational risk taker develops and introduces products and services that anticipate and even create market needs.

Let's clear up a common misunderstanding. Successful risk takers are *not* wildly passionate about risk per se. Before venturing out on a course of action, most innovators seek first to understand and contain risks. If at all possible, they try to turn leaps of faith into plays of percentage. Doing so makes them more confident as they move forward. And move forward they do. After making a reasonable assessment of both upside and downside potential, risk takers pursue opportunities aggressively. They are confident of obtaining necessary financial, physical, and human resources even if it takes considerable scrounging. Their driving purpose is to forge the new, not preserve the old.

The pure risk taker emerges when circumstances do not allow the odds of success to be determined with reasonable accuracy. Although most innovators like to use some form of risk calculus to optimize their risk-taking behavior, creativity may flow most freely when such analysis is not possible, when almost complete uncertainty exists. We would expect risk taking and innovation in extreme uncertainty to occur more frequently in a small entrepreneurial setting, in which there is usually less to lose. Promoting an innovation with unmeasurable risk is not common in large organizations, especially in circumstances in which the company's future could be bet on the outcome. Caretaker influence is too great.

A Design for Organizational Risk Taking

Risk taking, whether measured and contained or not, is linked to creativity and innovation. Entrepreneurs, in general, may be more prone to take on high risks than executives operating in an established organizational environment. Yet our central question remains: What can an organization do to encourage a desirable degree of risk taking, a level conducive to needed creativity and innovation? Here are some suggestions:

1. *Tension.* An executive must appreciate that a certain level of tension between company risk takers and caretakers is not only inevitable but desirable. How to preserve the best of the old while developing the new is a fundamental dynamic. For an organization to be stable, it must have some "unlosables," a core from its history that is protected and preserved. Yet for an organization to be vibrant, it must not ossify in its past. There must be some venturesomeness in responding to the environment. Organizational integrity and unity demands a general consensus among leaders as to how aggressive the innovative thrust should be. Resolving this tension is the starting place in developing organizational policy toward risk taking.

2. *Assessment.* In areas in which the organization seeks to be innovative, risks should be assessed and contained as much as possible. Doing so will increase the confidence with which leadership ventures forth. There may be some projects, however, for which risk cannot be assessed with any accuracy. In such cases the potential losses may be enormous or even total, but the potential gain may be equally grand. If the company is being bet, the leadership should at least know the stakes.

3. *Diversification.*   It is advisable to diversify away as much risk as possible. Modern portfolio theory argues that any premium in the required return of any equity issue is associated with nondiversifiable (systematic) risk. Risk that can be diversified away is not rewarded in the general market. Similarly, to have an efficient risk portfolio, organizations need to explore options for the diversification or sharing of project risk (and gain) from financial and psychological perspectives (e.g., joint ventures). The company must then concentrate on succeeding in the areas of nondiversifiable risk to which it has chosen to expose itself.

4. *Leadership and support.*   Select project leaders to head innovative projects and provide them with organizational support that encourages risk-taking behavior on their part. A project leader should be free to select project team members. (You wouldn't want to climb a mountain with people you couldn't count on, would you?) Team access to information relating to project success is vital. Mental and material support is vital for creative productivity.

5. *Promotion.*   To cultivate creativity in organizations does not mean that company policy should encourage all employees to be as unrestrained as free-form poets. However, in project areas in which top management wants risk taking to occur, it must promote risk as well as understand the failure that frequently accompanies it. Although mechanisms to minimize the chances of project dead ends should be established, failure in the context of working toward project success must meet with social acceptance.

6. *Commitment.*   Work to keep innovative people committed to the organization and to the specific projects on which they are working. If innovative success is to occur within organizations, individuals must be willing to make enormous psychological investments in company projects. It is highly unlikely that the intensity of effort typically required for creativity will be reached unless an employee is wholly dedicated to organizational and project goals. (See Chapter 17 for the connection between personal creativity and company commitment.)

7. *Appreciation.*   Remember that to promote organizational innovation, the mechanisms that encourage and support individual and group risk taking must be put in place. In order to prevent risk takers from evolving into company caretakers (or from leaving the firm), the central role that risk taking plays in successful innovation must be appreciated. Such appreciation applies across the entire risk spectrum, from showing overt recognition of risk takers (not just the successful ones) to understanding how risk exerts its subtle influence on every new idea or venture.

7

Whole Brain Creativity

Ned Herrmann

President, Applied Creative Services, Ltd. and
Chairman, The Whole Brain Corporation

What are the special qualities that engender chief executive success? How do CEOs achieve diversity in thinking when most of their careers were focused on single-function activities such as finance, marketing, engineering, or legal? Studies of how CEOs think show that they are in the small percentage of managers who apply their brain power relatively equally over the entire set of mental specialties, that they are "smarter" across a wider range of mental processes.

My research relates management, creativity, and CEO capability with a model of brain specialization. It was triggered by Henry Mintzberg's burning question: "Why are some people so smart and dull at the same time, so capable of certain mental activities and so curiously incapable of so many others?" The model was derived from research showing a division of function among various areas and sides of the brain. This distribution provides the basis for my metaphoric model of a person's preferred mode of thinking, knowing, and learning. I began the research when teaching at General Electric's Management Institute and subsequently developed an instrument for measuring these preferred modes. The instrument is an inventory (questionnaire) of personal information that, when processed, produces a profile of the individual's mental preferences. Over 250,000 questionnaires, representing several thousand companies and about 500 occupations, have been processed.

The Brain Model

The brain is composed of two separate hemispheres, left and right. Contained within the brain halves are two sets of major structures: cerebral hemispheres, connected by the corpus collosum, and the limbic system, connected by the hippocampal commissure. The cerebral hemispheres are the locus of cognitive and intellectual functions while the limbic system is concerned with affect and emotion. Critical limbic system functions include transforming input information for appropriate processing and the organized and emotional aspects of learning.

The concept of Whole Brain Management is based on a model that divides the brain into four quadrants. Going horizontally, the top two represent the more cognitive and intellectual modes that are associated with the two cerebral hemispheres; the bottom two represent the more visceral, emotional modes that are associated with the limbic system. Going vertically, two of the four quadrants specialize in left-mode thinking processes. These are the more logical, analytic, quantitative, and fact-based modes that are contained in the cerebral left quadrant and the more planned, organized, detailed, and sequential modes that are processed in the limbic left quadrant. In contrast, the other two quadrants make up right mode specialization; these include the more holistic, intuitive, synthesizing, and integrating modes that are associated with the cerebral right quadrant and the emotional, interpersonal, feeling-based, and kinesthetic modes that are associated with the right limbic quadrant (see Figure 7.1).

Personnel Profiles

People gravitate toward work that allows them to function most effectively. For example, an individual who prefers to think in logical, analytical, rational, factual, and technical terms might pursue a career in engineering. A person with a preference for planned, organized, structured activities, who thinks sequentially and is interested in administrative detail, might enter manufacturing. Individual responses to the 120 questions that make up the Herrmann Brain Dominance Instrument determine the distribution of mental preferences in each of the

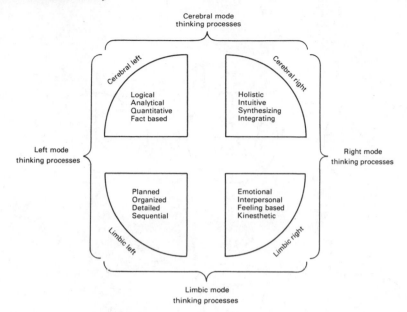

Figure 7.1 Four quadrants of the brain.

four quadrants that make up the metaphoric model. The resulting profile shows the most and least preferred modes of thinking. Displayed in Figure 7.2 are the profiles of typical business occupations. Brain dominance data indicate that individuals in similar occupations tend to have the same general profile; for example, accountants in one company have profiles that are similar to accountants in another company (even another country). Work is a common denominator of mental preferences, not only between companies but also between cultures.

There is direct correlation among a person's personal profile, occupational profile, and managing profile. The array of profiles, when correlated with the four-quadrant brain dominance concept, provides the bases for the Whole Brain Managing Model. Incorporated are key descriptors that differentiate each quadrant from the others in terms of major thinking modes, procedures, and processes. Using the model as a diagnostic tool can help allocate different "professions," "types," and special "interests" into the four brain dominance quadrants.

Chief Executive Profile

CEOs, by reason of the multifunctional work required, tend to have profiles that exhibit multiple preferences distributed across all four quadrants rather than highly focused preferences in only one or two

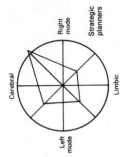

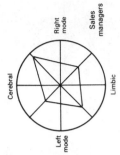

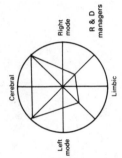

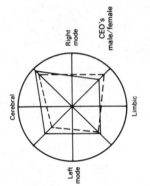

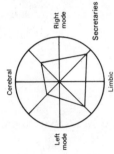

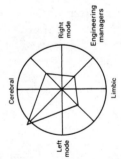

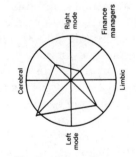

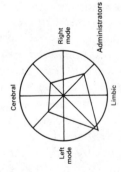

Figure 7.2 Profiles of typical business occupations.

quadrants. In other words, CEOs are frequently multidominant translators of these functional "languages." The center profile in Figure 7.2 displays the average of about 100 CEOs representing a variety of businesses. The relatively balanced distribution of preferences is in striking contrast to the sharply focused profiles of other corporate personnel.

CEOs exhibit profiles with multiple primaries—usually three and frequently four. The reason, I believe, is the nature of CEO work. The full spectrum of mental processing is required. The languages needed to function effectively in the logical, analytic, quantitative, and rational mode are different from the languages needed for planning, organizing, implementing, and administering—which are different from the languages needed for interpersonal, emotional, and humanistic issues— which are different from the languages needed for strategic thinking, holistic policy formulation, and integration of business functions. To speak these different languages requires relating to the functional "tribes" that originated them. The engineering, manufacturing, finance, legal, human resources, and strategic planning staffs all speak their own tribal dialects. The successful CEO, therefore, must be a "translator," capable of speaking these separate languages and translating from one to another.

An analysis of CEO work shows that in any given period there is a relatively equal distribution across all four languages, which represent the four quadrants of preferred modes of knowing. Studies of CEO calendars reveal that they spend about an equal amount of time in each of the four quadrants. Since the nature of the work is multidominant, the CEO who has a balanced profile is in a better position to deal with the variety of mental processes required. Furthermore, such a mental profile enables CEOs to become independent of their staffs in the final executive decision-making process.

Bibliography

Mintzberg, Henry: "Planning on the Left, Managing on the Right," *Harvard Business Review*, July–August, 1976.

8

What Managers Can Learn from Artists about Creativity

Brian Knowles

Editor, Butane-Propane News and Professional Artist

Pontifications on management abound. Libraries are stacked with books and journals and authorities traverse the planet conducting seminars and workshops. Formulas, theories, and approaches proliferate, and it's a life's work just to keep up with the utterances of gurus. Makes you wonder . . . . If the meaning of management is all that plain, why must so much be said about it? If management is more science than art, why must there be so many contradictory techniques for managing?

Management, in my view, is analogous to many other endeavors, one of which is childrearing. If you've ever reared three sons, as I have, you'll know that three children of the same gender, raised in the same home with the same parents who share the same philosophy, can turn out differently. Each child is a unique individual with a particular personality, and particular penchants and proclivities. There are no formulas that work equally well with any or all children. "Success" in childrearing is not something that can be guaranteed through the strict application of some technique or formula. So it is with management.

Not only is management more art than science, more subjective than objective, it also contains within its variables the essence of its own results. In this sense, management is analogous to painting.

In some forms of painting, the goal is strictly definable, just as it is in some aspects of management. In the latter, the specific goal might be, say, to up production by 15 percent or to increase market share by 4 percent. With such tightly defined objectives, a manager might be able to determine, more or less scientifically, just what would be required for achievement. He or she might therefore be able to approach the whole matter somewhat methodically. In painting, the goal of the artist might be to produce a specific image, say, of an apple, that looks exactly like the apple he or she is using as a model. In such cases the artist may be able to proceed more or less mechanically.

But most painting, like most management, is not that objective. Management, in the broadest sense, is not that clearly defined, nor should it be. Management, in this larger perspective, might be described as the creative manipulation of resources to achieve corporate objectives. Painting, in the same sense, could be described as the creative manipulation of resources to achieve the artist's objectives.

Many corporations exist simply because they exist. Somehow, they were started, became profitable, and grew. Now they are major forces in the business world. But, somewhere along the line they lost sight of their *raison d'être*. Yet, corporate executives continue to act in the way corporate executives act, even in the face of ill-defined, or nonexistent, corporate philosophies.

Painters paint because it has become a part of their natures to paint. They are not always certain just how their paintings will turn out. They are working with a large number of variables, and altering any one could change the ultimate outcome. Massaging the variables is not always an objective process. Often it is utterly subjective. Artists seek to bring into being "controlled accidents." They seek spontaneity. Yet they desire some sense of control, some feeling that they are in charge of the process.

Corporate management, following the analogy, is much like this. Executives work with a large number of variables: human resources, money, tools and equipment, and a constantly changing marketplace. On a personal level, executives operate on the basis of natural instincts. There is no sense of *absolute* control. They must work with ever-changing variables.

No human being is utterly predictable. The worth and availability of money is not fixed. Equipment and tools have their limitations. The marketplace is uncertain, even capricious, and does not react kindly to attempted prognostication. Like artists, corporate managers must work with variables. They cannot control all the factors involved. Rather, like artists, they must learn to manipulate, to turn fortuitous accidents into managerial advantage. Truly effective executives must therefore be sensitive individuals—that is, they must have the "feel" of those human and nonhuman factors they seek to use to produce a result.

Artists must also be able to feel their variables—paint, brushes, canvas. The canvas is like a living surface that responds to the pressure of the brush. Its "teeth" pick up the paint in response to the paint's consistency. If the paint oozes or dribbles when, according to the artist's intent, it should be reacting with an impasto effect, the painter must adjust the medium to produce the desired message. Corporate managers must also be able to feel the reactions of their human resources when they are directed to respond a certain way, yet do not. Every man or woman is existentially unique. There is no single formula for directing the productive efforts of people that works equally well for all. Every human resource must be handled in the context of his or her unique qualities. A person cannot do what he or she cannot do.

The painter knows that some colors are tinting colors and others are dyeing colors. And, from brand to brand, the tinting and dyeing qualities of the same colors vary in consistency. To achieve a desired result, the artist must become familiar with these variables and learn how to mix them to create the intended masterwork. The same is true with the management of human resources. All engineers, like all cobalt blues, are not identical. One engineer will not produce the same result as another in the same position. An artist might choose Reeve's cobalt blue for one painting and Grumbacher's for another.

High-handed authoritarian management is unable to deal with such subtleties. The more militaristic the management, the more rigid and arbitrary, the more constipated the results. It would be absurd for a painter to approach a new work in an authoritarian manner. The product would be bereft of spontaneity, of uniqueness, and of fortuitous accidents. Yet, what many executives fail to realize is that approaching management in a narrow, constrained way is equally absurd. A company is *not* an army.

This is not to say that the antidote to authoritarian rigidity is free-form anarchy. The very word "management" implies some sense of control—but that control should be to encourage creativity, move more toward *positive manipulation* than tight-fisted suppression. Returning to the imagery of the painter, artists do not seek unbending control over their materials and subject matter. Rather, they seek to manipulate their paints, brushes, medium, and painting surface in a largely subjective, yet knowledgeable, manner in order to produce an exciting result. The best corporate executives do something similar.

Authoritarian managers who seek to impose upon their managerial universes their own autocratic philosophies—their own inflexible goals and objectives along with their own martinet methodology—will have to explain a disastrous "canvas," a creative abyss. Authoritarian autocracy and creative management are mutually exclusive since the former stifles the latter. By the same token, executives who detach themselves may also have to learn to live with tragedy. Managers can no more divorce themselves from the processes they are orchestrating than painters can turn their backs on their paintings and expect them to create themselves. Yet, in corporate reality, delegation is sometimes a euphemism for abdication of responsibility. Effective management, like good painting, requires that a balance be struck between freedom and control. Too much of either will self-destruct. Good, creative management is anything but simple. It is a highly complex, utterly sophisticated effort, befitting the most sensitive manager.

Sensitivity should not be taken for weakness or indecisiveness. Quite the contrary. The creative manager must be able to render rapid, insightful decisions to capitalize on the convergence of fortuitous variables. Sensitivity here means the capacity and willingness to capitalize on options of the moment. People, machinery, money, and marketplace may all "line up" like planets in some astrological pattern. When this occurs, creative managers must seize the meaning of the moment and make it their own. Likewise the painter might suddenly be confronted with a running streak of burnt umber cutting a path through a cobalt shadow. What to do? Leave it? Eliminate it? Or bend it to serve the higher purpose of the painting? Standing before a "live" canvas is like witnessing an animated creature in formation. Painters are merged with their painting surfaces, pigments, brushes, and the symphonies of colors, values, shapes, forms, and light in their compositions. A moment's inattention can prove disastrous. The process of creating a painting is a dynamic one—one that demands concentration, involvement, and benevolent manipulation.

Ideally, management is much the same. The company—its personnel, financial and material resources, physical plants, means of communication, and transportation—is a living, vibrant canvas upon which the manager is attempting to bring into being a work of managerial art. External factors such as the marketplace may be viewed as an integral part of the process.

In today's postindustrial society, services are what make the business world tick. The professional is pivotal. The accountant, attorney, consultant, all command top dollar. The corporate ship is awash in a sea of computer printouts, legal briefs, and accounting forms, not to mention tax records, bills, market data, and advertising materials. The black-and-white world of the old industrial society has given way to the abstract universe of paper transactions and computerized money. Less and less do we see tangible products being marketed. More and more we sense the pervading presence of salespeople, brokers, agents, and other go-betweens. An army of consultants representing myriad specialties peddle their wares. The business world is no longer cut and dried, no longer easily understandable. Today's managers must be much more sophisticated than their older industrial counterparts. Today's business is both more complex and more subjective. Almost nothing is what it seems.

Modern painting—if you monitor trends since the slavish literalism of the Northern Renaissance—has followed a similar pattern. It is likely that Jan Vermeer would not have understood the sophistication of Picasso's *Guernica*. Bosch would have had a terrible time with Jackson Pollock's style, and Brueghel would not have had the wit to see the intended meaning of Monet's cathedral paintings.

One of the most unfortunate factors in today's management scene is executive turnover. "If the boss calls, get his name," is a familiar employee taunt. An artist cannot take over the painting of a previous artist and expect to make a success of it. Can you imagine a painter moving into a suddenly abandoned studio, donning the previous inhabitant's smock, picking up his or her brushes and pallette, and beginning to paint the unfinished canvas of his or her predecessor? Yet that's exactly what happens in the corporate world every day. Is it any wonder that chaos and instability often follow in the wake of such organizational traumas?

To compound the problem, we often find executives of radically different mentalities taking over positions of predecessors. Many top corporate executives, who came up through the ranks of marketing, are being replaced by accountants and attorneys. This is analogous to a Van Gogh taking over the unfinished canvas of a Constable or of a Turner taking up the brush to complete a Miró. The result is often chaotic. The managerial approach changes—from bells-and-whistles product pushing to bottom-line bean counting. All that flows from the executive suite takes on a new complexion. Continuity is lost. Wheels are rediscovered. Game plans change. Discordant notes are struck. Casualties inevitably result and, in the process of executive musical chairs, momentum is dissipated.

If an artist finds that his or her work is going badly, does it make sense that he or she should call in another artist who paints in a completely different style and ask him or her to take over the painting? Is it not better to abandon the painting and start with a fresh canvas, assuming that the work cannot be redeemed. Corporations are more likely to need new ideas than new personnel. Continuity is important. Executive work is highly complex, rather subjective, and cumulative. What is being contributed today is built upon what was accomplished yesterday. Managerial "artists" have become intimately familiar with their resources. While they may make occasional misjudgments in the use of those resources, it is likely that corrections will be made and the process proceed apace. Therefore, is it not better to allow managers their mistakes, knowing they will correct them and continue on?

Clearly this needs qualification. If it is discovered that a plumber, who knows nothing about painting, is standing in front of a canvas making an offensively blatant mess of it, should he or she be paid an artist's wage and encouraged to continue with such disastrous work? If a manager is incompetent, he or she should be removed from his or her position and placed at a level of competence.

The concrete corridors of the corporate jungle are still haunted by too many managerial dinosaurs left over from America's great industrial age. The key to successful evolution is appropriate *adaptation*. Such adaptation requires more than mere change; it involves making the *correct* changes, ones that move the company onto higher grounds of operations.

The corporate universe can be a rich canvas-in-process, one constantly coming alive with vibrant new life, one perpetually witnessing resource actualization. Or it can be a deadening, autocratic environment that is analogous to a painting rendered in bile yellow by a drill sergeant. Management, at any level, can be an exciting creative process exhilarating beyond compare, or it can be a stultifying, stress-laden chore that breaks even the best of executives. It's all a matter of hue.

9

Creative Characters: Entrepreneurs and Chief Executives

Robert Lawrence Kuhn

*Investment Banker; Senior Research Fellow, IC²
Institute, University of Texas at Austin; and Adjunct
Professor, Graduate School of Business
Administration, New York University*

Entrepreneurship is the driving energy of a new world of business, a broad-base universe of traditional organizations and innovative institutions of all sizes. The concept is no longer limited to small, start-up companies; its impact today is virtually pandemic. The widening scope of the field requires an expanded definition of the term. Entrepreneurship, to me, is the economic synthesis of human knowledge, the molding of physical substance and value out of mental form and concept. Entrepreneurship is the modern human analogue of the original Genesis creation, when chaos and void were transformed into heavens and earth. Entrepreneurship is the process that produces something from nothing. It is also exciting—the hope of the big hit, the tension of uncertain outcome, the suspense of hoped-for success. What makes entrepreneurship energizing to the individual is the fuel that empowers society and drives human progress.

The Entrepreneurial Spirit

All human beings are created equal, but only a few forge the future. We now explore the entrepreneurial mind. The excursion grafts us onto a main branch of business creativity and expresses the essence of success-ful companies. It sensitizes us to the corporate culture, catalyzing ongoing dynamism. For any top-performing firm to ride the fast track, creativity and innovation must be the driving engine. The key to stimulate creativity and fire innovation? Entrepreneurial motivation, the magnetic pull of proprietary participation. Incentive generation is vital because research and innovation are not the same thing. The former can be done on demand; the latter cannot. Research can be programmed from without; innovation must be generated from within. Research and innovation, we should stress, are not the private domain of technology-driven companies; they are essential components of all successful businesses. While large and mid-sized firms are not entrepre-neurships in structure, the best of them must be entrepreneurial in spirit. And to understand what makes these top performers tick, we must feel the pulse of the entrepreneur. (The traits are those of independent business people. They apply as well to "intrapreneurs," the new breed of corporate pioneers who work in untraditional ways within tradition organizations.)

Human beings are creatures strange. Just scribble a person's name on a contract giving legal ownership or proprietary position, and he or she will work longer hours, endure more hardships, suffer more abuse, absorb more stress, and earn less money. Why? Merely the prospect of making more money in the long run? That's part of the answer, sure, but only part. Most people would love to run their own businesses, to be their own bosses. They imagine going to work in the morning without superiors to serve or time clocks to punch. A rugged individualist is the image, a loner cutting a private path and shaping personal destiny. Of those who take the plunge, a few prosper, most fail, all struggle. And yet the glamor remains: It's the chance of a lifetime, the Great American Dream. More than dollars are involved. Personal achievement more than organizational security motivates the typical entrepreneur. The business must become the most important thing in the world. It must *be* the world, at least for a time. The sun must rise and set on the daily sales report, the monthly P&Ls, the new product introduction, the almost-working prototype. The entrepreneur must burn with the idea, be obsessed with its success, and consumed by its passion. Wholehearted commitment, monastic dedication, intense energy, great perseverance—these are the critical success ingredients. Running your own business has been compared to keeping an ever-demanding mistress content.

Entrepreneurial Characteristics

There are, of course, no cookbook recipes for entrepreneurial triumph. Add everything conventional wisdom requires, and failure is often the outcome. Leave out the commitment, dedication, energy, or perseverance, and disaster is almost surely the result. When dealing with new ventures, it is far easier to predict failure than prescribe success. Starting a new business is a life-affecting decision. It dominates every working hour and absorbs most waking ones. Research on entrepreneurs reveals some interesting, perhaps startling, characteristics. In general, independent successful business people are not necessarily the smartest (cerebral types are more interested in theory), not necessarily the best students (some had dropped out of school, some had even been thrown out), not the most stable employees (many had been fired from previous jobs), certainly not comfortable around subordinates (they only trust other entrepreneurs), and not viewers of spectator sports (they are active, not passive, and prefer to participate). Although people decide to break into business at all ages—the stories of toddler tycoons and geriatric giants are not uncommon—the early 30s is the most likely age of decision. Entrepreneurs seem to arise more from medium-sized firms than from very small or very large ones; the former may be too confining, the latter too restrictive. Many who go into business for themselves had fathers who did the same. Few entrepreneurs are ever ready to retire and fewer still like giving up the reins without a fight. All in all, an entrepreneur is one rare bird.

John Welsh, director of the Caruth Institute of Owner-Managed Business at Southern Methodist University, has identified eleven characteristics of successful entrepreneurs: (1) *Good health.* They maintain heavy work loads for protracted periods of time; they will themselves well, even those with chronic problems are sick less frequently. (2) *Basic need to control and direct.* They require freedom and authority; they enjoy creating and executing their own strategies; they are oriented toward results and consumed by achievement; attained goals are superseded by greater goals. (3) *Self-confidence.* They are relentless in pursuit of objectives as long as they are in control; they like to be held accountable; they believe that nobody can do the job better than they can. (4) *Never-ending sense of urgency.* They thrive on activity and excitement; they have high energy levels and are always directed toward accomplishing objectives. (5) *Comprehensive awareness.* They maintain constant vision of the big picture, how each event fits together; they see both forests and trees. (6) *Realistic.* They accept things as they are; they seek firsthand verification; they want to measure and be measured; they are honest and assume everyone else is also. (7) *Superior conceptual ability.* They sense relationships in the midst of complex and confused situations; they identify problems quickly and achieve solutions rapidly. (8) *Low need for status.* They focus externally, preferring praise for their businesses rather than glory for themselves; they are not embarrassed to admit ignorance; they willingly subordinate luxurious trappings of success to current business needs. (9) *Objective approach to interpersonal relationships.* They are more concerned with results than feelings; they maintain psychological distance; they eschew lines of authority; they are not good teambuilders. (10) *Sufficient emotional stability.* They have considerable self-control; they are challenged, not discouraged by setbacks; they have difficulty with personal feelings. (11) *Attracted to challenges, not risks.* They play for high stakes but prefer situations in which they can influence outcomes; they calculate risks and like odds to be interesting but not overwhelming.

Consider the relationship between the sharpness of focus and the vigor of creativity in successful entrepreneurs. Both are necessary, but neither is sufficient. Can focused energy and creative problem solving intersect, if not in the same person at least in the same firm? Extreme focus is a form of discipline, states Arthur Lipper III, chairman of *Venture* magazine and a venture capitalist. As a provider of capital, he is attracted to entrepreneurs who evince intense focus and strong self-discipline. While discipline per se does not correlate with ability, intelligence, or even integrity, it does suggest *predictability*, which Lipper stresses for investor comfort—since most venture capital surprises are unwelcome and unpleasant. Creativity, of course, is vital for the entrepreneurial process. A successful new business must do something different and better than others. Now the critical question: Are disciplined people usually creative? Are not the two traits contradictory? Do they not war against each other? Creativity requires "divergent thinking," and divergent thinking questions authority, often contemptuously, and flouts established systems and protocols. Would most traditionally disciplined people even consider ideas that, on their face, appear silly and contra-conventional? This is the paradox of the entrepreneur. "We'd all like to find super 'Patton/Picasso-like hybrids,' " says Lipper, "highly motivated, intelligent entrepreneurs who think divergently *and* are disciplined, commercial magicians who can predict cash flows accurately while walking on water."

A word of caution. Good entrepreneurs and good business people are not necessarily the same animals. There are substantial skill and personality differences between innovators on the one hand and managers on the other. Each group, of course, can produce its share of commercial successes. Indeed, some innovators make good managers, but this is often not true. To run your own show you need fire in your belly as well as brains in your head. To sustain an ongoing operation you must be skilled in organizational control and sensitive to human relations. We shouldn't get mixed up; we shouldn't blend the two together. If we become so intoxicated by the entrepreneurial side that we neglect the business side, we will be washing both good money and good ideas down the same drain.

Entrepreneurial environments are the fertile fields in which the best companies grow, and those key employees who indeed forge the future must be encouraged, protected, and secured. Whether through profit sharing, stock options, royalty rights, or personal recognition, those few must be kept. Many companies today, recognizing the need to attract and retain business innovators, are devising unusual methods of granting autonomy and giving ownership. These mechanisms are becoming an accepted part of modern corporate life—however messy the profit participations and cluttered the organizational charts.

Entrepreneurial venturing within corporations—known as intrapreneurship—is not without organizational trauma. Preserving real independence is virtually impossible. Jealousies run rampant. Simulating the high-risk, high-anxiety environment of true entrepreneurs is difficult, and withstanding 5 or more years of losses tests the fortitude and stamina of most large firms. Intrapreneurs themselves are a mixed bag: many are technical types not desirous or capable of running their own business; some come to realize how much they like the full resources and security of the mother corporation; others will never work for a "normal" company again.

Test Your EQ (Entrepreneurial Quotient)

Interested in starting your own business or managing a new corporate venture? Think you have entrepreneurial or intrapreneurial instincts? Check your EQ. Try answering the following questions:

1. *Which do I prefer, job security or personal independence?*   The entrepreneur is willing to risk abject failure—personal bankruptcy and public embarrassment—in order to play his or her own game.

2. *Is my business the most important thing in my life?*   If not, you could be in big trouble striking out on your own.

3. *Am I willing to work 60 hours a week for poor wages for long periods of time?*   You had better plan on working at least that— for a lot less pay. Work, for the entrepreneur, is its own reward.

4. *Can I take full responsibility for meeting my employees' payroll and paying my bills?*   If you answer No, you should work for someone else, not yourself.

5. *Do I like to think about business at home?*   You should if you are going into business for yourself since that is exactly what you'll be doing a lot of.

6. *Does my business product have something unique about it: some new technology to run it, some special method to make it, some different way to sell it?*   If not, you'll be forever running uphill.

7. *Do I have to be told what to do?*   If so, you need to be under a boss, not be one.

8. *How badly do I want to be my own boss?*   The answer should be "plenty bad." You have to put up with many aggravating problems for little immediate reward.

9. *Which is more important to me, achievement or power?*   A typical entrepreneur would rather market his or her own product or idea from his or her own garage than run a large corporate division from an eight-window corner office.

10. *If given a chance to go into my own business, would I hesitate?*   Most entrepreneurs wouldn't hesitate a microsecond, but, then again, most of them would fail.

Now, if you still want to start your own business but failed to meet any (or even all) of the above criteria, take heart. Entrepreneurs, remember, don't make the mold. They break it!

Chief Executive Characteristics

How to learn about companies quickly? Check out the chief executives. Imagine giving a Rorschach test to a company. "This is your next

CEO," we would say while showing a neutral picture. "Describe for me, please, his (or her) background and personality." The description evoked would give a good feeling for that company. Is the person progressive or conservative in outlook? Authoritarian or participatory in style? Dynamic or stodgy in attitude? From inside or outside the company? With what educational background? With what operational background— R&D, manufacturing, finance, marketing? The answers would be a quick read of present potential and corporate culture.

When in short order the new president of Apple was brought in from Pepsi and Atari's new chief arrived from Philip Morris, the meaning was clear. The entire industry, just 5 years old, was being transformed. Creative need had moved from technology to marketing; the home computer was now a consumer item. Pivotal issues were changing amazingly fast. The dramatic drop in price accelerated rapid public acceptance; selling computers was suddenly a marketing game, and it was no different from selling diet drinks or cigarettes. Technical specs were minor matter. Buying decisions were being controlled by buying behavior, and strategy had a new thrust: advertising appeal to end users, retail shelf space, perceived product differentiation, price point positioning, and the like. For Apple and Atari, new priorities required new skills, and new skills demanded new leaders.

Try a sample company. Check out the CEO. Is a science-based firm being run by someone other than from technical, say from finance or marketing? If so, you learn something quickly: Current priorities suggest current concerns. When the consortium of twelve high-tech companies chose Admiral Bobby Inman as president of their nascent Microelectronics and Computer Technology Corporation, they made a strong statement. Inman was one of America's most respected officers in the intelligence community, with three decades of experience getting competing agencies to work together. He was articulate and had excellent rapport in Washington (where, it was realized, help would be needed to surmount antitrust and other legal problems). When Harry Gray chose General Alexander Haig to be president of United Technologies, he had specific objectives in mind. International marketing, especially of its Pratt & Whitney jet engines and other industrial products, was a high priority. Haig had been commander of the NATO forces and was highly regarded in Europe. Inman and Haig were thoughtful choices for specific conditions.

While creativity is critical for CEOs to do their jobs, it is not so critical to *get* their jobs. Thus the paradox: Companies need creative CEOs, but boards do not make creativity a prime criterion for selecting CEOs. Gerard Roche, chairman of Heidrick & Struggles (a leading executive search firm), states, "In my 21 years of looking for major company

CEOs, I have never been asked, first and foremost, to find a creator/ innovator." The key, according to Roche (who has placed presidents at Apple Computer, CBS, RCA, GTE, and Allied among others), is an outstanding track record in profit-center line management—superb bottom-line performance. Functional area, industry experience, and educational background vary according to search. Breadth, flexibility, and adaptability are important. Roche highlights human sensitivity, communication skills, value structure, vision, and risk taking. Creativity and innovation, says Roche, are involved in all characteristics mentioned, including function and industry. When companies want someone from finance, for example, they want a person who has evinced creativity and innovation in his or her financial career. This is also true for marketing, manufacturing, mergers and acquisitions, and so on. But to isolate creativity and innovation as a separate requirement just does not happen.

Vision and risk taking, to be sure, are products of creativity. CEO selection committees seek candidates with an eye, ear, and nose for future trends. Where will the market be in 10 years, and how will our products (and/or services) be positioned for maximum competitive advantage? Search committees want a leader with a sense for what will be happening in the industrial environment in which the firm functions. They want a visionary who can look over the horizon, seeing beyond upcoming earnings reports. Risk taking, as well, is essential for turning innovative ideas into revenues and profits. One cannot be a CEO, according to Roche, and be afraid to take a foot off first base while looking to steal second. Few search committees seek a cautious conservative to direct their destinies. In fact, entrepreneurial thinking has been gaining greater weight in the selection process. Twenty years ago, Jack Welch could not have become CEO of General Electric nor Ed Hennesey the head of Allied-Signal. But today, such dynamic, daring creativity has become essential for corporate leadership. Roche likes Plato's description of creative people—not according to the fruits of their labor, but according to their effect on reality.

Bibliography

Smilor, Raymond and Robert Lawrence Kuhn: *Corporate Creativity: Robust Companies and the Entrepreneurial Spirit*, Praeger, New York, 1984.
Kuhn, Robert Lawrence: *To Flourish Among Giants: Creative Management for Mid-Sized Firms*, John Wiley, New York, 1985.

PART 2:

Stimulating the Creative Process

Making Strange and Making Sense

How do managers encourage creativity and innovation in their companies? What mechanisms to apply, techniques to try, methods to use? Experts have accumulated skill and experience based on experimental research and practical application. Helping organizations stimulate creative and innovative management has become a major business, virtually a new industry. Several consulting companies and research institutes specialize in understanding and enhancing creativity, and we present leaders in the field strutting their stuff. Stimulating creativity means "multiplying options." How to do it? By breaking bonds, shedding constraints, twisting common lines of thinking. "Make the familiar strange and the strange familiar" is Synectics' philosophy. "Going wild out on the fringes" is what happens when Innotech's diverse "BrainBankers" come together. In Part 2 we examine attitudes and approaches for augmenting corporate creativity: triggering new ideas, designing new products, solving thorny problems. We avoid "innovation death," and wonder whether religion, of all things, can teach business a thing or two. (You'll find the latter, linking personal meaning and company mission, a bit unusual.) Techniques for stimulating creativity are both fascinating and disturbing, invigorating and annoying, expanding and disorienting. Our contributors present many such techniques. Some seem sensible; some sound silly. All have worked for some; only some will work for all. How to choose? See the full offerings and experiment. But do not choose up front. It is impossible to decide in advance which technique(s) will work for your organization. The business of creativity, remember, is elusive and unpredictable. So play the field—and enjoy it.

10

Creativity in Problem Solving and Planning

Russell L. Ackoff

Anheuser-Busch Professor of Management Science,
The Wharton School, University of Pennsylvania

Elsa Vergara

Assistant Administrator for Planning,
Phoebe Putney Hospital

The accelerating rate of change is accompanied by a corresponding rate of obsolescence. An increasing number of problems have few or no precedents; hence there is a decreasing number of opportunities to solve them effectively in familiar ways. The greater the need for new ways of doing things, the greater the need for creativity. This attribute is in short supply and is inequitably distributed. All this has led to an increase in the amount of reflection, research, and writing directed at increasing its availability and improving its distribution.

This chapter has three parts. First, we consider what has been written about the nature of creativity. Second, we review a number of processes that have been proposed for enhancing creativity in problem solving and planning. Third, we present an operationally meaningful

definition of the concept and relate the creativity-enhancing processes
to it.

On the Nature of Creativity

There is no universally accepted meaning of creativity. There are well
over 100 definitions available in the literature. Furthermore, "creativity" has many synonyms; for example, "productive thinking," "divergent thinking," "originality," "imagination," and "lateral thinking."
As might be expected, definitions differ in some respects and are alike
in others. They can be divided into two main categories: origin oriented
and process oriented.

Origin-Oriented Approaches

Psychoanalysts and certain psychologists have been more concerned
with the origins of creativity than with what it is. For example, Freud
held that creativity arises from conflict within an individual. It is
produced when the energy generated by unfulfilled (and unfulfillable)
wishes involving forbidden primitive goals is diverted to goals that are
socially acceptable. The creative process, he claimed, involved external-
izing the internal products of imagination through the interaction of
primitive and more mature types of thinking. He distinguished between
a primary thought process characterized as generally unconscious,
random, impulsive, and not reality oriented and a secondary process
that is logical, purposeful, and reality oriented. The creative person is
one who can use the primary type of thinking (such as fantasy and
daydreaming) without being dominated by it and the secondary process
to convert the output of the primary to realizable proposals.

Humanistic psychologists such as Fromm, Maslow, and Rogers inverted the psychoanalytic perspective and claim that creativity arises
when there is no conflict within an individual. For them it is a product
of the interaction of healthy conflict-free individuals and healthy
enabling environments. The creative process is thus taken to involve the
release of natural creative potential through the removal of inhibitions
from individuals and obstructions from their environments.

Psychometricians like Guilford also take creativity to be a natural
potential that is realized under appropriate environmental conditions.
They believe, however, that each individual's potential is limited by
genetic endowment. Thus they maintain that a person's "creative
potential" can be measured by standardized tests. As in psychoanalytic

theory, the creative process is said to derive from the interaction of two contrasting types of thinking: "divergent," which converts information into a variety of unconventional alternatives, and "convergent," which aims at unique or conventional outcomes.

Process-Oriented Approaches

In contrast to the origin-oriented approach, Associationists, Gestalt psychologists, and those who take what might be called an information-processing approach focus on the thought process. Although they emphasize different aspects of this process, they all view creativity as a property of it that can be acquired and improved through instruction and practice.

The Associationists.   Here, thinking involves the exploration and evaluation of responses that are habitually associated with (linked to) the type of problem in hand. Therefore, the three elements in an Associationist theory of thinking are: the stimulus (a particular problematic situation), the response (a particular problem-solving situation), and the (mental) associations between them. The response may vary in strength because some associations are stronger (less remote, more familiar) than others. Then creativity is taken to be an association of remote responses with a particular problematic situation that produces a new response to it. Therefore, individual creativity is a function of an ability to invoke and explore remote associations directly or through mediating ideas (e.g., analogies) in selecting a response to a problem.

Gestalt.   Whereas the Associationists deal primarily with the "reproductive" or habitual aspects of thinking, Gestalt psychologists focus on "productive" or novel ways of thinking about a problematic situation. According to Wertheimer, thinking proceeds neither by piecemeal logical operations nor by disconnected arbitrary associations but by successively more determinate restructuring of the whole situation.

What goes on in the formulation of a problem and a response to it? Dunker identifies three major characteristics of the problem-solving process: (1) The problem solver considers the general nature of the problem, examines its requirements, and tries to identify a direction in which he or she might find a solution, (2) he or she tries to identify the functional requirements of a solution to the problem, and (3) he or she seeks a specific solution that meets these functional requirements. Dunker suggests that most problem solving moves from the general to the specific. He noted that when people either reached a tentative solution that did not meet the requirements as then formulated or were unable to make further progress, they were likely to retrace their steps, moving back either to reconsider a functional requirement previously formulated or even further back to a more general aspect of the problem.

Maier tried to show how creativity enters the problem-solving process. The way a problem is formulated, he claimed, determines which aspects of past experience and the current environment are selected as relevant and how they are combined into new and meaningful directions. He used the concept "direction" to explain the reorganization of the elements of a problematic situation. Something must happen to produce a change in direction. Failure to solve a problem is not enough because failures are often repeated. It is by reformulating a problem, Maier argued, that redirection occurs. In selecting a new direction the problematic situation is "fragmented" ("reformulated" or "reorganized" according to Wertheimer) in a new way. Redirection involves breaking perceptual or experiential constraints. By doing so, new objectives and courses of action are discovered. Thus creativity lies in the ability to redirect a line of thought taken in solving a problem. Because redirection is cognitive, it emerges from a specific problematic situation and it can be changed by instruction. Therefore, it can be learned.

Information Processing.   This approach involves the development of information processing models of thinking, many of which have been programmed for and tested on computers. Newell, Shaw, and Simon concluded that problem solving is creative to the extent that one or more of the following conditions are satisfied: (1) The product of the thinking is novel and valuable, (2) the thinking is unconventional, (3) it requires high motivation and persistence "taking place over a considerable span of time . . . or at high intensity," and (4) the initial problem is vague and ill-defined requiring the problem solver to formulate the problem itself.

Procedures for Enhancing Creativity

The following procedures for enhancing individual and collective creativity are, we believe, among the best known and most widely used.

Synectics

Synectics is a procedure developed by Gordon who defined it as "the joining together of different and apparently irrelevant elements" to resolve a paradox or a problem. It is based on the use of analogies. In such thinking similarities between apparently different things are sought. Metaphors are its products. A metaphor asserts the equivalence of two concepts taken from different domains. It does so by identifying, implicitly or explicitly, properties that both have. The creative use of metaphor arises from the invention or discovery of links between two previously disconnected concepts and the maintenance of the tension produced by their juxtaposition long enough to develop a new perspective on the problem.

The process of Synectics begins by identifying the "essence" of the problematic situation. The essence is a functional description of a desired outcome in which the conflicts or paradoxes in the problem are condensed. Once the essence is formulated, it is put into the form of a question that captures in general terms the uniqueness of the situation. For example, the essence of a problem in which one person wants to read in a quiet setting and another wants to listen to music at a high volume in the same setting at the same time could be: How can a loud silence be produced? Once the essence has been formulated as a question, a metaphor is sought that addresses it. For example: "A bullet that embeds itself in one body cannot strike another." This metaphor may suggest that the person who wants to listen to music at a high volume use a headset.

In order to create greater distance from the problematic situation, far-from-obvious metaphors are sought; for example, if the problem concerns hearing, an effort might be made to find a metaphor that involves sight or touch. In this way, Synecticians claim, assumptions concerning what constitutes a possible solution are broken.

The Synectic procedure can be outlined as follows: (1) *Essence.* Present the problem. Analyze the problem. Formulate the essence. (2) *Metaphor.* Reformulate the essence as an evocative question. Find a metaphor that "answers" the question. Analyze the analogy. (3) *Solution.* Find the functional requirements of a solution by force fitting the analogy to the problem. Find solution. This process can be repeated if necessary. (See Chapter 14.)

Brainstorming

Brainstorming is probably the best known and most widely used procedure for stimulating creativity in problem solving. It was invented by Osborn "for the sole purpose of producing checklists of ideas" that can be used in developing a solution to a problem. The technique is directed to generating unconventional ideas by suppressing the common tendency to criticize or reject them summarily. Osborn tried to separate idea evaluation from idea generation because he believed that if evaluation comes early, it reduces the number and quality of the ideas produced. Therefore, in a brainstorming session no criticism is permitted, and the free-wheeling generation of a large number of ideas and their combination and development are encouraged.

Brainstorming is based on the associative premise that the greater the number of associations, the less stereotyped and more creative the ideas of how to solve a problem will be. The procedure can be outlined as follows: (1) *Preparation.*   Select the participants and circulate a preliminary statement of the problem. (2) *Brainstorming.*   Conduct a warm-up session with simple unrelated problems. Present the relevant problem and Brainstorming rules. Generate and record ideas using checklists and other techniques if necessary. (3) *Evaluation.*   Evaluate the ideas relative to the problem.

Brainstorming has been embedded in a program at the Creative Problem Solving Institute. The following is a description of the program that was taken from Noller: (1) *Fact-finding.*   Gathering and analyzing data in preparation for defining the problem. (2) *Problem-finding.*   Analyzing problematic areas in order to define the problem. (3) *Idea-finding.*   Thinking up and developing various leads to solutions. (4) *Criteria-finding.*   Generating criteria for evaluating solutions. (5) *Solution-finding.*   Evaluating potential solutions using defined criteria. (6) *Acceptance-finding.*   Adoption—developing a plan of action and implementing it.

TKJ

TKJ is a group problem-solving technique developed by Kobayashi and Kawakita. It works from a set of facts generated by participants. These facts have to satisfy three conditions: (1) They should be relevant to the problem in hand, (2) they should be objectively verifiable, and (3) they should be important.

Sets of related facts are formed out of separately generated facts. Each set is given a name that all participants agree reflects its essence. This "fact essence" must satisfy the following conditions: (1) It can be verified by using the facts from which it was generated, (2) it should not be too general, and (3) it should not be a simple aggregation of the facts making up the subset.

This compacting process is repeated, forming sets of the sets and formulating their essences, until one set and its essence are obtained. The final set should encompass all the facts and fact essences previously formulated.

The solution process is similar to that used in compacting the facts, but it starts with suggested solutions to the previously defined problem. The individually proposed solutions are required to involve concrete actions that can be carried out in the near future. They are combined until one set is obtained whose essence encompasses all the previously generated solutions.

TKJ can be outlined as follows: (1) *Problem definition.* Identify the area of concern. Participants write on cards facts that are related to this area, one fact per card. Collect cards. Distribute cards so no person receives his or her own cards. Read entry on one card out loud. Participants select facts on their cards that relate to the fact that was read, thus building a set. Name the set so as to reflect its essence and put on a name-set card. Continue until all facts have been placed in a set. Continue with set-name cards until one all-inclusive set is obtained. (2) *Problem solution.* Write proposed solutions on cards, one per card. Collect cards. Distribute cards so no person receives his or own cards. Read entry on one card out loud. Participants select solutions on their cards that relate to the one read, thus building a set. Name the set and place it on a set-name card. Continue until all proposed solutions have been placed in a set; then continue until one all-inclusive set is obtained.

TKJ evokes different perspectives and experiences and tries to synthesize them into a definition of a solution to a problem that is acceptable to all participants. It places as much emphasis on problem formulation as it does on problem solving. Problematic situations "must be formulated in creative ways if they are to be moved to creative solutions" (Getzels).

Unlike Synectics, Brainstorming, and TKJ, the following three processes were not developed primarily to enhance creativity but, more generally, to improve the quality of problem solving and planning. Nevertheless, when used, they tend to stimulate creativity.

The Search Conference

F. E. Emery developed the Search Conference to enable organizations to find more effective ways of adapting to changes in their environments. Its purpose is to help a system's stakeholders develop shared perceptions of their current situation, a desired future, and how to get there. The stakeholders draw on their experiences and values and pool their knowledge of the system and its environment. Together they identify trends that are emerging in their environment and formulate new adaptive responses to them. They are encouraged to consider a wide variety of possible futures and ways of bringing them about.

There are three characteristics of a Search Conference that appear to enhance creativity. First, it focuses on desired futures rather than on current constraints. Second, it encourages participants to look at familiar problems from a new and broader perspective by starting with consideration of the environment rather than the system. Finally, it forces stakeholders to confront and synthesize conflicting views into a mutually satisfying design of and plan for the future.

The Dialectical Approach

The dialectical approach to problem solving is used to identify the assumptions on which such a plan can be based. It employs two research teams, both with access to the same data. These teams deliberately work out different and conflicting solutions to the same problem. A confrontation between these two teams and their solution reveals the assumptions underlying each. Then a creative synthesis of the opposing proposals is sought.

As with many competitive situations, the dialectical approach is dramatic. Each party in the culminating debate does everything to convince a third party, the decision maker, that one formulation of the problem and the solution derived from it are better than the others. After witnessing this confrontation, the third party reformulates the problem and finds its own solution drawing assumptions from both of the opposing viewpoints. The dialectical procedure reveals the arbitrariness of assumptions and exposes their consequences. It focuses on inferences drawn from data and shows that the same data can be interpreted in different ways depending on the assumptions made.

The following steps are involved in the dialectical process: (1) *Preparation.* The decision maker forms two (or more) teams that are provided with the same statement of objectives and set of relevant data. Each team develops a solution that is deliberately designed to conflict with the other's. It formulates the assumptions as explicitly as it can. (2) *Confrontation.* Each team presents its solution to the decision maker in the presence of the other team and defends its solution as strongly as it can. After the presentations each team attacks the other trying to weaken its position and strengthen its own. The decision maker may question either team at any time. (3) *Synthesis.* The decision maker formulates his or her own solution using the inputs provided by the two opposing teams and makes explicit the assumptions on which this "third" solution is based so they can be monitored when the solution is implemented.

Idealized Design

The use of idealized design or redesign of a system (e.g., strategy, new product, etc.) and its environment in solving complex problems or in planning was developed by Ackoff. Such a design is one that the stakeholders in the system would have *now* if they could have any system they wanted. The design must be technologically feasible and operationally viable—that is, capable of surviving if it were brought into existence—but it is prepared without regard to whether or how it can be realized. Additionally, the system should be designed to be capable of rapid and effective learning and adaptation. The product of such a design is not a utopian or ideal system because it is capable of being improved and improving itself; rather, it is the best ideal-seeking system that its designers can conceive.

The idealized-design process involves three steps: (1) Selecting a mission—a general purpose of the system to be designed that encompasses its relationship to the environment and to its stakeholders. (2) Specifying desired properties of the design—a comprehensive list of the functional properties that the system should have and to which the stakeholders agree. (3) Designing the system—determining how the specified properties should be obtained.

The resulting design should cover every aspect of the system: its social and technical processes, its organization, management system, inputs, outputs, and so on. Normally two versions of the design are prepared: one constrained (i.e., without changing the environment) and one unconstrained (i.e., changing the environment).

The process of idealization releases participants from even unconsciously self-imposed constraints because it eliminates consideration of feasibility. When such a design is completed, there is usually general recognition among participants that most of it is in fact obtainable and, therefore, that they themselves are the principal obstructions to the future they most desire.

Other Techniques

There are a number of techniques that take the form of rules-of-thumb, guidelines, tricks, or gimmicks, all directed at enhancing creativity, usually in some restricted way. They fall into the following three major categories: (1) ways of transforming ordinary ideas into ones that are less ordinary, (2) ways of finding new relationships between familiar things, and (3) ways of restructuring existing data into new patterns.

Transforming Ideas.   Perhaps the simplest of all proposals for stimulating creativity consists of using a checklist in the hope that some of its items will trigger new thinking. Some checklists are related to specific classes of problems. Others are quite general and can be applied to a wide variety of problematic situations, for example, Osborn's, which contains nine questions intended to alter an existing idea, object, or product: Put to other uses? Adapt? Modify? Magnify? Minify? Substitute? Rearrange? Reverse? Combine?

Searching for New Relationships.   Matrices have been used to explore the effect of altering the relationships between parts of a problematic situation. Attributes of an idea, object, or product can be listed and related to one another to facilitate systematic search for variations in overall design (Crawford). In some cases, attributes or elements are brought into forced relationships with each other in order to generate associations that suggest possible changes in a focal attribute (Whiting). Morphological analysis (Allen, Goldner) combines attribute listing and force fitting into a procedure for exploring new combinations within a defined solution space. A design problem is decomposed into a set of necessary functions and a full range of alternative means are generated for each function. Various combinations of these means are then explored to provide a set of alternative overall designs. (See Chapter 13.)

Restructuring Data into Alternative Patterns.   De Bono coined the term "lateral thinking" to describe the process of restructuring conceptual patterns and provoking new ones. He does not provide a procedure for such thinking but rather a collection of exercises designed to help a problem solver look at familiar data in new ways. His suggestions include techniques for (1) generating alternative ways of describing an issue, (2) making assumptions explicit and challenging them, (3) identifying the use of recurring themes and modifying them, (4) identifying the use of cliches and replacing them, (5) identifying recurring obstacles and circumventing them, (6) consciously directing attention to areas not previously noticed, (7) identifying those aspects of a situation first attended to and reentering from a different point, (8) identifying different ways of decomposing and recomposing a problematic situation, and (9) using a random stimulus to bring new elements into a problematic situation.

Toward an Operationally Meaningful Synthesis

Although there is considerable disagreement about the origins of creativity, most agree that it consists of the ability to break through constraints imposed by habit and tradition so as to find "new" solutions to problems. We have defined *creativity* in problem solving and planning as the *ability of a subject in a choice situation to modify self-imposed constraints so as to enable him or her to select courses of action or produce outcomes that he or she would not otherwise select or produce and that are more efficient or valuable than any he or she would otherwise have chosen.*

From this definition of creativity, it is clear that procedures for enhancing it must either prevent the self-imposition of constraining assumptions or facilitate their removal. Consider in this light the six procedures discussed in the last section.

First, note that they are all group processes. Since different members of a group often make different constraining assumptions, these are likely to be exposed in discussions of what appear to be feasible alternatives to different members. Once exposed, they are subject to questioning. This process is augmented in the *dialectical process* in which two or more groups deliberately set up to oppose each other and make a strong case for their conflicting proposals. Their confrontation makes the third party aware of the different assumptions made by the opposing teams and of the possibility of choosing between them.

By suspending evaluation and encouraging development and defense of unconventional ideas, *Brainstorming* relaxes self-imposed constraints, often without raising them to consciousness. If a creative idea is proposed that appeals to the group, the group seldom "goes back" and imposes constraining assumptions on it. The group tries to show how it can be made to work rather than why it cannot.

Synectics, by moving from one universe of discourse to another, looks for solutions in a domain other than the one occupied by the problem at hand, one that may not be as restricted by self-imposed constraints as the relevant domain. The move back from the irrelevant analogous domain to the relevant one is carried out in such a way as to reduce the chances of adopting those constraining assumptions normally imposed on the relevant domain.

TKJ paradoxically reverses the problem-solving process as described by Dunker by moving from the particular to the general—from particular facts to a general formulation of the problem, not the other way around. It is based on the assumption that in doing so fewer constraints are adopted than in movement from the general to the particular.

The *Search Conference* is a group process that involves enlarging the context of the problem and thus brings into question assumptions that might otherwise be made as to what constraints are imposed by the environment. Open disagreement and discussion of what the environment will and will not permit lead to identification of what are really self-imposed constraints and thus make their removal possible.

Idealization is based on the assumption that most self-imposed constraints derive from consideration of feasibility. It creates a task in which any consideration of feasibility other than technical is removed. Furthermore, by focusing on redesign of a system and its environment it enlarges the scope of what can be done from the usually constrained consideration of what the existing system and its environment can do if they are not changed. The process also overcomes the constraints that derive from reluctance to change because the exercise is engaged in without any commitment to produce change. In sets up a game-like situation in which the process is more play than work. Finally, the desirability of the finished design tends to make those who produced it try to remove obstructions to its realization, including self-imposed constraints.

Bibliography

Ackoff, R. L.: *The Art of Problem Solving*, John Wiley, New York, 1978.
Ackoff, R. L., and F. Emery: *On Purposeful Systems*, Aldine, Chicago, 1972.
Adams, J.: *Conceptual Blockbusting*, Stanford, 1976.
Allen, M. S.: *The Allen Morphologizer*, Prentice-Hall, Englewood Cliffs, NJ, 1962.
Crawford, R. P.: *The Techniques of Creative Thinking*, Hawthorn, New York, 1954.
Davis, G. A.: *Psychology of Problem Solving*, Basic Books, New York, 1973.
de Bono, E.: *The Mechanism of Mind*, Penguin, Baltimore, 1969.
_____ *Lateral Thinking*, Harper & Row, New York, 1973.
Dunker, K.: "On Problem Solving," *Psychological Monographs*, vol. 58, 1945.
Emery, M., and F. Emery: "Searching for New Directions, in New Ways for New Times," in J. W. Sutherland (ed.), *Management Handbook for Public Administrators*, Van Nostrand, New York, 1978.
Festinger, L.: *A Theory of Cognitive Dissonance*, Row, Peterson Co., Evanston, IL, 1957.
Freud, S.: "Creative Writers and Day Dreaming," in P. E. Vernon (ed.), *Creativity*, Penguin, Baltimore, 1970.
Fromm, E.: "The Creative Attitude," in H. Anderson (ed.), *Creativity and Its Cultivation*, Harper & Row, New York, 1959.
Getzels, J. W., and M. Csikszentmihalyi: "Discovery-Oriented Behavior and Originality of Creative Products," *J. Personality and Social Psychology*, vol. 19, 1971, pp. 47–52.
Goldner, B. B.: *The Strategy of Creative Thinking*, Prentice-Hall, Englewood Cliffs, NJ, 1962.
Gordon, W.: *Synectics*, Harper & Row, New York, 1961.

Guilford, J. P.: *Way Beyond the I.Q.*, Creative Education Foundation, Buffalo, NY, 1977.

Kobayashi, S.: *Creative Management*, American Management Association, New York, 1971.

Koestler, A.: *The Act of Creation*, Dell, New York, 1973.

Laing, R. D.: *Knots*, Pantheon, New York, 1970.

Maier, N. R.: *Problem Solving and Creativity*, Brooks/Cole, Belmont, CA 1970.

Maslow, A. H.: "Creativity in Self-Actualizing People," in H. Anderson (ed.), *Creativity and its Cultivation*, Harper & Row, New York, 1959.

Mason, R. O.: "Dialectics in Decision Making: a Study in the Use of Counterplanning and Structured Debate in Management Information Systems," Ph.D. thesis, University of California at Berkeley.

Mintzberg, H.: "Patterns in Strategy Formation," *Management Science*, vol. 24, 1978, pp. 934–948.

Newell, A., and H. A. Simon, *Human Problem Solving*, Prentice-Hall, Englewood Cliffs, NJ, 1972.

Newell, A., J. C. Shaw, and H. A. Simon: "The Process of Creative Thinking," in H. E. Gruber et al. (eds.), *Contemporary Approaches to Creative Thinking*, Atherton Press, New York, 1962.

Noller, R. B., S. J. Parnes, and H. M. Biondi: *Creative Actionbook*, Scribner's, New York, 1976.

Osborn, A. F.: *Applied Imagination*, Scribner's, New York, 1963.

Parnes, S. J., R. B. Noller, and A. M. Biondi: *Guide to Creative Action*, Scribner's, New York, 1977.

Prince, G. M.: *The Practice of Creativity*, Harper & Row, New York, 1970.

Reitman, W. R.: *Cognition and Thought: An Information Processing Approach*, John Wiley, New York, 1964.

Rogers, C. R.: "Towards a Theory of Creativity," in P. E. Vernon (ed.), *Creativity*, Penguin, Baltimore, 1970.

Synectics, *Making It Strange*, Harper & Row, New York, 1968.

Wertheimer, M.: *Productive Thinking*, Harper & Row, New York, 1959.

Wheelwright, S.: An Analysis of Strategic Planning as Creative Problem Solving Process, Ph.D. thesis, Stanford University, CA, 1970.

Whiting, C. S.: *Creative Thinking*, Reinhold, 1959.

Note: This chapter has been derived by the editor from Russell L. Ackoff and Elsa Vergara, "Creativity in Problem Solving and Planning: A Review," *European Journal of Operational Research* ,Vol. 7, 1981, pp. 1–12.

11

Change-Master Skills: What It Takes to Be Creative

Rosabeth Moss Kanter

Class of 1960 Professor of Business Administration, Harvard University

Corporate entrepreneurs are people who envision something new and make it work. They don't start businesses; they improve them. Being a corporate entrepreneur, what I call a "change master," is much more challenging and fun than being a nonentrepreneur. It requires more of a person, but it gives back more self-satisfaction.

Change masters journey through three stages. First they formulate and sell a vision. Next they find the power to advance their idea. Finally they must maintain the momentum. I discovered the skills of change masters by researching hundreds of managers across more than a half-dozen industries. I put change-master skills in two categories: first, the personal or individual skills and second, the interpersonal ones, how the person manages others.

Kaleidoscope Thinking

The first essential skill is a style of thinking, or a way of approaching the world, that I have come to call "kaleidoscope thinking." The metaphor of a kaleidoscope is a good way of capturing exactly what innovators, or leaders of change, do. A kaleidoscope is a device for seeing patterns. It takes a set of fragments and it forms them into a pattern. But when the kaleidoscope is twisted, shaken, or approached from a new angle, the exact same fragments form an entirely different pattern. Kaleidoscope thinking, then, involves taking an existing array of data, phenomena, or assumptions and being able to twist them, shake them, look at them upside down or from another angle or from a new direction—thus permitting an entirely new pattern and consequent set of actions to take place.

Change masters, or the makers of change, are not necessarily more creative than other people, but they are more willing to move beyond received wisdom to approach problems from new angles. This is a classic finding in the history of any kind of innovation—that it takes challenges to beliefs to achieve a breakthrough. A large proportion of important innovations are brought about by people who step outside of conventional categories or traditional assumptions. They are often *not* the experts or the specialists. Rather they are "boundary crossers" or "generalists" who move across fields or among sectors, who bypass what everybody else is looking at to find possibilities for change.

Kaleidoscope thinking begins with experience not associated with one's own field or department. Moving outside for broadened perspectives was the common foundation of every innovation I studied. A woman change master at a computer company began an important project this way. She got her assignment, and the first thing she did was leave her area and roam around the rest of the organization, talking it over with nearly everyone she could find, regardless of field, looking for new directions, new perspectives, new ways to approach it—so what she could bring back would be new and creative. She did not start with what she already knew. She started with what other people could bring her; she crossed boundaries to do that.

This is how many important changes have been seeded. For example, frozen vegetables were invented by Clarence Birdseye, owner of a produce business at the turn of the century. The conventional wisdom of his time, like that of our time, held that the best way to run a business (or a department) was to "mind the store"—managing one's field and only one's field, watching it like a microscope image, getting better and better at knowing and doing just one thing. But Birdseye was an adventurer, and so, like many change masters, he wandered away from his store and his scope; he passed beyond his territory, quite literally, and went on expeditions. On one of his adventure trips, fur-trapping in Labrador, he discovered that fish caught in ice could be eaten much later with no ill effects. He brought that idea back and transformed his business from a local produce store to the beginnings of national distribution.

Organizations that seek innovation ought to learn from this kind of experience: allow people to move outside of the orthodoxy of an area, to mix and match, to shake up assumptions. One chief executive believed that such thinking was so important to his organization's success in a high-tech field that he staged a highly imaginative top management meeting. He took his top fifty officers to a resort to hold their annual financial planning meeting. Though it started out just like their usual meetings, he wanted this year to be different. He was concerned that they were getting stuck in a rut and that he was not getting much creative thinking, though his company needed innovation for survival. He made the point symbolically. Halfway through his talk, the meeting was suddenly interrupted by a cadre of men dressed as prison guards; these rather realistic toughs burst into the room, grabbed everybody there, and took them out to a set of waiting helicopters, which flew the bewildered executives off to a second meeting site. "Now we'll begin again," said the CEO, "and we will bury all the thinking we were doing in the last meeting and approach everything from a new angle. I want new thinking out of you." He continued to punctuate the meeting with sets of surprises, like a parade of elephants on the beach. First there was a small elephant and it had the natural financial goal painted on its side, then along came a bigger elephant with a bigger number, and then a huge elephant with a huge number, and he said, "Go for it! Stretch your thinking! " The symbolism of the whole meeting was to stretch, move outside, challenge assumptions, twist that kaleidoscope.

Communicating Visions

The second conclusion I drew about change masters' individual skills was their ability to articulate and communicate *visions*. New and creative ideas and better ways to do things come not from *systems* but from *people*. People leading other people in untried directions are the true shapers of change. So behind every change, every innovation, every development project, there must be somebody with a vision who has been able to communicate and sell that vision to somebody else (even when the change begins with an assignment, not a self-directed initiative).

Though innovation is a very positive term, it is important to remember that any *particular* innovation is only positive in retrospect, *after* it has worked. Before that, because change by definition is something no one has seen yet (despite models that may exist elsewhere), it has to be taken at least partially on faith. For example, why a continuing education program now? Why use funds to develop a new product when there are so many already on the market? Why take the risk of decentralizing the accounting office? In short, unless there is somebody behind the idea willing to take the risk of speaking up for it, the idea will evaporate and disappear. One reason there is so little change in most traditional bureaucratic organizations, I argue, is that they have conditioned out of people the willingness to stand up for a new idea. Instead, people learn to back off at the first sign that somebody might disapprove.

This second change-master skill can be called "leadership." Martin Luther King's famous speech in the March on Washington personified this as "I have a dream." He didn't say, "I have a few ideas; there seem to be some problems out there. Maybe if we set up a few *committees*, something will happen." But when I see managers present their ideas in just this sort of well-if-you-don't-like-it-that's-all-right way, I can understand why so many are so ineffective in getting new things done. Each innovation, shift, or novel project—even the noncontroversial and apparently desirable ones—requires somebody getting behind it and pushing, especially when things get difficult, as they always do when change is involved. This kind of leadership involves communication plus conviction, both energized by commitment.

Persistence

Leaders of innovation persist in an idea; they keep at it. When I examined the difference between success and failure in change projects or development efforts, I found that one major difference was simply *time*—staying with it long enough to make it work.

To some extent, *everything* looks like a failure in the middle. There is a point or points in the history of every new project, every original effort, every fresh idea when discouragements mount, and the temptation to stop is great. But pulling out at that moment automatically yields failure. There is nothing to show just yet. The inevitable problems, roadblocks, and low spots when enthusiasm wanes are the critical hurdles in achieving a healthy return on the investment of time and resources. Without persistence, important changes never happen.

In large organizations, the number of roadblocks and low points can seem infinite, particularly when something new is being tried. There are not only all the technical details of how the new program is going to work, but there are also all the political difficulties of handling the critics. Naysayers are more likely to surface in the middle than at the beginning because now the project is more of a threat, more a challenge to their own perceived status. There is little incentive for critics to tie up political capital by confronting the project until it looks like it actually may happen. This is a reality of organizational life.

At one major consumer products company, this phenomenon was demonstrated all too well. Today, the company has a highly successful new product on every supermarket's shelves. But when this project was in the development stage, it was known as "Project Lazarus" because it "rose from the dead" so many times. Four times people at higher levels tried to kill it off, and four times the people working on it came back and fought for it, argued for it, provided justification and evidence for why it should continue: "Just give us a little more time; we know we can make it work."

Every organization has examples like this one. If the team had stopped, the effort would have been a total loss—confirming, in a circular way, the critics. But arguing for the additional time and money and confronting the critics transformed a potential failure into a ringing success.

Coalition Building

In addition to the personal skills of change masters, interpersonal and organizational skills are also required. The first of these is coalition building. At the point at which there is a creative idea, with someone with vision behind it willing to persist, it still has to be sold to other people in the organization in order to get implemented.

Though the literature on organizational politics has emphasized one-on-one relationship building, my research moves the emphasis to the coalition. What makes people effective in organizations is the ability to create a whole set of backers and supporters, specifically for projects of innovative activities, that helps lend the power necessary to vitalize those activities. In this sense entrepreneurs inside a corporation are just like entrepreneurs outside: They have to find bankers, people who will provide the funds; they have to find information sources; and they have to find legitimacy and support, people who will champion the project to other powerholders.

Multiple, rather than single, sponsors and backers make the difference. An attractive young woman who now holds one of the top six positions in an American corporation began as assistant to the chairman and was subjected to many innuendoes about their relationship. But she proved to be a highly effective change master in her organization, responsible for many successful new projects, because she is a superb coalition builder, drawing hardly at all on her relationship with the CEO. She brings others into projects; she works with peers and people below to make them feel included. She creates multiple relationships and teams around her by giving people "stakes" in each project, solidified by promised personal benefit. Because of her coalition-building skills, she led successful change projects that in turn brought her recognition and early promotions.

Coalitions are especially important when change is needed because innovation—new projects or developments—generally involve going outside of current sources of organizational power. My research found that managers who wanted to innovate, or try something new, almost invariably needed more resources, information, and support than they had. They often needed money above and beyond their budget (though sometimes not much)—because usually their budget was for the routine, things they were doing, and if they wanted to do something novel, they had to find extra funds. They also needed higher levels of support because innovations sometimes interfere with ongoing things in an organization. Change is often resisted because it can be a nuisance and an interference; it requires other people to stop what they are doing or redirect their thinking. And new efforts also tend to require special information, more data, new sources of knowledge. Thus, the change masters I studied *had* to build a coalition in order to find the backers or "power sources" to provide information, support, and resources for their projects.

Coalition building not only attracts needed power to a project, it also tends to help guarantee success. Once others are brought in and contribute their money or support to a project, they also have a stake in making it work. Their reputations (and egos) are now on the line. As a result, the innovator is not out there all by herself, trying to convince a reluctant organization to do something. There are now other people to serve as cheerleaders.

This process of coalition building is so well-known that some companies have invented their own language around it. They call the whole process one of getting "buy-in" or generating wider "ownership" of a project from key supporters. First is a low-key step of gathering intelligence and planting seeds—just finding out where people stand and leaving behind a germ of the idea to let it blossom. Then the serious business of coalition building begins in the process they call "tin-cupping." The manager, symbolically, takes his or her "tin cup" in hand and walks around the organization "begging" for involvement, seeing who has a little bit to chip in, who has a few spare budget dollars to invest, who has a staff member to lend, who will be on the advisory committee, or who has key data. In the process of tin-cupping, two vital organizational functions take place that guard against failures. First is the "horse trading" required. For everything that is dropped into the tin cup, people have to feel that they get something back. Thus, one person's project has to be translated into something of wider benefit around the organization—which helps ensure success because it has support. And, second, in the course of tin-cupping, an innovator also gets a "sanity check"—feedback from "older and wiser heads" helping reshape the idea to make it more workable. (The only failures at innovation that I saw in high-tech firms occurred when the manager thought he or she already had so much power that coalition building was unnecessary.)

Coalition building, therefore, provides not just personal or political advantage; it is also an important process for making sure that the ideas that do get developed have merit and broad support. It is a form of peer control, a way of screening out bad or nonimplementable proposals. For this reason, top management at one computer company is more likely to provide large allocations for ideas that come with a coalition already formed around them.

Working through Teams

Once a group of supporters has been generated, it is time to get down to the actual project work. Now the next interpersonal-organizational skill comes into play: the ability to build a working team to carry out the idea.

Very few ideas and very few projects of any significance are implemented by one person alone: Other people's effort makes it happen—whether they are assistants, subordinates, a staff, a special project team, or a task force of peers assembled just for this effort. But regardless of who the people are, it is critical that they feel like a *team* in order to make any new idea work. My research documents the importance of participative management when change is involved even if it is not necessary for managing the routine. Full involvement turns out to be critical when the issue is change.

For a routine operation in which everybody knows what they are doing high involvement and high intensity are less critical. But change requires above-and-beyond effort on the part of everybody involved. It requires their creativity and their commitment. Without such general cooperation, those trying to make something significant happen in an organization run forever uphill. Help is hard to find. Peers find other priorities; reports are late. When dependent on other people to get the job done, one must engage them. Everybody in an organization has at least one form of power—the "pocket veto." Even without directly challenging an idea, all one has to do is sit on it for a while, put it in his or her pocket, not respond, find other projects more important—and the change effort will be stalled. Loss of momentum occurs when other people are not motivated to do their part.

The development of a new computer at Data General illustrates the process of team building. Tom West, the middle manager behind this development team, worked extraordinarily hard to create a self-conscious sense of *team*—team play, ownership, and identification. He led young engineers who were just out of school to perform engineering "miracles"—record-time achievements that no one predicted. Their intense sense of ownership came from a team identity, symbolized by names (the "microkids" and the "Hardy boys"). The team genuinely had a mission. They also had fun together. They were given full responsibility and were always informed. They had room to make mistakes. West, the manager, supported by two assistants, did not impose his ideas on the team. Indeed, when he had solutions to problems, he sometimes went to the lab late at night and left his ideas on slips of paper for people to find in the morning—without knowing how they got there. Thus, he created an atmosphere in which people felt autonomous and in control and consequently became incredibly dedicated and committed to the project.

Sharing the Credit

Finally, bringing innovation full circle, people who lead changes share credit and recognition—making everyone a "hero." Instead of simply taking individual credit, change masters make sure that everyone who works on their effort gets rewarded. This behavior brings back benefit to the change master. I saw this dramatically illustrated in an insurance company. A manager had led a series of employee involvement projects that improved productivity in his region and boosted the firm's overall profits. At bonus time, his superiors were going to reward him with a fat check. He asked if he could also have bonus money for the people below who had also contributed to his efforts. Management, unfortunately, turned him down. So he took several thousand dollars from his own pocket, collected contributions from peers, and made up his own bonus pool for everyone down to the clerks who had contributed. That made people feel that their least effort was rewarded and they looked forward to participating in the next organizational improvement. Change became an opportunity rather than a threat.

For many people, projects of change and innovation become the most significant things they have ever done in their work lives. I have interviewed people who had spent 30 years in a big bureaucracy who said that the 6-month development task force was the only thing they were excited by and the only thing they would be remembered for—change was their mark on the organization.

Change, the development of something new, unleashes people's creative energy. It is exhilarating, stimulating personnel in a way that routine work cannot do. Giving people the opportunity for innovation and recognizing them for it fulfills both organizational and individual needs.

12

Toolbox for Practical Creativity

R. Donald Gamache

Chairman and Chief Executive Officer, INNOTECH Corporation

Caren Calish Gagliano

President, Services Division, INNOTECH Corporation

"How can I make my organization more creative?" This is a frequent, and often favorite, CEO question. "I know we have creative people, but I can't seem to get anything creative out of them." From another perspective, why do executives seem to get in the way of their organization's creative potential? Our answer might appear facetious: we must learn to make mistakes faster.

Most managers have a highly refined fear of failure. We talk about the downside penalty of trying something new versus the upside reward. In fact, there is often such a mismatch to the individual between downside and upside that it would be foolhardy to try at all; maintaining the status quo makes much more sense. Typically the older we get, the more we reject the discomfort and risk of the new and simultaneously accept the repetition and ease of the old. The bottom line: Organizations are designed to promote the steady state and are counterreceptive to change.

Could it be that top management demands too much when it demands outstanding short-term performance *and* creative open-minded thinking. Our experience shows that while there is fundamental understanding that every organization must change continually to meet the needs of a changing world, they have considerable difficulty in identifying new products and opportunities. Incredible as it may seem, one of the key obstacles is inexperience in doing the "entirely new." Looking at your own company or at others, ask what has really been done that is not merely an extrapolation of present capabilities, a gradual refinement of product or service. Isn't the prime day-to-day mission of a paint company to stay abreast of the fashion trends, colors, and technological developments in product performance and manufacturing? Most companies have done the same thing over and over again, with an occasional variation on the traditional theme. Most firms really do not know how to go about doing something other than what they are already doing.

A consequence of conflicting management demands is actually an indictment of most managers. We call it the "curse of the magic idea." Management sends out the clarion cry for new ideas. At the same time, it holds an ideal of a product or opportunity that has little or no risk, requires little or no change, little or no investment, and that can be completed in a shorter time frame than anything in its history, yielding profit returns at a rate far above present operations. Typically, after toying with various novel concepts—wasting time and money—management usually rejects them all for failing to fit this impractical template of the magic idea.

And why is today's management so impatient? Clearly, it is the pressing need to replace portions of their business that are being lost, aggravated by the insistent demand for constant growth. And, because of the rapid pace of change, older products are being lost at a faster pace as each year passes. Words and phrases such as "knowledge explosion," "technological obsolescence," the "rust belt," and the like have been in our vocabulary a very short time. The pace of change requires everyone to stay abreast of relevant developments in his or her field. If we neglect this responsibility, either the competition will pass us by or our markets will disappear. Also, every organization is designed for today's business. It hires the individuals with the technologies, processing skills, and marketing and sales strengths to support its ongoing businesses. Doing something new will require new information and new people that, by definition, we do not yet have.

Against this background, we see a frenetic pace of activity directed toward generating new products and businesses. Most is smoke—supported by preciously little fire. Someone once said that a zealot is someone who, upon losing sight of his or her other goals, redoubles his or her efforts. The activities of many companies seem to support the truth of this statement. In new business development, activity is not results.

The following "tools" have been derived from considerable on-line work in helping companies grow into new areas or revitalize existing ones. These techniques or mechanisms are not theoretical; rather, they are the practical embodiment of experience, much of it gained through painful failures and disappointments. Some may seem obvious, others insightful. But all deserve a solid place in your toolbox for enhancing the practical application of creative growth.

The Growth Team

No one functional area in your company can suddenly be responsible for future growth opportunities or their implementation. Yet, depending upon corporate culture, we see this responsibility vested in R&D, marketing, even manufacturing. Our early experience found us working intimately with one of these groups to produce a new product or opportunity, but inevitably, when it came time to implement the "new" thing, there was, at a minimum, a lack of understanding or support from the other functional areas. As a consequence, we soon began to insist upon a multidisciplinary team, whose members are the prime "owners" of the growth problem. Team members come, for example, from general management, marketing, sales, R&D, and manufacturing. These are frequently supplemented by specialty areas, e.g., the head of a design center who may be critical to matching products with consumer preferences. The participation of the key "problem owners" has multiple benefits. Each contributes something to the new opportunity, and leaving out one part will diminish the whole. We are no longer surprised to find that the top functional managers of most companies seldom function together and, even if they do, it is ordinarily within highly structured operational meetings. Rarely do they apply their collective intelligence and experience to the task of developing new opportunities. Rarely are they the prime movers for change. Rather, these senior executives sit in judgment of the ideas generated by others—which is a sad, simple reflection of their risk-avoidance attitude.

Almost every idea will have, to varying degrees, its supporters and detractors. Doing something new entails a degree of risk, and if top management is not unanimously committed to moving forward, the probability of significant action toward commercialization is minimal. Nothing short of the emotional and intellectual involvement of the people who will ultimately have to make the decisions and advance the project is critical to success. We like to think of it as "greasing the ways before building the ship." From a practical viewpoint, top functional management has overwhelming responsibilities running day-to-day operations and cannot be expected to spend significant amounts of time in "doing." However, it is critical that they set the direction and establish the parameters by which opportunities are assessed.

Because of the risks involved, management will, knowingly or unknowingly, push responsibility that is rightfully theirs down into the organization. This leaves them in the role of evaluators, in which they can frustrate the doers by rejecting proposals not fitting within their magic idea template. It's not surprising, then, how many middle managers and technical executives suffer from severe frustration. How to release this frustration? Senior management must take responsibility for clearly delineating the criteria they feel make sense for the organization. By setting honest, realistic corporate goals—whether financial, marketing, or other—they will realize that success need not come in the shape of the magic idea. Thus our first tool for drawing on the power of the organization—the multidisciplinary team of "growth problem owners" who will establish the parameters for realistic success.

Establishing Realistic Criteria

Establishing realistic criteria is probably the single most important factor in any attempt to generate new products or opportunities. Many companies *think* they have such criteria. These are often found buried in long flowery paragraphs and tomes of many pages. The actual number of stated criteria we in fact find in most companies ranges from four to six on average. Yet it takes approximately *twenty* very precise statements about the company culture and its goals before sufficient definition is attained to begin an aggressive search process. But it is virtually impossible for an executive group to accomplish this enumerating function unaided. Why? Strong provincial interest, total lack of perspective and reality, and oversights of existing strengths and weaknesses.

The cornerstone of creative criteria setting is made up of *size* and *timing* parameters. How big should the new activity be and by when? It is not useful to state these parameters in terms of minimums. What size of new product volume would be a sufficient critical mass to make an impact in your firm? A fifty million dollar company would have a different perspective than a five billion dollar company. Typically, we see numbers reflecting approximately 10 percent of total company sales. Anything is possible if sufficient resources are made available. But the difference between criteria and a "wish list" is that criteria reflect reality. Criteria can be developed to apply to all avenues of growth ranging from new products to acquisitions to new ventures. Basically a good set of criteria looks at functional areas in a company and defines their future importance. For example, a company with excess manufacturing capacity might feel that the new product should be made on their existing equipment. An organization with an overloaded manufacturing facility may be more concerned with transforming its culture and style to market-sourced products. A strong marketing organization may be an exploitable resource, whereas a weak one may be either ignored or strengthened. "Underexploited assets" embodied in a technology, process, or patented position may be reason enough to focus a growth search on opportunities for additional utilization. Many cultural, ethical, and moral considerations are often reflected in a company's criteria, and rightfully so. After all, companies are people, and it is people who will have to believe in and ultimately implement the required action steps. To be of optimal use, criteria should be ranked in importance. We use the simple but effective classifications: M, must, D, desirable, and B, bonus.

The biggest downfall of most lists of criteria are the "phantoms." A phantom criterion is one that is lurking somewhere in the organization—in the back of a senior manager's head—but is never expressed. Worse yet, the individual does not even realize its existence. Some examples might include: It should not compete with existing customers; it should not be directed to the military establishment; it should not be overly susceptible to government intervention. In short, a phantom is any unstated criterion that has the potential to kill a project. Phantoms are the primary reason projects are derailed or aborted after much time and money have been spent.

Criteria not only tell us what to look for, but they eliminate most of the world from our search. There must be a cultural fit between the new and the known. If this fit is lacking, many excuses may be proposed for not moving forward, though they are seldom the real ones. By eliminating most of the world from our search, we become more focused and productive in the small area that can realistically result in action. We call this smaller area the "domain," and it is only within the domain described by the criteria that dollars and human resources should be directed.

Meeting Dynamics

Synergy is a word that seems to have gone out of favor in our business culture. However synergy does exist in meetings and is illustrated when two heads come together for the purpose of idea generation. That two heads are better than one, and seven or eight better than two, reflects the fact that creativity is essentially the process of insightfully rearranging known elements into new ideas. We as individuals, or collectively as companies, cannot make good pictures if we do not have the relevant pieces—information. The more minds we have around a problem, the more pieces (information) we bring to its potential solution. If the vice president of marketing has X, and the director of technology has Y, their insightful rearrangement may well yield Z —the new idea. Therefore, much of what a group should do in a creative session is to fit together their collective bits of knowledge to arrive at insights and novelty. Thus, promoting free flow of information that can result in productive combinations is at the heart of creative group activity. The problem comes with the words, "free flow." If the organization, culture, meeting dynamics, etc., do not allow and encourage such free flow, the session is doomed to failure. You can effectively use groups of inside experts (from your company) or outside experts (consultants knowledgeable in the area you want to explore). We favor the use of outside experts to generate ideas that are then developed by the team of inside experts who "own the growth problem."

Some of the common difficulties with company creative sessions is that they are fraught with politics and power plays. An idea is like a baby in that it is extremely fragile and needs lots of love and encouragement to grow to its full potential. Yet, most business executives tend to judge ideas with the same standards they apply to fully grown businesses. From a human dynamics perspective, when an individual has an idea, that idea is a uniquely personal creation—in a sense, that individual's "baby." Any negative reaction—whether disparaging words or non-verbal signals—can kill it. Predictably, the individual either withdraws from the group, taking away his or her information and potential for contribution, or becomes aggressive toward others when they present their babies. In either case, the dynamics and climate preclude productive information exchange and creative insights.

There is much in the literature on unspecific creative techniques. At their core, however, are a few simple principles. First, creativity requires us to look at a situation in a different way. The fact that we often fail to do this is reflected in comments such as, "we've *never* done it that way," or "we've *always* done it that way." Ironically, both positions are presented as a reason for not moving forward with the new idea. In some languages, the phrase "home blind" is used to describe a situation in which something is so familiar that it becomes nearly invisible to the observer. Conventional thinking and habits are major enemies of new approaches and insights. Remember the pitfalls when groups gather to generate new ideas. Unless the proper ambience is established, new ideas (babies) will be killed before they can grow sufficiently to develop a life of their own.

Creative Sessions

The first step in running any company creative session is to identify its objectives. A group of individuals can be brought together to generate information, spawn ideas, or make decisions—though combining all three objectives causes confusion. If the purpose of the session is creativity, its end output should be ideas. Such a session is designed, staffed, and run very differently from one aimed at generating relevant information on a subject or making a decision on an issue.

Once the mission is established, the next step is to decide who should participate. The key consideration here is: Does he or she have relevant experience and information? Naturally creative people may be a bonus, but creativity without appropriate knowledge is seldom productive. We like to hold small sessions, involving those areas of expertise valuable to the mission. For example, a session to devise new approaches for extracting blood in sample quantities painlessly from a patient might include: an entomologist who is knowledgeable about the mosquito's bloodsucking apparatus, an electronics expert who understands the human nervous system and can produce insights on nerve impulse blocking, an oriental acupuncture master, and a magician who is an expert at creating distraction. Compare this to the more conventional approach of assembling doctors and researchers who, having worked in the field for years, will almost surely go no further than the tried and true.

Once the appropriate individuals have been identified, the next task is to prepare them for the session. The maximum productive time for such an event is about 3 hours. Because this is so little time, it shouldn't be squandered on briefing the participants. Also, because the subconscious mind is such a powerful factor in the creative process, the earlier someone begins work on the problem before the event, the greater his or her mental potential for meaningful contributions and insights. Therefore, the problem and mission should be communicated prior to the session event and should be accompanied by techniques that will trigger ideas and insights.

The session should be led by an individual who knows what is to be accomplished. It requires knowledge of session management techniques to fairly and productively allocate the available "air time," or a few individuals will dominate the discussion and the remainder will contribute negligibly if at all. The group must understand the core principle: Don't kill the other person's baby! Help it become better and stronger.

Every idea has flaws and if these negatives are focused upon, little if anything will survive. We want to cancel the traditional, off-putting, evaluative mind-set because the session is merely the beginning of the creative process. The sessions produce raw material—ideas—not finished products. The key is in the words "What's *good* about it?" This new mind-set, repeated often by the leader, will force people away from their normally judgmental modes into a creative orientation that fits the mission of the session.

After asking what's good about it, the next question might be, "How can I fix the obvious flaws, how can I make this idea better, does this idea give me other ideas? " In sum, the goal of the creative session is *quantity*. But there is no absolute number to shoot for as the creative productivity of a session is a function of its objective. Looking for commercial applications for a new material may lead to a hundred or more suggestions in a 3-hour session. We generated ten to fifteen new ideas for blood sampling. The session is over when ideas stop emerging and familiar ground is being replowed.

The Opportunity Area versus Ideas

One idea is one idea, but an "opportunity area" may contain dozens of ideas. To clarify this point, the idea for an inexpensive electronic thermometer may be a good one; but the area of home health care might contain that product—and hundreds of others. If focusing on an emerging market segment would make sense to your company's present capabilities, the place to start is with the area—not a simple product concept. Companies often fall in love with a single exciting idea. But from a broader business perspective, one idea, even with all its glamor, is not a business. It cannot support the requisite marketing, sales, manufacturing, etc. However a cluster of product ideas within a strategically focused opportunity area is the stuff of which businesses are made.

New business opportunities are created by change, and the same change that produces an opportunity for one company may produce a dislocation for another. A major problem in most companies looking for new products is that they begin by looking for ideas rather than trends. Try identifying the factors that produce the changes that, in turn, produce the ultimate product opportunities, e.g., the major change elements are new technologies, political factors, economic factors, and social attitudes. Ideally, an opportunity area should be insightful and supported by forecasting trends and relevant information.

Tools for Finding Information

Even an exciting idea unsupported by information will seldom be acted upon. Very few business executives are truly gamblers, and even those who are want a clear assessment of the risk of their gamble. When millions of dollars are involved, investment-level decisions require investment-quality information. Because of today's information explosion and pace of change, conventional approaches to accessing information are not enough. Though databases are excellent tools, a database search is no better than the quality of the database and the knowledge of the searcher. The real issue is how do I get as smart as I can as quickly as possible based on state-of-the-art knowledge. The following two tools are extremely powerful when effectively employed, and the key to both is accessing the appropriate individuals.

The Expert-to-Expert Session

Conventional information gathering is a slow and inefficient process: we read books and articles, attend trade shows, and fly around the country or world to visit knowledgeable experts. This is usually done by one or two individuals who represent a larger management group. But the single strongest tool to produce "step-function learning"—a quantum leap in knowledge—is to bring together the individuals with questions and the experts likely to have answers. The first step is to flush out the questions. After getting them on paper, they will begin to suggest the kinds of experts who should have the answers. The next step is to network through various channels to identify exactly the right participants. Since the creative sessions will be a group event and there will be much probing and talking, the maximum number of experts for one event should probably be limited to five. After agreeing to participate at a specified time and place, each invited expert should receive a carefully crafted briefing document positioning the event and containing the questions and areas to be explored. On the appointed day, the outside and inside experts meet, and a leader manages the dynamics of the process. The event should be recorded, preferably on videotape. The emergence of comments and issues, information and insights, will happen so rapidly that the postsession debriefing will be at least as valuable as the session event itself. Because company people are face-to-face with outside experts, the answer to a first-level question may trigger another on a second or third level, which still can be addressed because the participants remain together. We have used such sessions to assess the fit of a possible acquisition, the value of a new technology, the promise of an opportunity area, and many other tasks. The result, consistently, has been step-function learning.

The Expert Survey

This tool bears resemblance to the Delphi technique from which it was derived. It differs from the expert-to-expert session in that more outside opinions are heard and the event is not face to face. Further, more than one iteration can be used. The inside expert's questions are embodied in a meticulously crafted survey. The key here is to identify the right individuals to receive it and to get them to spend time and effort to complete the survey as thoroughly as possible for some form of compensation—a fee, executive-level gift, or the like. (We have used high-toy-value items such as a printing calculator, portable TV, or restaurant gift certificate.) Twenty appears to be a good sample size because we are dealing with vertical experts, not the general public. Consider the benefits your company would derive from the carefully thought out opinions of twenty cleverly selected experts in an area of potential promise.

Debriefing

White noise is not information. The output of any session event falls quickly into the category of unintelligible random sound. Much of the information is casual, superficial, disorganized, even incredible, making the processing of this information critically important. Processing entails supplementary research via databases, telephone interviews, and personal visits. Debriefing basically addresses the issue of "don't tell me what they said, tell me what they meant."

Champion and Sponsor

Ideas do not come to fruition by themselves. This seemingly obvious statement has not been recognized by many frustrated companies. Perhaps the problem begins with the fact that everyone has a full-time job. A new idea will require an extraordinary amount of work simply because it is new. And because the organization hasn't done it before, there will be many new things to learn—and inevitable mistakes and false starts will be made in the process. Creativity is not a part-time job, but the responsibility for opportunity implementation is often put into the laps of individuals who are already devoting more than full time to present responsibilities. Therefore, by design or default, these new ideas are often destined to a quick and quiet death.

Our first solution to the problem is to emphasize the critical importance of the champion—an individual who has the requisite knowledge and experience to fit and push the new idea. If the individual is presently in the organization, his or her job must be at least partially redesigned to provide him or her with the time to do the needed work. If not in the organization, find him or her. But even the most well-intentioned champion with sufficient time can fail. Champions tend to be located at middle management or lower and most often do not have the clout to accomplish their tasks, to get through the maze and mechanics of an organization obsessed with today's ongoing business. Thus the critical need for the sponsor.

The *sponsor* is an executive at the highest level with the responsibility of protecting the champion from management—and the company from the champion. As one executive put it, management wants to keep pulling up the young plant by the roots to see if it's growing. On the other hand, an unproven individual with *carte blanche* in a new area may lead the corporation toward drastic consequences both in the marketplace and on the income statement. Top management should have full confidence that the sponsor has the company's interests at heart while providing protection, support, and counsel for the champion.

Going for Creativity

The tools for practical creativity are analogous to the tools of an auto mechanic. Each tool has a technical purpose, yet to function properly requires the mechanic, the user of the tool, to be skilled and capable. This is true for product innovation and business development. The manager—the mechanic—must be skilled in the use of each creativity tool in order to maximize innovation and development. But how can a manager with short-term, bottom-line demands gain the skills necessary to be efficient in long-term, growth-oriented tasks?

The answer is two-fold. First, there must be a stated dedication by senior management that long-term, growth-oriented tasks are *good* for the organization. This implies that the corporate culture must move toward embracing change and accepting failure. Dedication is also needed by middle and lower-level managers. They must be willing to experiment with the tools in order to build confidence and expertise. Second, corporations must recognize that outside experience and expertise can augment their creative talent and complement their skills. If the organization's structure and culture are focused short term, input from outside the corporation is requisite to innovation and growth. Such an outside contribution is, in itself, a tool that can increase a firm's business development effectiveness. Outside input can come from many sources. Advertising agencies, investment bankers, independent consultants, large consulting firms, manufacturer's representatives—all can contribute. It is the manager's task to recognize and utilize wisely these sources along with his or her tools in business development. The toolbox for practical creativity is by no means easy to use. Its use requires practice and experience in an environment willing to accept the risks of change.

13

Techniques for Stimulating New Ideas: A Matter of Fluency

William C. Miller

Senior Management Consultant, Managing Innovation and Change, SRI International

Imagine that you are president of a major American oil company. Both retail and wholesale markets have changed dramatically over the last few years: Whereas it used to take 5 to 7 years for market structure to change—as consumer lifestyles and oil technologies evolved—now it can restructure in as little as 5 to 7 months. You feel strongly that your organization needs to respond more rapidly and more innovatively at all levels to keep its leadership position. But how? At your last two executive retreats, senior managers suggested many ways to promote creativity: "Teach brainstorming." "Set up internal venture teams." "Communicate our strategies and policies more clearly to our employees." "Install a new incentive system." "Hire more creative people." "Find better ways to implement ideas we already have."

The demands of the times are clear. You can't achieve significant new growth doing things the old way. You must foster more "ahead of their time" ideas that give people what they really want. You must also, as

CEO, change the climate for innovation to get a united effort generating new ideas. Thus you face the critical questions: "Can innovation and creativity be 'managed'? " "How can we promote new concepts for improving our products, marketing, and operations?" "Can creativity contribute to a productive rather than a chaotic environment for growth?"

The Climate for Innovation

Creativity for companies can be defined as "coming up with new ideas that can shape business and operational goals," and innovations, as "putting these ideas into action, producing something tangible." Innovation can occur in any company function. It can be *inward* when productivity and cost factors are paramount: Manufacturing, finance, purchasing, and other functions can all be ripe for innovations that affect the bottom line. (For example, quality circles are innovations aimed at productivity issues at decentralized levels.) Or it can be turned *outward* when increased revenues are critical: Innovation can focus on marketing, new product and/or service development, R&D, and other functions more commonly associated with "being creative."

Before turning people loose to generate new ideas, a climate that supports implementing those ideas is essential. Otherwise, a sense of frustration and betrayal will be the result of well-intentioned requests for employee suggestions and participation. But all too often, ways to improve the climate, such as those given by senior managers in the example above, only "heat up the room" rather than change the organization's "creativity thermostat" setting; after a number of months, the system works to bring the temperature back down to the setting, and the status quo resumes.

Innovation and creativity *can* be "managed." To change the thermostat setting itself, there are eight issues to address in a strategic approach to managing innovation: C = *Collaboration and communication.* How do people work together and communicate across department lines and within project teams? R = *Roles, risks, and rewards.* Who are the best initiators and implementers of new ideas, and how do they work best? E = *Environmental monitoring.* What trends and events signal threats and opportunities, and how is this information spread throughout the organization? A = *Administration.* How is innovation supported by the following systems: budget and accounting, information management, performance appraisal, reporting structure, and innovation process (steps)? T = *Transition management.* How are changes in organizational life planned, paced, communicated, and implemented? I =

Intuition and logic. How are both intuition and logic honored and utilized in defining problems, generating solutions, and making decisions? V = *Vision and purpose.* How do people agree with and unite around a central sense of purpose and vision and the subsequent priorities for innovation? E = *Evaluation methods.* How are the ideas evaluated—by what criteria and process at various stages?

The synergy of these factors produces an organization's creative climate for innovation. Shifting the thermostat requires changes in each factor, carefully planned to reinforce each other, to produce an organization able and willing to respond to new business environments, to generate and act upon new ideas from every level.

New ideas produced in this climate *can* be channeled into productive rather than chaotic effort. Many factors—including proliferation of microcomputers and a "gold collar" professional workforce—are promoting more decentralized decision making. Because traditional management controls do not work as well in this environment, there is a striking need for emphasizing leadership and vision rather than authority and coercion. Leaders should exercise power more through shared purpose, mission and values. After all, we can generate all sorts of creative ideas—but aimed at what purpose, to fulfill what mission, and with what values? More than ever, companies need to have a vision that gives meaning and direction to creative efforts. Organizations are not mechanisms whose precise functioning can be stipulated and manipulated; rather they are dynamic organisms that live by intuition as well as analysis, inspiration as well as control.

Creative leadership shifts from *motivating* to *empowering* employees to act in fulfilling the shared vision. Only then can leaders know that decisions can benefit the whole, that ideas tailored to solve specific problems are directed by an overall sense of organizational purpose. CEOs have many options to develop and communicate the company vision. In one model, the CEO has a personal sense of vision and sells it well, "enculturating" the organization. But more and more, CEOs can take advantage of diverse employee vision. Allowing these personal concepts to filter up as input can give life to creative efforts and realize a truly shared corporate vision.

Idea Stimulating Techniques: Linear and Intuitive

There are two general classes of human thinking and problem solving, linear and intuitive. The essential difference is that linear thinking is sequential, while intuitive thinking is holistic. Many great scientific discoveries occur when logical, orderly thought reaches its limit and intuition provides the insight—when sudden flashes jump rational analysis. Einstein once said, "I did not discover the fundamental nature of the universe using my rational mind."

Idea-stimulation methods can be classified in a similar way. Some give you a linear path, a pattern, a sequence of steps; others rely on a single intuitive image or symbol to provide a "whole" answer all at once. When you find an idea or solution by a linear method, you usually recognize the achievement casually: "Oh, there you are. Of course." But a solution arrived at intuitively is often accompanied by surprise: "Where did that come from? "

A common failing of many start-up businesses is an overreliance on the entrepreneur's intuitive feel for his or her market, without supporting data. Yet as companies grow, that failing can reverse itself: As decisions are made and ratified at multiple levels, decisions become data driven and lack intuitive energy. Managers who do use their intuition feel they must hide that fact and dress up their decisions in "data clothes."

Both intuition and logic or data are important in generating ideas to solve everyday business problems. Each is like a language, and *fluency* in each is required to take advantage of their unique contributions.

You can employ both linear and intuitive idea-generation techniques for a wide variety of business issues and opportunities. Different techniques can be mixed and matched for different topics. Some of the applications at SRI have included helping one division of a chemical firm establish a broader vision of the business (including specific market opportunities), developing a financial institution's strategy for the Asia-Pacific region, identifying 1990 to 1995 software opportunities for a Japanese company, establishing R&D priorities aimed at positioning an electronics firm for the 21st century, discovering new mixing methods for processing a consumer health product, formulating new business opportunities for using excess engineering personnel in a nuclear engineering firm, inventing a new portable printer, and so on.

Linear Techniques

Linear methods help us organize information in ways that give us new "entry points" for solving problems. They give new perspectives on *where* to look for innovations, which is often the key to finding the best solution(s).

Matrix Analysis.   Suppose you want to develop some new product

	MARKETS				
	A	B	C	D	... Z
1					
2			X		
3					
4					
... N					

TECHNOLOGIES
Figure 13.1 Market-technologies matrix.

ideas, and you have identified various market needs, available technologies, and product functions (what the product *does*). You could develop a two- or three-dimensional matrix to identify where to look for new ideas. For example, consider a market-technologies matrix, as shown in Figure 13.1.

At each cell of the grid (X), there may be a possible set of innovations that would use a particular technology for a particular market. If you were, say, developing innovative packaging products, your matrix might look like the one shown in Figure 13.2. Or you might prefer to use a market-functions matrix, as in Figure 13.3 and assume (for the purpose of idea stimulation) that you could invent or find whatever technology you would need to make the new product. Within each box, you can put new ideas for products. You can also identify all possible technologies to be applied, thus constructing a "working" three-dimensional matrix.

	MARKETS		
	Food	Chemicals	Health care
Adhesives	x		
Laminating			
Foam			
Pulp processing			

TECHNOLOGIES
Figure 13.2 Sample matrix for developing innovative packaging products.

	MARKETS		
	Foods	Chemicals	Health care
High strength	x		
Moisture-proof			
Usable in ovens			
Lightweight			

FUNCTIONS

Figure 13.3 Market-functions matrix.

Morphological Analysis. This technique allows you to deal with any number of variables and subtopics to spawn specific ideas. By listing all possible subtopics under each variable and then developing combinations chosen from each variable list, new ideas emerge (some quite outlandish and some quite practical). For example, suppose you wanted a new food product and the variables to consider were: forms, kinds, properties, processes, and packaging. Subtopics for each of these variables might include those shown in Figure 13.4. Pick one or two items from each list to make a complete idea. How about chips of fruits and spice with medicinal properties (antihistamines?), compacted and formed, and packaged in small sacks?

Nature of the Business Businesses are defined in different ways: by their products and services (a cutting and welding company), by their

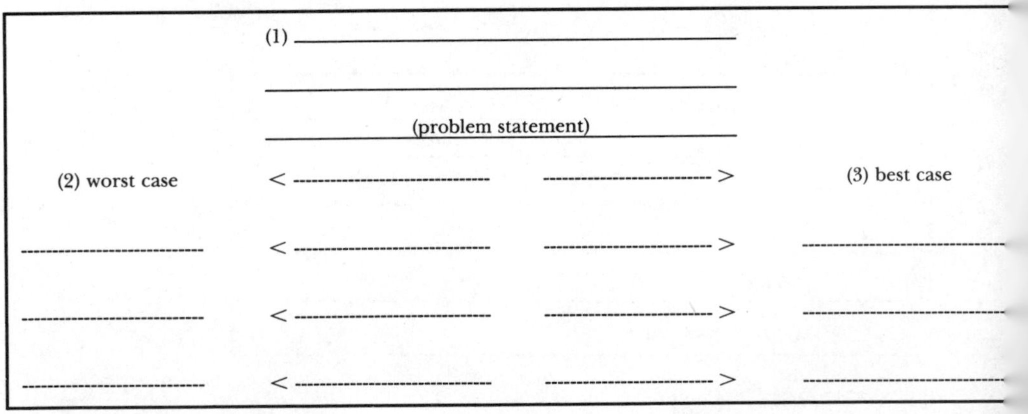

(1) _____

_____

(problem statement)

(2) worst case   < ----------------------------   ---------------------------- >   (3) best case

----------------------------   < ----------------------------   ---------------------------- >   ----------------------------

----------------------------   < ----------------------------   ---------------------------- >   ----------------------------

----------------------------   < ----------------------------   ---------------------------- >   ----------------------------

Figure 13.4 Force field analysis.

markets (products for the chemical industry), by the functions they serve (products for automated processing), or by their technologies (products based on artificial intelligence). The "primary unifying factor" is key. As an example, a bank might be in the financial business, the management assistance business (with financial resources to help implement decisions), or the transaction processing business. Each definition can lead to different ideas of products or services the bank might offer. For instance, as a financial business, you might offer trust investment services. As a management assistance business, you might include software packages to support financial decisions. As a transaction processing business, you might contact "back office" service for local insurance agencies or brokerage firms.

A variation of this technique builds on morphological analysis. You could piece individual ideas into whole business concepts. Suppose you were developing a new (or extended) food business. You could list all possible markets, functions, etc., in a "key word" index, as in Table 13.1. Every new idea could be expressed in terms of these key words, such as the fruit-chip idea. With all ideas expressed in terms of key words, a computer can sort all ideas for a given item, e.g., a business built around the chips or grains and nuts or nutrition or freeze drying or canning. This allows you to examine the possible businesses that could produce such products.

Attribute Listing. If you wish to improve a procedure, product, or process, you can write down all its attributes and see how to upgrade any or all of them. For example, to improve upon a decision-making process, you could generate new ways of accomplishing each of these steps (attributes), as shown in Table 13.2.

SCAMPER. Alex Osborn, a pioneer in creativity facilitation, developed

Table 13.1. Example of Morphological Analysis

Variables for Food Businesses*				
Forms	Kinds	Properties	Processes	Packages
Preserves	Meat	Cost	Ferment	Bottle
Drink	Vegetables	Convenience	Freeze dry	Can
Chips	Fish	Nutrition	Compact	Pouch
Flake	Fruit	Taste	Blend	Foil or Paper
Stew	Dairy	Texture	Form	Aerosol
Roll	Grains	Odor	Fry	Box
Soup	Nuts	Viscosity	Bake	Cup
Topping	spices	Medicinal	Stir	Sack

*SOURCE: Miller, William C., *The Creative Edge:* Fostering Innovation Where You Work, Addison-Wesley, Boston, 1986.

Table 13.2. Sample of Attribute Listing

Process attribute	Idea(s) for improvement
Perceive: What, objectively, is happening?	What new ways can gather information and input objectively?
Define: What is a consensus definition of the problem?	What new methods can gain consensus understanding of the problem's exact nature?
Analyze: What factors are contributing to the problem?	What new ways can determine all the factors and causes affecting the problem?
Generate alternate solutions: What is the range of options available?	What new methods can stimulate ideas and options?
Evaluate alternate solutions: What are the criteria and which options best fit the criteria?	What new processes can evaluate ideas and options?
Decide: What will be the choice for action?	What new ways can decisions be made to solve the problem?
Implement: Who will do what, when, and how?	What new methods can ensure the decision will be implemented?
Evaluate results: How well did the solution work?	What new methods can follow-up, feedback, and correct?

a list of idea-spurring questions. They were later arranged by Bob Eberle as the mnemonic SCAMPER: S = Substitute? C = Combine? A = Adapt? M = Modify? Magnify? Minify? P = Put to other uses? E = Eliminate? R = Reverse? Rearrange? This checklist could help, say, a firm trying to develop a new office procedure by spurring ideas for novel work flows or new policies.

Force Field.　Kurt Lewin, a social psychologist, developed this method. First, identify the problem to analyze. Then describe two opposite conditions: the best or optimum state you would like to be in and the worst state you can imagine (absolute catastrophe). To analyze the current state use the format in Figure 13.5 to represent a tug of war between forces pulling toward optimum or catastrophe. For example, suppose you want to explore "How to implement a new computer system" in your organization (see Figure 13.5).

With this force field, you can discover the relationship of goals to current situational strengths and weaknesses. To improve, "move" the line toward the optimum in three ways: strengthen an already present positive force, weaken an already present negative force, or add a new positive force.

---

1) PROBLEM: How to implement a new computer system

Complete Loss of Productivity   *All New Tasks Being*
with High Backlog   *Performed Well*

Frequent-last-minute changes   Commitment of management to
in the system   proper planning; to do what's
                                                   necessary in making it work

Insufficient time and   Adequate budget allocated for
resources to train people   developing training materials
fully

Employee fears of not   Good communications between systems
performing well on new,   development staff and user
long-term, highly complex   departments
tasks

NOTE: Each side is like an end of a continuum. The statements represent a tug-of-war toward
opposing ends.

Figure 13.5 Sample problem for force field analysis.

Alternative Scenarios. All too often, managers do their long-range
planning based on a *single* forecast of trends, on only *one* notion of
what their market and business will be like in 2, 5, 10, or more years
ahead. "Betting the company" on a single forecast can be risky. The
first question usually asked of a single description of a future—even
with "high, low, and probable" projections—is, "Given its assumptions,

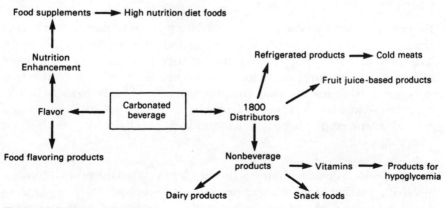

Figure 13.6 Design tree example.

how wrong might it be? " This practice can also be paralyzing, as managers refuse to act given the uncertainty of their business environment. Thinking through several scenarios is a less risky, more conservative approach to planning than relying on single forecasts and trend analyses; it can thus free up management to take more innovative actions.

In the early 1970s companies such as Royal Dutch Shell began using qualitatively different descriptions of the future, "alternative scenarios," to plan and position themselves in case of sudden "discontinuities" in the future. For example, one of their 1971 scenarios contained a description of an oil shortage and a corresponding rise in oil prices. They hadn't necessarily predicted the 1973 crisis, because they also had more conventional scenarios on their tables; but by positioning themselves across a number of plausible futures, they had broken new ground on how to direct their business activities. Partly because of this, they subsequently grew from seventh to second in their industry.

Scenarios are built around a specific decision to be made rather than being general "future histories." Once the key decision has been stated, critical factors for success are identified along with major environmental forces that affect the decision. Each force should provoke qualitatively different possibilities that are plausible, though they are not predictions from trends. For example, suppose the decision to be made is "How can we develop our consumer lending business in a deregulated environment? " Assume the major environmental forces might include economics, technology, competition, and customer satisfaction. With scenarios built around these forces, business opportunities can be identified within each scenario and then combined to lead toward a primary strategy for investment. Another advantage of using scenarios is that they help identify what environmental factors to monitor over time, and when the environment shifts, you can recognize where it is shifting *to*.

Forced or Direct Association.   Sometimes it helps to pair two concepts that seemingly have nothing in common and see what ideas emerge. In a workshop whose purpose was to identify new ideas for computer software architecture, participants were asked to make a connection between scuba diving and using computers. Wetsuits likened to user-friendly features—"insulating" the user from the "cold technology"—produced new ideas for employing artificial intelligence to help with on-the-spot programming.

Design Tree.   This technique is useful when you have a central topic— product, market, technology, process, etc.—on which you want to build. Suppose that you sell carbonated beverages and want to expand

that business. The design tree is a mapping of ideas as you consider
what else can be done with your related technologies and markets (see
Figure 13.6).

Intuitive Techniques

Whereas linear techniques structure information to focus where we
look for new ideas, intuitive techniques promote leaps of logic to
suddenly perceive whole solutions. Our intuition, however, is more
fluent in sounds, symbols, and images than in words. The following
techniques take advantage of superior insight that is often available
through intuition by purposefully eliciting such sounds, symbols, and
images. Successful practical solutions then depend on translating the
results into linear communication, i.e., words and formulas.

Imagery.   Images can be symbols, scenes, sounds, or feelings used as
windows to our inner intuition. The scientist Kekule had spent years
trying to find the molecular structure of benzene when, in a dream,
"My mind's eye . . . could distinguish larger structures of different forms
and in long chains . . . everything was moving in a snake-like and twisting
manner. Suddenly, what was this? One of the snakes got hold of its own
tail and the whole structure was mockingly twisting in front of my
eyes." (The result was the benzene ring—a pivotal discovery in chemistry.)
Imagery can be encouraged in guided fantasies conducted while
participants are in a state of deep relaxation. In one case, managers
wanted to identify core values for operating a joint venture—values to
communicate to employees and customers. To understand the meanings and conclusions of demographic data, these managers were asked
to close their eyes, relax their breathing, and "consult" their intuitions
for symbols representing core values for each of them personally. The
qualities underlying such images as "Thanksgiving dinners" led to
themes based on respect, service, and family. At first, mental images
may be hard to understand. You can always ask your intuition for
another image that might be clearer; your imagination is quite accommodating.
Some guidelines for using imagery are: relax your body and mind as
deeply as possible; make a clear request to your subconscious for images
that represent desired solutions; accept whatever image comes to mind
(surrender!); look for strong emotions and many sensory modes (imagine sights, sounds, tastes, feelings, and smells); if the image is not easy to
understand, ask your intuition for another one or for a "deeper"

meaning; honor all intuitive images, they come from a friend; look for qualities represented by the images, rather than getting caught up in the literal meaning.

Analogy. Analogies are a correspondence between dissimilar things. Analogies assume that if two things are alike in some respects, they may be alike in other respects. Analogies are a wonderful way to "make the familiar strange and the strange familiar," a key concept of creative thinking popularized by Synectics (see Chapter 14).

Personal Analogy. Identify with an object and see the problem from that perspective. If you were trying to invent a new electronic printer, you might imagine, "If I were a machine in a noisy office, how would I like to operate most quietly?"

Direct Analogy. Draw a comparison between events in different fields. The inspiration for Velcro came from observing how burdock burrs cling to clothing.

Symbolic Analogy. Take the function or purpose of a solution to a problem and imagine ways to fill in the following: "Something that [performs a function] like a [analogy]." You might want to invent "new photo film" that "tunes" colors like a TV set—perhaps a new electronics-based "film."

Fantasy Analogy. Use your imagination without reference to "objective reality," and see what real-world ideas you can get. To invent new species of grains, imagine shrinking down and taking a "fantastic voyage" through genetic structures.

Brainstorming. This is perhaps the most well-known—and *misused*— of all idea-generation methods, misused because people try to employ it either without understanding the ground rules or when other techniques would be more effective. To brainstorm, define a problem and give all your ideas as they first occur to you. Some ground rules for effective brainstorming (and for other techniques as well) include: pick a problem common to all participants, do not define the problem in terms of a preselected solution (instead of "How do I get John to do this job?" use something like "How can I get this job done?"), record ideas where everyone can see them, do not evaluate or judge until all ideas have been given, try for wild ideas, aim for quantity to help find quality, and encourage building on ideas. Brainstorming can also be applied within other techniques, such as matrix, design tree, and so on.

Dreams. This method takes advantage of our wonderful ability for both daydreams and night dreams. Often, solutions can come when you don't expect them, after some mental "gestation" period. You can actually encourage this: Ask your intuition to work on a problem and then give you an answer. The key is to write down whatever images or words come to mind *as soon as they pop up;* the insights can be hard to recall later. Look for *qualities* represented by the images and symbols rather than taking them too literally or interpreting them too mechanically ("this always means that").

Drawing. For people who have a hard time getting away from the world of words and into the world of imagery, free-hand drawing is often useful. Suspend judgment—especially those voices that from age 8 said you weren't good at art. Use colors or pens or even magazine cutouts in "automatic drawing": just let the image pictures (or even words) flow without conscious direction, as if the items on paper were self-directed, telling you how they wanted to be. For example, to restructure a workflow creatively, you might draw symbols of each type of work and observe which ones "wish" to be next to each other. Or draw a symbol for the outcome of a team-building meeting and see how team members see their own wishes for the team in the symbol.

Meditation. Meditation (or mind clearing) is perhaps the most effective and consistent method to tap one's creative potential. Meditation gives familiarity with states of internal awareness and deep relaxation that allow you to listen to the quiet, inner voice characteristic of intuition. Generating images can become easier, and there can be a stronger connection between your intuitive answers and your sense of meaning in life: your answers will feel richer, energized by a more profound commitment to make them real. (One talented chemist started his own company after getting an insight into a problem of molecular interaction while meditating.) There are various types of meditation you might experiment with: walking with special attention to your movements, sitting and paying attention to the flow of your breath (perhaps listening for the sound "so" on the inhale and "hum" on the exhale), watching or imagining a candle flame, following certain types of music (solo flute, etc.), and so on. For people unaccustomed to meditation, having someone guide them in a "walk on the beach," or some other fantasy, is often useful, especially in group problem-solving sessions.

Employing Idea-Stimulating Techniques

The guidelines given for brainstorming should be followed when using any of these techniques. A neutral facilitator helps, as does a recorder who keeps a group memory of all ideas. (Sometimes the facilitator also does the recording, but this can dampen the effectiveness of each role.) This combination of guidelines and special roles helps to keep the discussions constructive, the idea generation more divergent initially (and more convergent subsequently), the guidelines in force, the agenda on track, the participants focused on content not process, and the participants' attention focused on problems not personalities.

Some creative problem-solving meetings are measured in minutes, with little preparation needed. Others can last days and are preceded by a month or two or preparation. When SRI worked with Toshiba, the Japanese electronics firm, on positioning for the early 21st century, a three-day "innovation search" was conducted, preceded by two to three months of scenario development and technology analyses. This workshop, like many others SRI has conducted, involved the use of many of these idea-stimulation techniques, some planned ahead of time and some emerging on the spot.

There are eight steps for producing an innovation search (or business opportunity search): (1) identify goals, capabilities, and internal or external criteria, (2) develop technology or market, etc., scenarios, (3) select focus areas, (4) prepare and educate range of participants, (5) develop creativity exercises, (6) generate alternatives in a variety of workshop settings, (7) screen alternatives for top concepts, and (8) evaluate feasibility and promise according to criteria.

Idea-stimulating techniques cannot only discover goals, opportunities, and solutions to problems, but they also can find new ways of getting organizations to face the future and implement ideas. These techniques can contribute significantly to getting a competitive edge and giving employees fulfillment—when the creative climate for innovation supports the ideas they produce. Ultimately, creativity is a cornerstone in securing a prosperous future.

Bibliography

William C. Miller: *The Creative Edge: Fostering Innovation in Where You Work,* Addison-Wesley, Boston, 1987.

14

Techniques for Fostering Innovation

Richard A. Harriman

President, Synectics, Inc.

The turtle, after getting beaten repeatedly in road races by the hare, is getting discouraged. So he calls on the wise old owl to seek help. The owl says "Why didn't you come to me sooner? It's very easy. Just before the race, stretch your legs until they are long and you will win handily." The race is about to begin. The turtle, concealed behind a rock, tugs furiously on his legs. His efforts seem futile, and when he races he gets beaten badly by the hare. Distraught, the turtle returns to the owl: "I pulled my legs and nothing happened. How, wise old wise, do I make my legs longer?" The owl replies sagely, "Implementation is your problem; I just make policy."

And so it is with creativity and innovation for management today. Corporations, much like the owl, are setting policies: "We *should* be more receptive to new ideas. We *should* explore totally new approaches. We *should* have a risk-taking climate." And like the owl's advice, these policies for innovative action are frequently made without providing the practical means to achieve them. Many organizations are practicing "innovation by exhortation." The fact that directives are more prevalent is not bad news. Just a few years ago, the call for innovative action was relegated to only special problems or particular functions (like R&D). More recently, competitive pressures have caused corporations

to expect innovation throughout the organization. In a rapidly changing world, standing still is moving backward.

The challenge for today's manager is to move beyond the policies and
bridge the gap between directive and results. He or she must answer the
questions: What *are* practical ways to be receptive to ideas? How *do* I
insure fresh thinking? How *do* you direct the unpredictable? How *does*
the company embrace the zeal of a new product champion without
sacrificing teamwork and commitment from other people? How *can* a
10,000-person organization be nimble and responsive?

This chapter provides managerial techniques to translate policy
directive into meaningful action. The techniques address the most
fundamental characteristics of an innovative environment—being receptive to ideas and ensuring fresh thinking. The examples used are
drawn from the work of Synectics, Inc. and are disguised to maintain
confidentiality.

Receptivity to Ideas

The following example illustrates *"paraphrasing"* and the *"developmental response,"* two practical techniques that foster receptivity; they
can be used at any level in the organization, within any function as well
as between functions.

The goal for Linda, a branch group manager in a large bank, was to
improve customer service without increasing costs. A colleague suggested that she manage the branch like an automat cafeteria. No one
would then have to wait in full-service lines—behind, say, a customer
selecting a four-course meal (check cashing, balance verification, traveler's checks, and money market transfers)—when he or she only wanted
a cup of coffee (check cashing). Linda's immediate objections centered
on the high number of stations required, confused floor traffic, and
increased cost implications. She didn't want to waste time on an
imperfect idea and was about to reply "That's an interesting idea, but
we can't do it because . . . "

Had she done so, she would have hampered innovation in three key
ways: She would have lost a potential solution buried in the half-baked
suggestion, she would have discouraged her colleague from offering
untested ideas in the future, and she would have sent a signal—perhaps
unintended but widely seen and heard—that she really did not want
new approaches. Instead she paused and invested a little time by
concentrating on the essence of the idea and exploring its unclear
points. Together, she and her colleague transformed the cafeteria
analogy to that of a fashionable gourmet restaurant. The discussion

turned to the role of a *maitre d'* who greets customers while managing the flow of tables, waiters, and diners. As a result of this exchange, staffing during peak hours at the branches was rearranged so that a staff member directed customers (like a *maitre d'*). Customers were directed to different service areas, taking into account their needs, the number of people ahead in line, and the capabilities of tellers and officers on duty. Customer service was noticeably improved. Those requiring full service weren't shortchanged. In fact, there was a solid increase in customer enrollment for multiple services. Waiting time was reduced with no cost increase. And, the new setup provided job enrichment opportunities when responsibilities were realigned to meet customer needs. This in turn decreased costly teller turnover, a recurrent problem.

The pivotal point in arriving at the branch group manager's ultimate solution was the way in which she responded to her colleague's first idea. Linda knew that implementing a policy of being receptive to new ideas requires specific skills. She handled the fresh idea with two of these: *paraphrasing* and the *developmental response.*

Paraphrasing

When her colleague offered the automat analogy, Linda paraphrased back, "If I understand this, you are suggesting we have a separate line for each general type of service—such as having one teller cashing checks, one teller taking deposits, etc." Linda's goal in paraphrasing was to confirm that she *really* had listened and grasped the key points. Listening validates the individual and his or her initiative. It demonstrates that ideas are worthy of respect.

The colleague responded, "That's not quite it. Actually I was going for the idea of helping customers who have simple transactions avoid getting stuck behind those who take lots of time. I want to give customers more control over their experience in the bank." Linda paraphrased again, "So the core of the idea is that customers have a variety of banking needs. Some transactions are complex and time consuming; some are quick and easy. But right now all customers have to wait in the same long line, regardless of needs. They may not get everything done when it's their turn. And the wait is both frustrating and unnecessary for someone just cashing a check. You're suggesting we enable customers to go where their needs will be best met." The colleague responded: "Yes, that's generally what I meant."

Steps in Paraphrasing. Repeat back to the speaker what you have heard. Stay as faithful as possible to the *essence of the idea* and the *important specifics* using your own words. Check your understanding with the speaker. Continue paraphrasing until the speaker verifies your understanding. Keep the paraphrase free of evaluation or opinion— the job here is to establish understanding, a mutual starting point. Evaluation is handled separately, and it comes later. Paraphrasing allows you to hear the idea fully, to understand it, and to defer premature judgment on its possible usefulness. It also keeps the idea and the speaker engaged, which permits further development of the idea.

Developmental Response

Following the paraphrase, the developmental response guides the transformation of the idea toward a more workable solution. Linda, the branch group manager, continued, "Yes, it would be useful to have customers feel less frustrated by lines. And to know that whomever they were waiting for could handle all their transactions. Now, how would we avoid mass confusion? Customers must know where to go."

Steps in the Developmental Response.   Separate your response into positive components (pros) and negative components (cons). First state the pros, the elements of the idea you want to preserve. Explain how each pro is useful. Be specific and genuine, listing at least one more pro than comes easily. Often a valuable avenue of thought is opened by that last, hard-to-give pro. This process acknowledges the contribution of the speaker and creates a better understanding of the components of the problem.

Then state the major cons, one at a time. Phrase each one so that it invites solutions; beginning with "how to," which redirects discussion toward solving the problem, toward generating an end result. For example, if the con is "Floor traffic would be confusing," use the phrase "How can we make traffic flow easy to understand? " As you consider each con singly, the process of correcting it will transform the original idea. The final solution may not even resemble the original thought.

A developmental response is important for several reasons. It focuses attention on the parts of the idea to be saved—often missed in the rush to identify flaws. It is a transforming process that builds beginning notions into final concepts. The developmental response also motivates. It demonstrates a manager's intention to solve the problem and steers the discussion to what needs to be accomplished. Nobody likes to be summarily dismissed, especially innovators. By going through the above process you give the innovator credit for the initiative, irrespective of whether the particular idea proves to be useful. Such credit encourages creative thinking on the part of each person who experiences this approach.

Applying the Paraphrase and Developmental Response

The paraphrase and developmental response are skills for establishing receptivity. They do not imply accepting or spending inordinate effort on every idea that comes along. Nor are they a disguised form of consensus management. Their purpose is to ensure that managers invest their time effectively to increase innovation among subordinates and to maximize problem-solving contributions. If, for example, you are vice president of marketing, and a sales director asks for a special rebate on a new pharmaceutical product to be offered to a select list of the company's best prospects, your first response might be: "That's illegal." Using the above skills, however, you would instead paraphrase the idea. Then you would say something like: "You're right that we want our best customers to order immediately and stock up on the new product. Is there another incentive we could give them? How can we create an incentive that would be both legal and ethical, one that appeals directly to our best customers?"

Listening to Nonexperts and Drawing Out Ideas behind Questions

The next example illustrates two additional skills that managers can use to promote receptivity: *"Listening to nonexperts"* and *"drawing out ideas behind questions."* Jack was marketing director for the agricultural chemicals division of a mid-sized company. The technical people had invented a new product that was a combination fertilizer and weed killer. Because of a setback in another product line, pressures were intense to introduce it immediately for use in spring planting. However, there was resistance from the marketplace: Farmers wanted more proof (beyond the company's assurances) that the product worked. Stan, vice president of manufacturing, asked Jack if someone in another division could provide that proof. Unsure of what he meant, Jack asked him to elaborate. Stan suggested that if the sales force in Australia could get the product tested down there (in the earlier growing season), those results would validate the product. As with Linda, Jack's first thoughts focused on flaws: Jack knew that the planting season was already underway in Australia and that the test logistics would be complicated and expensive, and he didn't think that farmers would really trust those results anyway. However, instead of refuting the notion, Jack used two powerful and almost invisible skills to foster innovation.

Listening to New Ideas from Nonexperts.   Jack knew that Stan was not a marketing expert. He also knew that innovation is often sparked by beginning ideas of nonexperts. As a person becomes an expert in any field, he or she develops a great deal of knowledge on what *cannot* be done. Therefore, over time, particular avenues for exploration are choked off. Most of the time, this is an efficient way to operate. However, it is counterproductive to close out any source of new ideas when breakthroughs are needed. In these instances the naivete of a nonexpert is beneficial. A nonexpert (naive but not stupid), not encumbered by years of experience and entrenched thought patterns, can often make suggestions that are fresh and divergent. In "invention sessions" I have run, I have been impressed with how often naive resources have sparked radically new lines of thought. However, this has only been effective when the experts were as open minded as was Jack. Without an open mind, it is all too easy—and destructive—to dismiss the nonexperts' contributions. You can multiply your idea sources by welcoming beginning ideas that come from nonexperts.

Drawing Out Ideas behind Questions.   Stan's initial query was "Could someone in another division help with providing proof?" Questions, by their very structure, invite answers. Jack could easily have said, "No, I don't think so—farmers don't want proof from the company. They want verification from peers, independent data." Question asked. Question answered. Few would find fault with such a response. Yet Jack understood a fundamental fact for tapping into creativity: *People frequently couch their ideas behind questions*, sometimes obscured so well that they are hard to recognize. In the context of creative problem solving, I have observed hundreds of people introducing ideas in question form. Couching an idea in a question is a comfortable way to introduce it. The pattern occurs because people (like Stan) have been burned before by harsh rejection of new ideas or because people need to protect thoughts that are not perfect or complete. By asking a question that appears to seek information, the speaker can more safely float the "trial balloon."

Jack knew that by simply encouraging Stan to elaborate, he would get more material that might be usable. And he did, picking up the ideas of doing the test (in Australia) before the U.S. growing season, and of the sales force being involved in the test phase. Then through paraphrasing and developmental response techniques, Jack took this beginning notion and worked it into a final idea. His solution came directly from the process of overcoming the imperfections of Stan's original suggestion. Ultimately, the domestic sales force selected a sample of leading American farmers; they hand-delivered indoor window boxes, seeds, and the new product to the spouses of the farmers (who have great influence in this home-based business). One window box was filled with the farmer's own soil plus the new fertilizer and weed killer. Another window box contained the farmer's own soil with no additives or with a competing product currently used by the farmer. In short order, there was visible evidence of the efficacy of the company's new product. The product launch for spring planting was successful.

Receptivity to Innovation

The preceding examples illustrate often-overlooked dimensions of managing innovation. Receptivity transcends a "wait and see" stance; it involves actively engaging in the process of problem solving. The solutions that Jack and Linda implemented were not handed to them in neat packages in response to requests; they didn't come as glorious "Eurekas!" that only needed knowing nods of approval. Linda and Jack had to be open to unsolicited ideas, they had to probe behind questions, listen to nonexperts, paraphrase to keep the innovator involved, and handle ambiguity through the transformation of the idea via the developmental response.

Further, as a rule, more creativity is needed in overcoming cons than is needed in generating initial ideas. The path of innovation is *not* linear; it is not a process of state the problem, generate novel ideas, choose the best idea, and implement it. Instead, the process oscillates between open-minded analytical assessment and free-form creative expansion.

Generating Fresh Thinking

Companies need fresh thinking; rehash just won't work. Fresh thinking embodies entirely new approaches to old problems; it is the essence of inspiration and an integral part of any innovative organization. The process of developing original ideas requires unconventional techniques. To develop fresh thinking, a manager needs first to understand the nature of ideas themselves and to learn these techniques.

The Composite Character of Ideas

New ideas are the core of innovation. Most think of an idea as a single entity; for example, the Eastern Airlines Shuttle, night baseball, or Federal Express's overnight package delivery. These ideas evoke a vivid, singular image. This singularity is deceptive. In fact, ideas are created by aggregation. A new idea is the result of an unusual combination of material obviously related to the problem and material apparently unrelated to the problem.

Examine, for instance, the idea of the Eastern Airlines Shuttle, an hourly unreserved flight service linking New York with Boston and Washington. The concepts of unreserved seating, paying on board, and a regular frequent schedule were borrowed from local bus services. (The early shuttle airplanes were emblazoned, "Eastern Airbus.") A twist on the old railroad passenger days provided an enhancement; the trains added a section, one car or more, if there were more reservations than available seats. In the first years of the Eastern Airlines Shuttle, a new plane was provided for extra passengers—even if it meant flying only one person on that plane.

So what is often perceived to be one idea is, in fact, a composite of several ideas, built by connections made among previously related and unrelated material. (In fact, the term "beginning idea," used for initial and imperfect ideas, suggests the aggregate nature of a "final idea.") By recognizing this characteristic, we can avoid the common mistake of prematurely judging an idea in a binary manner—good versus bad, go versus no go, right versus wrong. Understanding that ideas have many components will deter us from inadvertently discarding promising elements merely because there are also infeasible elements. As the saying goes, "Don't throw out the baby with the bath water."

Connection-Making Material

Generating quality connection-making material is the foundation for fresh thinking. The process can be difficult to accept in the beginning. It may seem slightly out of control and counter-rational, and if there is one thing drummed into managers, it is "Be rational, use your head!" This conditioning discourages "irrelevant" flights of fancy. Senior managers may do some constructive dreaming on the side, being in a position to give themselves that freedom. But subordinates are pressured to stick to the rules and take no chances of looking silly. If we want them to develop fresh thinking, we must guide them in productive speculation. The stage for this can be set by modeling the behavior and by pushing ourselves to be a little more unconventional. For example, the president of a successful exercise shoe company said, "I push myself to be a little outlandish in front of my conservative staff. I want them to feel free to take more risks, to think more adventurously."

Developing connection-making material is aided by conjuring up *absurd ideas*. Directed absurdity can stimulate original lines of thinking—unwalked paths that broaden horizons. Two techniques are "wishing" and "generating distant analogies." Although such practices appear alien to serious business, they produce large payoffs in ideas and attitudes. As Einstein said, "If at first an idea does not seem absurd, there is no hope for it." Wishes and distant analogies are simply mechanisms of temporarily removing unproductive constraints that surround most problems. They stimulate novel, surprising beginning thoughts that can lead to new, practical final concepts.

Consider the senior scientist at a large paper products company who *wished* he could make a gigantic facial tissue as strong as cloth but softer. The wish was a start—a freeing leap that gave him the momentum to think past constraints of current technology. Later, as the scientist was looking at an old leaded window, he got the first inkling (beginning idea) on how to achieve this goal. In the early days of window making, lead was used as reinforcement for small panes of glass in order to create larger windows. The scientist saw a connection. After hundreds of experiments, he had his wish: large sheets of tissue with tiny filaments (threads) of inlaid nylon. It was as strong as cloth and very soft. Today, the product is used widely in hospitals for garments and sheets.

Wishing. The steps for wishing are elementary—the necessary frame of mind is more difficult. Imagine outcomes as you would want them. Visualize those scenarios. Then, while temporarily ignoring logic, verbalize and write down a series of headline statements that start with, "I wish . . . " For example, "I wish we could make facial tissue as strong as cloth." And, "I wish nylon could be as soft as clouds." The attitude and posture to take with wishing are quite different from the wishing that occurs in fairy tales. In fairy tales, "I wish" and someone else magically provides. In innovation, "I wish" and I must practically provide. Wish in order to set directions and remove constraints in problem-solving efforts. The act of visualizing and articulating solutions—however improbable— gives the wisher momentum to realize the wish. Wishing focuses through processes and resources on essential goals. It refocuses the process of invention on how to solve the problem rather than on whether it can be solved. Wishing galvanizes people's most imaginative thinking. Other techniques, such as the developmental response discussed earlier, can then be used to guide the process started by wishing.

Generating Distant Analogies.   Sometimes "distant analogies" provide specific ideas that can be transformed into relevant solutions. Just as often distant analogies stimulate a fresh approach to the problem, which then may lead to a specific idea. That was the case when Peter, a food science executive for a major consumer package goods company, faced the recurring problem of flock (organic debris) floating in flavored syrup. The flock detracted from the product's appearance. His problem was that the method of removing the flock wasted large amounts of syrup itself. Because this had been an ongoing problem, Peter realized that he needed a novel perspective. He generated distant analogies to develop new avenues for investigation. With a nonexpert colleague, Peter transposed an aspect of the problem to a foreign context. They chose to imagine "debris" in the context of nature. Peter's goal was to get mental distance from the problem in order to find a new route to its solution. This approach is not an obvious one, but it is critical for introducing original thinking when traditional wisdom has failed. (The strategy is analogous to a sailboat whose destination is directly into the wind—the fastest voyage is not the straight route ahead, which could take you backward, but tacking from side to side, zigzagging toward your destination.) First, Peter and his colleague generated some connection-making images from "debris in the context of nature": raking piles of dead leaves in autumn; orange peels on road sides; logging in the Northwest, with rivers swollen with logs; a canoe floating toward a lake's dam (where debris was piled up). Then they explored the canoe image for insights or interesting directions. Alluding to the pull on the canoe toward the lake's dam, Peter recalled that tidal currents changed the surface characteristics of sea water. He had once worked on a harbor clean up for which they had used this principle. The glimmer of an idea began with a mental connection: "Let's change the surface tension of the syrup—like the lake water at dams and sea water in fast tides. If we could decrease the holding power of the syrup's surface, the flock might be removed more easily and without as much product waste." Ultimately they solved the problem using an evaporating chemical to reduce the syrup's surface tension.

Distant analogies are analogies from unrelated contexts; they are rich sources of new connection-making material. Recall the analogy of bank branches to automats that led to Linda's success in improving customer service. A seasoned practitioner of this technique can generate an almost infinite source of material for the connections that lead to fresh thinking. The *steps for generating distant analogies* are to state the problem, beginning with a directional phrase like "How to" or "I wish that." Choose a key word or phrase in our stated problem. (In the previous example, Peter used "debris.") Then choose a field or world or phrase from that world. (A useful rule of thumb is that the greater the distance the selected world is from the world of the problem, the greater the chance for freshness. For example, Peter's choice of "debris in the world of nature" was richer in potential than "debris in the world of manufactured products." He could have chosen from an unlimited number of other distant contexts, such as archaeology, European history, athletics or politics.) Once you have stimulated several images, choose a rich one and work to make connections between that and the original stated problem. Ultimately you will not accept many of these connections but you can't prejudge which lines of thought will be fruitful. Don't expect the use of distant analogies to be clear and easy. Even for those familiar with this process, it evokes a sense of ambiguity, uncertainty, and discomfort. This feeling was captured by a senior engineer, who said, "I feel like a chameleon on a plaid rug!"

Uncertainty and Ambiguity.

A natural instinct in the face of uncertainty and ambiguity is to eliminate those feelings. This impulse is reinforced by corporate cultures that seek to minimize the unpredictable. So we plan, we organize, we lead, we control so that people know where we are going and how we are going to get there. We even plan how to handle surprises before they occur. Unfortunately, in managing innovation, if we orient ourselves to eliminate uncertainty, we cap the wellspring of ideas. We make our lives more comfortable, sure, but only short term. Temporary periods of uncertainty and confusion are so critical to developing real originality that we need to welcome and encourage them at key stages. Uncertainty is an integral part of creativity.

Summary

The pressure for innovation is becoming more intense, manifesting itself in increased exhortations. Managers at all levels need to develop a new set of tools to make these directives operational. The skills in the two policy areas discussed—receptivity to ideas, and generating fresh thinking—are fundamental to any effort. They are also synergistic. With active receptivity to new ideas we can speculate more widely, knowing that as we come across fragile germs of ideas the environment for developing these thought-seeds will be more nurturing than negative. The rich ideas generated by fresh thinking demand more of our receptivity skills, thereby strengthening them, which in turn allows even richer speculation. The skills and techniques are much like the nylon threads in the tissue mentioned earlier—they aren't the whole cloth, but enough of them in the right place provide strength and flexibility to increase innovation throughout the organization.

15

Human Factors for Innovative Problem Solving

Scott G. Isaksen

Director, Center for Studies in Creativity,
State University College at Buffalo

Management is increasingly concerned with responding to changing conditions and achieving higher levels of productivity. The need to convene problem-solving groups to deal with these issues means that management must become more effective in using human resources. There are many different types of problem-solving groups. This chapter focuses on the "innovative" type.

Problem solving is innovative in that it calls for novel and useful responses. In addition, there are no predetermined or single-correct approaches. "Innovative problem solving" (IPS) is a set of procedures that can be used individually or with groups to define and analyze problems and challenges, generate and select promising ideas or options, and develop and find acceptance for those promising solutions. "Human factors" are considerations relating to individual styles and preferences for certain activities, motivational variables, aspects of group dynamics and development, and other people-related concerns. These factors are important as managers seek to improve productivity and effectiveness.

There are a variety of ways to apply innovative problem solving. The first is to use the skills, methods, and techniques individually, on challenges and opportunities you deal with alone. Another way is with small groups and in setting up organizational structures and contexts conducive to innovation. This second type of application uses IPS to involve those with immediate ownership in solutions. Structures can be actual working groups and ad hoc task teams convened for specific charges, or the focus can be more permanent and pervasive like that of creating self-managing teams or other organizational contexts within which to apply IPS skills. Such process-oriented skills are more durable and long-lasting than the rapidly changing specific technical knowledge required by organizations. Technical training needs to be augmented and extended through deliberate development of creativity-related skills.

Using Innovative Problem Solving

There are at least five areas to consider in using IPS: first, orientation and readiness issues; second, how various levels of application call for different types of leadership and climate; third, how IPS challenges require diverse roles for group members; fourth, aspects of group selection and development; and fifth, meeting certain logistical needs to optimize IPS.

Orientation and Readiness

Effective problem solving relies on a balance of two different types of thinking. The first is "creative" thinking in which one makes and communicates meaningful new connections by devising unusual new possibilities. The second is "critical" thinking, in which one analyzes and develops mechanisms to compare and contrast ideas; improve and refine concepts; screen, select, and support alternatives; and make judgments and effect decisions. These two different types of thinking are more complementary than contradictory and should be viewed as mutually supportive aspects of effective thinking and problem solving. One should seek a productive balance or harmony, not choose one over the other.

Understanding your type of thinking and problem-solving strengths and weaknesses can help you select appropriate techniques. The same applies to groups. Establishing clear ownership for directions and approaches can increase involvement and commitment to actions that are developed. "Ownership" refers to the level of influence someone has in finding a solution to the problem. It also means that the individual has serious interest in actually implementing solutions. Finally, ownership suggests that the individuals are really looking for imaginative thinking, that they are not simply trying to manipulate the group to agree with a predetermined bias.

Levels of Application

There are at least three levels in developing and implementing an IPS program. The first is learning basic methods and techniques. This can be accomplished by attending programs or hiring internal or external consultants. The focus is on teaching or training to provide direct instruction in how to deliver technologies. The organizational climate needs to promote the importance of learning and applying creativity-relevant skills. (The more higher level support the better!)

At the second level of application we practice the process. Opportunities are provided for using the tools, combining them together to form the process. This combining needs to be practiced. The leader should orchestrate, demonstrate, familiarize, and organize. The participants need to feel safe. The group works on sample problems and begins applying IPS technology.

The third level deals with real-life concerns and opportunities. Outlets for application take shape. A corporate cadre or IPS task group begins to function. Leadership strategy is facilitation. The facilitator creates networks, forms teams, and helps guide the application process. (There should be several facilitators who share responsibilities of leading the actual IPS sessions. The level-three facilitator may be the individual with corporate responsibility for starting the IPS program.) Be aware of group dynamics and development. The environment must support real ownership for clients of IPS sessions. The clients need to know that they can apply the solutions developed, that they have the necessary freedom to implement originality.

Roles

The person who has the greatest degree of ownership of the challenge or problem is called the "client." The person who helps the client use the IPS process is called the "facilitator." Those who provide input and ideas are called the "resource group." Understanding clear ownership or clientship reinforces the separation of roles, which is essential when using IPS. The facilitator guides the client and resource group through the IPS process. The client makes decisions and provides background information. It is the client who will ultimately determine success, deciding whether the resource group has generated appropriate options. The resource group may not have direct ownership, but their idea-generation efforts provide raw material from which the client screens, selects, and develops solutions.

Group Selection and Development

The style of the leader should be consistent with group participation. It would be counterproductive if the leader were to autocratically order all group members to "enjoy" participation. In selecting a group, consider such factors as number of members; diversity of people, jobs, ages, and levels of expertise; appropriate people to play the three roles of facilitator, client, and resource group members. In a typical IPS session, the number would be limited to five to seven including facilitator and client. If the client is searching for an unusually novel approach or solution, bring together a diversity of people who do not have a great deal of expert knowledge regarding the challenge (or who do not view it as does the client). This would be especially true for generating many varied ideas. Use experts later for considering and analyzing those options. Of course the client maintains control of deciding which ideas or combinations of ideas to consider for implementation and may wish to gather many ideas from a variety of resource groups and IPS sessions.

Be sensitive to group dynamics. One of the classic leadership dilemmas is getting work done while at the same time maintaining positive human relations. Understanding groups increases effectiveness and productivity. Groups, for example, go through certain phases of development. According to the model in Figure 15.1, the stages a group goes through while moving toward some desired goal are relatively predictable and controllable. The two dimensions of the model are personal relations and task functions. Regardless of the group, people who come together progress from independent individuals to group members, to people who feel attachment to each other, to people who are able to link up in creative ways. Personal relations involve how people feel about each other, the commitments they make, and the problems they have. Task functions involve learning what the task is, mobilizing to accomplish it, and doing the work.

The two dimensions, personal relations and task functions, form a matrix that highlights the interaction between characteristic human relations and task-oriented behaviors at the various stages of group

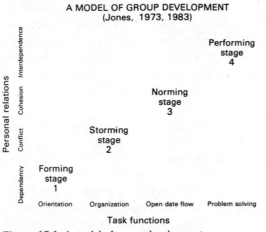

A MODEL OF GROUP DEVELOPMENT
(Jones, 1973, 1983)

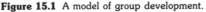

Figure 15.1 A model of group development.

development. The model provides a common language whereby members can explore the emerging characteristics and needs of their group.

Forming. In the initial stage, personal relations are characterized by dependency, and the major task functions concern orientation. In the beginning of the group's life, individual members tend to depend on the leader to provide all the structure, leaning on the facilitator, chairperson, or manager to set the ground rules, establish the agenda, and guide the proceedings. The parallel task function is the orientation of group members to the assigned work. The issues have to be specified. The nature of the work has to be explored to give common understanding of what the group has been organized to do. Expected behavior at this point is questioning. Why are we here? What are we supposed to do? How are we going to get it done? What are our goals?

Storming. Stage two is characterized by conflict in personal relations and organization in task functions. This stage is referred to as "storming" because interpersonal conflict inevitably ensues. The conflict may remain hidden, but it is there. People bring to small-group activity unresolved personal conflicts with regard to authority, structure, influence, dependency, rules, and agenda, and they experience interpersonal conflict as they organize to get work done. Who is going to be responsible for what? What are going to be the rules? The limits? The reward system? The criteria?

Norming. In stage three, personal relations are marked by cohesion and the task function is data flow. Here people begin to experience a feeling of "groupness," a sense of clarification at having resolved conflict. They begin sharing ideas and emotions, giving and soliciting feedback, and exploring actions related to the task. People feel good about what is going on; they like being part of a group, and there is emerging openness. Sometimes there is even abandonment of the task—and a period of play, an expression of the joys of cohesion, ensues.

Performing.   Stage four is not achieved without attention and effort. It is marked by interdependence in personal relations and problem solving in task function. Interdependence means that members can work alone, in any subgrouping, or as a total unit. Members are both highly task-oriented and highly person-oriented. Activities are marked by both collaboration and functional competition. The group's tasks are well defined, there is high commitment to common activity, and there is support for experimentation with solving problems.

Logistics

Materials should be made available—flipcharts, paper, markets, tape, etc. The room should be organized so that everyone can comfortably see the facilitator. There should be space to post the completed sheets of flipchart paper for easy review.

IPS Methods and Techniques

The IPS process is any problem-solving process that balances creative and critical thinking. Many are described in the literature; I have found one to be particularly helpful. Figure 15.2 depicts a six-stage model for innovative problem solving. Each stage has a divergent or creative phase and a convergent or critical phase. Again, it is the effective balance of these aspects that is sought. These stages can be grouped for effective application. "Mess finding," "data finding," and "problem finding" lead to an effective understanding of the problem. This grouping is "problem analysis." The outcome is a clear definition of the challenge. This could be the agenda of a meeting between the problem owner (client) and the process leader (facilitator). In the "idea finding" stage the resources of the group are absolutely essential. This is an "idea generation" meeting. All group members are concerned and given background information and a starting definition of the problem. The session emphasizes generating ideas and options for the client. Finally, the stages of "solution finding" and "acceptance finding" can be

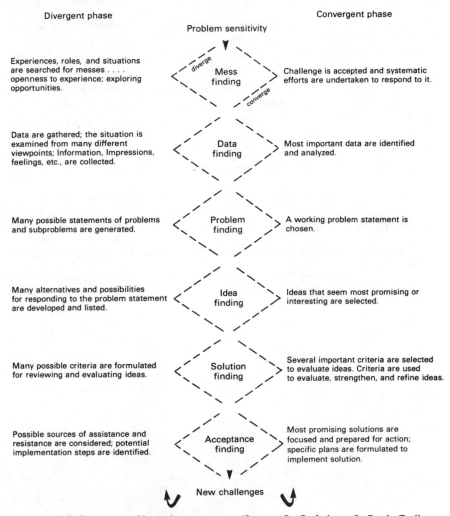

Divergent phase   Convergent phase

Problem sensitivity

Experiences, roles, and situations are searched for messes . . . . openness to experience; exploring opportunities.

diverge
Mess finding
converge

Challenge is accepted and systematic efforts are undertaken to respond to it.

Data are gathered; the situation is examined from many different viewpoints; Information, Impressions, feelings, etc., are collected.

Data finding

Most important data are identified and analyzed.

Many possible statements of problems and subproblems are generated.

Problem finding

A working problem statement is chosen.

Many alternatives and possibilities for responding to the problem statement are developed and listed.

Idea finding

Ideas that seem most promising or interesting are selected.

Many possible criteria are formulated for reviewing and evaluating ideas.

Solution finding

Several important criteria are selected to evaluate ideas. Criteria are used to evaluate, strengthen, and refine ideas.

Possible sources of assistance and resistance are considered; potential implementation steps are identified.

Acceptance finding

Most promising solutions are focused and prepared for action; specific plans are formulated to implement solution.

New challenges

Figure 15.2 Creative problem-solving process. *(Source: S. G. Isaksen & D. J. Treffinger, Creative Problem Solving: The Basic Course, Bearly Limited, Buffalo, NY, 1985.)*

grouped together as "solution development." During this time frame the client, with or without group resources, generates criteria and analyzes options. In addition, plans are made to overcome sources of resistance and utilize sources of assistance. This can be the agenda for a third meeting.

Employing a deliberate and explicit process during IPS tracks group resources to client needs. Group members can learn their roles and know what is expected of them during the various phases of the process. There are a wide variety of methods and techniques to be used during

IPS. Just as a mechanic selects certain tools for specific jobs, the facilitator will select right techniques for specific challenges.

The IPS process need not be applied in an overly-structured or monotonously linear manner. Real problem solving rarely occurs in a neat, step-by-step fashion. However, the process serves as an organizer for the vast number of available procedures. In a sense, learning IPS is like learning piano scales: One starts out practicing them in a particular order; actual pieces of music, however, contain the same notes, but in an entirely different flow and sequence. Learning IPS helps select and evaluate appropriate strategies for creative problem solving.

Bibliography

S. G. Isaksen and D. J. Treffinger: *Creative Problem Solving: The Basic Course*, Bearly Limited, Buffalo, NY, 1985.

J. E. Jones: An updated model for group development. A paper presented at the 29th Annual Creative Problem Solving Institute, Decker Memorial Lecture, Buffalo, New York, 1983.

16

Innovation Death Need Not Occur

C. Joshua Abend

President, Innovation America Group, Inc.

The connection between business failure and creativity failure became apparent in the early 1970s. I call it the "innovation death syndrome," and it is the most devastating of corporate diseases. Innovation, after all, is survival, and therefore innovation death and business death are synonymous. The bright spot is that we now know more about the syndrome and there is a greater likelihood of curing it. How to recognize terminal symptoms? What strategies can avoid them? Like other serious illnesses, prevention is easier than cure.

To begin with, think of innovation death as nature's way of clearing out old products, old ideas, and old companies. The death is the outcome of long years of avoidance or error in dealing with internal and external changes. Internal changes come in the form of new values, attitudes, organizational styles, and new patterns of operating and communicating. External changes come as a result of social shifts, economic dislocation, or technological substitution. Too often the corporate response can be "It can't be happening to us" or "It's just a fad and it will go away." Unfortunately, "it" never goes away—but companies do. External changes require addressing novel situations and understanding changing customer needs. Innovation death is not always apparent until it materializes as cutbacks, pink slips, layoffs, and factory closings. In the early stages it comes as giving up certain products and market share or withdrawing from funding new projects. These signs can be terminal, but they can be corrected. I offer several steps to healthier, more responsive and profitable business outcomes. Quick remedy is possible, but to apply these steps properly takes time and vigorous attention.

Checkpoint Innovation

A company must be serious about innovation and willing to undertake the preparation and commitment that it demands. Don't kid yourself: This is not like swallowing a pill; it means doing things very differently. Some aspects may be uncomfortable, so decide if you can handle disruptive changes in exchange for excellence. If the answer is Yes, develop a policy that assures implementation. A way to determine if you are *not* ready or *not* willing to proceed is to check if your current style matches the following: (1) everything you or your company does must return to center and everything must relate back to present policies, (2) you or your associates have only one plan or goal and dismiss examining all other alternatives or options, (3) you or your associates are withholding resources necessary for developing new directions, (4) you or your associates do not want to share the process with others.

Once deciding to move forward, begin by diagnosing your present situation. How can you improve it? Don't build a skyscraper on a mushy foundation. Here are some critical diagnostics—probes or tests of organizational innovation:

1. What is the general response time for assessing new directions and ideas?

2. Every organization shows inertia to new proposals, some a matter of years between first exposure and decision time. What is your inertia pattern?

3. Determine gestation time. Once approved, how long does it take an idea to get through your pipeline and manifest itself as a product, program, or system?

4. How do ideas get fertilized? Do they always come from the top? Are ideas artificially inseminated from outside?

5. What has to happen to gain acceptance? Who pushes forward and who pulls back?

6. What is the general level of resistance? (Resistance is functional in avoiding weird or improper behavior, but it can also block out good impulses.)

7. Who has the ball with respect to innovation? Is there only one source? Is innovation thought to be the exclusive domain and responsibility of R&D? (If so, that's one reason for innovation death.)

8. How is innovation encouraged and what kind of continuity does it have? Can you tell when it's being snuffed out?

9. What about slippage? Do your programs "stop and go?" If so, why?

10. What is the mechanism for raising questions? For resolving issues? For changing policy? For establishing collaborative undertakings?

11. Another diagnostic is recognizing what I call "Band-Aid projects"—minor undertakings to address losses, usually too little and too late. These projects dribble away resources and erode organizational spirit. If your strategy repertoire is short term, you are marked for certain innovation death.

12. Check meetings that never end. Many executives do not discriminate among purposes of a meeting; is it a think session, decision session, fault finding session, or reporting session? People tumble out 3 hours later wondering what happened and why they were there.

13. What about project aborts? Of all the projects authorized, how many bombed out, and why? Should go-no go criteria have been established earlier? Are people flying by the seat of their pants? They may be working on the wrong projects or laboring under the wrong priority. Enlighten them.

14. Don't overlook isolation from reality. It takes the form of reasoning that "we have always been in this business and we have always done it this way"—that too can be the kiss of death to innovation.

15. The last diagnostic is watching for desperation projects, the kind that get green lights at times of business or technological anxiety. The high-risk idea may come from the top or the middle, but somehow it gains endorsement because it seems the only hope. Up and down the line no one wants to defy destiny, and so they nod approval but they fear disaster—which is inevitable. Nowhere is

the fear greater than in the heart of the president, because he or she knows that nobody will confess serious misgivings—that would be disloyalty—and that the president is shielded from opinions below. Thus a project destined for death becomes blessed "dogma." The strange thing is that it occurs not out of conflict but out of inability to deal openly with agreement. Everybody wants to be on the bandwagon; no one wants to be a spoilsport or left behind. The antidote? Organizational dogma should be challenged; if the idea has merit it will be improved—and if it does not, let it sink.

Removing Impediments

Innovation is process for change. It is usually regarded as an intuitive, random, and uncontrollable event. Yet it has specific characteristics that can be played as predictably as one plays a musical instrument. Innovation is a *successful* solution to a specific problem; it is what nature gave us to survive, and it is natural, not strange. It affects the entire organization because if innovation health suffers, all aspects suffer. "Management by objectives," "productivity," "quality circles," and so forth are thought of as distinct and separate ideas; innovation is the drive shaft that can tie everything together. We are dealing with a manageable and rational process. It can be installed for generating new ideas, for evaluating them, for knowing where to start a project, and for measuring the innovation capabilities of individuals, departments, and divisions. Understanding how innovation works increases the likelihood of its success.

There are forces that seem to suck up every form of creative light. Good ideas and good intentions vanish mysteriously into a void and are never heard from again. "Corporate black holes" of varying sizes exist in most organizations and cause innovation death. One such hole is poor climate brought on by heavy-handed bureaucracy. Another hole is trench warfare, which prevents collaboration because of fractionalized, divided, and counterproductive competition among groups.

Next comes "Titanic" invulnerability—big, strong, and unsinkable. Wouldn't it be nice if we could recognize the Titanic the moment we stepped aboard? We can! Another form of invulnerability is the belief that somehow, sometime, someone is going to break down the door with the answer to our next new product or next marketing plan. It is fantasy to believe that some outside force is voluntarily going to waltz in, put together a successful concept, and hand it over. Only a deliberate innovation plan and process will make that happen.

To remove impediments, house clean. Get rid of *fear of ideas* because they could rock the boat; *inspirational bias*, which suggests that ideas spring only from mysterious places; and *professional prejudice*, an example of which is the quotation attributed to Admiral Leahy in 1941, "That thing will never go off and I speak as an *expert* on explosives." He was referring of course to the atom bomb. Regardless of evidence to the contrary, there is always someone announcing that it can't be done. Adaptation to change is apparently so difficult on the human ego that denying it is one way of coping with it. A vice president of a multinational company once told me that as long as "our competitors won't improve their product, there is not much point in improving ours." In 7 years that well-known division went from first to last in market share. Complacent statements are generated by vested interest or muddled thinking, and if you hear them often you can detect innovation death in the air; it usually smells sweet.

Everyone knows what brainstorming is, or do they? You meet sort of semiseriously and play a group game that has no ground rules other than "anything goes;" you address a problem for a few minutes and hope that perhaps some brilliant solution will emerge out of this craziness. Isn't that it? The word "brainstorming" was invented by Alex Osborne about 40 years ago, but unfortunately it never rose above the stigma of silliness. Properly applied it is really a rational approach to problem solving and controlling creative ideas by using brain patterns and images. Brainstorming as an undisciplined and random exercise had at least one main virtue—it permitted people to suggest "stupid ideas" without getting penalized for them. What I call "creative leveraging" has much to do with left and right brain functions; it means being able to see in new ways. In the western world the left brain, the sequential analytical side, has been the dominant style of problem solving. When we get an "ah-ha!" in a cold shower or driving to work, it's our right brain at work; silently, holistically, subconsciously it has been processing a solution. How to access the right brain, increase those ah-has, and magnify our ability for innovation? This is possible through a whole range of brainstorming concepts, methodologies, and processes (see Chapter 13).

Innovation Death—A Close Call

What service does your product actually perform for customers and why do they really buy it? That question got lost in the Singer Company some years ago. Foundaries and factories producing sewing machines for decades were left idle almost overnight. Yet those "in charge" seem to have been in a hypnotic trance as the market slipped away. Why? Singer was caught by social reorientation. Women were no longer at home sewing dresses and repairing garments. They were enjoying new income and earnings; it was easier to buy a $15 dress in K-Mart than struggle with stitches. Women were opting for cameras, televisions, and other more entertaining products. Few Singer insiders fully recognized what was happening—it was a puzzlement considering their historical success. It can't happen, right? So the message got through only when the ship actually hit the iceberg.

A product, after all, performs something that a customer wants performed; when that changes, the product must also change. Singer to its credit did develop the Athena, the first electronic sewing machine, which, although expensive, was successful because it did things that women no longer wanted to fuss with (such as automatic embroidery, stitching patterns, and other complicated sewing tasks). When a need is satisfied in a different way socially or by product substitution, the previous product may simply evaporate. Recall what happened when digital watches arrived. The new chip technology not only displayed the time, but the date and other data as well. Virtually overnight it displaced the old technology. But for many watchmakers innovation death needn't have occurred, because the analog watch still had innovative things to offer.

Could creative leverage have helped in these situations to explore alternative possibilities? Certainly. It could have sparked intriguing and perhaps annoying thoughts such as: "How else might the service be rendered? How else might the function be performed? How else might the product be threatened?" This approach does not guarantee that we can always discover the needle in the haystack—but proactive creativity has to be better than waiting for events to occur and then reacting to them. Isn't passivity the biggest dice roll of all? It amazes me that executives and directors do not insist that the destiny of companies and their products be placed under continuous creative scrutiny, if only as insurance that innovation death will not occur. Not to do so is a serious omission in fiduciary responsibility. If you think innovation is risky, try standing still.

Making It Happen

Let's talk about implementing innovation. Making it happen has to do with action. Here are some suggestions for applying positive counter-pressure to overcome inertia and normal resistance to change:

1. Give endorsement of innovation personally to people, not just through reports. It is not enough to make statements in the company newsletter or to take expensive ads in newspapers. The best way for a CEO to induce innovation is to parachute into operations. Stroll down the halls and "accidentally" encounter the first engineering staff member you find. Introduce yourself; say, "Hi, I'm out for excellence and innovation. I want to reward it and I want to see you do it. Are there any ideas that interest you now? What can I do to make innovation happen more frequently? " Do that about a dozen times and word spreads like wildfire; it should cost about one-tenth the price of a corporate PR campaign with 100 times the impact.

2. Develop a customized innovation strategy. Just because it works for IBM doesn't mean it's going to work for you. Find consensus within your company culture and apply what fits. The principles of innovation remain essentially the same but application and approach will change.

3. Make your innovation strategy a team action, and let the team help create the plan or policies. The team can pick the most creative players and recommend the best procedures. Use the peer group as a driving force for innovation.

4. Determine what happens after the boss "blesses it." Can it be killed later? Presumably if a project gets a green light at the top, it will fly, but those who want to slow progress can still shoot it down. Be prepared for flak.

5. Install rewards and incentives that promote innovation. Such incentives are not necessarily the same as for sales personnel; reaching creative minds is different. They want freedom and opportunity to explore; they want recognition; they want permission to fail.

Back to implementation. Never forget organizational politics as it relates to change. You may have to amend some ground rules. Add innovation to corporate and personal objectives. Rate managers and staff by their ability to find new opportunities and unconventional solutions—and do not reward managers who leave behind an impoverished legacy. We come from an era in which many product managers who sapped the system have been promoted. What a terrible model. Who can best correct this? The president. Only the CEO can really inspire people. He or she must modify the natural tendency for risk aversion and scrap the penalties that are frequently imposed upon change makers and risk takers. The CEO can say it's okay to take chances and can widen the boundaries of risk.

Be clear about expected results and announce your expectations. Employees should know it's okay to struggle for innovation and to be measured by it, even if their direct boss is dragging his or her heels. To maximize innovation, do it in a positive, confident way. Do not keep those aims a mystery. Innovation should be easy going, and successful. Innovation death need not occur; but if it does, one can only assume it is nature's final way of making room for tomorrow.

17

Building and Breaking Creativity: What Religion Teaches Business about Commitment

Robert Lawrence Kuhn

Investment Banker, Senior Research Fellow,
IC² Institute, University of Texas at Austin, and,
Adjunct Professor, Graduate School of Business
Administration, New York University

George T. Geis

Research Coordinator, Center for Human Resources
Management, UCLA

How does personal creativity develop within companies? What makes individual innovation productive for businesses? We believe that personal creativity must be linked with company commitment for beneficial innovation to work well in corporate environments. Personal creativity erupts from individual initiative. Commitment is the firm bond between individuals and organizations. The linkage is key: Only by joining personal creativity with company commitment can novel thinking promote corporate welfare. Our focus is managers—those who are creative themselves and those who manage the creativity of others. Both must understand the commitment-creativity connection. We explore it in a novel way.

Commitment is a primal force impelling employees to achieve company goals, and such commitment is tied closely to company creativity. The coupling is critical. We suggest that there is a direct relationship between the level of employee commitment and the extent to which that employee engages in creative efforts on behalf of the company. Creative acts demand a level of energy expenditure not commonly given by one who is only "routinely" attached to an organization. Personal creativity, we say, is proportional to company commitment. Furthermore, building and maintaining the commitment of people almost always involves a creative, even artistic, effort by leadership. To build commitment, managers must not only understand the needs and goals of employees but must also be sensitive to how their particular organizational society (culture) influences the individual level of commitment. Commitment is both vital and delicate, and care must be taken in its development.

Commitment

The commitment strength of employees determines the goal achievement of companies. Commitment makes personnel put out something extra—bust quotas in factories, close difficult sales, solve nagging problems. Personal reward is important; monetary and career gain is part of the story. But not the whole story. Human desire can transcend self. Group goal is magnetic. People want larger identification; we all want to see a big picture. Why does personnel commitment help companies? Efficiency, productivity, and creativity are each driven by employee motivation, and high motivation is a clear characteristic of successful firms. Personal fulfillment and company success are complementary targets, and we shoot at them both.

Commitment is the crux of "the firm bond," the affective bridge between individuals and organizations. What exactly is "commitment?" We define it as *the link between personal meaning and company mission*. Mission is the heart of company existence just as meaning is the soul of employee dedication. Each is driving energy and directing force—businesses seek to achieve objectives, employees strive to fulfill purposes. Personal meaning and company mission are the two poles of our axis, and around them this firm bond revolves. Commitment is the emotional lines of force that attract individuals to institutions, the mental might that empowers goal-directed work. Commitment is "purpose with action," an internal desire of employees to achieve an external objective of companies. Metaphors come easy: The "glue" that produces group stickiness? The "knot" that ties together independent individuals? (Knot, not glue, seems a better metaphor for the firm bond since ideally one should be "tied," not "stuck," to an organization.) Commitment signals emotional attachment, and it runs the gamut from self-sacrifice to adversarial attack. One way to examine commitment is to watch where it works best. This is our novelty. What we present about commitment is rooted in religion.[1]

Commitment in Religion

Don't mix business and religion? That advice, given for generations, we ignore. Why? To help companies improve employee dedication. Whatever makes commitment in religion so potent should make commitment in business more meaningful. We combine ecclesia and commerce in an unusual brew. Our concern is people and companies; we seek meaning and fulfillment for the former, mission and performance for the latter. Finding transcendence—a prime motivator in religion—is relevant, applicable, and necessary for corporate creativity. Vision is vital: Moving hearts and minds is more important than fattening wallets and pocketbooks; generating visceral support for policies and programs is what firm fortune is all about.

Most organizations, when viewed from within, consider themselves unique. But these same organizations, when observed from without, show remarkable sameness. Fundamentals affect them all: goals, strategy, structure, leadership, succession, politicking, finances, and related items. From company to congregation, management and motivation play crucial roles. How to make employees more committed and creative? How to make companies more productive and successful? Commercial demands parallel spiritual desires. Carl in his Bible school parallels Betty in her computer company. What each seeks is personal fulfillment. Life within any organization has spiritual overtones. People and organizations are surprisingly similar whether pushed by profits and positions or pulled by eternity and morality. The same mental processes are involved in business and religion. They run equivalent races, occupy parallel universes. The nature of religious commitment is merely a cleaner, more overt form of the same magical mental force that binds individuals to institutions and energizes goal-directed action. Understanding what commitment means in religious organizations helps explain what it means in all organizations.

Parallels between business and religion are stunning. Founders of firms are similar in character and style to founders of churches. When "truth" must change, the organization is shaken—truth to a church is "doctrine," to a company it is "strategy." Strategic change in the latter echoes doctrinal change in the former. In each the break is traumatic. Liberals strive against conservatives, young radicals against old guard— the infighting often putting politics to shame. Another example is hype: dated doomsday prophecies in a religion; unachievable earnings projections in a business. When doomsday fails to arrive on schedule or when earnings fall short of forecasts, faith is shaken and commitment eroded. This is a shame. Biblical belief far transcends misinterpreted prophecies just as company confidence should well exceed inflated projections.

A fascinating example of religion-business counterparts is the so-called "double standard," when leaders enjoy privilege, power, honor, wealth, and license that their followers do not. What the clergy (professional) can do, the laity (amateur) cannot. One reads with regularity reports of religious leaders involved in personal activities hardly religious. This morality gap is severely criticized by outsiders, yet the faithful do not complain. Such support of superiors, even when discovered in sin, mystifies observers and bewilders critics. Yet there is logic here, and the same social contract, believe it or not, binds executives and employees in companies. Differentiation in personal behavior, privilege of position, power to control subordinates, license to supersede rules, organizational honor, and degree of reward are all present. What executives are permitted, workers are not. The double standard is a two-edged sword. Cutting one way, it affirms the superior rights of leadership. Cutting the other way, it legitimizes the social position of workers. Not everyone can be a member of the ruling hierarchy, and the double standard justifies each end of the axis.

In our dual study of business and religion, we have experienced the parallels. The examples are real; the people we know. Fred W. really discarded his business because of his religion; Roger A. really discarded his religion because of his business. Steve L. really agonized when thrown out of his church; Alice R. really achieved when comforted by her church. Clarence S., though banished by his congregation, would not forsake it; Ralph R., though lateralized by his corporation, would not leave it.

How does religion highlight commitment? With ultimate things at stake, unusual things are done. How much sacrifice to preach the Word! How much inspiration in music, art, literature, law! Religious belief inflames human emotions; so to view commitment, religious organizations become a powerful "magnifying glass." Thus we use this "organizational lens" to focus on commitment, to understand how creativity is generated in companies. Can the attitudes of ministers in sects, for example, shed light on the effectiveness of managers in companies? Can understanding the fidelity of church members improve the loyalty of factory workers? What follows are conclusions about commitment in business; they are derived from examining commitment in religion.

Commitment Styles

From our work with both business and religious groups we categorize various styles of commitment: "Core" (when fervent group belief dominates—"partisans"), "calculative" (when personal benefit rules—"adherents"), and "cog" (when status quo dominates—"routiners"). Commitment also has its dark side, a nether world populated with "disengageds" (cog negative), "disaffecteds" (calculative negative), and "adversaries" (core negative).

Core commitment. This style fuses personal belief with organizational creed. It involves profound private devotion to publicly recognized goals and the melding of these group aspirations into one's own identity. It means that an employee wholly accepts company ideals and values and has internalized them. Such a person will adopt and reflect the style of the organization, the culture of the company, the attitude of the group. An individual with core commitment keeps the organization's welfare at heart; building the company determines general behavior and specific action. Individual creativity is motivated here, at least in part, by seeking collective benefit. This is the arena in which, for normal needs, personal creativity is most productive.

Calculative commitment. This one starts with the individual, not the organization. The prime consideration is personal gain. How effectively are one's total needs being satisfied? How does the employee benefit from the company or from personal creative achievement? How much is he or she "making" in the broadest sense of the term? Calculations, measurements, benchmarks, and yardsticks—these are important. What is one's total net income—financial and psychic, now and in the future? Comparisons are part of the equation, current company versus other opportunities. Creativity happens here, but only when the person perceives strong direct benefits.

Cog commitment. The last style is present when work is seen only as necessary routine. Little meaning is present, little emotion is felt. The job gets done but just barely. External pressures and constant controls are necessary for motivation. As for real creativity, forget it for cogs.

Aspects of core, calculative, and cog commitment can be found in most people. One style, however, usually dominates. This is especially true in response to organizational mission. At different moments in one's business career, commitment style may shift. To cross such a boundary is not without trauma. (Different commitment styles may be expressed in different situations. For example, a person may be core as a political volunteer in an election campaign, calculative as a part-time MBA student, and cog as a salesperson pitching accounts.)

Commitment Types

We can use commitment strength types to assess creative contribution on the job. Relationships, however, are complex. Standard journeyman creativity, such as incremental innovations extending current products, is likely to be strongest at both ends of the scale (core +/−) and weakest in the middle (cog +/−). (Compare, from the New Testament, the similar creative efforts put forth by the partisan Paul and the adversary Saul. Routiners and disengageds, cog +/−, will not likely expend the physical effort or psychic energy necessary for creative development.) Dynamic breakthrough creativity, however, is a different story. Generating ideas that challenge tradition and upset the established way, such as devising radically new products that render current products *obsolete*, often requires peculiar personal traits. Such creativity may be strongest when commitment is calculative, when corporate and personal interests blend, even by coincidence.

We postulate six categories of commitment types. They reflect varying degrees of willingness to exert personal effort to support (or hinder) organizational goals.

Partisans (core +).   They radiate maximum commitment. They are dedicated and persistent, the backbone of organizations. Unshakable in mind and deed, zealous in fervor and intensity, they are ready to sacrifice self for company good. Wholehearted belief, irrespective of personal benefit, is the key characteristic of a partisan. Such blind loyalty, however, can hinder the iconoclastic freedom required for revolutionary creativity.

Adherents (calculative +).   They are motivated to promote and protect the organization. Their motivation is typically a mix of internal and external elements. They behave proactively to support the system.

Positive organizational action is important to them, although the basis is often enlightened self-interest. Building the business for personal reward is the essence of an adherent. Vibrant creativity is often highest here since personal benefits are maximized within a clear context of company contribution.

Routiners (cog +). They are a shade more positive than neutral, requiring direct external motivation to fulfill company expectations. Work is done, but action is passive and consequences are of little personal value. Keeping the status quo is all the routiner wants. Don't look for much creativity here.

Disengageds (cog −). They are psychologically retired, slightly more negative than neutral. Jobs are done and tasks are accomplished but with no interest and marginal performance. There is no personal involvement. Their passive presence can produce a deleterious effect on other workers, depressing motivation, creativity, and productivity. Weighing a company down is the contribution of the disengaged.

Disaffecteds (calculative −). They may or may not still be associated with the company. Whether from within or without, they work to foil or frustrate the organization, especially when doing so will serve their own interests. Personal profit from obstructing a company is what the disaffected seeks. Unfortunately, creativity can prosper, if not flourish, under such circumstances.

Adversaries (core −). They are energetic foes of the company, operating actively and perhaps maliciously from either inside or outside. They seek dramatic change in the organization's goals, policies, structure, or leadership, and often nothing less than complete change at the top will suffice. Overthrowing the system, even irrespective of personal benefit, is the mission of the adversary, Creativity, here, may be blinded by emotion.

The trick for business? Build toward core while respecting calculative and minimizing cog—but always stay on the positive side.

Building Commitment Creativity

How can core commitment be strengthened, enhancing corporate creativity? Commitment builders are powerful. Each stimulates individual creativity in group settings. We focus on five mechanisms: "identification" (melding employee and company interests) , "confidence" (employee trust in company), "momentum" (company forward movement), "responsibility" (personal position), and "accomplishment" (attaining goals). These mechanisms can be used for improving "normal" corporate creativity, for stimulating the kinds of innovations required for competitive advantage. (Triggering "radical" creativity is less predictable and less related to employee-company bonding.) But theory is one thing, life another. Beware simple solutions and cookbook recipes.

Identification.   The fusion of interests between person and group; the extension of ego to include company; the expansion of empirical self. What makes an individual allocate ego to organization? Why do people exchange personal freedoms for group constraints and exert private effort to achieve common objectives? Why create for someone else? If reasons are ones of necessity, whether financial needs or administered coercion, the commitment is often calculative or cog and the creativity is often weak. To build core commitment, to rouse partisans, it is necessary to form structural linkage between personal meaning and company mission. This is identification, and in such an environment creativity (at least normal creativity) flourishes. Identification is amplified by importance or uniqueness. It is difficult to identify with a company if the individual does not perceive the presence of something salient. Identification requires significance, a resonance with what's important to the person. The process of identification has an invigorating effect. People fired up by causes are people empowered for creativity. Related concepts: "meaningfulness," the sense that group membership is important in some larger (perhaps transcendent) way; "participation," a personal stake in company ownership, whether literally or figuratively.

Confidence.   The belief that the company can be trusted in its stated policies and public pronouncements; a relaxed conviction that the organization is concerned with the welfare of the individual, that the group cares for its member. Nothing promotes creativity more than confidence. Nothing holds the firm bond steadier than the anchor of trust, the internal comfort of knowing that your company will promise what is right and do what it promises. Confidence underlies all elements of commitment and without it all else is for naught. Frequent organizational change, for example, inhibits high creative output. Leadership is critical: Confidence in the boss is confidence in the company. It is easy for a company to keep confidence when it is present, but it is difficult to regain it when lost. Employees have a natural tendency to believe the best but become suspicious once fooled. Confidence of employees is something companies must not take for granted. It should be developed actively and monitored constantly. Related concepts: "integrity," the honesty and fidelity of the organization; "consistency," the stability and reliability of its policies; "fairness," the company record in dealing evenhandedly without bias or prejudice. Stability and consistency, we should note, do not mean stagnancy and torpidity. Creative companies can be stable, and innovative ones, consistent. A firm that brings out highly original products can certainly generate confidence among employees. The excitement brings its own consistency, and the regular introductions its own stability.

Momentum. The forward motion of the organization; the energetic impulsion of growth and advancement; the sense of electricity and excitement generated by dynamic movement. Progress is vital; the thrill of high growth can catalyze creativity. Momentum is what happens when inertia is overcome through the application of constant force. Once started, it is hard to stop; once stopped, it is hard to restart. Corporate momentum is the exhilarating sense of company growth, with the payoff to employees coming in bonuses, promotions, and the special pleasure of being a winner. Related concepts: "innovativeness," the pioneering of process and content, a venturing spirit, the intent to be in the vanguard; "progressiveness," a general state of corporate mind, more attitude than action. A progressive company is never satisfied with the status quo but never makes changes just to make changes. It is always searching for better products to market, more efficient ways to manufacture and distribute the product, more effective systems of internal control, better programs and benefits for personnel. A progressive company always wants to push limits, to stay out in front. Momentum and progressiveness are usually related, but either can be present without the other. Momentum without progressiveness stimulates high commitment creativity but runs the risk of running wild. Progressiveness without momentum can also engender commitment creativity, but it is only a promise and will falter unless those promises are eventually fulfilled. There is little direction in the former and little punch in the latter.

Responsibility. The position of the individual in the organization; the degree of company trust given to the person; the expectational level of job performance. Responsibility is personal burden. It is being relied upon, being held accountable. People react differently to responsibility. Some enjoy it—they like the power to direct and control. Others do not enjoy it—it is weighty and onerous and taxes their freedom. In either case, however, when responsibility is given, commitment increases—but only when it is enjoyed is creativity enhanced. It is a curious thing, this responsibility. It carries with it more work and more anxiety, and all it can assure is more fear and more risk. If one does not have responsibility, there is no way to fail. Yet people pursue it with passion. Why? Responsibility heightens the exhilaration of achievement. Tasks are usually broader, stakes bigger. Preparing a successful business plan is one thing; building a successful business is something else. Responsibility is a recognized facilitator of creativity in organizations. Being responsible for a program or project triggers greater creative efforts; the ego is energized and the psyche swelled—irrespective of personal gain in finances or career. Related concepts: "respect," the social standing of the individual; "knowledge," information and feedback from the company. The more employees know what's happening, the more they feel part of the action.

Accomplishment. The person's sense of reaching and attaining a desired goal, whether broad and noteworthy or narrow and unassuming. The condition of bringing meaningful assignments to successful conclusions. Accomplishment is completing tasks of personal importance, with the process carrying its own reward. It is more mental satisfaction than physical reward. It is the act of fulfillment itself, irrespective of benefits derived, that generates joy. Feelings of accomplishment are generally proportional to the degree of effort. Accomplishment is the goal of creativity. Doing things right gives intrinsic kick. We all exult in a job well done, even if we are the only ones who appreciate it. This is especially true for creative jobs. In many situations, the reward can be eliminated without diminishing the exhilaration of triumph. Achievement is a unique mental phenomenon. Its independence from other desirables such as power and possessions is well established. Achievement, like creativity, is sought for its own worth. Achievers are dedicated to finishing their work, which is often self-assigned and self-motivated. Achievers are often compulsives, beset by self-generated passion to perfect and complete. Nothing makes them happier than to see the tough tasks done, but then again they are not happy unless working on tough tasks. (Ditto for creatives.) Related concept: "fulfillment," the specific sense of task completion.

Breaking Commitment Creativity

Why is commitment often destroyed and along with it corporate creativity? Breaking commitment may seem easy. It is not—it's just that companies work so hard at it, however unwittingly. It is surprising how frequently reputable firms sabotage commitment. Commitment is broken by disturbances between individuals and institutions; the firm bond is severed by disruptions between personal meaning and company mission. It does not matter which side triggers the disturbances or causes the disruptions. What is broken and severed on one side is broken and severed on both sides.

Though commitment is undermined gradually, the impact can emerge suddenly. The commitment of employees, remember, is something a company usually begins with; the firm bond normally starts out tied with some strength. For openers, commitment is a given, almost like having products to sell. Commitment, at least the calculative type, is something for companies to *lose*, not win.

What are ways of destroying commitment, of shattering the bond between individuals and institutions? Commitment breakers are potent. Each retards individual creativity in group settings. We examine five such negative mechanisms: "alienation" (employee-company estrangement), "powerlessness" (absence of personal control), "meaninglessness" (void of personal benefit), "worthlessness" (void of personal esteem), and "anxiety" (employee apprehensions of ill). Managers should be ever vigilant for first signs of these organizational cancers. Caught early they can be cured.

Alienation. The social separation between individual and institution; the estrangement between employee and company; the feeling that organization and member are moving in opposite directions with contradictory purpose; the active rejection of company goals, values, essence, and substance. Alienation implies distance and disruption. As with many of the breakers, it can more easily be defined in the negative: Alienation is the absence of identification. It is what happens when there is no positive relationship between employee and company. When workers are alienated, they feel isolated and apart. The culture and society of the company become, in a real sense, an "alien" world, a foreign territory in which they neither have nor want a part. Overt antagonism to goals and values is common, and ridicule of executives and managers is frequent. Alienated personnel—adversaries or disaffecteds—are a hard-bitten bunch to turn around. Never expect productive creativity from them. Organizations do not have to be evil to turn off employees. In most cases, a part taints the whole. Alienation usually begins as a small seed, but it is virulent and contagious and can spread anywhere. The opposite is identification.

Powerlessness. The belief that organizational events and outcomes are determined by forces beyond individual control; the feeling that what will happen to people is unknown and unknowable and they cannot change or influence future events. Powerlessness, in this context, is not the mere absence of power. Power is the capacity to command, alter, or influence the behavior of people and the course of events. It is not per se a prime commitment builder. Power motivates inwardly, feeding the ego. Powerlessness reaches beyond an individual's lack of capacity to command, alter, or influence people and events. Powerlessness is that airy, aimless sense of no control. Events seem to swirl around like a tornado without awareness or concern for the individual. Powerlessness describes the "helplessness" of a person within an organization; it is the inability to make any dent whatsoever in matters of personal concern, especially those within one's own sphere of influence. Powerlessness, say, for quality control supervisors is not the fact that they cannot change market strategy or modify compensation policy; it is the fact that they cannot make their own jobs more effective or their procedures more efficient. Their suggestions may be requested, but their voices are never heard. Social ostracism, however subtle, is debilitating. Creativity wilts under such heat. Furthermore, when managers are criticized constantly for performance (which, of course, can always be better), a "what's the use" attitude can develop. Enthusiasm is destroyed; energy is sapped—commitment slides to cog and creativity to zero. When companies teach employees to be helpless, however inadvertently, it is trouble.[2] The opposite is responsibility.

Meaninglessness. The sense that nothing about the company has any import or interest for the employee; the feeling of emptiness, the absence of significance in everything the organization is doing. Meaninglessness is more empty than the mere absence of meaning. Its emotion is negative not neutral, callous not caring. It connotes barrenness between individual and institution, an unbridgeable gulf between the purpose of the person and the mission of the group. It means that nothing the firm stands for or is doing carries any consequence for the individual. Meaninglessness is cold and gnawing. It eats away at resolve, undermining dedication, destroying motivation, dissolving the firm bond. Its poison works without haste, building its lethal power. Like a slow-growing malignancy, meaninglessness must be present internally long before its symptoms are apparent externally. No antagonism is implied; the company is a blank, a zero, as far as the employee is concerned. Emptiness and void prevail. Human beings are motivated by diverse factors but none as powerful or robust as the search for meaning, the quest for cause. An employee devoid of meaning will be, at best, a functionary (a routiner with cog commitment), doing assigned work with minimum involvement and maximum aloofness. Meaninglessness is hard to generate, but meaningfulness is even harder to *re*generate. Most people begin new work in new companies with a degree of enthusiasm and excitement. It requires progressive and persistent pressure to suck out substance and suffocate significance. Once present, meaninglessness is resilient and resourceful and extraordinarily hard to replace. Never expect creativity here. The opposite is import and significance.

Worthlessness. The sense that a person is engaged in organizational activities devoid of benefit or reward; a depressed image of self and group. Esteem and pride, though often overbearing, are building blocks of commitment and precursors of creativity. Humans need a positive sense of self-worth, as individuals and as groups. Nothing is more injurious to creative initiative than feelings of uselessness and irrelevance, a low opinion of self relative to others. Depression is common in such persons; no one cares, they think, and nothing matters. A person feeling worthless will neither see any importance in employment nor any reason to improve it. Worthlessness drains out energy and spews forth despair. It is a circular system of compulsive thinking, vicious and venomous and very difficult to break. Creativity is dependent on confidence, and anything that undermines the latter will inhibit the former. Worthlessness can be the most deadly of the commitment-creativity breakers as it is one of most subtle. It is highly protective of its existence, resisting contradictory evidence and seeking constant confirmation. (Extreme conditions of worthlessness can trigger suicidal states.) Managers are often unaware that unrelenting criticism of a subordinate, though done to correct and improve, can erode self-confidence, thus making correction and improvements harder to effect. Worthlessness packs a double punch. It is easy to be engulfed by overwhelming events *and* to see oneself as trivial and irrelevant within huge organizations. Worthlessness and creativity just don't mix. The opposite is esteem and pride.

Anxiety. The uneasy feeling caused by apprehensions of trouble, danger, or personal misfortune; an unsettling expectancy of future events, a general sense of foreboding. Anxiety is uncertainty about what might happen.[3] It is an unspecific apprehension that weakens commitment by breaking down stability, undermining confidence, and triggering unease. An employee so racked will be in continual fear of organizational attack. There may be expectations of criticism from superiors, failure on assignments, peer ostracism, even arbitrary termination. An anxious employee has little psychic energy available for productive purposes and none for creative ones. (Productive creativity is erased by high anxiety. Curiously, though, anxious people can be personally creative but almost always unpredictably and almost never programmable.) There is an inverse relationship between anxiety and security; anxiety makes little headway with a person grounded in a stable belief system and value structure. (Confidence and security are not the same as contentment and complacency; creativity will flourish with the former, not with the latter.) The opposite is confidence.

Commitment breakers at work? One church imposed so many regulations on members that physical trivia swamped spiritual motivation; comparable corporate trauma is caused by, say, making paperwork more important than actual work. Another church second guessed ministers so often that members became confused; the same thing occurs in business when supervisors' decisions are frequently overruled.

Implementing Commitment Creativity

Creativity cannot be coerced. Innovation must be nurtured not enforced. Encouraging the creativity of employees involves understanding and meeting their changing needs. As these needs evolve through the life cycle (and work span), personality variables shift in relative importance. Managers must understand what brings meaning to employees in order to develop optimum creative effort. The best companies develop commitment builders and avoid commitment breakers; they give commitment attention, thus augmenting creativity. How to apply? Start by making commitment priority one.

Managers need new methods to increase employee creativity and commitment. Religion teaches business how to enhance commitment, how to link personal meaning with company mission. With the magnifying glass of religious organizations, we see how commitment helps business corporations. The business-religion connection forges a strong tool. We hear much about how Japanese business methods motivate employees. The critical factor, however, may be more religious than Japanese.

Creativity is rooted in the human psyche and as such is affected by feelings and emotion. Creativity in companies is not the solitary acts of weirdos and those on the fringe; those strange sorts are more fictional stereotypes than real prototypes. *Productive* creativity accomplishes company goals, and its firm strength is dependent on organizational attitudes. Commitment counts, and creative companies will understand it and build it.

Notes

1. Material in this chapter has been derived from *The Firm Bond: Linking Meaning and Mission in Business and Religion*, Robert Lawrence Kuhn and George T. Geis (New York: Praeger), 1984. The authors build a model of commitment by combining organizational theory with extended case studies from both religious and business organizations. The thesis is that commitment can be best studied under extreme conditions and that by examining the link between personal meaning and organizational mission (the working definition of commitment) in ecclesiastical settings, one can apply the results in commercial settings.

   We seek to provoke corporate leaders to build employee commitment—which in turn is hypothesized to increase employee creativity. The model is designed to explain the dynamics of the commitment building or breaking process. Insight from the model can facilitate an intuitive and pragmatic understanding of the nature of commitment and, properly used, can enhance commitment building and retard commitment breaking.

   In *The Firm Bond*, the commitment model is built inductively through organizational theory combined with in-depth personal histories and then applied deductively to generate the commitment builders and breakers described in the above text. Religions are used as the "organizational lens" with which commitment is examined. The key elements of commitment are discerned under the "magnifying glass" of religious fervor and then applied to companies of common kind. Personal, organizational, and experiential factors are inputs to the model, which yields commitment strength and mission contribution as its output. The model is used in numerous personal studies to improve the relationship between individuals and institutions by bringing the benefits of commitment to both sides of the firm bond.

   Input factors follow: These are the elements from which commitment-creativity breakers and builders are derived. The most important relationships are formed between meaning-related variables ("personal factors"), mission-related variables ("organizational factors"), and meaning and mission-related variables ("experiential factors"). (Note that "group" can mean "company.")

   Personal factors.   Individual needs as well as other personal variables influencing commitment, independent of any organizational association. (The first five are meaning-related variables.) *Transcendence :* beyond self; interest in ultimates. *Autonomy :* independence from authority. *Achievement :* fulfillment in completing tasks. *Esteem :* sense of personal worth. *Power :* capacity to influence. *Affiliation :* sense of belonging and association. *Stability :* comfort of routine and status quo. *Structure :* dependency on form and system. *Materialism :* money, wealth, and associated trappings. *Education :* amount, level, and kind of schooling. *Generalized loyalty :* desire to belong; sense of duty. *Locus of Control :* how life is directed, internally or externally.

Organizational factors. Key factors of the organization affecting member commitment, independent of any personal association. (The first four are mission-related variables). *Goal structure :* group mission, purpose, grand design. *Permeability :* degree of flow between group and society. *Leadership :* nature and character of the boss. *Progressiveness :* degree of forward motion; momentum. *Cohesiveness :* group coherence; internal attachment. *Organizational esteem :* sense of group value and worth. *People valuing :* degree to which employees are treated as assets.

Experiential factors. Elements that emerge from interactions between individual and organization, the experiences that develop from group association. (The first five are meaning and mission-related variables.) *Importance and uniqueness :* distinguishing the group from others; setting it apart, making it superior. *Support :* group sustenance and self-help. *Reality congruence :* confidence in group pronouncements. *Status :* personal position in the group. *Task identification :* enjoyment of job. *Emotional Conditioning :* affective, nonrational elements. *Rewards :* psychic and material benefits. *Role strain :* job-related stress. *Investment :* degree of ego and effort sunk into the group.

The interaction between personal and organizational factors helps generate company commitment—and therefore enhances individual creativity. Following are some examples of how a company can increase its receptivity for creative expression: Creative mechanisms for achieving organizational uniqueness, creative structures for providing support for key people, creative company events that build a sense of emotional identification, and creative strategies getting employees to invest in (bet on) the firm.

2. "Learned helplessness" is a psychological concept discovered in animal experiments and applicable, virtually unchanged, to human organizations. Picture two cages of rats, each with a two-sided electrified grid for a floor. In one cage, whenever a light goes on, a pulse of painful (though not harmful) electrical current is passed through one side of the grid. The rats, in this situation, are conditioned to run over to the other side whenever they see the light, and they learn quickly to avoid the shock. In the other cage, the lights and electric current have no relationship at all; each comes on randomly and it is impossible to learn how to escape the current. Wherever the rats run, they get the shock and feel the pain. The interesting point comes when both groups of rats are placed in new though similar situations, this time, say, with a bell signaling the onset of the electrical shock. The first group, successful with the light, is successful again, perhaps even a bit quicker in learning time. The second group, those rats unable to learn with the light, is equally unable to learn with the bell—*even though it is now fully possible to avoid the painful shock.* The rats just freeze in a prone position. They have learned to be helpless.

   The same attitude is all too common among employees. "What's the use, it won't help anyway" is a typical response to many situations. When companies ask for new ideas, and none of them is ever considered much less tried, employees are learning helplessness. They will be less responsive to future requests, and, if the pattern continues, eventually not responsive at all. A cadre of routiners and disengageds will have been formed.

3. Anxiety can be defined as a present state of mind caused by the *possibility* that an action of the past, present, or future might conflict with the environment at some future date. Described in this manner, anxiety encompasses Festinger's theory of cognitive dissonance (*A Theory of Cognitive Dissonance*, Leon Festinger, Evanston, Ill.: Row and Peterson, 1957). "Dissonance" means that two or more concepts are logically opposed to one another. Simply stated, anxiety is the anticipation of possible dissonance.

In psychiatric conditions, an anxious patient will exhibit pathological alertness and tension. There can be extreme eagerness that results in inept or awkward actions. The person considers each thought proof that some dire event will occur. Sometimes this event will continually change; occasionally all signs point toward a single calamity. Say a person has organized a company picnic 3 weeks in advance. Many arrangements will have to be made. With the outing a few days away, the weather bureau reports storm warnings. The picnic planner is *now,* according to our definition, in a state of anxiety. There is a possibility that his or her actions of the past (arranging the picnic) might conflict with the environment at some future date (inclement weather). Anxiety would not be the present state of mind if the picnic had to be *definitely* postponed for one reason or another. The emotion might then be disappointment, irritation, anger—but not anxiety. Anxiety is present only when dissonance is *possible ;* if the feared event actually occurs, anxiety is consummated and another mood takes its place.

Anxiety is more serious when no immediate cause is apparent. The person is in a continuous state of expectancy, waiting for some disaster to befall him or her. The awful event might happen at any moment, it may assume any form. Perhaps financial loss will result from poor decisions; perhaps one will be fired; perhaps . . . the magnitude of anxiety can vary widely. Apprehension is part of our biological warning mechanism. A certain degree of anxiety is valuable. We function better when more alert. Students do better on tests and athletes do better in competition with *moderate* anxiety than with either high or low anxiety. With the ill-fated organizer of the picnic, anxiety can be beneficial. The organizer will now be more alert to weather reports and better prepared for alternative action. He or she, in fact, will be more creative with moderate anxiety. If, however, this alerting reaction becomes inappropriately strong, normal functioning can be interrupted. Creativity is slowed somewhat by low anxiety and retarded substantially by high anxiety.

Anxiety can be reduced by reducing dissonance since, by definition, anxiety is a function of dissonance. How to reduce dissonance? The simplest way, though not often practical, is to alter the action. Call off the picnic. Since anxiety is the anticipation of possible dissonance, anxiety decreases as possible dissonance decreases. Although bad weather was forecast, the person might check other reports for second opinions. A humorous article recounting mistakes in weather forecasting will be read avidly, while other articles dealing with increased reliability because of weather satellites will be ignored. News ofsmall craft warnings might be misinterpreted to mean that the storm was blowing out to sea. The person might begin to minimize the picnic by discounting the importance of social occasions for an "all-business" company.

Now for the strange part. An anxious person expecting calamity might be motivated to reduce anxiety by making the calamity *more* likely to happen. Dissonance would be reduced sharply since reality would then be in agreement with his or her feelings of imminent disaster. An employee overly anxious about being criticized for creativity, for example, might start choosing more bizarre projects or promoting off-the-wall ideas. The reaction of superiors would then confirm the initial apprehension and justify his or her mental state.

18

Creative Climate Checklist: 101 Ideas

Eugene Raudsepp

President, Princeton Creative Research, Inc.

In the present corporate thrust for manufacturing productivity and product quality, creativity and innovation have been relegated to a back seat. To be sure, creativity has moved from after-dinner podiums into executive weekend retreats, but it is rarely used systematically in the day-to-day corporate environment. Creativity is linked directly to productivity and quality enhancement in that it increases the soundness of solutions to organizational problems, helps bring about profitable innovations, spurs increased productivity by revitalizing motivation, upgrades personal skills, and catalyzes effective team performance.

How can executives harness and focus employee energies to achieve innovative results? Following are 101 guidelines and intervention ideas managers can use to improve personal creativity and organizational innovation. Try some.

1. Take personal responsibility for the development of an organizational climate for innovation. Subordinates may support and encourage one another's creativity, but they won't sustain it consistently unless their superiors support such behavior.

2. Experiment with new forms of organization. Search for ways of maximizing peer support for creativity.

3. Concentrate change efforts on those aspects of organizational culture—the traditional procedures and norms—that inhibit and stifle innovation.

4. Remember that innovative behavior does not happen spontaneously. Managers must explicitly communicate that innovation is expected.

5. Create an open, interactive climate in which subordinates can stimulate greater awareness, excitement, and ideas among one another. Alter the dominant mood of many corporations—isolation, frustration, apprehension, and vulnerability.

6. Free yourself from the hold of, and dependence on, traditional systems of governance. Do not overdirect, overobserve, or overreport.

7. Recognize that your change efforts will encounter the dead weights of inertia and resistance. By consistently and patiently demonstrating that you mean business and that you encourage creative behavior, you can surmount these roadblocks.

8. Formulate innovative objectives all employees can visualize and believe in. Communicate those objectives constantly.

9. Dramatize problems to which creative solutions are known to be needed.

10. Mercilessly houseclean "yesterday's" products, services, and ventures that only absorb limited resources and energy but do not contribute to growth.

11. Budget adequately for innovation.

12. Encourage and train subordinates to develop greater psychological openness to new ideas and new experiences.

13. Recognize differences in individuals. Have a keen appreciation of each person's unique characteristics—strengths and weaknesses. Treat each individual as a person of worth in his or her own right.

14. Match project tasks and objectives with the natural central interests of the individuals involved.

15. Determine and encourage those aspects of each individual's motivation that relate to his or her self-confidence and desire to achieve.

16. Promote responsible individuality and maturity. Maturity is characterized by high motivation, autonomy, flexible behavior patterns, action orientation, and strong commitment to goals. Organizations may publicly contend that they support these qualities, yet their policies evoke just the opposite: immaturity and dependency. Immature, dependent behavior results when people perceive that they have little control over their environment and are expected to behave in a conforming, passive, and subordinate manner. Rather than encouraging individuals who challenge assumptions and question the way things are run, organizations reward those who never question anything, who never rock the boat, who never propose challenging ideas that would threaten the status quo or require restructuring and risk taking.

17. Provide stimulating work that generates a feeling of personal and professional growth. These are potent motivators and without them people cannot get excited about their jobs.

18. Provide projects and tasks that give a sense of accomplishment that best matches employees' value systems.

19. Provide challenge by pitching assignments and projects just above the known capabilities of the individuals.

20. Enable subordinates to feel that the satisfaction they have enjoyed in the past will be repeatable and will provide a secure springboard for tradeoffs in new creative directions. Provide consistent form and pattern in assignments.

21. Help subordinates see problems as challenges. Instilling an attitude that problems are "opportunity potentials" helps them regard problems in a more positive light.

22. Make known that individuals' career successes hinge on their creative contributions.

23. Allow diversity in personal styles. Don't let your personality stifle those whose methods of doing things differ from your own.

24. Recognize that there is no one single managerial style that is appropriate and effective with all individuals. The creative manager is a situational stylist and can select either participative, laissez faire, or autocratic styles of managing, depending on circumstances and the individuals involved. The participative style, however, should be the favored style.

25. Utilize resources, methods, and subordinates in more versatile ways to achieve novel results.

26. Focus potential and skills on goals, not roles. Excessive preoccupation with roles saps creativity.

27. Create a free-flow task environment that encourages creative completión.

28. Encourage and motivate subordinates to come back again and again to the same problem until there is a breakthrough.

29. Set high but reasonable standards, knowing that even the most lofty ideas must eventually be subjected to the realistic technical and financial constraints of the organization. By setting high goals initially, you increase the chances of some people sparking revolutionary ideas.

30. Instill an attitude that "thinks quality" at every stage of a project's development.

31. While a measure of external structure and discipline has to be imposed, ideally they should resonate with the individual's own sense of responsibility and self-discipline. As one manager stated, "Authentic discipline is internal and is generated by absorption in inherently satisfying activity."

32. Discover in what ways individuals think they are most creative or would like to be most creative and what sort of creative contribution they would most like to make. Almost every organization has people who would be creative enthusiastically, frequently, and naturally. Find out who they are and form special "brain trusts" to develop their talents.

33. Actively seek out, develop, and encourage those with *special* creative talents and aptitudes.

34. Arrive at a sound problem statement and some vision of the desired end result. Set the initial directions. Zero in on the problem and determine to solve it in innovative ways. Involve people who can "own" the problem. Involve others who can offer their expertise or who can be idea catalysts or who can represent the problem in unique ways.

35. Lead and enthuse by suggestion and indirect persuasion rather than by specification or command. Frame objectives in clear terms but allow freedom for diverse approaches.

36. Define the problem broadly to allow maximum creative ideation. Broad definitions preclude the loss of potentially innovative solutions. Encourage more open-ended and less structured approaches to problem solving. For certain periods of time, tolerate messiness, mushiness, complexity, and even disorder.

37. Allow adequate time for ideas to develop and mature.

38. Allow more freedom for individuals to guide their own work. Provide them with specific areas of self-direction and increase these when appropriate.

39. Guard against subordinates' overinvolvement with putting out fires and coping with urgent, immediate problems.

40. Make sure that the most promising people are not bogged down with specific tasks all the time. Creative people need time to think, without having their thoughts always tied to a particular activity or task.

41. Make special organizational provisions for highly creative people. Have them act as special task forces for solving complex, intractable problems.

42. Make sure subordinates have ready access to resources, information, knowledge, and expertise.

43. Allow free play and encourage openness. Freedom to play and toy in thinking, feeling, and imagination encourages creativity. An attitude that looks favorably on exploration and experiment facilitates creativity. Develop a more permissive and accepting "open system;" this environment is invigorating and stimulating, allowing a free interplay of differences among people. Moving from a closed to an open system shifts interpersonal relations from political to collaborative, thus maximizing creativity.

44. Train yourself and others to respond to the positive parts of proposed ideas rather than reacting to the often easier-to-spot negative ones. As Charles F. Kettering aptly put it: "The typical eye sees the 10 percent bad of an idea and overlooks the 90 percent good."

45. Develop more noncompetitive and nonevaluative contexts in which mutual trust prevails.

46. Reserve special rooms in the organization in which people can "be creative."

47. Encourage calculated risk taking because it is an important ingredient in personal growth.

48. Develop greater frustration tolerance to mistakes and errors.

49. Provide a safe atmosphere for failures. In many organizations the penalties for failure far exceed the rewards for success. In some organizations the penalties for failure are in fact greater than the

penalties for doing nothing. Even one failure can brand an individual as a loser. Reward success and ignore failure as much as possible.

50. Reduce fear of failure and punishment if innovative ideas and recommendations do not pan out.

51. Project the attitude that if ideas are not accepted or do not work, they are not wasted. Highly creative types do not like to be associated with wasted effort.

52. Regard errors and mistakes as opportunities for learning. Organizations place heavy emphasis on avoidance of errors and mistakes. This contributes to a sharp perception of flaws or weaknesses in ideas and to a tendency to play it safe and avoid punishment for adopting any but the safest and often the least creative ideas. Companies sorely need to reverse this attitude and focus initially on the "what's good about it" aspects, the "pros" of an idea. There is plenty of time later to consider the shortcomings, the "cons" of an idea. Frequently, when the acceptable aspects are considered and strengthened, a way is found to modify the unacceptable particulars. If this cannot be accomplished, it is obvious that the idea should be discarded. But it is absolutely mandatory that a positive stance be adopted initially because if we give in to our natural tendency to focus on flaws and weaknesses immediately, we never really perceive all implications of an idea. One technique is to consider (or pretend) that the idea is workable and to list and outline all its positive benefits. After doing this exhaustively, switch to reality testing and fault finding.

53. Occasionally allow individuals to try out pet ideas without any criticism whatsoever. Provide a reasonable margin for error. Punitive action for every mistake or failure leads to excessive dependence on safety and tradition.

54. Always use mistakes and setbacks positively, for example as steps to future solutions.

55. Use even constructive criticism with caution and in small doses. Speak softly and carry a big carrot.

56. Be a catalyst not an inhibitor. Many managers are so overburdened with all kinds of requests that when someone comes up with a new idea or proposal, their negative mind-set confuses it with yet another petition.

57. Encourage candor and frankness. Have the curiosity and ego strength to find out how you yourself come across, how you are regarded—and how you can improve.

58. Help subordinates develop greater self-reliance by reducing their fears, inhibitions, and defensiveness.

59. Strengthen power by shifting power. Invent ways to generate collaborative momentum.

60. Be a resource person rather than a controller, a facilitator rather than a boss.

61. Be loyal to subordinates and know how to evoke loyalty from them. Loyalty cannot be created by gratitude, edict, or compulsion; it is the result of mutual respect and acceptance, which can be developed only through day-to-day interactions.

62. Be a sympathetic, friendly person who has high personal standards and integrity and who is able to be either serious and sincere or humorous and relaxed as the occasion demands. Listen to your people and laugh with them.

63. Know the difference between assertiveness and aggressiveness and act accordingly.

64. Act as a buffer between subordinates and outside problems or higher-up demands.

65. Make participative decision making real, not symbolic, at all levels. Allow individuals to make more of their own decisions. As one creative manager put it, "A good deal of my time is spent trying *not* to make a decision. The best decisions are made by those closest to the problem or most affected by the decision."

66. Allow creative people to take as large a part as possible in overall decision making and in the formulation of long-term plans.

67. Increase delegation and influence sharing throughout the organization.

68. Encourage, develop, and release initiative rather than inhibit, stifle, and thwart it.

69. Make sure that subordinates know where the organization is going and how their individual contributions advance that goal.

70. Upgrade and revamp both the tangible and intangible rewards and inducements for creative contributions. The time-honored incentives of increased power, status, and salaries encourage secretiveness, playing of politics, jockeying for positions, conformity, and the desire to please superiors. These discourage innovative thinking.

71. Modify the seniority tradition so that individuals can be promoted from any level strictly on merit.

72. Use creativity-related performance dimensions in personnel performance appraisals.

73. Individuals should be given time off for unusual creative achievements and/or more on-the-job flexibility.

74. Provide personal recognition for accomplishment. Emphasize the importance of the individual rather than his or her group or department.

75. Increase recognition of creative performance through formally established profit-sharing and similar programs, such as deferred compensation plans, cash or stock bonuses, and royalties. Reward financially for outstanding individual contribution, patents, and inventions, new products, money-saving projects, etc.

76. Use letters of commendation and appreciation from the company president and other members of top management for important contributions. Honors and distinctions should be established that reflect admiration for creative excellence.

77. The company's public relations department should provide deserving individuals with special recognition and publicity. There should be press releases on individual achievements to newspapers, journals, and college alumni magazines.

78. Analyze the company communication system—this is the way individuals get their perspective on the organization and their sources of stimulation or blockage of creativity.

79. Put creative people in touch with one another, particularly across interdisciplinary lines. Bring together people with diverse knowledge and viewpoints.

80. Organize brainstorming teams, using people from different backgrounds.

81. As critical incidents of success or failure in creativity occur, record and make use of them as subject matter for group discussion. Develop your own curriculum materials for creative activities in your own area.

82. Expand subordinates' creative potential through exposure to experiences that enrich their content awareness.

83. Encourage open communications and the utilization of more people as resources.

84. Devise an educational situation in which small discussion groups, made up of people from management and operational areas, openly explore problems and views.

85. Conduct meetings and face-to-face discussions about opportunities to be exploited. Achieve *commitment* to specific innovative goals.

86. Departmental structures should be made less rigid and encapsulated; this would encourage greater interdepartmental communication, which, in turn, would heighten individual creativity. Eliminate the "organizational box mentality": "If you'll stay out of my organizational box, I'll stay out of yours."

87. Appreciate the loner. Although creative, highly motivated teams are exceedingly useful, find a place for the creative hermit. Allow him or her freedom to follow leads that are contrary to group direction.

88. "Celebrate" individual contributors and deemphasize the anonymity of group rewards and commendations.

89. Welcome and encourage a diversity of ideas and opinions, no matter where they come from.

90. Make people aware, through lectures and other special communications, of the pressures they bring on one another to conform.

91. Import, for short periods of time, individuals who have a professional interest in teaching how to cultivate creativity. Provide creativity training and workshops.

92. Locate individuals in the organization who have a capacity for helping others realize their creative potential. Let these individuals become tutors and mentors to individuals who show promise.

93. Enhance your own creative ability through special workshops and seminars, specialized reading, and practice of creative exercises and games. This sets an excellent example subordinates will want to emulate. Enhanced personal creative ability makes it easier for you to recognize and relate to the creativity of others.

94. Encourage subordinates to offer ideas not only concerning their specific jobs but also outside their direct responsibilities.

95. Provide channels through which creativity converts into specific ideas, suggestions, and changes. You cannot wait for this to happen.

96. Introduce formal mechanisms for implementation and follow-through.

97. Make sure that innovative ideas are transmitted to top management with your support and backing; then insist on a feedback mechanism. Without feedback, the flow of creative ideas dries up because innovators feel that their ideas are not given a fair hearing or taken seriously. Get commitments from higher-ups to respond to creativity.

98. Recommend and encourage more informal contact between top management and individual contributors.

99. Analyze the creative potential of subordinates in their first year of employment and those who are in their prime (near the top of their promotional possibilities).

100. Analyze why some subordinates go stale, noting what they will not respond to and suggesting opportunities that might stimulate them.

101. Do not consider creativity as a gimmick but as the name for an integral aspect of total organizational policy.

One hundred and one ideas. Try some.

PART 3

Structuring the Creative Organization

Diversion and Conversion, Freedom and Control

Creativity within companies adds organizational complexity to an already arcane personal process. The demand is for a fine balance between freedom and focus, the former for idea generation (divergence), the latter for idea evaluation (convergence). Each has its own requirements, its own mind-set. What structural factors facilitate the formulation and implementation of original ideas, products, and processes? Structure, from biology to business, used to be the weak sister of function, something static not dynamic, mundane not vital. Times change. Today structure is important in all areas of knowledge; function can follow form and structure can determine function. Eastman Kodak, for example, established an "Office of Innovation" to channel and consider grass-roots ideas, primarily technical ones, germinating from individuals outside their assigned work areas. Though spawned in R&D labs, the office "networked" into marketing and manufacturing and soon pervaded the entire company. "We're in the idea-connection business," says its founder. Communications is the nervous system of innovation; successful firms simply do not allow creative people in different disciplines to remain isolated. Harold Guetzkow states that when an organization has little slack—when the ship is tightly run—the climate is unfavorable for innovation. Conversely, the greater the organizational slack, with its increased capability of absorbing errors and ethos for risk taking, the greater the propensity for innovation. In Part 3 we inspect how organizational structure affects corporate creativity: we note special characteristics of creative organizations, environments in which innovation flourishes, bureaucratic environments that can be changed, innovation impediments in large companies, creative culture as a competitive weapon. We conclude with two diverse cases: one company that mandates that no division can have more than 200 employees and another that centralizes creativity in one main building.

19

Designing a Creative Organization

Richard M. Cyert

President, Carnegie-Mellon University

The creative organization is one dominated by new ideas that are implemented and, as a result, is characterized by change. The creative organization may undertake problems that are different from traditional ones in standard fields and disciplines. It may attack these problems in original or interdisciplinary ways that do not respect conventional classifications of knowledge. It is difficult to characterize innovation, almost by definition, but it is clear that the creative organization looks for new means to achieve old goals.

Strategic Planning

Most corporate executives, in my view, miss the point of strategic planning. What should be creative is most often mechanical. The approach usually involves a simple model with a well-defined output. Instead true strategic planning should determine the long-run quality of the firm, embedding corporate decisions such as areas for research, kinds of products produced, method of production, regions for marketing, and the like. In other words, strategic planning touches the very nature of the firm.

Goals and plans interact intimately. Neither goals nor plans can be determined independently. Theoretically, we are dealing with a system of simultaneous equations. Practically, the system is solved by a series of trial and error approaches. Goals are selected and strategies chosen. When analysis determines that the goals cannot be achieved, the strategy is changed or the goals are modified.

The essence of strategic planning is a creative act: to find a distinctive place among competition, to achieve comparative advantage against competitors. The worst action a firm can take is to imitate another firm that it considers successful. *Uniqueness*, not carbon copy, is required for a company to establish permanent market position. The key to uniqueness is creativity.

Leadership

Many factors affect company creativity; leadership is perhaps the most critical. The objective of leadership is to get subordinates to behave in specific ways that are desired by the leader, to perform tasks and achieve goals that the boss deems relevant and important. A good definition of leadership is the ability to bring about conformity between subgroup goals and total organizational goals and between individual goals and company goals (see Chapter 17).

It is commonplace to distinguish between leadership and management, the latter being somewhat more maintenance oriented (and thereby somewhat inferior). Leadership and management are not always found together. There may even be tension between them. A firm can be well managed and not well led. Some believe that it is impossible for a single person to perform both functions properly. Creativity, we note, is enhanced by leadership, and it may be inhibited by "management" (using this restricted definition).

It is difficult to write a formula for leadership. The best approach is to concentrate on modifying the attention focus of subordinates in ways, formal and informal, that can achieve goals. Without leadership, the organization drifts, and creativity, if it exists at all, is aimless.

Organizational Theory

Organization theorists have been concerned with developing structure that would lead to a creative organization. The problem of achieving particular objectives has long fascinated students of organizational theory. Such theory leads to a recognition of variables that are important but not to specific ways in which they can have an impact on the organization to achieve desired results. As more knowledge has been gained, the capacity to design a creative organization has increased.

This chapter is based on my deductions from organization theory and the actions that I have come to believe, through experience and experimentation, are effective in structuring a creative organization. Much of my personal work has been in the context of academic institutions, developing new approaches to problems of education and research. The university, in fact, is an interesting model with which to consider the issues of creative design since all of its pressures are conservative ones. There is a tension, for example, between an administration that wants an innovative organization and a faculty that wants a conventional one.

The parallels to large corporations desiring to become more creative are direct, particularly when senior management seeks innovation and change while middle management maintains status quo and stability. This analogy is especially strong for those companies that have decentralized structures (e.g., separate subsidiaries in diverse industrial or geographic areas or autonomous functional departments such as R&D) or have substantial numbers of professionals and independent producers (e.g., scientists and engineers, lawyers and accountants, salesmen and marketeers, entrepreneurs and intrapreneurs) who consider themselves central to the firm's primary output. In making the corporate-university correlation, the decentralized structures are analogous to colleges within universities and departments within colleges, and the professionals and independent producers are analogous to faculty members. Ways and means of introducing organizational innovation are similar in academic institutions and business corporations.

Critical Variables

Leadership must be oriented toward particular variables if creative behavior is to be augmented. Sometimes leadership is exercised through changing the formal reporting structure. Often, however, current structure is so well established that it is difficult to alter. Further, it is not clear that structure is the most important variable. There are, undoubtedly, many structures that can enable an organization to achieve a particular set of objectives.

There are other variables of significance for inducing creative behavior. The first is the goal structure of the organization. A goal structure for a company must be developed with the participation of key producers. That goal structure has to include innovation as a major objective. Without formal recognition of the importance of creative activity, any organization has little chance of being an innovative place. The attention focus of participants, the items that personnel are thinking and speaking about, is another prime variable. The attention focus is closely connected with behavior, and activities influencing the attention focus can, thereby, influence behavior. The reward system, of course, is a well-known variable. Strangely enough, it is difficult to tie the reward system closely to behavior. Emphasizing only one variable may not produce a particular kind of activity. The designers of executive compensation systems have long experienced this frustration.

The connection between the variables with which we must work and actual behavior is tenuous. We can never be sure, in complex organizations, that a particular action will lead to a particular reaction. Our aim has to be to design organizational policies using those variables that will *tend to produce* the type of behavior desired.

Innovation as a Goal

In an organization that is being designed for creativity, it is critical that innovation be specifically listed as a goal. Furthermore, the reasons why innovation is a goal should be specified. There are many ways to establish a goal structure. The initiative must be taken by the president and a draft document must come from his or her office to initiate the process. At some point, key personnel must be involved. It is vital that they participate and accept the goal structure.

The president should make a point of stressing innovation as a goal of the organization and point to the established set of goals. As the point is emphasized in discussion, participants in the organization begin to accept innovation as a way of life.

Attention Focus of Participants

The attention focus of key personnel is generally on their own disciplines and departments. Yet, if the organization is to be creative, the attention must be focused on innovation.

Role of the President.   Important for changing the attention focus are the actions of the chief executive officer. If the president is committed to innovation, his or her behavior can so influence all participants in the organization.

The first action that can influence attention focus is oral communication with key personnel—on an individual basis, in larger subunits, or with all collectively. The president should aim in these talks to change attitudes. He or she must find ways to emphasize the importance of innovation. The concept of innovation must be recognized as an organizational goal. Informal talks are vital, as is the formal planning process. Even banter and jokes count. In all conversations, the president must stress innovation. These talks are ways of altering the more orthodox attitudes of the environment.

Second, the president must be receptive to new ideas and must demonstrate that receptivity. The environment the president creates must be one in which key personnel are able to speak with him or her directly. Bureaucratic deference to a chain of command can choke off new ideas and stifle new idea generation. When an employee presents a proposal for change, the president must be open minded and careful in appraisal. The usual reactions of "we're doing that already" or "that won't work" should never be used. No matter what the initial reaction, nothing should be said that would in any sense make the initiator of the idea feel foolish or frustrated. Getting key personnel to introduce new ideas may be difficult, but it is still only a first step. Once the idea is presented, the reception must be positive. Every idea must be treated as an important contribution, and feedback as to its disposition must be given ultimately to the person who generated it.

Third, the president must make sure that actions are taken to implement new ideas. If a proposal needs to be studied further to determine whether it has merit, that action should be taken as soon as possible and as visibly as appropriate. Frequently, it is desirable to appoint a committee and make a public announcement of the appointment and the reason for it. The committee should be chosen with care and should have members who have a reputation for receptivity to new ideas. As soon as possible, action should be taken to put the idea into motion or to have valid and justifiable reasons why the idea cannot be utilized.

To project proper attitudes, the president must avoid the reaction that a new idea is a criticism of the way the organization is being operated. Actions based on such assessments will tend to kill innovativeness quickly. Another emotional reaction that is antithetical to innovation is any resentment the president may feel at not having thought of the idea. Such reactions reduce receptivity and impair ability to evaluate the idea properly. The president must be a secure and confident person if his or her actions are to produce attention focus on innovation.

Finally, it is desirable for the president to be innovative. I mean that the president must initiate some innovations directly. There must be care, however, how the innovation is implemented. He or she must resist the effort to *impose* a change on key personnel but should not hesitate to initiate discussion of the proposal. Ultimately, as this process progresses, all will recognize an innovative president and administration. The president is a role model and is always "on stage." The net result is positive stimulation of attitudes and attention focus toward innovative activity.

Role of Senior Executives.   Senior executives have a role similar to that of the president with regard to innovation. They should reflect the same attitudes and values as does the president. They must have participated in innovative activity and be still interested in doing so. Their stressing the goal of innovation stimulates younger managers to give attention to creative ideas.

More important, senior executives must make certain that the results of creative actions of subordinates will be taken into account when evaluations are made. Such recognition of creative behavior will reinforce that behavior. Senior executives represent an internal reference group. Positive response to innovative actions encourages others to behave in ways that are desired by the organization even though the actions may not be in the mainline of the particular department. Clearly one of the obstacles to making an organization innovative is the conservatism of most disciplines. Young professionals or managers in particular must worry about deviating from the "party line" of their discipline or department since future jobs may depend on the extent to which they are accepted and evaluated by others. Thus, there is a tension that develops in the innovative organization and most of the burden falls on younger personnel. (Consider young faculty members who do not have tenure.) The behavior of senior executives can significantly help to reduce this tension.

Reward System

A third factor for enhancing creativity and innovation in an organization is the reward system, which should relate as directly as possible to innovative behavior. Oftentimes, organizations speak one way and reward another. This is disaster. Rewards must be given according to desired results. The university model is a good one to track here.

There are three basic components of reward—salary, promotion, and public recognition. Department heads and deans have the most authority in setting salaries. The usual criteria relate to publication performance and the amount of research money that the individual has brought into the university. The importance of teaching tends to be overlooked. The weighting of these factors for determining salary influences the behavior of faculty. For example, if teaching is really weighted less than publications and grants, faculty members will tend to put less attention on teaching. Too often, whether in academia or business, the concept of creative and innovative activity is not even looked upon as one of the variables determining salary.

In order to change this situation, the department head must give different signals. He or she must make it clear that innovative activity is important and must define what is meant by innovative activity. Then those who are receiving their increases must understand the role that innovative activity has played, one way or another. Word will spread. The president should also be involved, working directly with department heads to change attitudes from the conventional value system that would not include innovative activity. There has to be a number of direct meetings between the president and individual department heads, as well as with the department heads as a group. The attention focus and attitude must be changed. Most have spent their working lives in this organization (or similar ones) and have absorbed conventional values. Such values do not include an understanding of creativity nor a heavy weighting on innovative activity for setting salaries and allocating other rewards.

The problem of promotions is similar. It is critical that innovations be credited to personnel being considered for promotion and that such innovations be taken into account in making promotions. Again, this approach may require a change in attitudes. Traditionally, the heavy weight that is put on financial performance for managers (publications for faculty) swamps all other variables. If the organization is to be innovative, promotion decisions must give heavy weighting to innovative activity. An organization can never encourage creative and innovative people if it does not reward these people with salary and promotion.

Public recognition also works. Awards, including cash bonuses for innovative activity, can demonstrate that innovative activity is valued. The awards should be made in public, with a great deal of internal publicity. The aim is to influence behavior by showing that innovative activity is actually rewarded.

Upward Communication

Upward communication is difficult. The belief among participants lower in the hierarchy that they can speak to the president is an important value for innovative activity. Ideas can be killed by people down in the ranks. When upward communication exists, it is possible for almost anyone to bring ideas directly to the president. Similarly, the president must ensure that senior executives are equally available and receptive to new ideas. Increasing upward communication reduces uncertainty regarding organizational receptivity to new ideas. To work, there must be rapport between top management and employees that gives confidence and ease of mind as to upward communications.

Conditions that promote communication can be established. The president, in many cases, should have thorough knowledge of the business. Perhaps he or she has come up through the ranks. Such a person will have a strong identification with the workers themselves. Second, the communication must be initiated by the president. The president must go out to the divisions and the departments to meet with key personnel on their grounds. This kind of action can develop a familiarity that makes it easier for employees of all ranks to communicate ideas to the president without fear and with some assurance that their ideas will receive a good hearing.

Of equal importance is the way in which the ideas are handled by the president or department head. In all cases, the ideas should be treated with respect and seriousness regardless of one's first opinion. More good ideas are killed and more people are discouraged by phrases such as, "we already tried that"; "that's an old idea"; or other similar expressions. An individual greeted in this fashion may never again present an idea to anyone in the organization. The grapevine will soon report the roadblock.

Each idea should be treated as special and a serious attempt made to deal with it. Sometimes this can be done on the spot through further discussion, and the individual may decide the idea needs further work. On the other hand, with greater exploration, the senior executive may realize that what looks like a poor idea is, in fact, a good one. So, the first step is to consider virtually every idea brought to the executive's office. Second, there must be a way of clear disposition. Frequently, having a small group investigate the idea is effective. When an idea is to be examined further, the originator of the idea should participate in the process. The organization's reputation for receptivity will depend on how top management treats those ideas that are brought to the executive suite.

Some Specific Techniques

Funding to Support Innovation

One way to make creativity operational as an organizational goal is to make funds available for innovative activities. These dollars must be visible and dedicated to new ideas. One effective technique I have used is to establish an "internal foundation" (or venture capital group). The clear objective of the foundation should be to finance innovative activity. The novel ideas could be in a specific area such as for increasing productivity, new product development, or breakthrough technology research. An alternative is to have the foundation willing to support any activity that meets the criterion of being innovative irrespective of area.

Formation of the internal foundation gives the president another opportunity to emphasize the importance of innovative activity. This can be accomplished through the specification of creativity in the guidelines for making proposals. To highlight the program, the president should be one of the group making the selection for financing proposals, at least in the beginning. There should also be a great deal of internal recognition given the participants who receive grants and much should be made of the innovative nature of the winning proposals. The objective of the internal foundation is to emphasize the importance of new ideas within the organization, to show the president's interest in creative thought, and to prove that the organization is prepared to put its own resources into stimulating them. Activities of this kind will emphasize the importance of innovative activity to the members of the organization as well as stimulate the desired goal.

Information Gathering

One of the requirements for designing a creative organization is the inclusion of "antennae." The organization has to be alert to developments in the world, or more specifically, potential developments. There may be a tendency to rely upon senior employees to keep abreast of what is happening. Frequently, however, those who are the most experienced may miss the more dramatic or discontinuous portents. An innovative organization needs to be futuristic, looking for revolutionary as well as evolutionary events.

Another way for the president to emphasize innovation and to keep track of the world is to establish a series of seminars in which people from a variety of fields outside the organization are invited to speak. The objective of the visits should be to talk with a selected group of key personnel on the future of a particular area. Encourage speakers to forecast what is going to happen and to identify where new areas of importance are likely to be. In small seminars, which the president chairs, excellent discussion between expert visitor and key personnel can result. (The outsiders resemble antennae that sense developments in the world and bring back information.) Such meetings can help the organization determine areas in which it has comparative advantage or in which, by being first, it can establish comparative advantage. Ideas of this kind require much discussion.

Reporting Systems

Corporate controllers use reporting systems effectively. W. W. Cooper, for example, has pointed out the behavioral effects on the management of a subsidiary when required to submit financial reports. The documents become a written record of performance. A somewhat similar mechanism can be used within an organization to stimulate innovation. A periodic request to division and department heads for a report on their innovations can be stimulating. There is always a danger that such requests can lead to descriptions that are nothing more than window dressing. Thus the president must read the reports carefully and give feedback to the reporting unit. Significant innovations do not occur with predictable frequency nor do they occur often. Regular reports may lead to definitions of innovations that are not helpful. Thus a reporting system for innovations, in contrast to an accounting control system, should probably be done on an irregular basis rather than routinely.

High Points

Four variables can be manipulated to help make an organization innovative—goal structure, attention focus, reward systems, and upward communication. Attention focus, in my view, is the most important. If properly understood, attention focus leads to a whole set of actions, each of which is designed to point the organization in the direction of innovation. These actions generally involve communication, especially from the president. It is only by making the goal of innovation clear, and making its importance apparent, that an organization will begin to become more creative in deed as well as word.

To design a creative organization, the president must establish objectives within the system. For example, at Carnegie-Mellon we seek to be a major innovator in both research and education. This objective has been established in the course of a number of strategic planning sessions, it has been published in the strategic planning document of the university, and it has been discussed in detail with the faculty. The last-named discussion is critical if the attention focus of the participants is to be concentrated on innovative behavior.

Clearly, the most important ingredient for designing a creative organization is that the CEO consider the process necessary. In the final analysis, there is no organizational structure that can make an organization innovative. It is, rather, the actions in many dimensions, particularly communication, that effect the desired behavior.

Bibliography

Cyert, R. M.: *The Management of Nonprofit Organizations*, Lexington Books, Lexington, MA, 1975.

Khandwalla, P. N.: *The Designing of Organizations*, Harcourt-Brace, New York, 1977.

March, J. G. and H. A. Simon: *Organization*, John Wiley, New York, 1958.

McCorkle, Jr., C. O. and S. O. Archibald: *Management and Leadership in Higher Education*, Jossey-Bass, San Francisco, 1982.

Mohr, L. B.: "Determinants of Innovation in Organization," *American Political Science Review*, Vol. 63, 1969, pp. 111–126.

Simon, H. A.: *Administrative Behavior*, Macmillan. New York, 1948.

20

Change-Master Companies: Environments in Which Innovations Flourish

Rosabeth Moss Kanter

Class of 1960 Professor of Business Administration,
Graduate School of Business Administration,
Harvard University

Innovation and new venture development have no special origin. They may begin as a deliberate and official decision of senior executives, or they may be the more or less "spontaneous" creation of mid-level managers who take the initiative to solve a problem in new ways or to develop a proposal for change. Of course, highly successful companies allow both, and even official top-management decisions to undertake a development effort benefit from the spontaneous creativity of those below. But regardless of origin, for an idea to be turned into living reality capable of generating financial returns, certain organizational characteristics must generally be present. Those companies with high levels of enterprise tend to reflect these "facilitating conditions" for change more widely in their ongoing practices, as I show in *The Change Masters.*

Broadly Defined Jobs

Innovation is aided when jobs are defined broadly rather than narrowly, when people's ranges of skills to use and tasks to perform give them a "feel" for the organization, and when assignments focus on results or goals to be achieved rather than rules or procedures to be followed. This, in turn, gives people the mandate to solve problems, to respond creatively to new conditions, to note changed requirements around them, to improve practices—rather than mindlessly following "book" routine derived from the past. Furthermore, when less constricted definitions of jobs permit task domains to overlap rather than diverge, people are encouraged to gain the perspective of others with whom they must now interact. Such communication leads to employees taking more responsibility for the total task rather than simply their own small piece of it. This in turn generates the broader perspectives that help stimulate innovation. In areas that benefit from more enterprise and problem solving, bigger jobs work better. This is the principle behind work systems that give employees responsibility for a major piece of a production process and allow them to make decisions about how and when to divide up the tasks. Pay-for-skill systems similarly encourage broader perspectives by rewarding people for learning more jobs.

A proliferation of job classifications and fine distinctions between steps in what are really connected processes (e.g., the differentiation among many types of engineers specializing in only one step in a conceive-to-design-to-build process) has inhibited innovation in many large, segmented American companies. Individual jobholders need take no responsibility for ultimate outcomes as long as they perform their own narrow task adequately. When jobs are narrowly and rigidly defined, people have little incentive to engage in either "spontaneous" innovation (self-generated, collective problem solving with those in neighboring tasks) or to join together across job categories for larger, top-directed innovation efforts—especially if differences in job classification also confer differential status or privilege. Companies even lose basic efficiency as some tasks remain undone while waiting for the person with the "right" job classification to become available—even though others in another classification may have both skills and time. And people tend to actively avoid doing any more work than the minimum, falling back on the familiar excuse, "That's not *my* job"—a refrain whose frequent repetition is a good sign of a troubled company.

Examples of high-level entrepreneurial effort make clear this link between job definitions and the enterprise necessary for innovation. In some high-tech computer companies, people in professional and managerial jobs are regularly exhorted to "invent" their own jobs or are given broad troubleshooting assignments to "fix it" by "doing the right thing." Organization charts can be produced on demand, but by the time people add all the exceptions, the dotted lines reflecting multiple responsibilities, and the circles around special teams or task forces, the whole thing resembles a "plate of spaghetti," as one observer put it, more than a chain of command. While this situation can also appear chaotic and undisciplined, it does result in more people assuming responsibility to solve problems and make improvements, generating high levels of innovation in every function.

A major manufacturer of household products can cite numerous instances of spontaneous problem-solving effort by employees who are part of self-managed "business teams" responsible for producing their product in their part of the factory without supervision. Over the last 10 years, work teams have gradually taken responsibility for every function in the factory, and they conceive of themselves as "owning" and managing their own small business. To capture such benefits, New United Motor Manufacturing, the GM-Toyota joint venture in Fremont, California, has enlarged production jobs. Teams of five to twelve workers, guided by a team leader, get broad responsibility and divide up the specific tasks themselves; each worker is theoretically able to do any job. In contrast to the dozens of job classifications that existed when the plant was run by GM, there is just one classification for production workers and three for skilled trades.

Small but Complete Structures

When it comes to innovation, "small is beautiful," and flexible is more beautiful. Or at least small is beautiful as long as the small unit includes a connection with every function or discipline necessary to create the final product, as well as the resources and the autonomy to go ahead and do it. In order to get the kind of interfunctional or interdisciplinary integration that innovation requires, close relationships are required among those dedicated to a common business goal—working teams or venture teams that are functionally complete, on which every necessary function is represented.

This is why the idea of dividing into smaller but complete business units is so appealing to organizations seeking continual innovation. All the players are right there, linked closely in the innovation process. (And for all their cumbersomeness in practice, "matrix" reporting relationships acknowledging multiple responsibilities nurture interfunctional links.) In smaller business units it is possible to maintain much closer working relationships across functions than in larger ones—this is one of the reasons for Hewlett-Packard's classic growth strategy of dividing divisions into two when they reached more than 2000 people or $100,000,000 in sales. Even when economies of scale push for such larger units, the cross-functional project or product team within a single facility (captured in such ideas as the factory-within-a-factory) helps keep communications alive and connections strong. Similarly, the skunk works of creative innovators given their own charter and territory speed the development process.

Finally, it is important that those with local knowledge have the ability to experiment based on it—within whatever guidelines or limits are set at higher levels. Innovation is discouraged when those with the responsibility lack the authority to make those changes they feel will benefit their business.

Culture of People Pride

High-innovation organizations have in common the high value they place on people and their potential—what I have come to call a "culture of pride" that expects and rewards high levels of achievement and assumes that investments in people pay off. A mutual adjustment system of management, in contrast to a command system, requires a high degree of respect for people—not only on the part of the company but also on the part of all the players who must back and support one another's ideas.

The investment in people that characterizes high-innovation settings is slightly different from the more paternalistic principle of lifetime employment. While many high-innovation companies try to maintain lifetime employment policies that certainly offer security in exchange for loyalty, this by itself is not responsible for the level of enterprise found in them. Instead, it is the expectation of continuing growth of contribution over time that fosters more entrepreneurial stances. This is reflected in large dollar amounts spent on training and development—and in the emphasis on having the best human resource systems possible.

Operationally, a "culture of pride" is fostered through abundant praise and recognition—a proliferation of awards and recognition mechanisms that continuously hold up the standards for display and publicly acknowledge the people who meet and exceed them. High-innovation settings are marked by celebrations and award ceremonies and trophies and wall plaques and merit badges and awards (e.g., "local hero" awards, "extra mile" awards, "atta-boys") that visibly communicate respect for people and their abilities to contribute.

Merit reward systems (as opposed to automatic cost-of-living adjustments with little or no merit component) also convey the company's recognition of performance. And so does rewarding people by giving them new challenges. Data General engineers say the rewards are like pinball—you win a free game, a chance to do something on your own.

Low-innovation settings, by contrast, seem begrudging about praise; they operate in ways that signal that all important knowledge comes from outside the company, and they expect people's recognition for achievement to be the fact that they have kept their job. I have even found a company that gives significant monetary awards for above-and-beyond contributions—but keeps these all secret.

Power Tools

The entrepreneurial process requires three kinds of "power tools" to move ideas into action—information, support (backing or legitimacy, appropriate sponsorship or championing), and resources. Of course, when large projects are initiated at the top of the organization and handed a staff and checkbook, there is little issue about acquiring the tools to accomplish innovation—although even in this case, managers can run across problems of access to things they need, whether people or facilities. But for instances of spontaneous entrepreneurship, generated within the organization and still lacking the status of a major and official project, access to power tools can determine whether bold new initiatives are ever seeded. Access to power tools is easier in high-innovation settings because of organizational structure and practice.

Information

Information is more readily available in high-innovation settings because of open communication patterns that make data accessible throughout the organization. For example, operating data may be shared down to the shop floor or face-to-face communication may be emphasized or norms may bar "closed meetings"—all common practices in some high-technology companies. Both GE Medical Systems and Wang Labs have declared all meetings open to anyone. And Hewlett-Packard emphasizes online "real time" face-to-face communication through meetings instead of writing.

Support

Support or collaboration is encouraged in high-innovation settings by the dense networks of ties that connect people across diverse areas of the company—such as cross-discipline career paths, membership on task forces and cross-area teams, frequent conferences or meetings across departments, or even whole-unit parties like Silicon Valley's Friday beer busts that bring everyone together to rub elbows as equals. Easy access to potential sponsors or champions is also more likely when title-consciousness is minimal and the chain of command is not a pecking order. Tektronix, for example, has everyone on a first-name basis. Digital Equipment has its own helicopter service to allow everyone easy travel across seventeen New England facilities.

Resources

Resources are easier to get in high-innovation settings because they are decentralized and loosely controlled. More people have budgetary authority and can make commitments for "seed capital" for new activities. Or there are more sources of slack—uncommitted funds—that can be allocated to innovation. There are discretionary time and discretionary resources that can be managed flexibly, used for experimentation, or reinvested in new approaches. 3M is most noted for its internal seed capital banks and its 15 percent rule for technical people—up to 15 percent of their time can be spent on projects of their own choosing.

Overall, high-innovation companies are what I call "integrative"—pulling people together rather than apart. The jobs, structure, and culture all promote a wider feeling of responsibility and team consciousness that not only encourages the development of new ideas but also gives people the tools and the confidence to act on them.

21

Encouraging Innovation and Entrepreneurs in Bureaucratic Companies

Rosabeth Moss Kanter

Class of 1960 Professor of Business Administration,
Graduate School of Business Administration,
Harvard University

What do you do if your organization was not begun in Silicon Valley, if "entrepreneurs" are as foreign as Martians, if people compete to see who can take the toughest stance against new ideas, and if structures are so rigid that the only way to get into another department is to be born there? (The last item is not far fetched. An oil executive told me that in his company, "The only way to move into marketing is to be born there.") It is one thing to hear praise for "excellent" or "innovative" companies. It is another to face the daily reality of an organization that has operated for so many years in a bureaucratic, innovation-stifling way that it seems overwhelming to try to change it.

There *are* a number of steps to begin moving toward creative and innovative management, to undertake special programs that institute manageable changes. These steps involve removing roadblocks to innovation, adding incentives, and helping find new opportunities for innovation across usually separate business areas.

Removing Roadblocks

Make sure that current systems, structures, and practices do not present insurmountable roadblocks to the flexibility and fast action needed for innovation.

Reducing Unnecessary "Bureaucracy"

Among the hindrances to innovation are the layers and layers of hierarchy and piles and piles of rules that slow down action and encourage only cautious, conservative action. Among Roger Smith's first actions as the new chairman of General Motors was to "cancel" ninety-two formerly standard reports (thereby reducing corporate staff) and to insist that all one-to-one reporting relationships be eliminated, reasoning that still one more person in the decision-making chain was not needed. Then he launched a 2-year total organization study with revolutionary results: a new structure that would decentralize authority while adding efficiencies.

In less dramatic fashion, a major petroleum company has made a number of significant changes in order to remove roadblocks to entrepreneurship. Its exploration area reduced the number of approvals necessary for land acquisition, finding that each additional approval was associated with a 15 percent loss of productivity. Another division conducted a "hog law" review, soliciting views from employees about archaic rules and regulations that were impeding change. Still another department reorganized to remove levels of hierarchy after concluding that the additional levels did not "add value" to activities but simply slowed them down.

Reducing "Segmentalism" and Encouraging Integration across Departments and Functions

What I call "segmentalism" is an attitude, a style, a structural form that divides the organization into tiny territories and then tells all to stay within these confines. Management levels don't eat in the same cafeteria with subordinate levels, departments don't talk to other departments, divisions don't cooperate with (or care much about) other divisions. Instead, guarding territory is the name of the game. Development processes are linear and disconnected: Design engineers hand off to production engineers who hand off to manufacturing who hand off to sales—with each group grumbling that the others didn't give them the "right" stuff. And the whole thing moves too slowly.

Actions that improve communication and information flow across units and levels are one corrective step. Some companies with a legacy of excessive segmentation of activities are restructuring to create more business-specific, customer-specific, or product-specific teams across functions. Honeywell has been doing this in its residential division. Campbell Soup divided into over fifty "business units" to stimulate new product development. Others are stressing interdepartmental improvement projects or idea exchanges, as SOHIO's technical areas do. They are trying to ease the flow of information, support, and resources across areas—the key "power tools" (see Chapter 20).

Changing Internal Budgeting and Accounting Procedures

One large household products manufacturer has discovered that its internal financial systems may discourage investment in new technologies because all expenditures must be justified in terms of immediate cost savings. A leading bank decided to separate budgets for ongoing investment activities from new ones for just this reason, and they have started reporting levels of investment expenditure positively in department reviews as well as (in the aggregate) in their annual report. The bank has also begun to encourage the divestment of old or less profitable products and services in favor of new ones by allowing departments to retain most cost savings for internal investment.

Adding Incentives

Provide incentives and tools for entrepreneurial projects.

Internal "Venture Capital" and Special Project Budgets

People need to find resources *somewhere* if they are to innovate. But free dollars cannot be siphoned out of everyday line operating budgets that are geared toward turning out *today's* products and services. So, following the lead of 3M and now other major organizations such as Eastman Kodak, an increasing number of companies are setting up special "innovation banks" to fund new ventures or ideas outside of operating budgets. General Motors set up such a fund with the United Auto Workers in the 1984 labor agreement to seek new ventures that could preserve jobs in the light of job reductions with new technology. Through such special banks, large new ventures can be supported inside the company as separate businesses. But perhaps even more significantly, many small development activities can be undertaken that would otherwise find no place in a line-manager's budget (because of the typical requirement for immediate cost savings or ROI hurdle rates to justify expenditures).

Thus, efforts that are more experimental or may take more time to bring returns or do not fit neatly within existing areas can still find a home. This is useful not only for those innovations in products or technology that might normally fall within the scope of an R&D operation but also for numerous other special projects in marketing or information systems or personnel or dealer relations that can themselves net considerable payoffs. The large computer manufacturer I call "Chipco" in *The Change Masters* has funded innovative organizational improvement projects out of a corporate innovation council. They involved workers and first-line supervisors in a series of problem-solving teams that redesigned the assembly line for team assembly and tackled other creative projects.

Discretionary Funds and Discretionary Time

Simply leaving a portion of budget uncommitted, to be used as managers see fit, can stimulate innovation. Similarly with time. 3M is again the most noteworthy model because of their formalization of the 15 percent rule—that up to 15 percent of technical employees' time may be spent on projects of their own choosing. At lower levels of the organization, related moves might involve allowing production workers to spend up to 10 percent of their time on problem-solving teams (as at Chipco).

A "Dry Hole" or "Portfolio" Approach to Innovation

Top management can and should act as sponsors of innovation, devoting more of their time to new venture creation and innovation than to controlling ongoing activities. Senior executives should structure internal systems to support novel and original ideas. A portfolio approach means seeding many diverse projects and original experiments—smaller scale and at lower funding levels than traditional projects—with an expectation that some will fail, but some will pay off. The dry hole analogy is to oil exploration in which a large number of holes are drilled with the knowledge that only a small portion will produce yields. But the more holes drilled—and the increasing intelligence brought to each by learning from "failures"—the greater likelihood of major success. Of course, there is a balancing factor: the importance of good aim, of efforts focused in areas likely to pay off. Increased experimentation does not necessitate acting on *every* idea. Long-range planning and management priority setting can help focus local initiative so that more "drilled holes" produce yields.

Performance Review and Compensation Geared to Innovation

While many companies engage in the rhetoric of innovation, their methods of appraising and rewarding people may still be tied to short-term revenues and profits, which almost always discourage innovation. For this reason, companies are increasingly including the development of creative new activities as part of management by objectives and performance appraisals, and they are making it harder for people to "do well" if they simply continue the tried and true. Such path-setting firms are also considering much larger rewards for successful innovation, from phantom stock to a percent of the return from a new venture, in exchange for deferral of more traditional reward (such as assured bonuses) that can have a negative impact on longer-term projects or ventures. Indeed, the entire topic of compensation will be rethought in the decade ahead and will itself be the target of innovation, as a more "entrepreneurial" era brings with it the emergence of vehicles tying individual compensation to company performance. Techniques include everything from ownership-like devices (such as gainsharing) to actual employee ownership. Finally, some companies are also experimenting with ways to reward and recognize the sponsors and champions of innovators, not just the doers, thus encouraging more high-level support for innovation.

Integrating Areas

Seek synergies across business areas, so that new opportunities are discovered in new combinations while still allowing business units to retain operating autonomy.

Joint Projects and Ventures

Intercompany, interdivisional, company-with-supplier, company-with-vendor, etc. Joint ventures, requiring a partnership structure and governance by mutual adjustment, are becoming more common as companies discover the synergies that come from combining resources for specific purposes rather than acquiring a whole company—a route for new venture development that innovation experts such as MIT's Edward Roberts have been encouraging. (Howard Stevenson and David Gumpert point out that "trustees" feel they must "own" all resources themselves in order to better control them, whereas entrepreneurs are willing to "rent" them, find them through joint ventures, or turn to subcontractors.)

Even joint ventures across divisions of a single company provide promising avenues for business development. But often, traditional practices have discouraged this—for example, how performance is measured for divisions and how career rewards are given to managers. Some companies are now explicitly trying to encourage technology transfer or integrated product development within the organization, large-scale projects that could not be funded within one plant's budget. A decentralized computer and control systems company is working to combine devices manufactured by separate divisions into one large system geared to the needs of particular customers. Liquid Tide was developed by three different R&D units at Procter & Gamble working across national borders—in the United States, Japan, and Belgium. An important goal, then, is increasing the feasibility and legitimacy of such cross-divisional projects.

Conferences, Idea Exchanges, and "Blue Sky Institutes"

Facilitating better information flow across parts of the company and between the company and its suppliers or dealers is one simple way of allowing synergies to be discovered. Rather than the one-way information flow characteristic of the command style (a parade of speakers and reports, with highly controlled question and answer sessions), companies are trying to encourage dialogue and joint problem solving that can generate partnerships through retreats with open-ended agendas.

Overall Approach

In general, the ideal-typical entrepreneurial corporation would be characterized by an integrative culture and structure, one that creates teamwork across any relevant part of the organization; encourages identification with overall company goals rather than "turfiness"; and removes barriers to communication or cooperative action. It would minimize hard-and-fast rules and procedures governed by a rigidly defined command structure and emphasize instead flexibility and integration—broadly skilled sets of employees in adaptive units that can be grouped and regrouped as changing circumstances require or as they spontaneously take initiative to solve problems or create innovations.

In the ideal world, such flexibility and spirit of partnership managed by reciprocity and mutual adjustment would extend to suppliers and dealers as well as to departments "inside" the company. Joint undertakings in which both parties work together as a team and exert synergistic influence to ensure the best mutual outcome would be the norm.

22

Encouraging Innovation and Entrepreneurship in Diversified Corporations

Lewis W. Lehr

Former Chairman and Chief Executive Officer, 3M

Managing and innovation do not always fit comfortably together. That's not surprising. Managers are people who like order. They like forecasts to come out as planned. In fact, managers are often judged on how much order they produce. Innovation, on the other hand, is often a disorderly process. Many times, perhaps most times, innovation does not turn out as planned. As a result, there is tension between managers and innovators.

I am tempted to say that innovation at 3M works *in spite* of top management. For example, some years ago we had a researcher who was fired. But he still kept coming to the laboratory to work on his pet project—improved roofing granules. He persisted. He was rehired. And the project became a division. The stubborn employee ultimately retired as vice president of a very successful operation. Another young lab worker was having a good time experimenting with tiny glass beads, more a novelty than a product. He was ordered back to his regular work. But many a night he returned to his lab, after everyone else had gone home, to pursue his glass beads. Today those tiny beads are on reflective road safety signs all over the world. And a few years ago, he received an Oscar for another pet project, a bead-based front projection system for moviemakers. We keep these stories alive and tell them often for the benefit of anyone who feels discouraged or frustrated. We want them to know they are not the first.

It is tempting to believe that managers and innovators are natural adversaries. Tempting but not necessarily true. Innovation may be a disorderly process, but it need not be carried out in a disorderly way. There is much that management can do to create and foster a climate for innovation.

Renewing Large Organizations

Most companies begin with a small group of people who have strong drives for success. They build a team. There is no motivation problem, no communication problem. People deal with each other face-to-face. But then if it's successful, the organization begins to grow. Gradually, things change. Informal give-and-take becomes preoccupation with policy and control. New challenges and new ideas are walled off into separate compartments and surrounded by specialists—almost as if they were some kind of a plague. In a word, the organization becomes "segmented," to use a term favored by Rosabeth Moss Kanter. Boundaries emerge. Turf becomes all-important. Instead of designing for success, management begins to design against error. Opportunity is seen as threat. It's an attempt to channel thinking. It's what I call "fenced-in-a-pasture thinking," and it cuts across public and private sectors.

Is it inevitable, this hardening of an organization's arteries? I don't believe so. There are things that management can do to slow down the process, to turn it around, to prevent it from happening. The key is understanding the process of innovation. That means understanding who innovators are and what they need from management. Why focus on innovators? Quite simply, they are the key to renewal in an organization. How do we find them? We don't even need to look. They'll find us if we let them. But innovators are not easy to manage. Few organizations are structured or temperamentally adjusted to handle them. Managers need to understand how innovators think and what they want. Then we can worry about changing structure, policy, and rules.

Gifford Pinchot calls them visionaries. By that he means something quite specific. Innovators, he says, are people with the ability to make an extraordinarily clear mental model of the way things are going to be. And then they act upon that vision. Among marathon runners, they say that the edge between real competitors and also-rans is the ability to picture yourself crossing the finish line. Apparently there are many runners who simply cannot see themselves crossing that line. They are the losers. Pinchot shows how powerful such vision can be for innovators. There was an inventor, he says, who could build a detailed model of a new machine in his mind. Then he put it into the mental background and left it running for 3 weeks. At the end of 3 weeks, he dragged the machine into the forefront of his mind, tore it down, and checked the bearings for wear.

If innovators are visionaries, they are not dreamers. They spend a lot of time looking at potential obstacles and considering how to get around them. They work until they have their vision clear and complete. What does this all mean for managers? Innovators are driven—impelled by their own visions. They march to their own drummers. And quite often, they march across boundaries—onto someone else's turf—and straight into trouble. In a sense, innovation is as much political as technical. It is the manager's job to smooth the way, to protect innovators and get them what they need. Some innovators are quite adept at finding their way through the political shrubbery of the organization. Others are not. And that's where the manager has to step in. To renew an organization it is essential to set up a system for the care and feeding of innovators.

Encouraging Innovation

How do we encourage 3M people to be innovative? Following are eight ways.

Challenge Them

First, we *challenge* managers with aggressive goals. Our divisions shoot for a high target: In any given year, 25 percent of sales should come from products introduced within the last 5 years. Of course, not every division hits its target every year. But our managers are judged not only on their ability to make existing product lines grow but also on their knack for bringing innovative new products to market. So they have a built-in incentive to keep R&D strong.

Use Sponsors

Successful projects often have a sponsor, or protector, somewhere high in the organization. Someone has to help the innovator gain access to resources. Above all, someone has to be there to protect a project when it falters, as it probably will.

Acting as a sponsor for an untried project is no picnic. Most sponsors, I believe, tend to bet on people rather than on products. We have a saying at 3M that, "The captains bite their tongues until they bleed." This means they have to keep their hands off the project. The first virtue of a sponsor is faith. The second is patience. And the third is understanding the differences between temporary setback and terminal problem.

It is at this level—the level of the sponsor—that there is opportunity to plant the seeds of innovation. Make sponsoring an explicit part of the job description for every top manager. When managers come in for appraisals, they should be asked about the new projects under their wings. The economics of projects is not the first issue to raise. Stress, instead, the vision of payoff.

Give Proper Reward

With true innovators, the problem of rewards can be sticky. Most innovators seem to find gratification in seeing their visions turn into concrete reality. In his book *The Soul of a New Machine,* Tracy Kidder follows the development of a new computer at Data General Corporation. At one point, Kidder asks one of the young engineers what's in it for his team. The engineer replied: "It's like pinball. If you win, you get to do it again." So, the "pinball reward" is important for the innovator—the freedom to do it again. This may not be quite as easy as it sounds. The career track in many organizations leads many a successful innovator straight into management, a job that he or she may neither want nor be good at.

If an organization ranks its managers only by the number of people they supervise, you get empires not innovation. There has to be a career track for innovators separate from the management ladder, a corporate path that allows them to continue doing what they do best. Of course, there are many innovators, in both technical and nontechnical disciplines, who can hardly wait to get into management. But there are others who have no interest whatever in sitting behind a desk and worrying about budgets—and frankly, who have no talent for that kind of work. They would much rather be in the lab or out in the field working on something interesting. They need a separate career path— a series of stages that are equivalent in compensation and status to the positions of supervisor, manager, director, and so forth. For these people, promotion can then be tied directly to successful innovation rather than to their ability to manage others. Beyond that, there is what Pinchot calls "earned freedom." Successful innovators are given progressively more freedom to work on whatever interests them. IBM's corporate fellows, for example, are free to roam the company, working on whatever interests them most, for a certain period of time.

Guarantee Time

At 3M we *guarantee time* for people to work on pet ideas. We've learned a lesson from those persistent investors of earlier years. We encourage our technical people to spend up to 15 percent of their time on projects of their own choosing. Only a small percentage actually make use of this 15-percent option at a given time. But the guarantee is there. In effect, this is a way for 3M to allocate capital to entrepreneurs. Thus, they can at least begin a project without going through a series of management approvals.

Communicate

A pervasive element of our climate of innovation is *communication*—a constant flow of good information in our technical community. It is hard to overestimate the value of communication in a multinational company. We are a highly diversified organization, to say the least. We have about forty separate divisions. We have about eighty-five basic technologies. And we have literally tens of thousands of individual products. Because our product divisions are fairly autonomous, it is natural for technical people to stay squirreled away in their own labs, concentrating only on their division's technologies.

To prevent this kind of isolation, we maintain a massive and continuing effort to promote cross-communication among the various innovators. Through an organization called the Technical Forum, our people are in continuing dialogue with each other. The Technical Forum has more than two dozen chapters and committees. In one year they staged more than 160 events, with presentations ranging from "ion implantation in metals and ceramics" to "new therapeutic approaches to rheumatoid arthritis."

Some of our scientists speak of a kind of super-technology—the ability to combine two or more separate technologies into a unique application or product. The well-developed communications network in 3M's technical community often provides such opportunities. For example, our pavement markings combine retro-reflective technologies and pressure-sensitive adhesive technologies. And our Controltac films for fleet graphics are a combination of glass bubble, adhesive, and imaging technologies. We try to provide incentives and opportunities for innovators to discuss their ideas with kindred spirits and to reinforce each other.

Just as we try to minimize barriers between staff people in different research labs, we also work at keeping open communication channels between researchers and process or production people, between researchers and marketing people, and even between researchers and customers. Then too, we have sales representatives who don't stop listening when they don't have the product a customer needs. That's when they really start to listen. These salespeople share what they learn with our lab men and women; we like satisfying customer needs by developing new products or businesses.

The whole process of commercializing a new development is *not* like a relay race—in which the scientist completes his or her lap and passes a baton to production people, who in turn run their lap and pass the baton to a sales force for the final leg of the race. Ideally there is communication and consultation among all functions at every step. They often form what we call a business development unit to exploit the new product or business ideas. Such a team may transcend the existing organization structure and be loosely formed as a matrix system.

Recognize Them

One or two dozen times a year some new 3M project reaches the level of $2 million in profitable sales. You might think that drop wouldn't get much attention in an $8 billion ocean. But it does. Lights flash, bells ring, and cameras are called out to honor the team responsible for such an achievement. We see in these fledgling projects the future of 3M. We also have recognition programs for international business successes, for purely technical achievements, and for outstanding work in virtually every discipline within the company.

These awards rarely take the form of cash bonuses or trips to Hawaii. We have found that, especially for technical people, few things are more important than simply being recognized by one's peers for good work. Recognition is a powerful incentive for innovation.

Structure for Growth

Finally, we stress *structures* that assure innovators both support and stimulation. With about forty product divisions, various projects and departments, and about fifty overseas companies, 3M has close to one hundred major profit centers. Yet each one must feel much like a free-standing business. Basically, division managers run their own shops. They make their own decisions, develop their own new products—and take responsibility for the consequences. As teams within a division develop successful new products and businesses, division management is responsible for spinning them off into self-sustaining enterprises. We call this process "divide and grow." Our policy of dividing for growth is based on a discovery made years ago. We found that when a division reaches a certain size, it may spend too much time on established products and markets. It then has less time to spend on new products and business. When we break out a new business, we appoint a new management team. We give people an opportunity to identify with the new business. And we find, almost without exception, that the new unit begins to grow at a faster rate.

Take, for example, our tape business. From our original Scotch brand masking tape and transparent tape have come four separate divisions, with countless lines of tape for industrial, commercial, and home use. Also out of our tape laboratories came a new surgical tape and surgical drape in the 1950s. These products gave birth to our health care business and eventually to our Medical, Surgical, and Orthopedic Products Divisions. And out of those same labs came a line of electrical-grade tapes. These in their turn spawned several divisions specializing in electrical connectors, terminals, insulation, and so forth. Our corporate structure is specifically designed to encourage innovators to take an idea and run with it. If they succeed, they may find themselves running their own business under the 3M umbrella.

We have a structure and personnel practice whereby one individual can enjoy a series of different careers without leaving the company. The innovator who is so inclined can become the entrepreneur who goes on to build a business. He or she may become the product champion before senior management or even in the marketplace.

Advice on rearing creative youngsters states that you *don't* provide children with coloring books and then warn them to stay inside the lines of the drawings. For management to expect innovators to stay inside the lines is a paradox. Such inhibiting boundaries may be job descriptions, detailed instructions on how to do something, or any restrictive language. Long ago we learned that if you place too many fences around people, they can easily become a pasture of sheep. And how many patents are assigned to sheep?

Accept Mistakes (But Only If Original)

The cost of failure is a major concern for innovators—since that is what will happen to most of them at one time or another. We estimate at 3M that about 60 percent of our formal new-product programs never make it. When this happens, the important thing is not to crucify the people involved. They should know that their jobs are not in jeopardy if they fail. Otherwise, too many would-be innovators will give in to the quite natural temptation to play it safe. Few things will choke innovation more quickly than the threat of losing a job if you fail.

We have a tradition of accepting honest mistakes and failures without harsh penalties. We see mistakes as a normal part of business and an essential by-product of innovation. But we expect our mistakes to have originality. We can afford almost any mistake once. Those who choose to lead high-risk, new-product programs know that their employment will not be threatened. This attitude of management eliminates one of the major barriers to innovation in large companies.

3M's heritage of innovation was epitomized by one of my predecessors, who said in 1944:

> As our business grows, it becomes increasingly necessary to delegate responsibility and to encourage men and women to exercise their initiative. This requires considerable tolerance . . . good people are going to want to do their jobs in their own way . . . mistakes will be made, but if a person is essentially right, the mistakes he or she makes are not as serious in the long run as the mistakes management will make if it is dictatorial and undertakes to tell those under its authority exactly how they must do their job. Management that is destructively critical when mistakes are made kills initiative, and it's essential that we have many people with initiative if we're to continue to grow.

Summary

These eight points, taken together, constitute management's proper approach to innovation. Without real commitment from the top, however, real innovation will be defeated again and again by the policies, procedures, and rituals of almost any large organization. Even with a good track record for innovation, do not leave anything to chance. Certainly, the best way to lose an innovative edge is to spend too much time admiring a successful past. A good reputation is history, nothing more. Good companies must always search for excellence.

23

Conditions for Innovation in Large Organizations

Sandra Gerson Weis

Program Manager, Telecommunications Strategy,
Trintex

There are many examples of large, innovative corporations that repeatedly introduce new products, enter new markets, and enjoy solid financial performance. These include IBM, 3M, General Electric, Hewlett-Packard, and others. There are also countless examples of companies that have sought growth and diversification through internal development, external acquisitions, or joint ventures only to find disappointment in failure, excessive cost, or moderate success that hardly seems worth the effort. What do highly innovative companies do differently than other firms? Are there specific conditions absent in less innovative counterparts? How can a corporation become innovative?

A large, conservative communications company's experience in internal venturing and other efforts to achieve product and service innovation provides a framework to address conditions required to foster innovation. This chapter describes the company's experience and then compares the literature on innovation management and entrepreneurship. I conclude with an approach to introduce innovation management into large, conservative corporations.

The Comminc Experience

A multibillion dollar communications company, referred to as Comminc, has at different times engaged in internal new ventures, major acquisition, and internal development efforts for growth and diversification. Comminc is a successful company, but its self-assessed performance compared to a peer group of companies fell short in terms of new product and service development. The self-assessment revealed that Comminc's major source of new product and service revenues had come from acquisitions and that internally developed, new-to-the-world innovations were almost nonexistent. Comminc's revenues are primarily generated by telephone operating companies although Comminc has major positions in products and services markets beyond its telephone companies.

Since the late seventies, Comminc has withstood a series of external shocks including telecommunications deregulation, the breakup of AT&T, and vigorous competition. Internal senior management changes, uncertainty in CEO succession, numerous reorganizations, and business cycle contractions have also taken their toll. Comminc during this time has been formulating a new corporate mission. Comminc has actively sought growth and new business development and has employed internal ventures, venture capital investments, new style joint ventures and strategic alliances, minority equity investments, and intrapreneurism with varying results. Examples of Comminc's experiences are summarized below.

New Product Development

In 1984, Comminc's top fifty managers evaluated why the corporation's new product and service development performance was below expectations. These managers reached consensus that four primary factors inhibited new product and service development and innovation: (1) lack of incentives to encourage inherent risk taking and little tolerance for failure, (2) pressure of financial periodic performance, (3) insufficient senior management support, and (4) lack of market knowledge. The primary source of new revenues was through acquisitions. Successful internal product development efforts were almost always add-ons to existing products.

Internal Ventures

Several internal development efforts were sponsored but these were principally extensions of existing products, technologies and/or services. Of three internal ventures started up during the period, two were considered failures and one may be successful. Comminc started two ventures in 1979–80, both of which were ultimately divested for strategic and financial reasons. Following divestiture both start-ups continued to be managed by their original general manager and both became profitable businesses. They are described below as "Service" and "Products."

Service.   Service was started in 1980 to fulfill a perceived market need for a home medical alert service. The idea had evolved from an in-hospital medical communications product developed by a Comminc division divested in 1980. Upon divestiture, the start-up was retained because it had promise, and a vice president had a strong personal commitment to its success. Service did not have an obvious "home" in Comminc but was placed under the umbrella of the profitable telephone operations group. The general manager, who had been a marketing director in the divested division, began operations in April 1980 in a geographic location adjacent to a Comminc telephone company. Early marketing efforts demonstrated that the original concept of a medical alert service was not selling but that repositioning to offer security alarms, remote fire detection, as well as medical alert consumer service would sell.

The business grew rapidly in terms of number of subscribers and employees—and in its ability to consume cash. In 1982, senior management took notice and made a decision to divest. In November 1983 the business was sold to the security alarms subsidiary of a major corporation. At the time of divestiture, Service was losing one dollar for every three revenue dollars. Eight months after divestiture, the buyer reported that Service had turned profitable, the subscriber base had remained intact, and efforts were underway to retarget to a more profitable commercial subscriber base. Service, while unsuccessful for Comminc financially and strategically, was viewed by its competitors as unique because it had built one of the largest subscriber bases in its industry. The buyer purchased Service for its subscribers and marketing performance and as a strategic foundation for further acquisitions. The general manager continued to run the business and almost all Comminc employees stayed.

The general manager made a number of observations about Service's start-up.

1. *Commitment lack.* There was a lack of total corporate commitment. For example, the adjacent telephone company would not assist Service because it feared that rate increases might be held up by state regulators. The lack of commitment was also reflected in diffusion of staff functional support. Service felt itself an orphan, particularly after its vice president and sponsor retired in 1982.

2. *Corporate diversion.* Excessive time was diverted from managing the business to interfacing with Comminc corporate. The general manager reported up through the telephone companies' staff and had at least six different supervisors between 1980 and divestiture. The supervisors in turn had multiple levels of supervision.

3. *Limited criteria.* Successful performance was keyed to subscriber growth rather than to a mix of performance factors. In addition, the general manager's bonus plan usually was not finalized until well into the performance year, and the dollar bonus was only about 5 to 8 percent of the general manager's salary.

4. *Limited control.* The general manager had day-to-day responsibility but lacked control over broad strategic direction.

5. *Poor fit.* Service was never a good strategic fit with Comminc and no one at corporate really understood the business.

Following divestiture, the general manager commented that he now reported directly to the president (of the buyer's alarms subsidiary), had complete P&L and strategic responsibility, and his bonus, in place January 1, could be a significant percent of total compensation.

Products. Products was started up by an operating division of Comminc ("Division") in 1979 to provide a specialized product for telephone companies. Products was Division's third attempt to enter the telephone companies' market, and entry was deemed critical to distract a major competitor from entering Division's main business. There were substantial differences, however, between Products and Division's main business. The main business' product development cycle was 2 to 3 years, backlogs were 12 to 18 months, and prices were in the $100,000+ range. Products' product lines, by contrast, were developed in 30 to 60 days, backlogs were negligible, prices were in the $100 range, and customers often required overnight delivery. Because Division's two prior entry attempts had been unsuccessful and Products' business was so different, Division modeled its third attempt after Products' entrepreneurial competitors.

The general manager was recruited from another Comminc division and started operations in a western U.S. location away from other

Comminc sites in 1979. At the time of divestiture, Products was number 9 out of 70 competitors and had grown to 180 employees, none of whom were prior Comminc employees. Products turned profitable during the first quarter of 1984.

In 1982, Division was in dire financial straits and was reorganized out of existence. Products' general manager, who had reported to Division's president, subsequently reported to a corporate senior vice president. The senior vice president ensured that resources and support were provided to Products and maintained personal commitment to the venture. Products was divested in 1984 because it no longer fit Comminc's long-range strategic plans. Its products were niche-filling analog products when Comminc was going digital and marketing systems. In effect, Products was successful in developing and marketing "the last buggy whip."

The general manager, who facilitated divestiture by putting together a leveraged buy-out package, commented upon the inherent difference in needs, management style, and operations of a small entrepreneurial business and those of a large, complex corporation.

1. *Standardized compensation.* A system that requires jobs be equated according to current responsibilities proved to be the most significant hurdle in forming the core management team. The general manager wanted to hire a marketing vice president able to expand the business from nothing to a $50 to $100 million enterprise. He was forced by Comminc to comply with accepted "standards," had to hire at a lower-middle management level, and was unable to offer a bonus or other performance incentives. Since divestiture, the general manager has hired a new marketing vice president who is motivated by a higher salary, stock in Products, and other performance incentives.

2. *Inability to reward employee performance.* Products' employees were compensated as were any other Comminc employees. Competitors, by contrast, were small entrepreneurial firms able to hire and motivate employees through flexible risk-reward incentives. Upon divestiture, for example, the general manager abolished the $80,000 cap on the sales force and put in incentive compensation packages throughout Products. Top salespeople now are *expected* to exceed $100,000 annually.

3. *Corporate administrative requirements.* The general manager said that within a few months after divestiture his administrative costs had declined by 12 percent because he did not need the same reports, treatment of expense accounts, purchasing, etc., that Comminc did.

4. *Senior management commitment.*   The senior vice president's support was critical for Products' survival when Division was slashing budgets.

5. *Autonomy and budget separation.*   Products' success was largely due to its strategic, marketing, and management autonomy and to the separation of its budget from Division and later Comminc.

Other Comminc Growth Efforts

New Ventures Group

Comminc in the 1970s was among the many *Fortune 500* firms that tried internal venturing but failed. The reasons for those failures are documented by Norman Fast in his book *The Rise and Fall of Corporate New Venture Divisions.* The specific reasons for Comminc's failure are classic—too short a time horizon (3 years), poor investment selection and lack of relevance to corporate strategy, excessive corporate control, and management inexperienced in new business creation.

Acquisitions

During the 5-year period observed to assess new product and service performance, Comminc closed a major acquisition in a related business, acquired a young technology company that is now a $100+ million business, and made a few other small technology or filler acquisitions. The major acquisition, while perceived to be successful, has encountered a downturn in its markets and has required large infusions of cash. The technology acquisition has grown substantially but required 6 years to generate net income.

Venture Capital

In 1979, Comminc invested in a West Coast venture capital limited partnership for strategic visibility and financial return. The corporate development vice president, responsible for the investment, believed that Comminc would benefit through gaining a window on technology. In the early 1980s, Comminc's pension funds invested $29 million through its money managers in a portfolio of venture capital partnerships. By 1982, it was becoming clear that a high percentage of venture capital investments were being made in communications and related technologies and that several portfolio companies were of potential strategic interest. A new corporate development vice president with venture capital experience, recruited outside Comminc, concluded that such investments could be effective strategic tools and that Comminc should increase its venture capital presence. He proposed that Comminc invest $25 million to set up a dedicated *internal venture capital fund*. Comminc did not implement the recommendation. However, the visibility of the proposal served to open access for the pension funds to invest in venture capital. The ERISA barrier between corporate and pension management, while carefully respected, did not preclude information access. Corporate development then focused on opportunistic scanning and systematic building of informal networking relationships among Comminc marketing and technical people and venture capital professionals. These contacts were unexpectedly successful in identifying a number of potential strategic deals.

Innovation: Conditions and Barriers

Innovation can be broadly defined as the process of using any new, problem-solving, or opportunity-addressing idea to create purposeful, focused change in an enterprise's economic or social potential. An overview of recent literature on innovation is summarized below to present a backdrop against which to evaluate the Comminc experience.

Quinn analyzed a multiyear, worldwide study of small ventures and large firms known for innovation. He concluded that there are striking similarities between innovative small and large firms and among innovative firms in different countries: He identified seven patterns present in large, innovative companies:

1. *Atmosphere and vision.* Top managers manage their company's value system and environment to support continuous innovation.

2. *Orientation to the market.* Two elements are always present: a strong market orientation at the top and mechanisms to ensure interactions between technical and marketing people.

3. *Small, flat organizations.* Typical are 6- to 7-person development teams and divisions that do not exceed 400 people.

4. *Multiple approaches.* Using several parallel prototype efforts.

5. *Development shoot-outs.* This reduces risk but is difficult to manage. It is critical to create a climate that values high-quality performers irrespective of whether their projects win the shoot-out.

6. *Skunk works.* Development teams that operate like small entrepreneurial companies eliminate bureaucracies, allow quick communication and rapid turnaround, and instill high group identity, loyalty, and performance.

7. *Interactive learning.* There are numerous ways to tap into outside sources for information. They can include joint ventures, academic funding, limited partnerships, and venture capital.

Maidique, Roberts, and MacMillan and George conclude that there are clear, definable roles and functions associated with successful innovation (see Chapters 11, 20, and 21 for Kanter). Maidique argues that the entrepreneurial role is essential for radical technological innovation, that top management involvement is required, and that an executive champion is important. Roberts documents five roles critical for innovation to occur in industrial R&D organizations. In order of occurrence they are: idea generator; entrepreneur; three gatekeepers—technological, market, and manufacturing; program manager; and senior sponsor.

MacMillan and George articulate the responsibilities of senior management. They identify specific tasks for initiation and execution of new ventures. To *initiate* senior management must:

1. *Select the context.* This requires clearly defining the development strategy and pursuing a portfolio of ventures to diversify the inherently high failure rate.

2. *Design the appropriate structure.* This may require a specialized structure to avoid smothering the fledgling venture.

3. *Commit to providing adequate support.* Senior management must affirm its commitment by delivering financial and organizational resources necessary for the venture.

4. *Appoint a venture sponsor.* A senior level manager as sponsor plays a vital troubleshooting role and must be able to both inspire venture managers and represent senior management.

To *execute* a new venture, senior management must (1) *Impose discipline :* insist on output; (2) *demand milestones :* have clearly identified events and "kill" points; and (3) *shoot the wounded :* exercising the kill option is senior management's sometimes painful responsibility. MacMillan and George conclude that

> There is little point in aspiring to expand the firm's sales via new business development unless senior management recognizes and meets certain key

responsibilities . . . the chances are high that the whole process is doomed to expensive and demoralizing failure if these responsibilities are not met.

Sherman surveyed America's most innovative large corporations (nominated by business school professors, security analysts, and management consultants). He then interviewed managers in those companies to find out how they achieved sustained inventiveness. Ten common themes emerged:

1. *Fear.* This drives the commitment to foster innovation.

2. *Marketing devotion is universal.* These companies listen carefully to their customers.

3. *Corporate cultures are clearly defined.* Strategic aims are conveyed widely and convincingly.

4. *The search for new ideas is ruthlessly limited.* Restrict innovation to areas in which the company has competency.

5. *Top executives control risk and financial exposure.* Tough internal testing processes winnow ideas.

6. *Communication.* People in different disciplines are not allowed to work in isolation. If natural interaction does not occur, it is forced.

7. *Corporate mission is clearly defined.* One of the chief executive officer's most important responsibilities is to define overall goals so that even low-level employees can understand them.

8. *"Slack" time and money are available.* For example, in R&D, a certain percentage of budgets are set aside for new projects.

9. *Decentralization.* This permits proximity to the market.

10. *Failure is tolerated and success is recognized.* Promotion, awards, and recognition are among the techniques used to reward the innovator.

Drucker argues that at least 90 percent of all effective innovations result from analysis, system, and hard work. Entrepreneurship and innovation are a purposeful and systematic management discipline with policies and practices in four major areas:

1. *Receptivity.* The organization must be made receptive to innovation and must be willing to see change as an opportunity rather than a threat.

2. *Appraisal.* Systematic appraisal of a company's performance as entrepreneur and innovator is mandatory.

3. *Specific practices.*   Entrepreneurial management requires specific practices pertaining to organizational structure, staffing, managing, compensation, incentives, and rewards.

4. *The Don'ts.*   Don't mix entrepreneurial and established business units; stick to areas you understand because if you add diversification difficulties to the demands of entrepreneurship, the results are predictable disaster; build entrepreneurial management into your own system because acquisition may not work.

Learning from Comminc

How does the Comminc experience relate to the research? What lessons can other large, conservative corporations learn? The most compelling conditions required for innovation cluster into the following areas:

1. *Communication information.*   External market and internal integration

2. *Senior management responsibilities.*   Mission, atmosphere supportive of innovation and involvement

3. *Support and resources.*   Slack money, protection from budget cuts, peer and senior level support

4. *Managing for innovation.*   Roles, structure, incentives

Comminc's mixed experience in two internal new ventures and its senior managers' self-assessed performance in new product development are understandable when viewed against the conditions present in innovative firms. Comminc's self-assessment of the barriers it had faced in new product and service development identified shortfalls in each of the above clusters. Products and Service both illustrate the presence of these conditions. Table 23.1 arrays self-assessment, Products, and Service against the above conditions for innovation.

Comminc's self-assessment, in effect, concludes that the corporation's atmosphere and culture are not receptive to innovation and that systematic approaches to innovation management have not been present. While Comminc's acquisitions have been relatively successful and have been the major source of new product and service revenues, its returns to date are disappointing.

Products should have been a successful start-up. The bulk of the conditions required for innovation were present. Perhaps the explanation for why Products produced the last buggy whip lies in insufficient

Table 23.1.

Conditions	Self-Assesment	Products	Service
Communication and information	Not close enough to market	Good market knowledge; internal R&D and marketing communication low	Able to shift marketing focus fast; communication gap at corporate
Senior management	Insufficient support	Strong both at Division and Corporate	Early vice president support, then orphaned; managed too loosely
Support and resources	Pressure of periodic financial performance	Blessed by Division president and Senior vice president; protected from budget cuts	Support low; funding available
Manage for innovation	Incentives lacking; failure not tolerated	Treated as any other Comminc business; risk and reward and incentives not considered	Treated as any other Comminc unit; hindered by location in bureaucracy

communication between Products and other parts of Comminc because of geographic distance and Products' location inside Division. A senior venture sponsor was not active until Products had been in operation 2 years. Finally, Comminc was adjusting to deregulation, its senior management succession was uncertain, and its mission unclear.

Service, in contrast to Products, was a start-up that should have been "shot" by senior management long before Comminc acted to divest the business. Service fell short in each condition for innovation, and it did not fit Comminc's strategic direction. Communication and market information, senior management involvement, and managing for innovation were the major stumbling blocks. The general manager's comment, "they never understood the business," was borne out a few months after divestiture when a senior Comminc planning executive referred to Service as "that medical alert for old folks" business and looked in disbelief when Service was being compared to a security alarms competitor.

Perhaps the major lesson to be learned from Comminc's experience with Products and Service is that managing for innovation requires treating start-up businesses differently from established businesses. Service's ability to turn profitable after divestiture is an example of the effectiveness of managing for innovation: The general manager's compensation and that of other key people are pegged to overall performance; milestones are the basis for measurement; and the general manager reports to the president. Products' success after divestiture reflects the efficiency that independent, small entrepreneurial firms must produce. Overhead costs were pruned substantially, and employees were motivated by rewards and incentives commensurate with risk. Comminc thus provides an example of a corporation that, absent proactive efforts to develop the conditions required for innovation, cannot expect to derive significant future revenues from products and services it currently does not offer.

An Innovation Management Approach

Large, conservative firms that wish to become more innovative can begin by recognizing that innovation can and must be managed. Four steps create the conditions required for innovation:

1. *Top management commitment and involvement.* Senior executive personnel must resolve to manage for innovation; provide mission or context, appoint a senior sponsor, and ensure that resources are available.

2. *Separate management of innovation from management of established businesses.* Begin culture change by piloting independent projects for which rules are different (but confined to preset limits). Encourage multiple skunk works in which small investments can limit risks—and be sure that slack money is available. Enable internal entrepreneurs to be totally separate from existing businesses. Compensate managers of new ventures or product development efforts on a risk and reward basis and give venture general managers complete flexibility to meet preagreed milestones.

3. *Reinforce and deliver.* Establish "legends" by visibly rewarding an innovator with a meaningful event such as a major promotion, significant cash award, and/or important recognition and tribute. Tolerate failure by putting a good performer who failed on another important project.

4. *Instill innovation management principles.* Begin to apply innovation management principles systematically but gradually. Reorganize to minimize bureaucracy and get closer to the market. Encourage an integrative environment and insist on interaction between marketing

and technical people and others. Establish dual compensation systems if necessary whereby internal entrepreneurs can be rewarded on performance and project success while managers of established businesses are compensated on traditional measures.

Managing so that people and ideas that *can* succeed *will* succeed is the objective of these steps. Managing for innovation can set the stage for major breakthroughs, but it is most important to foster a climate in which seemingly small innovations occur routinely. The four conditions for innovation can be developed in an evolutionary manner to enhance the organization's ability to change with minimum disruption to ongoing businesses.

Innovation management requires hard work but need not be revolutionary to a first-rate, traditional corporation.

Bibliography

Drucker, Peter F.: *Innovation and Entrepreneurship: Practice and Principles*, Harper & Row, New York, 1985.

Fast, Norman D.: *The Rise and Fall of Corporate New Venture Divisions*, UMI Research Press, 1977.

George, Robin, and Ian C. MacMillan: "Corporate Venturing/Senior Management Responsibilities," Center for Entrepreneurial Studies, New York University, Working Paper.

Maidique, Modesto A.: "Entrepreneurs, Champions, and Technological Innovation," *Sloan Management Review*, Winter 1980.

Quinn, James Brian: "Managing Innovation: Controlled Chaos," *Harvard Business Review*, May–June 1985.

Roberts, Edward B.: "Stimulating Technological Innovation-Organizational Approaches," *Research Management*, November 1979.

Sherman, Stratford P.: "Eight Big Masters of Innovation," *Fortune*, October, 15, 1984.

24

Corporate Entrepreneurship at Three Levels

Karl H. Vesper

*Professor of Entrepreneurship, Graduate School of
Business, University of Washington*

Entrepreneurs should not be able to get away with building new companies. Established companies work constantly to provide whatever the market wants. So new companies should not have to be formed to offer additional products and services. Besides, entrepreneurs are not in a good position to compete. A new company is highly vulnerable during start-up, and established companies should be able to snuff it out. Established companies want, and vigorously pursue, the customer's dollar. Entrepreneurs should not be able to get it. Established companies have known brand names, employees with high job performance capability borne of long practice, and both suppliers and customers who are used to dealing with them. All these things entrepreneurs typically lack. Established companies can raise money cheaply because of their size and proven staying power. Entrepreneurs are severely handicapped in all these things.

But they manage to do it anyway because entrepreneurs also have some powerful advantages. These include innovative ideas and the initiative to act upon them. They do not have to wait for permission of committees and management layers. Their overhead is low because they can't afford anything else. They and their employees work hard and swiftly. They are spurred by the need to survive without the safety net of being able to transfer to another department or division. They are motivated by being part of a small team in which the maximum contribution of each member is essential and in which many members can see firsthand the effects of their individual contributions.

Wouldn't it be nice if established corporations could benefit from these advantages traditionally associated with entrepreneurs and from big company advantages as well? Some corporations think it a goal worth pursuing. So today we find companies experimenting with various entrepreneurial approaches. Broadly speaking, there are three organizational levels on which this quest can take place.

Level 1: Top-Management Initiatives

At the top-management level there are two forms entrepreneurial initiatives may take. One is environment, establishing a culture: Let it be known that entrepreneurial initiatives lower down in the organization are desired and will be favorably recognized. (More about this shortly.) The other is action, undertaking strategic departures: Lead the corporation into new lines of business and change the way the company does business. Strategic departure is represented by such things as entering new markets, initiating technologies new to the company, being viewed as a new entrant by customers and competitors, making near-term investment for the sake of longer-term gains, or combinations of such actions.

There are several possible approaches to strategic departure, including acquisitions, internal start-ups and joint ventures. Venture capital investment does not produce strategic departure by itself, but it may lead to strategic departure in the form of any of the three approaches. The trouble, of course, is that they are all fraught with problems and have produced failures. The record, in general, is not a good one. The record, however, is only statistical and only historical. Only statistical means that success has been poor *only on the average* , which is to say *not* in all cases. There are cases of success, and that means more successes are possible. Only historical means that was the record *in the past*. For the future the aim should be to learn from prior experience and perform better next time. That way the statistics of the future can be different and better than those of the past, particularly for *your* case.

In fact, there are some data from prior experience about where we should hope to wind up strategically and how we might best start out in undertaking departure. PIMS data of the Strategic Planning Institute on some 2500 businesses indicate that characteristics that set winners apart from losers are (in terms of ROI): (1) being in a market that is growing faster than the GNP, (2) having a differentiated rather than commodity product or service to offer, (3) being less capital intensive, and (4) having 25 percent or more of the market. These are objectives a strategic departure might hope to reach in the long run. Especially interesting is that they do not seem to depend upon the particular business in terms of product, whether consumer or commercial. What matters is whether it is differentiated or not. The claim that "our business is different and special" does not generally hold up. Remember, however, that the findings are only statistical hindsight. They may not apply in a particular case, and they could change in the future. But they have been consistent in the past and should highlight issues in considering alternatives. And absent better information about a particular case, they should be the best first guess about directions to take.

With the same cautions there are also data on the most promising initial strategy for new ventures. Based upon the history of some 200 corporate ventures, it appears best to bet on: (1) a growing market; (2) entering boldly rather than timidly in terms of high product quality, sufficient productive capacity, substantial R&D effort, and strong marketing push; and (3) emphasizing the pursuit of market share as opposed to rapid initial profitability.

Level 2: Business Unit Autonomy

Entrepreneurial characteristics to be sought at the business unit level are also those of boldness and shrewd directional choice, but, in addition, effective, opportunistic implementation is vital. How can independent entrepreneurial ventures operate opportunistically? By their autonomy. Autonomy seems to be a key reason why fledgling ventures can break into successful competition with established firms. Here are some of the *advantages* it gives:

1. The venture is not hamstrung by established company rules at times when departing from those rules is a more effective way to operate. When IBM wanted to get its personal computer on the market fast, it avoided the usual company departments. Rather the PC initiative was set up like an entrepreneurial venture with freedom from corporate constraints that would have, for example, prohibited it from purchasing components from outside vendors and from selling through wholesalers and retailers. When Borg Warner set up its chain of plastic service centers to sell in quantities smaller than the large amounts needed to

make a profit at its customary prices, those centers had to be free to carry other lines besides Borg Warner's own and to hire other than Borg Warner people to run its stores. Autonomy made this possible.

2. Autonomy means the person heading the venture can make more decisions without approvals from higher-ups in the organization. The limits of freedom still have to be defined with care. In one company it may be possible to add or drop lines without approval and in another it may not. In one the limits of capital expenditure discretion may be higher. One may be able to impose its own name and logo, while another may be required to use the parent's; in still another the parent company may not want its logo used by the new venture until it has proven viable. Generally, the greater the autonomy given to the venture, the faster its decision-making speed. Also, the quality of decisions may be better since they will be made by people closer to action.

3. Autonomy tends to enhance morale. Employees feel a greater sense of ownership for the venture and responsibility for being on their own. The venture can be more responsive to individual idiosyncrasies. Ability to recruit can be enhanced by the sense of joining a smaller and more intimate group. In short, the venture can come closer to imparting the kind of excitement, urgency, and responsiveness that characterize an independent entrepreneurial start-up.

Clearly, however, autonomy must be handled effectively, or there can be severe negative consequences. Independent entrepreneurial ventures can quickly fail, losing money for investors and jobs for employees. Similarly, when corporate ventures are managed ineffectively, they become heavy loss centers for their parent companies. One dramatic bad example was Exxon's foray into office machines, which allegedly lost billions. Loose purse strings and heavy spending, insensitive management practices that alienated key people, and an inadequate product focus all contributed to the failure.

For guidance in dealing with autonomous start-ups, following are *lessons* learned over the years by venture capitalists in dealing with independent start-ups:

1. The venture needs a clear business plan that makes good business sense. The heart of it will be financial projections, beginning with sales, backed up with details behind the details. Obviously, departures from plan will occur. The objective is not to stick to the plan but rather to make the venture a success.

2. For autonomy to work it is essential that competent, resourceful, dedicated people head the venture. They have to be trusted to make it

work. That is not to say that there should be no interaction with backers. Entrepreneurs are given counsel, coaching, and valuable connections by venture capitalists. Others helpful to the company can be recruited for advisory and director boards.

3. Autonomy does not mean "lone wolf." The venture is an organizational unit, not a single person. It should be headed by someone who can build a team to expand the business beyond a "one man band." How to be sure of this capability? Start out with balance among disciplines.

4. Outside as well as inside team members are important. The venture capitalist and board of directors and/or advisors can be vital sources of counsel, encouragement, and guidance for an independent venture. A corporate venture may similarly benefit from an advisory board that meets periodically with the venture's leading entrepreneur.

5. Playing the numbers with patience is a necessary part of venturing, whether inside or outside companies. No matter how carefully judgments are made, some ventures will be total losers and only a minority, major winners. (At 3M, which is noted for its innovative successes, a heavy percentage of ventures undertaken can be deemed failures.) It also takes time for most successes to occur. Patience on the order of 3 to 5 years for independent ventures, which tend to be smaller, and up to 20 years for corporate ventures, which tend to be larger, has been the historical payout pattern. Possibly with more venturing experience in the future, these times can be reduced, but they will likely still remain substantial in both cases.

6. Top management support of autonomy is crucial. Otherwise, attention will have to be diverted to "fighting off" intermediate layers of management who will be concerned about operating "right." Top management is responsible for the organization's structure and job appointments that allow autonomy to operate. Paradoxically, top management must both set the policy and supportive environment for ventures and at the same time not pay much attention to them. Data of the Strategic Planning Institute indicate that having ventures report to higher levels in the organization tends to correlate with poorer performance. Possibly it is because top management will be more tempted to meddle and undermine autonomy. Since top management is closer to shareholders, who tend to be bottom-line oriented, attention by top management may impose an overemphasis on short-run profits in ventures that need more time to mature. The whole business is top management's concern, and that concern should not be disproportionately applied to the tiny fraction of the business that ventures in early

stages represent. So top management's mission in ventures should be to establish the setting in which they can flourish but then leave them alone while they do it.

Level 3: Individual Initiative

The third level of entrepreneurial behavior in the organization is that of the individual employee, whose option it is to choose a path of initiative and innovation. Outside entrepreneurs who start new independent companies are not authorized or appointed by anyone. They may have all sorts of responsibilities, including jobs and families, but their entrepreneurial initiative is beyond the call of formal duty. They find a business idea, round up the wherewithal to make it happen, and push it into being.

An analogous pattern sometimes occurs inside established organizations and can be legitimately regarded as entrepreneurial employee behavior. The result could take alternative forms, including creation of new business units selling to outside markets or new internal units providing services to the rest of the organization. Individual initiative beyond normal expectations of the job can also result in reduced costs, higher quality, better organizational spirit, and other virtues that don't take the form of new corporate units. Whether to call such initiatives "entrepreneurial" when they do not create new units is a matter of arbitrary definition. It seems likely that a culture that encourages individual initiative will generate many types, some that produce new units and others that do not. How to encourage such initiatives while at the same time selecting those that are most constructive and avoiding those that might be only disruptive or wasteful is a challenging problem. Companies such as 3M and Hewlett-Packard are noted for exceptionally effective performance in this area. Note has been taken of policies that seem to help. But the roots of such organizational behavior seem to lie deeper than current policies, going back in company history all the way to the founders.

Companies attempting to make an entrepreneurial shift are pioneering a frontier of American management. Some approaches being tested include:

1. *Organizational rearrangements.* For example, establishing an office with a mission to encourage more venture initiatives, providing "greenhouses" in which ventures can develop during early stages independent of the mainstream organization, forming review commit-

tees to screen ideas for company backing, and organizing task forces to pursue particular ventures or to seek possible ventures within defined industrial segments.

2. *Incentive schemes.* For example, establishing a "third track" for career advancement (alongside management and research tracks) via entrepreneurial accomplishment, providing special bonus and compensation schemes for corporate entrepreneurs, and allowing stock buy-ins (either real or phantom stock) to allow ownership in corporate ventures.

3. *Support grants for new venture proponents.* For example, the Texas Instruments program wherein employees can apply for in-house monetary grants to pursue new product concepts.

4. *Training programs.* Improve entrepreneurial skills in activities such as venture idea screening and selection, venture design, and venture planning. This training is sometimes incorporated as part of existing in-house courses in management development or creativity skill improvement and sometimes taken through outside programs.

5. *Cultural shaping.* For example, hiring people who aspire to be entrepreneurs; reducing the penalties for failure; giving glory to employees who accomplish entrepreneurial feats; encouraging cross-discipline interacting, learning, and working arrangements; permitting employees wider latitude in moving around the organization; and participating in venture teams and trying new approaches.

Each company is a special case for such experimentation aimed at more individual entrepreneurial behavior. What is bold and new at one may be old hat at another. An experiment that might be part of the normal course of corporate tinkering and tuning at one company may be an act of desperation to reverse declining markets or obsolescing technology at another. Sometimes, unfortunately, the experiments are a short-run whim of new management, which may be replaced by newer management with different whims, erasing activities before they can pan out. At others, the commitment is longer term and includes systematic tracking and review.

Choosing Approaches

For many companies "business as usual," "sticking to the knitting," and evolving in conventional ways may be fully adequate. In those few companies in which bolder entrepreneurial approaches are being tried, a host of factors will determine which approaches work well and which do not. Those factors will be different in each company, so it will not be possible to learn with certainty from the experiments of one company how well a particular approach will work at another. But the experiments should give some indications of how best to beat the odds, provided some record of them is reported. Hence, a minimum effort for a management wanting to explore entrepreneurial approaches would be to follow the news of what other companies are trying and how good their results are. Some of this news will be openly published. Some will have to be discerned from more anonymous reports, particularly when results are unfavorable.

There may, however, be no adequate substitute for direct experimentation by management. By undertaking entrepreneurial pilots on a small scale, costs can be kept down. At the same time, the learning can be substantial and can put the company in a good position to make better decisions—especially when its own direct experience is combined with information exchanged with other companies. This exchange of entrepreneurial experience has been a powerful learning tool in the venture capital community. In analogous fashion, corporations may be able to share the "tuition costs" of becoming more skillful at managing corporate entrepreneurship.

25

Changing a Corporate Culture: Leadership through Quality

David T. Kearns

Chairman and Chief Executive Officer,
Xerox Corporation

Every good company has its own philosophy, its own set of values, its own way of doing things—in other words, its own culture. The best companies make a concerted effort to promote a strong corporate culture. They understand that an organization's basic philosophy has much more to do with its *achievements* than its resources, technology, or structure. Building a strong corporate culture means getting everybody to think and do things in a certain way—consistently. It's a long, arduous, and sometimes frustrating process.

Now, imagine, if you will, what it's like to *reverse* that process. Imagine making everybody in a company *unlearn* a particular set of rules and learn a new one. Imagine completely changing the culture of an entire company. That's what we're doing at Xerox.

Leadership through Quality

We have, in fact, decided to make *quality* the basic business principle of Xerox and, therefore, the job of every Xerox employee. Quality—I cannot think of a word or a concept more misused and misunderstood. Quality is fashionable. Everybody, it seems, claims to make a "quality" product or deliver a "quality" service. Obviously, it's the thing to say, but often it's still not the thing that's done. Quality is a word that has been weakened by overuse, much like an overinflated currency.

Why, then, did we choose quality as the linchpin of our new culture? We could have picked the "pursuit of excellence" or being "the most cost effective" or, simply, being "the best." But we chose quality, and for a simple reason—economics.

It's estimated that one-fourth of all work done in American industry is done to correct errors. And that spans the entire spectrum from executive office to factory floor. A secretary who types a letter with mistakes in it has to go back and retype the letter. A product designer who produces a faulty design has to redo that design, which adds the cost of retrofits. In manufacturing, there is the cost of scrap and rework because the product was not made right the first time. Think of it— one-fourth of all work corrects errors. That's a terrible track record, and at Xerox, we were only slightly better than the industry average. We were spending close to 25 percent of gross revenues—or $2 billion a year—redoing tasks that had not been done right. We were using one-fourth of our facilities, equipment, space, and people to make products that were not up to par.

By focusing on doing the job right in the first place and by making sure everybody knew what was expected of them, we thought we could eliminate much of that waste. But we needed a way to formalize the idea, make it understandable, make it tangible. In short, we needed a *process* to make it work. We call that process "Leadership through Quality." It is a goal and a strategy, as well as a process. It is a goal because we are not there yet. It is a strategy because we have made it an integral part of our business plans. And it is a process because we have set down specific actions to implement it. Leadership through Quality, then, is the tool we are using to profoundly change the culture of our company from top to bottom.

Defining and Measuring Quality

At Xerox, we define quality as *fully meeting customer requirements*. This implies understanding precisely what those requirements are and how to fulfill them in the most efficient, effective way. It also implies understanding precisely who the customer is for every piece of work that is produced.

Most people wrongly assume that quality is an intangible that cannot be measured. The fact is, quality can be measured by one of the oldest and most respected yardsticks in business—the customer. Indeed, the customer's degree of satisfaction with any company's product or service is in direct proportion to the quality of that product or service.

The traditional definition of customer is simply the end user of a product or service—the consumer. At Xerox, we have expanded that definition to include both internal and external consumers. In other words, every employee—white collar or blue collar, manager or worker—has an internal customer for his or her work. (That internal customer becomes especially important for staff positions that have no direct contact with the end-user consumer. In the final analysis, all are inextricably linked to the external customer by a quality chain that affects the bottom line.)

At Xerox, customers define quality. For us, quality means providing our internal and external consumers with innovative products and services that fully satisfy their requirements. This is not only clear, it is also *measurable*. We can gauge the quality of our products by the reaction of our customers, as expressed through their comments and buying decisions. If we deliver quality, we will do well. It's that simple.

Let me reemphasize that our definition of quality is *meeting* customer requirements—nothing more and nothing less. Everybody understands when customer requirements are not met. Usually, something breaks or stops working. The cost? Lost business, lost opportunities to gain new business, and lost respect in the marketplace. Those costs are elusive and incalculable and if left unattended, probably irreversible.

Not Doing More

Most people readily understand the effects of not meeting customer requirements. On the other hand, many people have trouble with the idea of *not exceeding* customer requirements, of *not* doing just a little more than they have to do. Indeed, the most common definition of quality is "providing the best," even if the best exceeds customer needs. I disagree.

If I ask someone on my staff for a sales analysis report on a single copier model and he or she comes back with a report on the entire product line, that is *not* quality at Xerox. I have gotten the best, but the best was *more* than I wanted. That staff person has put in extra time and effort to give me information I do not need. Then it costs me time and effort to wade through extraneous material, however good it is. And wasted time and effort translates into wasted money.

The concept of quality as strictly meeting customer requirements is the single most important part of Leadership through Quality. It is a concept difficult to accept because it is so different from anything we have ever had at Xerox and because most people have the urge to do a better job by doing a bigger job. And that is precisely what we no longer want them to do. (The emphasis on doing only what is required does not mean we have lowered our standards. They are just as high as ever. The difference is that we have focused and sharpened our efforts so that we can meet those standards more effectively and more efficiently.)

Past Culture

Whenever I talk about Leadership through Quality as an entirely new culture, I get a skeptical reaction. People cannot understand why a company like Xerox would not have been emphasizing quality all along. The fact is, we always thought we were.

Xerox was effectively born in 1959, the year we introduced the Xerox 914, the world's first plain paper copier. The 914 has been called the single most successful product of all time. It created an instant industry that today generates more than $27 billion per year. Almost overnight, it propelled Xerox from a small, marginally profitable company to a multinational corporation of worldwide prominence. In 1960, we had 3000 employees and revenues of $37 million. Twenty years later, Xerox had 100,000 employees and revenues of $8 billion. The company grew so much, so fast that management could barely keep up with demand for Xerox products. They built a highly successful, global enterprise—but with lots of loose ends.

It was management in the classic capitalist tradition. Twenty-five years ago, the people who ran Xerox sensed they had a revolutionary new product, and they risked everything to bring that product to market quickly. It was a decision that took faith, courage, foresight, and, above all, a strong spirit of entrepreneurship. Nevertheless, Xerox was ill-equipped to deal with the astounding success the 914 brought with it. The only way to keep up with the frantic pace seemed to be to hire more and more people. The company became top-heavy with too much overhead and too many layers of management. Vital functions, such as product development and manufacturing, became slow and inefficient.

Success also bred a sort of benign arrogance. At Xerox, we were living in what amounted to a corporate camelot. Our new dry copiers were so good and so different that we just could not make machines fast enough. We were able to sell almost everything we made at whatever price we wanted to charge. Xerox was the darling of Wall Street. Ours was the glamor of glamor stocks, the bluest of blue chips. We lived in an enchanted dream world in which we could do no wrong—or so it seemed.

What we had was a corporate culture isolated from any real competition, believing its own press. After all, the system had worked well for 20 years, and up until about 1975, Xerox was indisputably the world leader. It's no wonder that we had a hard time coping with competition when it finally hit us in the mid-1970s. Surprisingly, our biggest challenge did not come from giants like Kodak and IBM. It came from smaller, Japanese manufacturers that began nibbling away at the low-volume segment of our market. Before we could respond, those fast-moving, innovative companies had captured a sizable share of our business. And they were not just beating us on cost. They were marketing good machines with features customers wanted—and were not getting from Xerox. We were jolted back to reality the day we learned that the Japanese copier companies were *selling* their machines in the United States for what it *cost* us to make ours.

Culture Shock

Faced with shrinking market share and sliding profits, we had to react quickly and drastically. We cut costs, eliminated overhead, streamlined organizations, and shed unprofitable ventures. All those things had to be done, but they weren't enough. In order to prosper, we had to make several fundamental, long-term changes. *First*, develop more disciplined ways of working. *Second*, find ways of getting and staying closer to our customers. *Third*, make better use of the ideas and talents of our employees. And *fourth*, make a solid commitment to quality in everything we do.

In short, we had to change the entire culture of a worldwide corporation, and we had no time to lose. We attacked on all fronts, beginning in 1980. In the product development area, we created Strategic Business Units, with teams of versatile, multifunctional engineers who had the resources to take a copier from drawing board to assembly line. In marketing and service, we set up a Customer Satisfaction Management System, a systematic way of sampling customer opinions about the performance of our products and people, compared with those of our competitors. We equipped our service branches with a Field Work Support System, a computerized system that insures fast and accurate response to machine service requests. And we integrated our huge sales force so that a single Xerox person could represent the entire range of Xerox products and services to our major accounts.

But that was only the beginning. In 1981, we launched a business effectiveness program throughout the company. The program's two components—competitive benchmarking and employee involvement— are designed to make sure every Xerox organization knows precisely what its priorities are and how to achieve them.

Competitive Benchmarking

Competitive benchmarking grew out of competitive analysis, a common way of studying a rival firm's product—buy their machine and take it apart to see how it works. We decided to push competitive analysis one step further by taking apart not only the competitions' products but also their processes and organizational structures. We needed to know how it *all* worked.

Competitive benchmarking, then, is the approach we use to compare our products and services, function by function, with those of our toughest competitors or with those companies that are the acknowledged leaders in that function. The goal is superiority in product reliability, quality, and cost in every benchmarked area. Eventually, every Xerox unit will benchmark as a routine part of its work.

Employee Involvement

Employee involvement is the process whereby Xerox people at every level participate in teams that identify and solve problems. The objective is to get the very best from employees, not just in terms of labor but in terms of creativity. Like competitive benchmarking, employee involvement has clearly defined methods. There are six stages in the process designed to identify, analyze, and solve problems. Each stage involves specific procedures and analytical tools that the teams learn and use. As in competitive benchmarking, everyone at Xerox will eventually participate in employee involvement teams as routine.

Underlying employee involvement is an emerging psychology that is profoundly affecting the way people work at Xerox. It says that management does not have all the answers, that the people closest to a problem are the best ones to solve it, and that the traditional autocratic "top-down" approach to management does not always work. There are companies that practice the top-down approach quite successfully. But they have to accept duplication of effort and wasted resources. In such an organization, middle-level managers are typically not encouraged, or even expected, to ask for clarification of assignments from superiors. If they do not understand what's required, they have a couple of options. They can do what they think is needed, or just to be on the safe side, they can do the assignment two or three different ways—and hope that one of them is right.

Employee involvement, on the other hand, gives people a true voice in their work. It says: "If you're not sure, ask. Don't wait until after you've done it wrong. If you can fix it, fix it. Don't wait to be told." Ask any employee—white collar or blue collar—what he or she wants most from management, and you're likely to hear: "Just let me do my job." At Xerox, we're trying to make it easier for all employees to do their jobs.

Problem-solving teams have proven their worth many times over in higher efficiency and lower costs. The cumulative effect has been impressive. We have 2000 problem-solving teams operating worldwide. They are working on hundreds of projects that have saved the company from thousands to millions of dollars each. (I made a conscious decision not to keep track of the amount of money our problem-solving teams save because I did not want people to become preoccupied with saving money at the expense of good ideas. But just as an informal gauge, we randomly sampled 90 projects in 1984 and found that they saved us a total of $11 million.)

My favorite example is a group in our manufacturing plant in Webster, New York, near Rochester. They make the harnesses that hold the wires and cables together inside a copier. We had found a small company that could make those wire harnesses less expensively than we could make them in-house. But before we decided to subcontract that work out, we gave our own employees a chance to improve their operation. They came back with a proposal that took $3 million out of their cost base and saved 150 jobs. How? By treating that business as if it were their own.

Competitive benchmarking and employee involvement are the twin pillars upon which we have built Leadership through Quality. As good as those two processes are, however, they were just the beginning. They addressed important issues but on a narrow basis. What we really needed was a universal process that put the concept of quality, as we've defined it, at the forefront of all our plans and actions. We needed a process that would help us change our entire corporate culture.

Competitive Catalyst

The impetus to develop Leadership through Quality came largely from the serious Japanese competition. We were fortunate to have a Japanese partner, Fuji Xerox, whose experience and help we could access and build upon. Fuji Xerox was the first member of the global Xerox organization to face other Japanese copier makers. Until 1975, Fuji Xerox enjoyed the benefits of xerography and prospered. That year, its profits and market share began to decline rapidly, and its products started to become uncompetitive. In response to that challenge, Fuji Xerox implemented a total quality control process called the New Xerox Movement. The program's objectives were to meet customers' quality expectations, to work toward overall cost reductions, and to encourage creativity among all employees. But the ultimate goal, of course, was to make Fuji Xerox more competitive. Two years later, Fuji Xerox had engineered a remarkable turnaround with a family of new, highly competitive copiers that it designed and manufactured. One of those machines, the 3500, set a record for placements in Japan and would eventually be successfully marketed throughout the world by Xerox.

Xerox has learned much from the Fuji Xerox experience. But it was harder and slower for the rest of us. We were dealing with a much larger entity. We were also looking at attitudes and practices that were very different from our way of doing business. Japanese society is built on cooperation, harmony, and consensus. In the West, progress has more often been forged in the crucible of conflicting interests and individual initiative. While there were many techniques and concepts we could comfortably adapt from our Japanese partner, we could not simply "lift" their entire plan and graft it onto the rest of the company. We had to develop our own plan.

The Process of Change

Late in 1982, we created a special task force to work with senior management to formulate the general strategy that would become Leadership through Quality. Early the following year, our top twenty-five executives got together for 3 days to hammer out the basic principles and major implementation steps of that strategy. We split up into small groups to craft separate pieces of the strategy, a strategy that was so broad and so different that it would affect every aspect of corporate life. We were, after all, creating a new corporate culture for Xerox.

In the spring of 1983 we established a Quality Implementation Team of sixteen persons to formulate the specifics of Leadership through Quality. Nine members of the team were vice presidents of major operational groups. They worked for 6 months to set down detailed implementation guidelines, consulting every step of the way with senior management at the group and corporate levels. What emerged was a ninety-two page blueprint for action that left little doubt as to the size of the task before us. At the same time, we formed a corporate-level Quality Office, headed by a corporate vice president, to oversee the entire process.

Looking back, I can pick out several elements that were critical in making Leadership through Quality a reality at Xerox. I believe these same elements would facilitate cultural change in any large corporation.

First, we had to have the full commitment of top management. Everyone in the company had to see clearly that Leadership through Quality was not only endorsed, but also practiced, at the highest levels.

Second, we had to continue to drive competitive benchmarking and employee involvement, the foundation for Leadership through Quality. Without the pervasive and intensive application of those processes, Leadership through Quality would fail.

Third, we had to set down a tough but realistic implementation schedule designed to yield tangible, practical results. We had to convince our people that Leadership through Quality was not just a psychological campaign or a passing fad or an appendage to our existing corporate culture. Everybody had to see and believe that Leadership through Quality was an integral, permanent part of business at Xerox.

Forging a brand-new corporate culture is probably the hardest part of the entire process. How do you get 100,000 people to change the way they view their work and the way they do their work? It's tough because change is always difficult, especially on such a massive scale. The process involves taking three steps forward and two steps back. Still, it is working.

The process is logical. It asks some simple questions about the job or task at hand. They include: What has to be done, and for whom? What is wanted, needed, or expected? Is it measurable, realistic, and achievable? How will it be accomplished? What has to be measured to insure that the assignment is successfully completed? Those using the process are working better and more easily together in teams and groups. Problems seem to be solved better and faster. Even individuals are encouraged to follow the same basic steps.

There are definite signs of progress. We are starting to hear the question Who is the customer for this job, and what are his or her requirements? in offices and departments throughout the company.

"Customer requirements" is a phrase we did not have before Leadership through Quality. You did what you thought customers wanted, and if they didn't like it you went back and tried something else. Now, people are at least aware of what such an approach costs in wasted time and duplication of effort.

I've changed too. I've noticed a marked difference in the way I do my own job as CEO since I completed Leadership through Quality training. I find I'm more willing to listen, to tailor my work to my customers' needs—yes, CEOs have customers, too. For example, I conduct a regular communications meeting for all my directors. I found out that they did not think those meetings were very useful. So, we developed a questionnaire to find out why. It asked questions like: Was the content relevant? Were the presentations clear? Does the material help you do your job better? Now, we rate each meeting after it's over and make the necessary changes for the next one. As a result, the approval rate of those meetings has gone up from 55 to 95 percent.

Like many American companies, Xerox had embraced a short-term perspective tied to quarterly earnings statements and shareholder expectations for rapid growth. Leadership through Quality, on the other hand, requires profound and lasting changes in performance and behavior for every Xerox employee, and that necessarily calls for a long-term approach to business objectives. To implement that approach, we put together an orderly, step-by-step training schedule to put Leadership through Quality into place over 5 years, culminating in 1987. We created the Quality Training Task Force to lay out a comprehensive training regimen. It's a formal program, complete with a team of 140 professional trainers positioned throughout the company.

The first ones to go through that training were top management, beginning with me, my vice chairman, and the heads of several organizations reporting to him. The idea was to have the training cascade down through the corporation, with managers training their direct-reports in "family groups" (in conjunction with our professional instructors). Training for most employees lasts for 6½ days in a formal classroom setting, taken in three separate sessions. The first is orientation to the concept and strategy of Leadership through Quality. The second is problem-solving skills of employee involvement. The third is quality improvement training, a nine-step procedure that teaches employees how to determine what their output is, who the end-user or customer for that output is, what that customer's needs are, and how to meet those needs.

The Quality Goal

Leadership through Quality is designed to make all of our employees think quality in all of their actions. We are trying to get them to take the long view instead of the short view and to recognize that quality is never achieved by a quick fix but only by a permanent solution. And we are trying to change their concept of error from accepting a certain margin of error to striving for no errors and from correcting defects to preventing them.

Leadership through Quality means learning to work in participative, structured ways rather than in individual, free-form ones. And it means understanding that each of us has a customer to satisfy and that satisfying that customer is our primary job. It doesn't matter whether we make a material product that goes directly to an outside consumer or we supply information or a service to another Xerox person.

Our larger goal is, of course, to have Xerox become recognized as a quality company by giving our customers the products and services they need. Ultimately, we expect increased revenues and market share. We already see evidence with the extraordinary customer acceptance of our ten-series family of copier-duplicators, the first product line produced using the basic principles of Leadership through Quality. We think its success is a clear signal that we are on the right track.

Leadership through Quality is not revolutionary. Basically, it represents an orderly, systematic approach to business problems, with common sense codified and applied consistently on a large scale. Leadership through Quality is powerful because it gets to the heart of the most important issue for any business—satisfying customer needs. And that, really, is as sound and simple as an idea can get. What is not so simple, however, is turning that sound idea into a viable corporate culture.

Somebody once said that to live is to change, and to be perfect is to have changed often. Xerox is a company that has changed often over the past 5 years and, although we are far from perfect, we are most definitely a much better company than we were. And by applying Leadership through Quality, we will become even better. We must.

26

Designing a Corporate Culture for Creative Personnel

Eric G. Flamholtz

President, Management Systems Consulting Corporation and Professor, UCLA Graduate School of Management

H. Stephen Cranston

President, Knapp Communications Corporation

How does senior management define and maintain a corporate culture for creative personnel? "Creative personnel" refers here not only to artistic or scientific employees but to all those in a position in which innovation or imagination must be exercised. Opportunities for innovation may be found not only in adding new products or services but in all functional operations of the organization. All corporations have a culture whether they recognize it or not. However, not all corporations are aware that they need to manage it as a competitive variable. An understanding and appreciation of corporate culture is essential for the effective management and development of organizations. It is especially important in managing creative personnel.

The creative impulse lies in most of us and all human endeavor can be improved through creativity. However, we speak of creative personnel in the sense that their jobs *require* constant change and continuing originality. It is not so much that the creative process is different as it is that the creative process is always ongoing and always needed. An organization that has a significant percentage of its employees involved in creative endeavors will develop a different culture than an organization in which constant creativity is not required. Creative employees require an atmosphere that has a minimum of bureaucratic impediments, places to think as well as places to act, a high element of trust from managers, and a system of rewards based on results achieved rather than on time spent.

Corporate Culture

The term "culture" has long been used by anthropologists and has a variety of definitions. The term "corporate culture" is much more recent but has also begun to spawn different concepts. As used here, corporate culture refers to the values, premises, and accepted behavior patterns of people who are members of a particular organization.

Corporate Values

Values are things that people believe to be important. They are normative guides to behavior, ideals to which people aspire. All corporations have a set of values whether stated or recognized. Some organizations, such as IBM, consider values to be central to their company and overall success. They invest heavily in communicating the corporate value system and are most resourceful in managing the corporate culture. Although IBM is a company with more than 375,000 employees, its culture is well entrenched: "We believe in customer service, excellence in what we seek to do, and respect for the individual." These values have been the unchanging cornerstone for the development of IBM since Thomas Watson formulated them during the company's inception.

Corporate Premises

Premises are assumptions that people make about the corporation or things affecting the corporation. For example, in one company that serves the affluent market, people assumed that because their customers were well-to-do, they were "recession proof," and in turn, the company was recession proof. This assumption had a significant effect on people's behavior and decisions—and proved to be invalid during the 1981–83 recession.

Accepted Behavior Patterns

These are organizational norms to which people are expected to adhere. They apply to a wide variety of organizational activities, ranging from proper modes of dress to the accepted way of addressing people, from the way in which offices are decorated to the number of hours worked per week. (An IBM salesman would hardly dress the same as a hot-tub salesman.)

Distinction between Nominal and Real Culture

In any organization, the true or real culture is not always what management believes it to be. There may be a difference between the nominal or stated values of a company and its effective or real values. For example, management may profess that the company strives to produce high-quality products, that it is concerned for employee welfare, and that it seeks innovation. This is merely the nominal or stated culture. The real culture may be quite different. In actuality, the firm may produce shoddy products, not be concerned about its people, and find all sorts of reasons not to innovate. In determining the culture of an organization, we observe how people actually behave, not just what they say.

Development of a Corporate Culture

In most organizations, a culture develops as an outgrowth of the values of the founder. For example, the culture at Disney was very much the product of Walt Disney's beliefs. Walt wanted to create a very special kind of culture in his company and at Disneyland, and under his leadership, that culture was created. To this day, the people who patronize Disneyland are not called "customers" but "guests." Similarly, those who work at Disneyland are not "employees" but "cast." A Company's culture is often an extension of the founder's personality.

The values of McDonalds are those of Ray Kroc; IBM's very much reflect Thomas Watson.

Assessing the Existing Culture

In order to mange corporate culture one must determine the real culture. Although this may seem simple, it is often complex. It is not enough to ask members of an organization: "What is your corporate culture?" A blank stare may be the only response. It is possible to "read" an organization's culture if one is aware of the signs and symbols. We must interpret three different manifestations of culture: (1) *tangible* manifestations, (2) *intangible* manifestations, and (3) *behavioral* manifestations.

Tangible Manifestations of Culture.   Some aspects of culture are palpable. They include physical artifacts, such as furniture or equipment. Such things represent symbols or aspects of culture. The way an office is furnished, for example, makes a statement about the organization to employees and the world at large. The office may be furnished to suggest that "this is an important company," and, by extension, the people who work here are important. Alternatively, it may be furnished to suggest that this is a "no nonsense" company that operates "lean and mean" and without frills. There are other possible messages. Open office systems, for example, portray involvement and equality.

In addition to tangible things, such as furniture, that have an intrinsic meaning, companies often use a variety of symbols that have no intrinsic value. For example, Knapp Communications Corporation (publishers of *Architectural Digest, Bon Appetit,* and *Home* magazines) began to distribute a gold K for outstanding performance, and this became a prized and desired symbol of excellence. Some people came to the company's president and asked: "How can I earn a K? "

Intangible Manifestations of Culture.   Two of the most significant intangible manifestations of corporate culture are the organizational reward system and the communications system. The organizational reward system determines who gets what, how, and why. These indicate the kinds of things the organization values. For example, firms of certified public accountants tell their young staff managers that they will be evaluated on a variety of criteria, including technical competence, chargeable hours to clients, professional advancement, and the development of their subordinates. Yet when most compensation and promotion decisions are based upon chargeable hours, the firm's message about its value is clear.

A company's values are also reflected in its communication system. *Who* gets *what* information as well as *when* and in *what form* are an important manifestation of culture. The communication system reflects the importance of people as well as the company's management style, participative or autocratic. The nature and content of corporate communications also indicate something about the company's culture. Newsletters, for example, promote a spirit of "family" by informing people about fellow employees.

Behavioral Manifestations.   These can be found in the day-to-day social interaction patterns of people and in the kinds of corporate-sponsored events. Collective occasions such as beer busts, picnics, and Christmas parties are typically used to establish or reinforce a "family" culture. There may be vast differences between what a company says about how people behave and how they actually behave. The company may state that "we are family" when in fact people act as though each department were at war with all other departments—the family image may be only a rationalization of the "father's" authoritarianism.

Designing the Desired Culture

The most important step in changing a culture is to determine exactly what *kind* of culture you want, including what you are willing to give up to get it. Here we assume that a company seeks to develop a culture that encourages maximum exercise of useful creativity by many in the enterprise—even if so-called "efficiency" may be somewhat reduced in the process. Once you have determined direction, you should compare that with where you are in order to define and characterize the differences. Thus if you want some people to have more information than they now receive, determine what information and in what time frame. If you believe that your culture is too rigid, determine ways in which that rigidity is manifested. As you proceed through the analysis and note "where we are" as compared to "where we want to be," the differences in the elements discussed in the "Corporate Culture" section should become obvious. Now, the difficult part. What is to be changed? How, when, and in what order are the changes to be made? The selection process is to a large extent governed by the tools available.

The Tools of Cultural Change

A variety of tools are available to facilitate cultural change in organizations. Three of the major ones are: (1) corporate orientation programs, (2) educational programs, and (3) corporate role models or heroes.

Orientation Programs

Corporate orientation programs, whether formal or informal, are designed to "introduce" employees to the organization—its values, premises, and accepted behavior patterns. These programs, also called "socialization procedures," may involve presentations by company officers who tell the organization's history or stories about the company. (Such stories are called "myths" in the anthropological sense, without implying fact or fiction.) The purpose of recounting company history or critical incidents is to communicate corporate values. For example, one of the prized stories told at IBM is what happened when the company was given a large order for computers by the government on the condition that they be delivered in just a few days. According to the story (the myth), the organization mobilized its efforts and worked day and night over a weekend to fulfill the president's promise. Moreover, throughout the weekend as the computers were delivered, Watson would send a telegram indicating how many remained for delivery. This story symbolizes IBM's commitment to customer service. Disneyland has an extensive employee orientation program. This socialization process is carefully scripted so that critical aspects of the company's culture are communicated and not left to chance.

Educational Programs

Employee training and management development programs help people develop new skills and help the company reinforce its culture. Hewlett-Packard, IBM, and Price Waterhouse invest substantially in training and development programs that are explicitly designed to educate people not only to perform with greater skill but also to absorb the organization's culture. Just as orientation programs use stories to communicate corporate values, so can educational programs use problem-solving cases or critical incidents. At Knapp Communications a management development program was designed to help reestablish corporate values. The entire program was planned down to each detail, and every element from personnel selection for the class through the graduation ceremony was reviewed as to that element's use in changing the corporate culture. All levels of management could recommend candidates, but final selection was based upon the candidate's application. Great stress was placed upon the rigors of the course, which was designed to be difficult both in terms of ability and time required. The course was graded and it was possible to fail. Thus, one element of desired corporate culture—hard, smart work—was reinforced continuously.

Corporate Role Models

All organizations develop heroes, people who personify the height of achievement. These role models represent the values that the organization wants to inspire people to attain. Corporate role models are not necessarily only people in glamor jobs. Some may be recognized for innovation in relatively small aspects of operations. The organization needs to analyze what kinds of values it wants to encourage, seek out people who typify those values, and turn them into corporate heroes.

Threats of Change

Before you undertake to institute change, remember that all change threatens existing power relationships within an organization. In some instances the threat is minimal and more perceived than actual. In others, the threat is actual and of significant magnitude. Thus, each element of change will start in motion additional changes in people and relationships that are not part of your plan. Many of these "chain reaction" changes can be anticipated, at least in general. But you will always miss a few, or some will manifest themselves in unexpected ways. Because tinkering with a culture produces far more changes than would appear on first review, it is important to isolate as many reactions as can be anticipated and incorporate them into your plan. Outside assistance can be invaluable at this stage since a different perspective on both the existing culture and the proposed changes can increase the number of "chain reaction" changes planned for. Just keep in mind that any change introduced into a culture affects the *entire* culture, not just a defined piece of it. Your perspective must be holistic.

Timing of change, as mentioned, is critical. *When* you introduce something new, as well as how you introduce it, sends its own signal, even if a false one. Thus, each step of the change process must anticipate the perception of change from as many viewpoints as possible, and timing should be such that few unwanted signals are sent.

The Role of Education

Education, whether formal or informal, on or off premises, company or outside teacher, will be your most important tool to mitigate threats and effect change. The greatest educational burden is to convincingly explain your goals to direct subordinates and persuade them of the necessity and inevitability of your plans. For the rest of the organization, informal communication about proposed changes, in advance, during, and after the changes are introduced, will be critical.

The use of formal classes for selected members of your organization is a way to introduce, discuss, command, and persuade a small cadre of elite personnel. These image makers must be convinced of the need for, and the wisdom of, change. In a formal educational setting, executives have the opportunity through neutral outsiders (i.e., outside faculty) to teach what others are doing, how they started, why they achieved good results, and to compare these external experiences with those of your company. A well-conceived in-house educational program for a small number of employees, usually at middle or lower management, can be used more effectively than any other tool of change.

As ideas are internalized, the perspective of students changes, and this new perspective is communicated to others by the cadre's actions as well as their words. Thus, as you announce change formally from above, it is already being expressed informally from below. If managed properly, many cadre members will help "sell" your changes through these powerful informal channels of communication. To some extent you educate a cadre of people whom you then use to "colonize" the organization. The process requires much advance planning and lead time, and it is essential when contemplating changes that will affect creative personnel—since these people are those least likely to accept authoritarian pronouncements and most likely to require "facts" upon which they can base their own reaction to proposed changes. Bright and thoughtful employees will seek out and exchange opinions with one another. Make certain that they understand and support your goals.

27

Freedom versus Structure: The Lattice Organization

W. L . Gore

Founder , W. L . Gore & Associates

Human potential is underutilized by enterprises of society. Leaders can unleash more inherent creativity and productivity by eliminating the authoritarian aspect of organizations and depending on commitment and natural leadership as controlling forces. The simplicity and order of an authoritarian organization make it an almost irresistible temptation. Yet it stifles individual freedom and smothers creative growth. The complexity of enterprise in today's scientific-industrial environment makes the task of maximizing human freedom and potential a challenging one. At Gore Associates, one of our basic principles is to encourage maximum freedom for each associate (employee). This has triggered an avalanche of inventions, innovations, and ways of increasing productivity and reducing costs.

The Lattice Organization

Characteristics and Functions

The "lattice" organization rejects the use of authoritarian titles that denote a pyramid of command, and "leaders" are defined as those who have "followers." Such an organization is founded naturally by an entrepreneur (or intrapreneur) who persuades joiners to "sign up" for the enterprise (or project). There is no need for bosses, assignment of tasks, establishing lines of command, defining channels of permitted communication, and the like. The necessary functions are organized by voluntary commitments, universal agreement on the objective, and the few basic principles needed for effective group cooperation.

In a lattice organization transactions are basically one-on-one, with no requirement for intermediaries. The organization shown in Figure 27.1 is flat and Al (A), for example, interacts directly with Bob (B), Cora (C), Dave (D), and Eva (E), one-on-one. Each person in the lattice interacts directly with every other person. Lines of communication are person-to-person. Obviously, this organizational chart serves no purpose and is not used.

Certain attributes of a lattice organization can be defined: No fixed or assigned authority; sponsors, not bosses; natural leadership defined by followership; person-to-person communication; objectives set by those who must "make them happen"; tasks and functions organized through commitments. The structure within the lattice is complex and evolves from interpersonal interactions, self-commitment to group-known responsibilities, natural leadership, and group-imposed discipline. Some typical transactions within the lattice follow:

> Joe says to me, "Bill, I've a great idea for a project that I'm sure you'll want to do." I groan to myself. I've already made commitments that are going to use me up. There is a long list of things beyond these that I ought to do. There are many more I'd like to do. So I dutifully put Joe's idea on my list—but do not make any commitment. Jim says to me, "Bill, I've got a great idea I'd like to follow up." I relax. Great ! An idea *he'd* like to follow up. I applaud, express my pleasure, and encourage him to charge. Bob says to me, "Bill, I need your help." I listen. I strain to find a way to give the needed aid. A sincere effort must be made here. Another day I will be seeking Bob's help. His response will relate closely to mine. And I will be needing his help.

Special teams evolve within the lattice structure, usually led by someone particularly competent in the discipline or activity. One individual may participate on several such teams and have a leadership role in one or more. These multiparticipant people serve an important

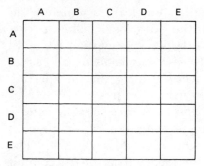

Figure 27.1

liaison function and are often involved in the planning and coordination of projects requiring a number of different teams.

Every (successful) organization has a lattice organization that underlies the facade of authoritarian hierarchy. It is through these lattice organizations that things get done, and most of us delight in "going around" the formal procedures and doing things the straightforward and easy way. The legendary subversion of official military procedures by the "non-coms" is an example. All astute military leaders utilize this subrosa lattice.

Problems and Difficulties

Is it feasible to dispense with formal authoritarian structure and operate entirely through natural lattices? There are obvious difficulties.

1. *Objectives.* Any coherent organization must have well understood and precisely defined objectives, the acceptance of which is imposed upon all who join and remain members of the organization. There is a "chicken or egg" situation here. An organizer must precede the lattice. The founder must establish objectives and then find joiners. However, the lattice will inevitably redirect the course and redefine the objectives. Stability and long-term constancy require a firm hand at the helm. If this hand is too firm, too authoritative, the ship may crash into the shoals or, equally serious, fail to find the fabulous islands of treasure. What is the proper balance?

2. *Decisions.* Decisions must be made. Complete consensus is never reached. Prompt actions are required. Crises occur. Can a lattice organization decide, act, respond to crisis situations? A possible answer is *natural leadership* that evolves based on knowledge, skill, courage, enthusiasm, dominance, dedication, historical situations, and other

nonobjective and perhaps mystical factors. But leaders somehow do evolve, leaders who have followers. It is the existence of followers that gives evidence of leadership. A mature lattice organization has well-defined leadership for a wide range of activities, problems, and situations. This develops through experience, including the unexpected. Decisions are made by and/or reached through leadership. Consensus is required only among those persons who must carry out the actions related to a decision. In a lattice (or any organization) a commitment must be obtained from each person who must do something. The nature of commitment is that it is self-generated. No person can commit another. All commitments are self-commitments. Authoritarians cannot impose commitments, only commands. The difference in response is enormous.

3. *Size.* Lattices accommodate only a limited number of persons—those who know each other. How can large and diverse enterprises be undertaken by the lattice? The answer is that they cannot. However, there are some mitigating possibilities. Just as it is natural to have multiparticipating liaison persons within the teams of a lattice, so it is feasible to evolve multiparticipating liaison people who operate within certain teams from two or more different lattices that may be widely separated in geography. The communication through these people maintains reasonable coordination between the separate lattices. Another device is systems. Most important is language. Not only English, but the special language that evolves in the course of enterprises. Key words, abbreviations, and acronyms may relate to complex concepts and agreements that are only understood by members of the organizational family. Financial systems help coordinate different lattices. Commerce between lattices also generates cooperative systems. An effort to establish a uniform set of systems throughout separate lattice groups, however, is certain to fail. Different people make different systems. Nonetheless, the natural desire to cooperate plus the good offices of liaison people can unify systems adequately so that effective communication and planning can be accomplished. The generation and maintenance of creative and flexible systems is a complex and never-ending activity for liaison persons, both inter- and intralattice groups.

4. *Compensation.* Can a workable system of rewards be devised without an authoritarian framework? It is obvious that the freedom to set the magnitude of one's own salary is unworkable. Therefore, the judgments on division of available income must not be made by the recipient. The authoritarian solution is largely that of proportioning compensation to levels of authority, though additional considerations have always been found necessary. The principle that compensation is

set in proportion to contribution to available income is generally accepted as fair and equitable. The propriety of the principle, however, does not entirely solve the problem. Judgment must be made of the relative contribution of each participant in the enterprise. In a lattice organization there is no natural structure adequate for reaching these judgments. Therefore, it has been necessary for each member of a lattice to have at least one "sponsor." The commitment of the sponsor is that he or she will be knowledgeable about the activities, well-being, progress, accomplishments, personal problems, and ambitions of the person sponsored. In compensation discussions, the role of the sponsor is that of a positive advocate. There is, however, the inexorable requirement for the compensation team to reach the fairest possible ordering of relative contributions to the success of the enterprise. Sponsorship is one of the crucial aspects of a lattice organization and involves the complexities of human interactions. A person who cannot find a sponsor is not a member of a lattice organization.

5. *Limited size.*   There is a limit to the size of a lattice organization. Everyone must know everyone else rather well in order to maintain cooperative communication. At Gore Associates, we have found this limit to be about 150, or at most, 200 people. As the size of the lattice increases, cooperation and communication become more difficult and, at some point, one hears "they decided" instead of "we decided." This change from we to they marks the limit to the effective size of a cooperating group.

Smaller groups cooperate better, but the need for synergy often forces us toward larger groups. There may be some tasks on which each person works independently and the output is simply the sum of the number of workers. However, in most enterprises, a variety of skills and knowledge is needed. The combination of engineers, chemists, computer operators, accountants, salespeople, production operators, and the like form a team that is synergistic—productive and creative far beyond the simple addition of like persons doing the same thing.

When we turn to the problem of optimizing human resources, the size of the organization is again relevant. As the number of persons increases, the synergy effect increases and the accomplishment per person increases. However, since there is an increasing concomitant loss in effective cooperation and individual identification, the negative drag soon exceeds the positive pull. Accomplishment per person plotted against number of persons is a bell-shaped curve, peaking at about 150.

But a group of 150 persons cannot afford expensive instruments, large computers, specialized machine tools, and the like. Also, a full range of specialized professional people cannot be supported. This difficulty is alleviated by building plants in clusters scattered over about a 10-mile distance. Then the electron microscope, long-bed lathe, infrared spectrograph, and the like can be shared among the various plants. Also, professional specialists can be shared since travel time between plants is short. The plant cluster concept solves many of the problems of keeping working groups small and still providing the specialized equipment and consultants not available within a single small plant.

Freedom to use one's talents, skill, and knowledge makes a stimulating and challenging environment. Creativity requires freedom—but freedom requires orderly restraints. In group endeavors, certain rules are always necessary. Indeed freedom requires responsibility for teamwork and cooperation. Freedom without responsibility is chaotic and threatens the enterprise. The restraints imposed by a need for cooperation are minimized in a lattice.

Governing Principles

There are basic agreements that must be kept in order to maintain a viable lattice organization. I believe five are necessary:

1. *Agreement on the objective.* The objective of our enterprise is to earn money and enjoy doing so. It is obviously necessary to earn money to buy raw materials and supplies, pay operating bills, provide facilities and equipment, and compensate associates so that they enjoy life and have long-term financial security. Enjoyment comes not only from friendships, social activities, and pleasure of working together on teams but, more important, in the conviction that what you are doing is important and worthwhile. It is also enjoyable to learn new skills and gain new knowledge. The "making money and having fun" objective is truly a single objective since, long-term, you can't have one without the other.

2. *Fairness.* Everyone will sincerely try to be fair in all transactions, with each other, our customers, our suppliers, and whomever we deal with. This is necessary to maintain good feelings among us. Deliberate or careless unfairness creates anger and resentment and destroys the communication and cooperation necessary for success.

3. *Freedom.* Everyone will allow, help, and encourage associates to grow in knowledge, skill, breadth of responsibility, and scope of activity. This is necessary to encourage creativity and innovation. Freedom to innovate entails risk. Therefore, freedom requires a tolerance for mistakes and failure.

4. *Commitment.*   Everyone will make personal commitments—and keep them. This is necessary for functions, projects, and group contracts. A leader's order without a follower's commitment is ineffective. Self-commitment operates absent of command and is enormously effective. At best, a command begets obedience. Commitment calls upon the total energies, talents, and dedication of the person making the commitment. Creative and innovative enterprises can only work through commitments.

5. *Waterline.*   Any action that has a serious risk to the reputation, financial security, or future opportunities of the enterprise is a "waterline" matter. The analogy is that we are all in the same boat. Everyone is free to bore holes in the sides of the boat—above the waterline. A hole below the waterline could sink us. Before taking any action below the waterline, an associate must take council with the appropriate associates and obtain their agreement to undertake the proposed action and share the responsibility for doing so.

The Associates Culture

Sponsors.   At Gore Associates, one important system is the sponsor network. An applicant for employment meets with several different leadership associates in search for one who will commit to bring the new person onto the team and sponsor him or her. The sponsorship entails instruction, training, and the commitment to help the new associate quickly reach the "quick win" point at which he or she is earning his or her pay. As time goes on, the new associate may find different or additional sponsors. The role of sponsorship is not only to help new associates get started but also to be a positive advocate who speaks for the accomplishments and contributions of the person being sponsored. When the income available for distribution as compensation is divided, sponsor groups judge the relative contributions of different associates so that the distribution is in proportion to contribution.

Leaders.   Leaders are discerned as associates who have followers. Leadership revolves depending on the problem, particular skill, or knowledge involved. Natural leadership emerges and evolves within any working team. This natural leadership is more effective than arbitrarily appointed leaders. Natural leadership is dynamic and flexible, changing with the issue or area of expertise.

Emergencies.   Emergencies require quick decisions and action. (Decisions, in general, are usually made by those who will implement the action.) Commitments and responsibilities are specified among associates. When an emergency arises, be it financial, injury, fire, or whatever, it is well-known who has responsibility for decision and directed action.

Success.   A successful event is always celebrated. Receiving a big order after long efforts requires a "bash." Everyone congratulates an associate who makes an invention or solves a problem. We all cheer when we accumulate enough cash to distribute it in profit-sharing checks.

Visitors.   Visitors from other plants are formally welcomed, and arrangements are made for their housing, transportation, and entertainment, and for their business purposes.

Intrapreneurs.   Intrapreneurs (associate entrepreneurs) undertake new businesses by inviting other associates to "sign up" for the new venture. If there are no signers, there is no new business. Experienced business leaders may advise, but signers are the basic requirement. The "yes, yes" test is applied to ventures and innovations. If best hopes are realized, would the outcome be worthwhile? If the worst comes to pass, can we stand it? The answer to both questions must always be Yes.

The lattice organization has evolved over almost 30 years at Gore Associates. The many inventions and innovations have generated many new products and businesses. When people operate in an environment of freedom with a minimum of restraints, their potential for creative innovation and productivity is released and spectacular achievements result.

28

A Place for Creativity: The Hallmark Innovation Center

Charles W. Hucker

Divisional Vice President, Public Affairs and Communication, Hallmark Cards

"I began to write short pieces when I was living in a room too small to write a novel in."

ANGELA CARTWRIGHT, AMERICAN WRITER

Environments *are* important to creativity. Some inhibit creativity by being too dark, too loud, or too cramped. It is hard to be creative if you are uncomfortable. The myth of the starving artist in the garret producing great works of art is just that—a myth. When great works of art are produced under such conditions, it is usually *in spite* of the environment, not *because* of it. On the other hand, creativity flourishes when tools, support, and inspiration abound. An environment can inspire creativity by being beautiful or unusual. It can foster creativity by allowing freedom or feedback. "Places don't create, people do," is an oft-said aphorism. True. But it is also true that a place can *help* a person to be more creative.

Creativity is of great importance to Hallmark. That's why in 1984 we decided to build a place for nurturing ideas, a structure for stimulating creativity, a center for innovation. That idea place, the Hallmark Innovation Center, was designed to foster creativity and innovation by providing a stimulating environment in which different groups of employees could easily exchange ideas. The two-story, 170,000-square-foot center houses Hallmark staff from Advanced Technical Research, Equipment Engineering, Product Innovation, and the Creative Workshop. The building is adjacent to the main Hallmark facility at corporate headquarters. It is accessible from the main building, but still, it is a separate structure—a place set apart. About 180 employees are housed in the Innovation Center permanently; others rotate through, staying for several months at a time to explore technologies and expand vision.

Mixing Ideas

Society's shorthand for the birth of an idea is a light bulb going off above a lone person's head. Often, though, the real process is neither sudden nor solitary. It involves people talking together—sometimes in an office, sometimes in a lab, sometimes over a cup of coffee. Such creative brainstorming is what the Innovation Center is all about. People from one discipline—say, engineering—work with people from another, quite different area—maybe design. They come up with new ideas. (Whether these ideas become new products depends on needs and demands of the marketplace.) Consultants who help corporations and individuals foster creativity say collaboration is necessary for innovation. "It's important to cross-relate the senses," says one creativity specialist. "When groups of people with diverse training work on a project, they mix their vocabularies as well as their ideas."

I like wandering through the Center. The last time, I met a project engineer who was experimenting with enamel glazes. We talked about an informal workshop he had led the day before to teach a group of artists how to use enameling. Then our conversation turned to creativity and how it is aided by such exchanges of ideas. "Creativity is basically finding the best solution to a problem," the engineer told me:

Here, you can walk one way and find a chemist or another way and find an artist or down the hall to find a press operator. With two or three spheres of knowledge, instead of just your own, you can find many fresh ideas to solve your problem. The more options you have, the better decisions you make. The more options you have, the more creative you can be. You hear a lot of "What about this?" "What about that?" around here. You've got no excuses when you're in this place. If you have energy to seek a solution, you can find it.

Designed for Communication and Inspiration

The whole atmosphere of this idea center has been to encourage collaboration—not only in formal sessions, but in labs, lounges, and lunch rooms. In designing the Innovation Center, we went to an architectural company known for creating structures that serve the function of the building. "We set out to design a building in which people mix as well as match," said Lewis Davis, one of the partners. "The Center is much like a very small town in which everyone understands what the other person does for a living. That sort of familiarity, mutual respect, and cohesiveness leads to more bright ideas and enhanced productivity."

The building encourages a free flow of information; communication is key to the design. That design is a constant, subtle reminder that the function of the building is the exchange of ideas. Conversation lounges and a small food service area promote employee interaction. The lower and larger floor consists of an open area the size of two football fields, adjoined by laboratories for traditional processes such as gravure, lithography, die cutting, and silk-screening, as well as electronics, lasers, ceramics, and plastics. Glass-walled conference rooms and work areas allow the Center's staff to see what others are doing. Doors—when they exist—are often open; many times they are literally holes in the walls. The Center's office walls are chest-high to encourage informal exchanges and drop-in meetings.

I once noticed three people sitting at a table in a glass conference room. Their coats were off; the meeting was informal. They were discussing jigsaw puzzles. How did I know? Through the glass I watched their gestures; through the open doors I heard their conversation. Then a fourth Hallmarker walked by and glanced in. One participant called to him. "You might know the answer," she said. A few minutes later, the meeting was over. Together, they had solved their puzzle problem.

"Too frequently a research facility looks like an ordinary factory. Little or no attempt has been made to produce an environment for innovation—to stimulate creativity or productivity of the R&D staff through design and setting." So states a call for entries in a laboratory design contest. Not so with this structure. The way things look is very important to Hallmark. After all, part of what we sell is beautiful design. It is essential that the structure of the Innovation Center support the function of its inhabitants. Light and color are critical ingredients in the development of our products. The Center reflects that importance with its teal-and-burgundy color scheme and its unique lighting system, which combines natural and artificial light. To achieve this, a corridor around the main work space allows all employees access to windows. In addition, ninety pyramid-shaped skylights provide even, indirect lighting throughout. At dusk, photoelectric cells trigger fluorescent lighting to give the illusion of daylight. "There's something about the atmosphere here," said an artist working on new products. "It's more than just the physical atmosphere, although the physical dictates the mental. You feel really free here. You feel that it's okay to do something that's never been done before."

Creativity Comes in Many Packages

The Innovation Center has evolved from years of searching, testing, and evaluating new ways to encourage the free exchange of ideas with the purpose of developing new products. Our Humor Workshop is a good example. Here, ten cartoonists work on projects of their own choosing in an office outside the main building. In a sense, the workshop operates like a freelance studio in which the cartoonists develop product ideas to "sell" to the company's product management staff. The workshop is filled with visual humor designed to stimulate the cartoonists' creativity. Take Earnestine, the workshop's receptionist. Earnestine is a life-sized soft-sculpture dressed as a 1940s telephone operator who sits in the anteroom by a welcoming sign that says "Go Home." Inside the workshop, cartoonists work on a variety of work surfaces ranging from roll-top desks to workbenches and wooden doors. An occasional stained-glass window, rubber chicken, or gorilla mask adorns the ceiling and walls. "In the workshop, it is creativity through inspiration, not requisition," said the Humor Workshop founder. "It makes a difference."

We have experimented with other methods for stimulating creativity through environment. For example, we occasionally send a group of creative writers to a hotel room to eat pizza and brainstorm for writing ideas. We also send creative staff members to cultural centers—such as Paris, London, Milan, New York, and Los Angeles—to soak up ideas that might lead to products down the road. And we offer stimulating "get-away" places right in the building—libraries, lounges, and fine art displays—in which people can talk about projects and exchange ideas.

The Hallmark Creative Workshop, which is now housed in the Innovation Center, has been around for almost 20 years. Many of the idea-place concepts from the Creative Workshop have been expanded and applied to the Center. Thirty-five permanent staff members work in the Workshop's Model Shop, Plastics Lab, Process Development Shop, and Design Staff. Their job is to develop new products and new ways to use the company's manufacturing equipment. The workshop is an idea place, a locus in which innovation is part of the job. It's a good example of how the Innovation Center works.

Three times a year, a "rotation group" of nine or ten artists enters the workshop. They spend 4 months there, working with permanent staff and experimenting with novel production techniques and product ideas. The workshop is *not* a pot in which artists and press operators are boiled together to make some sort of social expression stew. It is a mixture rather than a melding, in which each participant remains individual and identifiable, but in which all add their own flavoring to the whole.

With the average tenure of permanent workshop employees at 27 years, you might expect some job burnout. "The operators still look at the workshop with inquisitive eyes," said the shop section manager. "Being fascinated, being interested in new ways to do things, that's written into the job description." " 'No' is not a word we use here," added the workshop director. "If an artist asks, 'Can you run this wrench through the press?' the press operator will say, 'Yes, but if I do, the press will break.' Trying to see if something works is the best way to learn."

The right attitude aids innovation. There was an artist in the Plastics Shop who had a reputation for poking through workshop trash cans. She would take "ruined" projects and experiment with them, viewing them in different ways. Cracked plastic might look like trash to most people, but to this artist it was treasure: a new technique that could give a card a brittle, ancient look. That vitality, that sense of wonder, is part of the history of the workshop, where they say "a mistake is only a mistake if you throw it away."

Working with the technical staff in this compressed, miniature manufacturing department, artists expand their vision—seeing what they rarely see while hunched over drawing boards. And that's a two-way street. Technicians often develop a method or material for which there seems no use. But the artist will look at it from a strange angle and suggest possible applications. Suddenly, a new product idea emerges. A press operator and design supervisor, working together to produce a new kind of ornament, chatted about their "creative combustion" theory. "Two or three people will be thinking about a project," the press operator said. "We all build on each other's ideas. We stand around saying, 'This sounds crazy, but . . .' Somehow, out of all the craziness, we figure out how to turn an idea into a product." The design supervisor agreed: "These fellows have lots of ideas. We artists have lots of ideas. When we get together, interesting things happen."

In Virginia Woolf's essay *A Room of One's Own,* the writer asserts that people cannot write unless they have a place to write. Place. It is often so ignored and always so important. We want our people to have a place in which just looking around stimulates ideas and encourages pursuit. We want our people to have a place big enough to write novels as well as short stories.

PART 4

Creative
Strategies

Creative Accent on Strategic Management

Creativity in the service of strategy multiplies organizational options and transforms corporate character. Strategy relates a company to its environment and seeks to optimize company strengths and weaknesses in light of industry opportunities and threats. Strategy seeks competitive advantage by maximizing distinctive competencies. But competitive advantage can be elusive and ephemeral, hard to find and harder to keep. Original thinking is often essential; we need mental frameworks that adapt and move and shift and change. The thicker the competitive environment the more critical the creative need. Indeed, creativity should be the wellspring of strategy: effective strategic choice cannot be made without a large variety of strategic options, and a large variety of strategic options cannot be generated without the dynamic turmoil of creative thinking. Creativity in strategy focuses creativity throughout the company. It is important to an innovative firm to define corporate mission clearly so that executives can sift the wheat of potent, practical concepts from the chaff of random, raucous ideas. Ideas that do not fit corporate purpose must be killed quickly, ideally through the internal litmus test of mission comparison. In Part 4 we apply creativity to corporate strategy: strategy formulation and implementation, building corporate value, new ways of thinking in strategic management, specific ideas for large and mid-sized firms. Strategic failure, interestingly enough, is a prime theme. We also consider troubled companies, in which creativity is sorely needed and rarely considered. Merger and acquisition pricing, conglomerate building, and multiunit organizations are three special situations in which creativity weaves its magic. Also important are decision making and deal making. Here are ideas for all to apply.

29

Strategic Formulation: Pruning and Focus

Martin S. Davis

Chairman and Chief Executive Officer,
Gulf + Western Inc.

The second half of the 1960s was the heyday of the conglomerate. Large corporations such as Gulf + Western were built through the acquisition of numerous unrelated, undervalued businesses. The theory was simple: Different businesses respond differently to the same economic conditions, and, therefore, a highly diversified company could grow in almost any economic environment—and the debt incurred from acquisitions would be paid back with inflationary dollars. All one really needed was the right mix of businesses. For instance, in a difficult economy, the sale of automotive parts for new vehicles would certainly be depressed but the sale of replacement parts would be strong since consumers would hold onto their existing cars longer.

While the theory was sound, it was not always put into practice. To work, it required a careful balancing of businesses to cushion the impact of economic change. But Gulf + Western, as one example, was essentially a bargain hunter and purchased businesses mainly at a sharp discount from book value rather than picking companies solely to fit the conglomerate model. A number of the companies G + W acquired were heavily oriented to commodities such as zinc, sugar, and cement and therefore subject to wide swings in earnings. Their unpredictable pattern adversely affected overall consistency in earnings growth. Sugar, for instance, sold for a historical high of $.65 per pound in 1974 (contributing significantly to record earnings that year) but for less than $.04 per pound in early 1985. "Conglomerate theory" proves even more fallible today in a world dominated by accelerated change. We have moved from an environment of growth and predictability to one that encompasses high growth, mixed growth and no growth, constant threats, and limited predictability. Nevertheless, despite the problems of the current marketplace, a wide array of opportunities exist for aggressive companies that move away from conservatism and eschew the building of bureaucracies.

Large, diverse companies must become more innovative and sharpen marketing skills. Companies must learn how to obtain true value from the strategic planning process by recognizing that the objective is to get something done, not develop reams of data nobody reads. We at Gulf + Western are spending more time attempting to answer three fundamental questions: Where are we now? Where do we want to be in the future? What is the best way to get there?

Planning at Gulf + Western has undergone major changes over the past several years. Annual business planning was formalized back in the late 1960s, but strategic planning, though an integral part of the process, never received the emphasis or attention intended or merited. The process was financially oriented and concentrated on the near term. We subsequently realized that new responses were needed to meet worldwide competition, rapid technological change, fluctuating rates of inflation and interest, and changing consumer spending habits. Also necessary was the need to sharpen management skills and improve the lines of communication between corporate staff and operating managers.

Strategic Lessons

Our philosophy is to do what appears to be right today, not what was comfortable yesterday. The strategic planning process helps us identify trends, events, and critical issues facing our businesses and implement the actions necessary to take advantage of marketplace opportunities. Strategic planning also was used to re-evaluate all of our businesses. This process helped to identify operating units that could not ultimately achieve an acceptable return on investment, that were commodity related, and that were unlikely to obtain future competitive advantage—and, therefore, did not conform to our long-term objectives. At the same time, we completed an extensive assessment of our strengths and determined more precisely the businesses to which our future energies and resources should be committed. The process pointed out a number of fundamental lessons:

Cyclicality. It must be redefined. Some businesses once considered cyclical are in fact contracting or fading as they face declining product demand caused by changing competitive factors, technology, or lifestyles. Therefore, it has become increasingly difficult to achieve a truly advantageous fit among companies presumably operating through counterbalancing cycles.

Complexity. It necessitates an acknowledgment of managerial boundaries. There are limits to information that managers can absorb and operating details they can monitor. If spread thin, managers can overlook not only potential problems but areas of true opportunity. An overriding challenge of the information age is to obtain the most pertinent data and to use that data advantageously.

Capital. It requires a sharper focus. Broad diversification can dilute financial resources so that all company components cannot be funded adequately to meet dynamic competitive forces.

Compatibility. It is essential for managerial personalities and points of view as well as in operations. Some stretching may be acceptable but stretching too far results in greater strain, not greater strength. The effort to reach common ground dissipates managerial vigor. Acquisitions related to core operations are much more likely to succeed than acquisitions that merely add sales.

Centralization-decentralization balance. It demands independent decision making. There is no universal formula to arrive at the right mix of centralized controls and decentralized operations. The goal is to strike a healthy balance, letting each segment do what it does best. Every organization must develop its own model.

Cross-fertilization. It is not easily attainable. The premise that two plus two can equal five does not compute in practice. The proven advantages of profit-center concepts outweigh the limited successes achieved in the quest for synergy.

Comparative sales position. It has lost significance in ranking corporate America. The prime measure of a company's progress must be the growth of shareholder value.

Strategic Pruning

Strategic planning led Gulf + Western to a major restructuring, undertaken in two phases. Phase 1 was launched in 1983 when we began to sell some fifty business units with sales of approximately $1.3 billion that did not meet our performance criteria. These divestitures included our building products business, a number of manufacturing units, the natural resources businesses, video game operations, two racetracks, and our sugar growing and related operations. More than $600 million in cash and notes was generated from the sale of these assets over an 18-month period, and the proceeds were used to pay down debt and fund other more attractive businesses. Phase 2 followed in 1985, when we completed the sale of our Consumer and Industrial Products Group to Wickes Companies, Inc., for approximately $1 billion in cash and the assumption by Wickes of about $73 million in long-term debt. In addition, Gulf + Western received a 5-year option to purchase ten million shares of Wickes common stock at $6 per share.

Phase 1 necessitated a write-down against earnings. Phase 2 resulted in a gain. The companies sold in Phase 2, well-managed and solid performers historically, included units that dated to the roots of Gulf + Western—G + W Manufacturing (automotive, electronic-electrical and construction products) and A.P.S. (automotive parts distribution)—and consumer products companies acquired in the middle and late 1970s—Kayser-Roth (apparel and hosiery) and Simmons (bedding and home furnishings). The companies had contributed significantly to G + W's success; their combined sales in 1985 totaled $2.7 billion. Their divestiture reflected the corporate decision to concentrate operations in business areas the company's management believes can generate higher returns and accelerated growth. This restructuring has resulted in a "deconglomeration" of Gulf + Western into a more rational and focused enterprise, with a clearer sense of purpose and direction. The company now is leaner, stronger, more profitable, and more growth-oriented—and shareholder values have been enhanced.

We went about the transformation methodically. At no time did we overleverage or venture beyond cost-effective limits. On the contrary, we strengthened our capital foundation during the process, repurchasing stock and reducing our debt-to-equity ratio (from .90 in 1982 to .69 in 1986).

Strategic Focus

Our future is primarily in three distinct areas: Publishing and Information Services, Entertainment, and Financial Services. In 1986, these operations had combined revenues of $3.8 billion. Publishing and Information Services is an example of our long-term strategy. We started with the 1975 purchase of Simon & Schuster for somewhat more than $10 million, mainly in common stock. It proved to be one of Gulf + Western's best acquisitions; we earned back our investment in a relatively short time.

In any business there are four critical elements that I call the four Ps: people, performance, products, and potential. The people element is probably the most important, and with the Simon & Schuster acquisition came some of publishing's most outstanding young managers. Their capability translated into performance. The industry grew at an impressive 10 percent per year from 1976 through 1983; Simon & Schuster grew more rapidly during that period, at about 17 percent.

Good products—books the public wants to buy—helped spur that performance. Simon & Schuster publishes an average of twenty-five hardcover best sellers a year, making it one of the most commercially successful publishing houses in the world. Its best sellers in recent years have included: *All the President's Men, Looking for Mr. Goodbar, Blind Ambition, Kane & Abel, Jane Fonda's Workout Book, Hollywood Wives, The Sicilian, Wired, Mayor, Contact, Lonesome Dove, The Road Less Traveled, Wiseguy,* and *The Fitzgeralds and the Kennedys.*

Clearly, Simon & Schuster had established a foundation with strong management and a potential for even greater growth, but we were not fully capitalizing on that opportunity. A few small acquisitions were made during the 1976–83 period, but there was no real attempt to make publishing a more important part of Gulf + Western. The corporation mission—until we began to implement our strategic planning process—was to remain a highly diversified group of unrelated companies (the definition of a true conglomerate).

The decision to move into publishing more aggressively was made after I became CEO in February 1983 following the death of the company's chairman and founder, and our ability to act quickly was aided by a fortuitous investment made earlier. In 1983 Gulf + Western owned a large portfolio of marketable securities that included 27 percent of Esquire, whose major business was the publishing of elementary and high school ("el-hi") textbooks. Numerous studies of educational systems in the United States had reached the same conclusion: American educational systems must be improved. Gulf + Western's internal research showed that educational book publishers would benefit from this sharply increased demand for educational excellence, and we therefore proceeded in 1984 to acquire the balance of Esquire that we did not already own and to integrate the company into Simon &

Schuster. Meanwhile, we decided to liquidate the rest of the portfolio to reduce debt and fund our new strategic direction.

As a result of the acquisition, Simon & Schuster gained an important foothold in the educational publishing market with opportunities for long-term growth. It was now time to augment our new base of publishing activities, and our studies led us to Prentice-Hall, a company with an enviable track record (1983 revenues, $448 million; operating income, $75 million). The Prentice-Hall acquisition in 1984 moved us into a leadership position in college textbook publishing, established us as a major professional and business information services company, and enhanced our position in the el-hi market. We were now a major force in virtually every significant segment of the book publishing industry. And today, we are a multimedia information resource, capable of serving customers by whatever means best suits their needs—print in books, newsletters, magazines, and looseleaf files or electronically through software and interactive communications services. Films and videocassettes watched in the classroom, as another example, might come from the library of Simon & Schuster Communications.

Future acquisitions will be of the "niche" variety, filling voids in our publishing lines. For instance, we acquired Ginn, a division of Xerox's Information Resources Group, in 1985—the leading publisher of basic reading programs at the elementary school level. Reading is the largest subsegment within elementary textbook publishing. Moreover, the demographics of the elementary school market are favorable; between 1983 and 1990, the population of 5-year-olds to 13-year-olds is expected to increase almost 9 percent.

Gulf + Western is a different company today, more entrenched in attractive businesses. We have consciously moved away from the industrial sector to a higher-return services base. We are better prepared to deal with tomorrow's problems and opportunities. While we cannot expect precisely predictable growth, our managers are stronger, our controls better, and our marketing and planning skills improving. We believe that the future belongs to those who plan for it.

We have since completed sixteen other publishing acquisitions representing an investment of more than $230 million. In total, we have invested over $1.2 billion in publishing acquisitions since 1964.

30

Strategy Implementation: Consistency and Coherence Can Be Creative

Harry J. Gray

Chairman of the Board and former Chief Executive Officer, United Technologies Corporation

The need to identify, develop, and manage the risk-reward relationship in any business, large or small, demands creativity and innovation. But such creativity and innovation need not be a revolutionary roller coaster of perpetual starts and stops, shifts and turns. Imagination works best when implementing a consistent and coherent strategic plan.

United Technologies Corporation (UTC) was built by design. It is the result of identifying the problems and strengths of the company, determining what was needed to solve the problems and optimize the strengths, setting aggressive though attainable goals, and developing and implementing a constant strategy to achieve these goals. The corporation's performance against objectives is shown by comparison:

In 1972, the company had about $2 billion in sales; it passed the $16 billion mark in 1984. Nearly $6 billion came from outside the United States; in 1972 it was under half a billion. The net profit growth rate has been triple the rate experienced by the *Fortune 100*. United Technologies has risen to become the third largest U.S. exporter, the seventh largest U.S. manufacturer, and the thirty-fifth largest industrial company in the world.

Growth Strategy

The company's strategy has not been rigidly cast. It has been modified and adjusted as appropriate, permitting us to grasp opportunities that presented themselves and to create opportunities when none were present. The broad outlines, however, have remained constant since they were first developed in the early 1970s, constant during some of the most turbulent times in the economy and technology. This is the point.

In 1972 the company was called United Aircraft. Virtually all of its $2 billion in sales were in aerospace. Its principal products were Pratt & Whitney jet engines, Sikorsky helicopters, Hamilton Standard aerospace controls, and Norden military electronic systems. About half the company's business came from government contracts. This meant that the company suffered from being tied to wide swings in aerospace and defense business cycles. The company's problems were two-fold. First, it was overly dependent on government contracts. Second, its industrial base was too narrow. It is not healthy for a company to be so dependent on one customer or one product line. On the other hand, United Aircraft did have some considerable strengths. It was sound financially. Its products, though relatively few in number, were high in quality. Its research and development projects were well-funded; and its capabilities in aerospace technology were first-rate. This was a solid foundation on which to build.

We concluded that it was important to reduce the percentage—but not the volume—of business we did with the government. (In fact, we wanted to increase the dollar volume of the company's government business.) In order to do this we needed to expand our industrial base considerably so that our government business would shrink as a percentage of our total sales. Internal growth by itself probably would be insufficient to meet this goal. Consequently we made diversification through acquisition an integral part of our corporate development plan.

Acquisition Strategy

Other companies have also looked to acquisitions as an attractive avenue of expansion. Unfortunately, acquisition avenue is not an easy road on which to travel. It has many surprise turns. Many announced mergers fall apart before they are consummated. Even worse, the majority fail after the transaction is completed. Studies of past mergers indicate that most do not yield the financial growth benefits anticipated by the acquiring companies. Most of these failures can be attributed to the lack of an adequately stated acquisition policy reflecting long-term corporate goals or to the lack of a corporate acquisition team with the necessary skills to initiate and implement a successful acquisition.

An acquisition policy needs to define how a company plans to grow. It needs to identify a small group of industries or markets that represent logical expansion opportunities. The age of the random acquisition is over. Successful growth through acquisition is invariably *reasoned* growth based on current competencies. United Technologies used acquisitions to decouple the company from the cyclical aspects of its traditional markets. Specifically, we zeroed in on four industries: electronics, communications, transportation, and environmental systems. Though this list seems diverse, the technologies of these fields are all closely related to each other and to the company's aerospace base.

The company engaged in five principal mergers in the 1970s, along with a number of smaller ones. The first was Essex International in 1974. Though scarcely a household name, Essex was—and is—a top-rank producer of wire and cable products. This acquisition gave us a strong position in the automotive, construction, appliance, electric utility, and telecommunications industries, as well as an increased mix of nongovernmental revenues. Once the company entered into these businesses, the word "Aircraft" in the corporate name no longer fit; hence United Aircraft became United Technologies. Just as the old name reflected an almost exclusive emphasis on aerospace, the new name has come to symbolize the high-technology thrust now common in all our operations.

In 1976 came the acquisition of Otis Elevator Company. Otis founded the elevator industry and is its world leader. Otis had a particular appeal because of its global scope. In fact, it does more business outside the United States than inside. When Otis joined United Technologies, the corporation had an instant international profile, with manufacturing plants and employees around the world.

Ambac Industries merged with United Technologies in 1978, adding substantial presence in markets for diesel fuel-injection systems, small electric motors, fluid-power products, and medical and scientific instruments. In 1979 Carrier Corporation was acquired. Carrier founded the air conditioning industry and is its world leader. The Carrier merger firmly brought us into environmental systems and further enlarged our worldwide business presence. Also in 1979, United Technologies purchased a microelectronics company based in Texas known as Mostek Corporation. Its products were on the leading edge of semiconductor technology. Though later divested with large write-offs, Mostek's technology continues to be an integral part of our product development strategy.

These acquisitions and some smaller ones helped raise the company's nongovernment sales from less than half the total in 1972 to more than 70 percent in 1984. Commercial and industrial sales during the period rose nearly twelve-fold. Government business declined as a percentage of sales, just as we intended it to do—but it rose in dollar volume, quadrupling from $1 billion in 1972 to $4.7 billion in 1984.

Coherent Strategy

While the company was broadening and balancing its operations through diversification, it was also strengthening its original foundations. Pratt & Whitney has grown into a $5 + billion company. Sikorsky has passed the $1.5 billion mark. Hamilton Standard has reached $1 billion in sales. And Norden has approached the $1 billion mark. All these operations were part of the corporation before we began implementing our acquisition strategy.

A coherent business theme runs through all our acquisitions. The companies we have acquired have a pronounced technological bent. They are able to benefit from our skills at managing technology. They are market leaders in their industries. Typically, they are first or second place in terms of market share. They are profitable companies that have good growth potential, both domestically and around the world, and strong managements.

This common theme has enabled the corporation to capitalize on the growing importance of microelectronics in product development and on the transition of the business environment from one that is export-oriented to one that is global in scope. Our long-term strategy calls for further efforts fully establishing United Technologies as a global corporation, for a broader application of microelectronics in all our products, and for using this technology to create new markets. We are giving high priority to investments that will generate a competitive edge by adding value to our products and lowering the cost of manufacturing them.

R&D Strategy

Investing heavily in research and development is the only way to stay in the forefront of the technologies from which we will shape our forthcoming products. The corporation's R&D expenditures for the first 5 years of the 1980s totaled $4.2 billion, equivalent to 6 percent of sales. These investments in R&D are not intended to yield returns immediately but years hence in new products, improved competitiveness, and expanded job opportunities. We want to be in a competitive position with technology and products long before we actually have to vie in the marketplace.

Our high-technology thrust has created new products. It also has created new businesses. Our expertise in aerospace technology was used to develop energy management systems for commercial building complexes. Combining this energy management with Otis and Carrier has created the new field of integrated building systems and services. The United Technologies "building systems" approach uses microelectronics and optical fibers to create a data highway to carry signals for elevators, heating, ventilating, air conditioning, lights, burglar and fire alarms, and all internal communications, including voice and data. For the building developer, this systemized approach means a reduction in construction costs. For the owner, it means reduced operating costs. Moreover, the data highway makes retrofitting much simpler when the servicing systems reach the end of their normal 20-year life span. Perhaps the most significant benefit, however, is the advanced telecommunications made available to building tenants.

International Strategy

In addition to creating new products and diversifying the company's product line, UTC has expanded its operations around the world. United Technologies now has 75,000 employees and more than 100 manufacturing plants outside the United States. Sales of products manufactured outside the United States account for nearly 60 percent of international business, with the rest derived from the export of products manufactured in the United States. The company achieved this international growth by acquiring U.S. companies that had major foreign operations, by acquiring foreign companies, and by establishing partnerships with companies in other countries. UTC has formed many cooperative relationships in the 1980s, for example, joint ventures with West German electronics companies for the production of semiconductors and other microelectronic products. Pratt & Whitney is participating in International Aero Engines, a five-nation consortium developing a new jet engine for commercial airlines. Otis has acquired elevator companies in Britain and Italy and has established a manufacturing joint venture in the People's Republic of China. Carrier has formed joint ventures with major air conditioning manufacturers in Italy and Brazil. Sikorsky has set up joint ventures for the coproduction of helicopters in Britain, Spain, and Brazil. Hamilton Standard has acquired a Swiss producer of magnet wire and electric insulation materials and is cooperating with China on the production of telephone wire and cable.

We believe a company cannot compete internationally just by exporting. It needs to serve customers worldwide by manufacturing and selling standardized products worldwide. International partnerships are essential to achieving this goal. In fact, cooperative ventures in many cases offer the only practical way to gain a market presence in a country. They also provide economies of scale that strengthen capacity to compete with major foreign companies. And they provide additional experience that promotes further growth.

International growth, coupled with an increasing emphasis on microelectronic technology, is part of the corporation's strategy. We encourage each operating unit, however, to tailor its short-term objectives and long-term goals to its individual circumstances. Operating managers have the responsibility to achieve superior performance within their own competitive environment. Corporate management has the responsibility to assure the appropriate mix of business that will allow the corporation to reach its overall goals.

We adapt to changing technology, to changing competition, to changing demands and expectations of our customers. Our basic strategy, however, remains set. It has worked; it is working. Sometimes, creativity can be consistent and coherent, and consistency and coherence can be creative.

31

Creative Financial Strategy: Ideas for Building Corporate Value

Charles Hurwitz

Chairman and Chief Executive Officer, MCO Holdings, Pacific Lumber Company, United Financial Group

Robert Lawrence Kuhn

Investment banker, Senior Research Fellow, IC² Institute, University of Texas at Austin and Adjunct Professor, Graduate School of Business Administration, New York University

There are two general kinds of financial strategy, one designed to support business operations and opportunities and the other structured to stand alone on its own merits. The former is more oriented toward corporations, the latter toward investors—though they articulate together for maximum benefit. Following are twelve principles that we have watched work. They are building blocks for enhancing corporate value. Creative managers will keep them in mind constantly, looking always for ways and means of implementation.

1. *Examine long-ignored assets closely.* It is remarkable how often value is discovered in apparently dormant corporate assets—from real estate holdings to off-center businesses. Even ancient contracts can have worth. Assets ignored by top management will languish. Revitalize those areas by personal focus, by new management, by merger or divesture—by something. Sleepy management is often at fault, though we all tend to tire over time when plowing the same field. At MCO Holdings we found large residual benefits in a coal contract thought worthless. The presence of a net operating loss carryforward, often overlooked, adds incremental worth to many firms.

2. *Be sensitive to market and value swings.* The cyclical nature of business affects the relative worth of different assets at different times. There is constant flux. Whether hard assets (such as oil and gas, coal, lumber, real estate), business assets (plant and equipment), or intangibles (such as brand names, media franchises, patents, and technologies)—all values are changing continuously. Sell conforming assets (at tops of cycles) and buy contrarian assets (at bottoms of cycles). Creative financial strategy requires nonstop attentiveness to relative value.

3. *Compare value to you versus value to someone else.* Falling in love with a business can be dangerous to financial health. Never forget the primary purpose of for-profit companies—to generate maximum financial returns with minimum financial risks. If a division is losing money or is out of step with current strategy or is draining scarce corporate resources or is consuming excessive managerial energy, perhaps it should be divested. Businesses, in fact, should only be held when they are worth more to you than they are to *anyone* else—not someone else. That may sound obvious, but the implications, when one considers them, are profound. Use any valuation system you like (see Chapter 40), but come up with some dollar amount for each of your corporate units. Will another party pay more than this amount to buy it? If so, it makes no sense to keep it.

4. *Look for strategic premiums and special conditions.* When selling assets, there are usually one or more parties who will pay considerably higher than what appears to be the expected value. This is true whether marketing an independent company or hard assets. Why will a precious few pay more? Not necessarily the "greater fool theory"—though that sometimes plays a part. Often there are "strategic premiums" involved—when the acquiring company can generate incremental value because of synergy (whether real or perceived). At times, special conditions may prevail—when a buyer is hungry to invest. For example, in selling a well-respected industrial manufacturing company, there were numerous bids clustered within 10 percent of one

another and two outliers some 25 percent higher—one from an industrial company, the other from a leveraged buy-out fund. Each had a different reason for making a high bid: The industrial company needed the superb distribution network to peddle its own languishing products; the fund was willing to accept lower rates of return because it wanted to justify raising more money and needed to have its dollars out of Treasury Bills and invested in deals. Finding such premiums is hard work but almost always doable.

5. *The key to making money is not losing it.*   It is far better, as the saying goes, to pass a good deal than to buy a bad one. Never look back at the big fish that got away. There are always deals around, more in a week than you ever can do in your life. But getting laden with the proverbial millstone has buried not a few. Better to hit lots of singles and doubles than risk striking out swinging for the grand slam. Furthermore, it is often nearly impossible to judge beforehand the success of a speculative venture. If you are not letting some good ones get away, your hurdle rate is too low or your risk is too high. One general principle is to get back your capital rapidly, even sacrificing some longer-term benefits; a low rate of return is unpleasant, a loss of principal is disaster. (This applies more to investment situations than to corporate positioning, where long term often outweighs short term.)

6. *Bet with the odds, not against them.*   All business is a gamble; that is fact and nothing can change it. But business gambling is not like casino gambling with fixed probabilities set by the house against passive customers. Business is an active process with success outcomes and failure rates able to be influenced by owners and managers. "Betting with the odds" need not imply underhandedness or trickery. Since business is competition, one should not be in business without some sort of competitive advantage, some reason why your company is better at doing something than anyone else. It is naive (if not futile) to buy a business, for example, without any sense of how you will make more out of it than others could. There are innumerable reasons why some people bring more to companies. Know what they are and be sure some apply. Give yourself a chance to "get lucky": Take some no-risk gambles, such as equity kickers to boost a good purchase price. (It's like the chess adage: "Always check, it might be mate.")

7. *Skew the risk-reward ratio in your favor.*   All businesses cannot have the same risk profile, and many good opportunities may have higher risks than desired. Accepting higher risks is not wrong as long as the potential reward is shifted *disproportionately* higher. When having only one business, the decision to make it high-risk–high-reward is much more serious than when such speculative activities make up a

small part of a large portfolio (e.g., divisions of a diversified corporation). There are fabled stories of frenetic risk takers who amass huge fortunes out of seemingly absurd ideas. If you've got such an idea (e.g., Federal Express, Apple computers, high-yield bonds, cabbage-patch dolls, or talking bears) and you don't mind risk, go for it. But be sure the potential rewards are there. For the rest of us mortals, stick to basics.

8. *Look for leverage.*   Leverage is a highly charged term. Some love it; some hate it. The fact is that properly used, leverage makes sense; it enables you to shift risk-reward ratios and adjust the odds. Not *beat* the odds, mind you, just move them a little in your favor. You can't expect anything more, and over the long run, it's not bad. Financial leverage makes all situations riskier, of course, but the key is the dramatically higher increased rates of return on net investment. Leverage, by the way, comes in many forms—marketing, manufacturing, and distribution as well as financial.

9. *Stress strength, eliminate weakness.*   Do not allow familiarity with this common prescription to undermine its usefulness. It is especially vital when planning financial strategy. Note the word "eliminate"—we did not say "improve." Eliminating weaknesses means ridding yourself, if possible, of the entire area—not just trying to make it better. "Making better" is bad business—time consuming at best, catastrophic at worst. Business is not a game for the mediocre; it is far better to be great at some things and lousy at others than to be middling at everything—so long as you *do* the great stuff and *kill* the lousy stuff. We, for example, determined that our Houston-based savings and loan was not competitive in the traditional branch banking business; thus we sold off many branches. On the other hand, since we understand financial markets, we've built a successful investment business.

10. *Test ideas continually, get a multitude of counsel.*   Decision makers are lonely people; on their desk the buck stops short. Requesting advice from others is not a sign of weakness and indecisiveness but of strength and confidence. Executives should test ideas in the cauldron of smart associates, stimulating frank, forceful, contrary opinions. (Encourage those whose advice is eventually not heeded.) "In the multitude of counselors," say the Proverbs, "there is safety."

11. *Get, keep, and reward the best people.*   Having highly competent personnel is always important; it is especially so for formulating and implementing financial strategy. The leverage, here, is enormous: The ratio of incremental compensation costs for top people can be a minuscule fraction of the incremental financial returns for the company. Performance is key. How to keep the best? Motivating them is a

complex process. It surely begins (but does not end) with competitive compensation; some say that companies should pay its top producers *more* over the long run than they could earn elsewhere—the best control mechanism for keeping good people is those famous "golden handcuffs." Strive for innovative compensation packages (see Chapter 57). But compensation, though necessary, is not sufficient; lasting motivation almost always requires more. The best people like doing their jobs; they are committed to personal creativity and company success. The greatest benefit is working with people you like on jobs you enjoy.

12. *Focus, intensity, and hard work.* Obvious but vital. Smarts are fine, but you can't succeed in building financial value without dedication, persistence, drive, and determination. And don't forget integrity and reputation; a good name means better business.

32

Radical Innovation through Creative Leadership

Frederick W. Gluck

Director, McKinsey & Company

There is an almost instinctive tendency of companies to protect past success rather than decouple themselves from fading technologies. My colleague Dick Foster calls this "the defender's dilemma" in his book, *Innovation: The Attacker's Advantage.* He describes how NCR clung to its past, refining electromechanical technology, while the computer revolution was on the verge of overwhelming it. In 1967, NCR's vice president for finance told the press, "The base of NCR's revenues comes from cash registers and accounting machines. Computers both support and *protect* NCR's traditional product lines." He believed in a company "sticking to its knitting." Three years later, NCR said in its annual report, "NCR has continued to stress the future evolution of its wide line of basic business machines." Time was passing, but NCR chose to ignore the marketplace. It was, in Peter Drucker's words, succumbing to the deadly temptation to feed yesterday and starve tomorrow. The following year a small company called DTS brought out the first electronic cash register. NCR continued to dabble in computers, trying to use them to break into newer lines of business while leaving their traditional cash registers tied to the electromechanical process. In the early 1970s, the market for cash registers went through turbulent times as customers, worried by both the recession and product uncertainty, delayed purchases. Electromechanical cash registers sunk from 90 percent of the market in 1972 to 10 percent in 1976. NCR was forced to write off $140 million in equipment barely 1 year after making it. The next year the company lost $60 million, the board of directors ousted its chairman, and 20,000 workers were let go to avoid bank ruptcy.

Much of this trauma could have been avoided had NCR realized early on that the technology that drove its business was fundamentally changing and that it could not *incrementalize* its way into the future. NCR is not alone. Few large, successful corporations can really renew themselves when major shifts in the environment occur. When the basis of industry competition changes or when there is radical technology advance, they appear to be incapable of rethinking—from ground zero—the way in which they do business. Consider, for example, General Motors, AT&T, U.S. Steel, International Harvester, Caterpillar Tractor, as well as a long list of European companies.

To come to grips with this problem we need to appreciate the difference between what, at one end of the spectrum, we might call "suggestion-box" innovation (product-line extensions, cost reductions, and the like)—an incremental type of innovation best exemplified by 3M—and, at the other end, "big-bang" innovation (radically new products and processes)—a discontinuous type of innovation represented by the Apples and Intels of the world. We also need to understand what kinds of contexts call for how big a bang.

Suggestion-Box Innovation

When the context of a business—competitors, suppliers, distribution networks, markets, and so on—is stable, the search for competitive advantage is essentially an information-processing exercise. There are usually much history and data and some well-understood rules. Innovation is still necessary, but it is generally incremental, based largely on analysis of operations. Change, here, is not very disruptive. Suggestion-box innovation requires highly specific information on a particular business function or market. The new insights are generally limited to small improvements, and required changes can be carried out in a reasonably contained way. This is innovation along the lines of

McDonald's Chicken McNuggets—market responsive thrusts that have an impact on one function, with only minor ripple effects in the organization.

Big-Bang Innovation

When an entire business concept is threatened by severe turmoil in its environment—technological breakthroughs, exchange rate gyrations, global competition, regulatory impact—a company faces a dramatically different problem. History may be nonexistent, data contradictory, and rules yet to be invented. These kinds of situations require major innovation and that means tampering with the mainspring. For example, going outside the core organization—against the corporate culture—to acquire technological know-how via acquisitions, licensing, or joint ventures. Big-bang innovations require information that goes beyond the province of any one function, and in many cases, beyond the ken of general managers. New communication and information-gathering networks need to be established. For example, one company has made significant investments in on-site personnel to stay close to its foreign competition; another has created an outside board of advisors to provide external perspective on issues facing individual business units. Both these moves are simply efforts to circumvent the stultifying effect of bureaucratic processes and quickly bring relevant new information to the attention of line management.

Change wrought by big-bang innovation is *very* disruptive: People and skills are made obsolete, facilities redundant, large investments worthless. Most important, the culture of the organization—"the way we do things around here"—may be torn apart. Big-bang innovation is the business equivalent of political revolution. And success requires institutional courage as well as managerial smarts. The real dilemma for captains of industry is at what point do they forsake suggestion-box innovation and go for big bang? And how do they do it without undermining all that is good in their organizations? These are basic questions for creative and innovative executives when major change looms large.

Innovation and Creativity

The subject of creativity and innovation and how it relates to organization design has been at the heart of McKinsey's research into excellent companies and strategic management. How do we make companies more innovative? How do we help them create their futures? Is there a difference between entrepreneurship and being innovative and creative? Should analysis or culture dominate? There are instances in which the rational model ought to control, others in which organizational dynamics need to take precedence, and yet others in which they ought to be considered in tandem.

Generally, when we speak of a creative person, we picture someone who is aggressive, imaginative, single-minded, knowledgeable, talented, and energetic. But at the end of the day, I believe there are only two attributes that really distinguish a creative person: *the possession of a tremendous store of raw information and the ability to combine, order, or connect this information in a novel and better way.* True, creative people are often energetic and single-minded. But I know many single-minded people who are incredibly pedestrian and many energetic people who are downright ordinary. However, I do not know any people who have a wealth of information about a subject and the ability to combine, order, and connect it in novel or better ways who are not creative. And what holds for individuals holds also for organizations.

The lifeblood of the creative individual—and the creative organization—is raw, messy, undigested information. How far could Watson and Crick have gone without an encyclopedic knowledge of what was already known about genetics? Or Edison without a profound grasp of the properties of electricity? And Steven Jobs did not just walk out to his garage one day and invent the Apple II without extensive awareness of microelectronics. Creative people are what I like to call "buffs." They have vast memories and aren't too quick to categorize their knowledge. They want to know everything about their subject. They get the information first and figure out what's important later. Efficiency in the information acquisition process is not high priority. They use all sources available. They accept redundancy. They have little patience with other people's digests of what's going on.

Innovative Organizations

Companies that create are effective learning systems; they maximize both their capacity to acquire information about customers, competitors, and technology and their ability to process that information and understand the implications of change. So the first requirement for a creative company is a method or approach to information acquisition that puts a great deal of raw information in the hands of many people—planners, market researchers, designers, and especially line managers—

those who make things happen. Second, there must be organizational arrangements and decision-making forums that provide managers opportunity for wide-ranging, unstructured, playful, contentious debate—a rambling process that forms patterns and meaning from raw, messy, undigested data, a process promoting different interpretations of facts to arrive at creative solutions. If information is the lifeblood of the creative organization, the decision-making process is its heart.

But understanding design requirements is only half the story. New ideas in the abstract—however good—are not innovation. Innovation means making something happen. The most brilliant concept is doomed without proper implementation. So the third requirement—what enables an organization to convert creativity into innovation—is the ability to execute. No mystery here. We're talking about functional skills and the kind of culture reported in *In Search of Excellence*.

A Taste for Raw Data

Most executives are isolated from raw information and spend little time in creative debate. They view change as problem not opportunity. This I understand. Demands on time are monumental. Senior managers seek summary information and embrace methodologies that give the appearance of precision and insight but are simply digested abstracts of the status quo. Most forecasts, for example, are only the past dressed up in trappings of the future. Experience curves, growth-share matrices, economic value calculations, and the like may be useful for raising danger signals but are useless in helping executives make big-bang innovation.

Too many CEOs have no time to view undigested information. Nor can they tolerate contradictory and ambiguous information. They reach out to few sources rather than many. They want clarity. It is this fear of being overwhelmed by raw information that forces companies to create multilevel organization structures and procedure-ridden management systems. This is a far cry from what Jack Welch does at General Electric. He is obsessed with getting more candor, more constructive conflict, more raw facts about strategic issues facing each business unit. And he is willing to invest the time to make this happen. Strategy reviews have gone from 15- to 20-minute "pass-throughs" to all-day affairs. The genius of an IBM top-management team or a Lee Iacocca is that, despite the threat of raw information, they have found ways to make the hard decisions based on personal convictions about its meaning. Iacocca writes in his autobiography: "Obviously you're responsible for gathering as many relevant facts as you personally can. But at some point you've got to take that leap of faith. First, because the right decision is wrong if it's made too late. Second, because in most cases there's no such thing as certainty."

Building Better Innovation

All this has sobering implications for corporations that seek to be creative and innovative. First of all, tools and techniques for digesting information and making decisions must be questioned, especially when things are changing fast. The need for summary is not at issue. But it must be done with great circumspection. And it must be done by people with broad understanding of the factors that challenge the corporation and who have the responsibility to meet that challenge.

Second, many of the traditions that have grown up around planning should be critiqued: planning as a process reserved for "planners," strategic planning flowing gracefully into operational planning without disruption, buttoned-up details about action steps, and so on. This is not to deny the importance of good operational planning or attention to detail but simply to suggest that the level of uncertainty surrounding major changes militates against programmed decision making and excessive specifics.

Finally, the notion of big-bang creativity, with its need for radical departures from conventional wisdom and the way we do things around here, calls into question whether existing executives can see such programs through. The sad fact is that current management at several levels may not respond well to, or be comfortable with, dramatic creativity and innovation. The CEO may be put off by the drain on time, the affront to experience, and the confusion that raw information generates. The planner may just like to "analyze"—digest information—rather than create forums for free-wheeling discussion. And the business unit manager may prefer to concentrate on incremental innovation and hence carefully mete out information on future threats and opportunities.

Corporations concerned with increasing creativity and innovation face three demands:

1. *Discovering better ways of sensing, communicating, and appreciating "early warning signals" of impending change.* Immerse top managers in the specifics of how customers view value received, how customer groups are segmenting, how competitive cost positions compare, and how all these things may change. Tony O'Reilly, CEO of Heinz, manages what he calls a "tough nickel-and-dime business": "I

meet with my twenty-five top line officers between once a month and every 6 weeks, and there is a pretty formal agenda . . .The art of concealment is difficult to practice at Heinz" *(Fortune)*.

2. *Creating better forums in which new big-bang ideas are easily expressed and new leadership can begin to emerge.* Forget the annual planning review for nurturing big-bang innovation. The meticulous choreography associated with such exercises and the limited agenda devoted to real interaction is counterproductive to radical innovation. Large blocks of top-management time must be set aside for grappling with competitive uncertainties. Decision making based on lower-level analysis is too static and cannot lead to bold initiatives. Senior executives should speculate about the way things might be rather than simply listening to the way they are (or were). New voices must be heard throughout the organization. At Xerox, for example, an "innovation board" brings a group of marketing, production, and R&D executives together to evaluate and provide early funding for corporate ventures. IBM runs a 3-week innovation program that provides substantial content on creativity and change and, even more important, provides opportunity for fifty diverse managers to become better acquainted and share ideas. Control Data, GTE, Pepsico all have programs in managing innovation that involve cross sections of the company working jointly on innovation-related problems.

3. *Choosing top executives who view change as opportunity not problem.* Michael Tushman and David Nadler describe how executive leadership behavior can help (or hinder) innovation:

> Managing innovation requires visionary executives who provide clear direction for their organizations and infuse that direction with energy and value . . . . such executives frequently display three types of behavior: First, they work actively on *envisioning* or articulating a credible yet exciting vision of the future. Second, they personally work on *energizing* the organization by demonstrating their own excitement, optimism, and enthusiasm. Third, they put effort into *enabling* required behaviors by providing resources, rewarding desired behaviors, building supportive organizational structures and processes, and by building an effective senior team.

Corporations in search of innovation must ensure that a good sprinkling of top managers are champions of change and that they build executive teams with appropriate technical, social, and conceptual skills to take on diverse tasks.

The image of innovation as the shatterer of serene status quo is inappropriate—even dangerous. One would be hard pressed to find anything resembling serene status quo in today's tumultuous sweep of technological and social change. Change and uncertainty are the new nature of things. History is quirky, full of random events; there is no vector of progress that can be discerned. This should not be depressing or intimidating. We must seek radical, big-bang innovation. We must exploit the uncertainty that will be with us always.

Bibliography

Drucker, Peter F: *Innovation and Entrepreneurship*, Harper & Row, New York, 1985.

Foster, Richard: *Innovation: The Attacker's Advantage*, Summit Books, New York, 1985.

Iacocca, Lee: *Iacocca: An Autobiography*, Bantam Books, New York, 1984.

Louis, Arthur: "America's New Economy: How to Manage It," *Fortune*, June 23, 1986.

Peters, T. J. and R. H. Waterman: *In Search of Excellence: Lessons from America's Best-Run Companies*, Harper & Row, New York, 1982.

Tushman, Michael and David Nadler: "Organizing for Innovation," *California Management Review*, Spring 1986.

33

Innovative Thinking in Strategic Management

Robert Boynton Lamb

Editor in Chief, Journal of Business Strategy

Creative managers are strategic thinkers. They implement original organizational ideas to achieve clear organizational goals. What are the latest innovations in strategic management? Where are they leading practitioners in corporate planning, strategy consulting firms, and business schools? The answers may help determine directions of companies and industries. We explore three emerging aspects of strategic management: (1) *Strategic failure analysis* (problems in practice and theory), (2) *strategic arenas* (strategy maps of industries revealing gaps and niches), and (3) *strategic systems practices* (dynamic approaches to strategic forecasting).

Strategic Failure Analysis

Causes of Strategic Failure at the Company Level

"Failure in process" is a frequent framework for analyzing strategic failures. All too often the design, planning, and implementation of a strategic plan squanders management time and wastes valuable resources. Four reasons follow:

Plan misconceived. The basic strategic plan itself was faulty. In some cases the plan fails because it was simply inoperable. In other cases, it may have been inappropriate for the specific industry or company. Failures frequently can be attributed to a mismatch between the corporate plan and the underlying corporate culture.

Cookie-cutter approach. A rigid strategic management system (from either a consulting company or corporate management) imposes its generic "cookie-cutter strategic model" upon all businesses or all divisions within a company. Applying some supposedly all-purpose strategy to a range of companies with varying cultures, product mixes, and competitive markets is doomed to failure.

No follow-up. Another problem has been the unhealthy split between strategy design and its implementation, evaluation, and control. Each phase has become compartmentalized. In part this split has been caused by "hit and run" strategy consultants who prepare a plan and do not stay around to see it integrated into practice. In the final analysis, however, management must make any plan its own, structuring and scheduling action and control. Sometimes even minimal effort is not made. Failures often occur because pristine plans sit on dusty shelves or are only partially implemented when second thoughts set in.

Financial deterioration. The process of strategic failure from a financial standpoint has been examined by using Edward Altman's Z score bankruptcy indicator. From this perspective strategy failure emerges as purely the mismanagement of financial resources, and financial considerations take precedence over all other aspects of strategy. If strategy failure equals financial failure, financial turnaround equals strategic turnaround. Altman, Price Waterhouse, and others, have affected turnarounds by simply reversing the direction of the financial components of the Z score, driving the troubled companies back into legal and financial health. Such success raises the possibility that strategic management, when stripped to its essential, is no more than disguised financial strategy.

Macroeconomic Causes of Strategic Failure

The second major area of strategic failure is the inadequacy of most management systems to combat broad-scale macroeconomic shifts. Regardless of corporate techniques adopted, these external pressures dictate the vast majority of company failure. Rates of corporate bankruptcy correlate with shifts in monetary policy, fiscal policy, OPEC policy, or radical political changes (such as national expropriation, tariff barriers, subsidies, grant or incentive programs, and alterations in tax structures).

When companies with different strategies in different industries fail as a result of economic changes, an analysis may indicate: (1) the range of situations in which strategy is ineffective, (2) the areas in which strategy can most make a difference, and (3) the ways in which strategy must cope with environmental shocks. Proponents of the domino theory contend that the critical factor in bankruptcies is the effect of one failing industry upon another, i.e., suppliers' failures having an impact on finished goods or finished goods' failures having an impact on suppliers. This has led to various theories—interdependency, bottleneck, critical path, wave, and ripple effects.

One response has been the growth of *contingency planning*. In rapidly changing markets, with sudden dislocations in cost, supply, and demand, strategies designed to meet only one set of factors can quickly become inoperable. Such situations question the validity of long-range planning, suggesting instead contingency planning that continually shifts strategy focus or simply fire-fights crises. The issue is a broad one: the degree to which a corporation's strategy is purely reactive to external forces versus the degree to which it can shape its own destiny. Contingency planning must obtain advance warning of environmental threats using methods such as strategic intelligence, future scans, multiple scenario forecasting, trend analysis, and discontinuity studies.

Conceptual Analyses of Strategic Management Failures

The third type attacks the essence of strategic management. Is it a scientific method, a logical process of development and experiment? Critics say, No; they argue that strategy lacks replicability, and therefore it is impossible to test scientifically. Others view strategy as a logical process that cannot be disproved by whether it worked out in practice— i.e., failure is simply an internal inconsistency. Still others see strategy as an entire process and maintain that failure may arise from inconsistent ideas, from inexact implementation, control, and monitoring, as well as from external factors.

What does it mean to win or lose strategically? I believe we need to develop a new goal for strategy because traditional short-term ratios and rates of return have failed to be viable over the long term. (Studies of conflicting goals show that short-term financial goals can undermine long-term strategic goals.) Strategic targets must be redefined. General Electric and McKinsey's effort is to make "true economic value" the goal, instead of a narrow focus on financial returns, margins, or other standard ratios. My own work has integrated different strategy evaluation techniques from a variety of disciplines, including biology and war games as well as business. Selim Basoul of American Hospital Supply and I have sought to assess total value added by each strategic business unit, product, company as a whole and by various sectors of an industry as compared with similar units.

Strategic Arenas

The basic premise of "strategic arenas" is the recognition that industries are blurring together worldwide. The compartmentalization and isolation of specific product, geographic, and national markets is being undermined by technology advance and global competition. Companies are beginning to see themselves as part of larger competitive fields in which several industries interact. Product-market competitions are seen not as isolated battles for market niches but as struggles for footholds in areas such as an "island in an archipelago" or a "peninsula of a continent." Strategic arenas is the study of how industries are fitting together dynamically, somewhat like the geographic theory of shifting continental plates that move together or drift apart. The world, seen as isolated national markets, is fast shrinking.

The strategic arena is a specific tool for enabling a potential entrant to a market to spot trends and gaps. These maps help survey and assess the strength and direction of each player's movement in the new arenas and subarenas in which specific product market competitions are fought. Product markets, formerly rigid, are now dynamic entities shifting in their various relationships. Note that: (1) Arenas are massive combinations of many industries. (2) Arena maps are drawn by positioning each subarena, each present industry, each current competitor.

Maps can be global or national. (3) Gaps between industries are the spawning grounds for new industries to emerge. Assess each potential gap adjacent to current businesses. Is synergy possible? Which competitors or potential entrants are threats? (4) Shifts occur in the direction or thrust, shown by arrows, of each subarena or each industry into each gap. Plot on the map new industries in different colors to determine direction of subarena growth. (6) Computers can aid in plotting maps and finding gaps—the potential niches for new industries and markets.

Management must determine what is necessary in terms of resources, personnel, investment, manufacturing capacity, and strategic initiative in order to make it among world-class competitors. Jack Welch, General Electric's CEO, requires that GE only stay in those businesses that can remain (or become) number one or two worldwide.

Performance versus Positioning

Michael Porter's competitor analysis calls for an international perspective and full awareness of potential entrants to your industry, potential substitutes for your product, and the ability of suppliers and buyers to enter your product markets from either end of your production, sales, or distribution channels. Porter stresses global competitors versus national competitors and methods of strategic competition, urging companies to be alert to the entrance of totally new players. Porter, however, limits his framework with what he calls "industry structure." The pace of technological change, of industry shifts and blurring that William Rothschild's arena theory points out, makes Porter's sharp focus on industry structure and strategic groups too static a portrait of corporate strategy.

In contrast, several strategy analysts urge concentration on performance, not on positioning alone. When most companies and consultants plan strategy, all they usually mean is *position*. But in order to truly carry out strategic management—especially among global competitors—it is vital to shift stress to the *performance* aspects of growth. Strategic *positioning* analysis argues that there are only a few businesses that are good: most are bad. Strategic *performance* analysis, however, shows that *any* business can be good or bad depending upon the company's unique ability to perform better than its rivals. Bad industries can be very bad for the worst performers but very good for the best performers. Moreover, the best performers in that bad business will frequently perform better than a portfolio of blue chip companies, better than the average return of the S&P 500—not simply better than other companies in that industry. Hence, when company strategists focus exclusively on determining good or bad businesses by examining the median industry returns and thereby position their company as one of these so-called *good* businesses only to find out they cannot achieve that median average, they are learning the hard way that positioning criteria alone do not make successful strategy. Only by combining performance criteria with company position and portfolio can one gain a true picture of strategic strengths and weaknesses.

This refocusing on performance is important since the traditional portfolio reshuffling that many corporations did in order to reposition themselves—e.g., heeding the Boston Consulting Group (BCG) matrix of so-called "star, cow, dog, question mark"—has turned out to be an abysmal failure. Often, *none* of the businesses that these companies acquired or entered achieved the criteria for performance success. In fact these portfolio shifts, or changes in positioning, were often counterproductive because managers chose to enter businesses they did not understand, did not know how to run, and could not evaluate. Positioning alone is nearly worthless as strategy. In-depth competitor analysis for global arena planning requires in-depth *performance analysis* of your own firm and your global, national, and regional competitors—not just portfolio analysis of positions.

Unfortunately, most companies and consultants do not know how to do in-depth competitor analysis. Richard Rumelt builds strategic performance analysis into his competitor studies. Instead of simply testing positioning rules of thumb from either BCG, McKinsey, PIMS, or other positioning experts, Rumelt stresses comparative corporate performance. There are a range of methods for doing in-depth competitor analysis. All require a great deal of data and frequent updating of details. There are few short cuts (one example: a cost curve comparison of competitive margins to assess maneuvering room).

Competitor Analysis in Changing Arenas

In-depth competitor analysis, if done correctly, is hard work, requiring serious commitment of resources as well as top personnel time. Strategic innovations range from new types of market research on competitors' products to not-quite-illegal spying. The basic aim in competitor analysis must be clear and very specific in order to obtain relevant strategic intelligence. It is like cracking codes in warfare. Several new strategic intelligence techniques have in fact been developed out of military espionage methods. The reason? Companies need immediate, current, precise information about key decisions, timing, resource capabilities, problems, and personnel. This is virtually identical to the aims of military spying. The borderline between legal and criminal industrial spying on competitors is fuzzy—so be careful. Methods include hiring defectors, paying to destroy competitors' test markets, and camouflaging your behavior.

The second type of in-depth competitor analysis is the more long-range, general scanning of upcoming strategically important events in primary and related industries. The objective is to fill in the arena maps with strengths and weaknesses of competitors and calculate which firms are likely to move into targeted gaps between subarenas, industries, or product markets.

A significant Japanese practice has been the gathering of strategic intelligence on a continual basis. What they have done, for example, is hire out their employees to American companies and send them to American business schools so that they can learn firsthand about American management techniques, specific processes, strategic thinking, technological developments, product design, production capacity, etc. Virtually no American companies send their managers to learn in Japanese universities or to work in Japanese companies. In addition, the Japanese absorb all the latest information concerning their foreign competitors. They buy the products and dissect and analyze them from component, cost, marketing, and engineering standpoints. They do this constantly, not just "when necessary," and have done it for decades. Competitor analysis is deeply ingrained in them. Japanese companies habitually delve through all overseas trade journals in each industry in which they have competitive products. Their trade missions in New York constantly research competitors' costs, prices, suppliers, markets, new products, new technologies, and employees who are leaving. Their trade representatives in Washington go through the latest filings with the Securities and Exchange Commission, the Patent Office, and other government records to monitor how each competitor is doing. Japanese companies take foreign competitors far more seriously than do most U.S. companies. (Incidents of illegal Japanese industrial spying and payments for competitors' secrets can be seen as an overaggressive part of an extensive program of strategic intelligence gathering—most of which has been straightforward and legal.)

Strategic Systems Practices

"Strategic systems practices" may be classified in a number of ways: "generic systems" (the simplest), "computer-aided strategic decision support systems," "interactive contingency theories," "multiindustry strategic planning data coordinators," "strategic risk theories," "strategic technology theories," "strategic leadership theories versus followership theories," "strategic resource dependency theories," "strategic groups theories," and many others.

Generic strategic systems theories are revised versions of BCG's classic portfolio theory. Its growth-share matrix is a systematic approach to cash flow distribution or decision making on return on investment capital allocation. A similar but more complex portfolio theory and matrix grew out of a related system of market assessment and industry attractiveness employed by GE and McKinsey. A second classic generic strategy system theory would be updated versions of the "product life cycle theories" that suggest that every product and industry has its own progressive periods, each of which calls for specific strategies. A third and closely related generic system theory involves the experience curve or cost behavior of various products and industries over time; it suggests that maximization of experience curve effects for each product and industry will dictate which companies will dominate and earn steadily greater returns in relation to scale and quantity produced.

The new strategic systems theories do not totally undermine classic systems but place them in a larger context, integrating them into a more holistic systems theory. Computer-aided decision support systems, for example, extend the reach of the strategist via computer simulations. Decision support systems have become critical for strategy makers to organize long series of choices, to help discriminate between various options and paths, and to evaluate results of various alternative strategies.

A second example of new strategic systems theories are the "interactive contingency theories." Such computer models of company strategy afford easy numerical manipulation and quick change of components, resources, and alternative scenarios. There are, however, a number of drawbacks to such computer dependence. The first is that constant information gathering, filing, and storage is burdensome and frustrating. These complex and time consuming systems are thought counterproductive by many top-level managers. The second pitfall is that computers are useful only if the numbers plugged in—the raw data— are accurate. Many companies have found their projections and strategies unrealistic simply because the initial information was off. Some data are wrong because they represent estimates and some because they are not a correct count of current production or costs. All figures are subject to change and modification, and the range of error can frequently make the difference between a marginally successful strategy and an outright failure. Third, no strategy operates in a vacuum, and therefore, even if company figures are entirely accurate, its competitors may behave in ways not anticipated, or data on their production capacity, cost structure, experience curve effects, technological break-throughs, marketing clout, reserve debt capacity, and/or government connections may be faulty—any one of which can cause your own strategy to be noncompetitive. Mismeasurement is a major roadblock to advances in strategic management. No packaged strategic planning computer program can overcome data inaccuracies, especially when coupled with the broader problem of conflicting goals. In short, garbage in, garbage out.

Another problem with overreliance on packaged programs is that well-calculated numbers sometimes trick planners into forgetting the underlying assumptions. The business realities on which the strategy is based can be lost in the perfusion of data, financial projections, alternative scenarios, and contingency plans that spew out of the computer.

Inadequacies of Current Strategic Theories

My own method of "computerized strategic planning" highlights the economic value of each strategic business unit as it adds to, subtracts from, or otherwise affects corporate strategy. Instead of simply plotting returns on investment, assets, or equity, I believe that what really matters is the economic value added by each product, strategic business unit, company, and industry. Why this approach? Although many companies were increasing sales and profits on paper, they were in fact not getting anywhere. They were, in terms of real dollars, market share, and growth, standing still or falling behind—dying as businesses. They were using current accounting data to show progress, not realizing that their companies or specific divisions or products were decaying. The key is how much value added was provided. This benchmark can assess the best allocations of capital, personnel, and other resources and the proper directions of future growth. The approach addresses drawbacks in analysis of profits, margin, or rates of return and copes with defects in multiindustry strategic planning data (PIMS) in market-share strategies, nonsynergistic merger and acquisitions, and divestiture theories. It also confronts inadequacies of portfolio strategies that fail to perceive strong life in old products, serious risks in so-called star businesses, and substantial hidden costs in portfolio shifts—all undermining strategic value. These inadequacies are rarely anticipated.

Strategic innovations have emerged from these reassessments. First, there have been numerous critiques of PIMS and the panoply of prescriptive strategies that emerged from these extensive studies. The criticism has centered on the fact that strategic planning data, homogenized from a variety of totally different companies, industries, and competitive conditions, may be counterproductive when taken as gospel by any particular company facing specific competitive threats and opportunities. Second, overreliance on the experience curve and market-share growth has led to different problems. In many industries the experience curve effect is either minimal or nonexistent. It is by no means universal, as some proponents have contended. The market-share growth madness that has consumed many top managements has been shown to be poor strategy, often detrimental to corporate goals. Many companies have paid far too much to increase market share—for example, those involved in the beer wars and those in the auto and insurance industries. Market-share wars seldom benefit winners, losers, or the industry as a whole.

Narrow Strategic Systems Analysis

Some strategic systems analysts look only at specific, limited segments— for example, mergers and acquisitions, mid-sized firms, new ventures. There has been industry-specific strategic systems analysis in financial services, commodities, and retailing among others.

Mergers and Acquisitions (M&A).   M&A vogues have led strategic analysts to evaluate the price paid for acquisitions, whether realistic or unrealistic, in the effort to increase market share. Their fundamental conclusion has been that nonsynergistic M&A does not make sense. When a company acquires or merges with another company whose business it does not know, whose suppliers, customers, production methods, technological pace, or resource requirements it does not understand, it is almost inevitable that little real growth will occur. More likely 2 + 2 will equal 3 because there will be an attenuation of existing growth levels as novice management tries to learn the new business. When a management merges or acquires horizontally or vertically in a business that it already knows, there is usually a greater degree of productive growth and rational decision making, although here too the dual bureaucracies, conflicting cultures, competing requirements, and the many clashes can also undermine profitable expansion. Divestiture theories have focused upon strategic exit decisions and reasons for business sales. These studies, such as those by Kathryn Harrigan, cover the best ways to sell or manage a failing business, to forecast the chances of turnaround, or to assess the need for divestiture.

Firm Size.   Robert Kuhn's investigations into mid-sized firms and their strategic behavior patterns and options, distinct from those of either large enterprises or small ventures, suggest that company size and rate of growth or shrinkage are new avenues for analysis of strategic dynamics. Strategies for high- and low-market-share companies, as well as for small- and large-sized firms, all focus on particular and perhaps unique circumstances.

Service Industries.   The transition from manufacturing to service industries suggests profound sectoral shift. Production-run economies of scale will likely be reduced drastically. (What will happen to the experience curve?) A hot topic is the strategic management of service industries: banks, investment houses, accounting and law firms, hospitals and health care facilities, universities, and all forms of government service, including fire, police, post office, sanitation departments, and social welfare. Not-for-profit and high-technology service industries have been two conspicuous areas in which strategic management has lagged behind, but great strides are now being made.

New Ventures.   The study of venture capital firms and the creation of venture capital enclaves in giant corporations are also areas of strategic innovation. There is, however, a split between optimists and pessimists here. The former believe that corporate venturing is the wave of the future and all-sized firms must experiment and develop fledgling programs regardless of strategy or direction. The latter note acute difficulties encountered by old-line firms trying to work venture organizations into traditional structures. Is the problem in human resources? Is it in disparate rewards, incentives, and promotion paths? Or in capital allocation and strategic priorities? Wherever the problems, the fact remains that (1) corporate culture conflicts are likely to arise between new and old organizations; (2) the small size of most new ventures dictates that even if they are successful, they tend to be ignored and unappreciated inside a huge corporation; and (3) their high failure rate, combined with economic cyclicality, generates a boom-and-bust cycle, making long-term strategic management difficult or impossible. From the human resources standpoint, there are two nearly opposite issues here: How to instill innovative incentives and creative thinking into established firms and how to instill controls and structure into rapidly evolving start-up ventures.

Acceleration in the rate of technological, managerial, and resource change spotlights obsolescence and multiple contingency theories. The strategic questions that confront us are: (1) Can we adapt to this quickened pace of change? (2) What happens to those companies, industries, or individuals who cannot cope? (3) Are there domino effects so that one set of problems triggers others? We may now be entering an era of linked-contingency strategies or multiscenario interactions. Seat-of-the-pants management—guesswork—has become obsolete.

Bibliography

Harrigan, Kathryn: "A framework for Looking at Vertical Integration," *Journal of Business Strategy*, vol. 3, no. 3, 1983.

Kuhn, Robert Lawrence: *To Flourish Among Giants: Creative Management for Mid-Sized Firms*, John Wiley, New York, 1985.

Lamb, Robert: *Competitive Strategic Management*, Prentice-Hall, Englewood Cliffs, NJ, 1984.

Macmillian, Ian: "Competitive Strategies for Not for Profit Agencies," in Robert Lamb (ed.), *Advances in Strategic Management.*, JAI Press, vol. 1, 1983.

Porter, Michael: *Competitive Analysis*, The Free Press, New York, 1985.

Rothschild, William: "Surprises and the Competitive Advantages," *Journal of Business Strategy*, vol. 4, no. 3, winter 1984.

Rumelt, Richard: "Toward a Strategic Theory of the Firm," in Robert Lamb (ed.), *Competitive Strategic Management*.

34

Creative Management for Large-Sized Firms: Avoid Strategy Failure

William Ebeling

*Senior Partner, Braxton Associates/Touche
Ross & Company*

Quick fix business "wisdom" is often dressed up in strategy. Every element of business, it seems, is now prefaced or suffixed with strategy. The concept has become overused, abused, and confused. We are in danger of killing it once and for all. Yet sound strategy is vital, especially in today's competitive environment. The key to sound strategy? Avoid strategy failure!

There are two major types of strategy failures: "process failures" and "logic failures." Process failures are caused by problems with the development and implementation of strategy. Logic failures result from faulty thinking regarding the competitive position of a business or the options for improvement.

Process Failures

The Quick Success Syndrome

Many managers are overambitious and impatient. Beset by internal pressures from superiors and external expectations of stockholders, executives set unrealistic time schedules for jumping impossibly high hurdles. Many only accept projects that promise huge after-tax returns and "hockey-stick" business plans that promise ever-widening margins. Yet few large companies consistently earn a 20 percent after tax return on investment. In short, managers are encouraged to lie about what can be reasonably expected by a business or a project. We blame this behavior on Wall Street or excuse it by claiming that by stretching to attain such goals we do better than by setting more limited goals. However, unrealistic goals often encourage bad behavior. Inappropriately raising prices or forgoing R&D and marketing to achieve short-term financial objectives will undermine long-term business success.

The Strategy, Plans, and Budgets Confusion

A strategy is a vision of where the business is headed and how it will achieve competitive success. Plans are statements of 3- to 5-year objectives and include programs in each functional area needed to attain those objectives. Budgets are typically 1-year projections of sales and expenditures by line item. Needless to say, budgets are rarely realistic; seldom do they relate to plans, much less to strategy. A workable budget process must start with sound strategy. Strategy should not be developed casually every year, but carefully every 2 to 3 years. The plan should be *updated* every year and the annual budget tied to it. Uncertainty must be taken into account so that a company can be ready to respond to possible environmental and competitive changes.

Often, the roles in the budget process are reversed. A senior executive will decide what bottom line he or she wants from a business unit, forcing the unit manager to back into his or her numbers. This inverted "budget" process is at best a waste of energy and at worst a cause of poor performance.

The Right People Problem

Planners can plan and accountants can budget, but line managers must develop strategy. Internal staffs can assist, but all line executives from the CEO to the heads of marketing, sales, manufacturing, and R&D

must develop the strategy together. Often, however, line managers comment, "I'm too busy to plan" or "Let's stop all this planning stuff and get back to basics." This skepticism has been caused by confusing strategy with planning and budgeting and by reducing the strategy process to filling out a series of generally useless forms. Strategy must be separate from planning and budgeting, and line managers must periodically think deeply about their businesses. They should be assisted by strategists, whether internal or external, who bring creative ideas, concepts, and objectivity to the process. Distinguish between strategists and planners. Planners can help develop functional plans to integrate with strategy once it is developed; but only strategists can set future directions.

Analysis without Insight

Neither superb process nor super analysis will automatically produce good strategy. Reams of nicely filled-out planning forms will rarely produce anything but trite middle-of-the-road, cliche-ridden statements. Strategic analysis should determine which product-market segments are worthy of pursuit and how a company can uniquely configure itself to serve them well. All else is waste. Mission statements and objectives, industry opportunity and threat analyses, strength and weakness assessments are all useless unless they lend insight.

However, not all managers are equally capable of developing insights. Some may be great at implementation and motivating people but not at creating key insights. (The opposite can also be true: Those who can produce insights may be lousy managers.) At least one and maybe two idea generators are needed on the strategy development team. It may be necessary to import them from other divisions or outside the company. The notion that strategists have to know the business well to produce useful insight about it is not true. Smarts produce insight. Experience will help test the practicality of insights. Up front, however, experience may actually hinder developing counterintuitive, creative approaches. Therefore, involving at least one outside person is usually a good idea. (But beware of industry experts. They have inherent conflict problems in dealing with many companies in the same industry.)

The Internal Versus External View Problem

You have undoubtedly heard the joke about Joe, who lost his watch one night and was searching for it under a street light. When asked by a friend, "Where, exactly, did you lose it?" Joe replied, "Over there in the bushes." Exasperated, the friend asked, "If you lost it over there in the bushes, why are you looking for it here under the street light?" Joe replied, equally exasperated, "Because this is where the light is! " Like Joe, we often look where there is light but no answers. For example, we spend many dollars crunching internal numbers. While direct labor and materials are known in minute detail, little is known about customer needs and even less about competitor strategies. The procurement and analysis of external data are difficult but essential, especially for marketing and R&D. It requires getting people out of their offices and into the field.

The Strategy Versus Implementation Debate

Some say that good execution produces successful business, irrespective of strategy. Others say strategy drives all. Both, of course, are critical. Some companies, however, can limp along forever with acceptable returns (usually under a price umbrella) through decent implementation but lousy strategy. Non-IBM mainframe manufacturers are one such example. Other companies, such as DEC in its early days, perform well with good strategies but relatively poor implementation. The issue is tricky. If you already have an excellent strategy that will stand up over time, then implementation is the only issue left. If strategy needs to change, a well-oiled implementation machine may actually be a block. For example, if a firm's strength is in running a distribution business utilizing central warehouses but it must shift to decentralized warehouses, its strong implementation strength could thwart the new strategy as central-oriented managers "hang on."

Logic Failures

Incorrect and Misapplied Portfolio Theory

The biggest flaw in making resource allocation or even survival decisions based on business unit grid positions on simplistic matrices (such as the growth-share matrix developed by The Boston Consulting Group) is that the units may not be truly independent. If, for example, all of the businesses share some major underlying value-added element, such as common electronic components or a sales force, the grid position of each business unit is not likely to capture the *inherent* competitive position of that unit. The collective position of the whole group or corporation in these underlying value-added elements, or "activities" aswe call them, is the most important factor in estimating competitive position. A good example of a strong activity position is Honda. Honda's strength is in engines. They build engines for products ranging from motorcycles and cars to lawn mowers and snow blowers. Honda became strong in a key activity, engines, that allowed them to enter the lawn mower market in the United States—even though they hardly have lawns in Japan. They did not define their business as "motorcycles" or "cars," but rather as "engines." *This activity concept forces proper business definitions.* It also helps to explain how Procter & Gamble can enter low-growth product-market segments, like toothpaste and shampoo, gain share, and ultimately become number one against apparently entrenched competitors, how Black & Decker succeeded in power tools where General Electric failed (B&D ultimately bought out GE Housewares); and how the Japanese may yet prove tough in computers and telecommunications.

However, if corporate business units are relatively independent (don't share underlying value-added elements), the growth-share matrix is not a bad starting point for analyzing business units' strategic positions in a portfolio. But people forget the essence of the growth-share matrix. "Relative market share" (RMS) is a surrogate for the position on the experience curve of the business unit versus its competitors. High RMS means lots of experience and hence (it is hoped) lower costs, higher quality, or more innovative product features. All should translate into higher margins. If a business unit with high RMS does not have high margins, blame the management, not the concept.

Finally, there is confusion about the role of "cash cows." No competent practitioner of the decade-old art of portfolio theory ever said to kill the cow; they only said to milk it. Somehow, people got milking confused with killing. Cash cows should be able to throw off cash, but they also require continued cost-reduction capital investment and R&D spent on product featurization and on finding substitutes (see self-cannibalization below). What they often can use less of are highly paid salespeople—order-takers and bloated customer support groups (by now customers know how to use the product). Put these experienced people in new divisions and train new salespeople in the old products. Cash cows, remember, are to be milked, not killed.

Confusion between Business Unit and Corporate Views

Sometimes the act of representing whole business units as "bubbles" on grids and then inferring general strategies for these units can be devastating. The view hides the fact that even cash-cow divisions may contain high-growth, cash-hungry opportunities within them. Thus classifying whole divisions as "cows" can foreclose important options. Similarly, prescribing the same growth and return goals for every business unit is even more dangerous.

Market-Driven versus Technology-Driven Malaise (or What Business Am I Really In?)

If most of a firm's value added is in marketing, sales, and distribution (like Frito Lay), being "market-driven" is obvious. Market-driven means being "close to your customer." When most of your value added is in manufacturing, design, and engineering, being "technology-driven" is obvious. Technology-driven means using R&D and manufacturing functions as a major source of business leverage. (Industrial R&D has been defined as "patient money being spent by impatient people.") However, if your value is split equally between marketing, sales, and distribution on the one hand and R&D, engineering, and manufacturing on the other, you had better do both well. There is no law against doing both well. IBM and Procter & Gamble excel in both marketing and technology, as do Kodak and Polaroid.

However, there is an important, if subtle, difference between IBM and P&G, and Kodak and Polaroid. Even if a company does both well, it is either marketing or technology *focused*. Being focused is different from being driven. Driven means the function dominates success (marketing at Frito Lay); focus means the company orients itself in one direction or the other (IBM focuses on the information market while Kodak focuses on chemical imaging or thin film coating). IBM focuses on the market and lets the technologies pass by. If you are a magnetic core engineer, your future at IBM is not great. If computers ultimately go optical, you can bet IBM will make them. Kodak, however, focuses on the technology and lets the markets pass by. As body imaging moves from using x-ray film to things like NMR, Kodak would naturally slough that market off and find new ones for chemical imaging. In the past it was believed that whether a company was market or technology focused was not important as long as its strategy was consistent with its focus. Now the issue seems more complex. For example, chemical imaging makes up a large part of Kodak's portfolio and is threatened by electronic imaging. Even though Kodak is strong in marketing, they may have been too focused on chemical imaging and their technology has become obsolete. Kodak may have to compete in electronic imaging with companies like Matsushita and Sony who have strong activity positions in consumer electronics. To survive in electronic imaging, Kodak may have to play broadly in the highly competitive consumer electronics market. For Polaroid, focusing primarily on *instant* chemical imaging technology is even more problematic. Polaroid was formed by Edwin Land and focused on his technology. For years this focus was successful, but now Polaroid is suffering from "technology myopia," akin to Levitt's "marketing myopia" two decades ago. Unless there are numerous, large opportunities for Polaroid's technology elsewhere, its future may be dim.

Market focus is not a panacea either. Companies like Mercury and Evinrude that have focused on the marine engine market, when much value added is in the engine, are vulnerable to Honda with its broader engine technology focus. However, in businesses in which at least half the value added is in marketing, sales, and distribution, market focus is probably better than technology focus. Technology focus may only be appropriate in products with high value added in manufacturing and with low threat of technological substitution.

The Niches as Salvation Syndrome

Niches are close to ruts and ruts are close to graves. On one side, it is true that there are many companies not doing well slugging it out head to head with formidable competitors. However, there are also many companies that say they are in niches that are not doing well either because their niches are not really niches. Hasty devotees would define a niche as a subsegment of a market that has different customer needs (that they can fill) than the major segments of that market being served by larger competitors. But to be a "true" niche, the minor segment not only must have different customer needs but must also have a different "activity configuration" to serve those needs. The point is to create a protective barrier, keeping out the competitor that dominates the major segment. Portable computers are probably not a niche. The underlying value added activities to develop portable computers do not appear to be significantly different from those of the nonportable version. Hence, portability is not a niche. What about Compaq? Their success, I contend, rests not with portability, but with the fact that they quickly became the best second source of high-quality IBM-compatible machines at lower prices.

Customer Needs versus Wants Confusion

As the lady-of-the-night said in a Bob Dylan tune, "Your debutante knows what you want, but I know what you need." Understanding customer needs is crucial to success; however, there are some subtleties. First, mothers-in-law and design engineers do not constitute a sufficient sample of "customers" upon which to base new product development. Also, asking customers what they want (every feature and lower prices) is not very helpful—determining what they need (what they are willing to pay for) is far more important. It is amazing how much expensive product R&D is done without any adequate market research. However, market research itself is often flawed. For example, simple factor ranking schemes fail to distinguish the degree of importance of each factor or of each variable within the factor. In addition, discussions with potential customers often fail to determine the boundaries of "what's needed" and to share "what's possible" ideas. Nonetheless, competent market research is crucial.

Misunderstanding Relative versus Absolute Growth Phenomenon

High-growth markets are great since growth and profitability correlate through demand-supply relationships, overhead spreading, and investments in new plant and equipment. However, it's obvious that a large number of businesses must fall into markets growing at or below the GNP. Equally as important as absolute growth, therefore, is relative growth—a company's growth compared to competitors or a technology's growth relative to substitute technologies. If a firm grows at 5 percent in a market growing at 2 percent, it is increasing share and bettering its competitive position. Similarly, if a competitive technology is growing at 20 percent while another is flat, like transistors over vacuum tubes in the early days, the end may be in sight. One had better enter the new technology or have a well-defined exit strategy developed. If a company develops a new product using technology that can cannibalize its current products, they should exploit it as quickly and aggressively as possible. I'm often asked, usually by financial types, how fast a company should cannibalize a current product, especially considering the sunk investment. The notion is to gracefully recover the investment in the old before moving to the new. While this might work for IBM, mere mortals risk losing their position to a competitor exploiting the new technology. One reason people often do not choose gain-share or self-cannibalization strategies is that they compare these aggressive alternatives to a "status quo" forecast. The status quo usually looks better, at least short to mid term. The fallacy, of course, is that the status quo does not happen; competitors will take share with lower prices or newer products. A proper comparison is to match the aggressive alternative with another option showing share *loss* through inaction. Using this one planning device could help revive American competitiveness.

Global versus Domestic Competition Confusion

Most senior managers developed their business experience over a period when only a small percentage of American GNP was exported or imported. They did not have to deal with international markets or foreign competition. Japanese and European businesspeople, in contrast, have had to import and export all along, primarily to access raw materials and to develop markets large enough to recover R&D and capital investments. U.S. business has three major problems dealing with global challenges: (1) Domestic experiences are not adequate models for dealing with worldwide competition, (2) simple duplication of U.S. operations in foreign countries is not a sound way to expand internationally, and (3) accounting systems that focus on profit repatriation and asset protection stress wrong variables and can cause incorrect decisions to be made about foreign investments.

To deal with global competition we must go beyond domestic notions such as relative share and cost positions. The following principle drives global competition: *It is not how you do relative to your foreign competitor that matters but rather how you do relative to your economy versus how your competitor does relative to its economy* . The primary reason this is true is that there is an important buffer between U.S. and foreign competitors called the *exchange rate* . This is one area in which it is difficult to make proper decisions about things like prices and capital investment without the benefit of a model to take into account the complexity of numerous interactions. Regarding international expansion, the tendency of putting large plants in the biggest markets is often the exact opposite of what sound global strategy would dictate. Finally, much of the financial hedging done by U.S. companies to protect against exchange rate shifts actually exacerbates the real exposure when taking competition into account.

In conclusion, let's *kill*: strategy as buzzword and dreary bureaucracy, strategy as cliche and wish list, analysis of form rather than substance, unrealistic goals and budgets, incorrect portfolio theory, and hastily constructed notions about niches. What should large companies do? Use the right people in formulating creative strategy. Search for insight with creative approaches. Take an external view. Apply the activity perspective. Assess customer needs. And take a truly international perspective. Remember, whether you are confronting global competitors or new technologies, aggressive strategies are usually better than those that purport to "hold the line." Also, hiding within a "niche" can be tantamount to surrender. The meek may inherit the earth, but they won't gain market share.

35

Creative Management for Mid-Sized Firms: Ten Creative Strategies

Robert Lawrence Kuhn

*Investment Banker, Senior Research Fellow,
IC² Institute, University of Texas at Austin
and Adjunct Professor, Graduate School of
Business Administration, New York University*

Picture Gulliver beset by both Brobdingnagians and Lilliputians, not sequentially on separate islands but simultaneously on the same island. It is a land of monsters and midgets and our traveling hero is trapped. Without respite he is pursued by mighty giants and badgered by crafty dwarfs; desperately he avoids the lumbering ferocity of the former and eludes the darting torments of the latter. The giants step with pulverizing weight; the dwarfs revel in piercing arrows. How to escape and how to survive? The task is daunting, the outlook grim. Now switch mental gears from 18th century literary fantasy to 20th century economic reality and you cut an image of the mid-size firm—a company class, experts say, that cannot survive.

Comparative Problems of Mid-Sized Firms

Caught in the Middle

Stuck in between, goes conventional wisdom, is no place to be. The business of modest dimensions is just too small to confront the market power of huge enterprises and too large to outwit the opportunistic flexibility of tiny ventures. Medium-sized companies, mashed by multi-national mammoths and nipped by entrepreneurial gnats, are an imperiled breed. How to hide and how to swat?

Small and medium-sized companies are a critical component of modern capitalism. They assure the efficiency of the economic sector by thwarting monopolies and secure the pluralism of the political sector by disrupting the hegemony between big business and big government. But neither fine tradition nor social value builds a healthy bottom line, an objective, consultants warn, difficult to achieve and harder to sustain. However vital for the country, small and medium-sized businesses must not be kept alive by artificial means; for not unlike brain-damaged humans maintained by machines, they would become living vegetables, objects of dole and pity, relics of the past, wards of the state, drained of vigor and energy, losing resolve and life-force, slowly degenerating, devoid of merit and bereft of worth. The only thing more tragic than the failure of small and medium-sized firms in the market-place would be their counterfeit survival in the iron lung of bureaucracy and government handout.

Mid-sized companies must survive and prosper within the free-market system, not outside of it, facing its force directly, not protected by artificial barriers. Smaller firms must compete effectively and efficiently against mammoths and gnats, guarding and guaranteeing their own existence. Anything less is self-defeating for the firm and counterproductive for society. Life dependent on largesse is life dependent on wind.

Size and Profits

Perhaps the most widely repeated strategic axiom—and it is a mournful one indeed for smaller companies—concerns the relationship between profitability and market share. A difference of 10 percentage points in market share has been shown to be accompanied by a corresponding difference of about 5 percentage points in pretax profit. On both sides of the production-marketing coin, big companies simply wield more muscle: economies of scale in procurement, manufacturing, and other cost components and market power in bargaining, administering prices, and selling more units. The combination is potent, the results inevitable. For any given product, revenues received go up and costs per unit go down; individual items are made for less and then sold for less, further increasing market share and accelerating market control. The feedback here is positive, literally and figuratively, for firms that have dominant market positions and negative, exceedingly negative, for firms that do not. Large-sized firms, in the end, simply obtain higher profits for any particular product. A simple success formula to be sure, and a pathway to oblivion for firms at the other end of the stick. Mid-sized firms, proclaim MBAs with terminals flickering and statistics flowing, are being pinned to the economic mat.

Yet the hand may not be that pat, the script not quite that tight; for although the data on profitability and market share may be accurate, the conclusions may not be. There is a different tale to tell. Computer projection can cloud dynamic perspective. Some medium-sized firms are forging the future, achieving technological and business breakthroughs; they are organizations resonant with current trends; they are new leaders of a new age. It is nothing less than industrial transformation. Mid-sized firms, I proffer, have competitive edge, catalyzed by their capacity to commercialize original ideas more quickly and build novel structures more easily. A fertile climate now exists for smaller companies, for entrepreneurs and executives with courage and foresight, for a whole new wave of creative and innovative managers. Mid-sized firms can expect, if they recognize the challenge and position themselves properly, to share the revolution. Indeed they may trigger the revolution.

Positive Trends

Four forces are shaping this economic eruption: (1) *The role of innovation.* Scientific advancement widens markets, the expansion fed by both fulfilling current needs and stimulating new ones. (2) *The rapidity of change.* Responding with speed and intensity is vital. The ability to shift company resources and focus on new areas can create instant competitive advantage no large organization can match. (3) *The narrowcasting of demand.* A world weaned on cable television and specialty magazines will not be satisfied by generalized products and services. With individual preferences afforded high visibility in mass media and consumer outlets, the populace will require increasingly personalized items and options, each crafted for small segments of the market with particular wants and interests. The burgeoning number of different products and services in specific demand means that each will be manufactured or provided in smaller quantities. Such a diminished size of product run or reduced repetition of similar service skews the market toward firms that can produce fewer numbers more efficiently, firms that do not require huge production runs to fill massive plant facilities or absorb large personnel overheads. (4) *The new managers*. These are the risk takers, the gutsy types who have fire in their bellies as well as brains in their heads. They like smaller firms in which they can exercise leadership, be closer to action, and implement personal vision.

Strategy

Strategy defines the relationship between an organization and its environment. It is ideally generated by mapping the firm's strengths and weaknesses onto the market opportunities and threats in order to accomplish long-term goals and short-term objectives. *Creativity* is vital to strategy formulation just as *consistency* is to strategy evaluation and *structure* is to strategy implementation. Finding effective strategies is the search for competitive advantage, areas of distinctive competencies in which one firm has or can develop a comparative edge over others. Competitive advantage can assume various forms, most of which are firm specific. What we seek here are comparative strengths for medium-sized companies as a class. Are there elements of organizational structure by which enterprises in the middle can gain an edge? How can mid-sized firms get to the head of the pack?

Comparative Advantages for Mid-Sized Firms

There are at least three size-related characteristics in which medium-sized companies display initial advantage, three corporate constructs entering on the side of the underdogs.

X-Inefficiency

"X-inefficiency" is a technical term defined as the excess of *unnecessary* cost as a percentage of actual cost—and it seems to increase with increasing size. Why is this so? What mechanisms are involved? Try executive luxury nurtured by substantial profits (two corporate jets when one is questionable), managerial flabbiness spawned by hefty margins (swollen staffs), the bureaucratic burden of large organizations (massive personnel departments), the sluggishness of pure size (interminable "coordinating" committees). Thus the smaller firm can be inherently more efficient. Is this the beginning of competitive advantage?

Employee Content

There are other *dis*economies of pure size. "Worker satisfaction"—the nature of work and social relationships inside the firm—is reduced by increasing company size. Employees in larger companies have, in general, higher degrees of personal alienation and depressed levels of job satisfaction—both of which are tied to the rigid, unilateral type of power structure associated with large organizations. Employees in smaller companies have, in general, greater task variety, more individual responsibility, higher satisfaction from their work product, and an enhanced sense of local identity. Aggregating these elements together, psychologists who study organizations use the term "content," and this content is said to be inversely proportional to firm size; that is, content decreases as firm size increases. Other things being equal, therefore, workers in smaller companies will produce more abundantly, do it more efficiently, and be happier in the process. Is this also competitive advantage?

Innovation

Innovation, too, while often used to justify large companies garnering greater control of corporate assets, might be more compromised than compounded in a business environment populated only by behemoths. The argument that increasing size is necessary to focus high R&D expenditures on complex problems is answered by statistical analysis of the actual record. Innovations in the steel, automobile, petroleum, drug, and other industries show consistent (but not uniform) patterns of small-share firms leading and dominant firms following. Such research suggests that innovation most often emerges from medium-sized firms, those companies with roughly a 5 to 20 percent share of the market. It is common knowledge that revolutionary ideas germinate with high frequency from small firms, sociological structures that have neither mental constraint nor prior predilection. Is this again competitive advantage? Innovation, these data indicate, becomes a potential ally of small and medium-sized firms in their epic struggle to flourish among giants.

Other sized firms, for diverse reasons (whether financial and numerical or organizational and psychological), do not appear to produce as well. Firms with lower market shares are often too small to apply adequate resources, human and technical as well as capital and financial. Large firms, those with shares greater than 20 percent, while not necessarily laggards in innovation because of size *per se*, may tend to delay introduction of new ideas until forced by competitive pressures. Many of the largest companies—such as IBM, AT&T, Xerox, General Motors—have withheld announcing new computer families, communication technologies, copier lines, automotive models long after they were developed. Sounds implausible? Consider the motivation: to maintain the value of their present asset base and product offerings, thus minimizing internal competition and maximizing financial return.

Taking Advantage

What begins to emerge, then, is the social superiority of medium-size firms. X-efficiency, content, innovation—they all contribute. But public benefit does not *ipso facto* become transformed into firm-specific financial success. Nor does the initial development of innovative products guarantee jungle survival (much less prosperity) for the venturesome mid-sized firm. Indeed, a larger competitor may well be able to take advantage of the new product or technology by its vastly more powerful procuring, producing, marketing, and distributional capacities, leaving the original innovative firm only the dregs with which to cover its much higher costs of initial research and development. (The jungle analogy seems uncomfortably appropriate: The larger predator waits lazily until its smaller rival does all the work of seeking, finding, capturing, and gathering food—only then to steal it by brute strength.)

Mid-sized firms must therefore know their environment, what their large competitors will do, how their small competitors will react. It's a tight, tough game, with the results carrying meaning to society as well as the firm. Medium-sized firms are important—economically, politically, socially, technologically. Their self-determined survival and prosperity must be assured by the force of internal strength. How to make it work? Only with effective strategies.

In many industries, smaller companies outperform larger companies. More profits. Better performance. *Consistently.* In fact there are hundreds of medium-sized firms, and thousands of small ones, that year-in and year-out achieve higher returns on sales and equity than do their larger-sized rivals. Why do they? How do they? What goals do these magical companies have? What strategies do they use? Surely, for these successful businesses, self-determined strategy is more precious than government-imposed regulation. The former is hard and sure, the latter full of whim and caprice.

Critical Success Strategies

In an elaborate study of over 200 top-performing medium-sized manufacturing companies, I showed that firms need not be industry leaders to be successful companies. Indeed, one of my criteria for selection was that each top-performing firm had to be in an industry dominated by one or more mammoths many times its size. Yet these smaller firms consistently outperformed their massive rivals. The reasons are "critical success strategies," well within a small firm's control. The results of my analysis revealed ten general principles of management for smaller firms.

Ten Creative Strategies for Mid-Sized Firms

I've watched winners and losers, observed trends and patterns. What does it take for mid-sized firms to flourish among giants? Following are ten critical success strategies. They are listed in order of importance. Some apply universally; some are contingent upon other factors. All, I trust, are useful.

1. *Dominance: Control your corporate niche.* Segment markets. Narrowcast products. Achieve and sustain maximum share within minimum markets. Tailor products tightly; define domains toughly. Segment by specific item, customer, price, quality, brand, distribution, geography, service, etc.—do anything to segment. Seek control through perceived superiority. Be a big fish in a little pond. Remember, small can still dominate.

2. *Product emphasis: Be product-oriented.* Give primary importance to company output. Stress product focus, essence, name, reliability, service. Visualize products from customers' viewpoint. Never make products subservient, not to executive desire, not to financial comfort. See each product in its broadest sense; understand the need it fills and the desires it satisfies. Be service oriented.

3. *Distinctiveness-uniqueness: Be different.*   Make the firm overtly dissimilar to competitors. Strive for originality; find something to set the company apart in customer perception. Have an impact on the end-user. Seek differentiation in each functional area affecting buyers. Cater to customers; service them well. Be noticed. Be remembered.

4. *Focus-coherence: Strive for strategic tightness.*   Establish goals, objectives, and strategies with clarity of thought and coherence of content. Build new businesses on the central skills, resources, facilities, or managerial competencies of old businesses. Structure on managerial strengths. Set corporate coherence and business focus as means not ends. Relatedness is contingent on business and industry environment: A mid-sized firm in a declining or dying industry or market should not fear diversification, yet should build new opportunities on past competencies.

5. *High-profile chief executive: Have a committed boss.*   The CEO should be more than a CEO. Personal charisma, profound dedication, pulsating presence—these really count. The CEO should project high levels of commitment and radiate intense auras of energy. There should be desire, even compulsion, to involve oneself all-pervasively in every aspect of the business. Contingent somewhat on industry and company traditions.

6. *Employee opportunity: Satisfy and fulfill personnel.*   Exploit the comparative advantage of smaller firms to attract entrepreneurial people; offer executives and managers greater job content and individual satisfaction. Be people oriented. Give employees a real sense of self-worth and personal participation, both emotionally and financially. Develop meaningful ownership programs. Get the right executives, then give them what they want—on the job and in the bank.

7. *Efficient innovation: Optimize new products, services, methods.*   Develop and commercialize new technologies. Exploit the comparative advantage of smaller firms to introduce new products sooner and more swiftly. Encourage creative types to weave their wonders. Attack market leaders if they protect current position by withholding innovation (as often happens). Emphasize efficiency in research; optimize development for rapid, cost-conscious results. Never attack broadside; focus R&D for maximum effectiveness. Use rifles, not shotguns.

8. *External perception: Know the industrial and market environment.*   Monitor all opportunities and threats, current and potential. Stay attuned to market conditions and customer needs. Know your customers; develop personal relationships. Have a keen sense of competitors. Appreciate issues of industrial organization: market share,

concentration ratios, growth patterns and trends, powers of suppliers and buyers, threats of new entrants and substitute products. Observe long-term forecasts, and watch them change. Be prepared for sudden discontinuities and be ready to exploit them.

9. *Growth-profits tradeoff: Weigh top line with bottom line.* Eschew growth for growth's sake, but seek growth for business' sake. Market products forcefully. Visualize longer time horizons for profit return. The bottom line, not the top one, is what counts. Billion-dollar corporations have gone bankrupt, while many very small firms have made their owners and executives very rich. Highly contingent on firm's comparative position within its market. Weaker mid-sized companies should prize profits far more than growth. Stronger mid-sized firms should not fear sacrificing short-term profits for long-term growth. When top performers establish strong market position, ultimate profits become much greater and more secure.

10. *Flexibility and opportunism: Change direction and move quickly.* Develop dynamic decision making. Be prepared to react rapidly to changes in products or markets. Be ready to turn on a dime and beat larger competitors to new opportunities. Retreat when enemy attacks. Attack when enemy retreats. Contingent on industry or market position. Weaker mid-sized firms should emphasize flexibility and opportunity more than stronger firms.

A word of warning for the eager mid-sized manager. These creative strategies may seem obvious and easy. Do not allow the former to discourage you or the latter to fool you. The points are both powerful and pragmatic, founded on live data from hundreds of companies. On the other hand, any simplistic advice should not be used as a magic wand. Smooth aphorisms are no panacea for perplexed executives. Generalized prescription, never forget, is one thing; realistic recommendation quite another.

Bibliography

Blair, John M.: *Economic Concentration: Structure, Behavior and Public Policy*, Harcourt Brace Jovanovich, New York, 1972.
Kuhn, Robert Lawrence: *To Flourish Among Giants: Creative Management for Mid-Sized Firms*, John Wiley, New York, 1985.
————: *Mid-Sized Firms: Success Strategies and Methodology*, Praeger, New York, 1982.
Porter, Michael: *Competitive Strategy*, The Free Press, New York, 1980.

Scherer, F. M.: *Industrial Market Structure and Economic Performance*, Rand McNally, Chicago, 1971, 1980.
Shepherd, William: *The Economics of Industrial Organization*, Prentice-Hall, Englewood Cliffs, N.J., 1979.

36

What's Creative About Cost-Cutting

Jack Rutherford

*President, International Consulting Management and
Former Vice Chairman, International Harvester*

"Cost-cutting creativity" almost makes reducing costs sound high-tech or magical. Baloney! Turnarounds are tough. Cost reduction is commitment, involvement, and lots of hard work. If that's creativity, fine. Though we focus on the industrial environment (particularly capital intensive operations), many of the concepts and techniques are applicable to any type and size business. The frame of reference is survival. If the operation or company is to survive, costs must be reduced. As American industry moves from a price strategy to a profit strategy, cost reduction is a critical tactic.

Many corporate problems were created by the *price* strategy. In other words, cost plus profit equals selling price. Go ahead: Charge the consumer, protect profit. Well the consumer has rebelled, demanding lower cost and higher quality. To stop industrial erosion, we must develop a *profit* strategy. The price less cost equals profit. We must control cost to protect profits.

Cost reduction is a logical process. You gather facts, analyze options, determine a course of action and follow up, follow up, follow up. To be most effective at reducing cost, however, you must rely heavily on human relations and interpersonal skills. Costs are controlled or uncontrolled through people. All understand the necessity and the objective.

Innovative cost reduction is really managing change. The risk is the negative connotation it can leave. Change must be managed to give a lasting positive attitude to the people who work daily in the shifting environment and carry the new philosophy forward.

Management Principles

Get Mentally Prepared

The battle is uphill. Things must change if costs are to be cut. Changes in policies, procedures, work habits, job responsibilities, job functions, etc. The biggest resistance to change will come from emotion and ego exacerbated by instability. Thus the trials and tribulations. The first hurdle, and often the biggest, is getting management to accept change. They have long played the game with one set of rules. The second hurdle is getting all employees prepared for the new world. Again, this generates resistance; however, it will be more emotion and less ego than when dealing with management.

Set Clear, Simple Objectives

Cost reduction programs work best, and people are more receptive to new realities if there is an identified objective. Change will come if people understand and support that objective and each change makes moves toward achieving it. Don't make the task so big or complex that people cannot appreciate their personal role. Reduce the job to dollars. Review cost elements and make sure you have enough under your control. More than one company has started cutting labor cost only to discover that if labor were *free,* its products still would not be cheap enough! Do not become rigid. Redefine objectives and priorities as you progress.

Think Success Probabilities

Learn to be a risk taker; change always includes risk. Know your risk-reward ratio. The idea is to reduce operational cost and maintain business viability. If you aren't willing to take a risk, you aren't willing to change. Without change you won't reduce cost and your success probability will decrease. Even a 50-50 proposition is in your favor. If the concept and logic are sound and if people understand why, they will work hard to be a winner.

Be Involved—Be the Leader

Senior management must be personally involved to effect the magnitude of change required to turn around a company. Such commitment is needed for three reasons: First, to understand the risk-reward ratio as situations shift; second, to overcome resistance to change; third, it is always easier to follow the leader than to push the leader. Indecision at the top is death. Develop a "can-do" attitude.

Be a Good Listener

You have some scope of the problem but have yet to develop a plan or strategy. Listen to key staff and line management. You will hear emotion, ego, excuses, opinions, as well as facts. Success is being able to find those facts. The emotion and ego encountered will also be useful as you build a structure to implement your plan. People work better when working for their own interests.

Give Direction

You must develop common direction. There are two simple concepts that can explain any action and give positive connotation. *First,* acknowledge that a cost-reduction program almost always involves reduced spending. Explain that a troubled business operates like a family checkbook. When you're in financial trouble at home, you don't solve the problem by borrowing more money. You don't spend what you don't have. *Second,* people always want to know if things will improve. Will the "good old days" return? Is there hope? Are your programs "fair"? People must implement the cost-reduction program. Their attitudes will be more positive if they believe they can share in success. The simple idea of "you must produce it before you can share it" is powerful. There is no free lunch.

Know Your Budget by Functional Discipline

Understand all budget elements thoroughly. Each must be analyzed as a potential area for reductions. Expect resistance. The first step is to understand each area of the budget in detail. The second step is an in-depth probe with each area supervisor. Third, and most difficult, is the risk-reward analysis. At this stage, you aren't making decisions, you are merely looking for opportunities to save the most money with the highest success probability. Generally, the job is more complicated than just reducing one element of cost. Most programs will require assessing all costs: manufacturing, marketing, engineering, finance, etc. This is the time for detail, looking at trees, not forests.

It is critical to have a "budget person." You need someone who is solely responsible for operational budgets. This person may report to the comptroller, but he or she should have a solid working relationship with "the boss." His or her input is vital in the risk-reward analysis. (If you don't have such a person, that may explain the need for crisis cost reductions.) You must measure performance and make comparisons against yourself and others. The "best ball" approach is effective as a guide only. It is not feasible to take parts and pieces of different systems and patch them together. Ultimately you must meet your own standards.

Get Your Staff Committed

The commitment and support of your management staff is paramount to a successful cost-reduction program. They must operate as a team. They must realize that all budgets will be cut since no functional area can get out of trouble by itself. When a problem occurs (not if), each staff member will have to contribute workers or budget dollars to get the troubled function over the hump. In fact, you should keep a small reserve "kitty" to channel additional resources into problem areas. Problems must be handled on a daily basis. They cannot be allowed to snowball and contaminate other areas. The staff will have to resist emotion and ego and put team objectives ahead of their own. Always give credit for sacrifice.

Zero Base Organization

This is one of the most important tasks. It is a difficult "gut wrenching" experience. The task is a detailed review of every person in the organization. Why does he or she exist? What function does he or she perform? What does he or she contribute? Can the job be eliminated? Can the job be combined? Can the function be restructured? There are several purposes for such a review: (1) It forces a critical look at value added for each job in the organization; (2) it provides detailed insight into the working knowledge of staff members in their disciplines and how the disciplines function with one another; (3) it gives first-hand opportunity to analyze emotion, ego, and facts; (4) it gives detailed knowledge of disciplines and provides a better base for analyzing risk-reward issues; (5) it facilitates restructuring of the organization to fulfill cost reduction needs; (6) it enables reducing levels of management—usually by one or two layers; (7) in many cases you discover jobs that were created to compensate for outdated problems; (8) you can assess each manager, supervisor, functional discipline, direct and indirect employee—firsthand; such value judgment is essential to a successful cost reduction program; (9) it provides a unique opportunity to assess your managers' strengths and weaknesses.

The involvement of the senior manager, whether president or plant supervisor, cannot be overemphasized. He or she should make the commitment to participate in the analysis on a full-time basis. The exercise requires 6 to 8 intensive days. It also requires substantial follow-up to implement. Do not change too many systems too quickly. "Never take a step longer than your leg." Always be able to achieve predictable results. Do not move too many key managers. This zero base exercise is the best mechanism to instill the entrepreneurial spirit in key managers. You can communicate the need for teamwork. People will pull together in hard times.

Develop a Hypothetical Plan

Develop a simulated strategy that achieves the cost-reduction goal. This initial hypothetical plan can best be accomplished by the comptroller, budget person, and operational leader. It will include an analysis of all expenditures. Look first at quality and establish cost-reduction objectives. At this point, you are dealing only in percentages (e.g., reduce office staff 20 percent). Do the same thing for each functional area, estimating the potential savings and the probability of success. The bottom line should add up to the total cost reduction objective.

Involve People at All Levels

Establish an atmosphere of credibility and trust. You don't ask for it— you earn it. People will only buy what you are selling if they buy what you are saying. Credibility and trust must be established before people will take the traumas of turnaround with a positive attitude. This is often easier to accomplish in union operations. They have an established organization and chain of command. The communication channels are already established; they merely have to be used. Union representatives can attend staff meetings. A union official (high ranking) can sit on the Board of Directors.

Communicate, Communicate, Communicate

Continuous communication provides continuous reinforcement. People need to be constantly reminded of the need for cost reduction. All levels should have a general knowledge of the overall strategy and a particular knowledge of their own participation. Management, especially upper levels, should be visible; such visible reinforcement has a lasting impact on the work force. Small group meetings involving a cross section of employees establish two-way communication. They should be held in a casual atmosphere. Sit the people in a circle. The plant manager, president, etc., should conduct the meeting. Create an atmosphere that will encourage questions. This is an excellent way to communicate the need and logic for ever-changing plans. It is also good for receiving feedback on the effectiveness and impact of a program. It provides positive visual reinforcement. Furthermore, many good ideas are generated by employees. PIT teams, quality circles, employee involvement, etc., are other examples of communication techniques. Remember that listening is also a form of communication. Listen to customers and listen to employees.

The Cost-Reduction Plan

Any cost-reduction program should incorporate some version of the following concepts:

Quality

The fastest way to reduce cost is to eliminate quality problems. This hits the bottom line quickest. It also has a positive impact on employees. Nobody can argue about improving quality. A computerized quality tracking report is the best approach to isolate problems and costs. This helps establish priorities and identify problems with rifle-shot accuracy. (This can be expanded to a full statistical process control program if warranted.) Quality should be categorized into warranty claims, vendor quality, and in-house quality. Programs with Product Engineering can reduce warranties. There may be substantial recovery potential from outside suppliers for their defective materials. Manufacturing and Manufacturing Engineering can focus on in-house quality problems. Programs that are properly managed can reduce quality costs 50 to 75 percent.

Inventory

All companies have cash flow problems. Material procurement and flow must be synchronized with production build-and-ship schedules. Tracking average days' supply instead of inventory levels targets the problem of excess inventory. Also track retail and wholesale orders: to force-feed dealers and not track retail sales is certain disaster.

Stable, predictable schedules generate good production economics. With special sales incentives, you can get material procurement cycles in line with build schedules. However, you must constantly track retail sales. High field inventories create excess discounting and margin loss. Remember, the only thing worse than a plant running a low-end schedule is a plant shut down because of high field inventory. The fixed cost of a shut-down operation is catastrophic. Several techniques can assist inventory control. Most computerized and material procurement systems are products of several disciplines and are developed and modified over years. Be sure to review receiving, material disbursement, and service. Look for ways to reduce lead times.

Create a theoretical inventory just to set your reduction potential goal. Consider line thread, burden items, perishable tools, coolants, etc. This exercise often highlights systems problems that must be resolved to maximize reductions. Inventory should be categorized into manufactured and purchased. Parts should be ranked by dollar value class A, B, C, etc. Generally, the 80-20 rule will apply in both manufactured and purchased categories. Zero in on 80 percent of the dollars by controlling 20 percent of the parts. The highest value parts should be manually scheduled to protect against schedule changes or order cancellation.

Purchased lead times should be reviewed separately from fabrication lead times. Attempt to get purchase parts in daily or weekly "buckets" depending on economics. Vendors should be given up to 12-month schedules for their fabrication process but ship codes should be restricted to meet minimum needs. Purchased materials should go from receiving dock to point-of-use storage. This reduces damage and handling costs and promotes visual reinforcement. Overall inventory reductions of 20 to 50 percent are possible.

Manufacturing lead-time reviews are more complicated. Economic run quantities must be assessed. Look for high scrap adjustments; this can be funneled into the quality project. A level-by-level operation analysis will highlight extra inventory versus safety stock. Equipment relocation or batch scheduling techniques will improve lead times. Set-up times must also be reviewed. Tooling revision (gauging, standard tools, fixtures, etc.) can produce "quick setups" that allow further lead-time reductions.

Schedule

Schedule stability and predictability is necessary to achieve optimum cost reduction. Missed schedules produce unhappy customers, manufacturing variances, and cash flow problems. Furthermore, missed schedules induce negative attitudes among employees. The discipline of making a schedule builds positive attitudes.

When schedules do fluctuate—and they will—great care must be taken to minimize the negative impact on quality and productivity. Review work rules and practices. *Always* put a qualified person on the job. Proper qualifications shorten learning curves and provide better quality and higher productivity, which fall immediately to the bottom line. Furthermore, qualified people are more satisfied. On-the-job learning in an incentive shop can cost all employees money and generate frustration—definitely a negative.

Control Spending

Over the years, bad habits develop that result in spending dollars for items or safety margins that are no longer required. Perishable tooling is a typical example. In a large machining operation, the tool budget for perishable tools totaled about $10,000,000. By requiring the manager of Production Operations to sign for all perishable tooling, spending was reduced by 30 percent. This was accomplished by using excess tool crib banks, the foreman's safety stock, and the operator's safety stock. This same pattern can be duplicated in many other areas: burden items, office supplies, phones, utilities, advertising, salespeople's expenses, etc. Unfortunately, many managers rely on historical averages and budget ratios instead of a detailed analysis of why and how they spend dollars. Spending reductions of 10 to 30 percent are not uncommon. Across-the-board cuts, however, are dangerous. Each account must be analyzed and reviewed in detail. Progress with measurable objectives must be made and maintained. The functional manager involvement is crucial. His or her personal authorization makes him or her painfully aware of problem areas and reinforces the need to be conservative in spending.

Productivity

Productivity is a difficult subject. It is easy to be defensive: The lack of productivity is always the other person's fault. Productivity improvement programs must be for everybody. Generally, if there is poor productivity in the hourly work force, the problem can be found in management and salaried personnel as well. In fact, the root cause of poor productivity is probably the same for all functional disciplines— poor management over a long period of time. This issue is so emotional that it requires special commitment from the top manager of each functional discipline. Management must accept the fact that they are all at fault. It will take several sessions, in groups and even individually, to convince managers that they are the root of the problem and that only they can initiate the action to solve it. Increasing productivity falls into three categories: (1) work effort, (2) working smarter, and (3) new technology. Productivity can usually be improved 30 percent. The percentage gain is relatively equal for each category.

1. *Work harder.*   Poor work effort is the result of bad work habits and eroding work rules. Your new expectation of work effort should be committed to writing, then reviewed with human resource and legal areas so that there are no violations of contracts or laws. Each member of management must understand not just the new rules but how to administer the new policies. This will require more time than you think. Hold several meetings with open two-way dialogue. Discuss actual situations. In a union shop the committee must be advised and understand the need. The new rules should then be conveyed to each individual, either one-on-one or in small groups. If you have an obvious offender, always go one-on-one. The work rules should be posted. Don't lose sight of the objective: Improved productivity is what you are after, not work rule administration. It takes good judgment to improve productivity.

2. *Work smarter.*   Everybody can improve productivity by better planning and better follow-up. This may require slight modifications in procedure, tooling, equipment, etc. But the expense is not major; it is a better, more logical way to do the same job. The development of the "can-do attitude" is important in this phase. A foreman once reduced the setup time in his department by 75 percent. All he did was modify some tooling charts. The process is simple and can be duplicated in hundreds of areas. He had one group of eighteen similar machines that produced forty different parts. The parts configuration fell into six different categories. The machines were down approximately 30 percent of the time. The foreman merely made himself a matrix grid. He

categorized machines, parts, and drive tools. He then set a procedure that tool station 1 was always a roughing tool; 2, a semifinish; 3, a finish; and 4, a grooving tool, etc. Within 3 weeks he changed all the tool sheets and routings and instructed all operators and schedulers. The key was the decision to improve. He thought about his section logically. The hourly employees thought it was great. It made learning a job much easier. Again, positive reinforcement.

3. *New technology.*   This category requires the expenditure of dollars—sometimes for capital equipment, sometimes for rearrangement. One of the easiest ways to improve productivity is to create productive cells—a group of similar work elements. They then can be applied in any functional discipline (production, engineering, marketing, etc.). Generally, you have all the equipment or tools, so the costs go for planning and rearrangement. Often, much is covered in burden accounts so it is merely a prioritizing of existing budgets. In manufacturing, cells not only improve productivity but reduce inventory and improve quality. Always look for higher costs or scrap areas. Then perform make-buy studies. The results are always beneficial. Perhaps you find ways to utilize equipment. Perhaps by adding a few new machines, you make tremendous productivity gains. Frequently, you can buy more cheaply than you can make, especially if design and equipment are old and manufacturing has low productivity. You may also learn how to make things more cheaply by going through the outsourcing exercise. The most difficult way to improve productivity is by developing automated or innovative ways of production. Engineering costs, development costs, training costs, as well as capital costs, are all high. Almost always you need higher production quantities, a product that is early in its life cycle, and one that has few engineering changes. If you can find such a situation, you will save much money. But be careful. Changes are super expensive with high technology.

Nuggets

There are several areas that can yield significant returns in a hurry. Often you must take dramatic action in key cash flow areas:

1. *Supplies.*   Ask suppliers to extend credit terms. First, go through regular channels. Then go from key manager to manager. You may be surprised: If you are a valued customer, they might extend credit 30 to 60 days longer than normal for periods up to 1 year. Also, check excess inventory. Often it can be returned for full value. You could be ahead

even if you get 50 to 60 cents on the dollar if the inventory is "dead" in your current build schedule. Even consignments are possible.

2. *Concessions.*　Wage freezes and even "take aways" are common these days. People know when companies are in trouble and they will respond if they understand the need and the goal. Remember, people will "buy what you are selling if they buy what you are saying." These concessions don't just apply to union shops. Management, salary, and hourly labor must participate.

3. *Pensions.*　Check for an overfunded pension program. It can free up large amounts of cash. People must understand the need and the risk. Often, moving from a typical pension fund to annuities gives the recipient better protection. This is volatile and complicated. Get legal help.

4. *Insurance.*　Change brokers or even companies. This can give short-term relief. Many companies will "buy your business" up front. Again, this has elements of risk. But you have to take chances to turn around a troubled company.

5. *Price increase.*　Review your product cost strategy. You may have a product in a "niche" market that can exploit prices for a year or two.

The list of "gold nuggets" goes on. It will vary from company to company depending on product and situation. Keep that positive attitude. There is a way! It involves risk. But leave no stone unturned.

37

Creativity Under the Gun: Managing Bankruptcy and Turnaround

Sanford C. Sigoloff

Chairman, President and Chief Executive Officer,
Wickes Companies

When Wickes filed Chapter 11 in 1982 with $4 billion in annual revenues and almost $2 billion in debts (largely unsecured), the company was the second largest bankruptcy in American history and surely one of the most complex. Our emergence some 2 1/2 years later has been hailed as a triumph of turnaround. There was no magic but much sweat. Just very hard work and very vital principles. To what do I attribute the Wickes success? Which actions can be emulated by future Chapter 11s? I stress three general principles and eight important factors in the creative management of bankrupt companies.

General Principles

1. *Don't make new law.* Don't try to change the existing system. Other Chapter 11s, for example, have attempted to break unions. Wickes didn't try and I don't recommend it. We followed "Sigoloff's Principle": Banks, creditors, and labor (whether in unions or not), along with the company, all must contribute to a successful Chapter 11; they are truly partners to the proceedings.

2. *Don't become a cripple.* Feeble companies can't help anyone. If the company can no longer make it in the market and if liquidation is clearly in the best interest of creditors, go ahead. But if the company is viable, a severely weakened enterprise is counterproductive to all. Almost from the start we established that Wickes would not become an economic cripple when it came out of Chapter 11. I never allowed uncertainty on this issue; there was no debate in anyone's mind: I was not going to liquidate the company for any class of creditors. Dealing with large numbers of diverse interests, there was much to disagree over. But one thing was unanimous: Wickes was not being liquidated for the banks, the trade, or the creditors.

3. *Don't be nearsighted.* This principle depends on the basic intelligence of human beings who work together and are well-informed, even though they are cast in adversarial roles. As a fiduciary of a Chapter 11 company, I am an avid fiduciary—an advocate for the enterprise. I seek to preserve the firm, maintaining jobs, customers, vendors, etc. I do not want to liquidate to pay all obligations to all creditors. To a creditor, of course, this seems unfair, if not dishonest. A creditor is owed money and wants it back as soon as possible. The creditor is already in trouble and doesn't want more. The affair is unpleasant, and he or she would rather be doing something else. I understand: I surely agree that creditors deserve all their money. Yet I know that if I tried to liquidate the company, I could not pay them off totally. (Often in Chapter 11s, a quick liquidation would not pay 50 cents on a dollar.) So explain that short-term payoff often guarantees long-term failure. If the business is viable, show how investing money today will bring the company back to health, whether through bringing in customers, expanding markets, etc. Each of the creditor classes should share in the future rewards, including preferred and common stock as well as interest and principle on notes. You may have hidden leverage: trade creditors stand to make much money during and after the bankruptcy. Though all are not happy, many do not want you to disappear. This may also apply to banks.

Important Factors

Planning.   Planning is always vital for organizations but especially so for troubled companies in or on the verge of Chapter 11. You have all the normal problems of business, plus the enormous burden of financial strain coupled with unhappy, emotional creditors. At Wickes, I formed ten "crisis teams," each with specific assignments. We created a chart in our executive offices, color-coding every Wickes division—red (must sell fast), gold (must keep), shades of gray (undecided). Don't forget to consider the enormous time, effort, and money that will be consumed in the Chapter 11 wranglings. (Wickes' Chapter 11 expenses—legal, accounting, and other—hit $3.5 million per month.)

Time.   Time is an important factor in a bankruptcy. Usually there isn't much of it to spare. Creditors usually are not well-organized. From the company's viewpoint, this is good at the beginning (allowing a strategy to be formulated, cash to be accumulated, etc.) but not so good later on. There was a danger point at Wickes at which if agreement was not reached quickly, we could have had all 250,000 creditors pursuing their own court actions—pushing legal proceedings to the end of the century.

Cash.   Cash is king, they say, and the old aphorism is especially true in Chapter 11. Use every means possible to conserve cash. The term "war chest" refers to the need to accumulate cash before filing Chapter 11 so that salaries and immediate expenses can be paid after filing. Without such minimum operating room, the company can be declared insolvent and the game lost before it begins. If possible, work with a noncreditor bank. Accumulating cash gives the company its greatest chance for regained health, which, ultimately, is in the best interest of all concerned—including creditors.

Pruning.   Stop the hemorrhaging at all costs. Close divisions that drain cash no matter how difficult. Closing Aldens, Wickes' catalog retailer, was agonizing. As a professional, I was disappointed not to find a viable solution. Aldens wasn't just a business; it was a way of life for about 3000 human beings. It had its own post office, its own health center. I've attributed most of my gray hairs to the decision to close Aldens. That decision couldn't be delegated. It was mine alone. I had to fire 2600 employees (mostly long-term) just before Christmas. I had to face those people; it was like annihilating a family. Yet Aldens was the linchpin of our whole case. It was losing $40 million per year, and we estimated it would take $60 million to get it into competitive shape.

Closing Aldens was critical for our cash consumption, our receivables liquidations, and most important, our going-forward investment strategy. (We asked the court to approve our giving Aldens' employees their full severance benefits, to which the creditors, to their credit, did not object.)

Sacrifice and Hard Work. Make no mistake: Chapter 11s are grueling; emotions often run raw and work never ends. All, for openers, must sacrifice. There is no alternative for debtors-in-possession. My famous "Six Days' Work for Five Days' Pay" speech triggered the exit of many people—but those who remained were more dedicated and ready to produce. Employee morale is critical. Sometimes the sacrifice and toughness improve morale—fighting for survival does that. But don't forget the upside, especially at the mournful beginning. Show those who remain what the future may hold—and how they may share in it. Don't forget to include creditors when considering hard work. Wickes' creditor committees worked extraordinarily hard, and I cannot compliment them enough.

Toughness and Fairness. The combination is important. You will be respected for both. We came close to filing a nonconsensual plan, thus confronting creditors in court. You always have an imaginary line. It is a point of honor beyond which you will not go, and most negotiations have that point. It can be construed as insulting to a creditors' committee to say, in essence, that we think the smaller creditors believe us and the larger creditors do not. It may be intimidating to threaten to go to court alone. But there is a time when negotiations are effectively over, and management must be about the business of rebuilding the company and emerging from Chapter 11.

Communications and Information. Creditors want—and deserve— to know exactly what is happening. They want data, especially financials. Be active and forthright with the numbers. If you err, err on the side of too much data, not too little. Seek frequent meetings and send regular reports. This will build confidence and rapport. At Wickes we had several simple ground rules for working with creditors. We asked them to set up subcommittees to assess our physical assets and to "review" our requests for capital expenditure. We would take their representatives to the various operations of the company. The key word is "review"; we didn't ask creditors to make decisions but to review them—there's a difference. We gave them all the raw data packaged with managements' recommendations. When we went for decisions, we expected them to be a learned body. Creditors and debtors-in-possession are, by force, adversarial—but communication and information put a more positive cast to the relationship.

Rebuilding. This sounds obvious but is not easy. Why should creditors allow "their money" to build your business? The answer, of course, must relate to an increasing likelihood that rebuilding the company will enable more (desirably all) of their money to be paid back. But there's no denying the higher short-term risk. During Wickes' Chapter 11, we closed about 600 retail stores and opened 200 new ones. We spent about $180 million for renovating existing stores and upgrading plant and equipment. We also acquired a nine-store chain for $11 million over creditors' objections—this was a decisive battle over who really runs the company and we could not afford to lose it. One factor often at work is that the bankrupt company usually has a significant net operating loss carryforward (NOL) that can be used to offset future tax liabilities. Thus the acquisition of profitable businesses can make sense by increasing company value for the benefit of all interested parties. Rebuilding continues, of course, after emergence from Chapter 11. Wickes' $1-billion acquisition of consumer and industrial-products units from Gulf + Western fit our strategic plan while it optimized our NOL position. The gratification is the proper payback for everyone, from initially hostile creditors to always loyal employees.

38

Reviving Troubled Companies

Marvin Blumenfeld

President, April-Marcus and Eagle Clothes

"Our sales are dropping and cash flow won't cover expenses." Those were the words with which my grim comptroller greeted me one not-so-bright April morning in 1970. I had taken four children, a wife, and a mother-in-law to a small upstate New York town to try my luck as a retail entrepreneur, and I had worked 7 days a week for 8 years only to have the economy (and some dumb decisions) leave me in an untenable position. File Chapter 11? Unthinkable. Sell off inventory and run? Worse. What to do? If ever one needed creative management. . . .

It was then that I discovered promotional management for companies in cash trouble. The idea was simple. You supplement inventory with discounted merchandise of the same quality you already carried, run a hard-hitting promotional sale, and pay off creditors as much as possible. The extra merchandise adds cash gross profits that more than make up for the discounts needed to move older inventory. (My sale was so successful that I was able to make an informal settlement with creditors and keep the business going. I subsequently joined Mr. Mortimer April, the man who conducted that promotion, and together we built a company that specializes in reviving troubled companies.)

One thing I learned is that *insolvency doesn't mean bankruptcy*. All it means is that you have to be more innovative in solving problems, such as finding fresh cash to pay new bills. Those who give up when confronted with adversity end up on the trash heap of discarded executives. Those who adopt the age-old philosophy of "don't let the bastards grind you down" always seem to survive. Some of the phoenixes that have risen from the ashes became fantastic success stories: Interstate Department Stores (Toys R Us), Miller Wohl, Unishops, Penn Central, United Merchants, and others.

Today's champ might be tomorrow's chump; the only permanent thing in business as in life is impermanence. Grave cash concerns can sneak up on any company, and all should be prepared to deal with the condition. The usual reaction of companies in crises is brush-fire management. Creative management is better. Though normally applied to upbeat, new-product, high-tech situations, creative management can resuscitate failing businesses. Following are various ways to solve problems that appear overwhelming. They can make the difference between companies that collapse and succumb and those that revive and prosper.

1. *List problems.* Put all problems on the table, analyzing and listing them in order of importance. Then reorder your list, enumerating the easiest-to-solve problems first, followed by the more difficult ones, until finally you arrive at those for which there seems no solution.

2. *Face reality.* Look at your list and realize its gravity. Recognition is the first step toward rehabilitation. I call it "coming to the party." Sound simplistic? It's amazing how many people let unbridled optimism cloud sober reality.

3. *Protect assets.* Troubled companies are threatened from all sides. Creditors won't supply materials; customers won't pay bills; employees lose loyalty. Your first order of business is to safeguard what you've got. Build cash reserves. Monitor collections. Watch company property. Be vigilant.

4. *Force a positive attitude* . It's tough after facing brutal facts, but try. Be strong, a bit arrogant if you must. Beat back discouragement. Destroy despondency. There's an answer out there somewhere. Eliminate negativism and generate a "can-do" aura: "I'm as smart as anyone and I'm going to find it." Transform "It can't be done" to "How can we do it? " Be aggressive not passive, proactive not reactive. Play the right role. In Rocky's immortal words, "Go for it! "

5. *Establish a braintrust or network.* Set up a group of close

professionals and associates (even friends) who have critical expertise and experience. Lay out your list of problems. Brainstorm. One
pivotal idea might be key. Test alternative strategies with the
group.

6. *Recognize strengths.* Forget weaknesses—they're obvious. You
   have assets beyond cash, those foundational elements on which
   your business was built. Don't ignore them—they're usually still
   there, if hidden by red ink. Whether specific expertise or personal
   dedication, bid your long suit.

7. *Position personnel.* It is especially important, though more difficult, to get the right person for the right job in a troubled company.
   Strive for positive people. A sales manager, for example, must be
   particularly buoyant to motivate the sales force while fielding
   customer complaints.

8. *Search creatively.* Look for ways around seemingly insoluble
   problems. Develop alternatives and options, especially when they
   seem few and limited. A moribund clothing manufacturer, for
   example, cheated death by prospering as a "factory outlet" retailer.
   Stone walls can be circled if they can't be scaled.

9. *Communicate constantly.* Keep in touch with all constituencies,
   both internal and external. Open, regular, and direct contact with
   creditors goes far in mitigating fears and softening attitudes. Give
   frank, frequent updates to employees. All associated with the
   company are at risk, and nothing defeats uncertainty better than
   current, honest information.

10. *Implement in order.* Granted, everything must be done at once in
    troubled companies—expenses cut, new funds found, customers
    mollified, creditors pacified. Nonetheless, implement in order of
    problem difficulty, easy ones first. Attack the more solvable prob-
    lems just as you listed them. In this manner, you will begin to make
    some progress. First steps will be small, but they will encourage all
    (including yourself). Often, solving easy problems sooner helps
    solve harder ones later.

11. *Maintain strict discipline.* Once deciding on a course of action,
    implement with decisiveness and conviction. Be resolute, There are
    always extenuating circumstances, but remember that if the com-
    pany vanishes no one is helped.

12. *Seek quick lifts.* Look for opportunities to boost the company
    rapidly, even if only short-run. The added cash from a special

promotional sale, what we do for clients at April-Marcus, sparks improved employee attitudes as well as buys better creditor relations.

13. *Be persistent.*   Don't close any doors. Never take No for a final answer. It's difficult to be rejected, when your sales pitch is turned down. But that's the time for rethinking and repackaging. Why did your original approach fail? What did you neglect to offer? Try, if all fails, an end run.

14. *Be courageous.*   Financial difficulties are the most grueling of business problems. Everyone, it seems, is coming after you. Don't let them get you. Stand tall. Show confidence.

15. *Have vision.*   Do not allow adversity to fog foresight. Sure you must think short term, but look long term: Have ultimate goals for which you reach. They will impel you forward.

39

Applying Innovation in Multiunit Organizations

John P. Thompson

Chairman of the Board, The Southland Corporation

An innovative environment fosters the exchange, development, and implementation of new ideas. Continued success is contingent on three principles: (1) Innovation is the result of a constant search for opportunities, (2) innovation is wasted if it does not fulfill specific company goals, (3) innovation is hard work.

Southland has dominated the convenience store ("c-store") industry since we pioneered the business in 1927. We started as The Southland Ice Company. Today Southland operates and franchises more than 7500 7-Eleven convenience stores, nearly 20 percent of the industry total. We also operate Citgo Petroleum Corporation, a dozen regional dairies, 450 Chief Auto Parts stores, and several light manufacturing plants and distribution centers. Being the industry leader has forced us to be more innovative, more creative. Our competitors are constantly searching for ways to whittle away at 7-Eleven's market share. Our business environment must encourage innovative performance. In addition to competitive pressures, we are also challenged by more than 8 million customers daily. It's incumbent upon our marketing personnel to devise new ideas to meet the ever-changing needs of this large, diverse population. Customers are fickle; if we don't meet their needs, they'll leave us and shop other c-stores that give them what they want.

The spirit of innovation has always thrived at Southland. My father, Joe C. Thompson, Jr., was one of Southland's first officers. It was through his vision that convenience retailing mushroomed from a creative remedy for slow winter ice sales to a worldwide phenomenon. Our management environment remains different. Our field structure is decentralized, providing great autonomy to division managers and their staffs. They have the authority to try new ideas, new processes. It's almost as if they are given the opportunity to fail. Now, I certainly don't want our employees failing. But I also don't want their creativity stifled because of fear of failure.

Our creative energies are not wasted on ideas, products, services, or practices that are not in tune with company goals. Every new product or service must satisfy a specific consumer or user demand. My father used to say that 7-Eleven is in business to provide customers what they want, when they want it, and where they want it. Such commitment to meeting customers' demands is the root of our prosperity. Undergirding this attitude is a willingness to take risks. But innovation must never be pursued casually. Consider the following four principles.

1. *Don't avoid risky but potentially rewarding ideas. But if the idea falters, don't hesitate to admit mistakes and move on.*   The obvious risk in trying new ideas is failure. Although our marketing processes have matured since my father directed the company, our product development group still adheres to his business attitude: Don't be afraid to explore a potentially rewarding idea, but if that idea does not succeed, don't be slow to pull the product or service and try something else. In 1954 we speculated that the emerging retail hardware business might be a successful diversification for Southland. Our first open-front drive-in hardware store, called 88 Hardware Store because of its 8 a.m. to 8 p.m. operating hours, was also our last. Our competitors offered major appliances and credit, which we did not believe belonged in hardware stores. The store closed within 18 months. We took a gamble, but we got out quickly when it became apparent we did not know hardware the way we knew convenience.

An early innovation is still our best known. Slurpee—the frozen carbonated soft drink—was initially an uncertainty because of consumers' unfamiliarity. A Dallas inventor approached 7-Eleven in the early 1960s with his "Icee" machine. We thought it had potential, coined the more catchy "Slurpee" name, and gave the concoction a try. We conjured up crazy names for the Slurpee flavors and backed the product with substantial media support. Slurpee still reaps large sales by exploiting numerous marketing and promotional ideas.

For the past several years we have been trying to appeal to more women and affluent customers. We offered competitive prices and more fruit, juices, and health-type foods. These items worked but more was needed. What we sought was a new product or service that would attract many new customers to our stores and keep them coming back on a steady basis. In the early 1980s automatic teller machines (ATMs) were becoming an alternative to on-premise bank tellers. Our product development group recognized ATMs as a possible solution to the challenge of broadening our customer base. But banks resisted convenience stores as prime ATM locations. Too few customers on a daily basis, we were told. Our ATM coordinators explained that our stores average more than 1000 customers daily. In a market with 50 to 60 stores, this makes for a daily customer count of up to 60,000. They also explained that ATM users could complete their transactions in a 7-Eleven-based ATM much faster than in a supermarket. Once initial contracts were signed and word spread, further negotiations were easier. Today we have ATMs in more than 4000 7-Eleven locations throughout the United States and Canada. Not only have we attracted thousands of new customers, but these customers have also purchased millions of gallons of milk, loaves of bread, six-packs of soft drinks, and other impulse items. ATMs were an industry innovation. The result of blind luck? No. It resulted from good intuition combined with the gumption to take risks and change others' attitudes. The right place at the right time? Maybe. But add an abundance of hard work, the determination to seek the best opportunities, and a field-tested mechanism for evaluating potentially innovative products and services.

Many new products and services have evolved from our new product development group. Most of our staff began their careers with 7-Eleven in field management or operating a store. That store-level experience developed a keen awareness of customers' needs and desires. Each 7-Eleven store is a miniature test lab, with thousands of customers as a test base. Each store operates in accordance with its own market preferences. At any point we are trying out many new products, services, or efficiencies. If a product is successful in one or two stores, a test program might be expanded to include several dozen stores. If successful at this level, a test will be expanded to several hundred stores. At each level of the test program several controls and variations determine the best possible combination of factors for success. We also examine alternative advertising and marketing strategies to determine what, in the event of a market rollout, will have the greatest impact on sales. Once a decision on a particular product or service is made, we move quickly to place it in our stores. This system provides the flexibility that many large companies lack. As trends are detected, we act. Indecisiveness is death.

2. *Listen to front-line employees and franchisees; they know the customer best.*   Innovation is impossible without knowing what customers expect. The best way to learn is by listening to front-line managers; they talk to customers day in and day out. Several years ago a sales promotion manager was searching for a way to attract new customers. The manager conducted a market study featuring decaffeinated coffee in several markets. His study revealed that caffeine-free coffee represented 26 percent of all coffee sales. There was a visible demand for the product. The manager knew that competing convenience stores offered only packets of instant decaffeinated coffee. He reasoned that if customers would be interested in freshly brewed decaffeinated coffee, just as they were in freshly brewed regular coffee, it would offer a competitive advantage for 7-Eleven. A test program was commissioned and today freshly brewed decaffeinated coffee is available in more than 5000 7-Eleven stores.

Because our more than 3000 franchisees are independent operators, they can make merchandising decisions they believe best reflect neighborhood customer preferences. This flexibility has added many new items and services, such as deli sandwiches and video cassette movie rental. If such products are profitable to the franchisee, our corporate marketing managers may then consider them for the entire chain.

We provide incentives for managers and franchisees to seek avenues of innovation that address consumer need. Informal incentives are competitively driven. The better their stores perform, the more sizeable their bonus. There are also formal incentives. If a manager introduces an idea that makes his or her store, district, zone, or division more profitable, then he or she might share in additional bonus possibilities.

Operation WIN—*W*inning *I*deas for *N*ew Products—is a program created by a marketing manager as a means for getting good ideas from the field to top management. Creators of the best, brightest, and most feasible ideas gleaned through WIN are given hefty awards for their innovative thinking. Example idea: a carton cigarette rack. Full cigarette cartons had always clumsily occupied shelf space under the sales counters. Store managers could not place the cartons in store aisles because shoplifters could too easily pilfer the products. A 7-Eleven franchisee devised a self-serve cigarette carton rack. The specially designed rack aggressively merchandises carton cigarettes, generates additional display allowances from cigarette manufacturers, and reduces the risk of theft by allowing customers to remove only one carton at a time. Potential profit increases: $2000 per year per store.

3. *Listen to customers—we're in business to serve them.* In the late 1920s, a Southland ice salesman, responding to customers' requests, began to sell milk, eggs, bread, and other staples during his operation's weak winter months. That ice dockman's foresight demonstrated the benefits of listening to customers and responding quickly to their changing wants and demands. In the late 1930s 7-Elevens offered curb service and sold staple items such as canned goods, ice cream, and salt. In the 1940s frozen foods, fresh fruit, and picnic items were popular. In the 1950s we added products such as television tubes, money orders, magazines, and shotgun shells. Through the 1970s and 1980s we added self-service gasoline, video games, and check cashing. By necessity we have had to offer creative remedies to changing buying patterns.

In the early 1960s our customers introduced us to a revolutionary concept—24-hour convenience shopping. We had a store near the University of Texas campus in Austin. After a football game one evening the store was so busy the manager could not get it closed. The store stayed busy—all night. Soon thereafter we extended operating hours at other stores located near college campuses. The population was changing; people were more restless, more active, and more likely to need products and services at all hours, not just normal shopping times. Since convenience stores were already providing services during extended hours, they were the obvious candidate to fill this new customer demand.

Southland satisfied customers' requests for food on the go with cold sandwiches in the 1960s, which were followed by microwaveable frozen foods in the 1970s. With the 1980s came an increased demand for fresh, quality fast foods. We were hearing that customers were frustrated by long lines at traditional fast-food outlets. They wanted a quality product, but they wanted it in a hurry. From this input we developed our fresh deli program, which was an instant success. Listening to customers is not difficult. The difficulty is being humble enough to recognize that your customers know some things about your business that you do not.

4. *Exploit ancillary businesses to bolster core business.* Our 7-Eleven c-stores account for a little more than half of Southland's annual revenues. 7-Eleven is our core business; it's our bread and butter. Our other businesses were initiated or acquired to provide economies of scale for 7-Eleven. These businesses have used innovations to create competitive advantages for 7-Eleven. They have also blossomed to become healthy profit centers in their own right.

C-stores in the past were tagged with a high-price image. This was due in part to the high cost of stocking products. Because stores are small—about 2500 square feet—they don't have room to stock a large supply of products. And some items, say bar soap or canned dog food, do not turn quickly. It is therefore necessary to order products in odd-lots quantities, which is expensive and inefficient. In 1969 Southland began developing a regional merchandise distribution system. The computerized inventory system delivered to the stores exactly the number of items needed. Items delivered are price marked before they reach the store, which enables store personnel to place them directly on the shelves. The quantities supplied represent actual sales requirements. Previously a store had to buy an entire case of a given product, storing excess products in the back room or on the shelf. Because of this computerized distribution system, stores were able to reduce inventories substantially, which freed up valuable shelf space, thus enabling stores to add new merchandising programs. (The company's five regional distribution centers sell products to many different businesses in addition to our 7-Elevens.)

We have capitalized on our petroleum marketing and refining subsidiary to provide an entirely new service to the c-store industry. 7-Eleven customers can purchase gasoline and other products with a Citgo credit card. Historically, consumers purchase gasoline from c-stores in relatively small quantities, usually less than 7 or 8 gallons, cash being the only method of payment. Because we own our own petroleum marketing and refining corporation and have a national presence—two advantages our competitors lack—we have the exclusive ability within the c-store industry to offer a major gasoline credit card. This increases 7-Eleven's average transaction size.

Innovative management systems must limit corporate controls, thus eliminating the danger of punishing risk takers or steering them toward mediocrity. But innovation alone does not guarantee success. Managers must also be action oriented. Doers. With drive and persistence they implement new ideas and take calculated risks. If several stores in an area, for example, are hit by a sales slump, management does not overthink the problem. They try something; if that doesn't work, they try something else. Total success rests on finding the right people and achieving a balance between creativity and control.

40

Merger and Acquisition Prices: Creativity through Multiple Mechanisms

Robert Lawrence Kuhn

Investment Banker, Senior Research Fellow,
IC² Institute, University of Texas at Austin and
Adjunct Professor, Graduate School of
Business Administration, New York University

Brian Saffer

Vice President, Swergold, Chefitz & Sinsabaugh

"Your price, my terms," said the buyer to the seller. "You get my money, I get your company." Mergers and acquisitions (M&A) characterize much of modern business. Reasons are many: *financial* M&A (e.g., stock enhancement, balance sheet earnings improvement, leveraged buyout, management buyout, going private), *strategic* M&A (e.g., horizontal and vertical integration, market share growth, product-market protection, plant utilization, overhead amortization, technology leaps, diversification), and *managerial* M&A (e.g., company restructure, desired growth, CEO interest).

The key to every merger, acquisition, and divestiture is *price* . How often we have heard someone say that everything has been worked out in a deal "except the price is too high." (That's like saying that you like everything about Buddhism except Buddha.) We focus on price—how to determine what businesses are worth, how to value companies. What methods are used, when are they used, where do they work, and where do they fail? (We do not focus on terms and conditions—the type, timing, and constraints of consideration used, such as cash, notes of all kinds, stock of all kinds, earn-outs, participations, personal contracts, and the like.)

Most literature on valuing companies for acquisition stresses one particular approach; it is highly quantitative and proffered as the "true method"—the "correct" route to the "right" answer. The approach is often a derivative of *discounted cash flow* (DCF), which calculates the internal rate of return or net present value using the stream of expected cash from the business compared to the initial cash investments. Experience proves, however, that no single method of valuing acquisition targets is entirely correct or truly comprehensive. The acquisition process occurs in the real world where multiple forces interact, not sheltered by the highly controlled, idealized models of academic theorists and computer analysts. Regardless of the pure economic validity of DCF, the real world uses, in addition, other standards for evaluating investments. And when results differ from those produced by DCF, they are impossible to ignore. To deny the existence of other forces or other avenues of analysis is to deny potential sources of value or potential areas of risk that must be included in a thorough M&A pricing analysis.

We present two kinds of approaches to setting M&A prices. The first deals with specific techniques, numerical valuation models that determine price; they are quantitative. The second lists "modifiers," nonnumerical elements that affect price; they are qualitative. Never assume numbers are inviolate; they may be precise without being accurate. Everything in business is contingent.

Where does creativity come in? How can you be "creative" about the price of a merger, acquisition, or divestiture? Price can right or wrong, high or low—but how creative? Terms sure, but price? Do not underestimate the role of creativity in M&A pricing. To make good deals, you have to *find* the right price, that exquisitely fine line interfacing the maximum the buyer can pay with the minimum the seller will accept. Finding that line, from either the buy or sell side, is a creative process. Creativity is enhanced when options are expanded, when choices are multiplied, when issues are addressed from diverse angles. Thus we provide numerous ways, numerical and judgmental, for valuing a business. Each offers its own view, its own cut of the problem. Choosing the right techniques, and deciding which modifiers apply and how, is part of the process. Seeing a problem from multiple perspectives is the essence of creativity. All major techniques and factors should be considered as components of a broadly comprehensive analysis that blends all relevant forces in determining price. Such "blending" is creativity. Used effectively, creativity in determining price can go far in facilitating mergers and acquisitions.

Techniques for Determining Price

The following methods for assessing business value are listed in approximate order of usage. The large number of techniques is designed to stimulate creative thinking. Though some are similar, consider the nuances.

1. *Discounted cash flow.* DCF is generally considered the most economically accurate; it is much discussed, though relied upon less. DCF works, as we've seen, by comparing the amount of cash invested for acquisition with the stream of all future net free cash generated over the life of the investment (net of depreciation, capital expenditures, working capital needs, etc.) to generate an *internal rate of return*. Alternatively, the future cash flows can be discounted to present value and compared to the initial investment (using interest rate expectations as the base discount rate, which is then increased by a risk factor related to the industry, company, financial structure, etc.); this yields a *net present value* , the difference between what you paid and what you expect to make (in present value terms). DCFs require that a terminal value be estimated, normally about 10 years out. The major problem with the DCF, of course, is the inherent uncertainty in forecasts and projections. Indeed, the numerical elegance of the method can be its greatest danger—i.e., the *illusory* accuracy and control of future estimates can be both deceptive and intoxicating. Nonetheless, one should use DCF in every situation; it's a good exercise if only because it focuses attention on the uncertainties. If one finds that even if actuals would track projections (which they never do) and rates of return are still only modest, the price is surely too high. Sensitivity analysis is a critical part of all analytical evaluation exercises. Here various scenarios are explored by assessing how "sensitive" your valuation is to changes in input. Since DCF is founded on the time value of money, it is

exceedingly dependent on the timing of cash inflows and outflows. Because of competition, momentum, tax, etc., no symmetry will be obvious: A decrease of 15 percent in margins will not, you can be sure, cause a 15-percent decrease in value. (One must be aware of the peculiarities of time in determining rates of return; the compounding curve accelerates benefits and costs. In almost every situation anticipated rates decline after the first few years—this is more a conceptual shortcoming of the method than an actual loss of value. It is most improbable to maintain high rates of return over extended periods of time as the base swells large—as is custom with most projections.)

2. *Market value.* The current market capitalization of public companies is central to M&A pricing—share price times number of shares outstanding, factored up by an appropriate premium (generally ranging from 20 to 100 percent or more). Premiums are paid for control positions; they overcome foot-dragging by incumbent owners or managers and thwart potential rivals from cranking up competing offers. Market price is obviously necessary for buying a public com.pany—since it is almost impossible to buy a company below its market price given the need for independent "fairness opinions." But market price is usually not sufficient. The share pricing mechanism is grounded on the efficient market theory: that the market is continuously evaluating all information about each company and expressing its current conclusions in up-to-the-minute cash bids and offers for the company's shares. Yet for acquisition analysis, there is a fatal flaw here: Stock market investors are not buying whole companies; they are buying small, liquid minority investments. The investor hopes to gain from market forces, not managerial influence, and can close out the position at any time. The buyer of an entire company does not enjoy such liquidity and flexibility but can, conversely, dictate future operations through managerial control. These are different concepts. The fruits of control usually command a hefty premium, but that premium may be more or less than the "real" value of the company. Hence the need for other techniques. Market value obviously applies to public companies but can be used to assess nonpublic companies by comparison (see technique 4).

3. *Price/earnings (P/E) ratio.* The capitalized earning power of the company. An industry-appropriate income statement number— such as earnings before interest and taxes (EBIT) or net profits after tax (NPAT)—is multiplied by an appropriate P/E factor to calculate price. The P/E factor is determined by both industry and company characteristics, with anticipated growth rate being the key variable. P/E ratios for acquisition purchases are usually applied to average earnings over a period of time, say 3 to 5 years. This will not work, of course, for young

companies. Here, the P/E may be applied to current or even projected earnings. Higher P/Es can only be justified (using strict financial criteria) by higher anticipated growth in earnings. P/Es work best when assessing steady-state companies in industries that have similar public firms.

4. *Merger market value* . These are comparison prices, the array of reasonably similar transactions that are used to judge the relative worth of the target company. Investment bankers favor this technique, generating long lists of comparable transactions to advise clients on both buy and sell sides. In theory, the M&A market is the true reflection of current interaction between willing sellers and willing buyers. In the real world, however, this is rarely the case. Corporations are not yellow pencils; it is difficult to make true comparisons of complex situations— in one way or another virtually every M&A sale can be considered special or extraordinary. Furthermore, the M&A market often evinces aberrations—companies selling too low when in distressed condition; companies selling too high when faddish or foolish buyers are overeager to acquire.

5. *Book value* . The classic accounting determination of net worth. Book value is a definitive "snapshot" number reflecting a firm's value at a particular time; it is valuable because it is produced by standardized generally accepted accounting principles and prepared by independent third parties. Yet it is just this apparent precision that makes book value so deceptive and therefore so dangerous. Book value often means nothing; it can be terribly misleading. When Maxxam Group bought the Pacific Lumber Company, the value of its world-dominant position in old growth redwood trees was carried on its books for less than 5 percent of real worth. On the other hand, many companies maintain ancient plants and worthless inventories, fearing the consequences of large writedowns. Book value may occasionally be used to add tax benefits to a transaction; for example, if the purchase price can be structured below book, additional cash may be·generated through tax loss carrybacks or carryforwards—the economic value of the transaction to the seller may then be sweetened in other ways (such as consulting contracts).

6. *Breakup value* . Some companies are worth more dead than alive. The value of the individual parts can be higher than the combined sum. This often occurs when companies have mediocre track records for generating healthy returns. Many conglomerates fall into this category. Breakup value estimates anticipated prices one could get if the various subsidiaries or divisions were sold off independently as viable businesses. Often these businesses are highly desirable to potential

acquirers who would pay a substantial premium for them (but who would not be interested in buying the entire company). The ideal goal is to recover most or all of the full purchase by selling off parts of the target company and thereby wind up keeping some desirable parts for a nominal investment.

7. *Liquidation value* . The benchmark, or lowest value, for any company is its realizable net asset value: all assets are sold individually for best obtainable prices and all liabilities are paid off—with both sale of assets and payment of liabilities assumed to be conducted in an orderly fashion. What remains, theoretically, should approximate book value—but variance is wide and one should not be surprised if there is great disparity. Here the analysis does not assume maintenance of any division or subsidiary as a going concern. The company is simply liquidated for its raw assets: receivables are collected, inventories are sold off, fixed assets (including advantageous leases) are brokered—all assets are converted to cash (including intangibles such as patents, trademarks, etc.). Debts are then netted against the likely gross cash generated to determine purchase price. Don't forget hidden liabilities such as underfunded pension plans and other contingencies. Also never underestimate the costs of liquidation—running the company as it is being closed down—from poor collections of receivables to managing unmotivated personnel. (Watch the vultures circle.) Remember: Debts are sure; assets are questionable. The difference, please note, between "orderly" and "fire sale" can be shocking. Always use liquidation value for calculating downside when acquiring troubled companies. It's a worthwhile exercise when evaluating all companies to give some sense for the ultimate floor. DCF and other going concern techniques do not contemplate sale of assets and therefore provide no sense whatsoever of liquidation value. Liquidation analysis is usually the domain of appraisers, brokers, and actuaries.

8. *Perceived growth.* Here's where forecasts and projections really matter. We must pay a price higher than historical or current earnings can support. What can we offer, and what's the worth? Assumptions are key; numbers on computer screens mean nothing of themselves. Numerous possibilities must be considered: market growth, competitive position, potential substitutes, and changing technology are just a few.

9. *Synergy value* . Assess the operational and financial impact of the proposed acquisition on our current business. Ask if the combination can yield benefits to either or both. Can the target's sales force sell our products? Can our plants produce their products? Can our overhead support their needs? Can our management help them, their management help us? Will 2 + 2 = 5—or 3 as often happens?

10. *Real asset value*. Determine the market value of all "hard assets" of the company—what you could get for the plant, property and equipment, any natural resources or reserves, etc. This gives a baseline. (Compare to book asset value, initial cost minus accumulated depreciation.)

11. *Going concern value*. Take net asset expectations (whether break up or liquidation value) and add any excess rates of return anticipated for operating the business. This technique hedges assets and earnings.

12. *Investment value*. This takes a more passive look at the acquisition and evaluates it as if it were merely a small stock purchase to be put into a large investment portfolio. Though the analysis will use many of these same techniques, the *attitude* and *approach* will be different. Passion will be less, as will assumptions of managerial magic.

13. *Competitive value*. The amount the company might be worth to competitors. How much would they pay to lessen competition, to gain share, to shore up prices—to thwart you? Magazines, for example, are occasionally bought and immediately closed—the point being to fold in acquired subscription lists of competitor publications in order to enhance the acquirers' existing properties.

14. *Reproduction value*. The cost of totally replacing target company in exactly its present form. Similar plant and equipment are assumed to be bought in their current condition, personnel must be hired and trained, new product names must be established, etc. This technique, along with the following two, are used primarily by industrial buyers who are considering entering target's business. Build-or-buy analyses should accompany all corporate acquisition programs and determine the relative advantages of buying going companies or starting similar businesses from ground up. Time delays, asset availability, personnel training, and market recognition may be as important as cost comparisons.

15. *Substitution value*. The cost of buying the same *output* as target company without having to buy any of its specific elements. Ends not means are judged—which is obviously less expensive.

16. *Replacement value*. The cost of replacing the target company with *all new* plant, equipment, materials, etc.—which is obviously more expensive.

Each of the above techniques for determining price are used in conjunction with prevailing rules of thumb that convert numerical output into actual prices. These rules of thumb, almost by definition, are creatures of the market to be discerned by common knowledge. They are generally expressed in multiples—industry-specific integer multipliers of operational data such as after-tax profits, earnings before interest and taxes (EBIT), net free cash flow or industry-specific integer multipliers of unit values such as price per barrel of oil reserves, price per bed for a health care company, or price per subscriber for a cable concern. Rules of thumb are tricky, perhaps unreliable. Figures and multiples change, and one must keep ear to the ground or listen to Wall Street Jungle tom-toms. Even more important, not all companies in a given industry are equal. Differences in market share, cost structure, reputation, management, and a myriad other elements are critical, so that the same multiple paid willingly for an industry leader would yield an excessive price for a follower. The bottom line is that numerical techniques are necessary to get some sense of the situation but inadequate to fix a final price.

Factors that Modify Price

Price is the universal key to create exceptional value. A "too high" or "too low" price, calculated by microprocessor model, does not, of itself, generate exceptional value for M&A activists on either side of the buy or sell. In general two categories of factors affect value—operational and financial. The two, of course, are interrelated and in most transactions acquirers look for both sets of benefits. Operational factors—such as market position and presumed synergy—tend to relate to specific companies at specific times and are less susceptible to general rules. Following are financial considerations that have an impact on M&A price. Each must be evaluated in specific context of acquirer and target.

1. *Risk.* For the buyer: What is the likelihood that business and financial expectations may not be met? How volatile is the industry and company? What are the environmental and competitive threats? For the seller: If the transaction is not all cash, what is the probability of not receiving full payment? In any case, what is the likelihood of closing?

2. *Financeability.* The ability to finance an acquisition—borrow or issue equity—is dependent on two factors: the general credibility of the acquiring company with lenders and/or security holders and the specific confidence of financial institutions that the proposed deal is a good one. The initial financial strength of both acquirer and target are

critical: e.g., history of earnings, quality of assets, absence of encumbrances. Projected streams of income, from which cash coverage of interest and amortization of principal will be derived, must be scrutinized. (Debts are paid with cash not earnings, so cash flow is always more important than accounting income.) "Haircuts" will be taken on company projections so that lenders can be confident that their loans are safe even under untoward conditions.

3. *Financial structure* . Acquisition price, independent of financial structure, may be misleading. How deals are financed can greatly affect appropriateness of price. An all-cash payment financed with only 3-year senior debt would constrain a very low price, while the use of owner-carried notes, zero coupon bonds, and preferred stock would support a much higher price for the same transaction. Sometimes a deal is really worth more than the new company can afford to pay. In a well-known billion-dollar acquisition of a natural resource company, interest charges ran twice the pre-acquisition cash flow. The deal could not have been done without substantial use of zero coupon notes that would mature as the target's assets could be converted to cash over a 15-year period. Much of the advance in modern M&A involves the creative development of novel financial instruments that match company cash flow with debt requirements and balance risk and return for various levels of lenders and investors. The three traditional levels— senior debt, mezzanine, equity—are often segmented into a dozen or more "strips" in larger and more complex transactions.

4. *Tax considerations.* This is a massive area in all M&A, fraught with opportunity and threat—and incurring high professional costs. For the buyer: How do tax considerations affect the net free cash available for operating the company and amortizing debt? What will the new tax basis be? Are there any special tax considerations in the industry or company? Any hidden tax liabilities? Any recapture? Any net operating loss carryforwards? For the seller: What is the realizable, after-tax, net free cash generated? What is the most efficient structure to minimize tax liability? What about tax-free exchanges, taxable transactions that generate losses, installment structures, capital gains treatment, contingent payouts, consulting arrangements, liquidations, spin-offs, and blanket tax exemptions? It is usually important to control timing, such as when taxes would become payable on exercise of options or on constructive receipts of dividends; the worst case is to mismatch the receipt of cash and income so that a tax liability is incurred without money to pay it. The key to many deals is to find the win-win structure

that minimizes the collective tax liabilities for both acquiring and acquired companies. In this manner, more value will be available to allocate between the parties.

5. *Liquidity.* For the buyer: What are the immediate cash requirements for operating the business, including working capital (seasonality) and capital expenditures? Many new owners have found themselves desperately short of operating cash the day after closing, having calculated only the direct acquisition costs. What are prospects for turning the business into cash? Can it be sold easily? Taken public? Refinanced?

6. *Cost of capital.* Hurdle rates differ. Rates of return must be evaluated in light of the acquirer's cost of capital. A company selling for a high P/E in the market can well afford to pay a higher price (in cash as well as stock) than a comparable company selling at a low P/E. Similarly, if corporate or investment fund money is languishing in low-return, short-term instruments, hurdle rates for a potential acquisition might be lower.

7. *Business timing.* For the buyer: Is this the right part of the cycle to acquire this company? Are you paying top dollar? What are the firm's immediate prospects? What are trends? What is likely to happen to target's relative cost of doing business over time? Will labor, for example, become progressively more expensive relative to foreign competition?

8. *Payment timing.* For the seller: How important is cash up front? Are you willing to take back notes? Even when equating price with market rate interests, a seller who waits for full payment can demand a higher (present value) price because of inherent risks.

9. *Acquisition timing.* For the buyer: How fast can you move? Must money be raised or is it available? For the seller: How quickly should the transaction be completed? Who's under more time pressures—buyer or seller?

10. *Synergy.* For the buyer: What are benefits to my current company if combined with target? What are the procedures, time frames, roadblocks, and dangers of generating the planned-for synergies between acquirer and target? What could happen to destroy such hoped-for incremental benefits? (Especially critical if synergistic increases in revenues or decreases in costs are part of projections supporting the purchase price.)

11. *Control.* For the buyer: Are there any special positions that target company controls—such as stock of other companies, market

share, long-term contracts, key real estate? Is there any value in buying a control position in the target but not buying the entire company? If so, different analysis is required. Control, of any kind, is often of high worth, and control premiums are common.

12. *Defensive*.   For the buyer: Would target make the acquiring company *less* risky, say by being countercyclical, protecting key markets and customers, or securing sources of supply? Would target be dangerous if acquired by a competitor?

13. *Competitive bidding*.   For the buyer: How strong are competitive bidders? How serious? What are their primary motivations? If complementary, might there be some cooperative effort—such as agreeing to break up target so that each partner would obtain a desired division while keeping the overall price within reason? If not, how likely are other bidders to remain interested (and hence be available to buy the business should acquirer change its mind or seek a quick profit)? What about risks of getting out bid after incurring high costs, primarily in a contested public arena? Can you get a "lockup" on some stock or key asset of target? For the seller: Can the price be jacked by competitive bidding? Is a formal auction appropriate?

14. *Desirability*.   For the buyer: How strongly is target wanted or needed? How far will you reach to get it? How important is it for business position? How important is it for CEO and executive interests? We delude ourselves if we think that personal desire does not wield substantial influence on M&A decisions. The gamut runs from incremental salaries and perquisites to opportunities for nepotism and tax shelter. Never underestimate the importance of enhanced power and prestige.

15. *Understandability*.   For the buyer: How well do you know the industry? Could you take over if current management walked out? The history of M&A is littered with good deals going south because the acquirer did not understand the business.

16. *Doability*.   No matter how attractive a situation, no matter how right the price, the deal has to be "doable." There are virtually an infinite number of reasons to make a deal un-doable—even after terms and conditions are generally agreed. How to unhinge a deal? Anything from bad chemistry and personal piques to overeager lawyers and potential lawsuits to changing business conditions and interest rates. Deals bust up, even at the last moment. It is much easier to uncover one hundred "terrific" situations than to consummate one good one.

Applications

In determining the "best price" for a business, from either buyer's or seller's side, creative analysis is prescribed. Such an analysis must reflect responses to a wide variety of stimuli; only a cyclical, looping, systems, organic approach can protect against simplistic or misleading conclusions. For example, one could do a DCF analysis based on best-guess forecasts. But should an astute buyer be tied to the price that emerges from the computer model? Not necessarily. The DCF value may be twice the stock market value—so why offer double up front? On the other hand, the DCF may be far less than the break-up value (other companies may put strategic premiums on various divisions)—so why lose the deal?

Alternative valuation approaches can be correlated to assess acquisition pricing strategies and concomitant risks. An "if-then" analysis seeks an array of recommended actions based on generally known conditions. Example: If comparable M&A market prices are below liquidation value, my risks are minimal, but if market prices are above DCF and break up, my risks are substantial. If-thens are not new and not magic. They rather reflect the creative process that goes on among acquirers examining a potential transaction. Serious buyers will always use sophisticated quantitative techniques—but the canny ones will not be bound by them. They will always plug a diversity of intuitive factors into the valuation process.

Buyer and seller should each attempt to assess the other's position—absolute worst case, probable minimal requirements, desired deal level, and realistic best case. Other companies should be included in the analysis. The buyer can evaluate what competitors might pay for target (and why), as well as what other companies might make a better candidate for acquisition. The seller should do likewise, exploring all possible suitors. Sensitivity analysis should be conducted across many of the techniques, testing what happens under various scenarios (e.g., sales down 15 percent, margins eroded by 7 percent, interest rates jump up to 18 percent, etc.).

A creative best-price analysis would include using many of the techniques that determine price and factors that modify price in various combinations. Matrices can be developed by mapping one onto the other, the techniques against the factors, so that each cell of intersection has the potential for generating new thinking. Then multidimensional matrices can be designed so that cells include several techniques and factors working together. In this manner, a fuller appreciation for price can be determined. Additional insights into the business will also be gleaned.

41

Creativity in Building Conglomerates

J. B. Fuqua

Chairman of the Board, Fuqua Industries, Inc.

Creative management is a continuous process. Building a business takes an extended period of time. In conglomerates, management must move into and out of markets according to opportunities and conditions. A conglomerate, by its form and character, is not bound to a particular industry. Being sensitive to changing conditions and having the courage to commit to new opportunities (and divert others) represent the foundation of long-term prosperity. Creative management for conglomerates means adapting to the times, matching company strategy to market structure. The stock market provides one measure of the payoff.

Fuqua Industries was created in the "conglomerate era," in 1965 when, with mostly borrowed funds, I acquired control of the smallest company on the New York Stock Exchange. The company, then named Natco, was not profitable but had a strong balance sheet. I discontinued the unprofitable product lines, reduced expenses, and made it profitable in 1966. The value of the shares rose. I changed the name to Fuqua Industries, Inc., and began to acquire new businesses. The original operations of Natco became our first disposition.

Conglomerate Era—1960s

The period 1966–1969 was the height of the conglomerate era. The basic formula of the conglomerate was as follows: (1) Acquire successful companies and retain the management that had made them successful. (2) Limit the corporate staff to a small group that would provide nonoperating services such as insurance, treasury, legal and tax—but avoid operational involvement, holding local management responsible for operational success or failure. (3) Diversify into several industries to reduce the risk of large fluctuations in cash flow and earnings.

The stock market became fascinated with the concept, especially the amazing capability of conglomerates to raise their earnings per share (EPS). With the stock market's focus on EPS growth, conglomerate management, including us at Fuqua Industries, became creatively proficient at providing what the market wanted. We knew we could add to EPS through acquisitions in two different ways:

1. *Acquire with borrowed cash (a purchase transaction)*. As long as the return on investment (reported earnings) exceeded the cost of the debt incurred (interest expense), there would be an increase in net earnings and EPS. In this type of transaction, sales and earnings would be reported beginning with the date the acquisition was consummated and when blended in with our other operations, would provide the high profile of growth that the stock market sought. The market seemed to ignore the increasing amount of debt that was building on conglomerates' balance sheets (perhaps because most was long term).

2. *Acquire by issuing common stock to the seller (a "pooling" transaction)*. During this era, conglomerates' stocks were priced at relatively high multiples of their current EPS. By acquiring companies with lower price/earnings (P/E) multiples, the transaction would cause the acquiring conglomerate to add to its EPS, as can be seen in Table 41.1. The conglomerate has to issue only twenty common shares at $15.00 each to acquire all of the common shares of the pooling

Table 41.1.

	Conglomerate	Pooling candidate	Pro forma combined
Net earnings	$100.00	$30.00	$130.00
No. common shares	100	30	120
EPS	$1.00	$1.00	$1.08
P/E multiple	15	10	15
Price per share	$15.00	$10.00	$16.25

candidate whose market value is $300 (thirty shares times $10). As a result of this acquisition, which involves no cash, the pro forma combined EPS would rise to $1.08 from $1.00 and, in the absence of any change in the P/E ratio of the conglomerate, the price of its stock would rise to $16.25 from $15.00. The greater the difference in P/E multiples, the more impact the acquisition transaction would have on the acquirer's EPS. Another interesting aspect of a pooling transaction was that it would cause the financial history of the acquiring company to be restated as though the two companies had always been together. Such statements gave the impression to investors that the acquiring company had been responsible for the pattern of historical growth; it also provided a rationale for projecting future growth.

At our peak in 1969, Fuqua common stock was priced at over 20 times the earning for that year. For nearly 4 years, we had made a creative response to an environment that endorsed the concept of the conglomerate and focused its attention on a single measure of value, earnings per share. By recognizing the opportunity, we created in those 4 years a company having over $300 million in sales and $13 million in net earnings.

The recession of 1970–1971 burst the bubble of the conglomerate era. Rising interest rates and declining P/E ratios curtailed acquisition activity, and some conglomerates also began to have operating difficulties. The investment markets, too, began to take a more thorough look at how conglomerates had generated much of their EPS performance in the 1960s through "creative" acquisition structuring.

After a brief respite during the boom years of 1972–1973, Fuqua Industries and many other conglomerates (as well as most segments of corporate America) fell into difficult times with the recession of 1974–1975. Operations vulnerable to swings in economic conditions became unprofitable. The price of our common stock declined by nearly 90 percent from its 1969 peak. The creative opportunities of the conglomerate era had, for the time being, come to an end.

Resource Allocation Strategy—1970s

The situation gave birth to a new approach. The downside of the economic cycle had exposed the relative strengths and weaknesses of our business units. We decided to dispose of the weak operations, even at a loss, and to allocate our resources only to areas having a high return on investment. We shifted our focus from EPS to return on equity (ROE) and, for our operating companies, to return on net assets (RONA).

As soon as the announcement was made in early 1976 that we would provide for losses of up to $20 million in disposing of the weak operations, the price of Fuqua's common stock began a major upward move. So successful was our disposition program, and so rewarding was our strategy in terms of stock market appreciation, that we began a search to acquire an undervalued conglomerate to which we could apply the same formula. In 1978, we acquired National Industries, Inc., a $1-billion (sales) conglomerate bogged down by some marginal operations. Within a year we had sold enough of these weaker business units to recoup the entire equity price of the acquisition ($67 million). Among the jewels that we retained (until 1981) was a petroleum distributor that earned $124 million (pretax) in 1979 when oil prices doubled.

We took some pride in developing our concept of resource allocation. Basically, we allocated financial resources and encouraged operational growth only in businesses that had good prospects (principally by demonstrated performance) for earning a return on capital (net assets) that exceeded the cost of capital. We limited growth or disposed of operations that were unable to meet our standards of RONA. In simplest terms, we cultivate our winners by providing them encouragement and resources for growth; and we had the courage and commitment to withdraw from unprofitable or unviable situations.

Leverage—1980s

Conglomerates have always been aggressive users of leverage. In the conglomerate era the heavy use of debt was seen as essential in building a diversified base of businesses. We became comfortable with a capital structure mix of about 50 percent debt and 50 percent equity by considering the following factors: Operating profits covered interest expense by a comfortable margin; diversification reduced the risk of illiquidity; maturities of most of our debt would come far into the future, and we would refinance long before the debt would come due; and as a conglomerate we would sell business units, if required, to meet financial obligations. We also have always recognized debt as being the least expensive source of capital, principally because the government picks up a major portion of the cost by the tax deductibility of interest expense.

Table 41.2.

(Dollars and Shares in Millions)

	1982 actual	1982 less leverage
Sales	$608	$608
Profit before interest	61	61
Interest expense	28	4
Income before taxes	33	57
Income taxes	16	27
Income from continuing operations	$17	$30
Number of common shares	4	13
Earnings per share	$4.16	$2.28
Debt	212	32
Equity	75	255
Return on equity	23%	12%

Fuqua Industries entered the 1970s with 50-50 debt to equity. During the decade we grew from $300 million to over $2 billion in annual revenues, and we ended the decade with about the same 50-50 debt to equity ratio. We have found that capital is not the limiting factor. Companies whose management has creativity, capacity, and courage can find the capital.

We are always searching for creative ways to enhance value. Sometimes this is done by buying, sometimes by selling. In 1981 we concluded that the developing oil glut might depress petroleum prices, and so we sold our petroleum distribution subsidiary, receiving about $180 million cash. In the search for how best to use this cash, we chose our own stock. In a public tender, Fuqua Industries bought back 73 percent of its outstanding common shares. The shrinkage of our equity left us temporarily with a debt-equity ratio of about 80-20.

The shift illustrates why leveraged buyouts became so popular during the 1980s. Increasing the amount of debt (leverage) tends to increase both earnings per share and return on equity, thereby creating value for shareholders. Consider how differently our company performed in 1982 as compared to how it would have performed if we had used the $180 million to reduce debt instead of purchasing our own stock (see Table 41.2).

Although we subsequently rebuilt equity to our long-range target of parity with debt, principally through retained earnings, our example shows the power of leverage on EPS and ROE. Such leverage, combined with the availability of funds and a resurgence of entrepreneurial spirit, has reshaped American enterprise in the 1980s.

42

Decision Making and Deal Making: How Creativity Helps

Robert Lawrence Kuhn

Investment Banker, Senior Research Fellow,
IC² Institute, University of Texas at Austin and
Adjunct Professor, Graduate School of Business
Administration, New York University

Louis Kuhn

Founder and former President, Chief Apparel, Inc.

Executives are consumed by making decisions and making deals. If they're not wrestling with one, they're struggling with the other. It's virtually an executive job description. Managers make decisions constantly—from allocating company resources to apportioning personal time. They also make deals constantly—not only the flashy external kind (e.g., financial transactions) but the quiet internal kind (e.g., personnel shifts). Keeping subordinates and peers working well can demand negotiating skills as creative as those required for complex acquisitions. We seek to understand the processes of decision making and deal making and then suggest ways to make each more creative.

Creative Decision Making

How do executives make large-scale decisions? Though attention in recent years has focused on tools of decision technology—data processing, information analysis, modeling, forecasting, expert systems—the real story is what happens next. How can enormously complex problems, involving competing and interwoven social, cultural, ethical, and personal issues, as well as economic ones, be integrated into coherent wholes? Considering the large numbers of people often involved and the compressed periods of time for finding solutions, the question becomes baffling.

Decision Theory

Mechanisms and techniques of decision making are studied by psychologists, economists, mathematicians, and statisticians. The basic concept is a person's "utility function," a numerical representation of how individuals rank alternative choices. Decision making can be thought of as "sequential choice behavior," the phrase embodying cognitive processes such as encoding, chunking, and hypothesis testing. "Probabilistic judgment," or "intuitive statistics," drives the personal decision-making process; the process is not, of course, simple arithmetic, considering the complex influence of risk adjustments, biases, and heuristics (nonspecific search and discovery).

Decision making by groups can follow predictable patterns, as emotional and task-related elements assume differential importance at different stages. Emotional elements predominate at the beginning and end of each problem discussed, while task-related elements predominate during the actual discussions themselves. As the group progresses, two different kinds of leaders can emerge—one, the "task leader," assumes leadership during task-related discussions; and the other, the "play leader," takes over during emotional periods. These two leadership roles are quite distinct, are rarely filled by the same person, and can be even antagonistic toward each other.

Computers versus Brains

Can computers help? Will they be making more creative decisions? For operational issues, computers are essential: record keeping and database management, minimizing costs of ingredients and inventory levels, maximizing efficiency in component scheduling and travel routes, and so on. Even for the organization and integration of long-range planning, computers are vital. The desk terminal or personal computer has become the new executive status symbol, symbolizing the control of data not money and representing the new wealth of a new world—information. But who wants all that data? Who needs all those numbers? Today's most critical need is not more information but *less*. We need data reduction techniques, systems of selection and discernment, the intelligent search for meaning. We have enough numbers; what we need is understanding. True creative decisions demand insight and imagination.

Computers are deterministic, preset by circuit and code; though the software may be most intelligent, electronic pathways are still hard wired to spark predictable output. Brains are probabilistic, patterned by design and chance; in the gray matter of the cerebral cortex semirandom processes can trip new thresholds. It is impossible to program computers, however large the database and however expert the system, to make creative decisions—that is, decisions that are original in essence and unique in vision, independent of previously known algorithms. The two dimensions are, at least today, incompatible. Computers can crunch vast numbers and sift complex programs by brute force and clever code, but only brains can search imaginatively for order and innovation amidst chaos and tradition.

Brains do one conscious thing at a time, generally not more. But they can shift rapidly from one to another, like time-sharing in a computer. The neural apparatus, called the reticular activating system, is the brain's arousal system; it controls the level of brain activity, highlights fresh or essential information, habituates (represses) repetitive or nonessential information, and directs mental focus and attention. (The reticular activating system, for example, determines why you do not feel your watch on your wrist but do feel the fly on your face.) Electric splashes of sensation can be traced throughout the brain, appearing not only in the specific conscious areas of the cerebral cortex but also in the unspecific (or association) areas of the cortex and in the lower subconscious centers. Among these brain areas, data pass back and forth furiously and incessantly, being synthesized and transformed in the process. Waiting some time to make a crucial decision could give these subtle systems a chance to work their loom-like magic.

One theory associates ordinary thought with medium levels of overall brain activity or arousal and other kinds of consciousness (great mental excitement, ecstasy, meditative states, etc.) with very high or very low levels. Information is processed according to different rules at different levels of activity or arousal so that we are bound to specific states of consciousness as a result of specific states of activity or arousal. This theory associates creativity with an ability to shift or combine diverse levels of brain activity or arousal. (While interesting and perhaps illuminating, all current brain models must be considered simplistic.)

Alfred Adler, the Austrian psychiatrist, hypothesized that dreams are rehearsals or trial solutions to current problems. Common support for this belief comes from introspective observations, especially from writers. Some experimental evidence lends credence. Subjects scored higher on tests of both problem solving and creative thinking after sleep when "rapid eye movement" (REM) was present than after sleep when REM was absent. REM is always associated with dreaming; but does dreaming actually "cause" improvement in problem solving and creativity? Strict scientific logic cannot determine whether it was the dreaming per se or the psychophysiological state associated with REM that enhances subsequent problem solving and brings to mind creative new thought combinations that can be put to use the next morning.

Rational versus Nonrational

Rational inquiry and nonrational insight should be complements, not antagonists, in seeking solutions to complex problems. Brain research has shown that one side of the cerebral hemisphere, usually the left, is logical and cognitive, while the other side, usually the right, is holistic and affective. The left brain, the one that speaks, dissects the pieces; the right brain, the one that visualizes, synthesizes wholes; the left operates deductively and rigorously, the right by patterns and images. Creative decision making involves the exquisite interweaving of programmable logic and nonprogrammable impression. An executive requires both hemispheres active; he or she must see forest and trees. (Although popular, the brain lateralization model is highly stylized and simplistically stark. In fact, both hemispheres of the brain are actively involved in most mental functions. Nonetheless, the left brain–right brain dichotomy is, at least, a good *metaphor* for representing contrasting modes of the life of the mind.)

Personal opinion and values used to be dismissed. "Irrelevant" was its kindest appellation. Of course, executive desire could never be avoided. Now we take a different tack. We consider individual want perfectly respectable input for decision makers. Intuition has come out of the closet. There is new appreciation for the art of conceptualizing decisions amidst the science of analyzing them. A manager's subjective feelings should not be intimidated by objective tests. Executives should not be afraid to contradict the computer. But neither should they leap to arbitrary conclusions with wild abandon.

Procedure for Creative Decision Making

First assess the problem intuitively. One should not call expert advice too quickly or track traditional trains of thought too willingly. Isolation is vital: It allows the psyche minimum constraint and coercion, lessening the likelihood of interference from preset concepts and long-standing lines of logic. On the other hand, wholly intuitive decisions can be dangerous if quantitative input is ignored. Executives should make a nonrational decision—that is, a "creative" one—only after they clearly understand rational alternatives and logical implications of the "innovative" choice. Intuition and analysis must be tested against each other repetitively in a recursive process, with each iteration gaining greater confidence. But remember the key: Never begin by checking the experts, and always use insight and intuition *before* logic and analysis.

Decision Modifiers

What is creative management? More, to be sure, than external analysis and internal intuition. Psychological motivation and political positioning are also involved. "Stakeholder analysis" is a qualitative technique that segregates out relevant parties and projects personal attitudes of each. What's everyone's driving motivation, his or her "stake" in the matter? Crucial here is an assessment of individual feelings and hidden agendas. What's the private bottom line? Potential political standing and perceived career paths are often lurking beneath the surface and must be considered in all creative management decisions.

Are most executive decisions made rationally? If Yes, that's not necessarily good; if No, that's not necessarily bad. Decisions are made by people, and people are constrained by company traditions and manipulated by political bargaining. The inertia of functional departments to do things the way they have always done them, according to standard operating procedures, is a potent regulating mechanism, just as the influence of powerful personalities is a reality of the corporate hierarchy (Allison). The pervasive strength and profound pressure of long-set bureaucracies—formal staffs, assistant to's, budget directors—is more a focus of serious study than the butt of sarcastic humor. "Networking" a company—discovering channels through which influence flows— often shocks top management. How real power patterns are structured can differ markedly from official organization charts. (Watch the executive secretary!)

Decision Settings

Making creative decisions must take into account the nature of the organization. How to "cut a company" is essential for understanding the creativity-generating process and making the innovation ring right. Numerous dimensions are involved. Decision making, especially when strategic, is a function of social structure and corporate culture. Is the sector profit making or not for profit? The organization large or small? The product original or repetitive? The level of managerial decision top or middle? The personalities assertive or passive? The procedure individual or collective? For example, in a high-technology company, how should the chief operating officer direct the key research scientist? In a charitable foundation, what dollar value should be placed on subsidized concerts for poor children? In a manufacturing firm, what level of losses can be sustained before a division is dispatched? In the media, should a magazine publisher stop his or her editor from printing a story critical of a top advertiser? Each of these creative decisions, while similar in superficial form, differs in fundamental substance. The scientist is a creative sort, perhaps not receptive to close supervision. The artistic enrichment of the poor children defies quantification. The manufacturing division may become a vital resource in future years. The magazine may not exist without editorial freedom.

Compromise, said to be golden, is sometimes a weak manager's failure to choose between contradictory positions or people. As such, the "in-between" solution can be worse than either of the extremes—and be no solution at all. To allocate to each of two competing projects half the money requested dooms both to disaster. Confrontive collaboration, on the other hand, brings opposing parties together, encouraging interaction and establishing conditions for innovation. The dialectic of dissent, carefully controlled, is a marvelous antidote for the poison of group-think.

Models can be used as classification frameworks, as long as one doesn't take them too seriously. For example, consider "information required" and "dimensions of thinking." If decision makers use low information and think in only one dimension, they are decisive and independent, "dictators." If they use high information and think in one dimension, they're analytic and rigorous, "computer programs." If they use low information and think in many dimensions, they're flexible and fleeting, "scatterbrains." If they use high information and think in many dimensions, they're transformational and synthetic, "alchemists." (The integrated attitudes of the last type would seem to make the most effective executive under normal circumstances—although a company nearing bankruptcy might need a dictator, a mutual fund might want a computer program, and an advertising agency might fancy a scatterbrain.)

Creative versus Strategic

Creative management decisions begin novel in character, vague in structure, open ended in process, and ambiguous in context. Complex decisions in unfamiliar areas must be factored into simpler subdivisions in familar areas. Only then can strategic routines and procedures be applied: Problem recognition, diagnosis, solution search, alternative generation, alternative analysis, preliminary screening, serious evaluation, final choice, authorization, feedback, and review. The critical test of strategic management is *internal consistency*. Does the overall plan make sense? Does it resonate well with all issues and areas? Is, for example, the decision to launch a new product consistent with all functional departments: Is production ready to make it, marketing ready to sell it, financing ready to pay for it? (How often do ever-eager sales forces promise delivery before plants can produce the stuff!)

One often associates "creativity" with the arts and "innovation" with science and technology. While wholly appropriate in these contexts, creative and innovative management attains its potential as a *strategy-making* mechanism even more than a decision-making one. Thus a difference emerges between strategy making and decision making, the former subsuming larger scope and complexity. More than traditional tradeoffs between "optimizing" and "satisficing" reside here. Corporate power and prosperity are the chips being bet. Creative and innovative management, desirable for decision making, becomes essential for strategy making.

Creative Deal Making

Business has but two parts, managing people and making deals. Deal making should be a means not an end, a mechanism to achieve goals not a showcase for advancing ego. All participants should be satisfied on signing, committed during execution, pleased on reflection. Solution sets optimizing nonconflicting objectives are always present and should be sought. Good deals enhance reputations of all deal makers.

Getting the Edge

The popular press harangues us with predatory propaganda. If you're not a "gamesperson," you're a pushover; if you don't "win through intimidation," you're a pansy; if you don't "look out for Number One," you're a fool. Beating your customer, squeezing your supplier, pinning your partner—all too often these become goals. Too many businesspeople pride themselves on besting their buddies; they must twist an advantage to enjoy success; they must feel the turn of the screw. You know the type. A fair price is never fair. Grinding never stops. Agreements are made to be broken. Power plays are always made. A done deal is altered on signing. Simple meaning is perverted by arcane language. Some like to bully, others prefer to hoodwink—the former want to see you squirm, the latter relish the painless kill. Priorities are inverted, objectives pulled inside out. An edge-getter is often vain, more turned on by clever kill than by extra meat. What counts is not the spending power of bigger payoffs but the puffing power of smoother strokes. It's the edge itself that's sought, not necessarily the amount.

But crafty deal makers fool themselves more often than opponents. Distorted egos make sure deals less sure, closed deals not closed. Playing the ego game is fugitive and short sighted. Today's quick buck chokes off a thousand tomorrow. Streams of dollars that could flow in the future are never seen. The irony is that what is not seen is not known; no negative reinforcement ever occurs, no long-term consequences of short-term actions are ever appreciated. The edge-getting deal makers strut blithely on their pompous ways, smug that they've played the perfect games, won through intimidation, and looked after Number One—whereas, in reality, they have lost the game, flubbed the deal, and flattened Number One. What happens here happens often: new problems erupt, commitment drifts, time is lost, deals rupture, relationships tear, reputations ruin—all silly sacrifices on the altar of oneupmanship. Building the business takes a back seat when personal ego does the driving.

The Good Deal

Being a sharp businessperson means being a shrewd deal maker, someone who formulates, structures, and implements transactions and arrangements with skill and finesse, someone who plans, organizes, and executes the interchange of products, services, and monetary considerations. Such an animal, it is assumed, lives by wit and scheme, claw and fang, with only raw cunning providing cover. Yet the best businesspeople live by reputation, the evidence of track record, and the image of integrity.

A good deal, of course, does not require each party to play an equal role or even to make money. Natural power is distributed according to pre-existing patterns. For example, a liquidator may buy end-of-season merchandise below cost; but although manufacturers lose money on these particular lots, they convert unsalable inventory to cash, and if their overall costs have been covered, the transactions, in a real sense, produce pure profit.

Stages of Deal Making

Creative deal making involves understanding critical issues at each stage of the process. Deal making can be dissected into sequential stages, and although boundaries between them may be fuzzy, critical issues are usually clear.

Deciding. Too many people forget preliminaries and lose the ball game before it begins. Determining *whether* and *what* to deal often controls more of the outcome than all strategy and tactics. What are your long-term goals and short-term objectives here? Verbalizing the "obvious" often reveals it wasn't so obvious.

Preparing. Doing all your homework is essential. Complete, relevant information should be generated early on—and then boiled down before actual negotiations begin. Discern superficial stances and underlying necessities. Get your hands on all numbers, public statements and reports, private opinions, and interests. Treat both sides alike: Do self-analysis from your opponent's point of view.

Initiating. Postures and positions are established up front. Power plays of office venue, seating arrangements, first proposals, and immediate deadline setting are all well-known. But such subliminal irritations are more disruptive than useful. Effective deal makers establish people rapport at the outset, trying to discern bottom-line needs of opponents. Often such needs are not incompatible and win-win solution sets can be found.

Continuing. Persistence and patience are assets in any deal-making situation. Progress will never be linear so don't expect smooth rides. Ratcheting forward—two steps ahead, one step back, even one step sideways—is terrific. Be satisfied to continue the process even if the direction appears temporarily wrong. Overcoming frustration is important. Impasses may be surmounted by retreating to first principles. Why are we here? Sticking points are almost always the result of artificial hindrances (e.g., face saving) not fundamental fact barriers. Novelty is an effective win-win tactic; try generating fresh sets of alternatives to overcome inertia, even in the middle of protracted negotiations.

Concluding.   Have the sense to finalize when finished. Nothing is more creative than to know when the deal is done. Many deals have broken down after having been made because one side continued to press for advantage, which is invariably more psychological than substantive. Having an attitude of genuine pleasure at seeing your opponent achieve goals and fulfill needs is a marvelous test for the creative deal maker.

Deal-Making Strategies

The following principles produce good deals but not necessarily self-importance. They are creative in that they work, making the deal and enhancing the deal-maker's image.

1. *Show quiet self-confidence* .   Personal faith is perhaps the most vital trait for deal makers. But self-confidence that is effective is self-confidence that is understated. Show your surety with unruffled composure. Fortitude and tenacity do not exude conceit and presumptuousness. Be circumspect and very careful: Pomposity and arrogance are powerful turnoffs. Boasters and blowhards alienate more than they influence. Chips on shoulders cut opponents and splinter deals. Antagonizing the other side is a definite downer.

2. *Know what you want; don't worry what others get.*   It's self-defeating to judge by comparison. Jealousy and envy are diversions and become obstacles to successful business. With proper preparation and self-confidence, a deal maker can segregate needs and wants from what others ask and get. For instance, if you sell your company with fair price and terms, you should have no gripe if the buyer makes more money over time.

3. *Understand the other side* .   Project yourself into the place of those with whom you are dealing. What are their real requirements? Hopes? Plans? What are they looking for now, bottom line, and how important is it? Often, giving others what they want will not detract from what you get. If, say, the owner of a closely held firm wants to sell

in order to retire or for estate-planning purposes, price can become secondary to terms and conditions. Such a person might well sell his or her business—his or her beloved baby—to a buyer offering a lower price if he or she believes that these new managers will take better care of his or her legacy (employees, products, reputation, customers, etc.).

4. *Seek win-win solutions.* Search for areas in which each side can achieve certain of its goals, desirably primary ones, without adversely affecting the other. These optimal regions of win-win intersection can be surprisingly broad if one has insight to seek them and perception to recognize them. When one structures deals with imagination and intelligence, win-win solutions emerge. For example, the purchase price of an acquisition often can be allocated so that a greater percentage of the proceeds are taxed at better rates for the seller without altering cash requirements from the buyer; or similarly, parts of the purchase price can be deferred to a time of lower tax bite. (The buyer can in fact pay less, and the seller can in fact receive more!)

5. *Be comprehensive in representation and conservative in projection.* Hype sometimes helps sell a first deal but never a second. If all you have is one deal to do, have at it. But if you plan a career not a caper, give heed. Hype always hinders subsequent deals. Exaggeration is a short-term, rapidly depleting asset—and a long-term, quickly accruing liability. Don't be afraid to admit uncertainty about parts of your package—nothing can be that "perfect" and that "precise"—honesty enhances credibility and such admissions can be most disarming. Develop alternative scenarios: allow the other side choices; give room and keep options open. Use sensitivity analysis to show what might happen "if" various internal surprises or external shocks have an impact on the proposed transaction (such as sales up or down 10 percent, 20 percent, 30 percent; gross-margin problems; escalating interest rates). Make a conservative forecast of your most likely result; strive to exceed a somewhat pessimistic projection rather than fall behind a more optimistic one. Also, use sensitivity analysis to test the other side's options. Are they really at the breakpoint, or can they move a bit further?

6. *Answer questions nobody asked.* Nothing makes more impact than one side bringing up sensitive subjects about its own proposals that the other side never considered. For example, in negotiating bank financing a company should enumerate all assumptions, pointing precisely to areas of difficulty or ambiguity. The honesty shown will cause credibility to soar. Potential problems should be exposed by design, not hidden by default.

7. *Be fair but be frank.* Do not seek the upper hand—but do not play doormat either. Let others realize that you know game, rules, and players. Being fair does not mean being weak. (Weakness, in fact, encourages disruption by tempting the other side to expand its position.) Some of the toughest deal makers are also some of the fairest. If you decide to do business with certain suppliers even though their prices are not the lowest, be sure they know that you know the score.

8. *Act as if the other side will become your public relations agents.* Act this way because they *will.* No matter how confidential the negotiations, no matter how secret the deal, other people will hear about it. Word of your deeds and conduct will reach important ears. Regardless of how you envision yourself, what circulates is how others see you. Above all, never boast about besting. Reputation is a deal maker's most valuable asset. Protect it.

Bibliography

Allison, Graham T.: *Essence of Decision: Explaining the Cuban Missile Crisis*, Little, Brown, Boston, 1971.

Kuhn, Robert Lawrence: "Creative and Innovative Management—A Challenge to Academia," in A. Charnes and W. W. Cooper (eds.), *Creative and Innovative Management: Essays in Honor of George Kozmetsky*, Ballinger, Cambridge, 1984.

———— "Negotiating," in Lester R. Bittel and Jackson Ramsey (eds.), *Handbook for Professional Managers*, McGraw-Hill, New York, 1985.

PART 5

Innovation in Functional Management

Creativity throughout the Company

Managers make a mistake if they assume that creativity does not venture out of the R&D lab or the advertising studio. Creative and innovative management should not be restricted by functional bias. Corporate creativity must overcome long-standing prejudice. It should be free to pervade the organization—that's the point here—offering potential breakthroughs to all areas of business. Creative ideas in inventory control, for example, may have greater bottom-line impact—even in a science-based company—than in new product development. Creative and innovative managers look for novelty, freshness, and originality throughout their purview. They are never satisfied. Successful innovation, by the way, does not have to be revolutionary or "new to the world." All that's needed may be "new to the firm," if enhanced profit not puffed ego is the objective. The best companies do not gamble: They rigorously restrict new idea search to areas of distinctive competency, and they often define these areas in terms of customer need not company interest. In Part 5 we show what creative managers do, can do, or should do in various functional areas of business. Readers should appreciate the particulars and apply the principles. Creative management means specific application. We choose examples where you might expect (e.g., advertising and finance) and where you might not (e.g., accounting and interest rates). Innovations in various functional areas are considered: product quality, new financial instruments and ideas, advertising and public relations, computers and information. The use of personal computers for managerial creativity and strategic information as a competitive weapon are important new concepts, and we explore them in depth.

43

The Magic of Product Quality

Colby H. Chandler

Chairman of the Board and Chief Executive Officer,
Eastman Kodak Corporation

Walking through Explorers' Hall in the National Geographic Building in our nation's capital some years ago, I came across a quotation from author Tom Robbins: "Science gives a person what he wants. Magic gives him what he needs." It conveys a vital truth behind the strong interest in quality: Science and technology can provide only partial human satisfaction. It is the magic of human judgment that underlies quality—and it is *quality* that really meets human needs.

There is magic in quality—in the design, manufacture, and marketing of first-rate goods and services. And most often today, it is the CEO who must be the magician, who must lead a team of skilled professionals working behind the scenes with technology and timing to create something new, something different, something that challenges the mind while satisfying the heart.

That is not an easy task for those accustomed to relying on formulas and data. And yet, when tomorrow is characterized by ambiguity and surprise, yesterday's solutions may be neither appropriate nor relevant. Rationality must be balanced with intuition, information must be weighed against "gut feelings," and, in the end, it becomes the CEO's role not to reanalyze the data but to synthesize diverse opinions and supply unique insight.

Insight is often based on market research—but research that predicts customer behavior has at least one significant limitation: *People determine what they want . . . by what they think is possible.*

By ignoring market guidance, we miss an essential point: We must design what the *customer* wants to buy, and that may be somewhat different from what we want to produce. But by following market guidance too closely, we limit ourselves to incremental improvements and deny the breakthroughs that become revolutionary stimulants to market growth. For the CEO, the challenge is to listen to customers' "words" but to hear the underlying "music" and to base decisions on the enduring rhythms of the marketplace.

Kodak Camera History

In the late 1960s, we took the pulse of the photographic marketplace and found it strong. Our introduction of Kodak Instamatic cameras in 1963 had come at a time when consumers in the United States were taking about 2½ billion pictures per year. Some people were astonished at those numbers and felt they could never rise appreciably. But our introduction of cartridge-loading cameras quickened the pace. By 1968, annual exposures in the United States more than doubled. Photography was still growing. From the consumers' point of view, photography was more convenient than ever and they were satisfied. But Kodak management saw a different vision.

We believed then—and we continue to believe now—that the most successful products simply set higher standards and tougher challenges. Leadership consists of building on those standards and meeting those challenges. And so, in 1972, we moved forward again by taking all the convenience built into the Instamatic products and making a pocket-sized camera. It was the right product at the right time and the market responded. By 1979, U.S. traditional exposures more than doubled again—to 9 billion. But, even as we introduced the pocket-sized products, we knew we must eventually go beyond them—and we knew that this time, the criteria for success were rising.

Changing Concepts of Quality

In the 1950s, 1960s, and even into the early 1970s, the equation for success was straightforward: *Quality = technological innovation =*

market growth. In other words, people perceived "newer" to mean "better," "different" to mean "more advanced," and "high tech" to mean "more desirable." Quality was in the hands of engineers, and marketing's task was simply to deliver the newest invention to receptive customers. But by the late 1970s—as we devised, designed, and developed the replacement for pocket cameras—people's perceptions began to change. Quality became a far more complex equation.

Engineers still played a critical role because innovation was still the essence of quality, but consumers began to question: Was the product really better or was it just *cosmetically* different? And equally important: Did it fit their lifestyle? Could it enhance their self-image? Would it provide good value? Would it be convenient to obtain and to use— and easy to understand? Could it . . .? Would it . . .? Should it . . .? It was clear: Those intangibles needed to be factored into any equation of quality. And that equation also had to include the concerns of our research, manufacturing, and marketing communities. A traditional approach to quality would not be sufficient. No longer could we judge quality by the product's appearance; no longer could we measure quality by calculating defect rates; no longer could we "inspect quality in" at the end of the line. Because those criteria simply determined whether a product looked different and worked consistently. Customers would take those factors for granted. Quality—for them—meant much more.

But if consumers wanted cameras that would meet their lifestyles, we needed to know as much about their personal lives as we knew about our manufacturing lines. If they wanted a camera that was easy to use, we needed to know how they expected to use it. If they wanted a camera to provide good value, we needed to know what *they* (not we) thought "value" meant. And we needed to know all that *before* we designed the product. Because if we did it right the first time, we could not only satisfy customers' needs, but we could meet our own expectations of profitability and growth.

Quality was no longer the narrow domain of the manufacturing community; it was, in fact, the responsibility for every division and every operation throughout our enterprise. And, what had been an informal approach to quality would now need to be more formalized— everyone, everywhere, from vendors to employees to distributors, had to understand this new meaning of quality.

Our policy contains three key points: In quality, (1) the customer is the arbiter, (2) everyone is the owner, and (3) quality cannot be a program; it must be a way of life.

Kodak's Quality Elements

The Customer is the Arbiter

In the 1950s we first set up finishing operations to make prints from our Kodacolor film. One laboratory was in Rochester, New York, another in Palo Alto, California. But it was our scientists in Rochester who set the aim points for the right color balance for prints, and they established these standards using strictly scientific criteria. It was not long after we began sampling Palo Alto's prints for quality that we noticed that their printers were out of adjustment. The flesh tones in their pictures looked far too "warm"—but surprisingly there were no customer complaints. When the color was changed to be technically correct, that was when customer complaints started to arrive! We had discovered a basic truth: Customers wanted what they *liked*—not what was *technically* right—and what they liked were warm pictures because warm pictures made them appear healthier, as if they had a tan.

In the years since, we have impressed upon our people that their customers may be outside the company or they may be inside—but it is every person's job to know the customer and to meet his or her needs. Everyone has a customer. And it is the customer—not you—who sets your course, measures your progress, and, ultimately, determines your success.

Everyone is an Owner of Quality

But the CEO must be quality's ultimate champion—supporting new directions and encouraging new approaches. And don't forget the passion and persistence that occasionally make us a pain in the bureaucracy! It is not enough to give a once-a-year speech on quality. It is not enough to allow managers to pay lip service to the latest fad. Quality must be woven into the very fabric of day-to-day operations. We have taken up that challenge by asking all of our people to define the meaning of quality in their jobs—and to set tangible, measurable, and achievable quality goals. These goals must be relevant for their positions and organizations. Quality plans are part of our annual operating plans. Quality considerations are at the heart of research allocations and capital budget programs. Quality is the basis for all staffing plans. And targets for quality are reviewed—and challenged—on a regular basis by top management.

Quality is a Way of Life

But quality is also a moving target. Just as the consumer's definition of quality changed from the 1950s to today, so, too, it continues to change. In fact, customers seem to see quality not as an absolute but as a continuum of trade-offs. For example, people may trade off high quality for low price, or they may trade off some features for other benefits. The challenge is to anticipate where consumers will place your product on the continuum, determine what they will trade for what they want, and set your own quality targets accordingly.

Yet we reach for more complex levels. Quality is often based on customers' perceptions. But perceptions become reality when customers select from a variety of alternatives. And, of course, customers translate perceptions. Why else, for example, would airlines wash their airplanes? Why else would we pay as much attention to packaging as we pay to products?

New Product Quality

As we began to design the camera that would be a step beyond pocket cameras—and as we weighed and balanced the customer's definition of quality—we in general management set two targets for the program: We would first determine what was desirable from the customer's viewpoint —*before* we determined if it were possible from our viewpoint. And second we would try to make it right—*before* we determined how we would make it profitable.

There is risk in those objectives, but there is almost certain failure in the alternatives. Those who do only what they are certain is possible seldom stretch themselves to discover what is desirable. And those who set out to do only what is profitable almost never do what is right. We were confident that, if we could engineer *in* what the customer wanted, we could engineer *out* the costs we could not afford.

But what did the customer want? To determine that, we looked at their pictures—thousands of them, taken by people of varying photographic ability, with various cameras and films, in all types of situations. As we began to sort those pictures—and categorize them according to camera-to-subject distance, light level, and number of pictures taken— it became obvious that people wanted to take good pictures in many situations that were beyond the capabilities of their cameras, their film, or their accessory flash equipment. And when the picture did not come out as well as they hoped, they did not blame the camera, they blamed themselves.

We knew other factors were at work. But we knew also that to provide the results the snapshooters wanted, we needed to provide more than a camera: We needed to provide a new system that would be designed, manufactured, packaged, promoted, and delivered differently from any before. The magnitude of the project required *management* from many people throughout the company, but it demanded *leadership* from us. The CEO would set the tone, establish the mood, and provide a unique viewpoint.

Change often consists of innovating from among the same parameters of technology. Quality—the giant leap—requires a discontinuity, a real break with the past. To achieve our discontinuity, managers began playing with wooden blocks cut in various shapes. As we tested the various shapes, we asked: Would a camera like this be comfortable to use? Would it fit in a pocket or purse? Could it be durable and dependable? And, in a series of market research tests, we asked snapshooters the same questions.

As we were settling on a design, our engineers were inventing the circuitry and optics that would enable these wooden blocks to take pictures where and when our customers wanted to take them. Our job became one of encouraging those engineers to be limited only by their imaginations. We told them: "Just because something is impossible does not mean we should not do it. And just because it has not been invented does not mean we do not need it."

As the product took final shape, we put early production models to the ultimate test: Were they simple enough for corporate officers to use? Our cameras, and our corporate officers, passed the test, and on February 3, 1982, we announced our system to the world. We called it disc photography from Kodak.

Looking back on that process, at least one point becomes clear: For many quality targets, our aim was true. We did design a system the customer perceived to be innovative, convenient, affordable, and fun to use. And as those customers continue to tell us, they get more good pictures with this camera than they got with any previous model. We received a vote of confidence from the media when *Fortune* magazine named the Kodak disc camera one of the ten most innovative products of 1982. And our competitors liked our system so well that nearly a dozen of them introduced disc products of their own.

From a research point of view, the innovative concepts in optics and electronics that were designed for disc are now finding other applications in product ideas that are still on the drawing boards. And we are using the T-grain emulsion that is the basis for current disc film in other sensitized goods ranging from x-ray films to printing products. From a manufacturing viewpoint, defective products are virtually nonexistent.

The disc camera is the most reliable camera we have ever offered to the marketplace. But there were other targets of quality for which our aimpoint was out of sync with the speed of the targets.

Quality in a Complex Environment

Our products entered the global marketplace at a time of worldwide recession. At the same time, the overvalued dollar through the early 1980s put pressure on a multinational company's ability to produce in the United States and market abroad. What may have been affordable at yesterday's currency rates could be too expensive at tomorrow's.

This means that the quality equation has become even more complex. Quality is not only a function of customer needs and manufacturing capabilities. It must be measured against a background of political and societal considerations that change at ever-increasing rates. For all those—including CEOs—involved in the design and delivery of new products and services, such market dynamism should be more invigorating than discouraging. Because it simply says that technology is not enough. For true quality, we must look beyond technology—to ourselves. We must do more than generate information, analyze data, and scrutinize successful formulas. We must rely equally on the business experience we have, the changes we sense, and the trends we foresee. Unless we provide *quality leadership* in whatever capacity we serve, unless we become the champion of new directions and new approaches, unless we stop comparing ourselves against yesterday and start measuring ourselves against tomorrow, unless we shape strong values and set high targets, we are not discharging full responsibility to our organizations, to our customers, or to ourselves.

44

Manufacturing Quality for the Creative Manager

Philip B. Crosby

President, Philip B. Crosby & Associates

Henry Longton came into the president's office, a worried expression on his face and a crumpled paper in his hand. "I have had it with this stuff. Complaints, problems, lost sales—it's just more than I can take."

The president waved him to a chair. "Take it easy, Hank. I'm sorry I don't have a bowl of hot soup to offer you. That's what my mother would do if she were here."

"I don't need soup," muttered Longton, "I need products that don't always have problems in them." Hank leaned forward. "The new ones aren't a bit better than the old ones. We make lousy stuff."

"Now it can't be that bad," the president smiled. "We have to meet market needs. Sometimes there just isn't enough time. Quality costs money. But we are as good as our competitors."

"Think so?" Hank asked, reaching into his pocket. "Take a look at this." He laid the device on the president's desk, where it was examined critically. "This looks like our model 329."

"With three exceptions," commented Hank. "One, it does what 329 does and six more things; two, it costs 40 percent less to make; and three, it works forever."

The president shook his head. "I know that company. They aren't any better than us. Are you kidding me?"

"They're a new outfit now. They've been concentrating on quality, and it's paying off. Also, their new products development is creating like crazy."

"But we work on quality; we have a Quality Assurance Department, and the manager can see me anytime. I put something about it in the annual report. We discuss quality at almost every executive meeting."

"We only talk about it in terms of the problems we have with quality, and we've been firing the quality manager every year or so. They wouldn't come tell us about a problem if we insisted."

"Well, what else can we do? Quality control is a technical problem, and it is inexact. Nothing is perfect and it would cost a fortune to make it come close. All the rules and regulations would destroy the innovative process that has made our company great. I worked in research for years, and you just can't do it on a schedule with a lot of controls."

"We have to do something about quality," insisted Hank. "The place to begin is with a new understanding of it. The solution lies in changing the way we manage the company rather than the way the quality manager runs the QA Department. Let me come back with a plan. And it won't be expensive."

Many such conversations, with modifications, have been taking place in recent years. Executives and managers are struggling with quality. The more creative they become, the worse the quality gets; the more innovation they put into control and motivation systems, the less employees think they are serious. It is, as Yul Brynner used to say, "a puzzlement."

To be successful, a company has to have an environment in which people feel they have permission to do things right and in which management is on their side. People don't work for a company; they work for their boss and what that position represents. The boss who leaves quality up to the quality department, human happiness to human resources, compensation to finance, and so forth is in trouble. People just do not respond to the impersonal. Programs don't change people or companies.

Quality is the result of a lifestyle that can be created by one department or a whole company. That lifestyle grows out of an understanding of what quality is and how it is accomplished. The understanding forms a foundation for communications inside the organization. Then people can work together in harmony because they know what they are supposed to do. They begin to have confidence that management is on their side and wants to help.

Absolutes of Quality Management

The concepts of quality are contained in what I call the absolutes of quality management. There are four of them:

1. *Definition.*   Quality means conformance to the requirements; it does not mean goodness.

2. *System.*   Prevention is the means to accomplish quality; not inspection and test.

3. *Performance standard.*   Do it right the first time (symbolically, zero defects); reject "acceptable quality levels."

4. *Measurement.*   The price of nonconformance; no indexes.

If we want employees to do it right the first time, we have to make certain they know what "it" is. They must have requirements they can understand and accept. It is management's job to cause these requirements to exist. That doesn't mean stopping everything while a whole new set of paperwork is drawn up; it means doing what we have now, though clarity and improvement may be necessary.

Clear requirements help make the process come out right each time. Prevention is vaccinating the operation. Prevention by vaccination lets us deal with a disease by *not* having it rather than learning how to cope with its effects. In business situations, this means setting up processes, whether in manufacturing, administration, or services, that will do the job properly if followed. Then we assist people in learning how to follow them. When it comes time to improve the processes, that too must be done in a controlled manner. That way, everyone knows what they are supposed to do differently. A performance standard of less than "do it right the first time" puts the manager in the position of spending time saying: "This is okay; that is not okay," all day long deciding what is good *enough*.

Most purchasing is done to "acceptable quality levels"—which implies to the supplier that it is not necessary to produce materials or services that are in agreement with stated requirements. Instead, a portion is permitted to deviate. A policy of zero defects eliminates the need for deviations. Management must make this clear by saying that the quality policy of the operation is "We will deliver defect-free products and services on time to our customers."

Measurement has to be related to money, or management will not take it seriously. The "price of nonconformance" (PONC) approach is the way to make that happen. The comptroller's office has to determine where all waste is spent. In addition to obvious things like blue- and white-collar rework, scrap, warranty, field service, customer service, and such, there are other categories. Excess inventory, software debug time, lost sales, overdue accounts receivable (most are caused by problems produced by the organization that sent the bill, not the one that received it), and dozens of others. After a procedure is developed, regular financial reports should cover this item. The stakes are large. In hardware companies, the PONC is over 25 percent of sales; in administrative or service companies it is 45 percent of operating costs. A real opportunity for improvement in every area of operations.

Implementation of Quality Management

Implementing quality management requires setting up a "quality improvement process" in a volunteer but formal way. The whole thing has to become part of the "woodwork" of the company rather than an add-on. This requires several years of doing it until everyone finally believes management is serious. During this time, individuals learn their personal responsibilities. Improvement comes rapidly and satisfactorily but can retreat just as quickly when the earnestness of the commitment is suspect.

There are three phases in making it happen:

1. *Conviction.*   When the manager begins to wonder how come nothing really works or is reliable. As a result, there comes a period of study and reflection and the desire to make changes that will really make the right things happen.

2. *Commitment.*   When the manager begins to take action, to get help and learn, to bring people into the equation: when policies and processes change, then integrity begins to be seen. It is like a diet in that improvement is visual and obvious, but individuals have to remind themselves minute by minute of things to do and not to do.

3. *Conversion.*   When quality becomes natural and people don't even ask "Is this good enough?" anymore.

Bibliography

Crosby, Philip, *Quality without Tears—The Art of Hassle-Free Management*, McGraw-Hill, New York, 1984.
———— *Running Things, The Art of Making Things Happen*, McGraw-Hill, New York, 1986.

45

Proper Positioning Is Creative Advertising

Jack Trout

President, Trout and Ries Advertising, Inc.

Al Ries

Vice President, Trout and Ries Advertising, Inc.

If one word marked the course of advertising in the 1970s, and 1980s, it was "positioning." Positioning has become the buzzword of advertising and marketing people, not only in this country but around the world. How did the concept get its start? It all began in 1969 in an obscure magazine called Industrial Marketing. The article, written by us, was entitled, "Positioning Is a Game People Play in Today's Me Too Marketplace." It named names and made predictions, all based on the "rules" of a game we called positioning.

The question most frequently asked is "why? " Why do we need a new approach to advertising and marketing? The answer today is the same as it was then. We have become an overcommunicated society. With only 5 percent of the world's population, America consumes 57 percent of the world's advertising output. The per-capita consumption of advertising in the United States today is about $375 a year for every man, woman, and child. If you spend $1,000,000 a year on advertising, you are bombarding the average consumer with less than ½ cent of advertising, spread out over 365 days. To talk about the "impact" of advertising is to overstate the potential effectiveness of your messages. It's an egocentric view that bears no relationship to the realities of the marketplace. In the communication jungle out there, the only hope of scoring big is to be selective, to concentrate on narrow targets, to practice segmentation. In a word, positioning.

Mind Changing

Millions of dollars have been wasted trying to alter opinions with advertising. Once a mind is made up, it's almost impossible to change it. Certainly not with a weak force like advertising. "Don't confuse me with facts, my mind's made up." The average person cannot tolerate being told he or she is "wrong." Mind-changing is the road to advertising disaster.

Back in 1969, we used the computer industry as an example of the folly of trying to alter attitudes. Company after company tried to tell people its computers were "better" than IBM's. Yet that doesn't "compute" in the prospect's mind. "If you're so smart," says the prospect, "how come you're not rich like IBM?" The computer position in the minds of most people is filled with the big blue letters, IBM. For a competitive manufacturer to obtain a favorable position in the prospect's mind, the company must somehow relate to IBM's position. In other words, don't try to change the prospect's mind at all. Accept what's up there and work around it. It's the only hope in today's overcommunicated society.

The classic example is the famous Avis campaign. "Avis is only No. 2 in rent-a-cars. So why go with us? We try harder." This program was extremely successful for Avis until corporate egos got in the way. Then the company launched a campaign that said "Avis is going to be No. 1." No way. In the ensuing years, Avis has run many different advertising campaigns. "The wizard of Avis," "You don't have to run through airports," etc. But what is the single theme that leaps into your mind when someone mentions Avis? No. 2, of course. Yet Avis in the last few years has consistently ignored this No. 2 theme.

We call this the "F.W.M.T.S." trap—forgot what made them successful. If you want to be successful today, you can't ignore the competitor's position. Nor can you walk away from your own. In the immortal words of Joan Didion, "Play it as it lays."

Another advertiser that fell into the F.W.M.T.S. trap is 7-Up. With the Uncola campaign, the company successfully positioned its 7-Up drink as an alternative to Coke and Pepsi. (Almost two-thirds of all the soft drinks consumed in the United States are cola drinks.) But then they dropped this idea and started to say, "America is turning 7-Up."America was doing no such thing. 7-Up was advertising their aspirations. No different conceptually than the "Avis is going to be No. 1" campaign. And no more effective.

Name Pushing

No aspect of positioning has proved as controversial as the "importance of the name." Our 1969 example was Eastern Airlines. Among the four largest domestic airlines, Eastern ranks consistently at the bottom on passenger surveys. Why? Eastern has a "regional" name that puts them in a different category from the big nationwide carriers (American, United, TWA). The name "Eastern" puts the airline in the same category with Southern, North Central, Piedmont, Allegheny. After many years of effort, Eastern still ranks at the bottom of the big four. You see what you expect to see. The passenger who has a bad experience on American or United says "It was just one of those things." An exception to the good service he or she was expecting. The passenger who has a bad experience on Eastern says "It's that darn Eastern Airlines again." A continuation of the bad service he or she was expecting.

Take any two abstract drawings. Write the name Schwartz on one and Picasso on the other. Then ask someone for an opinion. You see what you expect to see. Pour a bottle of Gallo into an empty 50-year-old bottle with a French burgundy label. Then carefully decant a glass in front of a friend and ask for an opinion. You taste what you expect to taste. Were it not so, there would be no role for advertising. Were the average consumer rational instead of emotional, there would be no advertising. At least not as we know it today.

One prime objective of advertising is to heighten expectations. To create the illusion that the product or service will perform the miracles you expect. And presto, it does. But create the opposite expectation and the product is in trouble. The introductory advertising for Gablinger's beer created a feeling that because it was a diet product, it would taste bad. And sure enough, the advertising worked! People tried it and were convinced it did taste bad. Allegheny Airlines saw the light and changed their name to U.S. Air. Since then they've taken off.

Yes, but don't industrial customers buy on reason not emotion? On logic and fact? No way. Ask IBM's competitors. Or Xerox's or General Electric's. Especially for high-priced technology products such as computers and copiers, the average industrial buyer tends to be far more emotional than your average Charmin-squeezing housewife (who, more often than not, is downright practical).

Industrial customers are also cursed by a "play it safe" attitude. You can't blame them. No housewife ever got fired for buying the wrong brand of coffee. But plenty of industrial buyers have been in deep trouble over a high-technology buy that went sour. The trend in industrial products is toward more sophistication, more use of integrated circuits, fiber optics, lasers, etc. So you can expect the industrial buyer to buy more on feelings, hunches, and especially reputation. And less on objective product comparisons. Which is why "factual expository copy" is getting less important in industrial advertising and positioning more important.

Line Extension Trap

Line extension has swept through the marketing community. And for sound reasons. Logic is on the side of line extension. Arguments of economics. Trade acceptance. Customer acceptance. Lower advertising costs. Increased income. Reduced costs. The corporate image. As we said, logic is on the side of line extension. Truth, unfortunately, is not.

The paradox of marketing is that conventional wisdom is almost always wrong. Xerox went out and bought a computer company that had a perfectly good name: Scientific Data Systems. And what was the first thing they did? They changed the name to Xerox Data Systems. Then they ran an ad that said, "This Xerox machine can't make a copy." Any Xerox machine that couldn't make a copy was headed for trouble, believe us. When Xerox folded its computer operations, it cost more millions to sweep up the mess.

Singer went out and did the same thing with the old, respected Frident name. One of their introductory ads said, "Singer Business Machines Introduces Touch & Know." Get it? Touch and know, touch and sew. This is the ultimate positioning mistake. To try to transfer a generic brand name to a different product sold to a different market. And then to top it off, to knock off your own sewing machine slogan! "Touch and Go" would have been more appropriate. When they folded this operation, Singer set a record—one of the largest single-quarter write-offs ever reported, $341,000,000.

You can't hang a company on a name today. You need a position. So if your corporate name is inappropriate for the new product you intend to market, create a new one. And a new position to go with it.

No-Name Trap

Of all the positioning concepts outlined back in 1969, this one generated the most instant acceptance. A strong name is superior to a meaningless set of initials. The "initialitis" that struck American business in the late 1960s and early 1970s abated. Some companies even went back to their original names.

Flanking Maneuvers

"A company has no hope to make progress head-on against the position that IBM has established." Perhaps the most quoted sentence from the original article. As true today as it was then. IBM has an overwhelming position in the broad middle range of computers. So, how do you compete against IBM? The big computer successes have been the companies that avoided going head-to-head with IBM. Digital Equipment Corp. and Compaq, in particular, at the small end of the market. This "new front" idea we call "flanking warfare." You avoid the competitors' high ground by outflanking them.

In 1968, Goodyear had sales of $2.9 billion while B.F. Goodrich's sales were $1.3 billion. Ten years later, in 1978, Goodyear had sales of $7.4 billion while B.F. Goodrich had $2.5 billion. So the rich get richer. But what is odd is that the loser's advertising continued to get all the publicity. "We're the other guys" got much favorable attention in the press. But not much favorable attention from the tire-buying public.

Eclipsing Creativity

But what really rattled the cages of Madison Avenue gurus was positioning's implied attack on "creativity." Even though creativity was not mentioned in the 1969 article, we didn't hesitate to attack it later on. By 1972, we were saying "Creativity is dead. The name of the advertising game in the '70s is positioning." In truth, the decade of the 1970s might well be characterized as a "return to reality." White knights and black eyepatches gave way to positioning concepts such as Lite Beer's "Everything you've always wanted in a great beer. And less." Poetic? Yes. Artful? Yes. But also a straightforward, clearly defined explanation of the basic positioning premise.

The Customer King is Dead

Since positioning has been around a while, it might be appropriate to ask, where do we go from here? If creativity belonged to the 1960s and positioning to the 1970s and 1980s, where will we be in the 1990s? Would you believe us if we told you that in the next decade we will be *burying* the marketing concept? Probably not, but we'll tell you anyway. For at least 50 years now, astute advertising people have preached the marketing gospel. "The customer is king," said the marketing moguls. Over and over again they used their wondrous presentations to warn top management that to be "production oriented" instead of "customer oriented" was to flirt with disaster. And plenty of companies who have dutifully followed their marketing experts have seen millions of dollars disappear in valiant but disastrous customer-oriented efforts.

Who do you suppose masterminded those classic positioning mistakes? Not amateurs but full-fledged marketing professionals with briefcases full of credentials. General Electric in computers. Singer in business machines. Sara Lee in frozen dinners. Of course, these marketing executives had excuses for failure. "Product problems." "Not enough capital." Or the ever popular, "Not enough distribution." Can it be that marketing itself was the problem?

Many managers are beginning to realize that something is wrong. That the traditional definition of marketing—to be customer oriented—is becoming obsolete. To get perspective, go back to the 1920s, when industry started its dramatic march forward. It was then that business first became production oriented. This was the heyday of Henry Ford and his Model T. You could have any color you wanted as long as it was black. Mr. Ford was more interested in keeping his production lines rolling (and his prices down) than keeping his customers satisfied. Advertising was an important ingredient in the scheme of things. Advertising's first commandment was, "Mass advertising creates mass demand, which makes mass production possible." Neat. Except that General Motors tooled up its production lines to please its prospects rather than its production engineers and quickly grabbed sales leadership from Ford. Things haven't been the same since.

In the aftermath of World War II, business became customer oriented with a vengeance. The marketing person was in charge, no doubt about it, and his or her power base was marketing research. But today, *every* company has become marketing oriented. So knowing what the customer wants isn't too helpful anymore if a dozen other companies are already serving his or her wants.

A small but growing number of experts believe that the customer isn't what he or she used to be. Confusion has set in. In many categories, customers no longer perceive any large differences in products. Thus, brand choice will not be based on a rational search of all brands in the category but on a brand previously tried. Or on the leader or the one positioned to the prospect's segment. It is becoming more and more difficult to change buying patterns once they are established. The customer doesn't really want to accept any more information in a category in which he or she has already formed an opinion, no matter how dramatically or how creatively this information is presented.

Competitor Oriented

To be successful today, a company must be competitively astute. It must look for weak points in the positions of its competitors and then launch marketing attacks against those windows of vulnerability. For example, while others were losing millions in the computer business, DEC was making millions by exploiting IBM's weakness in small computers.

Aren't competitors always considered in a well-thought-out marketing plan? Sure. Usually toward the back of the book under a heading entitled "Competitive Evaluation." Almost as an afterthought. Up front with prominence is the major part of the plan. The details of marketplace, the various demographic segments, and a myriad of "customer" research statistics carefully gleaned from endless focus groups, test panels, concept, and market tests. That's a mistake. Priorities are reversed.

The future marketing plan won't be called a marketing plan at all, but a competitive analysis or battle plan. In the battle plan of the future, many more pages will be dedicated to competition. The plan will carefully dissect each participant in the marketplace. It will develop a list of competitive strengths and weaknesses as well as a plan of action to either exploit or defend against them. There might even come a day when such a plan will contain a dossier on each of the competitors' key management executives, which will include their favorite tactics and styles of operation. (Not unlike the ones the Germans kept on the Allied commanders in World War II.)

And we're not talking about the distant future. It's old news that management hasn't caught up with yet. In the August 1978 issue of *Management Review* is a report entitled, "Customer or Competitor: Which Guideline for Marketing? " Alfred R. Oxenfeldt and William L. Moore spell out six weaknesses that can make a firm vulnerable to an attack from a competitor: The article's basic premise was that switching to competitor orientation can provide better payoff. In the August 1978 issue of *Business Horizons*, Williams S. Sachs and George Benson state the issue directly. "Is it time to discard the marketing concept?"

Marketing Warfare

What does all this portend for the marketing people of the 1990s? (Or whatever they're going to be called.) In simple terms, it means that they have to be prepared to wage marketing warfare. That's the new name of the new game. Successful marketing campaigns will have to be planned like military campaigns. Strategic planning will become more and more important. Companies will have to learn how to attack, defend, and flank their competition. And when to resort to guerrilla warfare. They will need better intelligence on how to anticipate competitive moves.

On a personal level, successful marketing people will have to exhibit many of the same virtues that make a great general. Courage, boldness, loyalty, and perseverance. The winners in the marketing battles of the future will be those men and women who have best learned the lessons of military history. The marketing people who have learned to plan like Alexander the Great, maneuver like Napoleon Bonaparte, and fight like George S. Patton. They will also know their competitors better than they know their customers.

46

Clarity and Creativity in Public Relations

Peter Hannaford

Chairman of the Board, The Hannaford Company, Inc.

Several decades ago, pioneer Edward Bernays defined public relations as "the attempt by information, persuasion, and adjustment to engineer public support for an activity, cause, movement, or institution." The definition is apt today. It will fit any contemporary public relations situation, such as marketing a product or service, a charitable fund drive, management of a crisis situation, or an initiative to modify public policy at the federal, state, or local level. How does a creative manager put this definition to work? What makes an effective public relations program?

Goals and Strategies

Before examining the many public relations "tools" available, one must have a *clear communications objective* . What is the *single* most important concept to establish? It should be set clearly and concisely. There can be secondary objectives but only one primary idea to which all others must relate. To have several different objectives of equal weight is to guarantee that the PR program will only confuse the audience it was intended to persuade.

Identifying the communications objective and describing it in a concise statement is the "why" of an effective program. Next, identify the target audiences, the "who" of the effort. Only now, with both the "why" and the "who" articulated, comes the "how," the strategy—which is the inventory of the tools to use and the ways to use them. (Don't confuse strategies with objectives. Communicating a favorable impression about a new product to a new market is an *objective* . Getting a photograph of the mayor using the product in tomorrow's newspaper is a *strategy.*)

Tools and Techniques

Many vehicles are available for crafting a public relations program. Here is a sampling: *Press releases* (for print media), audio and videotape releases (for broadcast media), and media information kits. *News conferences* (to introduce a product or service or announce an important business development). A variation, the media briefing, has a less formal format. *Direct mail* (used especially for fund raising and for generating support for a public policy position). *Magazine and newspaper articles* (including opinion articles for the "op-ed" page). *Letters to the editor; Conferences, seminars, and forums. Special events* (e.g., a reception to introduce a new product line). *Advertising* (e.g., advocating a position on an issue). *Books* (Lee Iacocca's best selling autobiography helps popularize Chrysler products and, as a by-product, a potential political personality). *Speeches and speaking tours. Interviews on radio and television* (e.g., to promote a new book or to counter a crisis as Johnson and Johnson did after the Tylenol poisoning cases by making its senior executive readily available for interviews).

Whatever combination of tools is used to devise a public relations strategy to achieve a communications objective, keep in mind the importance of three factors—integrating the various elements of the program, constructing a carefully paced timetable, and assessing performance at regular intervals. Ideally, a thorough program should "benchmark" public opinion by a market survey prior to commencing, then use "checkpoint" surveys to determine any changes in public attitudes about the product, service, or cause. Short of such investment, there is temptation to measure the program's success by simple bulk, say by the number of column inches of news clippings it produces. While this is one criterion, resist considering it the definitive one. Sample the opinions of key influencers, such as dealers and distributors (or other known "constituents" of your program). Take such samples from time to time to detect movement or trends for better or worse. If selling a product or service, sales results over time is the best gauge of success. In the public policy arena, measurement may be easier. When, for example, the objective is to kill a particular piece of legislation, the objective is achieved by the failure of the bill to pass by the end of the legislative body's term.

Integrating public relations elements is a creative task and critical for the senior executive. Elements of the program should be so selected that one extends the reach and coverage of another. For example, when embarking on a nationwide speaking tour, schedule interviews in each city with local editors and radio and television talk show hosts. Amplification and leverage are key. Rarely be restricted to just a speech to the local service club or chamber of commerce. The message will be the same but will be greatly enhanced when the media are brought in. Bear in mind, however, that live coverage of business speeches to local service clubs is not common. If your name is a household word or there is genuine news to communicate—if so, let the media know in advance—your speech may be the exception. Otherwise, assume the speech will not be covered.

Always try to help journalists do their job. They cover many stories, and by supplying them with information, you could push your story to the head of the line. Give, for example, an advance copy of your speech to interviewers for better questions and coverage. Have reprint booklets of the speech mailed to select audiences your organization wishes to influence. Thus, the leverage: One speech may influence much larger and more diverse audiences through print and broadcast interviews and by direct mailings to target groups such as customers.

Case 1: Media Relations in Corporate Crisis

Most "marketing" PR campaigns are a case of putting one's best foot forward, and the difference between failure and success often rests on careful planning: setting clear objectives, employing the right tools, integrating the program, and maintaining consistency and focus. Crisis management, on the other hand, is a sudden, sustained effort to contain negatives and control damage.

When a company makes products or performs services that could be involved in life-threatening situations or environmental dangers, it needs a standby crisis management program. Indeed, whenever a company sells things to the public or otherwise meets the public in any numbers, it requires such a contingency program. The creative manager plans for the unexpected.

The basic rules of crisis management are simple. It is the execution that is difficult. First, designate a single senior spokesperson for the organization. He or she may have deputies (someone may have to be on duty around the clock for several days, so shifts may be necessary), but there should be no confusion about whom the news media should contact. The spokesperson must be readily available and as forthright as circumstances permit. He or she should stick to the facts. No speculation, no hypothetical situations, no erroneous or misleading information. While not all the facts may be available at any given moment, what is said must be factual to that time.

How does it work in real life? After the much-publicized Tylenol poisoning event, a number of "copy cat" cases broke out. The Hygrade Food Products Corp., Southfield, Michigan, which makes a popular brand of frankfurters (Ball Park) and other meat products, did not expect a crisis. Few firms ever do. When one hit, it had the suddenness of a cyclone and, for a few days, imperiled the future of the company. What saved Hygrade, as it turned out, was outward calmness in responding to the crisis, along with centralizing all media contact with a single spokesperson. Underlying this approach was the fact that Hygrade, a mid-sized firm in the $200-million-a-year sales range, took pride in turning out good quality products and had healthy labor relations with its employees.

Hygrade's management was dismayed when in October 1982 it was flooded with reports of consumers in its home market area (Detroit) who claimed to have found foreign objects in their Ball Park frankfurters. There were fourteen such reports, and they were frightening. The first was from a housewife who claimed she found a razor blade in a frank she had taken fresh from the package. Two thoughts crossed the mind of Hygrade's Charles Ledgerwood, Vice President of Operations. One was that a chip of plant machinery might somehow have gotten into the frank accidentally; the other was that an irrational employee might have sabotaged it deliberately.

Ledgerwood visited the housewife the next day and saw that it was, indeed, a piece of razor blade that had been in the frank. Chipped machinery was ruled out. He reported his findings to the company president. They made two crucial decisions: they would be open with the news media, and there would be only one company spokesperson during the crisis, Ledgerwood. They made another decision, one that later proved to be a mistake. Having ruled out chipped machinery, they assumed what they thought to be obvious, that the tampering must have been done by a disgruntled or deranged employee. They put out a press release. The charge not only hurt employee morale but also encouraged a round of copy cat reports of product tamperings. The news media covered both the "discoveries" of foreign objects and Hygrade's response. Within 2 days there were so many incidents reported that the company shut down production and recalled 350,000 pounds of frankfurters from retail stores.

Two days after the initial discovery, management began to doubt their disgruntled employee theory. None of the discovered items was the same. Because Ball Park packages are age-dated, management reasoned that, had the objects been inserted at the plant, some would have been corroded by the time they were discovered. Yet, none was corroded.

They acted quickly. Ledgerwood was dispatched to meet with employees and apologize for implicating them. The apology was accepted and the work force volunteered to come in the next day—Saturday—to run hundreds of thousands of pounds of frankfurters through a metal detector.

While this was going on, one woman who had "discovered" a razor blade in her package of Ball Park franks the day before admitted her report was false. By Sunday, Hygrade's employees had inspected every last frank in the plant and found no trace of metal in them. Management concluded that all the reports were hoaxes and went public with its conclusions. The media played this story as strongly as they had the original discoveries, and Hygrade was vindicated. In fact, a month later, Livonia, where Hygrade's main plant is located, turned out for a "Livonia Loves Hygrade Week" and consumed 148,000 pounds of franks in the process.

According to Ledgerwood, the lessons to be learned were that if you make a product that can be tampered with, you need a crisis management standby plan and regular product security checks. In addition, Hygrade, which was already active in its communities, broadened its involvement in gratitude for the community support it received during the crisis.

The elements of a crisis management standby plan will vary from company to company. What should be common to all business is that they should review crisis scenarios periodically. Beyond that, a company with good employee relations and committed to its community is going to have more friends when disaster strikes. The creative manager makes friends for rainy days.

Case 2: Public Relations and Public Policy

Three decades ago it was common to hear executives say, "Business and politics don't mix. I'll stick to business." Today, most corporate leaders acknowledge that government policymaking affects daily life in hundreds of ways. A decision on a single paragraph of a tax bill may change an industry's profit-and-loss picture by millions of dollars. A new regulation may cost large sums for compliance, thus causing prices to rise. If a bill is introduced in a state legislature or the U.S. Congress that would result in heavy new regulatory burdens or costs to a particular industry, it is not uncommon for the affected parties to band together in an ad hoc committee to fight such legislation.

This was the case with a bill proposed to Congress in early 1983 to forbid insurance companies from using gender as a determinant in setting policy premium rates. Dubbed the "Unisex" insurance bill, it had as its major proponent the National Organization for Women (N.O.W.), which sought a legislative agenda item in the wake of the failure, in 1982, of the Equal Rights Amendment to be ratified by enough states to become law.

In early spring 1983, representatives of several insurance companies met to discuss the implications of the bill. Their actuaries had concluded that passage of the bill would mean that women, as a group, would pay some $700 million more a year in insurance premiums (some would pay more, some less; this was the net). The group was also concerned that market factors would be replaced by political ones in what were private business transactions. They reasoned that while insurance companies used actual experience as a guide in setting rates, this involved using gender to make distinctions, not discrimination against women as the bill's proponents charged. Women, for example, have fewer auto accidents than men, so pay less in insurance premiums. As a group they pay more for health insurance because they use it more.

A canvass of Congress revealed that the issue was considered to be positioned as a "civil rights–women's rights" issue, almost impossible to oppose publicly despite the bad economics of the bill. The committee was advised that lobbying at that stage would serve no purpose. It was necessary to shift the grounds of the argument, from civil rights–women's rights to one of economic dislocation, especially for young working women.

Calling itself "The Committee for Fair Insurance Rates," the group—headed by women insurance executives—went to work. In concert with its outside public relations counsel and industry lobbyists, the committee identified approximately three dozen members of the

Senate and House committees then considering the bill who had not yet made up their minds on the issue. The home districts and states of these legislators were targeted for a three-stage information and education program. First were radio announcements, drawing attention to a large newspaper ad that would run later in the week. The newspaper ad set forth the economic arguments and urged readers to watch for a special mailing. The mailing consisted of a letter from the woman insurance executive who chaired the committee; it argued for the fairness of the existing system and against the economic disadvantages of the proposed Unisex insurance bill. It urged recipients to express their views to their elected representatives in Washington. Enclosed was a suggested response letter along with a postcard to be mailed back to the committee indicating that the members of Congress had been contacted.

Response was very heavy. Ordinarily, 1 to 4 percent returns are considered good in direct mail. This case routinely ran 20 to 25 percent. Over the next 10 months, three more rounds of multimedia bursts were targeted to fewer and fewer swing districts, as the members of the relevant congressional committees made up their minds.

It is axiomatic in politics that if a piece of legislation is so controversial that a legislator's vote will draw nearly equal fire from both sides, he or she will tend to vote against the measure or hope it never comes to a vote. No elected politician wants to alienate a large number of voters. The Committee for Fair Insurance Rates knew from the reaction of staff members of the targeted members of Congress that the issue was shifting from an easy one (civil rights–women's rights) to a difficult one (civil rights–women's rights versus economic hardship for many women). The fact that the issue had moved into the controversial category was demonstrated by the many delays in bringing it to "markup" (final consideration) in either the House or Senate committee studying it.

Women insurance executive teams fanned out across the country to be interviewed in cities and towns in the targeted districts and states in order to amplify their position and rebut proponents. In addition, they wrote opinion articles and letters to the editors of publications that had quoted extensively from proponents.

A little over a year after the industry committee began, the House committee considering the bill brought it to markup, but the grounds of argument had changed. And when an amendment was added that virtually turned the bill inside out ("gutting" it, in Washington parlance), even the bill's original sponsors voted against the final version. The Senate committee never took action after the adverse action in the House. Nor has the bill been heard from since.

Why, When, Where, How

There are no "magic bullets" in public relations. There is no one approach that will solve all public policy problems; no one appearance on television or story in one magazine that will insure positive recognition for your company. Creativity involves the use of a range of activities and tools, applied consistently and persistently. Programs must be maintained. Continuity is much less expensive than pulling back, then being forced to re-solve all your communications problems again a year or two later. Creativity in public relations is not the result of the discovery of some secret communications tool. Rather it is the product of a clearly established objective matched with a strategy using several well-timed, carefully applied techniques that are already available. Creativity, in short, is knowing why, when, where, and how.

47

Creative Concepts for Corporate Finance

Robert Lawrence Kuhn

Investment Banker, Senior Research Fellow,
IC² Institute, University of Texas at Austin and
Adjunct Professor, Graduate School of Business
Administration, New York University

For all its hypermodern complexity, corporate finance has but three essential elements: (1) obtaining the lowest cost of capital (financial strategy), (2) obtaining capital that most properly matches and times sources to uses (financial structure), and (3) obtaining optimum value for investments (financial returns). The fundamental principle of linking risk with return applies to all three: Seekers and providers of capital each desire to obtain highest returns commensurate with acceptable levels of risk. Financial strategy, structure, and return all benefit from creativity.

Creativity in corporate finance stresses securing low cost of capital and/or finding innovative sources for particular uses. Creative finance devises financial instruments and tailors financial structures for complex, difficult, or adverse conditions. The last decade has witnessed an explosion of new financial products as major financial institutions (especially investment banks) compete for power and prestige (not to mention fees). We note five catalysts: (1) the volatility of financial markets, especially the unprecedented swings in interest and exchange rates; (2) the broadened deregulation of financial markets in the United States, Europe, and Japan; (3) the desire for higher liquidity for holders of small debts (such as mortgages, car loans, etc.); (4) the need for greater financial flexibility; and (5) the demand for financial support for aggressive corporate ventures. No longer can companies be satisfied with simply locking in long-term rates at some local low point. Now they must hunt continuously for optimum borrowing conditions, exchanging old instruments for new ones as though trading in used cars for new models.

Understanding the bewildering assortment of new products and structures demands constant study; choosing which to use under what conditions is even more daunting. The easy answer is rely on professionals. Yet it is a mistake for corporate executives to abrogate responsibility—or even initiative. The more senior managers know about creative finance the better they can work with experts. Never allow financial complexity to undermine executive leadership. Creative management flourishes with knowledge—and no one knows your business better than you do.

The purpose of this chapter is to introduce general categories (concepts and uses) of new financial instruments. The context, remember, is strictly corporate finance. The objective is comprehension not comprehensiveness (if the former is difficult, the latter is impossible). The more executives appreciate ideas behind instruments the better they can consider and choose which ones make sense.

Categories of New Financial Instruments

1. *Options.* Buying the right to purchase a security is a "call"; buying the right to sell a security is a "put." Companies can use options to offer greater flexibility and leverage to investors and thereby attract more investment at lower rates. Companies also use options to hedge their own investment positions. Sophisticated mathematical models (e.g., Black-Scholes option valuation formula) are used to evaluate the current worth of options. Program trading—using computers to exploit minute differences among stock prices, options, and indexes—can produce guaranteed returns (and can cause market perturbations).

2. *Futures.* The promises to deliver certain items, usually commodities, at specific times in the future are bought and sold. Uses: Companies buy and sell futures to hedge exposure to fluctuations in commodity prices, interest rates, and exchange rates. For example, a

company can hedge its long-term bond position by buying Treasury bond futures. Futures can stabilize any company depending on the price of commodities, whether a seller (e.g., a food producer of wheat, oranges, etc.) or a buyer (e.g., a textile firm using cotton or an electronics firm using expensive metals).

3. *Indexes.* Indexes link financial rates to the price of certain indicators (Treasury bills, prime, LIBOR, currency exchange rates, stock exchange indexes, etc.) or commodity prices (gold, silver, lumber, etc.). Uses: Companies employ indexes to hedge their positions. Issuers can pay lower guaranteed rates since they will gladly pay higher rates if the chosen indexes rise (which would mean that their products would be generating more profits). Example: an oil company bond paying a premium at maturity if the price of oil exceeds $25 per barrel.

4. *Swaps.* The exchange of obligations among two or more entities, often through a third party such as a major bank (see Chapter 48). Uses: Locking in interest and exchange rates, e.g., converting floating to fixed rates. Swaps exploit the relative borrowing strength of different borrowers. Swaps can produce complex variations in defining specific constraints for interest rates. This can be linked, for example, to sinking fund debentures. A variant is a note that resets interest rates in the *opposite* direction from the market (i.e., goes up when rates drop and vice versa); such an upside-down reset formula is used to hedge other interest-sensitive instruments.

5. *Zero coupon instruments.* Debt instruments whose repayment, interest and principal, is deferred for a number of years. As accrued interest is compounded, the principal amount increases ("accretes"). Zeros are essentially bonds stripped of their interest coupons and selling at a deep discount to face value (say 60 percent off for an 8-year maturity—an implied interest rate of about 12 percent per year); the deep discount reflects the present value of the principal at maturity discounted by the implied interest rate. On the one hand, zeros provide investors with a guaranteed rate of interest reinvestment (which current pay instruments cannot). On the other hand, zeros have higher risk since current interest is accrued and not paid. Zeros, therefore, command higher interest rates. Uses: Zeros match company current financial needs with its future payback capacity. Many financings in recent times, particularly leveraged buyouts, could not have been done without zeros. A variant allows investors the option of investing interest with the same terms and conditions (the bond may have warrants as well). By transferring the reinvesting option to investors, interest is lower than on a normal bond for the same reasons that interest on a regular zero (no option) is higher.

6. *High-yield debt ("junk bonds")*.   High-yield debt is issued with ratings below investment grade and consequently higher coupon rates. Spread premiums have more than compensated for the heightened risk, giving investors better long-term returns. The impact of high-yield debt on corporate America has been dramatic. Uses: By paying higher coupon rates on notes, companies previously unable to raise capital have raised billions for both restructuring and growth. Controversial, though perhaps misunderstood by the mass media, high-yield bonds catalyzed the explosive increase in mergers and acquisitions (especially leveraged buyouts). Interestingly enough, the failure rate of junk bonds has been surprisingly small. This has translated into a higher overall return for investors compared to investment grade notes.

7. *High-yield commercial paper*.   Junk bonds' success has invaded the commercial paper market in the form of "unrated paper." Uses: Such commercial paper provides low-cost, fixed-term sources of cash previously unavailable to unrated companies. Borrowings can be custom tailored, by maturity, to the firm's precise cash flow needs (literally to the day). The borrower can access the market at its discretion, with almost no advance notice. All transactions are net of transaction fees, so comparisons can be made easily. Issuing commercial paper offers companies continuous exposure to institutional investors in money and capital markets. This visibility can enhance success of future debt or equity offerings. Commercial paper can also provide benefits in future negotiations on bank pricing.

8. *Interest-rate protection*.   Interest-rate fluctuation on floating notes can be bounded with upper and/or lower limits by setting floors, ceilings (caps), and collars (combined floors and ceilings or minimax). Uses: Companies can set absolute limits on interest-rate exposure while getting benefits of floating rates. Issuing companies, of course, pay a premium for caps on floating-rate notes. A variant are floating-rate bonds that convert into fixed rates when market rates fall below a certain level.

9. *Asset-backed instruments*.   Debt instruments supported by real or hard assets have multiplied. The most common use is the pooling of small-denomination debt into instruments that look like traditional bonds. By packaging receivables into publicly traded securities—"securitizing" them—a company can attract a broader investor market and hence lower rates while enhancing liquidity. Mortgage-backed securities (real estate receivables) are perhaps the best known; they permit savings and loans to sell their mortgages and gain liquidity. A proliferation of products uses a variety of other assets to back securities: car

loans, credit card obligations, receivables of all kinds, etc. In theory, securities can be written on any asset whose cash flow and risk can be predicted. Uses: Liquidity is enhanced for the issuer by packaging previously illiquid debt, and collateralization can reduce interest rates.

10. *Convertible instruments.* Debt (usually subordinated) and preferred stock that can be converted into common stock at a preset price have increased in popularity. Uses: Issuers reduce interest or dividend rates by offering investors upside participations. Convertible instruments are often used for "mezzanine" levels of finance, i.e., debt layered in between senior bank lending and equity investments. Such high-risk debt, common to venture capital and leveraged buyouts, demands rates of return between 20 and 40 percent. Since few companies can afford to pay such rates in interest, the convertible feature allows some equity-level participation to augment the stated interest rate.

11. *Exchangeable instruments.* Some instruments under certain conditions can be exchanged for others, e.g., a preferred stock that can be exchanged for a subordinated debt (with similar features, interest rate, and convertibility). Uses: Optimizes rates by taking advantage of particular tax situations, e.g., preferred stock may be better in the near term (when the company is not a taxpayer) while subordinated debt may be better in the long term (when the company becomes a taxpayer).

12. *Debt with kickers.* Debt instruments (or preferred stock) with additional benefits—e.g., warrants, royalties, profit participations, premiums, etc. Uses: Issuers reduce interest rate and current risk by sacrificing some upside. Warrants are rights to buy securities at predetermined prices for a period of time. They can be detachable (able to be used or sold independent of the original note) and therefore more valuable to investors. Warrants may give the bearer rights to purchase common stock (at some premium to market) or additional bonds (with same or different terms). "Usable bonds" are bonds that can be used at par in lieu of cash to exercise specific warrants. When linked with these underlying warrants, these bond units have been called "synthetic convertibles." Usability can give bonds added value when investors seek to exercise the warrants. In this case, no price is too high for the usable bond as long as it can be purchased below par (including forfeited accrued interest) since this is the cash exercise price. Companies have used these bonds to convert debt into equity by "flushing out" warrants; the company simply reduces the warrant exercise price below the underlying stock trading price (throwing the warrant "in the money").

13. *Changeable-rate instruments.* Instruments whose yields change under certain conditions. Fixed-rate notes can have rates readjusted at one (or more) specific times or triggered by specific events. Floating-rate funds are tied to various indexes such as prime, LIBOR, etc. Even long-term bonds can have interest rates set each day. Numerous formulas can be used; typical are spreads over specified Treasury bills. Uses: Increasing-rate notes are bridge financing facilities. Refinancing is forced since the increase is punitive, growing at, say, 50 basis points per quarter (or month) until full repayment. Reset (debt or equity) instruments can change any feature such as the conversion rate. Exchangeable variable rate notes are reset regularly (e.g., quarterly) and can be exchanged at the issuer's option into fixed-rate notes with predetermined characteristics (price relative to Treasuries, maturity, call price, sinking fund, etc.); often after 5 years, the "fix" becomes mandatory.

14. *Off-balance-sheet financing.* Moving assets and liabilities off the balance sheet (usually fixed assets) improves the balance sheet. Uses: Reducing the debt-equity ratio can augment financing capability and bring down rates.

15. *Asset-based financing.* A new breed of financial institution offers companies greater options, especially when financing requirements exceed traditional creditworthiness. Finance companies deliver fast turnaround for aggressive or troubled companies. Reward must be matched to risk; they charge higher interest rates (perhaps 3 to 6 points above prime). Credit is "asset-based," with formulas for lending based on a percentage of receivables (e.g., 80 percent), inventories (e.g., 50 percent), and fixed asssets (e.g., 25 percent). Newer thinking gives credence to cash flow, especially when proprietary products and services or franchise positioning is involved. General Electric Commercial Credit (GECC), though not a traditional bank, has become one of the largest and most influential financial institutions. GECC often takes substantial equity warrants to finance leveraged buyouts, but the deal gets done.

16. *Limited partnerships.* A business structure that can offer tax benefits directly to owners. Uses: increasing tax benefits diminish required returns. Master limited partnerships can efficiently distribute income to shareholders while enabling partnership interests to be traded on stock exchanges (thereby giving liquidity). Current U.S. tax law makes "passive income" desirable for investors (to offset passive losses) and therefore efficient for companies to use in raising debt capital. Good for companies with stable, predictable cash flows.

17. *Credit enhancement mechanisms.* Corporate guarantees, principal insurance, and other credit-enhancing mechanisms are becoming more common. Uses: Obtaining financing under difficult conditions and reducing rates.

18. *Equity levels and classes.* Common stock with diverse voting and valuation participations. "Supervoting" classes (e.g., 100 votes per share). Uses: Enables control to be assured while selling equity to raise capital.

19. *International markets.* Perhaps the greatest explosion in financial flexibility has been the globalization of financial markets. Even companies that do not have foreign operations now access money overseas. Uses: Companies can raise capital and hedge risk wherever optimal irrespective of geography. Borrowings from commercial paper to long-term debentures can be in eurodollars, Swiss francs, or Japanese yen almost as easily as U.S. dollars. Bonds may be denominated in one currency (e.g., Swiss francs) and interest paid in another (e.g., U.S. dollars). Foreign-currency denominated bonds may be sold to investors in that foreign country or in other places. By taking advantage of fleeting opportunities in foreign financial markets, Exxon, for example, has even been able to borrow at rates lower than even the U.S. Treasury.

20. *Tax-advantaged instruments.* Debt that offers tax benefits can produce financial efficiency. Uses: Lower taxes for investors means lower rates for issuers. Industrial revenue bonds (IRBs) have long been used to reduce cost of capital by giving investors tax-free interest and therefore lower coupon rates. Dutch Auction preferred stock (DARTs) enables corporate investors to exclude 80 to 85 percent of dividends with rates close to market through a frequent auction process. Multinational companies with profits in numerous countries should consider borrowing in those countries that have higher relative tax rates (although repatriation of funds may not be so simple).

48

Innovative Financial Mechanisms: Interest Rate Swaps

Francis X. Stankard

Chairman, Chase Investment Bank

We live in a world of continuous flux in financial markets. Interest rates shift and currencies move—and management's role has become far more complex. Not only must the chief executive or chief financial officer decide how much funding the company needs, but he or she must also decide when and how funds should be raised. An error in timing or miscalculation of the source could cost dearly.

As the job has increased in complexity, the number and types of tools to aid the funding-decision process have also multiplied. The zero coupon bond, for example, has become an accepted way for corporations to borrow funds without hindering short-term cash flow. Another relative newcomer, futures are now commonly used to provide companies with ways to hedge against interest-rate and currency risks.

One of the most innovative corporate finance products entering the global marketplace was interest-rate and currency swaps. Originally developed to exploit the credit-spread differential that existed between fixed and floating rate funds, interest-rate swaps became important tools for treasurers in asset and liability management programs. Negotiated around the clock, around the world, these interest exchange agreements provide an excellent example of how an innovation can solve what had been a major problem—namely, staying locked into an interest rate that made sense last month but not next month.

The Basis for Swaps

The flight to quality in the fixed-rate public and private markets has resulted in spreads of 200 basis points (2 percentage points) or more between coupons of AAA issuers and BAA issuers. However, such a differential does not exist in the floating-rate markets in which the spread between AAA and BAA credits is less than 40 basis points. This credit spread differential provides better credits with a relative borrowing advantage in the fixed-rate market and lesser credits with a relative borrowing advantage in the floating-rate market. It also creates an arbitrage opportunity that results in lesser credits obtaining lower-cost fixed-rate funds and better credits obtaining lower-cost floating-rate funds than if each borrowed directly in its basis of choice.

Assume a AAA credit wants to borrow money on a floating-rate basis while a BAA credit wants to borrow on a fixed-rate basis. Each could borrow directly on its basis of choice; however, as discussed, the capital markets provide better credits with a relative borrowing advantage in raising fixed-rate funds and lesser credits with a relative borrowing advantage in raising floating-rate funds. Instead of each party borrowing directly on its chosen basis, each would do better by obtaining funds in the market in which it has a relative borrowing advantage and then swapping its obligation. The effect of the two parties swapping liabilities can be a combined savings of over 100 basis points annually.

Certainly, the scenario described is only possible if each party is willing to assume the credit risk of its counterparty. However, most companies are not in the business of assessing and assuming such risk. As a result, a number of major commercial banks, whose business it is to evaluate and assume credit risk, have become quite active as intermediaries in the swap market. Today, corporate treasurers who want to swap cash can execute a swap with Chase and be assured of the credit quality of its counterparty.

While swaps were originally developed as an arbitrage tool, they now play an important role in interest-rate asset and liability risk management. Swaps today can take a variety of forms on both the asset and liability sides of the balance sheet. They are not only used to convert a cash flow from fixed to floating-rate basis (or vice-versa) but also to convert cash flows from one floating-rate basis to another. The possible uses of swaps is limited only by the imagination of the corporate treasurers who utilize them.

Swaps as an Interest-Rate Risk-Management Tool

Swaps are a powerful tool in managing a company's exposure to rising interest rates. A company with a large amount of floating-rate debt might want to convert some of its obligations to a fixed-rate basis. By doing so, the company reduces the likelihood that its earnings will be devastated by a dramatic rise in short-term rates. In addition, swaps can be used as a speculative vehicle in interest-rate risk management. A company with a large amount of fixed-rate debt but with the view that short-term interest rates are going to decline might wish to convert some or all of its fixed-rate debt to a floating-rate basis. Once the company believes that rates have reached bottom, the company can execute a reversing swap that offsets the effect of the initial swap transaction and returns the company to its original borrowing basis. Such a strategy can prove extremely profitable for the company whose treasurer is able to correctly predict the direction of short-term interest rates.

However, since most companies are not so lucky, Chase has developed an interest-rate protection product ideally suited to the needs of a company that maintains a large amount of floating-rate debt: the Floor/Ceiling Swap. This swap enables the company to put a ceiling on the maximum rate of its floating-rate borrowings while simultaneously permitting the company to benefit from a future decline in interest rates. Chase put together a Floor/Ceiling Swap for one of its corporate clients in financing a major acquisition. The company was forced to finance its acquisition primarily with floating-rate debt tied to a short-term index. While it believed short-term interest rates were trending downward, it could not afford the risk that interest rates would rise to the point at which interest on the debt would exceed the cash generated through the company's operations. To reduce this risk, the company entered into a Floor/Ceiling Swap with Chase. Under terms of the swap, the company limited its exposure to rising interest rates and was still able to benefit from the predicted decline in short-term rates.

Short-Dated Swaps as an Asset and Liability Management Tool

A recent development in interest-rate swaps has been in applications for debt instruments that have maturities under 2 years. These short-term or short-dated swaps are direct competitors with the interest-rate future contracts, but they offer more flexibility. Chase offers a product that effectively hedges short-term interest-rate exposure without the inherent risks associated with futures. This short-term product, called CHESS, or Chase Electronic Swap System, allows customers to electronically access short-dated swap quotes, issue securities where they have their greatest relative rate advantage, and lock in fixed interest rates for 6, 9, 12, or 18 months.

Most active commercial paper issuers sell their paper in the 1-month area and rarely issue in maturities longer than 3 months. This hesitancy is understandable given the illiquidity and consequent relative cost of issuing commercial paper in the 3- to 8-month maturity area. For example, the difference between 1-month LIBOR and 1-month commercial paper may be 60 basis points while the difference between 6-month LIBOR and 6-month commercial paper may be only 30 basis points. Commercial paper's historically steep slope has kept issuers in the very short maturities (1 or 2 months) and forced them to use other financial instruments in lengthening their time horizons.

Interest-rate futures contracts offer corporate treasurers one means of lengthening their commercial paper maturity positions. For example, if a corporate treasurer wants to lengthen his or her 1-month position to 6 months or 1 year, he or she could sell futures contracts. This futures position would become profitable as interest rates rose, thereby offering the corporate treasurer a hedge against such rising rates. Using futures contracts as a hedge, however, creates several problems. First, futures contracts settle only four times per year. This means that the maturity position created with futures contracts will rarely match the treasurer's desired maturity position. For example, if in July the treasurer wants to lengthen the maturity of his or her commercial paper from 1 month to 6 months, he or she will not be able to create an instrument with exactly a 6-month maturity using the futures market. The second problem with futures is that a commercial paper futures contract does not exist. Therefore another contract such as the Treasury bill or eurodollar futures contract will have to be used. Since the spread between Treasury bills or eurodollars and commercial paper can widen or narrow, an exact hedge cannot be constructed. A third problem is that the futures position must be marked to market every day. That is, if a futures position lost a significant amount of money in the course of a day, at the end of that day the holder of that position must deposit funds with his or her broker equal to at least part of the loss. The accounting maintenance costs can be substantial. These problems can be partially solved by devoting a great deal of time and effort to managing the futures position. This means that the costs of hedging in the futures markets extend well beyond the initial price paid for the particular futures positions.

Short-dated swaps have evolved as an alternative to the futures markets. Unlike the futures contracts, the short-date swap can provide treasurers with exactly the hedges that they want to create. A commercial paper short-dated swap exists and can be tailored to exact maturity specifications. For example, suppose the treasurer of ABC Corporation has a double A bond rating with an A-1, P-1 commercial paper rating. Further suppose that 1-month commercial paper is selling at a discount of 7.50 percent to yield 7.55 percent and 1-month and 6-month LIBOR are at 7.80 percent and 8.0 percent, respectively. To fix a 6-month rate the treasurer has two alternatives: Enter into a 6-month LIBOR-LIBOR swap or a 6-month commercial paper-LIBOR swap. If the treasurer decided on a 6-month LIBOR-LIBOR swap, the company would pick up the differential between the 1-month LIBOR and 1-month commercial paper yields yet pay the fixed 6-month LIBOR rate. The customer would pick up the 25 basis point spread between the 1-month LIBOR and 1-month commercial paper rates while paying out a fixed 8 percent for the 6-month period. Thus, in the first month of the swap the customer would be paying a net 7.75 percent [8.00 − (7.80 − 7.55)]. The problem with this swap is that the basis-point spread between 1-month LIBOR and commercial paper could narrow over the 6-month period, which would raise the effective cost of the net 6-month payment.

To solve this spread problem, a commercial paper-LIBOR swap can be constructed. In this case ABC would receive 1-month commercial paper from Chase and would pay Chase 6-month LIBOR minus a basis point spread. The spread subtracted from the 6-month LIBOR rate would depend on such factors as the current commercial paper-LIBOR basis point spread, the current and expected volatility, and the market's expectations for future interest rates.

Liquidity and return have always been overriding concerns of corporate treasurers deciding where to invest excess cash. Unfortunately, the financial instruments with the most liquidity are often of short maturity and offer relatively low returns. Short-dated swaps offer a solution to the high-liquidity but low-return dilemma. By entering into a swap, an investor can keep his or her principal invested in short-term assets yet receive longer-term interest payments for purposes of yield pickup. For example, suppose an investor wanted to keep his or her assets in 1-month obligations because the funds might be needed on short notice for acquisition or project financing. The investor, however, wanted to earn the current 6-month return. This case is just the reverse of the previously discussed liability swap. The investor keeps his or her principal in short-term assets yet earns the higher interest rate from a longer-term asset. If he or she has to sell off his or her 1-month asset, he or she can either keep the swap in place or reverse the swap and thereby close out the swap position.

The above examples illustrate the complexity of financial decisions being made by senior corporate managers. Treasurers are shopping the world's financial markets for cheaper capital or restructuring their debt on the international securities markets. As this occurs, you can be certain that the world's investment banks will continue to develop more innovative options, more products from which corporate financial officers can choose.

49

Creative Finance for Young Companies

Arthur Lipper III

Chairman of VENTURE magazine, and New York & Foreign Securities Corporation

One skill that most successful entrepreneurs have in common is pattern recognition. They sense the existence of a set of circumstances from which some benefit may be derived. Frequently, entrepreneurs are divergent thinkers, more intuitive than analytic. In developing new techniques for financing young companies, I practice "reality recognition" to accommodate the conflicting needs of entrepreneurs and investors. It is a new mechanism for resolving such conflicts.

Characters and Characteristics

Those seeking financing almost universally believe that their businesses will improve and that they will be more successful in the future. They desire financing on terms most favorable to themselves. Furthermore, these seekers of capital usually are overly optimistic and greedy.

Those having money to invest in other people's businesses are generally skeptical of rosy projections and future idealism. They desire to obtain the highest return or greatest profit while assuming the least amount of risk and trouble. The providers of capital usually are overly fearful and also greedy. ("Investors" herein refers to corporate as well as individual investors.)

Greed

There is nothing wrong with being greedy. Greed is human. It is simply the desire for more; it is also the fear of not having enough relative to the perceived opportunity to have. Some desire to obtain all, and for those, there will never be enough. For most, however, there is a sense of proportion, and greed does not have to become gluttony. The proportion is based on the balancing of resource availability or shortage, the risk inherent in achieving the projected return, and the availability of alternative asset utilization on comparable terms. ("Measured greed" becomes institutionalized—for example, when pension funds become limited partners in a venture capital fund—while those with "unrestrained greed" may find themselves institutionalized.)

Optimism

There is nothing wrong with those seeking capital being optimistic about their future. Were they not to so believe, they would not have the motivation to strive and build. The nature of things, however, is that entrepreneurs often will be wrong in their projections of progress. Paradoxically the more strongly they believe, the more likely they will be wrong. This is very human and perhaps necessary for "entrepreneurial spirit." But long-term survival requires balance.

The Function of a Financier

An effective financier tries to satisfy the perceived, and therefore, the real needs of the parties to a transaction. To do so he or she has to understand and empathize with the interests of the parties, the providers of capital and consumers thereof. He or she has to know the fears of each side. The financier must understand fully the present and future areas of conflict between the entrepreneur and his or her investors. This understanding should be reflected in the deal structured, including flexible clauses that can be invoked if disagreements arise. When certain assumptions provided by the seeker of capital are reviewed by a more experienced provider of capital, adjustments are certain to be necessary. With imagination and insight, the process of making these predictable changes can be improved. A good financier is both actor and director in the drama of investing in dynamic business opportunities. (It also helps to have a sense of humor; the maintenance of perspective is always desirable and with entrepreneurs is frequently difficult.)

The Two-Part Investment Process

Before devising creative financing, the investor should first be exquisitely sensitive in selecting which deals to finance. Creativity here can enhance the ultimate probability of success. Deal evaluation is a two-part decision-making process.

The *first* part occurs to everybody—will the company be successful? Success or failure is 90 percent of the average investor's decision-making focus, whereas it should really be no more than 60 percent.

The *second* part, all too often played down, concerns the worth of the deal the investor gets for his or her money. What will the investor have to pay for the projected success? What is the cost of admission? What is the sacrifice of liquidity? How much of his or her time will it take, with how much travel and worry will he or she be burdened, and to what risk will he or she be exposed? Will the investor have to provide additional funds? What is the valuation? How much is this business worth today in terms of currently available alternatives?

Take a start-up business that has a typical business plan, one that predicts losses in the first through third years, a small profit in the fourth year, and a big profit in the fifth. Suppose that the entrepreneur's projections are correct and that a profit of $500,000 after taxes is made in the fifth year. Using as a guideline a publicly traded stock of a comparable company being worth 12 times its annual after tax earnings, a public company with earnings of $500,000 would be worth $6 million. However, private companies are often valued at a fraction of the value of public companies. Suppose, therefore, that the private company is worth $3,000,000 or 50 percent of the public company's market valuation. Remember, of course, that the investor is not being offered 100 percent of the company in exchange for the investment; if the offer is for 50 percent, the projected value of that share of the company in 5 years will be $1,500,000. Now figure present value, with a risk-adjusted discount rate. Is $1,500,000 5 years hence worth the investment in current dollars, considering the risk, illiquidity, time, and effort that will be required? (A minimum requirement or "hurdle rate" of 35 percent compounded annual return would only permit $335,000 as an initial investment.) Of course, if it is realistic to assume that the private company will go public within less than 5 years, a higher valuation probably is warranted.

Investing in young, private, entrepreneurial companies involves the sacrifice of liquidity in addition to the assumption of risk, both of which justify a return significantly higher than that for a publicly traded investment. An astute investor knows that stocks can double or triple their value in a single year and that he or she can sell down-trending public stock in order to cut losses. Another option is to put money into second mortgages where a high current return with good security can be secured. Having considered numerous alternative opportunities, the investor will expect a much higher rate of return from a private company investment because such an investment lacks an easy way of cashing out. The relative success of an investor, therefore, has more to do with the structure of the investment and pricing of the deal than with the company's ultimate commercial success.

A New Mechanism

The user and the owner of money want much the same—the greatest upside with least downside. This is the reason most private company investor-entrepreneur relationships become adversarial (and perhaps must be). One way of reducing the friction between them is to shift the focus of the reward factor (that which is used to induce the acceptance of risk) from projected future profits to projected future *revenues*, a measure easier for the entrepreneur to predict and over which he or she may have more control. If both owner and user of the money have increased revenue rather than net profit as their shared objective, an important area of potential conflict is removed immediately. Of course, the entrepreneur must be concerned with the ultimate generation of profits, but this focus can be less intense, and less short-term oriented, if the investor is not similarly concerned.

Consider the concept of investor royalties, or as we call them, revenue participation certificates (RPCs). With RPCs in place to satisfy investor return requirements, owners can manage the business differently and frequently more constructively, especially for longer-term objectives. Assuming the recipient of the revenue participation is in a position (from the perspective of income tax considerations) to accept ordinary income (an issue made moot by the current tax law eliminating capital gains advantages), there are no drawbacks from the royalty recipient's point of view. (The paying entity must be certain the RPC payments will be allowed as ordinary deductions for tax purposes.)

RPC arrangements can be as flexible and imaginative as the parties want. The RPC can be secured or unsecured; it can have either a revenue minimum or a maximum and either for each year or for a period of years; it can start immediately or only after an agreed upon revenue level is reached annually or in an aggregate amount; it can be perpetual or for a fixed period; it can be convertible at either or both parties' initiation; it can be terminable upon agreed conditions. The RPC can be specific currency denominated and can have as its beneficiary entities located domestically or abroad. The RPC can be cut into as many pieces as the parties agree and could even be offered or reoffered publicly. The terms of the RPC may be guaranteed by third parties, including the entrepreneurs managing the business. The RPC can stand alone as the inducement for risk acceptance or be used as an additional incentive. Also, the timing of RPC payments is flexible. For example, payments can be daily, monthly, annually, or as the revenue is received by the issuer. RPCs can be granted in return for loans made directly by the issuer or guaranteed on the issuer's behalf. RPCs can be granted in return for services, as is done routinely in the entertainment and publishing industries with author, actor, and director royalties. Also RPCs can be used in acquisitions of stock and/or assets. Many industries and activities—for example mining, petroleum drilling, patent licensing—make extensive use of royalty payments. Frankly, I see no great attraction in purchasing equity when there is no immediate capacity to trade the shares obtained.

Another of my favorite mediums for creative investing is through the provision of bank guarantees (or supplier indemnifications) rather than through accepting a similar risk by lending a company money directly. My rationale is that it is better for a company to establish credit (even if only third-party supported) than to have no credit at all. Also, from an investor standpoint, I would rather have another party interposed between myself and risk, even on a pass-through basis, since that party then also has a reason to try to assist the company. Another benefit of this form of financing for the capital provider is the borrower's increased reluctance to renege on a loan involving a supplier or an institutional lender.

Regardless of the form in which they are received by the company, investor funds should always have a priority in both dividends and liquidation over the promotional ("free") interest in the company earned by the entrepreneurs ("sweat equity"). It must be remembered that the entrepreneur's opportunity to create wealth and receive current income during the uncertain period of development is made possible by investor building and risk. Investing in entrepreneurial companies is capitalism at its best and is most constructive for society. Financing entrepreneurs is a wonderful way to develop creativity, structurally as well as commercially, for individuals and corporate investors.

50

Accounting Support for Creative Management

Robert S. Kay, CPA

Senior Partner, Touche Ross & Company

Many executives do not regard accountants as creative or innovative. They may even conjure up the sinister meaning that "creative accounting" means "cooking the books." Such "creativity" is fraudulent. Our focus is on the positive connotation: What CPA firms can do for creative managers beyond their legendary facility with numbers.

As the language of business, accounting aims to portray financial statement numbers for what they are and not what presenters might like them to be. Too often it is presumed that the accountant is the embodiment of the cold figures he or she presents or attests. This stereotype may have had some basis in fact years ago but has little relevance today. Accountants in the practice of public accountancy provide—as they have for more than 80 years—accounting and auditing, tax, and management consulting services. But now the panoply of financially oriented services obtainable from a major CPA firm is almost limitless, provided that their uniquely distinguishing feature—*objectivity*—is the essence of that service. Most accountants know that the more successful the client, the more rewarding the arrangement, both financially and psychically. Accountants have thus metamorphosed into business and financial advisors, doing everything possible to be a part of the client's team, yet bringing along always-needed objectivity and independence.

Some CPA services mandated by regulation (e.g., SEC audits) have become price sensitive. To diminish the impact of depressed rates and to win the confidence of clients, CPA firms are providing "value-added" special services that tend to average fees upward. Admittedly, this approach does not depict accountants as altruists. However, such economic initiative catalyzed the accounting profession's creative broadening of its service offerings, which benefits clients as well. The accountant genuinely wants a client's business to be successful and wants each of the owners, officers, managers, or employees he or she serves within the client to be equally successful. Alert always to novel ideas, that accountant will work with client personnel to turn these ideas into pragmatic reality.

Accountants' Services

There are many variations among CPA firms—some specializing in areas others eschew. In a major accounting firm (some are called the "Big Eight") you might find the following areas of service: accounting and auditing, taxation, management consulting, actuarial and benefits consulting, advanced technology consulting, business interruption consulting, corporate finance advisory services, government contracting services, liaison with government, litigation support, regulatory consulting, reorganization advisory services, and small and private company services. Only the first three areas listed are traditional and then only if regarded narrowly. Table 50.1 lists more detailed examples of typically available services.

Every major public accounting firm has found that, to please clients, it must speak their language and feel their concerns. This ordains an industry approach, and many of the listed services can be obtained from practitioners versed in specific industries, both domestically and internationally. Indeed, some firms declare as many as sixty industry programs. This industry orientation means the right advice for *your* business, not something that works "on average." It is hard to imagine so many specialties in business and finance in a single organization, but consider that the major CPA firms will have 7000 to 12,000 personnel domestically—double worldwide.

Table 50.1. A Sample of Major CPA Firm Services

Traditional

- Accounting advice
- Financial statement auditing
- SEC and similar regulatory agency filings
- Computer-based auditing
- Tax planning, advice, and representation
- Business and financial planning
- Organizational analysis
- Computer hardware and software systems

Not So Traditional

General services:

- Policies, objectives and goals, profit opportunities, and business plans
- Strategic planning and control
- Organization plans and structure
- Personal financial management

Actuarial services

- Actuarial valuation of pension and benefit plans
- Design of capital accumulation plans
- Personnel cost containment studies
- Design of health care delivery system
- Design of flexible compensation plans

Advanced technology and systems services

- Strategic systems planning
- Planning, design, and implementation of management information systems
- Systems development and implementation
- Computer security review and improvement
- Automation design and implementation
- Advanced engineering systems design
- Information center implementation
- Technological impact studies

Business interruption insurance services

- Insurance coverage review
- Claims preparation and presentation
- Claims negotiation and settlement
- Expert testimony

Financial services

- General accounting, financial planning, budgeting, capital expenditures, cash management, cost accounting, and related systems and procedures
- Financial projections for planning purposes
- Financial forecasts and reporting thereon
- Evaluation of specific business practices or operations

Financing advisory services

- Locating merger and acquisition partners
- Valuation of the business
- Structuring transactions
- Development of antitakeover strategies
- Alternate financing sources
- Financial "engineering"
- Advice on new financial instruments

Table 50.1 A sample of Major CPA Firm Services (Continued)

Human resource services
- Management development and training programs
- Executive compensation programs
- Personnel practices and procedures

Litigation support
- Discovery assistance
- Deposition assistance
- Trial assistance

Marketing services
- Marketing plans and programs, product profitability, pricing, and performance measurement
- Marketing controls and procedures

Operations services
- Production planning, scheduling, and inventory management policies and procedures
- Control and efficiency of operations
- Improved transportation and distribution methods

Reorganization advisory services
- Operational restructuring
- Cash flow management and cost reduction
- Negotiations with creditors
- Debt restructuring assistance
- Liquidation and analysis and monitoring

Small business services
- Assistance in finding financing
- Management information systems
- Strategic planning
- Reorganization and merger and acquisition assistance
- Mini- and microcomputer advice

Using the CPA Firm's Services

How can an individual manager take advantage of these diverse services? No one, not even a company's CEO, can possibly get involved in everything the CPA firm offers. Success is obtaining the service you need, when you need it, from the best qualified persons available, and at a cost commensurate with benefit. This is good theory, of course. How is it done in practice? A company's main relationship with the CPA firm that audits its books and records is often through the chief financial or chief accounting officer. In some companies, operating management may also work extensively with the audit firm. If there isn't a known link in your area, talk to a colleague who has one. Ask the controller's office for the "ground rules" to explore a problem with your CPAs.

Perhaps what you need may be better provided by a CPA firm other than your auditors. This is often the case with consulting projects, for which the expertise both of the firm and specific personnel are paramount. Again, companies usually have guidelines for engaging an outside consultant. When the right choice is a CPA firm that is not your company's auditor, you will still benefit from the distinctive objectivity and confidentiality that is the stock-in-trade of all CPA firm professionals.

Long ago engagements simply walked in the door, but today the CPA profession is highly competitive in all facets. CPA firms want to tell what they can do for executives and their businesses. Representatives will arrive on cue at your office or at lunch because they can prosper only if given a chance to sell. You will expend only your time to discover whether a complex or pesky problem can be solved by one or another accounting firm. If you already know that your problem is regularly dealt with by CPA firms, the initial encounter will allow for more specifics or for actually shaping the engagement.

The greatest fear of most managers is the possible cost of special accounting firm services. Stories abound of professionals—lawyers, accountants, consultants—charging hefty fees for work that seems mundane. The press is not the place to find testimonials to tough jobs well done at fair prices. Realistically, it will cost more than a pittance to engage CPA firm professionals, who almost invariably charge according to the amount of time expended. To provide a degree of comfort, many arrangements are "capped" at an estimated amount, and occasionally there might be a fee that is essentially based on the success of the engagement. For example, a CPA can set a fee in tax representation matters based on the outcome of a dispute with the IRS. In general, the CPA firm is not permitted to charge a "contingent fee" based on present canons of professional ethics. However, consideration is being given to lifting this embargo to some degree. Creativity and innovation never come without risk. Thus, there is always uncertainty in using outside services: cost versus value, need, timeliness, effectiveness, and so on. CPA firm services are essential for companies, but they must be used properly.

Knowing When You Need CPA Firm Services

Almost anything financial is within the purview of a major accounting firm. With the principal exception of financial statement audits, it is true that non-CPA consulting firms and specialty boutiques can provide many of the same services. But when objectivity is a *sine qua non*, CPA firms by definition have this advantage. Further, many services have as their logical output a report that makes assertions about company information. CPA firms can attest to the meaning and reliability of such data, and the association of the CPA firm's name carries additional weight. You can rest assured that attestation standards are well-developed in the accounting profession, which has its origins in adding credibility to financial information. Of course, many of the services listed in Table 50.1 will have only internal applicability; even so, the same care will usually be taken as if external release is possible.

When all suppliers of a professional service are being considered, criteria for making a rational choice might include reputation of the firm, expertise in the area of specific need, proposed engagement staffing and credentials of the partner in charge, estimated elapsed and total time, and proposed fee versus anticipated results. As with any professional services, the "chemistry" should feel right. You should ask for a written proposal and for specifics of similar engagements performed for others. The CPA firm will be pleased to tell you about them within limits permitted by confidentiality rules. And, regardless of the firm, be sure to get (and check) references if you don't have prior experience with the firm.

Consulting Ground Rules

All consulting is done in keeping with professional rules that assure performance. A thumbnail sketch of these rules follows: (1) There will be a clear understanding with the client as to the nature, scope, and limitations of the service to be performed. (2) Proper planning will include understanding client need, assessing the client's present knowledge of the issue, and defining what specific steps will be necessary. (3) Staffing will consist of personnel with proper expertise, adequately supervised. (4) Relevant data will be assessed as to its sufficiency and credibility. When basing results on client-provided data, the advice given will be qualified as dependent on the accuracy and completeness of such data. (5) To secure its objectivity, the CPA firm will perform an advisory role and will not assume managerial responsibility. (6) Engagements should not be undertaken if the consultant perceives little potential benefit, unless the client is informed of such reservations and asks the CPA firm to proceed. Results should not be implicitly or explicitly guaranteed. (7) Conclusions and advice must be clearly communicated, and the degree of reliability of the advice specified.

Examples of CPA Firm Support

How can the unique skills of CPA firms be used to support management creativity and innovation? Without delving into specifics of complex consulting engagements, a few examples should be instructive.

Advice for the Asking

Most CPA firms publish information on events and forces affecting your business, industry, and administrative and operating problems—not to mention a steady stream of technical accounting, auditing, and tax information. In larger firms, this amounts to a veritable deluge that rivals the output of many proprietary business publishers. Why pay for it when you can have it gratis? Be sure to ask for the entire list of a CPA's firm publications, usually updated at least annually, and select items of interest. If you don't see what you want, make special inquiry. You will find many ideas that you might self-implement. The publications, however, are unlikely to tell you how to perform complex projects simply because professional judgment is the prime ingredient that cannot be readily formulated in print. When you want further information, just ask. (It is easy to overload your in-box with publications from many CPA firms, so be selective.)

Financing the New Business

As owner of a fledgling business, you need more capital to begin production of that long-waited product. There are bank lenders, to be sure, but perhaps they are shy of new companies in your industry. Venture capital investors are available, but they seek a large ownership stake. Your investment banker friend says you can't sell equity or debt in an initial public offering (IPO) because you have no track record. Besides, the expense of a public offering is substantial, as is the cost of complying with all the periodic disclosure rules that ensue. What to do? Many CPA firms provide a service that analyzes your business from a financing perspective, comparing alternative methods of obtaining capital funds. Indeed, the CPA firm can advise you where to shop, or which investment banking houses to visit, based on a knowledge of how those providers of funds have performed in the past for your type of business. If, for example, an IPO is the appropriate route to funds, the CPA firm will help you use the least onerous registration form; the SEC keeps simplifying the process for smaller businesses, and this route might be tolerable if done efficiently. If you decide that venture capital is the approach, the CPA firm will help you negotiate terms and understand their implications.

Audits for Financing Purposes

Perhaps you haven't been audited before. Banks will want to see audited financial statements if any appreciable amount of money is to be lent.

You will also need projections showing how the loan will be paid off. And considerable care must be taken to assure that the lender doesn't extract overly onerous covenants that can hamper future operations. CPA firms do audits, of course. But accountants will also assist in dealing with lenders, work out projections based on future business assumptions (which will be challenged to assess contingencies), and advise on covenants that might be excessive based on their knowledge of similarly situated clients.

Financing the Established Business

Companies already public, from Davids to Goliaths, need financing as they grow or roll over prior funding. Funds are required for countless reasons, not only for business expansion. "Financial engineering"— realigning debt to equity ratios and matching terms of funds obtained with assets intended to repay—is often a motivation for accessing capital markets. Investment banking houses have developed financial products that amalgamate numerous basic materials (leases, debt, preferred stock, common stock) and will even invent a new financial instrument if appropriate. "New Product Groups" at major investment banks are constantly trying to outdo their competitor's last coup. Lamentably, the accounting rule makers, including the SEC, simply have been unable to keep current with the flood of new financial instruments and transactions, and those in the user vanguard are sometimes in peril that the rules—when they later arrive—will require an unanticipated and undesirable financial presentation. The IRS also has many murky regulations that often require temerity—and written tax opinions. To guard against this peril, investment bankers seek the accounting, tax, and regulatory advice of CPA firms, often in writing, passing this advice along to those they hope might use a new product. Because accountants are cerebral, differences of opinion are bound to occur. Use your CPA audit firm to evaluate the high-tech financial instrument or transaction proffered by investment bankers to assure that it will be accounted for and taxed as represented.

Government Contracting

As a government contractor, you are concerned by reports of serious overcharges. This business is vital, and you want assurance that no such problems lurk in your operations. The CPA firm can perform "vulnerability" and "risk assessment" studies, review your systems and estimating procedures, and help develop stronger internal auditing methods. Policy and procedure manuals can be developed so that everyone in your organization will know what to do, when to do it, and how.

Taxing Matters

There is nothing wrong about legitimately saving taxes or at least postponing their due date. Indeed, it is wasteful to pay any more, any sooner, than needed. The complexity of our federal and state tax codes and regulations requires that expert advice be obtained when contemplating any major move. Most financing decisions have tax implications that are a moving target. CPA firms are consummate experts in income taxes and should readily save you the cost of their tax services. Personal financial planning (PFP), today's upscale perk at many companies, is heavily tilted toward income tax minimization. All major CPA firms offer this service, with the advantage to you that the CPA will appreciate your business interrelationships and not deal with PFP in a vacuum.

Feasibility Studies and Break-Even Analysis

What will it cost to make the new product? What are its variable costs, and how much might it contribute to fixed costs? Is there a market? What can go wrong? CPA firms have developed the feasibility study area on all levels ranging from individual new products to the viability of an entire enterprise. Public offering documents often contain a CPA firm's opinion regarding financial feasibility—such as on the development of a hotel or sports arena—and this type of expertise can be tailored to your specific need.

Facilitating Introductions

It is prudent to build as many business relationships as time permits; you never know when you will need one or another. Networking is vital for some, important for all. You should utilize your CPA firm as a mainline to many professional and business leaders you are not able to cultivate on your own: attorneys, investment bankers, possible merger partners, government officials, accounting and tax rule makers and more—international as well as domestic. CPA firms often have someone specializing in what interests you only occasionally. By linking with several leaders at the CPA firms, you can request—and get—the entrées. The CPA firm is not a public relations firm, however, so have a well-formulated rationale when asking for this service. The CPA firm will desire to please you in any reasonable endeavor, as their future business comes from today's goodwill.

Overseas Needs

Foreign manufacturing may lower cost and/or improve quality. CPA firms can point out government incentives, tariffs, taxation, restrictions on funds flows, and a host of other problems you might take months to investigate. Again, the worldwide scope of major CPA firms facilitates such feasibility analysis.

Opportunity Knocks

CPA firms will be around whenever you need them. In this sense opportunity knocks more than once. Creativity and innovation emerge from ongoing processes. Thus be proactive more than reactive. Keeping abreast of your CPA firm's service offerings through cultivating several firm representatives is far better than calling for help when beset by problems. CPA firms no longer wear the "green-eye-shade" image. Don't think of them as simply "number crunchers" but as all-around business advisers.

51

Creating Competitive Advantage with Information Technology

John A. Cunningham

President, Competitive Technologies, Inc. and former Senior Manager, Corporate Information Systems Staff, General Electric

David Bendel Hertz

Distinguished Professor and Director, Intelligent Computer Systems Research Institute, University of Miami

The deployment of information technology to gain competitive advantage tests the depths of executive creativity. What is it about the strategic use of data that suggests a new brand of creative leadership? What drivers propel diffusion throughout business and industry? How can the creative use of information systems influence strategic thinking? Key is the changing purposes of computers.

Man-Machine Decision Making

One large airline revamped its entire fleet planning process on a large-scale spreadsheet. Airlines have had difficulty maintaining satisfactory profitability under deregulation. Aircraft utilization has fluctuated widely because of price and schedule competition and because of seasonal and intraday usage patterns. A computer-based model was developed that could examine the effects of fleet composition and scheduling on short-term operating costs and long-term costs. Depending on the particular problem focus, cost data and decision "heuristics" were used to develop tentative schedules, provide guidelines for fleet development, plan aircraft acquisition programs, and evaluate competitive policies on specific flight routes. (Heuristics represent an approach to problem solving that is different from algorithms in that the steps do not guarantee "a best solution," but only "a solution"—which is then assessed and used to improve subsequent attempts until an acceptable solution is reached. Heuristic methods are dependent on human guesses whereas algorithmic methods use fixed sets of rules and relationships.) The computer program "simulated" (i.e., represented symbolically in the computer) the airline and provided management with an opportunity to visualize what alternative courses of action might yield. This is not artificial intelligence but rather a profitable symbiosis between man and machine.

Most managers like methods that do not threaten their exercise of managerial judgment. The use of the computer for financial, marketing, and manufacturing data processing seems perfectly safe to them. But when innovative ideas have an impact on their decision-making domains, they are reluctant to embrace them. But computers played a major role in Citibank's drive to the top of its industry (see below). And company after company has found that the manager-computer alliance can mean the difference between mediocre and outstanding performance.

Risk Analysis and Computer Simulations

A major task in most businesses is assessment of the risk involved in making a commitment of resources to a product, plant, or acquisition. Risk taking is the job of the creative manager. Developing analytical information about the nature of risks is a task on which managers and computers work well together. The enlightened manager has always investigated the effects of assumptions on decision alternatives. Now the computer can assess the entire range of possible outcomes in evaluating whether a particular investment, new-product proposal, or corporate strategy should be approved or turned down. Computer simulation permits estimates of future uncertainties attached to such factors as market size, selling prices, market growth rates, market shares, investment required, useful life and residual values, and operating and fixed costs. These estimates can be combined so as to test the many possible alternative variation combinations, and outcomes. The number of simulations can be made sufficiently large to provide realistic estimates of the odds on specific outcomes, say for return on investment. Clearly the reliability of results depends on original input factors. The more reliable the inputs the more confident the outputs. It is like the difference between betting in a dice game (if the dice are not loaded, the odds are known in advance), and betting on horse races (the track odds are guestimates of expected performance).

Management of a large oil company has applied the risk-analysis simulation process to assist in the development of exploration strategies. Strategies are defined as the selection of a portfolio of opportunities to be pursued from among those that are available to the company. Potential reserves, costs, and yields are utilized to help determine such factors for alternative exploration plans as feasibility, contribution to corporate objectives, and risks. They have found that the following key elements are necessary for useful simulation results—they are included here since they represent the kinds of information that should be used in any strategic comparison, particularly those carried out by computer programs: (1) All significant opportunities must be included. (2) Opportunities must be defined in a consistent manner. (3) Uncertainties must be included in the expected outcomes of opportunities. (4) Performance tradeoffs of alternative strategies must be clearly presented (remembering that each alternative strategy is a package of opportunities and cannot be ranked in order of highest payoff, or other criteria, since each not only has an expected payoff but a risk distribution as well. The tradeoff is between higher and lower return and higher and lower risk). (5) Programming must permit flexible and rapid evaluation of strategies as new opportunities arise and as the return-risk relationships of old ones change in light of new information.

Computer simulation offers easy assessment of alternative actions, policies, and plans. Managers can establish ceilings and targets in various investment categories with increased understanding of the risks involved in each. The computer can be a partner in helping describe the criteria and policies to make choices. It can help managers stay in the driver's seat. This is true symbiosis. We don't expect the computer to have a social sense or be very original—that's the manager's job. But to run all those calculations in a simulation, the creative manager can count on the trusty and patient (but demanding) computer.

General Electric's Information Systems

To differentiate strategic competitive advantage from other information technology gains, General Electric's Corporate Information Systems uses a four-circle explanation: (1) Circle number one reaches back 20 or 30 years to the first productive uses of computers—routine detail, such as payrolls, accounts payable, and similar labor-intensive record-keeping tasks; these are called "pro forma" functions. (2) The second circle contains many ways to cut costs and improve productivity with computer-based processes (e.g., linear programming); this is called the "cost improvement and productivity" circle. (3) In the third circle are the applications that embed computers and microprocessors right into the product, to yield novel features that achieve real gains in market share; call this circle "product innovation." (4) The fourth circle leads into new territory—where competitive advantage is reaped from creatively cultivating better ways of handling business information; it comes by integrating information across functions—marketing, engineering, manufacturing, finance, customer service, and the like; this is the "strategic information" circle.

Information Technology as a Competitive Weapon

American Airlines

The AAdvantage incentive program for frequent flyers is a good example of the fourth circle. American created it by leveraging their passenger reservation system. Eighty percent of revenues, they found, came from 20 percent of travelers. Armed with these insights, they refined their data collection and reporting procedures, pinpointed prime customers, and mounted a campaign. As a result, they created competitive advantage that delivered greater market share and disrupted competition. They changed the marketplace. AA created a brand image for a commodity product. Their move was strategic. They made no changes in product, no change in service, no alteration in routes, no reduction in prices, no rescheduling. They simply made smarter use of their data through top-level synergy among marketing, customer service, and information resources.

American Hospital Supply

Creative use of information technology can also erect high barriers for competitors to scale. American Hospital Supply (AHS) is a classic illustration. The company won its dominant position during the upswing in hospital services during the 1970s and early 1980s. AHS made it easy (and accurate) to enter supply orders via card readers placed in administrative offices of major hospitals. As these devices became more sophisticated and were backed up with AHS computers for managing warehouses and sourcing, hospitals preferred to purchase from AHS's 117,000 stocked items. AHS terminals, network, and computers became an entrenched asset that competitors found difficult to dislodge; hospitals were locked-in, the cost of switching to catch-up systems offered by other firms were huge. AHS had changed the structure of the market by using computers to facilitate customer service.

Citicorp

When the computer revolution was just starting, John S. Reed, now Chairman and CEO of Citicorp, began his career as a systems analyst with an abiding faith that these machines were a key factor for the future competitive success of financial organizations. That this faith was not misplaced is written into the record growth of Citibank, surpassing the Bank of America in assets, earnings, and global activities. Reed pressured managers in all departments to engage actively in the change strategy. He pushed the creative process along by placing computer-savvy individuals in pivotal positions. But Reed's rise to the top, as a systems analyst, in a field in which marketing, loan, and trust officers had long held sway, did not come about just because Reed led Citibank into the forefront of internal and external computerized banking. Walter Wriston was the CEO whose aggressive foresight structured the imaginative dream of being number one. Part of that dream was having Reed, a technologist, at his side as Citibank took the competitive edge in the application of computers in banking finance. When Wriston retired in 1984, he put Reed, the computer expert, in charge of the commercial banking empire they had created.

General Electric Appliance

Nothing is forever; sustaining positions of competitive advantage draws heavily from the bank of executive energy and creativity. Parts and service of GE's appliance business illustrates the point. GE's strategy is to deliver first-class service in order to enhance the attractiveness of its appliance purchases, influencing not only the buyer's current purchase decision but also the next one. The consumer sees only a serviceperson and a company van; invisible is a massive, computer-based logistics system that handles 60 million pieces per year, ships 47 tons of parts daily, and maintains a catalog of some 50,000 items. And the distribution center fills 93 percent of parts requests without reordering and ships 85 percent the same day the order is placed. This is the kind of back-up service needed to answer the calls of consumers in their homes—to keep the basic strategy well and working. At no time did the concept appear as a sudden flash of brilliance nor was the implementation achieved overnight. It took two decades and is being improved continually. The staff believes that every review, every study, every probe from higher level offices is an opportunity to spark new ideas and find better ways of serving the consumer.

How is information technology leveraged in an operation like this? First it takes commitment of top management; the responsible executive must be convinced that first-class parts and service is a key strategy element. Second, it takes continual analysis of data from the marketplace, always evaluating calls for parts to determine customer needs and wants; "staying close to the customer" is very real. And third, it requires constant re-examination of all aspects of logistics: costs, vendor prices, repackaging labor, shipping alternatives, automated billing and credit checks, automatic data capture at receiving, and inventory investment levels; the purpose is to seek more cost-effective service.

"Smokestack" Company

This old-line manufacturing business produced small electrical devices, high-quality products made for equipment assembled by other firms. At one time the company enjoyed a 60 percent market share—but now it was only 40 percent and slipping. The purchasers were treating this product as "a commodity," which negated its differentiating strengths. The management team found themselves in a worst-case scenario, with few options left. Could information technology make a difference in a smokestack company like this? First off, they had to change their focus from internal criteria to external markets. For instance, when annual contract renewal talks came around, it was clear that customers kept track of missed deliveries—as well they should. Think how useful it would be for the company to keep track of the occasions when they were on time, ahead of schedule, or saved the day with an emergency shipment. Value chain analysis suggested fewer products and faster service. The structure for competing was changed. Internal information processes and logistics were redesigned for rapid response to short-turnaround orders.

Merrill Lynch

In this case imaginative leadership used information technology to introduce a new product. That new product stunned banks and the investment community, and to the dismay of competitors, it captured a new multibillion dollar market. The Cash Management Account (CMA) of Merrill Lynch came out of creative work sparked by an innocent-sounding study, jointly funded with Stanford Research Institute (SRI) by some fifteen firms. SRI studied the interests of emerging investors. How might they pick investment instruments? All sponsors of the study, of course, received the report. A couple of staff members of Merrill Lynch, however, were the only ones to catch the glimmer of a new kind of market and product—a checking account that would combine a high-interest money fund and a stock trading facility. Processing the voluminous information from over 1 million participants was a herculean task. Needed was the creative thinking of a variety of talents. Pivotally, this included an upbeat, can-do information systems leader whom they found in the data services operation of Bank One in Ohio. The CMA hinged on support services. The 18-month lead gained with this information system was all it took to make spectators out of competitors.

Information Systems Today

Information and information technology constitute a resource, not a tool. They are on a par with other resources: human, capital, plant and equipment, materials. Firms should appoint an "information systems executive" who reports directly to the general manager—making sure it's the right person.

What does this new approach mean to the role of information systems (I/S) managers? Cultural shock. At one meeting of I/S managers a corporate executive answered the question this way: "Imagine reporting to your general manager. List those things meaningful to him or her and compare it to the things that you have been doing. Any disparity? I think you'll be asking yourself, what does the business need, . . . how can I support it, . . . how can I get out ahead?" I/S managers must become leaders not laggards.

Historically I/S led the way as *the* large-scale computer user—pioneering the first pro forma applications discussed earlier. The logical home was with finance. For many years I/S managers were given a "support service" role. Today, the role is less support and more *leadership*. In most industries finance is the lowest leverage spot for information systems to report to. Leading-edge advice is to report the information systems function to the top executive. If that's not doable, then move I/S to the function that has the greatest leverage, the biggest driver in the business.

In this new role, the I/S manager becomes interpreter, educator, advocate, and stimulator—an aggressive, innovative member of the management team, consumed with the passion of making the business a creatively successful user of its information resources. In many instances it means new blood, in others, educational programs and some mentor guidance. It means incorporating information technology into executive education programs. And still further out, it means devising ambitious career programs for junior people.

How does all this change the work style of general managers (GM)? They have new dimension in their leadership. They have a major role in information management planning, particularly in early stages in which orchestration of strategy and positions of team members take place. To emphasize the point: Information management is not a spectator sport. If I/S reports to the GM, he or she will have to make the intellectual investment to think about the function, to think about its leader, to attract the best people, and to force those reporting to him or her to do the same.

What about management information systems (MIS)? Senior executives often prefer to leave their company's MIS to someone else. The creative manager, however, never opts out of MIS design and control. The goal of MIS is to get the correct information to the appropriate manager at the right time. This information should be decision oriented, organized, and efficient. A manager's success can be affected seriously by MIS structure. So, if the system is being designed, he or she should influence it. If it is already designed and does not fit his or her needs, he or she should change it. Managers have too much at stake in the flow of information to allow MIS to develop by default.

How does the new vision of information technology affect the work force? This is the most exciting part. Experience shows that when you share information—needed or not—with personnel, they do their jobs better. Individually and in concert. Ownership is the key concept. Employees need a personal stake in the fortunes of the business, an opportunity to be players in the action. The premium is on good ideas—not rank in the hierarchy. It's the people that make it work—

who can generate competitive advantage by using information technology. The leadership role is to catalyze that generative force. It's almost as if the "information revolution" is starting all over again—this time with a quantum jump.

52

How Personal Computers Enhance Executive Creativity and Creative Strategy

Edward M . Esber

President, Ashton-Tate, Inc.

George T. Geis

Research Coordinator, UCLA Center for Human Resource Management

Robert Lawrence Kuhn

Investment Banker, Senior Research Fellow, IC² Institute, The University of Texas at Austin and Adjunct Professor, Graduate School of Business Administration, New York University

Is the personal computer (PC) an elixir able to turn a common executive into a creative dynamo? Do innovative solutions to organizational problems reside inside that desktop box, waiting to be released by gentle keyboard massage of executive fingers? While few executives have such lofty expectations, a number of myths have developed about what PCs can do for managers. Some industry promoters have perpetuated the mystique. So let's be forthright. The truth is that you can't go out today and buy a machine that will make you creative. You won't find software in the stores, as of yet, to tell you how to design or introduce an innovative process or service.

A computer is a very literal machine, understanding what you say but not what you mean. It features the rational, not the intuitive. Since creativity fundamentally involves generating a novel response to a problem that doesn't have a clear, cookbook-like solution, we must not overstate how computers can aid the executive in innovation. Little purpose is served by feeding the personal computer mystique. To raise false expectations is to engender later frustration. We provide a realistic appraisal of how *today's* personal computers can enhance executive creativity.

We keep stressing *today* because advances in both hardware and software capabilities are being made rapidly. Central to the process of continual product development is input from executive PC users. What types of things would you like to be able to do? Watch the field of artificial intelligence. When breakthroughs occur, the way personal computers and executives work together will substantially change. True artificial intelligence will (1) enable the computer to focus on what we mean and not just what we say, (2) facilitate the development of expert systems capable of transferring state-of-the-art knowledge and experience in a field, and (3) erode the barriers of computer use for the computer nonliterate. With the advent of artificial intelligence, the possibilities for executive creativity and innovation will expand dramatically. For now, however, let's return to today's world and examine both the pitfalls and the place of PCs in executive problem solving.

Potential Pitfalls in Executive Computing

Before we make specific suggestions about how personal computers can aid executive decision making and creativity, in the spirit of realism championed above, we examine some computer limitations.

1. In spite of the claim of some industry leaders, it is not clear that PCs always help executives make better decisions. While application packages such as spreadsheets have allowed executives to examine more alternatives, to manipulate information in more minute detail, an

abundance of output can create bottlenecks in organizational decision making. The business leader has so many more alternatives to consider that decision paralysis can occur. Information is so abundant that it has sometimes thrown people off the right track. (Remember the extraneous data placed in business school cases for the purpose of distracting students? The purpose was to teach the importance of finding and using the essential information. However, in the corporate setting, a professor is not around to help steer the way through an information maze.) Current packages are of little help in the *evaluation* of alternatives. For example, spreadsheets tend to examine the impact of changing one or two variables at a time, with little sense of the priority of variable importance. Worse, these packages can do little, if anything, to assess the importance of variables not subject to quantification.

2. Computers will not magically make bad managers into good ones. A PC will not make an accountant out of a financial novice. A computer is a tool in the hands of a skilled executive; it cannot take the place of formal training, apprenticeship, and experience.

3. The executive must guard against feeling that the computer or its output is "beyond reproach." Some managers assign raw intelligence to computers and attribute a definitiveness to computer input. Such executives, however subconsciously, ascribe a touch of infallibility to spreadsheet models and forecasts, assigning more validity than had the same output been cranked out manually.

How Personal Computers Enhance Creativity

Here are some ways in which personal computers can be used as a tool to support executive decision making and creative problem solving. Our emphasis is on using the machine as a tool, not viewing it as an oracle.

1. *Immediate feedback.* A PC can help capture your own thoughts and process your own assumptions almost instantly, enabling you to see creative possibilities in a situation more quickly and efficiently. No longer do you have to work with a programming analyst, trying to get someone else to track the implications of your business plan. Communication and feedback come directly from the machine and not from an intermediary programmer who may not understand the "guts of the business" or what you want to model and test.

2. *Alternative analysis.* A PC can reduce the riskiness of decisions by allowing you to look at more alternatives. You can experiment more cheaply and faster, examining alternative "what if" scenarios using the most recent data. If you avoid the decision paralysis we talked about earlier (caused by an overload of information or plethora of options), examining alternatives will allow you to proceed with more confidence. Venturing forward and taking risks are linked with executive creativity. However, before taking a major risk, the innovative executive first understands the possible risks and works to structure the situation so that the downside is contained. PCs can be your ally in this process. Simulating possible outcomes using sensitivity analysis can increase confidence in your leap to action.

3. *Database Development.* PCs can allow for the selective sharing of company information. As an executive, you probably have need for at least three types of databases: (1) *Personal* database containing information central to your specific responsibilities and areas of interest. More details are given later. (2) *Departmental* databases holding information required by employees of a given department or division. (3) *Corporate* databases with information utilized by more than one department or division. Evidence exists that companies that foster employee creativity and innovation provide for sharing of information needed to solve problems, with requests for such information requiring only minimal justification. Building departmental and corporate databases and making them available to company PC-users through networking can help meet this information-sharing goal. A true multiuser system allows interdepartmental sharing of important information, such as mailing lists. One executive noted that his most critical need was a unified master corporate mailing list for a key product, instead of the current fifteen separate departmental lists. (More effective decision making would result from having access to the complete list. Special purpose lists could also be maintained for specific department purposes.) Widescale availability of data can have a cultural impact on a company. PC networks can facilitate the sharing of information and can help prevent the selective hoarding of information by a territoriality-obsessed manager in an attempt to maintain hierarchical control. Such organizational tyranny is surely not conducive to employee creativity. Availability can also lead employees to discover organizational problems that need solution. Research has shown that an employee is more likely to come up with an innovative solution if a problem is discovered rather than assigned.

4. *Graphic excitement.* The graphic imagery available on personal computers can spark innovation. Creativity is associated with a keen

sense of imagery in a field, and recasting information in graphic form can trigger creative ideas. Graphics interfaces and their ability to provide, expand, contract, and rotate predrawn figures help those who do not have native artistic skills in creative design. For artists, advertising designers, architects, or others working regularly in the graphic arts, native skills are enhanced by computer graphics.

5. *Verbal communication.* Let's not ignore what word processors can do to help you become a better communicator. Many professionals have long argued that the essence of effective writing is rewriting. Notable writers such as E. B. White and James Thurber estimated that eight or nine rewrites of a piece were necessary before it met their standards. While you need not be a White or Thurber, the convenience of rewriting with word processors can make writing more accurate and effective. One executive described word processing as adding a sense of excitement and exhilaration to his writing: "The best part of it is the ease with which I can clean up my documents. I had little motivation to improve the quality of my memos when they resided on a yellow pad, with lines, arrows, and scratch-out marks filling the paper." Software with outlining functions that enable idea processing are further steps toward enhancing executive creativity. Some of these application packages provide for two-dimensional visualization and manipulation of ideas or concepts, much as spreadsheets allow for the two-dimensional portrayal and analysis of numbers.

6. *Personal information.* Personal databases can give executives quick access to information in those domains central to their responsibilities. Personal executive databases deserve special attention. A necessary component of executive creativity is to stay on top of the facts and methods necessary to solve problems in one's area of expertise and responsibility. An individual database, structured to meet your own specific informational needs, can assist you to access concepts and knowledge in supporting decision making. For example, one executive built a personal database on corporate taxation. Using key phrases, this executive can immediately access up to 3000 specifically targeted articles or other pieces of information in this area. Personal databases can also provide a strong catalyst to get and stay organized.

7. *Staying in touch.* PCs enable you to keep close to key data, to have your fingers (quite literally) on the pivotal indicators of your business. The best executives keep right on top of the raw data that is important to their company—new product sales, markdowns, competitive pricing—the list is long. Many creative executives find the PC invaluable as an aid in touching such primary data. They feel it, select it, reduce it, present it. The PC can keep track of what competitors are

doing. Closeness to unfiltered, unreduced data for the company, industry, and economy is especially important in making creative moves in a market environment. (See Chapter 32.)

8. *Playfulness.* Personal brainstorming. The opportunity to play around with data on a PC can be a marvelous inducement of creativity. Playfulness, free from external control, is a key element in creativity. So in the privacy of your own office, don't be reluctant to fool around (on your microcomputer, that is). Sift and shift data central to your company's future. Build templates that break away from traditional ways. Playing with information on your PC may lead to a fresh, perhaps revolutionary concept about where your company should go. (But, remember, don't believe it just because it pops up on that screen.) Don't be deceived: your PC won't turn you into a creative genius. Using your computer as a personal tool, however, can help facilitate creative insights and aid you in becoming a more effective executive.

How Personal Computers Enhance Creative Strategy

If there is any area deemed "off limits" for computers, it is the creative development of strategy. Such is conventional wisdom. Personal computers are changing this perspective. It's not the machine's new capacity; it's the user's new thinking. Even the most intuitive executives are put at a disadvantage if they are not using PCs for strategic planning, formulation, and control. Following are things to think about when using PCs in creative strategy making.

1. *Using tension.* What should managers do themselves, and what should they assign subordinates? The age-old dilemma triggers new anxiety in a PC world in which so much more can be done by one's self. This tension is good: Managers need to feel and use it—especially in areas that affect creative decision making. Take, for example, the writing of a strategic plan—the simple application of word processing. The extent to which an executive polishes words, phrases, and ideas on his or her PC can often increase impact of an important document. Yet there's a cost for this personal wordsmithing—and here's where the tension arises. The executive is now doing some of what used to be considered secretarial work, and most effective use of executive time emerges as an issue. Another example is model making: Should an executive allocate effort, often substantial, to construct and debug complex spreadsheets? The task can be easily assigned to bright, young MBAs. Yet something strange happens when an executive is forced to

go through the rigorous thinking of the model-making process: There is unexpected advantage—raw data is assessed anew; assumptions are questioned, relationships explored, alternatives considered. General creative confidence, even more than particular detailed content, is a special benefit.

2. *Giving direction.* Executives should have working knowledge of PCs in order to properly manage subordinates. What do executives need to know to assign and manage PC tasks relating to strategic planning? How can executives seek creative development through others? Only by being personally capable of building models. A PC-literate manager will be far more effective in directing others: The executive will be more assured and the subordinates more secure.

3. *Decision-making meetings.* There is an increasing role of personal computers in formal meetings ("decision conferences")—e.g., executive committees or board meetings in which real-time scenario building and alternative analysis can take place. (This is actually occurring in a Swedish banking group.) Such high-powered meetings require advance preparation: Participants must study the subjects and the computer must be operated by a skilled model builder and manipulator. (Note how new technology demands new structure.) Once again an executive with hands-on familiarity will be better able to offer alternatives in this pressured, real-time environment.

4. *Quick information.* PCs generate swift, comprehensive answers to data-oriented questions, thus facilitating rapid response to strategy formulation issues. Creative ideas are ephemeral: They cannot wait for leisurely support. PCs enable the construction of personal databases (see above) in which one is not constricted by how information is formatted by the MIS department. The capacity to structure information in free-form ways is especially helpful for the idea-generation process of alternative strategy formulation.

5. *Competitive analysis.* Creative strategies cannot be formulated in a vacuum. There is no isolated idealism in highly competitive markets. Understanding competitor positioning is critical for all strategic planning, especially when novel corporate moves are being considered. What, for example, are the alternative scenarios if our company took an aggressive tack with higher advertising and lower price? What is each competitor likely to do and how would such counterattacks affect the overall market? Only a sophisticated, interactive model can suggest a solution to such a multidimensional problem. Furthermore, possible responses are so varied it is impossible to test all combinations and permutations. This is the arena in which creative executives shine:

Selective search with personal insight can choose likely sequences of events. Such game playing is critical when assessing innovative ideas in strategy, where decisions affect the entire enterprise.

6. *Brainstorming.* Using PCs in brainstorming and idea exchange sessions (formal and informal) promises a fascinating structural shift in such meetings. Group decision support and collaborative problem solving can be made more efficient while personal creativity is enhanced. The system combines the best of group process and interaction with individual freedom and privacy. Ideas from group members' desktop machines pop out on a common screen where they can be ordered and organized. Yet individuals remain insulated from insult, thus promoting free expression.

7. *Convergence.* PCs energize the iterative process of focusing in on a particular strategy. The formulation of models is the generation of a series of discrete, interrelated steps representing real-world relationships, each one of which can be real-world tested by knowledgeable people inside and outside the organization. Such "sequential processing" forms a new decision-making environment that supports the creative process.

8. *Collective creativity at a distance.* Networks of PCs, across the hall or across the country, can greatly enlarge numbers of participants in idea-generating sessions as well as ease their means of participation. Brainstorming, for example, can now involve dozens if not hundreds of people unencumbered by constraints of geography. Delphi techniques, in which experts are repetitively polled on specific issues, can be intensified by virtually instant feedback in real time.

9. *Human resources.* Personal computers are altering the character of personnel—the way they think, how they work, even where they work. The transformation is inexorable as new kinds of managers, hired to enhance competitive position, continue to develop personal computers for creative strategy making.

Bibliography

Geis, George T., and Robert L. Kuhn: *Micromanaging: Transforming Business Leaders with Personal Computers*, Prentice-Hall, Englewood, NJ, 1987. This book/disk package presents the personal computer revolution in terms of the four basic functions of management: planning, organizing, leading, and controlling. Each is discussed in light of the transforming concept of information, the transforming character of organization, and the transforming nature of thinking.

53

Thinking Internationally

Bertram S. Brown

Senior Vice President,
Healthcare, Inc.

Gerald Rosenthal

Professor, Department of Humanities and Social
Sciences, and Coordinator of International Activities,
Hahnemann University

Gunter David

Journalist and Free-lance Writer

Thinking internationally requires major changes in perspective. Cultural differences may demand mental overhaul. These differences have a crucial impact on doing business. Success or failure depends on your ability to adjust to new circumstances. Flexibility, then, is a key to doing business in other countries. You need not only a geographic map, but a mental and conceptual guide to travel and thrive in foreign territory.

Creative thinking also requires flexibility. When you think creatively, you may change your goals in ways you had not considered or imagined before. As in strategic thinking, you must research your market thoroughly, study the competition, and so forth. The difference lies in shifting objectives when better, more promising ones come along.

Therein lies the creativity. For example, some years ago NASA developed a nutritional product containing multiple vitamins. The product, a liquid, was capable of staying intact through extremes of hot and cold, jarring, and other physical assaults. An R&D manager was asked to find a market application for the product, beyond use on space flights. He did, not in the food or health care industry, but in the paint business. The characteristics of the liquid solved the problems of paint storage and distribution in the tropics. The creativity was in developing a use that had not been anticipated.

World Views

Global Flows

One can view the world as a global system, a series of flows of money, material, information, and people across boundaries, oceans, and air. Technology facilitates the flow of information and the speed of transportation, while politics and turbulence affect the movement of people. Tastes are homogenizing, making Americans kings of culture. Jeans, the American uniform, are worn in Hong Kong and Tel Aviv, as well as in Dubuque. You can eat at a Burger King in Zurich, as well as on Route 66. If your product has an American look, the world is your market. Television, movies, and the American traveler have presold it. At the same time, the masses of immigrants moving from one country to another bring their individual cultures with them. This had to be faced by the HMO in Denver, which now operates three clinics in Vietnamese, and by some supermarket chains in Washington, D.C., and Los Angeles that cater to various oriental groups. While thinking internationally is taken to mean exporting domestic goods or establishing American business overseas, it includes today the internationalization of parts of our country and thus parts of the domestic market.

Anthropological Variety

One can view the world as an enormous collection of anthropological entities, of thousands of tribes, languages, and nearly 200 countries. Each subculture may form a country, and sometimes different entities create a political union. Consider India, China, and the Soviet Union as giant conglomerations of heterogeneous states and cultures. On the other hand, the Flemings and Walloons squeeze together in little

Belgium. Such diversity means marketing in a different way. A nation may not be a market unto itself. A whole part of the world may be your market, or perhaps only a particular tribe. Market definition can supersede geography. You may sell a product, for example, to all English-speaking people or, conversely, you may sell only to urban Australians.

Socio-Economic Classes

One can target products to specific strata of society, to working, middle, or upper economic and social classes. Different classes of people and nations have different needs, and you must fit supply to demand. For example, you may have a product that will appeal to Third World governments that are trying to meet the diet deficiency of their people.

Political Alliances

One can view the world in terms of east-west and north-south relationships. It is a political perspective in which the United States and allies are poised vis-à-vis the Soviet Union and allies: east and west facing each other. The north-south confrontations are between the "have" countries of the north and the "have not" countries of the south, such as those in Latin America, Africa, and portions of Asia. Companies must understand how different political structures affect the way business is done. Political tension can affect business, and one must be prepared for possible fall-out from an American embargo to certain countries. Political and economic instability can be devastating. Consider the freezing of foreign currency by revolutionary governments.

Why Think Internationally?

At Home

In many American industries foreign production is no longer an option; it is a cost-driven necessity. Even uniquely American products, in demand around the world, are no longer produced in the United States—or they may be made in America but with imported material. The shirt you buy in Philadelphia may carry a well-known label but most likely was made somewhere in the Orient. In short, you are wearing a foreign product with an American label.

Abroad

Manufacturers who export goods soon discover that they must also manufacture abroad in order to grow. Europeans have known this for some time. For example, the LaCoste alligator shirt, manufactured by a French company, is not made solely in France. It is often made in the country in which it is sold. To achieve volume, a company must often produce locally: (1) Production costs are lower abroad than in the United States; (2) foreign distributors or retailers will not tie up cash in large inventories; (3) frequent and fast deliveries are required.

Abroad at Home

The flow of immigrants, legal or otherwise, into the United States is turning this country anew into a microcosm of the world. If you do business in an area whose population is turning Vietnamese, Korean, or Mexican, you must think cross-culturally. When neighborhoods change, Mom and Pop stores can move out. But large chains cannot. They must adapt to the new customers. They may bring in Chinese cabbage. But more than that, they need a new mentality. This means changing the mix of personnel and hiring workers from among the new constituents. Adjustment to changing conditions may be especially difficult for national chains and franchises, which are operated according to a single set of rules. Senior management will have to modify those rules. The pool of management also will have to reflect the market change. As different cultures invade the executive suite, the company character will change. Thinking internationally at home must permeate the entire company if it is to succeed.

Principles of International Business

Suspend Opinion

Rules for doing business may differ from one country or even one culture to another. The way to do business in New York won't hold in New Delhi. Therefore, suspend opinion until you have collected information. The proper moment to take action is when you have enough knowledge to determine the impact of actions not only on the corporation but also on the environment. For example, in many cultures people are quite accommodating. That does not mean they agree with you. You must suspend the usual presumption that positive feedback means you are doing well in a deal. What you hear is not always what you get.

Consider the case of the American consultant hired by a Latin American government. Eagerly he arrived, armed with a contract signed by the assistant secretary of health, stipulating conditions the government had accepted. He soon learned that not a single condition would be met. While this surprised the consultant on his initial assignment, it was old hat to people experienced in doing business in that country. "They wanted me to go and knew that if they said the right things, I would," he explains. "So they said the right things and I went."

Establish a Beachhead

To move your product in a foreign country you must sell it in an acceptable way. This will differ from culture to culture. It will pay, therefore, to establish a beachhead, a presence in the country you have selected as a market before you try to do business on a large scale. The person chosen as your representative must be flexible and willing to learn and respect foreign ways. His or her job will be to understand how the market works, to find the frustrations of doing business. He or she must identify important people with whom you must eventually negotiate. He or she should join the local Rotary or similar club in order to meet local businessmen and women, rather than only associate with fellow Americans who think the way he or she does. It could be helpful to learn the language. Your representative should seek out people with a similar predisposition, who have been through the experience. Most companies underinvest in the training of executives they send abroad. Give your representatives some exposure to anthropology as well as to marketing. What they face abroad are not just new markets but new rules. You are going to try to make a profit by domestic standards, doing what you always have done, but doing it in another world, with other rules, other constraints, new problems and a different history.

All this takes time, and financial payoffs will not be immediate. Often you will collaborate with local businesspeople: partners who have a different outlook may be indispensable for successful entry into a foreign market. Maintaining representation will help protect against counterfeit goods. Many foreign countries are not very concerned about patent rights established outside their boundaries. As a result, and depending on volume, you may have to establish a presence in the foreign country to make sure that you get your fair share as the market develops. Establish yourself in a market before it gets hot. For example, many American executives maintain that China will be a big market. Currently, however, China is poor, especially in rural areas, and is a small market for American products. The potential lies in the country's demographics, its ability to grow and develop economically. Therefore, to enter the China market, you should position there now, not because of the money to be made in the near future but because those who establish early and learn how to function in the Chinese culture are going to have a better opportunity to succeed than those who do not make this kind of investment. Not every good market is a good market for you. Your firm has its own cultural context, a style in which you like to work. And even if your product is accepted in the foreign market, your style may not be.

Rules Can Change

This is a primary truth of doing business abroad. A sudden shift in government, especially in a totalitarian state, is bound to have a negative impact on business and investment. Nationalization, a rarity in this country, can subvert you. A 100 percent ownership of a factory or business will make you vulnerable. Several countries require businesses to have at least 51 percent local ownership. The nationalization of banks makes matters even more complicated. In these instances, dollar accounts can be frozen, which means that money cannot leave the country. To avoid being damaged seriously by nationalization of banks or freezing of currency, carry very low cash balances in the country. Operate with transfers into the country as needed, or make payments from a third country. For instance, the company could locate in Uganda and pay bills out of Belgium. When planning to enter a foreign market, you must assess expectations based on locally prevailing wage rates, access to markets, and other factors. But you must also determine how much change in those conditions can be tolerated. How vulnerable are you? For example, you may have set up a successful distribution network in Turkey, when suddenly the government changes the rules and sets up an official distribution board. Could you survive such a change?

Among the rules that can change rapidly is that your market is in a land of peace. Peace can deteriorate into war in a short time either through an outside aggressor or civil war. Examine the history of the potential market. Not too long ago Lebanon was considered the jewel of the Middle East and Beirut, a banking mecca. In a market with potential upheaval, you must consider personnel risks as well financial and business risks.

Agreements and Relationships

In many countries, such as China, Japan, and Latin America, agreements go beyond quick contracts. That is the American way, which includes a brief courtship over lunch or drinks or perhaps dinner and a show, depending on client importance. An American buyer will switch from one supplier to another, depending on exigencies of the moment. But abroad, agreements are often relationships that last for years. Cooperative or collaborative relationships with foreign manufacturers or licensing agreements in other countries are not a single transaction with a single transfer of resources. They are ongoing relationships. Their continuity makes the market. This means two important things. First, negotiations with a potential business contact abroad must be seen as a learning process—do not make commitments early; get a feel for the territory. Second, agreements often won't contain or specify all expectations because many will be culturally implicit. As a result, stay flexible and consider foreign agreements as downside risks. For example, plan alternatives should a condition or an expectation not be met by your counterpart abroad. Often you cannot treat agreements as absolutes. Do not, therefore, program your thinking for absolutes. Use your imagination, not your bias. It may be best to pick initial ventures that test the relationship in a small way. Gain some cross-cultural experience before moving into higher-risk ventures. For example, to distribute existing products to a buyer in Istanbul, all you have is a shipping problem. But if you must retool your product line, you would be taking an even bigger risk. Should the product fail or should you and your new foreign partners not get along, you stand to suffer big loss.

Fundamental Differences

There are cultural gaps that affect the way various groups do business. For example, Americans consider it fair for a buyer to put money up front. Others, including the Chinese, consider such a practice unreasonable. They question why they should give you money in advance before they have seen what you can produce. In the United States, there are contractual obligations, subject to court action if they are not kept. That is why the court system is overburdened with many thousands of business law suits. Some issues specified in contracts in this country are not even discussed in many other countries. For example, take a contract with a company in Paris or Rome that depends on the conduct of a third party. In the United States, if the third party does not come through, you bear the responsibility of an alternative supplier for your client. In many other countries the producer may disclaim all responsibility by blaming the third party. Though wording and conditions sound similar, contracts in many countries are little more than a series of agreements to be kept only if things go well. The next example happens often enough to merit mention. There are areas of the world, such as Latin America, in which the person with whom you have signed an agreement may suddenly go back to his or her village for several weeks because of local problems. This can happen even if he or she is a senior government official who carries a briefcase and speaks business jargon. Deep inside he or she has a different set of priorities, and trouble in the village takes precedence.

The form of government can affect marketing and distribution. In a Western democracy, the law of supply and demand dictates how to distribute merchandise. Consider the shoe business. You move shoes from plant to stores in which inventory is low and in which certain models are in demand. In a centrally controlled country like China, marketing may be dictated by the leadership's own considerations, having to do with party loyalty and production efficiency. If your line does not sell in Outer Mongolia, you may be through.

Management Differences

While management in the United States is hierarchy oriented, there are responsibilities as well as authority on every level. This is not the case in other countries in which people on one level must be wholly subservient to those over them, without interaction. Every assignment from above is accepted without question. This means that a superior never learns from a subordinate anything regarding an assignment. Local subordinates may therefore just follow whatever instructions you give, even if your planning is incomplete because of lack of knowledge in a new land. Moreover, your local subordinates may be uncertain about an assignment, but in many cultures they won't discuss their questions or qualms because this would reveal uncertainty and they would lose face. You have no way of judging from their response whether they are capable of doing the job, and they won't ask you or anybody else either. Your representatives will just do the job and take their chances. (The Japanese have found a way around this problem. They use local executive talent but form a Japanese shadow management to work with local managers.)

Foreign Workers

The issue of dealing with foreign workers is a major consideration when going abroad. You may do business with a Peruvian boasting an MBA from Harvard, who cuts a purely American deal. But remember that when he or she gets back to Peru, he or she must deal with Peruvian workers who have different standards and ways of life. As a result, quality control specifications in your contract will require a greater range of flexibility. When the Japanese operate in Mexico or Peru, their firms function with predominantly local management but with Japanese counterparts who focus on quality control and work processes—and the Mexicans or Peruvians get credit for the final product. As a result, the Japanese have much greater success in Latin America than others who have large plants there. Rigidly pursuing their own methods, the Germans and Swiss, for example, experience much conflict, frustration, and waste. Work habits differ among countries and cultures. Keep this in mind when hiring a local manufacturer's representative. You cannot assume that he or she will go out on the road every day. You don't really know what he or she is going to do. Learn as much as possible about his or her environment, the way people in his or her culture think, in order to know what to expect from him or her within the context of his or her environment. People vary, of course, but usually within the parameters of their society and culture.

Foreign Governments Deal Differently

Flexibility is especially important when dealing with foreign governments. Your expectations must be predicated on the way the country runs. In some countries, such as China and the Soviet Union, negotiations can take years because you are working with government officials rather than with businesspeople. Take the experience of the Philadelphia carpetmaker who wanted to build a plant in China to manufacture rugs. The Chinese were eager to have him build a plant in order to provide employment. Yet it took the Philadelphian many trips to China before he got to the serious talking stage and even longer to figure out an agreement, partly because of the question of plant ownership. The city was not going to be in the manufacturing business. Yet it did require certain control, which had to be considered and honored. Each foreign government has its own way of doing business. The Chinese may be slow paying their bills upon completion of delivery or service. In dealing with the Soviets, you will find the contract a subject of protracted argument and trading, complete with showdowns. Once the contract has been signed, however, the Soviets have a good track record of keeping commitments. In many countries, be prepared for bureaucratic delays. Finding a key government functionary away on vacation just when you need him or her is not uncommon.

Marketing Variance

Testing the market is different abroad. Let us say you want to try a new line of kitchen gadgets in a Latin American country. You test them in the capital, and sales are great. That may be because the upper layer of society likes new things, especially from the United States, and can afford to pay for them. But urban testing may not give true estimated sales. You may have to test smaller towns and villages, especially if the market has large agrarian and rural areas. Merchandising is also different. In Mexico, for example, the public buys a great deal in small general stores, in which inventory control is not a priority. Unlike in the United States, where you can reach an agreement with a chain to display your item independently in a special place of each branch store, the Mexican merchant will put your gadget with everybody else's. While there is much advertising on television, there is little or none within the store through the use of displays. Also, customer profiles are hard to get—often you don't know who buys your product. Can your products sell under such circumstances?

Extend Time Horizons

The old saying, "Time is money," exemplifies the lack of patience so typically American. A former vice president of Asahi Mutual Life Insurance Co. noted, " . . . Americans are more short-term oriented than Japanese . . . Americans easily divorce their spouse when they are not satisfied with their marriages. They change jobs when they don't get along with their bosses." Considering the fact that in many parts of the world agreements are relationships and negotiations take a long time, you will have to widen your time horizon. This may be frustrating and will take adjustment, but it can be rewarding.

There are instances in which you can do business and realize quick profit. Suppose you want to buy 50,000 glasses in Czechoslovakia for import into the United States. You only have to get them through customs, and making use of an established means of distribution, you will complete this transaction, it is hoped, on the plus side of the ledger. But if, for the sake of argument, you are considering building a glass manufacturing plant in Czechoslovakia, remove the words "quick profit" from your vocabulary. You probably will have protracted negotiations with state authorities, perhaps also with local authorities. Numerous issues will emerge and chances are you won't make a profit for years. Your time frame must be realistic. Even if you know the technology, if plans are the same, your experience building a plant in Pittsburgh will be of little use in Prague. The Japanese approach to time frames is that investments do not have to pay for several years. When they go into a new market, they are long-term market-share players. Former British Prime Minister Edward Heath says the difference in marketing techniques between Japanese and Americans is that Americans want to sell the potential foreign customers their specific product, while Japanese ask, "What do you need, and how much can you afford? " Americans recognize a market. The Japanese create it. Thinking internationally is a creative challenge.

PART 6

Creative Approaches to Human Resources

Creative Care of a Company's Most Valuable Assets

Ask chief executives about their primary problems. On what do they spend the most time? The answer is similar irrespective of industry, size, or status. *People* occupy a CEO's time; dealing with personnel is a full-time job. Human resource management is becoming a prime discipline of management, and we promote it for creative and innovative managers. Human assets are a firm's most current and liquid assets. Mitch Kapor, founder of Lotus (1-2-3), sees high correlation between running a good company for employees and managing a profitable company for shareholders. How to keep a balance between bureaucracy and creativity? He stresses *real* job descriptions—focusing time, energy, and attention.

Team personality is also important. In most organizations, he says, "stars" can be forgiven all folly. ("You can be an outrageous idiot to people and still be a hero.") Not at Lotus. Disruptive personalities get a quick exit interview. Kapor believes that if people are treated fairly, they will give back full measure. Jobs are important, getting things done is required, but burned-out employees are counterproductive. Family life is not be neglected. Lotus has a dual requirement: People should live balanced lives, and the company should be profitable. You cannot treat people badly or allow people to treat themselves badly without its having deleterious effects. What goes around comes around. In Part 6 we examine leadership in creative management, how human resource accounting puts dollar values on people assets, how environment and personality affect creative productivity, new approaches to compensation, how caring for people is a real service, how counseling can be a creative resource, and a new concept of work. Take special note of Chapters 55 and 58: The former presents proper *methodology* for creativity research; the latter describes a company founded on providing human resources.

54

Creative Management Demands Creative Leadership

Barry Munitz

*President, Federated Development Company and
Former Chancellor, University of Houston*

A creative and innovative team, whether in public or private sectors, large or small companies, always needs a combination of skills at the top that weaves together leadership and managerial requirements. In Abraham Zaleznik's historic description, leaders are active not reactive; they shape ideas instead of responding to them. Leaders adopt a personal attitude toward goals; they exert influence in altering moods, in evoking images and expectations, and in establishing specific desires and objectives that determine corporate direction. The net result of this influence is to change what people think is desirable, possible, and necessary.

It takes neither genius nor vision to be a manager, but rather persistence, tough mindedness, hard work, intelligence, analytical ability, and, perhaps most important, tolerance and goodwill. Paraphrasing Zaleznik again, in order to get people to accept solutions to problems, managers need to coordinate and balance continually; they use shifting power to sift solutions and effect a compromise among conflicting values. To be a successful leader, one needs to project ideas into images that excite people and only then develop choices that give those images substance.

Talents for Top Management

Limitations

The talents required to reach the top are not necessarily those required to remain, or even to be effective, at the top. Just as in national presidential politics in which three different challenges—achieving the nomination, winning the election, governing the country—require fundamentally different strengths and instincts, so the characteristics found in successful executives and managers at the division level can be fundamentally different from those sought for chief executives. Indeed, one critical requirement for creative and innovative managers in the exercise of leadership is an ability to recognize the limitations of their own skills. Whether examining the qualities of operating staff, the nature of compensation policies, or the priorities for planning and analysis, productive executives are always looking over their own shoulders to test patterned assumptions and to adjust all-too-comfortable habits.

Uncertainty and Ambiguity

Top managers of an innovative organization should cultivate the art of weighing probabilities; they exist in a state of steady uncertainty and their success rests upon constant exploration of uncharted waters. Though expressing an external air of uninterrupted confidence, they will nonetheless feel frequent internal tuggings of instability and doubt. Learning to live with ambiguity in a world that respects firm certainty, to probe and to check in a culture that expects rapid decisions, requires a bizarre combination of patience, bluster, and daring.

Commitment and Trust

Leadership in this environment must use interpersonal strategies and negotiating styles that build trust while enhancing stability. Wherever personal credibility can be the ultimate value, manipulative gameplaying will quickly undermine any stature. Integrity, confidence, tolerating ambiguity, and timely testing of personal biases comprise the humanistic side of corporate leadership and represent intangible but crucial aspects of creative management. What makes the difference in the long run is quality of people—how they are chosen, why they stay committed, and what they do to bring success. The absence of fundamental trust and credibility—principles for which leadership is responsible—cannot be overcome by sheer hard work and gamesmanship. For example, playing off subordinates against each other as they fight for the executive's ear and struggle to deflate colleagues may temporarily heighten individual position, but in the long run all sense of teamwork and cooperation is destroyed. Responsive leadership requires commitment to an honest and caring attitude toward human resources. Although periodic individual accomplishments can fly in the face of these principles, ultimate consistent success cannot.

Team Building

One must learn to rely upon people who have other perspectives. Reaching the top of an organization usually reflects superb instincts, but those should never be confused with infallibility. The finest leaders often work against their own orientations when establishing a senior corporate staff, choosing individuals with varying styles, strengths, histories, and biases so that those responsible for overall administration will comprise a productive balance of corporate attitudes and personal attributes. Any temptation to clone a single style throughout top management must be resisted strenuously. This is particularly true when selecting one's potential successors since the nature of new challenges and ever-changing conditions often requires substantial shifts in skills for the next generation's managers.

Humility

One accidental success or isolated victory may cause an individual to consider himself or herself omnipotent and therefore impervious to conflicting advice. The danger for those who have been successful early in their careers, especially when they have opposed the guidance of mentors in achieving those victories, is that they often believe that their own instincts are far superior to any advisor's wisdom. The healthier framework is always to remain aware of hidden challenges confronting any complex organization, to recognize the need for diversity and contradiction, and to build modesty not majesty out of idiosyncratic accomplishments. One should never assume that because one is quicker or brighter than most people most of the time, one is righter and better all the time—one mistake derived from such overconfidence can be extremely costly and the general attitude itself will inhibit others. One should recognize that serendipity and happenstance, luck and chance, are often stronger determinants in the mysterious world of creative management than programmed analysis and research—and then be grateful for the luck without depending upon it or confusing it with skill.

Rewards

Executives should establish an overall fabric of innovation which combines hard work and careful preparation with sound people instincts and personal integrity so that life's unexpected openings are afforded best opportunity to work. A specific application of this principle is the absolute need for delivering reward once goals are achieved. Creative and entrepreneurial employees must feel a material stake in an organization's overall success. Promoting a feeling of participation encourages them to behave more like owners than hired help. Allowing them to receive a portion of the organization's equity establishes a direct link between individual productivity and corporate progress. This is particularly important for those who tend to work in isolation or on longer-range or more speculative projects. The provision of internal investment, and the consistent distribution of substantial reward when deserved, strengthen morale and heighten productivity.

Credit and Recognition

Many clichés have achieved their status because of transparent truth. One such time-honored phrase emphasizes how much can be accomplished if one need not take personal credit. An executive's ability to share, laugh, listen, and display self-effacing recognition of other's talents creates an effective setting for generating widespread creativity. On the other hand *everyone* needs recognition and support from someone—colleague, superior, friend, family. The pure, selfless manager who distributes credit like Johnnie Appleseed throughout the organization, without enjoying support in return, is rare if not nonexistent. Furthermore, such extreme self-dependence can even be dangerous. These aspects of recognition and reward, focusing on modesty, money, and motivation, once again establish that the humanistic side of corporate leadership is more difficult to define but, like many things harder to grasp, is also more vital to maintain.

Incentives and Alerts for Creative Managers

The following "do more" and "do less" suggestions are neither comprehensive nor conclusive. They are proposals to consider and refine.

Do More

1. Impose hierarchy by insight and accomplishment not by status symbol pretense and posture.

2. Understand the required distance of a leader that puts an automatic barrier between the chief executive and even those colleagues who are close friends, but do not establish the false mystery of royalty; there is a vital distinction between awe built upon accomplishment and aloofness imposed by status.

3. To best make one's self wealthy at the very top, make those closest around you almost as wealthy—and all become more productive; this requires sharing the reward and perquisites in order to build a first-rate team.

4. Appreciate what someone has called "the splendid, ethically neutral calculus of personal profit."

5. Recognize that the retention of bright people often requires rewarding instincts counter to one's own.

6. Be genuinely curious and responsive when others suggest "far out" ideas about leadership style.

7. Show willingness to get hands dirty, by messing in the muck where nuts-and-bolts work is done.

8. Learn how to use (but not be captured by) those staff and service roles (consultants, planners, lawyers, accountants, etc.) essential to any contemporary corporation.

9. Enjoy laughter; have a sense of self-humor, particularly with some irony.

10. Appreciate private-life expectations and pressures on employees—

respect their quiet time and family sense; encourage their personal
growth.

Do Less

1. Do not mistake superficial and unpleasant toughness for strong fiber
   or real talent; it is a serious mistake to assume that interpersonal
   awareness and caring instincts reflect managerial weakness or that
   impolitic authoritarianism and combative confrontation indicate
   resourceful strength.

2. Do not measure the value of a person by the volume of his or her
   vault. The endless pursuit of greater power and money is never an
   accurate expression of personal success, nor is a strong personal
   balance sheet necessarily an indication of true "net worth."

3. On the other hand, do not assume that extremely successful people
   have automatically sacrificed their personal values or private lives in
   building personal wealth.

4. Do not expose subordinates to unnecessary tension and heat; building a buffer between pressure and one's own position can discredit
   leadership.

5. When tempted to garner self-credit, do not forget sharing the kudos
   and supporting others.

6. Believing one's self to be irreplaceable undermines the next generation of leadership; management succession must be planned carefully, and efforts to identify potential successors shows strength not
   weakness.

7. Gameplaying may be enjoyable and the source of manipulative
   satisfaction, but such political maneuvering can introduce a dangerous level of hypocrisy and competition.

8. Do not ascribe exclusive value to one kind of talent; this sends wrong
   signals to employees regarding relative priorities and personal
   worth; creative management means good team building.

Summary

In the end, forceful speeches, articulate essays, and lengthy memos
cannot substitute for the reality of productive management and operating skill. Leading by example, creative leaders use their own perfor-

mance to establish successful role models. Jack Welch, General Electric's CEO, puts it well: "I can't stand predictions. What I have to do is try to visualize the world, and I have to be agile enough to live with it and to win in it. It doesn't mean a thing to say I'm going to do something; it only means something to do it."

Bibliography

Zaleznik, Abraham: "Managers and Leaders: Are They Different?," *Harvard Business Review*, May–June 1977.

55

Human Resource Accounting: New Thinking About People Assets

Eric G. Flamholtz

*President, Management Systems Consulting
Corporation and Professor, UCLA Graduate School of
Management*

The year is 1995. Susan Freed stares at her computer screen, proofing a status report, when the phone buzzes. The human resource director's face materializes on her screen. "Susan, this is Jim Lee. This is short notice, but I need the 1996–1999 Human Resource Plan by Friday."

"Not a problem," she answers in an even voice. "I have my HRA (human resource accounting) manager working on it now. I'll report back." She disengages the videophone wondering how far along Mary is on that report. She buzzes Mary's office.

"Mary, this is Susan Freed in Spatial Engineering. I'm calling regarding the status of the human resource plan for next year. How far have you gotten with the mobility analysis?"

"It's done. I'm networking it to you [Tables 55.1 and 55.2]. Note that for every eight level I engineers we recruit, one makes it to GM [group manager]. At the current turnover and promotion rates, we'll have to

Table 55.1 Human Resource Mobility Probabilities*

Year T			Year T + 1			
	Project manager	Group manager	Technical consultant	Engineer II	Engineer I	Exit
Project manager	.90					.10
Group manager	.18	.62				.20
Technical consultant		.30	.55			.15
Engineer II			.45	.30		.25
Engineer I				.70	.20	.10

*For example, the probability that a group manager will be promoted to project manager (in the next year) is 18 percent. The probability that he or she will remain a group manager is 62 percent, and the probability that he or she will exit the firm is 20 percent.

replace three GMs next year. Since we're growing at 14 percent per year and it takes 4 years to reach GM, we'll need six additional managers 4 years from now. To account for both replacement, 3, and growth, 6, we must hire 72 level I engineers (nine group managers times eight level I engineers needed per group manager). Do you want a sensitivity analysis?''

Table 55.2 Recruitment Planning Summary

Job level	Level I engineers needed to gain 1 person on this level	Turnover* rate	Years to reach this level	Promotion* rate
Project manager	17.6	.10	7	.05
Group manager	8.0	.20	4	.18
Technical consultant	5.2	.15	2	.30
Engineer II	3.0	.25	1	.45
Engineer I	1.0	.10		.70

Critical position = Group manager; Current number at critical position = 8.
Expected replacements at critical position = 3 (1.6 exit + 1.4 promoted) = (# at critical level) × (turnover rate + promotional rate).
Rate of growth = 14%; group managers needed to reflect growth = 6.
Total needed at critical position = 9 (6 for growth + 3 replacements).
Planned recruiting efforts = 72 new hires (9 managers needed × 8 level I engineers per manager).

*From Table 55.1

"Please. Run it with 12 and 16 percent growth rates. Also, I have some ideas for reducing GM turnover. Let's see what happens when we drop that rate by 3 percent. Oh, have you measured GM replacement costs yet?"

"I have the direct recruitment, selection, development, and separation costs, but we're still compiling the time sampling data to measure the opportunity cost of on-the-job training. Should have it tomorrow."

"Good. One more thing. Do you have the valuation for the people we got in last year's merger?"

"Sure, the figures are on file in the HRA database."

Susan brought the HRA database up on her workstation. According to the analysis, she would be able to amortize about 1 million dollars in human assets in the next year alone, a significant tax saving for her department. Then she examined the balance sheets for the last few years and the projections for the next. She smiled when she saw how the value of human assets had increased in the 3 years she had been department head. This would put her in line for promotion—maybe even Jim Lee's job when he moves up. The buzz of the videophone brought back her all-business face and Don Harris, one of her group managers, appeared on the screen and requested a meeting. He looked distraught.

Susan surmised that Don was fed up with his job and possibly had been offered more money to work elsewhere. She couldn't really blame him—he'd been a manager for 4 years without promotion. Still, she didn't want to lose him. She checked last year's replacement cost report and compared it to the average compensation for group managers. She could justify a substantial raise in Don's salary considering what it would cost to replace him. She noted the effects of staff attrition on the full replacement cost (as opposed to the marginal cost which does not reflect attrition). Perhaps he might like some pay in the form of training, thus increasing his value to the firm. That amount, of course, would be treated as an investment in human capital rather than as an expense.

Susan hoped that by analyzing human resource problems with all available data, she could reduce turnover in the next few years. This would be included in her human resource plan. The plan would increase out-of-pocket human resource costs but would reduce opportunity costs significantly (the cost of on-the-job training and inefficiencies caused by a person's separation). In addition, there was the unquantifiable value added to the department's morale brought about by people staying with the firm. Taken together, the long-term benefits of her policies should outweigh the short-term cost.

Human Resource Accounting

Human resource accounting has developed in response to the fundamental restructuring of the economy from manufacturing to service. Increasingly, firms consider their primary assets to be people rather than plant and equipment, and new techniques had to be developed to account for these "human assets." Human resource accounting recognizes the importance of human capital. Its techniques are used for resolving legal disputes and tax issues as well as for management decision making. It is a necessary tool for creative and innovative managers.

Definition

Human resource accounting involves the application of accounting concepts and methods to the area of personnel management. *It may be defined as the measurement and reporting of the cost and value of people as organizational resources.* It involves accounting for investments in people through calculation of their cost and economic value. Human resource costs are costs incurred to acquire or replace people. Like other costs, they have expense and asset components, they may be composed of outlay and opportunity costs, and they may have both direct and indirect cost elements.

Original Cost

The original cost of human resources refers to the sacrifice that was actually incurred to acquire and develop people. This is identical to the concept of original cost for other assets, e.g., the original cost of plant and equipment is the cost incurred to acquire these resources. The original cost of human resources typically includes costs of recruitment, selection, hiring, placement, orientation, and on-the-job training. Some of these costs are direct while others are indirect. For example, the cost of a trainer's salary is a direct cost of training, while the cost of a supervisor's time during training is an indirect cost.

Replacement Cost

The replacement cost of human resources refers to the sacrifice that would have to be incurred to replace human resources presently employed. The notion of human resource replacement cost can be extended to individuals, groups of people, and to the organization as a whole. At present, however, personnel managers typically think in terms of acquiring a substitute for a single specified position rather than in terms of replacing an individual per se. The former type of cost is known as "positional" replacement cost, while the latter is termed "personal" replacement cost. Positional replacement cost refers to the sacrifice that would have to be incurred to replace a person occupying a specified position with a substitute capable of rendering equivalent services in that position.

There are three basic elements of positional replacement cost: (1) acquisition costs, (2) development or learning costs, and (3) separation costs. Acquisition costs refer to the sacrifice that must be incurred to "acquire" a new position holder. They include all of direct and indirect costs of recruitment, selection, hiring, and placement. Development costs refer to the sacrifice that must be incurred to train a person to bring him or her to the level of performance normally expected from an individual in a given position. These costs include both direct and indirect costs of formal orientation and training as well as on-the-job training. Separation costs are the costs incurred as a result of a position holder leaving an organization. These costs include: (1) separation compensation cost, (2) differential preseparation cost, and (3) vacant position cost. Separation compensation cost is severance pay. Differential preseparation performance cost refers to the lost productivity prior to the separation of an individual from an organization, as there is a tendency for performance to decrease prior to separation. Vacant position cost is an indirect cost resulting from less effective performance in positions that are affected by the vacant position or from reduced revenues accruing to the organization as the result of the vacancy.

Human Resource Value

The economic *value* of people, like all resources, rests on employee capacity for rendering service potential. More precisely, the value of people is *the present worth of their expected future services*. This notion of human resource value can be extended across the organization's entire stock of human resources—its "human organization." While measures of human resource value need not be restricted to financial constructs, monetary measurement of human resource value should be performed wherever feasible. This is because money is the common denominator on which many organizational decisions are based.

One method of measuring the monetary value of human resources views the movement of people among organizational roles over time as a stochastic process with service rewards. This method regards the movement of people from one role to another as a probabilistic process depending upon the service states previously occupied. The model defines "service states" as organizational roles and the state of "exit." Rewards represent the services rendered to the organization as people occupy organizational roles. Since future states are an uncertain phenomenon, the model measures the mathematical expectation of a person's services. Thus, the measurement of an individual's value to an organization involves: (1) defining the mutually exclusive set of service states an individual occupies in the organization, (2) determining the value of each service state to the organization, (3) estimating a person's expected tenure in the organization, (4) determining the probability that a person will occupy each possible service state at specified future times, and (5) discounting the expected future cash flows to determine their present value.

This procedure results in a monetary measure of the person's expected value to an organization. The information obtained can be used to calculate the "expected conditional value" and the "expected realizable value" of an individual to an organization. Expected conditional value is the mathematical expectation of an individual's potential value to an organization, under the assumption that the person does not exit from the organization. On the other hand, the ultimate measure of a person's value to an organization is expected realizable value—the present worth of service actually expected to be derived during an individual's anticipated tenure in the organization.

The act of measuring and reporting human resource accounting information should influence management to develop an "enlightened style" in which people are recognized as long-term assets to be maximized rather than short-term expenses to be minimized. Using human resource accounting as a managerial tool makes possible the evaluation of proposed investments in human resources on a cost-value basis. It also provides information for decisions involving optimum allocation, development, and compensation of people.

Bibliography

Flamholtz, E. G.: *Human Resource Accounting,* Jossey-Bass, San Francisco, 1985.
Flamholtz, E. G., G. T. Geis, and R. J. Perle: "A Markovian Model for the Valuation of Human Assets Acquired by an Organizational Purchase," *Interfaces,* November–December, 1984.
Flamholtz, E. G., "Human Resource Accounting: State-of-the-Art and Future Prospects," *Annual Accounting Review* (1979) pp. 211–261.

56

Creative Human Resources in the R&D Laboratory: How Environment and Personality Affect Innovation

Teresa M. Amabile

*Brandeis University and Center for Creative
Leadership*

Stanley S. Gryskiewicz

Center for Creative Leadership

Our approach to creativity in R&D has been a simple one. We interviewed a large number of scientists from a wide variety of corporations and gave them questionnaires. Our immediate goal was to identify major factors of environment and personality that influence creativity positively or negatively in R&D. Our long-term goal is to develop a reliable and valid method for assessing the environment in any given R&D lab, indicating how particular individuals in that lab would be affected by that environment and suggesting specific approaches for improving the creativity climate. To our knowledge, this is the first study that examines real-world "online" creativity through detailed content analysis of interviews with a large number of people actually involved in R&D work. We believe these results to be especially useful for understanding and promoting creativity in R&D.

Prior Research in R&D Creativity

A number of researchers have addressed questions about the R&D laboratory (Taylor and Barron; Badaway; Burgelman and Sayler; Miller). Two reviews exemplify the range of approaches (Scherer; Andrews). Both point to the late 1950s as a starting time when dramatic increases occurred in the attempt to understand the nature of technological innovation in the R&D setting. Scherer's review offered a macroeconomic framework, focusing on technology push and allocation of resources; Andrew's review stressed social and psychological issues since "most modern R&D is performed by people within an organizational setting." Accordingly, one would expect the nature of that setting to have an impact on the creativity of individual scientists working there. This is our orientation.

One research group concluded, after a study of 1300 American scientists and 1200 research teams in six European countries, that the management of innovation was a multidimensional phenomenon that included individual and organizational factors (Pelz and Andrews; Andrews, 1979). Of the nine factors listed (motivation, diversity, adequacy of human resources, technical skill of group leader, communication, quality of research planning, time pressure, influence exercise by scientist, age of research group), all show consistent relationships to innovation, but any one alone is not very strong. When considered together, they can account for 30 to 40 percent of the observed variance.

Andrews (1975) found four factors that, when present simultaneously, show good correlation (.55) between creative ability and innovation: (1) Scientists are responsible for initiating new activity, (2) scientists have substantial influence, (3) scientists have a strong sense of personal security, (4) scientists are relatively free from interference by administrative superiors (independent to act). When any one of these factors was absent, the correlation was close to zero, thus suggesting a social and psychological model for understanding and managing the innovation process. One such example of environmental impact on innovation is what Andrews calls the "security dilemma." A scientist rather secure in his or her position is likely to produce creative and sometimes risky ideas. These risky ideas in turn unsettle the organization and may elicit responses from the organization that erode the security; the scientist may then be inhibited from generating subsequent creative ideas.

Ekvall postulated four climate variables that have an impact on innovative ability of the organization: (1) mutual trust and confidence, support of ideas, open relationships; (2) challenge and motivation, commitment to organization's goals and activities; (3) freedom to seek information and show initiative; (4) pluralism in views, knowledge, and experience; the open exchange of opinions and ideas. The Ekvall studies suggest a climate (and organization structure) that has an impact on the innovativeness of organizations.

Zannetos focused on latter stages of the innovation process—the mature stage of the business cycle. His perspective offers a backward glance into factors that inhibit innovation and, in his case, the process of renewal. Members of the organization who report that their creativity is being stifled and who cannot convince superiors of the value of their new product ideas must overcome some "critical fixities" that emerge in the mature organization. These impediments to the adoption of innovation include fixed investment, threat of obsolescence of current producers, less economic and psychic cost if existing path continues, and ideas outside the organization specialty. All of these fixities in the work environment mobilize people to resist change and innovation.

Bailyn uses interview data to separate out apparent conflicts between the autonomy of the original contributor and the goals of the organization. At one time the autonomy of the R&D employee was seen as paramount to innovation. R&D was to be done by highly creative people unencumbered by the involvement of top management. An obvious weakness in this view was that such a framework played to "the technical interest of the R&D employees and not the technical needs of the companies" (Faas). According to Faas, there has been a move away from the autonomy of individual contributors toward the autonomy of R&D departments—but still this may not be enough.

Bailyn asserts that the assumption that all scientists work best when left alone carries over to assumptions about R&D employees. This model may fit the academic scholar type who is motivated by the activity itself with science being its own reward. However, Bailyn's interview data suggest that many R&D professionals *do not* seek this complete autonomy. The irony here is that a completely autonomous R&D management fits neither the needs of the organization nor the desires of its technical employees. Bailyn concludes that what R&D scientists want is to be given some discretion in the process of solving assigned problems.

It is at the level of implementation that they want autonomy. They do not want to interrupt their creative process to receive an authorization or to seek sign-off by managers. The notion is similar to Schein's "autonomous anchor"—the need to produce and do it your own way once organizationally imposed and agreed-to goals have been set.

Bailyn proposes a more sophisticated understanding of autonomy by separating out strategic and operational autonomy. While successful R&D organizations seem to deny the former (freedom to set one's own research direction), they do provide the latter (discretion to decide how to pursue this goal). It is just such important climate issues that we address with interviews of R&D managers.

Research Methods of Assessing R&D Creativity

Sample Characteristics

Of the 129 participants in our study, 83 were scientists in various laboratories of a large *(Fortune 50)* American chemical company. They were tested with questionnaires and interviewed on-site in their workplace. Of the remaining 46 participants, 18 were tested and interviewed on-site in another company, and 28 during their enrollment in a week-long course for R&D managers at the Center for Creative Leadership. This latter group represented two dozen corporations (mostly large) from the United States, Canada, Mexico, and Europe. Of the interviewees, about 90 percent were male, 10 percent female. Our average participant was 40 years old (range: 26 to 60 years). Most participants (83) had Ph.D. degrees; there were 21 with Master's degrees, and 15 with Bachelor's. On the average, they had been working in their occupations for 12 years (range: 0 to 40 years). Most participants had some managerial responsibility but not at the highest levels.

Creativity Questionnaire

A short self-report creativity inventory was given to all participants—yielding four interesting results. First, the respondents emphatically stated that creativity is an explicit goal in their work. Second, although the level of creativity called for in their work is reasonably high, they wish it were higher still. Third, much could be done to improve the work environment to facilitate creativity. Finally, respondents feel that they have not yet realized their full potential for personal creativity.

Interview Procedure

Each participant was interviewed individually in a 20-minute session with a single interviewer. Several days before, they received a written description of the question to be asked:

> Think of something that stands out in your mind as an example of a creative idea or product in your work experience. Creativity is whatever you see as creativity. The example does not have to be from your current work setting, and it does not have to involve you personally (although it certainly can). In general, during the interview, tell us anything you can to completely describe the event and the factors contributing to the creativity. What made the difference between this and other, uncreative events? Touch on these points in your answer: What was the creative idea or product? (Describe in *nontechnical* terms and give no proprietary information.) What was the context? What characteristics or abilities of the people involved contributed to the creativity of the event? What features of the work situation contributed to the creativity of the event? Were any obstacles in the work environment overcome in the process? Think also of something that was a disappointment in terms of creativity in your work setting: an example of an uncreative idea or product. What made the difference between this and other, more creative events? Touch on the same points in your answer.

Interviews were recorded (with permission), transcribed, and subjected to rigorous content analysis by two pairs of independent raters who had generally good agreement on assigning statements to particular themes and subthemes.

Content of the Creativity Stories

Nearly all interviewees had both a high and a low creativity story to tell. The events described covered a wide range. The high creativity stories tended to fall into four distinct categories. In descending order of frequency, the categories are: (1) *Product work* (either the development of a completely new product or the improvement of an existing product). Some examples: the invention of a hand-held vacuum cleaner; the design of a new light tire for trucks; developing new materials for making microfilm images. (2) *Process work* (the development of new processes, the improvement of existing processes, and the discovery of new uses for existing products). Some examples: a new process for crude oil refining, a system for detecting defects in making film, a new technique for forming solidified sulfur. (3) *Basic research* (theoretical or exploratory, not directly tied to a specific product or process).Examples: mathematical modeling, research on surface forces, new combinations of organic and inorganic chemistry. (4) Other (nonspecific or miscellaneous).

The stories of low creativity also fell into similar categories—with some interesting differences. Participants seemed to have more difficulty recalling or relating the low creativity stories. In addition, a new category appears here. A fair number of stories did not concern scientific work but rather matters of management or personnel administration.

Although we did not ask participants to give definitions of creativity that guided their choice of stories, many offered definitions spontaneously. Of these, nearly all said that, to be considered creative, a product must be novel or unique ("nothing else like it," "didn't exist before," "no one else thought of it before"). In addition, many said that a product must also be useful or successful to be considered creative (though some expressed a dissenting view). Finally, some saw creativity more as a process than a feature of products; they described it as the process of taking a new perspective, combining things in a new way, synthesizing opposites.

Major Themes of the Creativity Stories

The majority of comments concerned environmental or personal influences on creativity. Specifically, these are the four major themes that emerged: (1) *Environmental stimulants to creativity.* Factors external to the problem-solver(s), including other people, that served as stimulants to creativity. This was the most frequently appearing theme, encompassing 35 percent of all comments. (2) *Environmental obstacles to creativity.* Factors external to the problem-solver(s), including other people, that served as obstacles to creativity. This theme also appeared frequently, with 31 percent of all comments. (3) *Favorable personal characteristics.* Factors of ability, personality, mood, etc., within the problem-solver(s) that served as stimulants to creativity. Approximately 25 percent of comments concerned this theme. (4) *Unfavorable personal characteristics.* Factors of ability, personality, mood, etc., within the problem-solver(s) that served as obstacles to creativity. This was the least frequent category, accounting for 9 percent of the comments.

The Environment for Creativity

Environmental Stimulants to Creativity

Content analysis identified 10 subthemes within this theme. They are listed in order of relative frequency.

1. *Freedom and control.*   We defined this subtheme as freedom in deciding what to do and/or how to do it, a sense of control over one's own work and ideas, freedom from having to meet someone else's constraints, a generally open atmosphere. Freedom was the most frequently mentioned specific factor in the work environment that served to stimulate creativity in the stories told by our interviewees; it was mentioned by 74 percent of them. Here are some examples of how freedom and control were mentioned:

> "Management did not believe that there was a solution to the problem; that's why they assigned me. I was new in the field, and since they didn't believe anyone could solve it, they didn't want to waste their senior people. As a consequence, I was left alone more than normal. And since I didn't know the problem couldn't be solved, with this kind of freedom, I just went ahead and solved it! "
>
> "The boss said, 'If you have free time, work on whatever you like.' That's when I came up with my best idea."
>
> "This was not something imposed on them, but a problem they generated themselves. There were no specific deadlines but a sense of internalized urgency. In order to get creativity, you can have large, well-defined time targets for the overall project, but individual targets for the parts have to be left flexible. People must feel they have control."

2. *Good project management.*   This theme, concerned specifically with the management of individual projects, included a wide range of factors involved in managing projects effectively. Some examples: the project manager's ability to gain political support, to shelter his group from outside pressures and distractions, to serve as a good role model, to match the right person to the right job, and to adjust management style depending on the individual being supervised. According to stories told by our interviewees, a successful manager must also foster good communication within the project team and, more important, must set clear goals and provide coherent problem definition. Not surprisingly, considering the importance of freedom as a stimulant, the good manager must also maintain a sense of self-direction in those working on the project:

"As manager, I gave the people involved a clear idea of what the end product was going to be. I attempted to get all people involved in those aspects of their expertise, and I asked them how they would go about doing it. I let people set their own goals and manage their own business."

In many high creativity stories, the project manager served as a valuable resource in terms of experience or information. Generally, successful project managers had good personal and social skills, were open to ideas, and led team members to feel that each person's individual contribution was essential. Clearly, the overall sense by scientists that their project is being well-managed can be crucial to its creative success.

3. *Sufficient resources.*   Access to appropriate resources—facilities, information, funds, and people—is vital:

"Something very important was the support provided. There was an allocation of people and capabilities throughout the organization. We got lots of diverse information."
"This place has tremendous resources, and I had no problems with access."

4. *Encouragement.*   This subtheme, mentioned by nearly half the participants as a stimulant to creativity, included three major points: management enthusiasm for, interest in, and commitment to a research idea; a nonevaluative atmosphere, one without destructive criticism or excessive concern over failure; and an orientation toward risk on the part of management:

"The project was a risk, so a willingness to gamble was important."
"Our proposal was submitted to management in our division, where it got support. Then we had meetings with other divisions, and there was a lot of interest. People wanted us to start right away."
"What helped here was people feeling secure—having an environment where they could say anything and not feel dumb."

5. *Various organizational characteristics.*   These factors concerning the organization as a whole might be called "corporate climate." A mechanism for considering new ideas was a necessity:

"What encouraged me? The company had set up an innovation office (or research proposal system) that was promoted by division management and recognized by people on the bench as something worthy of interest."

The organizational climate was most conducive to creativity when there was a cooperative and collaborative atmosphere within and between divisions, with good communication throughout:

> "Having other scientists to talk to is important. When it came time to introduce the product, support from different areas such as marketing enhanced its success."

6. *Recognition and feedback.* For scientists to do their most creative work, they must believe that they will receive appropriate responses and rewards. This sense usually comes from an "organization feel," not from experience on one isolated project:

> "To be a good manager, you have to reward creative people if they are successful. I mean giving them publicity, allowing them to spread the idea around, as well as giving them financial reward."
>
> "Do not compare people with one another. People should be compared only against expectations and prior performance."
>
> "It was good to hear management say, "You made the discovery, and you will make the presentation." The pat on the back, the recognition, felt good."

7. *Sufficient time.* Time, like resources, must be available for creativity to flourish:

> "On this particular project, there was a small number of people, but their time was 100 percent dedicated."
>
> "He was insulated from day-to-day firefighting, so that he could step back and take the time to think."
>
> "What made a difference was that we felt we could take the time to work without worrying about schedule."

8. *Challenge.* A sense of challenge fuels creativity—often coming from the intriguing nature of the problem itself. Sometimes, however, the needs of the organization provided the challenge:

> "The work has not been done in the way we propose to do it. The novelty is very attractive."
>
> "We knew we were taking a chance, but the area had such potential that it was compelling. If we found something, we could really develop it."
>
> "People said it couldn't be done; other companies had turned it down. That challenge gave us our motivation."

9. *Pressure.* Some sort of pressure within the work environment was occasionally cited as a stimulant to creativity. This conducive type of

pressure must be generated internally, not by some external force; individuals or teams feel driven to prove that they can succeed:

> "There is a high level of stress, but not in a bad sense. What you are doing is important and timely, so you feel some compulsion. Adding a little bit of pressure stimulates creativity more than having all the time in the world."
> "There was much parallel effort; there were competing groups seeking solutions. This contributed to creativity; it was not viewed as destructive competition, but as more of a challenge, since everyone wanted a workable solution."

10. *Miscellaneous other factors.* Most comments concerned not the environment of the laboratory or the organization but of the field itself:

> "It is an integrated science, and that's where things happen."
> "Not much was known and people were free. There wasn't a path that had already been beaten down."

Environmental Obstacles to Creativity

Content analysis identified ten subthemes, listed in order of relative frequency:

1. *Poor organizational climate.* Nearly two-thirds of participants mentioned some feature of the organizational atmosphere as an obstacle. Comments were relatively general rather than focusing on a particular work event. The most striking detriment to creativity was the reward system—either too much emphasis on rewards or insufficient or unfair distribution of rewards (including recognition of good work):

> "The problem is that there is a tendency to drive people toward management—that is, how to move up—and no drive to keep them on the technical side. There is a dual ladder system, but one is shorter than the other."
> "Not providing special recognition when due can really hurt."
> "I didn't get as much credit for the project as I should have, but that's kind of immaterial—I have a tremendous amount of self-satisfaction and that's what I'm looking for, not some monetary reward. I wouldn't reject cash, but it is a measure of success—not a motivator."

Lack of support or cooperation from other areas within the organization was cited frequently:

> "Marketing is the biggest obstacle to our creativity. They don't want us to be first with anything; there's too much risk involved."

> "When we bring an idea to manufacturing, we have to overcome the NIH syndrome—not invented here."
>
> 'We have an unproductive patent department. They are so slow in processing patents that by the time our new developments get written up, they are essentially useless. This is extremely frustrating."

The formal structure, procedures, and communication channels can also be detrimental:

> "Management must determine what information we can share and what we cannot. This hinders sharing."
>
> "The structure I'm working in is matrix *mis*management. I report to too many different organizations all at once."
>
> "Here, instead of ideas really flowing, we have a more formal approach. You wait until you have a complete package of information and then present it to a formal meeting."

Political problems were prevalent, which perhaps inhibited mechanisms for encouraging and developing new ideas:

> "Technical success came quickly. But getting the invention out the door as a product became very political. No one person controls a creative process from inception to implementation."
>
> "The real tragedy is that the environment seems deliberately stacked against anything creative. The whole organization is designed to 'put out fires'—to tweak up current products and make them better—but never to look at something that may be new."
>
> "We have a harmful atmosphere—I call it 'I've got a secret.' As you go up the corporate ladder, managers do not share information—which might be vital for the creation or execution of a product line; they think it prestigious to have hidden knowledge."

Comments were made about the physical environment, goal setting, and mobility within the corporation:

> "The people in management change their minds a lot, shifting goals. You don't want to focus on a problem because you know it will be changed."
>
> "The constant transferring of employees is disruptive. There's too much mobility, too much disorganization."
>
> "Creativity is something that management wants to buy; they want someone who will get bolts out of the blue. But you've got to put in time to understand the field. People aren't allowed to stay in a job long enough."

2. *Constraint.* Constraint is defined as a lack of freedom in deciding what to do or how to do it; lack of control over one's own work—nearly half mentioned constraint on work as a negative influence on creativity:

"There have been times when I felt I was on to something and people would actually tell me I shouldn't think about the problem. The only thing important for my creativity is the freedom to own my ideas and to exploit them myself. If an idea is mine, I very much want to work on it, but I know it is going to be taken away from me."

"That was a low creativity situation because they wanted me to follow a particular path without adding any of my own ideas. To be creative, you can't be told the exact way something should be done."

3. *Organizational disinterest.*   This subtheme includes a lack of psychological support within the organization, a lack of faith in a project's success, a lack of enthusiasm and interest, a general apathy or complacency toward research:

"Our major obstacle was that a similar program had failed at a different site. We had the stigma that it couldn't be done even before we started."

"In management's viewpoint, research creativity is not as important as product development."

"From the beginning, it was a defensive strategy; instead of looking one step beyond what was currently available, we settled for coming out with a 'me too' product."

4. *Poor project management.*   Frequently cited features included an inability to set clear goals, provide good problem definition, or give a strong sense of direction to the project team; poor scientific or managerial skills; and the allowance of too many distractions or fragmentation of effort:

"It's hard to work without specific goals in mind. The supervisor wasn't good at making decisions."

"There were too many people involved in the project and too many inputs determining what it should be. The inputs kept changing so there was never a well-defined goal."

"We fragment our time—20 percent on one project, 10 percent on another, etc."

"There were too many people, too many meetings, too much overlap. Everything went in circles; decisions were made by committee. The ideas generated didn't go anywhere."

"Our manager was against the project because he didn't understand it."

5. *Evaluation and pressure .*   Participants mentioned what they perceived as inappropriate evaluation or feedback procedures, unrealistic expectations, pressure to produce something (anything) appropriate, and a general concern about criticism and external evaluation of work:

"The project was in its third year when one group said they had found the answer. It turned out to be a disaster. Part of the problem was that everyone was looking for a breakthrough. Expectations were too high. Upper management was busily involved in the work and would constantly ask for results."

"Management had a very heavy hand and over-reviewed the project."

"Extreme pressure stifles the freedom to pursue things that might be a little more risky. It spawns 'safe' research rather than something truly innovative."

"It's hard to be creative when you have people pounding on you to solve something quickly."

"It is important to be encouraged. Nothing squelches creativity as fast as someone saying it is stupid or just ignoring it. After several such encounters, you aren't going to bother anymore."

6. *Insufficient Resources.* Lack of necessary facilities, materials, information, and personnel is certainly a hindrance:

> "Our main problems were time-sharing of the production process, and limited resources. It's demoralizing to be told you can't buy something you really need."
>
> "About 10 years ago, young scientists were promoted to management. This accomplished two negative things: It deprived the staff of good researchers, and it put into place poor managers."

7. *Time pressure .* Here, again, there is parallelism between the environmental stimulants to creativity and the environmental obstacles. Just as one-third of participants mentioned sufficient time as an aid to creativity, one-third mentioned insufficient time—or too great a workload in an unrealistic time frame—as a hindrance:

> "There was pressure to get the product produced quickly. It was a long-range product, but this is a short-range company."
>
> "When you are pressed with a problem and told to come up with a new X within a short period of time, you start looking at what has been done before. Really new things aren't going to come from pressure."
>
> "Neither creativity by timeline, nor invention by decree, can work."

8. *Emphasis on the status quo.* There is reluctance to change modes of operation. Emphasis is on keeping things the same, not wanting to take risks, avoiding controversial ideas, and taking a generally conservative course. All are detrimental to creativity:

> "There's so much inertia to keep things going the same way, it is almost impossible to turn things around."
>
> "They weren't willing to consider a major change; they wanted a 'quick fix.' "

> "People in manufacturing have been doing the same thing for 20 years, and when research comes along with a new product or process, they resist."

9. *Miscellaneous other factors*

> "Working by myself turned out to be an obstacle."
> "Things are being computerized that don't have to be, and it ends up more of a hindrance."

10. *Competition.*   The competition described here seems to be different from the competition mentioned as an environmental stimulant to creativity (under the subtheme "Pressure"). There, the helpful competition seemed to come from an internally generated desire to meet the challenges of the problem. Here, the harmful competition seems to come from interpersonal rivalry within the organization:

> "We had two groups trying to achieve the same thing. It became a win-lose situation, and we all ended up losing."
> "The key problem is that the managers, being young, still want to do research, and they compete with the technical staff."
> "We had difficulties with people feeling that we were treading on their turf. They thought themselves experts in the area."

Personal Influences on Creativity

Favorable Personal Characteristics

Content analysis identified ten subthemes under this main theme:

1. *Various personality traits.*   Special qualities in the personality of the problem solver, including persistence, curiosity, energy, and honesty, contributed to creativity:

> "I studied the unrelated system and began to see how it could be successfully applied to the problem. From there, it was just a matter of being persistent and hammering out details."
> "I was very dogmatic about working on what I thought was important, which turns out to be what *was* important, so management started backing off and giving me some freedom."
> "Hard work makes all the difference."
> "Important traits are those that go along with not stealing ideas, such as honesty, ethics, and an ability to take and give criticism without taking it personally."
> "Creative people tend to be more inquisitive, more prone to investigate options before they act."

2. *Self-motivation.*   Being self-driven, excited by the work itself, enthusiastic, attracted by the challenge of the problem, having a sense of working on something important, and a belief in or commitment to the idea:

> "I find that having an idea, putting something together, testing, experimenting . . . is just very exciting."
>
> "The difference between high and low creativity? I think 75 percent is the person. Self-motivation is key. The person has to have inner drive. I don't know how a manager can motivate someone if he or she doesn't have that inner drive already."
>
> "What's important to me is feeling that I've made a difference, seeing that something I've worked on has turned into a product. It's not getting pats on the back for my own management but having the self-satisfaction of seeing my work come to fruition, feeling that I've made a contribution to company profit and consumer usage."
>
> "People felt ownership of the problem; they felt responsible for it."

3. *Special cognitive abilities.*   These factors included special talents in the scientist's particular field, as well as general problem-solving abilities and tactics for creative thinking:

> "Good problem-solving smarts were important, as was the ability to take an idea from one field and extend it into another."
>
> "A certain amount of intuition can help."
>
> "It's important to zero in on key issues, to think unconventionally, to discard the known approach and keep only essential principles."
>
> "Creative people tend to look at problems in a more general way, to look for broad alternatives as opposed to narrow definitions."
>
> "I never let too much theory get in my way."

4. *Risk orientation.*   This range of creative qualities suggests that a creative person has unconventional attitudes, thoughts, or style; deviates from usual paths; doesn't just adapt; doesn't do the standard thing; is risk oriented; takes chances; is not overly cautious; is rebellious or brash; is courageous; is attracted to challenge; is willing to take risks with ideas and money:

> "I think along different directions. I'm always looking for the interesting twist that something might have. I'm always more interested in the variations, the deviations that might result in something novel."
>
> "People were not afraid to step over boundary lines. Because this is a frontier type of chemistry, your mind-set has to accept new results without knowing what to do with them."
>
> "He had a way about him that got around obstacles simply by creating his own environment. He was a true eccentric who didn't fit in."

5. *Expertise in the area.* Our interviewees often noted the importance of talent, experience, and acquired knowledge in the particular field:

> "The breakthrough was really based on my knowledge and understanding of the problem. Creativity requires natural ability, intelligence, awareness, and command of the literature—a good knowledge base."
>
> "One of the people was familiar with a new technique just being published; it had a definitive influence."
>
> "It's a talent. Like singing."

6. *Group qualities.* Most subthemes of favorable personal characteristics were concerned with qualities of an individual scientist. This subtheme, however, stressed the synergy of the group—intellectual, personal, and social qualities that emerged from members of a project team. Among the qualities noted were trust, free communication, good teamwork, being mutually helpful, diverse, flexible, self-reliant, and taking a fresh perspective:

> "The high-creativity situation was a small cohesive group of people working together. There was very good interaction. It was a self-directed group."
>
> "Consensus governed. People sensed immediately what should be done next whenever they looked at previous results."
>
> "Ideas were not stifled; we were not there to grab claim that we had the greatest thing in the world. There wasn't much competition between us to take credit."
>
> "We had similar abilities, but different backgrounds—thus different ways of looking at the problem. Also, we had mutual respect for one another and a willingness to listen but not hang on to someone's idea— we'd say, 'Well, that's a good idea, but here are some problems. . . . ' "

7. *Diverse experience.* In addition to having expertise within one's area of specialty, many scientists stressed broad general knowledge and experience. In this sense, some saw older, more experienced scientists as being better able to produce a creative synthesis of ideas:

> "Having strong backgrounds in two different fields was very important."
>
> "He was creative because he was able to draw on virtually every aspect of his previous experience."

8. *Social skills.* These include good political sense, good rapport with others, being a good listener and team player, and being broadminded or open to others' ideas:

"The major obstacle was winning support of development engineers. They thought it was their job to work out this new process. There was competition, but it was overcome by technical success and our willingness to run joint experiments. That helped achieve their buy-in."

"You need to interact with peers and exchange ideas. This includes respecting the input you get."

9. *Brilliance* . A high level of intelligence was mentioned by only about 13 percent of our participants. It appears that other qualities, such as self-motivation and area expertise, are seen as more important than raw native brilliance:

"The people in the creative group were highly intelligent, very sharp."

"What was important? The ability to look at existing information and draw on general knowledge to suggest a solution."

10. *Naiveté*. Several commented that a creative idea or solution came about because the scientist involved was, in some sense, naive or new to the field and was, as a result, not biased by preconceptions or bound by old ways.

"The best thing about us was that we didn't feel we already knew the right answer."

"I was new with the company. I was not so deeply involved with the on-going development. I could step back and look at things differently."

"I knew enough about the mechanism to give me the ideas. But I didn't know too much about the theory to inhibit me from going further."

"Which of my characteristics most contributed to creativity here? Ignorance. I had no preconceptions or prejudices. I was rather naive."

Unfavorable Personal Characteristics

Content analysis identified six subthemes; they are listed in order of frequency:

1. *Unmotivated.* Just as self-motivation was the most frequently cited favorable personal characteristic, being unmotivated was the most frequently cited unfavorable personal characteristic. Included are a wide range of factors, all focused on lack of motivation for the work: not being challenged by the problem, lacking courage in overcoming environmental obstacles, having a pessimistic attitude toward the likely

outcome, being overly cautious and unwilling to take risks, being complacent, being unhappy about the work, or simply being lazy:

> "People had trouble making sparks—generating the necessary enthusiasm for the project."
> "We had no inherent interest."

2. *Unskilled or inexperienced.* A scientist's lack of ability or experience can contribute to a project's failure. Either the scientist was lacking in necessary skills, education, or knowledge; was low in conceptual problem-solving ability; or was too narrow in knowledge, interest, or experience:

> "I couldn't be very creative there because I lacked ability and knowledge in the area."
> "People tend to believe the data they get irrespective of common sense."
> "He got bogged down in the details. He spent time analyzing things that were intuitively obvious and working from a too-narrow point of view."

3. *Inflexible.* Being set in one's own ways, opinionated, unwilling to do things differently, or too constrained by one's education and training, are no help to creativity:

> "Intelligence is often a disaster. We have preconceived notions based on our experience or education, and we form blind judgments rather than informed opinions."
> "He seems to have a little too much pride. He is slow to admit mistakes."
> "My own preconceptions served as an obstacle."

4. *Externally motivated.* The favorable personal characteristic of being self-motivated really signified a type of *internal* motivation— being motivated by one's own interest in the problem, one's sense of intellectual challenge. By contrast, being motivated by *external* factors (factors outside the problem itself) appears to be an unfavorable personal characteristic. Some examples: being motivated primarily by money, recognition, or other factors aside from the work itself; responding primarily to restrictions and goals set by others; being competitive and jealous of someone else's success:

> "The people involved responded too rapidly to management's pressures."
> "In some uncreative cases, the thinking is, 'Well, this might not solve anything, but it is one more compound I can make, and that will make someone happy.'"
> "The enjoyment wasn't there because this guy really felt constrained."
> "If there was a fault, it was not wanting to make waves in the face of a management directive."

"If you limit yourself to what is expected by your supervisor, creativity is lost. Most people do not question original directives. Everybody spins their wheels trying to please management and gets nowhere."

"The major obstacle? Ego. Everyone wants to be the high-tech magician."

5. *Miscellaneous.* Most had to do with unfavorable personality traits or inadequate cognitive approaches to problem solving:

"Many people go for complex solutions rather than simple ones."

"He was methodical and a perfectionist. He had the 'bookkeeper mentality.' "

"People get tired; and when you are tired, you tend not to be creative."

6. *Socially unskilled.* A lack of social or political skills—for example, being a poor team player—is an obstacle to creativity:

"When several people working in close proximity all have their own way of doing something, it is difficult. They didn't make enough effort to lower barriers, improve communications, and act like a group."

"His personality gets in the way. He is so prolific with ideas that he tends to put people off."

Nature of R&D Creativity

Given the popular mythology that creativity is simply something that comes from creative people, it is intriguing that these interviewees concentrated more heavily on environmental factors than on personal factors in their descriptions of creative and noncreative events. This suggests that, at least within the R&D laboratory, scientists see the work climate as more instrumental than personal characteristics in making the difference between high and low creativity.

Creativity appears to depend on three general classes of factors: domain-relevant skills (or skills and talents in the work domain), creativity-relevant skills (or skills in thinking and working imaginatively and productively), and task motivation. Perhaps the screening process in high-powered R&D laboratories is so stringent that only the most skilled, most highly talented, and most productive scientists are allowed to enter. With this sort of baseline, the strongest effects on creative output might indeed come from the work environment and the way it influences motivation.

The high level of consistency in the types and frequency of comments made by scientists in different companies suggests that the factors identified really are important influences on creativity. Identification of the *most* important factors is aided by noting parallelism between stimulants and obstacles: freedom versus constraint, self-motivation versus external motivation, sufficient resources versus insufficient resources, encouragement versus organizational disinterest, recognition versus evaluation pressure, sufficient time versus insufficient time, good versus poor project management, good versus poor organizational climate. Those pairs of factors suggest a central theme: Scientists who feel motivated primarily by their own interest in and sense of challenge toward the project are more likely to produce creative work than those who feel they are working primarily to meet the constraints placed on them by their work environment. We call this the "intrinsic principle of creativity."

In his autobiography, Albert Einstein said, "It is a very grave mistake to think that the enjoyment of seeing and searching can be promoted by means of coercion and a sense of duty." And a Nobel-prize winning physicist, Arthur Schawlow, observed: "The successful scientists are often not the most talented but the ones who are just impelled by curiosity—they've got to know what the answer is." These comments suggest that, given a certain requisite level of talent and experience, intrinsic motivation is the key to creativity—desire to do something for its own sake, because of passionate interest in the work, because it provides its own challenge and satisfaction. In other words, given a particular level of skill and ability, intrinsic task motivation can make the difference between what a person *can* do and what he or she *will* do.

Intrinsic motivation can be undermined by the imposition of external constraints on a person's work. That is, people who are initially interested in doing some activity will subsequently show less interest if they have been made to do that activity under some externally imposed constraint, such as a promised reward or an explicit deadline. According to the intrinsic motivation principle, then, these external constraints should, by reducing intrinsic motivation, also impair creativity. Creativity researchers investigating brainstorming and related techniques have long suggested that evaluation of ideas can undermine creative thinking in problem-solving groups (e.g. Osborne). In experimental studies, expected evaluation has been shown to have negative effects on both intrinsic motivation and creativity. Promised reward, competition, and restricted choice have shown similar negative effects. (See Amabile.)

The results of the present study support the intrinsic motivation principle in four ways: First, the interviews revealed freedom from constraint as the single most prominent environmental factor stimulating creativity; constraint was also a prominent environmental factor undermining creativity. Second, the interviews presented self-motivation as a major personal stimulant to creativity, and lack of motivation as the single most important personal obstacle. Third, questionnaires which we administered on cognitive and motivational style revealed that scientists who have a more "innovative" creative style tend to be more intrinsically motivated. Fourth, intrinsically motivated scientists tend to be interested in even more opportunities for creativity in their work.

The minimal differences between different scientists in their patterns of responses (interviews and questionnaires) was intriguing. For example, although many people might believe that age would be a significant factor, no clear differences emerged. Indeed, although many comments suggested that young scientists should be at a creative advantage because they are more fresh and flexible, just as many suggested that older scientists should be at a creative advantage because they have both more freedom and more experience.

Implications for Managing Creativity

The role of management in facilitating or undermining creativity appears to be crucial at two levels. Both project management and organizational management were categories that appeared frequently in the creativity stories told by our participants. Interestingly, project management seemed a more generally positive force and organizational climate a more generally negative force. Perhaps this difference is caused by a pervasive dissatisfaction that many of our interviewees felt, not so much with the management of specific project teams, but with what they perceived as the general organizational attitude toward research.

Clearly, the most important direct utility of this study comes from the prescriptions it can provide for stimulating creativity in the research environment. We focused interviewees' responses *not* on their abstract notions of what *should* influence creativity but on their best recollections of what *did* influence creativity in two very specific events from their work experience. Descriptions of those events drive our prescriptions for enhancing creativity in the R&D setting.

The most immediate source of advice on managing for creativity is the direct roles of our participants. The creativity stories elicited specific suggestions about stimulating creativity:

> "What makes the difference between high and low creativity? It's freedom from management. Freedom and autonomy are the key points. Yet, this is opposed to what managers are supposed to do—'manage' people. There is no good way to manage professional creativity; you are better off leaving them alone if you hire good people."
>
> "The important thing is to work on what I enjoy."

"I was free to explore anything. I had the freedom to go in the lab and play. That was very helpful. But a manager must be careful. He must balance freedom with what's required."

"The best managers are those who ask questions. The role of the manager is to make clear objectives, directions, and purposes—then allow creative types to discern their own ways and means to achieve them. Once the operation is under way, the manager should provide an environment where many questions are asked. He should be nonjudgmental—the people working on the project should make judgments. Managers should assure completeness of the work and understand ramifications of different procedures. Sometimes it's necessary to ask 'dumb questions.' "

"The manager should know the field and make it challenging and fun. Try to turn creativity into a game."

"There should be a reward system. To maximize creativity, the organization needs some way to recognize those who have given it a good shot, not only those who have been successful. The generation of new knowledge is a frustrating, failure-ridden effort. Most new things won't work. So people who are doing exploratory work may need to be rewarded on the basis of their creative output and not on whether it is successful. On the other hand, there is nothing wrong with identifying the invention or creative product of the year. Most would prefer recognition over monetary awards."

"Good managers get good people, and then give them room."

The following set of guidelines can be used for managing the creative process in R&D:

1. Pay at least as much attention to the quality of the work environment as to the quality of the persons placed in that environment.

2. Develop specific stimulants to creativity in the work environment, most notably: freedom, sufficient resources, encouragement, and recognition.

3. Remove specific obstacles to creativity in the work environment, most notably: constraint, lack of enthusiasm by management, threatening evaluation, and other forms of pressure.

4. Implement a project management style characterized by: the amplification of specific stimulants to creativity and the removal of specific obstacles to creativity. The manager should: set clear overall goals and problem definitions, have the ability to "champion" the project within the organization, speak for the project's merits and protect the project team from unnecessary distractions and pressures, create an atmosphere of free communication and collaboration, and have necessary scientific abilities to be used as a resource to guide the project and not as a controlling intrusion.

5. Implement a general organizational-level management style characterized by: the amplification of specific stimulants to creativity and the removal of specific obstacles to creativity *and* by the appropriate reward systems (equitable, generous recognition and awards on a general, organization-wide, continuing basis—as opposed to a system in which specific rewards are offered or withheld only on the basis of specific pieces of work); clear and efficient mechanisms for encouraging, considering, and developing new ideas; a cooperative and collaborative atmosphere between departments and divisions; clear organizational structure, without excessive movement of research personnel.

6. Choose able people, and then match them to appropriate jobs—keeping in mind (and nurturing) the special motivational orientation of unusually creative scientists. In other words, it is important to determine each scientist's area of ability *and* interest and then provide opportunities for that individual to work on projects that are personally enjoyable, challenging, and satisfying—within an atmosphere that allows the enjoyment, challenge, and satisfaction to be experienced.

Bibliography

Amabile T. M.: *The Social Psychology of Creativity.* Springer-Verlag, New York, 1982.

Andrews, F. M.: "Social and Psychological Factors Which Influence the Creative Process," in I. A. Taylor and J. W. Getzels (eds.), *Perspectives in Creativity,* Aldine Publishing, Chicago, 1975.

Andrews, F. M.: *Scientific Productivity.* Cambridge University Press, Cambridge, England, 1979.

Badaway, M. K.: *Developing Managerial Skills in Engineers and Scientists: Succeeding as a Technical Manager.* Van Nostrand, New York, 1982.

Bailyn, L.: "Autonomy in the Industrial R&D Laboratory," *Human Resource Management,* Vol. 24, no. 2, 1985, pp. 129–146.

Burgelman, R. A. and L. R. Sales: *Inside Corporate Innovation,* The Free Press, New York, 1986.

Ekvall, G.: *Climate, Structure, and Innovativeness of Organizations* (Report 1). The Swedish Council for Management and Organizational Behavior, Stockholm, Sweden, 1983.

Ekvall, G., J. Arvonen, and I. Waldenstrom-Lindblad: *Creative Organizational Climate* (Report 2). The Swedish Council for Management and Organizational Behavior, Stockholm, Sweden, 1983.

Faas, F. A. M. J.: "How to Solve Communication Problems on the R&D Interface," *Journal of Management Studies,* Vol. 22, no. 1, 1985, pp. 83–102.

Miller, D. B.: *Managing Professionals in Research and Development,* Jossey-Bass, San Francisco, 1986.

Osborn, A. F.: *Applied Imagination,* Scribner's, New York, 1986.

Pelz, D. C. and F. M. Andrews: *Scientists in Organizations: Productive Climates for Research and Development,* John Wiley, New York, 1986.

_____: *Scientists in Organizations,* Institute for Social Research, Ann Arbor, MI, 1976.

Scherer, F. N.: *Innovation and Growth.* MIT Press, Cambridge, MA, 1984.

Schien, E.: *Career Dynamics: Matching Individual and Organizational Needs,* Addison-Wesley, Reading MA, 1978.

Taylor, C. W. and F. Barron: *Scientific Creativity,* John Wiley, New York, 1966.

Zannetos, Z. S.: "Strategies for Productivity," *Interfaces,* Vol. 14 no. 1, pp. 96–102.

57

Executive Compensation Creativity: What's New and What Works

Robert C. Ochsner

Senior Vice President, Hay Management Consultants

All executives need a sense of personal worth as well as financial motivation. A good compensation package helps provide both. Creativity in compensating executives is neither obvious nor easy. Three dimensions of thinking are needed for breakthroughs: amount, form, and fairness.

Amount

Creative compensation usually means *more*—in one way or another; it always means *different*. To be creative, compensation packages must really "grab" the executive. Why do astute owners pay more than competitors? Because they know how to maximize the value of their executives. They select people who know how to succeed. They provide a climate that expects success. And they eliminate organizational barriers that frustrate managers and muddy accountability. This usually means a lean organization, built on simple lines with mostly direct reporting relationships. The savings in lower total compensation cost, plus the greater freedom of action, will go far in paying back the higher compensation costs of executives singled out for special treatment. There is a great lesson here. *Excellent executives should make more because they are worth more.*

Executive value arises from the ability to plan, organize, direct, and control. In the postwar era of growth, American businesses became enamored of management. The myth grew that, since additions to management could be shown to pay for themselves, all management was free. Middle levels proliferated, their main function being to gather, evaluate, and process information on its way to the top. Those functions are increasingly done by machine. The savings in compensation costs from reduction of now-unneeded staff can be applied to breakthrough levels of compensation for the real executives who remain. We must not forget, however, that higher pay for fewer people puts added pressure on the selection process. Contemporary companies rely heavily on variable compensation systems. This is a healthy development, emphasizing goal setting and performance orientation for managers. However, there is a subtle tendency to let the compensation plan become the "silent supervisor" of employees further down the ladder, where top management cannot observe the action directly. Yet this is where the real selection of future executives takes place. As we learn to operate in a "lean and mean" environment, with less staff around to rely on (and occasionally hide behind), we must be even more sure that the people we have are the right ones so that those at the top are and will be worth the larger sums we intend to pay.

Form

The form in which compensation is delivered must also be different. There are five basic types of executive compensation: salary, benefits, perquisites, short-term incentives, and long-term incentives. Salary and benefits, of course, are paid to all employees, not just executives. The other three types of compensation tend to be reserved for management positions, although short-term incentives are being used for increasingly wider ranges of jobs. In most organizations, receiving perquisites and long-term incentives practically defines who is considered an executive. Creativity in compensation mix can be shown in two ways: in the selection of compensation plans or devices within each of the five areas and in the relative amounts of value provided by these five "pieces of the pie." Creative plan selection uses many factors to make executive compensation more interesting and more rewarding. New forms of compensation practices appear within each of the five types, and old ones disappear. This change process reflects evolution of tax laws, as well as business and social norms. For example:

Deferral of compensation. This popular benefit comes and goes in response to the steepness and structure of the graduated individual tax rate table.

Long-term incentives. These financial motivators have grown in size and variety over the years, along with the increased use of long-range planning and the need to look well beyond quarterly earnings. The long-term incentive vehicle of choice has varied with the state of the stock market, the relative tax advantage of capital gains, and the latest theory on what factors drive the value of a company.

Personal perks. For decades, perquisites like yachts and hunting lodges were a prized status symbol for executives. When a substantial part of American society began to take a less favorable view, other types of perquisites more in line with the prevailing social ethic of democracy took their place. Only when most of the change had occurred and the old perquisites had few defenders was the tax law changed to put a penalty on their use.

Tax-advantaged benefits. A perennial favorite. Executives are captivated by ways they can receive pay at lower than "normal" tax rates. This is especially true if they have recently climbed atop the graduated brackets or if they anticipate a forthcoming drop in rates, such as at retirement. Plans offering capital gains opportunities used to fall into this category; plans that use tax-favored investments such as individual life insurance may still do so. Benefits and perquisites are often justified as being "tax effective." This is only good if the executive needs what they provide. In general, however, the new tax law effective in 1987, with its lower rates and fewer loopholes, mitigates tax-advantaged benefits in favor of current income.

Ownership. An offer of real ownership usually meets with a positive response from executives. There is a sounder ring to real stock than to the various "phantom stock" plans that can be built around the book, market, or other formula values. However, be cautious when the stock is marketable. Executives should not be forced to hold stock unless the yield it offers is commensurate with any investment they make to acquire it. The method of determining the stock's value should be fair but not too unwieldy to be applied annually. (The majority owners should be able to control executive stock for purposes of making major corporate decisions, including mergers, divestitures, recapitalization, and the like.) Every discussion of executive pay should center around performance, where the level of pay given depends on level of results achieved.

Leverage. Leverage adds "sizzle" to executives compensation programs. Simply put, this means affording upside money-making potential that is much larger than the accompanying downside risk. The ever-popular stock option is the best example of high leverage; in practice, it can offer infinite leveraging because the executive does not have to accept any downside risk until the option is exercised. A second leveraging technique is the "carried interest," offered to executives in the oil and gas and other extractive industries. A third is the opportunity to participate in investment partnerships (venture capital, R&D, and so on) along with the employing company. Some established companies will incorporate a new branch or operation separately, then offer executives and other employees a percentage (typically 5 to 15 percent) of its ownership. All of these devices can be fashioned out of real stock or through the use of "phantom" shares. These produce the same economic results, but the psychological impact, as well as the tax and accounting treatment, will vary.

Fairness

The third type of creative thinking needed in executive compensation is fairness to existing employees. Over and over, we see the big compensation packages and rich incentives go to a "Mr. Right," just hired from the outside. It is somehow easier to see executive abilities in a new hire—a relative stranger—than in those already employed. Sometimes this happens because we associate existing employees with prior (and smaller) positions or with past mistakes. The new hire does not have such visible blemishes. But if we had x-ray vision, the same blemishes would appear underneath. A new hire at the top gives opportunity to take stock of the size and shape of a company's executive compensation package. It is often shocking to find that the amount needed to attract someone from the outside is 30, 50, even 100 percent above current executive pay levels.

There is a natural tendency to pay executives only about "as much as it takes to keep them." After a few years of this practice, there is a gradual loss of the most capable—the biggest risk takers. As long as the remaining executives are promotable, the loss is hard to detect. There will still be enough managers to avoid hiring-in at the top because the organization is shaped like a pyramid. There are fewer positions at each successive higher level. Even with the loss of some, others remain to promote. The difference is that the organization is *being* selected rather than *doing* the selection. As this insidious erosion continues, organizational vitality decays and goal setting becomes less ambitious. More successful organizations, who can pick among capable candidates for promotion, actually have to "outplace" those who are not selected for the next level.

When executive hiring-in requires a tremendous break with existing structure, it is probably a sign that current pay practices do not reflect earnings levels of the best quality talent. The organization has likely lost the privilege of selecting its top people. And it may mean that the firm is no longer an exciting place to work. If this is the case, new hires at the top may be badly needed to re-energize the place, and the sums needed to attract them are well spent. Experience has shown that one new hire per ten executives is about the most an organization can tolerate without turning evolution into revolution.

For most companies, the situation is not so pronounced. There is little difference between current executives and new hires, either in quality or motivation. (Pay of the new hires may reflect a differential of up to about 30 percent, which is the premium required to recruit them.) Infusion of "outsiders" into the executive structure usually brings with it new ideas and methods and a certain amount of conflict. A healthy organization turns this into new strategies and goals. These provide the focus for reviewing and revamping pay.

What to do without increasing current pay levels? Leverage can be increased. This offers upside opportunity to the whole executive group. The atmosphere of increased challenge, coupled with increased opportunity, forges the group into a team working together toward a common goal. Acceptance of newcomers is thereby quickened.

Compensation Revamping

Compensation revamping involves two steps. First, existing pay practices for the executive group should be examined. Be sure to include all five types of compensation: salary, benefits, perquisites, short-term incentives, and long-term incentives. There should be no sacred cows.

Three categories should emerge: (1) A number of compensation programs will be retained as is. They are working and serving a useful purpose. (2) Some programs should be retired. These are the least useful, the most abused—the last CEO's pets. Momentum is vital for commitment. The feeling of "going someplace" in the compensation program may require leaving where we are. (3) Existing programs should be rebalanced. Identify their legitimate purpose, and accomplish it in a different way—possibly at lower cost. "Folding in" is a useful technique here. Often the short-term incentive has spread to become an expensive prerequisite for classes of middle management jobs for which measures of performance cannot readily be devised and administered. This is really just an expensive salary supplement. It is better to fold the average award into the salary structure, identify those jobs for which performance is critical, and establish a new incentive plan for them.

Second, a new series of programs should be designed. They should carry a clear message about the organization's strategic direction, performance demands, and "membership list" of the various levels of management. Normally, the economic value of the new programs will reflect the firm's economic goals and involve leverage. However, some programs can be designed to increase executives' financial security. If the realistic future outlook is for hard times, too much leverage can be a mistake.

Creativity in executive compensation can be as simple as remembering three rules: (1) Make the reward as big as the challenge. (2) Dare to be different; if you treat executives like a commodity they will perform like one. (3) Bet on people, and let them know it.

58

Incentive Compensation: Making Innovation Work

F. Kenneth Iverson

President, Nucor Corporation

Nucor's success in steel—revitalizing a basic industry and taking market share from the Japanese—is founded on advanced minimill technology, efficient operating methods, and innovative personnel policies. I concentrate on the latter, which creative managers can apply, in principle, in other companies.

Management-employee relations revolve around four principles: (1) earnings tied to productivity, (2) job security for proper performance, (3) fair and consistent treatment, and (4) easy and direct avenues of appeal. Money, we believe, is the best motivator—but money is paid only for performance, not for promises. No one is immune. I know: Several years ago I was the lowest paid CEO among the *Fortune 500*.

Incentive Compensation for Production Workers

All employees have a significant part of their compensation based directly on productivity. Incentive systems are designed around groups, not individuals. This applies to everyone, from production workers to middle management, secretaries to senior executives. Base salaries are low, but productivity bonuses can add between 50 and 100 percent in total compensation—with no upper limit. When plants are running at full capacity, workers can make over $35,000 a year in a region in which half that might be the norm. (We do not believe in raising standards when workers beat them consistently.) High productivity works, yielding critical competitive advantage.

In the production incentive program, the groups range from 25 to 35 people who are working as a team on some complete task. We have nine bonus groups in the steel mills—three each in melting and casting, rolling, and finishing and shipping—and there is stiff competition among them. Let's use the melting and casting group as an example. We begin with a base of 12 tons of good billets per hour; above this base, each person in the group gets a 4 percent bonus for every ton per hour produced. If, over a week, they average 30 tons per hour—which is considered low—they earn a 72 percent bonus [$4 \times (30 - 12)$] for that week. This bonus multiplier affects all pay, overtime as well as regular.

Our program is easy to understand—it must be—and the rewards are received rapidly. Group operations are definable and measurable, and bonuses are paid promptly, right along with regular checks. If you work hard and produce well, you get your money—not at the end of the year but at the end of the *week*. It's the best kind of conditioning: You work hard and receive the benefit. In this manner, employees can tie increased effort and productivity directly to increased reward and compensation. We do not impose ceilings on compensation, and it is not unusual for production bonuses to double base pay.

We assume that each bonus group is, in a real sense, a business unto itself. The company provides the building, equipment, technology, and direction—but what each group earns is entirely dependent on how much they produce. In one operation (the joist production line), bonuses are based on roughly 90 percent of the historical time it takes to make a particular product. If, during a week, a group makes the product at 40 percent less than standard time, they receive a 40 percent bonus—with the *next* pay check.

Don't mistake our system for paternalism. We're tough. We insist on strict production rules—for mutual benefit. If a machine breaks down, all pay the price. Workers revert to base pay until it is fixed—which, I might add, is quickly. Tardiness is penalized heavily since the group suffers. If a worker is more than 5 minutes late, he or she loses the day's bonus; more than half an hour, the week's. (We do allow four "forgiveness" days a year.) Such an incentive system is not for everyone. It is made for workers oriented toward high performance. Those who won't work so hard don't last so long—the group just won't let them foul up their productivity. The problem is more acute when starting up new facilities. We might experience a 200 to 300 percent turnover over the first year, but once we find performance-oriented employees, turnover drops dramatically.

Incentive Compensation for Managers and Executives

Productivity tests are not limited to workers. Nucor maintains a lean executive staff (housed in rather unassuming offices). There are only four levels of management, just three steps from president to factory worker. Corporate staff is minuscule for a three-quarter billion dollar company. The entire corporate staff including secretarial and clerical is seventeen people. A security analyst once said: "Jack Benny would like this company. So would Peter Drucker." We subscribe to Drucker's philosophy that "it is a symptom of a sick organization to rely on coordinators, assistants, and other such whose job it is not to have a job."

How do we pay managerial bonuses? The critical test is return on assets. Since Nucor is a capital-intense business, this seems the best measure of managerial productivity. In an operating division, bonuses are based primarily on the return on assets of that particular division, and bonuses for department heads can go as high as 74 percent of base pay. For senior officers they can be higher. Our executives put their money where their philosophy is. First of all, top managers do not have employment contracts. We receive no guaranteed or discretionary bonuses, profit sharing, pension plans, or other executive perks (no company cars, planes, country-club memberships, executive dining rooms, not even reserved parking spots). Base salaries are set at about 75 percent of what executives would earn in comparable positions with other companies. If the company produces below par, that's all we get. Par has been defined as a 9 percent return on equity, above which the bonus kicks in. For every pretax dollar earned above this base, 5 percent goes into an officers' pool that is divided according to salaries. If earned, half the bonus is deferred. Don't feel too sorry for us. If return on equity reaches 24 percent, which it has, we can wind up with up to 270 percent of our base in salary and an additional 180 percent in stock. (Officers do not participate in Nucor's profit-sharing plan.)

I confess that when I had the lowest compensation among *Fortune 500* CEOs, I was a little proud. During that period, to avoid layoffs, we had to cut back to 4- or even 3½-day work weeks. With fewer work days per week, employee pay was cut to 20 to 25 percent lower than normal, but few complained: They knew that department heads were cut more and officers still more—and that's by percentage (35 to 40 and 60 to 70 percent, respectively). I call it our "share the pain" program. If a company is not successful, the reasons are irrelevant. Management should take the biggest cut because they are the most responsible. (By the way, I have never found our compensation system to be an obstacle in hiring anyone.)

Problems with Incentive Compensation

We do not have any discretionary bonus program, say to reward excellent managers whose divisions, through no fault of their own, just didn't hit the right numbers. All bonuses are based strictly on performance. No one, I believe, should be sitting in arbitrary judgment—I don't know how it could be fair. I don't want to be influenced by what happened in the last 3 months; maybe someone did well for the first 9 months and then fell down because of family problems. You cannot sort those things out and be fair. And fairness is our touchstone.

Can Nucor's incentive compensation be applied in other companies and industries? There are limitations. To implement such a system, two elements are necessary: (1) It must make sense to break out small groups of people who work as a team on a particular function, and (2) that particular function must be both self-contained and measurable.

When applicable, it really works. All employees prosper and suffer together; they receive the same insurance, holidays, and vacations. Everyone, including the CEO, flies coach. There is a profit-sharing program that is mainly deferred (some cash is paid to make the point that the money is real). Nucor provides a scholarship of $1500 per year for 4 years of college or vocational training for every child of every employee. (We have more than 200 children enrolled in more than 120 learning institutions. When they graduate, many come to work at Nucor.) We have not laid off a single employee for lack of work for more than 15 years. It's hard enough to get good productive people. When we get them we want to keep them.

59

Can Human Resource Service Be Creative? Why Not!

Elmer L . Winter

Cofounder and Past President, Manpower, Inc.

Back in the late 1940s, I met Clifford Sawdo at our summer home. Cliff was a jack-of-all-trades. He had worked on steamships, plying the Great Lakes, tackling tough, hard-to-fix jobs. Cliff helped me in the construction of large bumper sculptures, a personal hobby. Often I'd ask, "Can we make this weld? " It seemed insurmountable. His answer was "Why not? " Over the years, I never heard Cliff respond with a flat No to any question; his response was always "Why not? "

I strongly recommend the "why not? " philosophy for creative managers. It avoids "cop outs"—going along with the tide—the "let's not make waves" attitude. By constantly asking "Why not? " a manager is forced to look for new ways to meet changing conditions.

Founding and Building Manpower

"It won't work—no one will bring in temporary workers not familiar with the company's work." That was the initial reaction from Milwaukee managers when my law partner and I conceived the idea of starting a temporary help service in 1948. While these companies went through peaks and valleys in their businesses, they believed they could meet their needs by having extra employees on hand, working employees overtime, or letting work pile up. But this method of operation caused overstaffing or delays in getting the work out—producing high cost. We asked ourselves, "Why not provide a service that could permit businesses to operate a planned staffing schedule, with temporary help used when needed? Why not set up a company to take care of personnel emergencies, peak seasons, and vacations? "

Our experience as business lawyers had taught us that oftentimes initial reaction to a suggestion is negative. As a result, we had learned to ask the question "why not" when analyzing business propositions. Taking the why-not tack forced us to think in positive not negative terms. Answers were then easier to generate.

Despite the naysayers, we organized Manpower, Inc., rented offices in Milwaukee and Chicago, hired two managers, and started advertising a range of temporary help services such as typists, stenographers, bookkeepers, sales help, warehouse workers, etc. Manpower's first year was discouraging. We lost $9000, a lot of money back then. Were the original critics correct—were we at a deadend—should we wind up Manpower and concentrate on our law practice? But looking over Manpower's customer list, we found heavy repeat business. We must be doing something right; there must be value to our service. Why not continue for one more year?

We broke about even in the second year and then, after becoming profitable, decided to explore other cities. I called on six executives in Minneapolis and asked them whether they would use our services if we had an office nearby. The answer was uniformly No. They would not consider calling a temporary help service for rush jobs, peak seasons— not for any reason. I received no encouragement. But I saw no real difference between Minneapolis and Milwaukee.

After we had opened thirty-two branch offices in the United States, we asked ourselves, "Why not develop a franchise program? " This would enable us to expand more rapidly. Competition was developing and we wanted to make certain that we would get a number one position in smaller cities. Again, the doomsayers warned: "Franchising won't work for a service organization—franchising will impair Manpower's reputation and destroy its image."

Despite the doubts, we went ahead. We found that our franchises worked hard to maintain our reputation since they were putting their life savings on the line. They wanted to build equity and followed our programs in detail. We reciprocated. I constantly asked our home office staff, "Why not provide more services to our franchises than were required by contract? " Some franchising companies were being confronted by disgruntled franchisees who claimed that they were not receiving promised goods and services. I thought we should "pour it on" and provide services *beyond* our agreements—to assure success of our Manpower franchises. We formed a Franchise Counseling Committee to resolve problems before they became serious. Honest give-and-take builds mutual trust and respect.

Why not carry the Manpower concept abroad? Two bright young Englishwomen were working for us in the United States as part-time secretaries. We hired them to start an office in London. They wrote a success story. In short order we opened offices across Europe. Why not South America, Australia, and Japan? The needs for temporary help were the same in every major business center worldwide. It was not easy to introduce the concept of temporary help in these foreign countries, but by employing local managers we were able to bridge the cultural gap. Today, Manpower operates over 1000 offices in 32 countries. A fundamental change is occurring in the workplace as more companies rely on temporary part-time workers on a planned staffing basis.

Ask "Why? "

The "why theory" means asking managers, "Why are we doing it this way? " It is surprising how many management practices become ingrained, mostly by force of habit. "We're doing it this way because that's the policy of the company" was the unacceptable answer I'd often receive. It was the answer of a person who took the easy course, who didn't bother to question the wisdom of the policy, who didn't seek new approaches to new conditions.

Milliken & Company found itself losing out to foreign competitors. They responded by installing a total quality improvement program. This included a customer responsiveness effort that cut development and delivery time by up to 90 percent. I am sure that someone at Milliken had asked, "Why is it necessary to have a 6-week delivery cycle? " By probing, they were able to cut this cycle to 5 days. Milliken also established more than 1000 customer action teams to find new market opportunities in partnership with existing customers.

I believe that the why theory can reverse the "hollowing" of many American corporations. Why have the Japanese been able to open factories in America using American labor, while so many American companies have gone to the Far East claiming that they cannot operate profitably at home? Not enough managers are questioning conventional wisdom. Japanese managers get employee cooperation by presenting themselves as equals. Employees are associates. Workers are not mere extensions of machines. Japanese philosophy is to make employees feel important.

Involvement with Personnel

The relationship that the CEO establishes with employees is vital. In most corporate annual reports, the president will conclude by stating, "Our employees are our greatest asset." Do they genuinely believe this or is it just an empty phrase that has become required management jargon?

I tried to develop a family feeling in Manpower. Our employees knew that I would do everything possible to provide opportunities for advancement as well as assure continuity of their jobs. Complimenting employees is important. It helps cement strong relationships. I wrote frequent "well done" personal messages. I tried to give a pat on the back in the presence of others. Each Christmas I called over 300 Manpower managers just to say a quick "Merry Christmas, I've been thinking of you—I want to thank you for helping make our company very special." This was one of the best things I did as president. I genuinely cared about our corporate family.

I traveled a great deal for Manpower. I wanted to be out where the action was. I couldn't get the feel of the force and flow of our business by sitting in my office. I wanted to visit with branch managers and franchisees in *their* offices. During these visits, I learned a great deal. I also visited managers and franchisees in their homes. I wanted to meet their husbands or wives. I wanted their children to get to know me. Many of these kids are now working for Manpower. This gives great personal satisfaction.

Putting Ideas into Action

How does one go about using the why not and why theories? I am a great believer in the "yellow-pad concept." This may well be a habit of my lawyering days. There is something about a yellow legal pad that compels me to write down a problem and pour over it. I generate a number of possible answers—not all valid, of course—but of the list some will provide new views and clues for solution.

Try these suggestions: (1) *Keep a yellow pad in your briefcase.* When you have a spare hour, just start writing. The results will surprise you. (2) *Use a yellow pad on airplane trips.* It beats playing cards with your seatmate. (3) *Take your yellow pad along on a vacation.* Get up before the family, get out on the beach or over to the pool, and come up with new ideas. You may argue that when you need a change of scenery, you must leave the office behind. I suggest that you will feel more refreshed from your vacation if you have taken a few hours each day to think through pressing problems and come up with possible solutions. Most executives do not have time for creative thinking at the office. When you get back after a "working" vacation, you will be exhilarated with fresh feelings and clear direction.

Some parting thoughts. I am not a devotee of tight job descriptions. I never liked to put people in boxes on organizational charts. Generally, job descriptions and boxes are too confining. They provide an easy out for the complacent. I prefer executives to do some free wheeling, even if the results do not fit their job descriptions. Also, it is fashionable to state, "We are running lean and mean." I don't mind the lean part: I encourage it. I object, however, to the "mean" part. Does running mean suggest that the company has lost its interest in people, and jobs will be lopped off without regard to the employees' family life? Running mean is the antithesis of creative management.

60

How Creative Managers Use Counseling and Psychotherapy

David L. Antion

*Clinical Psychologist and Marriage and Family
Counselor*

A corporation's primary resource is its people. But people have personal problems that interfere with productivity. A great percentage involve substance abuse (alcohol and drugs). Alcoholism is especially widespread and costs American industry over $50 billion each year. The creative use of professional counseling and psychotherapy enhances productivity as well as shows social responsibility and humanitarian concern. The best corporations are a breed apart from earlier counterparts, evincing care for employees. Yet executives, for all their technical sophistication, are often unaware of advances in behavioral science.

Psychology first entered the workplace with the use of intelligence and aptitude tests to help screen job applicants. Since that time the application of psychology to work-related issues has expanded enormously. Industrial psychologists design job-enrichment programs, attenuating routine and boredom that yield poor performance. They also build training programs for employees, set up evaluation systems, supervise selection of new employees through interviews and testing, and administer various kinds of counseling programs. Behavioral scientists advocate that a proper objective of corporate enterprise is to create fulfilled and happy employees who will, therefore, be loyal and productive. Research in organizations proves that people are profitable if they are able to use their abilities to the full and find satisfaction in their work.

Over half of *Fortune 500* companies have employee assistance programs. These programs identify, assess, assist, and support employees and their dependents when personal problems interfere with job performance. The goal of counseling and psychotherapy within the organization is to increase both personnel productivity and personal fulfillment. Corporations have substantial investments in employees through years of training and experience. Thus it is financially practical to help people and it builds morale to do so. (Creative personnel, in particular, may be more susceptible to psychological problems.)

Creative managers should know how and when to use counseling. And while managers need not understand technical aspects of psychology, they should understand what psychologists do, signs and symptoms of trouble, and what types of problems would be best referred to professional care. Psychotherapy must not be an embarrassment. It is an important new tool for creative managers.

Detecting Personnel Problems

There are four primary signals suggesting a need for help. They are listed in order of importance.

1. *Absenteeism.*   This is the most serious sign of trouble and the most costly to the company. Absenteeism may indicate severe physical, emotional, or substance abuse problems. It is usually the trigger that calls attention to alcohol or drug dependencies. Job performance alone can never tell the whole story. The task may be difficult or easy and the employee underqualified or overqualified. Watch job attendance: It's the most frequent indicator of problems.

2. *Deteriorating job performance.*   This is the second most obvious signal. But it too may involve factors other than personal problems. Something must be done about inadequate work product. Whether the employee is suffering from physical, emotional, or substance-abuse

problems is yet to be determined. But deteriorating job performance is a red flag that must not be overlooked.

3. *Deteriorating personal relations.* When people are involved in substance abuse, their relationships (especially close ones) deteriorate. Emotional problems can also affect the quality of relationships. Depression, high anxiety, severe stress, brain tumors, or marital problems, as well as substance abuse may contribute to irritability and isolation.

4. *Deteriorating physical appearance.* If an employee shows an increasingly disheveled appearance in dress and grooming, it is usually a sign of personal problems. If the deteriorating condition consists of changes in facial appearance (lines, dark circles, red eyes, etc.), loss of hair, stooped posture, halting or unsteady walk, it may be caused by a disease that may or may not be tied to emotional problems or substance abuse. However, employees having substance abuse problems will eventually show a deteriorating physical appearance.

What To Do

Whenever these signs are evident, a manager has a duty both to the firm and to the employee—whether peer or subordinate. This duty begins with approaching the person in a *caring* attitude reflected in facial look and tone of voice. With this posture the manager presents what he or she has observed. For instance, "Joe, I've noticed that you've been absent from work 7 out of the last 15 working days and that your production has declined from 18 to 12 widgets per day. What's happening? " If the employee says nothing is happening—"everything's all right"—then it is best to again present the observations. "I hear you—but you've really missed a lot of work and your production is way off. Do you want to talk? " While temptation toward denial is strong in people having problems, a caring, nonthreatening, understanding approach will often open the door to discussion of the problem. Consider two examples of personal problems that affect the workplace.

Examples of Personal Problems

Joe, an executive in your company, comes to work with pains in his stomach. He pops down antacids to settle gastric juices. He is nervous and irritable; his breakfast is not digesting well. He takes care of corporate "brushfires" and reacts to emergencies. However he neither plans nor innovates—the main work for which he is paid. He is a crisis manager, not a creative one. As long as he is reacting to a problem, he does a passable job even though he snaps at people brusquely. No one realizes that Joe's upset condition is caused by marital problems, perhaps not even Joe himself. These troubles have been going on for months and have caused much suffering and anguish. This particular morning Joe and his wife had a bitter argument that included verbal attacks and threats of divorce. Joe can't forget the look on his boy's face when he and his wife fought over potential child custody. Thoughts of divorce and its consequences go through Joe's mind at every lull in the work day. He thinks about how relatives, friends, and his boss will react. Such preoccupation drains Joe's creativity and efficiency. His energies no longer go into his work except in response to crises. As Joe's peer, you notice that he lacks the spark he used to have. You mention your observations to him in an understanding and concerned way. He tells you about his domestic problems and that he doesn't know where to turn. At this point you explain the advantages of marital therapy for him and his wife. There are psychologists who specialize in relationship therapy and improving communications between spouses. You assure Joe that seeking help is a courageous and positive move. There is no need to feel embarrassment in seeking professional assistance. Joe takes courage and accepts your admonition. He decides to call for an appointment, which immediately gives him some comfort—at last he has some place to turn and some positive action to take. Joe and his wife enter therapy. They are helped with issues that have become sore points between them. They are shown how to argue properly. They are educated on the nature of human relationships. They are taught how to express needs, wants, desires, dislikes, etc., in positive ways that do not harm their bond. Resentments are dealt with and eliminated. Both Joe and his wife feel their point of view is understood by another caring person. Because of this they can more readily accept each other. (This is an abbreviated description of what this author has seen time and again. Exceptions are when there are other personal problems or hidden agendas on the part of either husband or wife that sabotage therapy.)

Another company employee, George, comes to work with increasing numbers of excuses for being late. George is having alcohol problems. These problems affect his family as well as his work. When George drinks, he is violent and disruptive at home. His wife reacts badly to his drinking, which in turn further angers George. He responds with threats and acts of violence, which is often the case when alcohol or drugs are mixed with marital problems. There may be the potential for child abuse—and in George's case it has happened more than once. Sober, George lives with the pain and shame of his unlawful behavior against his child. He tries to escape and forget on every occasion. As soon as personal or work stress gets severe, he seeks relief through alcohol or drugs. These have become his best "friends" and the addiction makes George even more inefficient at work. You see the unmistakable signs in absenteeism coupled with deteriorating job performance. You approach George caringly but firmly. You present the facts regarding his behavior at work, letting him know that it is unacceptable. You also ask, in a compassionate way, if he is having a problem with drinking or drugs. At first, George denies it. You again make him confront his behavior—what has been happening. You let George know that it is safe to confide in you and that you are interested in helping him. You tell him how valuable he has been to the company and of the past good work record he has had. At this point George tells you about his drinking. You refer him to the psychologist or alcoholism counselor. George makes an appointment because of your encouragement and firmness. He knows that the way to keep his job is to do something about this problem. He knows that doing nothing will not be tolerated. George keeps his appointment. He is sent for a brief detoxification period at a local hospital—5 to 7 days. He then returns for outpatient treatment that includes individual, family, and group therapy. George is encouraged to join and follow the Alcoholics Anonymous program and to attend regular meetings. George should be kept as busy as possible so that his life begins to be full and interesting again without the use of alcohol. Other goals would be to build George's sense of self-esteem, strengthen his marriage and family life, and improve his social skills. With George's desire to have a better life and regain work competence, improvement is usually dramatic and pleasing for all who know and interact with him.

Managers are confronted with such situations frequently. Often they have outstanding people skills that may help the employee. However, when the problem is beyond their competence and training—involving interpersonal, marital, childrearing, substance abuse, legal, or health problems— the creative manager will refer the troubled employee to proper professional care.

What Problems Do Psychologists Treat

Psychologists use a variety of methods and techniques. They possess good listening abilities and are skilled at developing therapeutic rapport with clients. They clarify, support, empathize, confront, and facilitate. They give insight into emotions, thoughts, and behaviors. A common result of therapy is improvement in the client's relationship skills. The majority of people's problems arise out of their interaction with other people. Thus, explaining the nature of human relationships plus helping with effective communication is of utmost importance. This enhances on-the-job relationships as well as those in private life.

It is important to understand the principle of confidentiality. Confidentiality covers what is said between therapist and patient and even the fact the client has come to the session. The psychologist must maintain the confidence. The only person privileged to break the confidence is the client (unless there is clear danger such as child abuse or potential suicide).

Alcohol and Drug Abuse Problems

Alcoholism is the third leading cause of death in the United States behind heart disease and cancer—ahead of traffic fatalities, suicide, and murder. The alcoholic in the workplace causes multiple problems: chronic absenteeism, changes in behavior, physical deterioration, spasmodic work pace, lower quantity and quality of work, partial absences, lying, avoiding supervisors, on-the-job drinking, on-the-job accidents, encouraging others to drink. The alcoholic lives in a constant state of denial. With apparent sincerity, he or she assures colleagues that bouts of overdrinking were "because of" job tensions or "because of" domestic problems or "because of" financial worries, ad nauseum. The truth is that any reason will do as an excuse for drinking. Usually everyone knows the alcoholic has a problem. They can see the detrimental changes. But people are reluctant to say anything to the person. This is the sad part. Early detection and intervention could do so much to save lives and prevent accidents and domestic abuse. Remember, before telltale signs show up at work, the alcoholic has already done damage at home. In treating alcoholism the psychologist may recommend hospitalization in severe cases. Adjunct community resources such as Alcoholics Anonymous are valuable. Individual, group, and family therapy are also needed as are alcohol education and information. Since there is no single treatment modality for chemical dependence, a combination of approaches must be used. Of course, the alcoholic must desire life improvement to end the enormous pain lived with constantly.

Stress

Stress is something almost all Americans live with to one degree or another. The main symptoms are depression, anxiety, and bodily complaints (headaches, tiredness, digestive or cardiovascular problems, etc.). Stress is caused when active coping or readjustment is demanded. Primary life events that produce stress are "separation and loss:" the death of a spouse or close family member, marital separation, and divorce. "Occupational stress," while usually not as severe, occurs more frequently. Executives and managers live and work under a great deal of pressure. Deadlines, the squeeze between higher and lower authority, office politics, rivalries, monetary competition, competitive lifestyles, personal and interpersonal conflicts all contribute to stress on the job. Two major sources of occupational stress are "time pressure"—constant worry over deadlines whether self-imposed or set by others—and "role conflict"—when one job-related task interferes with another. "Relocation" is another widespread cause of stress. When an employee is transferred, the family faces uncertainty. Spouses may react with depression; children often experience a period of poor peer relationships.

Since avoiding stress is nearly impossible, the important thing becomes how stress is handled. "Stress management," a major concern in industry, is usually approached from several perspectives. Following are some common techniques.

1. *Anxiety management training.*   The use of imagined scenes and relaxation techniques. The procedure first arouses anxiety through a combination of methods including visualizing the anxiety-producing situation. Anxiety is then reduced through the use of competing responses such as relaxation or visualization of success outcomes.

2. *Biofeedback.*   The reduction of blood pressure and heart rate through systematic reinforcement of desired behaviors whenever they occur. Treating tension headaches illustrates the technique. Electrodes, applied to forehead and body, pick up minute amounts of electrical activity each time the sufferer's muscles contract. The biofeedback equipment amplifies this small charge and emits a tone. Gradually the client learns to stop the tone by maintaining a relaxation response.

3. *Stress inoculation.*   The capacity to cope with anxiety states by increasing self-control and adapting skills. This procedure involves three phases: "education"—understanding cognitive and behavioral responses to stressful situations; "rehearsal"—learning to control physiological arousal through direct-action techniques (e.g., physical relaxation, arranging "escape routes") and cognitive techniques (e.g., monitoring negative self-statements and replacing them with adjusting statements); and "application"—using coping skills in imagined as well as real-life stress-producing situations.

4. *Thought stoppage.* A way to gain control over irrational thinking that increases stress. Here clients are instructed to stop irrational thoughts by yelling "stop, stop, stop," by pinching themselves, or by snapping a rubber band around their wrists. Once the interruption takes place, the client is taught how to relax and turn attention to positive mental imagery.

5. *Mental imagery.* The use of a number of techniques for combating stress. It is also used with meditation and hypnosis. Try this yourself. Take three deep breaths, concentrating on the air going in and out of your lungs. Now let your eyelids close down. Begin to imagine that you are in a most pleasant location—one that you have thoroughly enjoyed. See it in your mind's eye. Hear the sounds. Smell the smells. Feel the atmosphere. Let yourself experience all the beauty and tranquility. Immerse yourself. Soon you will feel the muscles of your body growing loose and limp. As this happens, your cares and tensions begin to fade.

6. *Exercise and Nutrition.* The benefits of physical exercise have been well documented. A regulated program builds a healthier mental outlook and increased feelings of self-control; a well-conditioned body is better able to cope with stressful situations. A nutritional approach concentrates on two aspects: avoiding junk foods and high sodium diets and providing the necessary nutrients that may be lost because of stress. A good diet consisting of natural foods—whole grains, raw fruits and vegetables, fresh dairy products, fresh fish, poultry or meats in wide variety—contributes to general health as well as mitigates stress.

Marital and Family Issues

Marital problems range from verbal arguments over money, in-laws, and recreation to infidelity and sex. Marital problems bring pain and distress. Symptoms are not obvious. They may manifest themselves in depression, irritability, tension, or bodily complaints. The surest signal that a marriage is in trouble is the breakdown of trust. Here's why. All human relationships have conflict. It is impossible for two people to live together and not experience some sort of conflict. Even if a couple likes the exact same things—tennis, classical music, camping—they may not like them at the same time or in the same amounts (e.g., "Let's stay longer." "No, I want to go home now."). Since conflict is inevitable, the individuals must develop conflict resolution skills through good communication. And good communication requires trust. There is no communicating if everything one says is doubted or questioned by the other. Trust, on the other hand, is maintained and strengthened by the truth. Furthermore, trust encourages the expression of truth. If I don't trust you, I am not likely to tell you the truth—for I fear what you will do with it and how you will react. When I don't tell you the truth, it causes you not to trust me. And that's a vicious, trust-busting circle. However, if I trust you and tell you the truth and you prove trustworthy by the way you handle it, the truth will cause you to trust me—and your handling the truth will cause me to trust you again. And that's a trust-truth building cycle.

When a marriage is in trouble, several symptoms occur: (1) There is a lack of open communication. Often this shows up in the tendency to avoid issues—a pseudoconviviality. (2) Resentments manifest themselves either in overt attacks and bitter arguments or in veiled threats and cold war tactics. (3) Communication becomes so out of step that every time the couple begins to solve a problem, the problem gets worse. The sooner employees avail themselves of help the more successful marital therapy is likely to be. Naturally it is desirable for the couple to work out their own problems if they can. However, when every attempt at resolving issues makes matters worse, then professional help is indicated. But too many couples wait until their problems have become so painful that they lose their love for each other. In effect they go through an emotional divorce and have no desire to put further energy into the relationship.

In marital therapy, the psychologist or counselor acts as an impartial, concerned friend. He or she is trained to spot and repair faulty communication patterns in the marriage. In effect the therapist becomes a communications facilitator in helping each partner understand what the other is saying and how the other feels. Old patterns will be disrupted and new ones established. Assignments are given that help the couple work together to build trust.

Marital therapy is part of family therapy. Family therapy is indicated when the symptoms of pain and distress affect all members of the household. Family therapists (whether psychologists or marriage and family counselors) see the family as a powerful system that both causes and sustains psychological disorders. Symptoms in one member may indicate that the family as a whole is disturbed. The goal of the family therapist is to change the often rigid and destructive ways in which family members interact. This is often done through direct interventions in communication patterns. There is also emphasis on making family members aware of family rules (usually unspoken), family secrets (what everyone knows but won't talk about), and family modes of interaction. As rigid rules are broken, much emotion may occur. Family members become aware of styles of interaction that cause their problems. With the therapist's guidance, they are encouraged to adopt more open, flexible, and mutually supportive relationships.

Nonassertive and Aggressive Behavior

These behaviors bring about poor human relations and low self-esteem. The "nonassertive" person is usually self-denying, inhibited, hurt, anxious. Such people allow others to choose and control. Needs are not met and rights are not protected. The nonassertive person does not speak up on behalf of self and as a consequence feels guilty, angry, and bad about self. The "aggressive" person is usually self-aggrandizing at the expense of others. These people get what they have coming but end up hurting others in the process. The aggressive person generates so much hatred and frustration that he or she feels hurt, defensive, and lonely. In effect, nonassertive people let others walk all over them while aggressive people walk all over others. The psychologist first assesses the degree of nonassertiveness or aggressiveness and then trains the client in complementary skills. For the nonassertive person, for example, these include: how to ask a waitress to bring the rare steak you ordered in place of the well-done steak on your plate; how to take an item back to the store and ask for your money back; how to give a compliment to others; how to say No to salespeople, etc. Anyone can learn these skills. The result is often increased self-worth and improved relationships.

Phobias

These are conditioned fears and can be treated through systematic desensitization. This behavioral process consists of teaching the client deep relaxation and then presenting scenes of increasing anxiety regarding the phobia. For example, if the client were afraid of elevators, the first scene presented might be walking into an office building that had an elevator. The psychologist would then elicit from the client the amount of anxiety experienced. Systematically the scenes are presented over and over until the client reports no anxiety even with the strongest anxiety-provoking scenes. Oftentimes employees develop phobias as a result of an industrial accident. They become fearful and anxious about returning to the job or place where the accident was experienced. The phobic person knows that there is no logical basis for the fear but cannot control it. He or she must be deconditioned from the phobia and gotten back on the job as soon as possible.

Brain Damage

Brain damage may be suspected whenever there is marked and sudden change in personality or behavior that may involve: explosive temper outburst, sudden crying, or other emotionally volatile behavior; impaired impulse control such as poor social judgment, sexual indiscretions, shoplifting; marked indifference, especially in hobbies; suspiciousness of others. Other symptoms caused by injury or disease include: fear, anxiety, panic, irritability, angry outbursts, delusions, restlessness, hyperactivity, insomnia, learning difficulties, impaired memory, confusion. If an employee were to exhibit sudden personality changes or violent behavior, most people in the surrounding environment would be perplexed. Few would suspect possible brain damage. Neuropsychologists and neurologists are trained to assess such symptoms. They can determine the disease or injury and prescribe appropriate treatment.

Obsessive-Compulsive Disorders

These are marked by persistent and usually irrational thoughts, impulses, or actions—frequently an urge to engage in a behavior while at the same time desiring to resist that behavior. Examples of obsessive thoughts include the wish that someone were dead, the image of a forbidden sexual act, or the thought of committing suicide. Examples of compulsive behaviors are going back time and again to check if the door is locked, washing one's hands time and again to be sure there are no germs; pacing back and forth for hours; counting papers in a report over and over; arranging items by size, color, etc., over and over. Depressive thoughts probably underlie obsessive-compulsive behaviors. Thus the psychologist might first use a treatment such as "flooding," also known as "deliberate exposure." Once the detrimental obsessive-compulsive symptoms have been controlled, long-term psychotherapy would deal with the underlying issues. The manager often sees mild forms of obsessive-compulsive behavior in the workplace, such as the perfectionist who spends excessive time and energy on a task. Every little detail must be without fault. Sometimes an employee will go over and over a piece of work—almost refusing to let it go. This is of no great consequence unless it interferes with work production. At that point the executive may recommend professional help.

Depressions

About one in twenty persons in America suffers from some form of depression. Abraham Lincoln and Winston Churchill had recurring bouts. F. Scott Fitzgerald described depression like this: "In a real dark night of the soul, it is always 3 o'clock in the morning." *Physical* symptoms often accompanying depression are: digestive problems, insomnia, headaches, loss of or reduced sexual desire, dizziness, heart palpitation, loss of appetite, and disturbances in vision. *Emotional* symptoms are: gloom, sadness, inability to experience pleasure, crying spells, apprehension or panic, irritability, feelings of guilt, and major decline of self-esteem or worth. *Mental* symptoms are: poor memory, indecisiveness, difficulty or inability to concentrate, loss of interest in work or play, dramatic reduction in self-confidence, thinking of life as dull, flat, and meaningless and, therefore, brooding about death. While causes of depression may be many, a prime trigger is stress. How is depression treated? When the symptoms are sadness, hopelessness, and interest loss, cognitive-behavioral psychotherapy has shown impressive results. But when a depression is so severe as to disturb sleep, shut down normal functioning, inhibit appetite, and reduce energy, antidepressant medication may be indicated. The psychologist would then refer the client to a psychiatrist.

Suicide

More than 25,000 deaths each year in the United States are caused by suicide. The single most common cause of suicide is depression. Women attempt suicide three to one over men. However 3 times more men actually succeed in killing themselves. Before individuals attempt suicide, they usually give subtle messages to those around them. In the work environment a person may tell colleagues that he or she has attempted or is planning suicide. Such threats should be taken seriously, and a professional or local psychiatric emergency team contacted immediately. They will assess the danger and decide urgency and appropriate action.

Preparation for Retirement

The time of retirement is a major readjustment and ought to be one of satisfaction and contentment. However, some are not so blessed. When an executive or other employee has devoted a lifetime to a corporation, retirement can be traumatic. Many workers enter retirement totally unprepared to cope with a variety of changes. Many don't live long thereafter. Creative managers are caring people. They understand the need to develop new social supports critical to a smooth adjustment. For most people work is their major interest. Their work career is part of who they are—their personal identity (e.g., "I'm an accountant," "I'm an electrical engineer," etc.). Inadequate preparation can turn retirement into nervous isolation with loss of identity. An employee who is being retired may feel unneeded or, worse, unwanted. There may be resentment. If you encourage subordinates approaching retirement to seek counsel and help, they can look forward to it with joy and anticipation. The employee then feels good about the step, loyal to his or her company and appreciative of his or her boss.

Overcoming Reluctance

There are a host of life's problems that can be helped by a psychologist. However, there is sometimes reluctance to refer employees to a psychologist even though most corporate insurance plans contain coverage for outpatient mental health services. The first reason is the imagined stigma. In modern America this ought not to be. People feel that they should be able to handle their own problems. Yet scientific knowledge is as relevant in psychology as it is in medicine. And when problems arise, a trained professional is needed.

The second reason for reluctance to refer is the belief that the cost of insurance premiums will increase should many employees avail themselves of this service. This is not true. The *Harvard Medical School Mental Health Letter* (June 1985) reported a University of Colorado study in which 85 percent of patients showed *less* use of medical services—mainly hospital services—following psychotherapy. It was shown that even "modest mental health intervention" was able to reduce hospital stays significantly. Similar results were reported for the Blue Cross-Blue Shield Federal Employees Program's medical claims for the 1974–1978 period. Average medical costs for people who had mental health treatment were lower than the control group. Other findings show cost reductions greatest for people over 55. Thus psychotherapeutic services will not only benefit companies by increased employee morale and job performance but also may help *cut* hospital costs and insurance premiums.

Managers influence the lives of hundreds: subordinates and their families are a large responsibility. A prime goal should be to keep the lives of workers as trouble free as possible so that all contribute their very best. Employee fulfillment and company productivity is a win-win match-up. Creative managers make marvelous use of impersonal, electronic computers; they should do likewise with personal, human care.

61

The New World of Creative Work

Philip R. Harris

Management Psychologist and Author

Innovation is the act of introducing something new into the established order or way of thinking. It need not be limited to novel products or processes alone but can also apply to the way we view and act in our roles. Those in international management have unique opportunities to exercise creative leadership and contribute to the larger cultural and social transition underway.

Leadership here means the transformational leadership that moves beyond daily concerns to create awareness and stimulate constructive actions (Burns). Transformational leaders sense the need for planned change, then share their vision to inspire others (Kozmetsky). Our information society calls for synergistic coexistence with nature and with each other; it offers an unprecedented chance for self-actualization and human emergence. Yoneji Masuda reminds us that this emerging civilization will be global in scope, founded on information productivity using communication and computer technologies; its goods will be often invisible, not material; its products will consist of signals, symbols, and images (Didsbury). Another characteristic of this information civilization deserves attention, especially from those involved in global management. Masuda, an eminent Japanese futurist, predicts the new culture will result in the sublation of the oriental and occidental (preservation and enhancement by integration of both). I expect to see, by the end of the century, the convergence of two contrasting expressions of human culture—the oriental, with its emphasis on the spiritual and intuitive, harmony with nature, and seeking interior peace or nirvana and the occidental, which accentuates the material and rational, control of nature, and the obtaining of life's pleasures and joys during our earthly existence (Masuda). In formulating the information culture, east-west leaders should foster synergy in the societies and organizations they influence.

The research of anthropologist Ruth Benedict on synergistic and nonsynergistic societies and groups was refined by humanistic psychologist Abraham Maslow. Their combined observations offer an ideal to promote in corporate systems. The key concepts are: "high synergy," which fosters mutually advantageous cooperation, encouragement of both individual and group development and a "win-win" philosophy or group victory, a sharing for the common good and collaborative leadership, while avoiding destructive competition and aggression. This is in stark contrast to "low synergy," which emphasizes rugged competition and individualism, often at the expense of the whole; a "win-lose" philosophy of victory over nature and others at all costs; and a "competitive atmosphere" of self-centeredness and single-minded actions without regard to consequences for others, a leadership focused upon private advantage and gain (Moran and Harris). If we are to be truly creative and innovative managers, let us cultivate, practice, and spread high synergy in our organizations! This is the way to build bridges from twentieth to twenty-first century management.

Global Managers as Cosmopolitans

Management activities center around the organization of ideas, people, and things so as to achieve objectives (Mackenzie). The management of change can be defined as stimulating creativity and innovation in the achieving of goals. Today, the focus is on the effective managing of *resources*—information and human, as well as material. Peter Drucker views management in the context of performance—economic to enable an institution to achieve its mission; making work productive through human capitalization and achievement; managing the enterprise's social impacts and responsibilities. Drucker's basic message is that business, in any form, is people, while management is responsible for their use and service.

Management is increasingly intercultural and global. We are in the midst of passage between two work cultures, in transition from the familiar industrial work culture that conditioned most of us. The industrial revolution recast our physical world and cities through mechanization, quantification, and consolidation (Didsbury). We are now moving toward a postindustrial work environment, an information culture marked by "mediation" (describing and interpreting our world), "simulation" (recreating perceptible experiences with heightened fidelity), and "circularity" (events whipping around us, interacting and shaping experience or history). All this contributes to rapid alterations in our images of ourselves and our social institutions.

Consider human development in the context of work culture. As we know, culture expresses the customs, traditions, viewpoints, practices, and life style of a particular people at a point in time. I like AT&T's designation "metaindustrial" to communicate that we have moved beyond the industrial way of thinking and acting; this requires a new management and organization. All assumptions upon which management practice was based during the receding industrial culture are becoming obsolete. That is why administration today is altering both leadership style and managerial activities.

One result is the global manager. Advances in communication, transportation, and other technologies have broken barriers that separated people and cultures. The concept of the global village or Spaceship Earth is a reality. We operate in a global economy that is increasingly interdependent. Thinking managers no longer view management activities in terms of domestic and international, but on a global scale. Louis Korn, CEO of an executive search firm, maintains that organizations should seek, train, and reward leaders who are forward looking, can deal effectively with different cultures, and can manage the results of technological change. "Tomorrow's executives," Korn said, "must possess a broad understanding of history, of culture, of technology, and of human relations. They must be as comfortable with history, anthropology, sociology, mathematics, and the physical and natural sciences as they are with cash management."

There is growing consensus that schools of business are not preparing such leaders. How can future executives be so transformed? Here are some ways: (1) Promote more interest in transnational enterprises, stressing synergistic leadership within the corporation and the communities in which it operates. (2) Conduct conferences, workshops, or seminars on global management issues for multinational corporation (MNC) executives. Produce learning materials from such sessions, including audio/video cassettes and other self-instructional aids, as well as sponsor videoconferences between eastern and western executives and entrepreneurs. (3) Encourage MNC leaders to take up temporary residence on sabbatical leave as lecturers and researchers in business schools or cross-cultural institutes (IBM has such a program). Middle managers should experience lateral growth, while top managers should have professional development. Another idea would be a "year-abroad" project for first world executives to serve as consultants to third world business or government enterprises. We can make more room at the top for aspiring managers by spreading out existing executive talent in new forms of constructive service.

Transnational executives have unique opportunities to effect economic and social change, to influence culture. My own experience with Westinghouse and N. V. Philips confirms that it is already happening, so why not formally examine how executive development can enhance greater corporate responsibility? The International Corps of Retired Executives and SCORE have demonstrated the value of executive voluntary service.

There is a basic need for creative managers to think more in terms of concepts and then to act upon such paradigms or models, especially in the formulation of management strategies. Ten such concepts should be incorporated in the human resource development of global managers. Since culture gives people a sense of who and what they are and how to behave appropriately, knowledge of these ten concepts can promote excellence in global managers.

1. *Concept of the cosmopolitan.* Learning to be a sensitive, participative leader capable of operating comfortably in a pluralistic or global environment; one who is open and flexible when dealing with differences.

2. *Concept of intercultural communication.* Learning to be aware of one's self-image and cultural influences and being willing to revise and expand this image with new input and intercultural experiences; one who is capable of entering into the world of the other, acquiring cross-cultural interaction skills, both verbal and nonverbal.

3. *Concept of cultural sensitivity.* Learning to empathize with those from different backgrounds, thus translating general cultural awareness into specific intercultural relationships.

4. *Concept of acculturation.* Learning to adjust and adapt to an alien culture, whether within one's own country or abroad; able to delimit culture shock and to use intercultural experience to enhance one's sense of identity.

5. *Concept of effective intercultural performance.* Learning to apply cultural theory and insights to specific cross-cultural work situations, to sustain high job performance in a strange environ-

ment; understanding intercultural peculiarities that effect work productivity.

6. *Concept of cultural management influences.*   Learning to appreciate the impact of cultural conditioning on the management of natural, material, information, and human resources; able to adapt management process to indigeneous situations and to cultivate a cross-cultural leadership style.

7. *Concept of changing international business.*   Learning to cope with the interdependence of world business activity and to operate globally within the managerial subculture; able to adapt multinational business practice to diverse cultural situations.

8. *Concept of cultural synergy.*   Learning to build upon cultural differences in people for mutual growth and development; able to identify similarities and common concerns, to combine the best, and to promote collaboration or cooperation.

9. *Concept of work culture.*   Learning to apply general theories of culture to how specific groups of people work; in the macro sense, able to analyze the hunting, agricultural, industrial, and metaindustrial stages of work culture, while in the micro sense, being able to study the work cultures of specific industries, organizations, or professional groupings.

10. *Concept of world culture.*   Learning that a unique world culture is emerging, abetted by new communication and transportation technologies; global managers must serve the commonality of human needs with strategies that are transnational.

There are other dimensions to global management, particularly the ability to direct, integrate, and control large, complex organizations and activities (Davidson & Cox). Such world leaders think in global rather than local terms and develop strategies that influence the future of a system as a whole. They deal with a variety of organizational stakeholders while encouraging autonomous operating units that develop individual and group talents. They are masters of planned change and of the new information technologies. But above all, they are global cosmopolitan managers capable of implementing the above ten concepts in their programs and projects. It is this type of twenty-first century management that will renew this planet's infrastructure while building tomorrow's space station and lunar base.

At another level, the global manager is a mind-set, a way of looking at the world and its people. Such persons are not provincial or ethnocentric in outlook but effective in intercultural communication, negotiation, and synergy. The global manager is a person empathetic to human aspirations, especially of women and minorities, emigrés and refugees, unemployed and underemployed; a person attuned to equal development opportunity, particularly for those who feel uncomfortable in the new technological workplace. In such circumstances, the global manager uses both work and organizational cultures to enhance human performance and potential. When dealing with organizational change—such as mergers, acquisitions, joint ventures, or consortia—the seeking of synergy can facilitate the process and ease the pain of paradigm shift. It is only through effective collaboration that we can renew existing institutions as well as create more relevant ones. In an atmosphere of mutual respect and creative interdependence, global leaders should promote cooperation among neighboring nations in the use of complementary assets, skills, and expertise. Prototypes have been created, for example, among Japanese and American automakers.

Global Managers in the New Work Culture

The metaindustrial work culture is a work environment oriented to information processing and new technologies. It is producing a service economy and knowledge workers, as well as a more diversified work force. Creative and innovative managers should focus attention on features and developments of this emerging work scene. But these trends can be threatening to some and cause considerable resistance. The impact of new technologies on organizations undermines bureaucratic structures and demands reconfiguration.

Every aspect of organizational culture is being transformed. That is why *new* management or leadership is necessary (O'Toole, Peters). It is why the practice of cultural synergy is essential (Corning). It is why entrepreneurialism is so central to corporate creativity in robust firms (Smilor and Kuhn). Organizational innovators are experimenting with new structural form and some of their efforts will become standard practice in the decades ahead. Following are ten indicators of tomorrow's work culture.

Autonomy and control over work space .   People seek more freedom of choice, more self-responsibility, more authority (especially at lower levels of the organization). They want more ownership of their work, psychologically and/or literally. They want to transcend traditional boundaries that constrict, separate, or regulate work. They also expect to be human at work, to err when taking risks, and to learn from failure. The drive for autonomy may even extend into the ownership of businesses, either directly as stockholders or through profit sharing. When corporations decide to close down operations, employees (such as in the Weirtown Steel Company) may combine resources and buy the company; hundreds of firms have been purchased by their workers. The trend is also exemplified by industrial democracy, worker ownership, and contract work. The latter is where expensive, full-time workers are turned into cheaper, independent subcontractors. By "turfing" them out and signing contracts, companies not only cut costs but retain relationships with personnel they trust. Britain's Rank-Xerox, for example, sold computer terminals to twenty employees and gave them contracts to work from their homes. ICI, a British chemical giant, supported former employees in their own businesses and initially guaranteed their income. Many European firms are doing the same. British government agencies and the European Common Market are funding consultants to train unemployed managers on how to raise venture capital and get their own enterprises going. Five thousand American companies have some form of employee ownership plan.

Participation and involvement in the enterprise. People seek more democracy in their work organizations. For knowledge workers this may mean sharing in management problem solving, planning, and decisions. For management, it may mean obtaining consensus or negotiating power sharing and compromises. The trend is manifested in team, project, and product management, as well as in various attempts at collegiality, such as networking. Sweden has pioneered a worker participation system for protection purposes. It features a worker safety ombudsman in every plant, a safety committee of employees and employers, worker-risk educational programs, and consensual decision making. Westinghouse instituted a participatory management approach that featured extensive use of quality circles. Ford Motor Company involved employees in improving productivity and quality.

Communications and information orientation. People seek more open, authentic, and circular communications at work. They want to have input and give feedback; they like attitudinal surveys—interviews, questionnaires, inventories, opinion polls. They expect to use a variety of media in transmitting messages at work, including electronic devices. Management information systems are now both centralized and distributed. But abundant data must be translated into useful information; thus information management will be the principal concern of all managers in metaindustrial organizations. Communication planning and coordination should become a senior management function. New telecommunication technology is being utilized to link together an organization's widely scattered facilities, subsidiaries, and total workforce. Lincoln National Life Insurance in Fort Wayne, for example, unified its telephone system using private microwave pathways. It caused dramatic improvements in productivity and customer relations, while decreasing operating costs by 15 percent. Increased microwave capability enables the company to accommodate computer terminals, high-speed facsimile transmissions, and video conferencing. Atlantic Richfield Company has a private internal satellite communication network that permits video conferencing among its many locations. ARCO uses this technology to discuss exploration and drilling prospects. AETNA has held thousands of video conferences between two remote sites since mid-1981 and plans to link up thirteen more sites throughout the country. Many companies, like Ford and IBM, use public video conferencing to introduce new products (Lazer, Pope).

Informal and synergistic relationships.   People seek work relations that are more cooperative, meaningful, caring, and respectful. Knowledge workers resist hierarchical or status relations and prefer those that are more informal and interdependent, marked by equality and integrity. Such organizational relations may be intense but temporary, as in ad hoc task forces, and more pluralistic (including women and minorities). Regarding "worker-machine" relationships, many welcome robots and computerization. Others suffer from either cyberphobia (fear of technology) or cyberphrenia (addiction to technology). The very complexities of metaindustrial organizations and their missions require more synergistic relations such as collaboration among people. The matrix organization is more adaptive, cross-functional, and task oriented. It features temporary work groups and relationships instead of permanent departments, decentralized authority, decision making dominated by technical concerns, complexity, and reporting to two or more supervisors or project managers. It thrives in smaller, entrepreneurial, innovation-oriented cultures but often has difficulties and turf battling when the company grows larger—such as happened at Intel and Texas Instruments. In a sprawling organization, a matrix can only work when people understand their professional relationships.

Enhanced quality of work life .   People seek work that is more self-fulfilling, more meaningful, more mentally rewarding. Knowledge workers want a creative corporate environment that energizes them. They have higher expectations regarding entitlements such as wellness programs and sabbatical leaves and physical surroundings such as campus-like plant facilities. Often, they prefer leave time or incentive travel over increased pay; they are concerned about corporate support services and fringe benefits that permit them to function effectively on and off the job. As middle management shrinks, the role of first-line supervisors is enhanced by computer-based technology and participatory managerial style. The change is illustrated in the new foreman type of automobile assembly lines. Ford Motor Company and the United Auto Workers have inaugurated a worker participation program to improve product quality and production as well as worker environment. Under the program called Employee Involvement (EI), foremen at Ford's Edison (New Jersey) plant chat with employees, solicit their ideas, and encourage them to use buttons to stop assembly lines when defects are spotted. The new foreman has an "enabling function" rather than a "control function," thanks to the computer. The supervisor facilitates worker problem solving and job analysis, tests out employee suggestions, and fosters self-management teams. The new foreman is more human—smiles and jokes with workers, helps workers analyze what went wrong when they make mistakes, and promotes family-like harmony. As a result, quality has gone up for everybody, hostility against bosses is down, absenteeism is reduced, authority is constructive, and disciplinary hearings are held less often and are more helpful. People maintenance is the primary activity of the new foreman, and personnel are happier.

Creative organizational norms. People are supporting new work standards that emphasize competence, high performance, entrepreneurship, risk taking, venturesomeness, audaciousness, and creativity. Knowledge workers prefer managers of change and transformation who are flexible and adaptable. Standards of work behavior and performance must reflect such sentiments whether they appear in personnel manuals, union contracts, work conventions, or management pronouncements. Metaindustrial organizations avoid publishing too many standards that constrain innovation. New norms encourage flexibility, ultrastability, and management by exception. In rapid-growth firms, accommodations are made for those on the "fast track." Intel sprouted when it cultivated an environment of innovation that excited and energized its technical personnel; when the company hit crises, some of their best talent jumped ship—a few starting their own companies and threatening Intel's technical prowess. At Xerox, executives had to fight their own entrenched system to become more competitive. Managers, conditioned by old norms, were reluctant to use their new-found authority for fear of being second guessed. Top executives found some managers vacillating because of concerns over reprisals if they failed in their new use of authority and risk taking. At Xerox, the corporate culture change is huge. (See Chapter 25.)

High performance and productivity. People in metaindustrial organizations are achievement oriented and develop a work ethic of "professionalism." Knowledge workers use technology to become more productive—they work smarter! Their sense of time is different, and they are not confined to the 9 to 5 syndrome. They work beyond the 8-hour day if project deadlines demand it; they work weekends if a tight schedule requires it. Concepts such as "excellence," "quality," and "service" motivate high performance in what is a career, not merely a job. They seek self-approval for top performance, not just organizational recognition. By videotaping outstanding employees or supervisors in a problem-solving conference, we found that recorded insights could be used not only as powerful feedback to top management but also as a training tool for average performers. New norms can be set by high achievers who become behavior models. A training manager for General Telephone holds that human resource development should not be used to maintain existing work practices. He recommends that we train toward maximum performance and use top performers in developing job criteria.

Entrepreneurial orientation. People in the new work culture value pluralism, competent performance, and innovation. They espouse entrepreneurial or intrapreneurial attitudes. Entrepreneurial types focus on where opportunities are going to be, then create concepts, processes, products, or structures to capitalize upon them. These promoters match people and resources with opportunities for greater choice, self-expression, and profit. This spirit energizes people to create and take responsibility for their own futures by making the most of knowledge, talent, and change. With large and complex corporations, the entrepreneurial revolution is extending the concept of small, high-risk workplace ventures. At Baker International, participants in new division ventures receive incentives in the form of "shares" that are later convertible to regular corporate stock at a lush price if the venture profits. Multinational corporations such as General Electric are setting up corporate entrepreneurial teams, giving employees a sense of owning the business. That means they spend less time worrying about treading upon toes and more time focusing on building "their" business.

Technological orientation. People are engaged in work of a more technical nature, often related to information processing. Technology and its tools are artifacts of culture, and in the new work culture their use is increasing. The trend is toward microfabrication and microelectronics—smaller, faster, more energy-efficient machines. It is manifested in microchips, lasers, and miniwonders of all types. By the year

2000, one-third of the work force in industrialized countries will be teleworking, using telecommunications rather than transportation to link themselves to central work sites, while half of management will be using electronic work stations. A computer-literate population will use electronic devices to conduct both business and personal life activities.

Research and development orientation. People in metaindustrial organizations will have greater R&D orientation. Research will be used to identify people, products, processes, and markets; it will promote technological innovation and advantage. It will affect "bottom-line" mentality and balance short-term returns against long-term pay-offs. Knowledge workers will employ research skills for human-factor data gathering to improve organizational effectiveness, for enhancing risk analysis systems, for responding to user and customer needs. Management by information will require technological forecasting and futures research and greater use of internal and external resources. This may mean utilizing outside research groups, putting together research consortia, and establishing synergistic relationships between corporations and universities.

For managers who aspire to be creative and innovative, the incorporation of the ten concepts described earlier must articulate with the ten trends just enumerated. When such strategies are applied to every aspect of organizational culture, our corporations and systems will be transformed.

Bibliography

Burns, J. M.: *Leadership,* Harper & Row, New York, 1978.

Casse, P.; *Training for the Multicultural Manager,* SIETAR International, Washington, DC, 1982.

Casse, P. and S. Deal: *Managing Intercultural Negotiations,* SIETAR International, Washington, DC, 1985.

Corning, P. A.: *The Synergism Hypothesis,* McGraw-Hill, New York, 1983.

Davidson, F. P. and J. S. Cox: *MACRO: A Clear Vision of How Science and Technology will Shape the Future,* William Morrow, New York, 1983.

Didsbury, H. F. (ed.): *Communications and the Future: Prospects, Promises, and Problems,* World Future Society, Bethesda, Md, 1982.

Drucker, P. F.: *Innovation and Entrepreneurship,* Harper & Row, New York, 1985.

Harris, P. R.: *Management in Transition: Transforming Managerial Practices and Organizational Strategies for the New Work Culture,* Jossey-Bass, San Francisco, 1985.

————— *New Worlds, New Ways, New Management,* Masterco Press/AMACOM, Ann Arbor, MI, 1983.

Harris, P. R. (ed.): *Global Strategies for Human Resource Development,* American Society for Training & Development, Washington, DC, 1984.

Harris, P. R., and G. H. Malin (eds.): *Innovations in Global Consultation,* International Consultants Foundation, Washington, DC, 1980.

Kozmetsky, G.: *Transformational Management,* Ballinger/Harper & Row, Cambridge, MA, 1985.

Mackenzie, R. A.: "The Management Process in 3D," *Harvard Business Review,* Nov./Dec. 1969.

Masuda, Y.: *The Information Society as a Post-Industrial Society,* World Future Society, Washington DC, 1981.

Moran, R. T.: *Getting Your Yen's Worth: How to Negotiate with Japan, Inc.,* Gulf Publishing Co., Houston, TX, 1985.

Moran, R. T., and P. R. Harris : *Managing Cultural Synergy,* Gulf Publishing Co., Houston, TX, 1982.

O'Toole, J. (ed.): *New Management,* Wilson Learning Corp., Eden Prairie, MI, vol. 1., no. 1, Spring 1983:3.

Ouchi, W.: *The M-Form Society: How American Teamwork Can Recover the Competitive Edge,* Addison-Wesley, Reading, MA, 1984.

Peters, T., and N. Austin: *A Passion for Excellence,* Random House, New York, 1985.

Schein, E. H.: *Organizational Culture and Leadership: A Dynamic View,* Jossey-Bass, San Francisco, 1985.

Smilor, R. W. and R. L. Kuhn (eds.): *Corporate Creativity: Robust Companies and the Entrepreneurial Spirit,* Praeger, New York 1984.

Toffler, A.: *The Adaptive Corporation,* McGraw-Hill, New York, 1985.

PART 7

Creative Culture for Knowledge Organizations

Emerging Sectors and Blurring Boundaries

The melding of industry, government, and academia is a monumental socio-economic movement. The emergence of "intellectual institutions," organizations whose primary product is new knowledge irrespective of profit-making intent, epitomizes the coming age. Intellectual institutions, therefore, are the purest form of "knowledge organizations" and are totally dependent on the generation and control of information. Indeed, leadership here is increasingly defined in terms of stimulating, focusing, leveraging, and implementing novel ideas and original concepts. This is fertile ground for creative and innovative management. Public, private, and not-for-profit worlds are converging. The contrasting settings and strategies of these diverse institutions comprise an endlessly changing kaleidoscope on the surface, yet cover surprisingly consistent goals and objectives just underneath. There are common principles to follow and common missions to fulfill. Creative management is a necessity here, not a luxury, as boundaries blur among sectors. Part 7 focuses on needed cooperation among industry, government, and academia to accomplish the macro projects that characterize contemporary civilization—such as advancing state-of-the-art science, building national infrastructure, and encouraging intellectual development. Topics include: creative management of intellectual institutions, science-based businesses, and universities; how technology has an impact on traditional business and promotes economic growth; broader constituencies of companies including social and environmental issues; new linkages of business, academia, and government; new directions for business education. We conclude with the place and importance of creative and innovative management in culture and society as we look to the future of enterprise. To nurture creative and innovative management among sectors is to engender humanity with the power to prosper.

62

The Emergence of Intellectual Institutions: Producing New Knowledge in Industry and Academia

Robert Lawrence Kuhn

*Investment Banker, Senior Research Fellow,
IC² Institute, The University of Texas at Austin and
Adjunct Professor, Graduate School of Business
Administration, New York University*

Barry Munitz

*President, Federated Development Company and
Former Chancellor, University of Houston*

The convergence of for-profit corporations and not-for-profit institutions is one of the great social shifts as we approach the twenty-first century. In an age of increasing economic complexity, when such corporations and institutions cross sectors as easily as they cross continents, a new form of organization is arising and a new demand for leadership is emerging. Creative managers see the trend and exploit its impact.

Intellectual Institutions

"Intellectual institutions" is our rubric for classifying certain modern organizations from which knowledge is the primary product. We like the term because it speaks neutrally regarding the profit-making intent. The taxonomic division into "for-profit" and "not-for-profit" categories misses the contemporary essence and has become mushy and archaic. Institutions are more alike if their primary product is based on generating new data, knowledge, technology, mechanisms, or ideas—irrespective of whether the legal structure is designed to reward stockholders financially. A computer software firm, for example, is more akin to a university science department than it is to, say, a metal stamping company.

An intellectual institution, therefore, is the most highly focused form of "knowledge organization." It may be a for-profit corporation, a not-for-profit university, a quasi-profit research organization, or a public-sector government agency. The nature of the output is the key determinant. If they are generating original information, seemingly disparate organizations have more in common than mere sector classification would suggest. Common characteristics pervading intellectual institutions include the nurturing of creative personnel, catalyzing scholarly synthesis, promoting interdisciplinary or interdepartmental flow, and pioneering intersector innovation.

The media like to portray conflict among corporate, educational, and government worlds, but, in reality, consonance is louder than dissonance. Our struggle is to break down traditional boundaries and concentrate on how each sector can contribute insight and experience to the others. We need institutional flexibility, quick response time, new combinations of talent, and new interpretations of regulation. Much of this visionary responsibility, we believe, belongs to governing boards. They must search beyond their lengthy long-range plans and learn how to provide independent imaginative support. Creative management is a team effort for all knowledge organizations.

Economic Convergence

The old adage "The reason academic politics is so great is that the stakes are so small" is suddenly wrong. Intellectual output is as much the raw material for the information age as energy output was for the industrial age. Society does not yet recognize the university's critical role in the economic reconstruction of the future. Progressively more of our goods and services are knowledge oriented, and knowledge is the primary product of academic institutions. We now see corporations courting universities for joint ventures in genetic engineering, energy, computers, and biomedical research. The trend will continue. The advent of personal computers will make information the world's primary medium of exchange. Universities must not become the passive recipients of corporate largess, performing service, if you pardon the analogy, for money. Fundamental intellectual inquiry is the essence of human progress. The university, sitting at the fulcrum of our information-based society, should take a leadership role in defining relationships and catalyzing interactions with both industry and government.

Managerial Convergence

We're familiar with traditional corporate structure. Hierarchical control is strong and authority is clearly delineated at each managerial level. In universities, the prototypical intellectual institution, it's not so simple. Here the richness and freedom of individual intellect is confronted by the collective necessity for order and control. Everyone in higher education—faculty, students, trustees, alumni, community—feels the right and the duty to participate in virtually every decision. Academic administrators are always overwhelmed by constant expectations of ultimate democracy as faculties seek the highest commodities: flexibility and innovation. The irony, of course, is that when everyone ponders every decision, flexibility and innovation falter. Where we should find imagination, we often hit brick walls. Form and structure are problems in academe; we've found more originality and innovation in the private sector.

Management styles in private and public sectors are changing, and credit must be given to media and government, the former for focusing public attention, the latter by legislating rules and regulations. Yet tradition remains strong. A corporation is founded on the principle of executive responsibility; although a decision maker needs the agreement of those who will implement policy, the actual decision and subsequent control are firmly hierarchical. Academic organization is almost the opposite: a flat or inverted structure in which the faculty feels that the administration is there to provide mere service and support and that real decision making takes place at the level of the dean, the department chair, and the individual faculty member in classroom and lab.

How does a flat or inverted structure affect the university CEO's capacity to run the institution? For one thing, enormous amounts of time are spent in meetings. When authority is shared, personal interaction consumes most of the working day. Collegial conversation is the critical bonding mechanism in educational institutions. When moving from university chancellor to corporate president, meeting time decreases tenfold and telephone time increases tenfold. Timely and effective decisions can be made without having to test them repeatedly against a dozen different constituencies. Such constraints leave little time for thoughtful reflection of institutional leadership. Leaders are often more thoughtful in the private sector, even though, contrasted to the university, the priority is action over introspection.

Society expects the university to be the focus of fresh forms and functions, the setting for new concepts and directions, the place where the future is supposed to be forged—and yet, paradoxically, university governance structure fosters rigidity. The problem is acute. Over the past decade, while university presidents have moved out of the public spotlight, corporate presidents have moved into it. Twenty years ago, educational leaders participated in almost every social decision in this country. Now it is hard to find a university president who is recognized as a national leader outside education. Yet more and more corporate executives are achieving exactly that status.

It's relatively easy for a university administrator to move from a decentralized, shared decision-making environment to one with the great luxury of stricter authority and control. Time, our primary asset, is freed for reflection. On the other hand, it's uncomfortable to travel in the other direction, from a strong hierarchical position, with clean lines of decision making, to an organizational structure in which most proposals are subject to wilting critique from multiple camps. The vision that universities should lead the way toward new management styles and intersector linkages would most benefit the campuses themselves.

Changes are coming, forced by circumstances. New social expectations, the postindustrial service economy, recent economic trends—all have forced bizarre role reversals. For example, given the financial battles academic administrators have fought, higher education is developing some hard-nosed budget cutters—quite unlike the vacillating eggheads of popular stereotype. Computer applications, mediation techniques, and management by objectives have all transformed the new generation of education leaders, while at the same time, corporate executives are strengthening communication skills, legislative insight, and psychological strategies. Each world has invaded and reshaped the other.

Convergence is coming. Universities are more control oriented, beset with financial constraints, while corporations are more creativity oriented, needing competitive edge. If business is the economic synthesis of human knowledge, employee ideas are the substrate from which new products are generated. What environment is most conducive for nurturing such invention? Not the policy-manual pigeonholing of the corporate pyramid. Universities, for their part, must learn the lesson of tough-minded business. Resources are not free nor are society's needs unlimited, and educational institutions must fight for place and position. The "academic industry" has become a competitive jungle, and university chief executive officers must be as skilled in long-range planning as their profit-making counterparts.

Strategic management is as critical for universities as it is for corporations, perhaps more so. Academic institutions have high levels of inertia; it takes time to alter course. In our tightly wired world, geography is less important. Compounding the problem is the flux and flow of modern society. Needs flip without warning, and what was valuable yesterday may be worthless tomorrow. What is the solution? The same one pioneered by leading businesses. Strategic thinking: socioeconomic forecasting, alternative policy formulation, rigorous policy evaluation accented by insight—the constant testing of institutional mission. Long-range planning is not a gimmick; it is life. Programatic positioning—the matching of organizational resources to environmental opportunities—is vital. Academic institutions, no less than business corporations, must develop particular strengths so that their distinctive competencies can generate competitive advantage.

A primary issue affecting both corporations and Universities is the balance between centralized and decentralized decision making. The administration of a multicampus system—such as the University of Texas—is similar to that in a corporate holding company or conglomerate. Each organization must be constantly checking and refining the division of responsibility and the level of control. What responsibilities should be assumed at top levels? How to encourage rapid and novel response to new opportunities and changing conditions? There is growing consensus that the multicampus system in the academic world, like the conglomerate in the business world, is presenting increasingly serious obstacles to efficient operations in a complex and dynamic environment.

Relevant here is the concept of entrepreneurship in academia and not-for-profit institutions. Though normally considered as only in the domain of business, entrepreneurs are the driving energy of intellectual institutions from all sectors. They are no less vital, though more difficult to accept, in university than in corporate environments. In the business world, where highly motivated, achievement-oriented folks can walk out and start new companies, innovative corporations are designing special structures to keep these invaluable human resources (intrapreneurs) within the organization. Although entrepreneurial types within universities cannot walk out and start their own schools, they can leave academe or allocate creative energies to outside endeavors. This is a tragedy. Intellectual institutions, in order to remain at the leading edge of modern society, must encourage their entrepreneurs. They are the means by which organizations maintain vitality and energy; they are the ones who design new frameworks and build new structures. They are the future. How can universities attract entrepreneurs without the corporate opportunities for profit sharing and stock options? It must be remembered that true entrepreneurs are motivated more by accomplishment than by remuneration (though the latter quantifies the former in the business world). Therefore, universities and not-for-profit institutions should foster creative initiative; they should allow their most talented personnel the opportunity to develop, for example, new institutes of interdisciplinary studies or to pioneer intersector interaction—even if the activity bucks traditional boundaries of authority. Corporations are beginning to understand that they need entrepreneurs. Universities and not-for-profits must come to the same realization.

Running Intellectual Institutions

The chief executive officer of an intellectual institution is a special person. He or she must earn the respect of the academic or research staff. The CEO should be able to converse fluently—virtually at the state-of-the-art of current thinking (at least qualitatively)—with each of the content areas in his or her purview. He or she must be able to make independent judgment as to the long-term implications of the information being generated and should have the self-reliant capacity to devise innovative structures and marketing concepts in order to optimize development. Similarly, to generate comparative strategic advantage, the CEO must have exceedingly broad intellectual reach and be able to sense interdisciplinary and cross-sector relationships before they reach the professional publications and well before they hit the mass media. Yet in order to make long-range decisions regarding organizational priorities and product position, the CEO must be able to distance him or herself from current paradigms and from common ways of thinking. What will the environment require in 10 to 15 years, and how can he or she prepare the organization to provide it? That's the strategic trick.

The management of knowledge organizations is a fascinating subject. Optimizing intellectual resources is vital, and increasing recognition is being given to executive leadership. Directing creativity and innovation is no textbook task. Great feeling and empathy—not sympathy or apathy—are required. One must have a special sense for the priorities of an academic, the concerns of a scientist, the intensity of an inventor, the rage of an artist. Managing mental types demands content knowledge and process sensitivity. People who produce original output have little concern for anything else, not managerial issues, not organizational problems. Their work is their world, and upon it alone does the sun rise and set. Creativity is impossible to coerce. It must be coaxed, stroked, massaged, shaped. The leader of an intellectual institution must get his or her people to *internalize* whatever they do or their tasks just won't get done. Though management is becoming a science, it will never cease to be an art.

Probably the greatest challenge we face in merging the art with the science is having people who are most effective in an environment in which their skills are appreciated and their weaknesses complemented. The requirements for new private and public sector leaders can be met only if they depend on each other's expertise to reach maximum managerial expertise. What's troublesome is that when the job market gets tight, those who hire entry-level professionals look for technical skills, even though what is required to move up the management ladder is a broader human and political orientation. We should recruit leadership skill and creative potential.

There is a distinction between management and leadership. Management is much more than nuts-and-bolts administrative operations, and leadership is even less tangible. A first-rate leader can hire excellent managers, but a first-rate manager has difficulty keeping high-quality leaders. At the top of any organization, the primary responsibility is to motivate and improve people.

As corporations become more information oriented and universities become more business oriented, there emerges a novel class of human organization: intellectual institutions. As premier knowledge organizations, the new category demands new criteria for leadership. We need executives with insight and guts, the former to discern what to do, the latter to determine how to do it. CEOs of intellectual institutions must be versed in the content of their charge, visionary in forecasting external opportunities and threats, and inventive in formulating strategic response; yet they must also be tough minded enough to assess internal strengths and weaknesses, establish unpopular priorities, unify their diverse constituencies, and lead the organization to implement coherent policies. Society calls our best and brightest. If ever America needed "the right stuff," it's for the creative management of knowledge organizations and intellectual institutions.

63

The Creative Management of Intellectual Institutions

William F. Miller

President and Chief Executive Officer, SRI
International

Teddy Roosevelt once said, "If you want to play a role in history, place yourself in the path of destiny." Intellectual institutions can play an important—even decisive—role at this critical time. But to do so they must first identify the path of destiny. To begin, we define "intellectual institutions" as organizations in which knowledge is the dominant and characteristic output: schools, universities, research institutes, consulting organizations, high-technology companies, and certain government agencies at the state and federal levels. I use this narrow definition not in an elitist sense but rather to focus on certain managerial issues, some of which—but not all—apply to any organizational endeavor.

I suggest that there are four factors that determine the success of effectiveness of knowledge organizations in general and intellectual institutions in particular: (1) a clear understanding of the environment in which the organization operates—"the path of destiny"; (2) a clear understanding of the organization itself—not merely its intellect but its

heart and soul; (3) a shared vision that fits well with the macroenvironment ("the destiny") and appeals to deepest values of the organization
("the soul"); (4) the will to act. Understanding, vision, and two-way
communication are all necessary conditions, but they are not sufficient.
The will of the leaders to act is the catalyst. They must communicate
such commitment to the entire organization. The sign on Harry
Truman's desk—"the buck stops here"—is a timeless phrase.

Trends in the Macroenvironment

"The path of destiny" is, in essence, the macroenvironment. It is
characterized by (1) extraordinary technological change, (2) pervasive
value changes, and (3) a new global economy. Leaders need to understand these three important changes in a profound way.

Technology Revolution

This is the outgrowth of extensive investments in basic and applied
research following World War II, particularly following Sputnik (1957).
Those investments in science are bearing fruit, yielding new technologies now ripe for commercialization. Today, even more investments are
being made in scientific research and they will generate new technologies at an ever-increasing rate. Furthermore, almost every nation in the
world has learned that lesson well and is increasing its R&D. Technology is clearly one of the basic driving forces of the macroenvironment.
Joseph Schumpeter coined the phrase "creative destruction," which he
described as a process that "incessantly revolutionizes the economic
structure from within, incessantly destroying the old one, incessantly
creating a new one." A key point about the new technologies is that
their major impacts have come through qualitative changes such as the
speed and carrying capacity of aircraft, the switching capacity of
telephone systems, the data processing power of computers, the greater
strength and lighter weight of new materials. The result is step-function
improvements in products and services, increasing the productive
capacity of industry and, therefore, making the economic pie larger.
New technology is not, in Lester Thurow's phrase, a "zero sum" game.
　　Wassily Leontief, the Nobel prize winning economist, said, "Past
experience has shown that society and the economy, even moral
standards, adapt to technology, not vice versa." This is an important
lesson. It may be irritating; it is to me, who started life as a humanist. We
sometimes feel locked in the grip of technology. But the real leaders are

those who adapt and utilize the new technologies, who make science serve their purposes. The good news is that the new technologies are decentralizing, disintermediating, and liberating.

Changing Values

American society and, for that matter, the societies of most developed nations, are undergoing profound changes in basic values. Shifts in societal values today are as pronounced and dramatic as those from the Middle Ages to the Renaissance. The significance of that change has been described neatly by Lewis Mumford, who pointed out that the seven deadly sins of the Middle Ages—pride, rage, greed, envy, lust, gluttony, and sloth—became virtues during the Renaissance. (That is, all but one: sloth never became a virtue.) These new virtues powered the later industrial revolution, engendering the desire to do things, achieve things, acquire things, even show off. All those values are part of the aggressive, competitive, materialistic value systems.

Today, I see more attractive values evolving. There is an increase of inner-directed people who are more interested in personal development, more concerned with societal issues, but who nonetheless have a strong work ethic. They derive high satisfaction from their employment; indeed, their work ethic is so strong that job satisfaction becomes a major value, even more important than sheer financial reward. Perhaps the greatest need in our new hierarchy of values is personal productivity—to do something worthwhile, to make a difference. The new technologies and these new values are mutually reinforcing. In a recent SRI annual report, my message was recruitment. I wrote: "We seek people who want to make a difference. We are building an organization that will make a difference on a global scale. We commit ourselves to create a corporate culture which will attract and nurture those individuals who can and want to make a difference."

Global Economy

After World War II, the United States became the dominant force, producing more than 50 percent of the world's goods and services. That dominance ended in the 1970s. Today we produce about 25 percent, still a major position. We are big enough to influence the world economy but not big enough to dominate it. That changes the game. Foreign trade has become an increasingly important part of the U.S. economy. Imports and exports represent twice as large a proportion of our GNP as in 1970. The implications are far reaching. Our attitudes toward the design of products, the structure of industrial companies, the process of international finance—all must change.

A dramatic, even dismaying change is that the United States has lost world market share in seven of ten major high-technology sectors, including electrical equipment, instruments, drugs, synthetic materials, and industrial chemicals. The United States is faced with the reality of a new global economy that forces both business and government to respond in new ways. Meeting the challenge of fierce worldwide competition will require both value and social changes. We must adopt the new technologies, and we must make changes in our basic institutions of business, government, and education. Global competition, then, is the force impelling us to speed the commercialization of new technologies. Most major companies are now conducting worldwide searches for such products and processes. Most encouraging is the decline of the "not invented here" syndrome. Formerly many American companies developed only those technologies that were emerging from their own laboratories. Now we see a more eclectic attitude. Eclecticism, incidentally, is an important reflection of the health and dynamism of a company or country. In economic history, the most dynamic period in the life of an individual company or country has coincided with a willingness to pick and choose externally. When a company or a country only looks within, it becomes less dynamic. Today, no company can afford to look only within for new technologies.

Understanding the Soul of an Organization

SRI is made up of a diverse group of highly skilled knowledge workers. These are among the most individualistic people in the world, and they are often endowed with well-developed egos. The leadership at SRI has to respond to their need for individualism, to their desire to make a difference, to their goal of achieving high personal productivity.

Integration

At the same time, however, our research at SRI into values and lifestyles indicates a growing desire for more integration in personal, business, and social life to balance the increasing fragmentation in society. Almost every SRI employee wants to be part of something bigger than himself or herself. Personal productivity without broader contribution does not have sufficient meaning. This suggests that we need leaders who can encourage individualism and, at the same time, create a vision that can be shared. It is no small task to integrate highly productive, inner-directed individuals with the more traditional "belonger" types, getting such diverse groups to buy into the same organizational goals.

Values

Of course, the leaders of an organization can, to a degree, shape the values of the staff. But goals and actions must be articulated in terms of employees' basic or core values, which cannot easily be changed or manipulated. For example, at SRI we need to become more competitive, to increase our profitability, and to grow. These economic goals of our organization are acceptable to most of our staff but only marginally so. Many employees might think, "That's top management's problem; I've got my own problems to solve." Might that be an appropriate response since we are an organization of intellectual entrepreneurs? No. The most deeply held value among SRI employees is to "make a difference"—to do something far reaching, worthwhile, and mentally exciting. Senior management's task is to articulate the connection between the economic goals of competitiveness, profitability, and growth on the one hand and our professionals' desire to make a difference, to experience intellectual excitement, and to work on the leading edge of science, technology, management consulting, and public policy on the other hand. We must explain that the first hand feeds the second, not the other way around. This is not manipulation but the stony truth. What use is there in being intellectually exciting if it leads to Chapter 11? "Show me a bankrupt organization that is intellectually exciting," I frequently exhort our staff. "Show me a competitive, profitable, growing organization, and I'll show you a lot of excited intellectuals." To be specific, we developed a simple model of our business, expressing the relationship between our performance on the bottom line and our ability to invest in new programs, new equipment, and new facilities. Such investment supports the vitality and professionalism of our staff. I said, "The model shows that if we double our bottom line, you will have x million dollars to invest in your new ideas." In the real world, the bottom line and new ideas are directly connected.

Knowledge

It has become fashionable to describe the contemporary macroenvironment as "the information era" (as opposed to the previous industrial era) and to view information as the key strategic resource, replacing land, capital, and labor (the strategic resources of the industrial era). These are useful concepts if not taken too literally. However we also need to probe deeper and ask: Who produces this new strategic resource? Who uses it? The answer to both questions is that people do. People produce the new information, and people use it to make the economy into a positive-sum game. The fact is that three-quarters of the U.S. workforce is now employed in information-handling jobs, and this proportion will increase. I argue that the ultimate strategic resource is not just information but the human resource that creates it and uses it. More and more of our endeavors are becoming information or knowledge intensive. We are increasingly dependent on skills of knowledge workers. In a democratic society, an organization can own land, capital, and equipment, but it cannot own the human resource. This is an important difference underlying the way in which we must manage in the information era. A knowledge worker, if mismanaged, can always walk out of the door and find another challenging job, perhaps with a competitor. That is why it is so important to understand the soul of the organization and to accommodate the deepest values and needs of its knowledge workers who are the ultimate strategic resource of an intellectual institution.

The Shared Vision

Internal surveys of SRI employees indicate that nearly three-quarters are inner directed. One of the most important characteristics of such people is entrepreneurship in the broadest sense. I define entrepreneurship as creativity, willingness to take a risk, and expectation of recognition or reward for that creativity and risk taking. Such entrepreneurship is the engine that drives the ship in an intellectual organization. Leadership is the hand upon the tiller. The challenge for leaders is to channel creativity and risk taking into directions that resonate with the strategic goals of the organization. Undirected creativity and risk taking lead to chaos and selfish manipulation. Jimmy Treybig, CEO of Tandem Corporation, has described the challenge as "directed creativity." I agree: Creativity requires direction; otherwise the organization will be deluged with whims or ideas that have no bearing upon the organizational strategy and mission.

A shared vision is vital for a knowledge organization. It involves each employee knowing about the organization, its goals and aspirations, and the risks and benefits of a particular idea. Leaders need to create a shared understanding of what the organization is trying to achieve by: (1) both a bottom-up process of encouraging ideas and a top-down process of peer review, (2) allocation of resources to back up promising ideas, and (3) a shared commitment to progress with plans and milestones (specific performance requirements over time).

Successful leaders must also find the correct balance between intuition and analysis. Too much analysis builds bureaucracy and slows action whereas too little spawns whimsy and caprice, decision making that is not based on sound, well-thought-out principles. In encountering new ideas, leaders need open minds but not empty heads. This is no easy task. Finding the right balance among individualism, consensus building, and direction is not a matter of the "scientific management" of the industrial era. Leaders must recognize that management in the information era is more a subjective art than an objective science. The job of leaders is to sense when the time for an idea has come—to grasp it, shape it, give it reality. Leadership is all-important, but leaders cannot implement a strategy without the support of "the governed." Leaders cannot fabricate directions out of whole cloth. The directions have to relate to the basic beliefs or perceived needs of the people being led.

As leader of an intellectual organization, I realize that the CEO has to set the tone and lead by example. But I do not buy the "man on the white horse" model. We depend not on a single leader but on a network of leaders. We need to decentralize leadership in the information era within the context of a shared vision. A better analogy for the CEO is the modern football coach with a strong staff, assistants, field captains, and an array of stars. But these stars have to be part of a cohesive team. A good team needs outstanding performers, but to succeed fully, outstanding performers need to work together. My definition of a leader is one who can capture and concentrate the rays of light—like a lens—upon a point in space and time to make something happen when it is ready to happen. In other words, the leader captures a shared vision that all people can see because all know that it is right and needs to happen. This is both a bottom-up and a top-down process, and it involves much talk. Ideas and values bubble up from the bottom, but the leader (and peers) selects and backs those consonant with strategic goals. He or she then articulates what Rousseau called the "general will" of the organization. A positive resonance among the general will, the macroenvironment, and the shared vision is essential. We at SRI structure these dialogues through a systematic process of settling and announcing agendas, indicating processes and forums for discussion, and publishing implementation actions after decision are made.

The Will to Act

In the industrial era, some successful corporate leaders ruled by power, manipulation, and fear. This was possible because the theme of that time was to triumph over the condition of scarcity or need. The challenge was to produce enough goods and services to satisfy the basic requirements for food, shelter, and enough income to survive and perhaps prosper. The industrial era was an economy of scale. It was characterized by the accumulation of ever-larger amounts of capital to finance ever-larger factories, transportation, and communication systems and ever-larger governmental and social institutions. Bigger was better in almost every sector of society. The industrial era was one of centralization, top-down command and control, bureaucratization, standardization, and mass production. Tasks on the production line were specialized, and people served the machine that created the wealth. And people were grateful to have a job.

I believe that we have now left the economy of scarcity and scale and are entering the economy of choice. Technology has made it possible to serve the needs of an increasingly diverse set of values and lifestyles among consumers and employees. Industrial-era technologies succeeded in creating an affluent society. Today, however, organizational success stories will depend less on massive concentrations of capital, technology, and human resources on a single product in a stable market than on combinations of different skills, technologies, and organizational arrangements serving highly segmented markets or needs. Narrowcasting of demand is the new world.

Entrepreneurs are a key factor in the economy's ability to serve such diverse new markets. We are in an entrepreneurial revolution. The figures are awesome. Back in 1950, the United States created 93,000 new companies. In the last 5 years the number of new incorporations have averaged more than 600,000 annually. In other words, the economy of choice has created more than 3 million new companies in the past 5 years. And nearly half are headed by women. Female entrepreneurs and CEOs—what a remarkable barometer of social change! The entrepreneurial revolution extends into large organizations, both in private and public sectors. These are called "intrapreneurs"; they are the ones who make a real difference to their organizations.

Entrepreneurs—or intrapreneurs—are the key resource in an intellectual organization. Bright, creative people are essential, but entrepreneurs are needed to make things happen. They are the ones who recognize those ideas whose time has come and who have the courage to take risks and transform ideas into business realities. It is difficult to manage such people. In fact, the phrase "managing entrepreneurs" is almost an oxymoron—a self-contradicting phrase. We cannot manage them in the conventional sense; they do not respond to the carrots and sticks of the industrial era. We can and must lead them, however. But we cannot lead unless we build respect and credibility. And that depends on what I call the "integrity of our people decisions." Leaders must be ready to move people into different positions in which they can be productive. We at SRI devote much time and energy building a corporate culture that views professionals and managers as equals, as different sides of the same coin. We make professionals into managers and managers into professionals without these moves being regarded as evidence of failure in any sense.

Developing managers in knowledge organizations is difficult; in intellectual institutions, it is particularly challenging. Professionals are not hired for their managerial skills; they are hired for their particular knowledge and expertise. They are good with ideas, but their professional development does nothing to develop people skills. Moreover, their most deeply held values stress personal productivity—new ideas, creative content generation, and the like. People management and the systematic part of professional management are not "fun" compared to the creative or problem-solving side. Therefore, it takes dedication and perseverance on the part of senior managers in an intellectual organization to identify and develop new management talent. Mentoring is important to help new managers learn how to be leaders and how to turn creative talent into creative management. First instincts are to do a task oneself rather than teach subordinates to do it. Learning to help others achieve and to develop pride in the accomplishments of others is an acquired talent that does not come easily to knowledge professionals. With good mentoring some, but not all, learn to enjoy the reflected glory of their group's accomplishments just as an athletic coach basks in the performance of a great team or a maestro in a great orchestra.

Professionals in knowledge organizations—especially intellectual institutions—tend to associate in disciplines or subject areas. No matter how the organization is structured it is important to establish collateral, issue-oriented task groups or projects that cut across disciplines or subject lines. Active participation by senior management provides opportunity to interact with the professional staff. Effective leadership of intellectual institutions means engaging the minds of its knowledge workers. This does not mean that management abdicates its responsibilities or its leadership to the staff. Quite the contrary, management sets up the task groups, calls the meetings, sets the agendas, and reviews the recommendations. But in the process management gets valuable advice and "buy in" by the staff. Much has been said about management by "walking around." There are many ways of walking around. Just dropping in on a group may not be as effective as working together on a project, such as a new marketing plan, investment program, or personnel policy. Another way to walk around is to have several forums for discussion or advice. These forums provide mechanisms for two-way communication as well as cross-disciplinary interaction. It is a way to relax the rigidity of hierarchical structures.

It is much easier to maintain stability than to effect change. Changing intellectual organizations is inherently difficult. Any new idea is likely to be rejected on first suggestion, especially if it comes from a senior executive. Persistence is critical. Often the best course is to get the idea before the organization: Put the new policy into effect even though not in perfect form, and then ask the staff to participate in improving the policy as experience with it develops.

Decisions affecting careers are never easy, especially when the decisions involve people who are talented and who have made real contributions to the organization. As leaders, we must recognize that some individuals cannot adjust to a change in corporate direction or a new challenge requiring different skills or management styles. We try to reassign such individuals within our own organization and, if we cannot, we try to help them develop new careers elsewhere. When we have to make "the tough decision" about an individual, we try to do so in a forthright way, with compassion and guidance.

I do not believe that "the leader"—the CEO—is the only one who must have and display the will to act. Because we are dealing with knowledge workers and new technologies that decentralize decision making, we should create the will to act throughout all levels of the organization. The willingness to make the difficult but sensitive decisions about people must pervade the organization; they must not be "kicked upstairs." The buck must stop at the desk of every manager at every level.

I believe that the organization of the future will resemble a network—a decentralized information system with nodes and connective channels—more than a hierarchy. The successful leader of the future will understand this change of perspective in a profound way. In this sense intellectual institutions of today are forerunners of most organizations of tomorrow.

64

Creativity and Innovation for Science-Based Businesses

Robert Lawrence Kuhn

Investment Banker, Senior Research Fellow,
IC² Institute, University of Texas at Austin, and
Adjunct Professor, Graduate School of Business
Administration, New York University

Science-based businesses are economic transformers of discovery; they are the modern mechanism for converting sophisticated new ideas into interesting new products. Human curiosity and desire drive the discovery, and human need and want build the business. Technology companies enrich civilization; they are the fulcrum of human progress.

Nature of Contemporary Science

Science is both process and content, the technique of discovery as well as the thing discovered. The scientific method is our core paradigm; it is the shortest distance and surest route to factual truth, the line of thinking most logical and reproducible. The scientific method is perhaps our finest conceptual tool: Unbiased data collection, creative hypothesis generation (induction), rigorous analytical reasoning (deduction), comprehensive hypothesis testing, and independent repetition and confirmation—all are necessary irrespective of content area, whether "science" in the traditional sense or any other facet of human awareness. Science teaches logic, how to use it, when to overrule it. It catalyzes enthusiasm for investigation and analysis; it teaches respect for proper rationale and confirmed proof; it offers the thrill of exploring the unknown, of using insight, of making discovery, of touching truth. Science replaces rote by rigor and repetition by reasoning. Science is no longer the exclusive domain of the elite; it is the language of all.

In the twenty-first century information will be the new medium of exchange. (Money, that archaic commodity, will be bytes in computer memories and numbers on computer screens.) International leadership will be framed in terms of cerebral skill not military prowess. A nation's prestige will be built by its intellectual endowment, not the number and sizes of its bombs and rockets. Scientists from all disciplines will contribute, from philosophy and astronomy to mathematics and music; new information will be prized and virtually all fields of knowledge will generate direct economic benefit.

A word, here, for *pure* science. Basic research is the foundation of science, the platform for progress, the precursor of revolution. One cannot know in advance where seminal breakthroughs will come and what application technologies may have. Instinct and intuition, not program and project, are the requisite sources of energy. Basic research is a stimulant for creativity; it is, in all fields, an absolute necessity.

Sensitivity to scientists as well as appreciation of science is vital for optimizing output. Scientists, by personality, are not easily coerced, not easily directed. Indeed, such is their strength. Scientists must be free to wander and explore, to confront blind alleys and to shatter tradition. Companies must establish incentive systems to encourage scientists, giving them maximum motivation to imagine and construct. A firm must nurture and develop its premier asset.

Evaluating Science-Based Companies

Forget high tone in this section. Our appeal focuses on your back pocket, the one with the wallet in it. How do you assess economic "value" in science and technology companies? Can one fathom what the "hot ones" are really worth and why? It's about firms that fly through the roof, then fall to the floor. It's about initial public offerings generating more market capitalization in 1 day than billion-dollar corporations could in 50 years. Science-sounding names add spice to self-image and multiples to stock prices and, all too often, little else.

The basic idea is simple: Business is business, and don't be swayed by the science. The game is the same and the rules must be followed. Products must be needed by customers; they must be manufactured properly, distributed efficiently, serviced easily, sold profitably (after all costs), and renewed or replaced regularly. Just because the product is founded on technology doesn't change the fundamentals. The primary question is: What really is the business? Not the external form, but the internal substance.

Take a new drug. There are various businesses here, all different. (Though often embedded within the same company, we separate out the different businesses for ease of analysis.) The company developing the drug and owning the patent is the real pioneer, investing hard years and big bucks in the laboratory, in preclinical animal tests, and finally in clinical human trials. This company is surely the riskiest player, and potentially, though by no means surely, the most profitable. Owning the patent could generate extremely high profits through extremely high margins (manufacturing costs are usually minimal). Getting approval from the Federal Drug Administration, however, is arduous and costly. It can take $50 million to create a new molecule and bring it through all the regulatory procedures up to commercial introduction—with real risks of costly delay or outright failure at each stage. Even if this pioneer brings out the new drug, financial success is not guaranteed. The market can be minimal; other drugs may do similar things; newer drugs may cause early obsolescence; unexpected side effects may pop up— there is no end to potential problems. Yet the bottom line is clear: Major pharmaceutical firms generate some of the largest returns of industrial companies.

The company manufacturing the drug is no different than a food or chemical producer, and margins are reasonable at best. If the company has a long-term contract with the patent holder, there is some value. If not, the "exciting drug" means little. The company distributing the drug is a distributor plain and simple, and the procedures for handling technology products are generally no different from those for handling more mundane products such as paper or tools. Margins are low; inventories absorb high carrying costs; customer service is critical. The urgent care center dispensing the drug is different still. It is a service business delivering distributed health care outside traditional channels. Targeting people who won't wait in hospitals, these centers have physicians available to treat patients immediately. The business, here, is all convenience, service, and quality of care. They have no loyalty to any brands or products and can switch whenever technology or cost so dictates. Their reputation is based on experience and trust, and there are no contracts or patents to assure continuity.

Why do technology companies command such high multiples in public markets? Price/earnings (P/E) ratios should reflect anticipated growth in earnings, discounted to give a present value capitalization estimate—nothing more. The faster the growth rate is expected to compound, the higher the P/E is likely to be. Often with science companies, however, market perceptions are distorted; whether by glamor, publicity, or fad, the results are disruptive. (Try some calculations with stratospheric P/Es. In order to maintain such luxurious multiples, company products, whatever they are, would have to be bought by everyone on earth in a couple of decades and by everyone in the universe in the next century.)

Such unrealistic hype does disservice to fine companies. When stocks are rising, there is a constant surge of energy. Expectations are created, unfortunately, that can never be fulfilled; when prices fall, both investors and employees become disillusioned, some permanently. It doesn't matter that the stock may still be double what it was 3 years before, the issue is *relative* movement and *relative* price. If the stock is higher today than it was yesterday, you feel good; if it's lower, you feel bad.

Importance of the Strategic Framework

Per share data, based on historical growth, are incomplete indicators of company prospects—especially in industries shocked by frequent discontinuities in technology and market. Only a *strategic* framework can deal with uncertainty.

Strategy links mission and goals above with operations and functions below. It is the mechanism for arraying alternative choices and for driving the resource allocation process. Strategy seeks competitive advantage, business segments in which the firm has or can develop the strongest market position compared to all other firms. Competitive advantage capitalizes on the distinctive competencies of the company, those fundamental areas—whether products, technology, distribution, brand name, customer loyalty, finance, etc.—in which it excels or can excel relative to competitors.

The formulation of corporate strategy maps a firm's strengths and weaknesses onto industry opportunities and threats in order to formulate alternative policies; these various options are then evaluated for probable outcomes relative to assumed risk, and the best are chosen for implementation. The strategic framework, of course, is exceedinglyvaluable for managing all kinds of companies, especially those that compete in volatile product-market industries. The faster the turnover of product generations, the more vital the planning imperative. When the strategic analysis is complete, however uncertain, management can make critical choices for corporate direction. Investors, as well, can make assumptions about growth and projections about profits (though with less information). Only then, after adding insight to analysis, can they tag a proper multiple and suggest reasonable worth. (But who does all this when your cabdriver has a hot tip!)

Commercializing Defense-Related Technology

The first step on the moon was made in a boot fabricated from silicon rubber, the same new material now used on office buildings for structural glazing. This example is one of thousands in which a technology, product, or process, originally designed for military or aerospace purposes, has made significant impact in the commercial marketplace (other examples are microelectronics, the Boeing 707, and composite materials). When tens of billions of dollars are allocated annually in government-sponsored R&D, the civilian potential for economic leverage is enormous. What we are dealing with is no less than America's chief asset in the world battle for competitive advantage and fertile ground for investigation by many companies.

"Commercialization" is defined as the process by which the outputs of defense-related R&D become the inputs for civilian-related products and services and are thus transformed into economically viable elements of the marketplace. The benefits to society are obvious: Commercial industry can gain substantial advantage from the technological advances (and breakthroughs) of military R&D programs. Critical issues include: policy considerations such as the declassification of data, foreign access to technology and export control, and proprietary interests of contractors; the technology transfer process itself; procedures to maximize economic returns and minimize national security risks; the appropriate role of federal and state government in catalyzing the process; the infrastructure required for private sector commercialization of public sector science; and developing the new partnership among industrial companies, academic institutions, and federal agencies in producing economic value from state-of-the-art technology. The United States should broaden its concept of "national security" to "*comprehensive* national security," which would encompass economic strength and independence as well as military power and preparedness.

Commercialization will not happen by itself; indeed some of the obvious approaches—such as large defense contractors forming civilian divisions to market spin-off technology—have not been successful. Several principles can facilitate effective commercialization:

1. Technology transfer will most often not be of "things" but of know-how, the demonstration of feasibility, the process of planning, and the mechanism of manufacturing. The concept is more attitudinal than tangible, more principle than product. Manufacturing technology, for example, should be encouraged in cooperation between industry and government.

2. The commercialization process demands particular expertise not necessarily transferable directly within the same organization. It is not required that a defense-oriented firm bring its own technology to the commercial marketplace. Corporate cultures are different; market sense and feel are often unfamiliar to military contractors, and market competition may not be a corporate experience—and it may be inefficient for some firms to develop such sense, feel, and experience. It's a similar story in manufacturing; military contractors are high-cost producers since military specifications stress product reliability substantially more than cost efficiency (compared with commercial counterparts). Alternative approaches should make frequent use of technology licensing and the subcontracting of marketing and manufacturing. Partnerships between large defense contractors and small-to-medium-sized market specialists could be mutually beneficial.

3. Mechanisms must be developed to maximize individual entrepreneurial motivation within government and industrial defense establishments. Incentive generation is vital. Inventors in all sectors—industry, government, university—must receive full rights to their creations; anything less will constrict the process and retard the economy. Defense scientists and engineers should be educated as to spin-off potential.

Ideas for Running Science-Based Companies

Science-based businesses are a new organizational form, now growing to prominence (even dominance) in the economy. These firms, in a sense, are quite schizophrenic, part science and part business, and must be managed with appreciation for both personalities. Following are some thoughts for managing science and technology companies. They are not comprehensive, organized, or terribly original; they are just my ideas designed to trigger your ideas.

1. Never forget that science businesses are still businesses and are constrained by financial statements, organizational structure, policies, and procedures. Do not neglect mundane matters such as inventory control and receivable collections.

2. Make extensive use of sensitivity analysis and scenario planning; companies with highly volatile products and markets must mitigate surprise, whether up or down. "What if" simulations are serious stuff. What happens (to finance, production, marketing, etc.) if the new product exceeds expectations by 50, 100, 200 percent; if the new product stagnates, bombs or dies; if . . . ?

3. Know the speed of new product introductions; track time between generations. The game is leapfrog; so you had better know the rules. Worry that your upcoming product is about to be trampled by competitors' products.

4. Give yourself a chance to be lucky. Always try some leapfrogging R&D; it will at least keep you aware of what competitors might do, and you just could connect.

5. Never wander from competitive advantage. Stress technological strengths. Build new products on current competencies. Have extremely high thresholds for invading new areas. The "grass is greener" syndrome has derailed many science-based companies.

6. Watch substitutability. Many technology products, while dominating their own market segments, fall victim to a new class of product satisfying the same need in a different way.

7. Be driven by market demands and customer needs. It's frighteningly easy to be suckered into supporting a fascinating technology that has no hope of ever building a commercial market.

8. Never assume that technology alone, no matter how great, will sell products. The world beats a path to very few doors, even those with better mousetraps. (What if there are no mice . . . or too many cats!)

9. Always know how new products will be marketed and distributed. It is a mistake to spend heavily in R&D without simulating *in advance* the complete cycle of marketing and distribution. Count-

less superb products have collapsed because of simple gaps in the chain.

10. Never go to market before you are fully ready. Reputations for poor performance, mediocre quality, or shoddy workmanship are awarded with frightful rapidity by an unforgiving market. Poor quality is a stubborn stigma that is exceptionally difficult to wipe off.

11. Balance R&D between focus and freedom. Maintain clear economic goals for programs and projects, yet encourage scientists to explore areas of personal interest.

12. Examine potential applications of all new technologies, products, and processes across diverse markets. Be venturesome in exploration (on paper): High economic value is often found far from areas of original intent.

13. Isolate and focus on key distinctive competencies in R&D, whether technology or markets, products or processes. Areas of clear competitive advantage must be the base; then expand outward from this sure source.

14. Strive for efficient, targeted R&D with insights and clever heuristics; when in areas of comparative competencies, however, do not fear a "brute force" approach to R&D.

15. Consider combining several technologies but only when the company has competitive advantage in at least one of them.

16. Use portfolio theory in the resource allocation process for diverse and competitive R&D projects. High risk must be accompanied by high return. Obvious, right? Recognize, however, that in high-tech R&D the "high risk" is far easier to assess than the "high return," especially for market acceptance. Skew the risk-return ratio, therefore, and demand even greater potential returns for uncertain projects.

17. Assess returns on R&D investments carefully. ROI is more difficult to calculate in science-based companies considering the broad range of possibilities—total market rejection on the downside, uncertain obsolescence in the middle, and expanding new product lines on the upside.

18. Never underestimate the importance of customer support—especially service and training. The more complex the product or process, the more important the support. Superior service and/or training can surmount competitive weakness in price and/or per-

formance. It can surely erect high entry barriers for potential competitors.

19. Establish brand-name identification. Industrial technology products are not consumer-package goods, but some of the same human tendencies apply to both. It's always easier for a purchasing agent to justify a brand-name decision. (If the choice was wrong, at least there is a good excuse.)

20. Influence the diffusion process for new products or technologies. Focus initial marketing efforts on industry or professional leaders. Be more concerned with getting the right initial users than the right initial prices.

21. Study price positioning. A new product may justify a premium price only if it offers incremental features, service, or value. (Yet, conversely, a premium price may support the pitch of technological breakthrough.) Price is relative to competitive methods of satisfying customer need, irrespective of technology.

22. Try to have a chief executive fully conversant with products and technology. The attitude of the boss permeates the organization and can, to a surprising degree, bring out the best in creative personnel.

23. Monitor costs carefully. It is easy to be blindsided by excessive costs and get priced out of the market by adding "good things" to products. Balance quality and cost, features and cost, technology and cost. Bells and whistles are good only if customers pay for them willingly.

24. Never be smug. Always look over your shoulder. Even when dominating a market segment with technology and profits, watch out. The better your product or process, the greater the danger or threat. Don't gloat over large margins—worry about protecting them! Many hungry competitors are observing your success; they are envious and jealous and eyeing your markets. So sleep lightly.

25. Track personnel productivity and turnover. Consider human resource accounting techniques to ascertain real costs of R&D employees. Valuations are often shockingly high so that even healthy raises become highly leveraged by the savings generated by even a small decrease in turnover.

26. Motivate R&D personnel by giving "ownership" of projects, psychological more than financial. Tie personal ego to upside success not downside failure.

27. Establish separate career tracks for R&D types who should not (or will not) go into management; provide equal salary and status.

28. Do not establish, even inadvertently, scientists as superior corporate citizens; do not relegate marketing, manufacturing, and financial types to second class. A for-profit business, remember, is not a not-for-profit research institute.

29. Always consider new structural relationships to maximize strengths and minimize weaknesses. Joint venture partners can be important for science-based companies, especially smaller ones. Yet controlling one's own destiny is hard to discard.

30. Promote espirit de corps. The business of science is a team effort.

Bibliography

Konecci, Eugene and Robert Lawrence Kuhn: *Technology Venturing: American Innovation and Risk Taking,* Praeger, New York, 1985.
Kuhn, Robert Lawrence: *Commercializing Defense-Related Technology,* Praeger, New York, 1984.

65

Innovative Science and Traditional Industry: New Visions in Agritechnology

David G. Eller

*Chairman and CEO, Granada Corporation and
Chairman of the Board of Regents, Texas A&M
University*

Agritechnology is a broad descriptor of the array of emerging products and processes applicable to food and fiber production. It is an example of the creative and innovative impact of high technology on traditional industry.

New Technologies

Biotechnology

Genetic engineering (recombinant DNA techniques) is one of the major scientific revolutions of this century. In agriculture, as in medicine, basic research can have profound practical benefits. Research at the Texas A&M University System exemplifies what will be emerging in agricultural biotechnology:

1. *Plant water relationships.* Develop drought-tolerant plants that can produce the same yields with 30 percent less water and plants that can use a brackish water.

2. *Plant productivity.* Manipulate plant metabolism; alter chemical composition of plant products; improve processing quality, and produce plants resistant to stress or herbicides.

3. *Plant disease resistance.* Develop inherent resistance to plant disease and insects. Reduce cost of production and enhance quality of environment through use of fewer chemical pesticides.

4. *Nutritional quality of plants.* Correct nutrient deficiency or prevent loss of nutrients during storage as well as eliminate or modify undesirable nutritional properties of plants, such as saturated fatty acid composition.

5. *Biological control of insects.* Produce highly specific organisms that adversely affect insect pests that attack crops and livestock. These organisms will be used in lieu of chemical pesticides.

6. *Biologically active materials.* Produce large quantities of biologically active materials such as hormones used in growth and reproduction, new vaccines, and diagnostic tools.

7. *Diagnostic and immunologic products.* Produce new vaccines and diagnostics that will have major impact on animal agriculture. For instance, a new vaccine for brucellosis in cattle is under development as is an improved diagnostic test to differentiate infected and vaccinated animals.

8. *Animal disease resistance.* Ultimately, the reduction of disease impact through introducing inherent resistance to disease rather than through administration of vaccines is desired. Though a more complex problem, work is underway to understand the genetics of disease resistance and to use embryo transfer to introduce recombinant DNA into livestock.

9. *Animal reproduction and development.* Augment natural breeding programs to enhance productivity in livestock. Modify animal genetics to reduce levels of saturated fat in meats while retaining palatability.

Computer Technology

The computer revolution comes at a time when agriculture, like other industries, must find new methods to cope with the information explosion. Management decisions by farmers and ranchers previously dealt with on a largely intuitive basis no longer work. The vastly larger information base as well as the need for better risk management requires new methods and capabilities. Computer-based information and decision systems for agriculture employ: (1) biological models, which portray the impact of various management decisions on crop or livestock performance, and (2) economic models, which permit evaluation of production alternatives, marketing strategies, and resource management options. Intrinsic to both kinds of models is the need for a real-time database that includes factors such as market forecasts, futures prices, weather conditions and predictions, cost of production inputs, and current federal farm policies. Current microcomputer programs provide new capability; for example, integrated pest management that allows farmers to make important choices on strategies involving crop management, biological control, scouting to determine thresholds of pest prevalence, cost of chemical control measures, and crop prices. Such methods have reduced pesticide usage in Texas cotton production by as much as 80 percent in the last 15 years. The development of artificial intelligence and expert systems for crop and livestock production will expand management capability to use current information in near real time. Exploiting computer technology for agriculture is creating a new area of research called "farming systems." Such research is targeted at putting together, in a total integrated system, the complex array of biological, economic, and management tools available to an agricultural enterprise. Farming systems ensure that individual pieces of new technology fit into the context of a total management operation.

Robotics

Substantial new precision and cost savings are being achieved by improved sensors for operations such as planting, irrigation, harvesting, etc. "Chemigation" systems, for example, introduce fertilizers, pesticides, and other chemicals into irrigation sprinklers with optimal quantity and timing. Similar systems can reduce compaction of fields from tractor operations. Tractors capable of operator-assisted or remote operation are in development. Systems that may even eliminate tractors in agricultural operations are being studied. Similarly, harvesting of horticultural crops using automated equipment to replace stoop labor is evolving, as are combines using automated guidance, header settings, and speed control. Automated devices are now available to permit electronic identification of individual livestock and to regulate the intake of concentrated feeds for individual animals. Robotics will increase efficiency of future agricultural operations, optimizing energy and minimizing waste.

Remote Sensing

Farming systems operations depend on current management information to make good decisions during the course of a crop season. Remote sensing, using either satellite imagery (e.g., Land Sat) or aerial reconnaissance, can help farmers and ranchers. Early detection of crop disease through infrared thermography is a current capability. Soil moisture measurements through remote sensing provides accurate irrigation needs. Estimates of population density of noxious plants, livestock and wildlife populations, and forage cover and status facilitate extensive ranching operations. Remote sensing estimates crop yields, improving key marketing decisions well in advance of harvesting. Information analysis, transmission, and delivery systems are needed to exploit satellite imaging for private users.

Practical Implications

How will these revolutionary technologies be best used, and what are their implications? First, agritechnology can return American agriculture to a robust and healthy industry. We must examine consumer preferences and trends and give end users what they want. For example, genetic engineering can accelerate programs to produce a lean beef product that is tender and tasty and that removes health concerns presently in the minds of many consumers. In addition, increasing demand for convenience in food preparation will stimulate development of innovative processing and preservation methods. Agritechnology will improve the safety, storage, and nutritional value of many foods and will, in fact, generate entirely new food products. New crops will be created, particularly in horticulture, through genetic engineering and somatic cell fusion.

Expansion of geographic production areas of existing crops, including cereals, may emerge. For instance, resistance to freeze damage in citrus could stabilize production, and tissue culture techniques can accelerate forestry development. Other possibilities include aquaculture production systems, remedying disease problems and seasonallimitations, and reduced dependence on agricultural chemicals, enhancing food safety as well as environmental quality.

How might a multiple set of new agritechnologies be employed in a 10- to 20-year time frame? Consider a possible beef-forage production system. Animals in such an operation would be inherently resistant to many infectious and parasitic diseases; embryo transfer techniques would disseminate desirable genetic material, including that produced through genetic engineering. Beef cattle would inherently have muscle tissue with sufficient fat to assure taste quality demanded by consumers, but the composition of that fat would minimize dietary impact on cardiovascular disease. Calves will be weaned at weights of 800 pounds. Forage will be drought tolerant, capable of producing useful nutrients for cattle at rainfalls of less than 15 inches per year. Forages will fix nitrogen, removing the expense of fertilizers; they will also be resistant to many grass pests. Yields of forage would be increased by 30 percent, and forage species would have enhanced ability to extract nutrients from the soil. Through genetically engineered enhancement of the photosynthetic process, the efficiency of forage production would be increased by 30 percent. To meet consumer preferences for a leaner beef product, cattle would be carried to heavier weights on forage and would spend much less time in feed lots. Less grain would be required to achieve the same quality of product. There would be a substantial market for grass-fed beef as quality improved and consumer preferences evolved.

Federal, state, and industrial relationships in research are undergoing great change. Industry, in particular, is making large investments in basic biological research. We need better methods for industry and academia to collaborate, to share science and resources to achieve common goals. Early involvement of business in cooperative efforts with universities speeds commercial product development and marketing and also moves new products or technology through regulatory hoops more quickly. Such partnerships should facilitate technology transfer from academic institutions to producers and consumers of food and fiber.

66

Creative Management in a Changing Environment

Meinolf Dierkes

President, Wissenschaftszentrum Berlin für Sozialforchung

Ariane Berthoin Antal

Wissenschaftszentrum Berlin für Sozialforchung

Adjusting to complex and rapid changes is a constant challenge to business corporations. Managing these changes has therefore become a task of central importance. We examine three key questions: What does environmental management involve? Why do certain firms handle this challenge more successfully than others? What constitutes a creative approach to environmental management?

The socio-political environment in which corporations function is increasingly dense and interrelated; therefore intuitive, informal mechanisms for monitoring changes and designing responses no longer suffice. It has become necessary to collect and analyze information about the environment in a systematic fashion in order to develop and implement effective policies. More than ever before, economic success now requires the integration of comprehensive and detailed information about the social, political, and ecological environment of the firm. To recognize trends, to establish priorities, and to respond to challenges, new strategic instruments are needed. Environmental management involves gathering necessary data, analyzing its consequences, and developing appropriate policies.

In the course of socio-political changes in the 1960s and 1970s, conceptions about the role and function of business in society underwent significant revisions. Fulfilling economic goals alone was no longer considered sufficient. Business had to redefine the basis of its legitimacy to include the societal component. Rising social costs of economic growth as well as value changes questioned the desirability of basing business decisions exclusively on economic criteria. Assessments of business based on short-term economic performance alone were criticized as being too narrow and, in effect, misleading. Society's reorientation also influenced management thinking and resulted in a new awareness of societal responsibilities. This implied that it would be necessary to collect information about, for example, who suffered what consequences of business activities and to decide which negative impacts should be reduced first. In sum, new management functions demand: the expansion of forecasting to include socio-political trends, the integration of such information into business planning, and the expansion of information systems to collect data systematically on the social and ecological impacts of corporate behavior. Dealing with these new functions requires innovation in management practices.

Innovative tools for environmental management were not slow in coming. Research focused on developing specialized instruments for environmental scanning, for modeling changes in the firm's social and political environment, and for integrating such information into strategic planning. Business schools taught these methods, and corporations experimented with them; examples include assigning new functions to the board or introducing new task forces at different levels of management. After these innovative tools had been developed and put in place, however, it was found that the experience of business with them in practice showed uneven performance. The innovation did not guarantee high sensitivity to environmental challenges nor success in meeting these challenges. Several factors can explain these differences in the effectiveness of using environmental management tools: first, the traditional economic and manager-specific explanations and more recently, cultural explanations.

Differences in sensitivity to environmental challenges have usually been explained by a narrowly defined concept of economic interests.

According to this view, business responds to challenges only when it perceives a close link to profits. This simple model, however, leaves basic questions unanswered: Why do some firms sense that a situation offers opportunity while others see only threat? For example, while European automobile manufacturers perceived economic burden in the demands of environmentalists for cleaner cars, Japanese manufacturers developed catalysts. Or, within a single national culture, why does one food chain invest early in producing "natural foods" while others do not recognize the market opportunity? Perhaps this kind of decision is based on different time horizons in defining profitability. But "once the notion of long-term profitability is introduced, only paucity of imagination and a short time-horizon limit one's capacity to justify expenditures with no direct, immediate business benefit" (Ackerman and Bauer). Doubtless, short-term costs of developing new technologies are often higher than lobbying costs to prevent the new technologies from being mandated. But this begs the question: Why do some companies use a more long-term perspective on profits while others see more short term?

Company-specific differences are usually related to the qualifications and characteristics of management. Some managers are more sensitive to changes in the environment. However, individual managers can neither be credited with nor blamed for the overall responsiveness of the entire company. Organizations cannot be viewed so simply. Their complexity makes it impossible for a single manager to influence the whole scope of decision making. Besides, a good manager in one context is not necessarily good in another: the myth of the manager apt for every company and function has not held up in practice. Apparently, characteristics of the individual company itself must be taken into consideration. "Standard management practices" are not universal. Neither "good managers" nor "good techniques" have had the same level of success in every situation.

Corporate Culture

In attempting to understand company-specific characteristics, researchers have taken recourse to anthropological work on groups, borrowing the concept of "culture" to explain the behavior of businesses as a specific type of "clan." Corporations, after all, like other definable groups, are units whose decisions and behavior are guided by many tacitly accepted beliefs and values developed over time. Culture is a "collective programming of the mind" that is "relatively stable over time and leads to nearly the same behavioral pattern in similar situations" (Hofstede). The concept draws attention to the importance of values and beliefs for organizational structures, procedures, and behavior. It throws light on how "shared values (what is important) and beliefs (how things work) interact with a company's people, organizational structures, and control systems to produce behavioral norms (the way we do things here)" (Uttal).

The concept of corporate culture has attracted much attention, but it remains fuzzy, difficult to define, and hard to operationalize. Its attractiveness has led to a flurry of popular publications (e.g., Peters and Waterman, Deal and Kennedy) that have indicated that cultures can be typologized as "excellent" or "strong" and that companies having such excellent cultures also excel in economic performance. Such a simplistic, cookbook view has serious drawbacks. It implies that cultures can be manipulated at will to integrate selected characteristics of "excellence" in order to ensure top economic performance—a suggestion that is untenable and impossible to implement. The usefulness of corporate culture as a concept lies more in the differentiation of a company's decision-making and implementation style, its very recognition of individuality.

The essential question for environmental management is: How does organizational culture influence a company's ability to deal with change? Culture can be seen as a filter that has inherent strengths and weaknesses affecting business' ability to respond to the entire range of environmental challenges. Understanding corporate culture can therefore help explain why a company might be sensitive or insensitive to certain types of issues and effective or ineffective in dealing with them. How can creative management shore up weaknesses and build on strengths? This task requires, first, assessing company responsiveness across the board and identifying the influence of corporate culture and, second, improving performance in all areas, assuring comprehensive and well-balanced environmental management.

The recognition of the role of corporate culture in environmental management reveals the weakness of previous approaches that did not take the inner corporate environment into account. Creative managers must therefore search for innovative tools that are designed to meet these requirements: In addition to the demands of an increasingly complex environment and the demands of new roles and responsibilities of business in society, managers find that they must also come to grips with the demands of specific corporate cultures. In order to meet these needs, modern companies need an *integrated socio-economic management system* that combines the following three key elements: a corporate socio-economic planning function; an internal and external reporting function on socio-economic performance; and a goal-oriented evaluation function for the performance of individual managers, profit centers, and the company as a whole.

Corporate Social Reporting

One tool that provides a comprehensive and systematic approach to integrating relevant social, political, and ecological data into the regular corporate information system is "corporate social reporting." Internally, this process supports management decision making; externally, it facilitates dialogue between management and its various constituencies. The "corporate social report" represents a means of institutionalizing the consideration of business-society interrelations into standard operating procedures and serves as a basis for evaluating performance.

Corporate social reporting is therefore somewhat of a misnomer for a far-reaching approach that includes planning, reporting, and evaluation. Seen from this broader perspective, the instrument appears to be particularly well-suited to meeting the demands of environmental management. For planning purposes, data are required on changes in the socio-political environment of business on the one hand and on the impact of business on the socio-political environment on the other. In addition, the various constituencies of the firm demand greater accountability, which means that they need detailed information about social, political, and ecological consequences of business behavior. The concept behind corporate social reporting is intended to satisfy both types of information demands. It is designed as an integrative management tool, linking goal-setting and planning functions to information and reporting systems, to performance appraisal, and back to the revision of goals and plans. What can be learned from the experiences of companies about the successful application of an *integrated socio-economic management system* such as the inappropriately labeled corporate social reporting? How have successful companies organized the process, and how is this instrument suited to different organizational cultures?

There are common characteristics of several advanced experiments with an integrated socio-economic management system. *First,* CEO commitment was high from the outset and maintained visibly throughout the process. *Second,* the staff responsible for the work combined members from throughout the organization with external academic consultants. Experience shows that such a diverse combination is particularly effective. The manager of the process was appointed by the CEO. The internal members of the committee assured that the process became an integral part of their traditional management functions. The inclusion of academic consultants maintained methodological quality and provided external objectivity. *Third,* the annual or biannual report, like the entire process, was goal oriented. The companies evaluated their activities in the reporting period in light of the goals they had set at the outset, thereby providing the transparency demanded by external constituencies and at the same time establishing the basis for determining the goals for the next period. The creative managers who actively sought feedback from their constituencies and involved them in the assessment of results found that they achieved greater credibility and made better progress toward satisfying the demands of the business-society relationship. In sum, the experiences of companies that have introduced such comprehensive and demanding approaches to environmental management show that: The support of an innovative CEO is crucial; the process requires team effort, including managers from different areas of the company and external consultants; the interaction between goal setting, implementation, and evaluation functions necessitates a goal-oriented reporting process.

How does an integrated socio-economic management system contribute to optimizing the culturally determined strengths and weaknesses of a company? By requiring the systematic treatment of all areas inside the corporation and inside the relevant stakeholder groups, such a system enables management to review its position comprehensively and critically. It documents those areas in which the company has traditionally responded more successfully to challenges and reveals those to which the company has been less sensitive. It makes the concept of corporate social responsiveness more manageable by disaggregating it in practice rather than treating "responsiveness" as a singular characteristic that a company as a whole either has or does not have. Companies applying this instrument have discovered that they had goals and corresponding policies in some areas but did not have them in others. On the basis of this "cultural audit," management can establish goals and policies that suit the particular features and interests of the corporation. Management must ensure ongoing monitoring, putting pressure on the organization to implement policies. Culture has a significant impact on implementation. Some areas are slower and have a more difficult time. The experience of managers was that the reporting instrument helped them keep track of the progress made over the entire range of environmental challenges. In those areas in which the company was traditionally strong, it served to heighten responsiveness and identify emerging issues that maintained and enhanced specific strengths. And in those areas where responsiveness to change was underdeveloped because of cultural blind spots, the systematic approach to information collection and planning helped to correct weaknesses.

Bibliography

Ackerman, R. and R. Bauer *Corporate Social Responsiveness: The Modern Dilemma,* Reston Publishing Co, Reston, VA, 1976.

Deal, T. and A. Kennedy: *Corporate Cultures,* Addison-Wesley, Reading, MA, 1982.

Hofstede, G.: *Culture's Consequences: International Differences in Work-Related Values,* Sage Publications, Beverly Hills, London, 1980.

Peters, T. J. and R. H. Waterman: *In Search of Excellence: Lessons from America's Best-Run Companies,* Harper & Row, New York, 1982.

Uttal, B.: "The Corporate Culture Vultures." *Fortune,* Oct. 17, 1983, pp. 66–72.

"Who's Excellent Now?" *Business Week,* Nov. 5, 1984, pp. 46–55.

67

Growth through Technology: A New Framework for Creative and Innovative Managers

George Kozmetsky

*Director, IC² Institute, the University of Texas at
Austin and Cofounder, Teledyne, Inc.*

Technology is a basic motor for economic growth. The management of
technology for industrial development and wealth generation is a recent
phenomenon. The lessons are clear. Only those who manage technology creatively and innovatively will reap sustained benefits. They can
also pioneer new issues of competition and cooperation.

A New Economic Development Strategy

To help companies meet the challenge of a hypercompetitive environment and to maximize the contributions of technology to general society, the promotion of new business growth has become an important facet of economic policy at the federal, state, and local levels. Building new companies on the one hand and expanding existing companies on the other have become the cornerstones of competitive strategy for economic development.

Creative and innovative managers must establish a new framework for economic growth through technology. There are four dimensions of this framework: (1) R&D linkages with public and private institutions, (2) institutional infrastructure for economic development, (3) support activities for entrepreneurial elements and innovation and manufacturing centers, and (4) economic wealth generation, resource development, markets and job creation. They are discussed below.

R&D Linkages with Public and Private Institutions

This dimension deals with elements of creative management. R&D linkages involve new ideas, directions, concepts, methods, and modes of operations. For R&D to occur and then be transferred and diffused for economic growth requires a supportive infrastructure. This means both new types of institutions and newer types of institutional relationships.

Innovative management requires the application of technology to generate new products, markets, and jobs. These, in turn, increase productivity, profits, and taxable bases to fulfill public sector responsibilities that contribute to a higher standard of living and quality of life. The transfer and diffusion of technology has become the central driver for local and regional economic development and diversification. Successful transfer and diffusion could, in the past, take place over a long period of time. Today the diffusion must be more rapid. This requires a level of collaboration among those institutions that generate the technology, those that develop new products, and those that provide the infrastructures for building competitive advantage.

There have been successful transfers to selected industries such as aerospace and electronics. Such transfers have been better between government labs and larger corporations than between the labs and small and medium-size firms. Increasing the number of successful transfers requires better innovative management and perhaps the development of more innovative institutions for diffusion. (The linkages between university basic research and the private sector are in much the same state. There is need to extend the abilities of universities to commercialize research and capitalize on intellectual properties.)

The linkages are best seen when viewed from a community perspective. Economic growth requires linking the education base with public infrastructure, private infrastructure, financial institutions, and business networks—locally, regionally, nationally, and internationally. Success requires conscious design and cooperative efforts.

Institutional Infrastructure for Economic Development

Making technological innovations commercially viable is a process that is independent of origins—a firm's R&D lab, a government-sponsored research project, the intellectual property of a university, an individual inventor, or licensing of foreign patents. Economic growth from technological innovations is dependent on capital funding. Capital is a critical infrastructure element.

Private Capital.   Capital formation consists of those private institutions that have been established to generate profits and those technology venturing institutions that set up new companies. There are three types of private capital institutional forms:

Traditional Venture Capital.   The industry consists of independent partnerships, corporate financial forms, corporate industrial firms, and small business investment companies. They provide a benchmark as to what technologies are fueling innovation as well as which states are involved in new institutional arrangements.

Emerging Venture Capital Sources.   This category includes international venture capital companies, business development corporations, and R&D partnerships. International companies have been the fastest growing source of venture capital in the United States. They comprise some 18 to 20 percent of new investment.

Special Funds for Corporate Restructure.   The desire for capital gains characterizes special funds dedicated to leveraged buy outs (LBOs) and mergers and acquisitions (M&A). There has been dramatic increase in LBOs. LBO investment in principle can secure capital gains in less time than investments in start-up or take-off stages of growth companies. The explosive amount invested in M&A signals another major transformation. Current M&A differ in many respects from past periods. Previously they represented either vertical or horizontal combinations for manufacturing or market control or for financial purposes (conglomerates). Today's M&A are more for purposes of capital gains, increasing managerial effectiveness, or providing special investment opportunities. Many of them focus on telescoping the time to commercialize innovations because of accelerated life cycles of products, processes, and services.

Technology Venturing Institutional Developments.   Technology venturing is a collaborative strategy for economic growth. Newer institutional developments fill in gaps in the traditional venture capital and economic development process. There are at least eight such new arrangements: industrial R&D joint ventures and consortia, academic-business collaboration, incubators, industry-university research and engineering centers of excellence, small business innovation research programs, state venture capital funds, commercialization of university intellectual property, and risk capital networks. These newer institutional developments are generally collaborative efforts. They are more than partnerships. Partnerships mean working together. In these technology venturing arrangements, each institution maintains its own independence.

Developing Emerging Industries.   Institutional relationships here are academic and industrial collaborations and industrial R&D consortia. Because basic research is carried out in universities and colleges, collaborative efforts between academia and industry can accelerate the commercialization process. Electronics, computers, and biotechnology are prime industry examples.

   Newer institutional structures are emerging in the "megabuilding business." These structures include domestic and foreign companies as well as multiple governments. Innovative financing pulls together banks, institutional investors, export credit agencies, and international development organizations. Megabuilders carry on basic, generic, and engineering research and keep up with technological advances in new materials, products, and processes. Their marketing strategy includes more than competitive winning of contracts. It involves longer-range planning, forecasting of markets, and constructing commercial-size demonstration plants.

Providing Seed Capital for Small and Take-Off Companies.   Institutional developments such as incubators, state venture capital funds, and risk capital networks are providing seed capital for small and take-off companies. Increasing state support encourages economic diversification through small technology firms.

Incubators provide a suitable environment for "hatching" new technology ventures. These are funded by both public and private sources. (See Chapter 68.)

Risk capital networks are structured to organize capital pools held by individuals. Some of these investors derive psychic income by putting resources back into their communities while they seek the high financial returns required for high-risk venture capital.

Achieving Economic Preeminence.   Institutional developments include national centers of research and engineering excellence, government-business-university collaborative arrangements, and industrial R&D joint ventures and consortia. They enable the creation of broad-based research programs that are too large for any one company to undertake alone; they stress multidisciplinary research to meet industry's needs.

Success in technology venturing depends on creative and innovative managers in the institutions involved. Through acts of management, they must link together organizational forms, motivations and incentives, cultures and environments, and strategies and structures.

Support Activities for Entrepreneurial Elements and Innovative and Manufacturing Centers

Innovation and manufacturing centers are the results of linking support activities and entrepreneurial elements. Support activities consist of formally constituted state, local, and private agencies such as chambers of commerce, industrial development commissions, and international offices; science, research, and innovation parks; and informal groups such as ad hoc bodies for goal, foreign investment, and future-oriented task forces. The entrepreneurial elements are talent, technology, capital, and know-how.

In many respects, how well these linkages are managed will determine the pace at which innovation and manufacturing centers are developed. The first step emphasizes creative management, devising new ideas. The second step is innovative management, especially in transforming sources of capital. Innovative management must implement successfully (private capital development) as well as move successfully in new directions (technology venturing).

Economic development problems cannot be solved in a short time. There are no quick and easy responses to various crises. Strategic planning is necessary to determine the multirelated requirements for innovation and manufacturing centers, the resources needed, and development of both short- and long-term action plans necessary to accomplish goals.

Economic development as a creative and innovative managerial activity is based on linking four critical factors: (1) talent—people, (2) technology—ideas, (3) capital—resources, and (4) know-how—knowledge. Entrepreneurial *talent* results from the perception, drive, tenacity, dedication, and hard work of special types of individuals—people who make things happen. Where there is a pool of such talent, there is the opportunity for growth, diversification, and new business development. But talent without ideas is like a seed without water. When talent is linked with *technology*, when people recognize and push viable ideas, the entrepreneurial process is underway. Every dynamic process needs to be fueled. The fuel here is *capital*. Capital is the catalyst in the entrepreneurial chain reaction.

One other element is indispensable. "Know-how" is the ability to leverage business or scientific knowledge by linking talent, technology, and capital in emerging and expanding enterprises. It finds and applies expertise in a variety of areas, making the difference between success and failure. This expertise may involve management, marketing, finance, accounting, production, and manufacturing, as well as legal, scientific, and engineering skills.

Economic Wealth Generation, Resource Development, Markets and Job Creation

The output of innovation and manufacturing centers generates economic wealth for their owners. Others also benefit, including employees and community. The centers also help provide tax revenues to support the public sector infrastructure.

The relationships between economic wealth generation and resource development, markets, and job creation involve more than making capital investments. Just as important as the usual economic standards of effectiveness and efficiency are two other dimensions. First, *flexibility*. If we do not invest, will we still have sufficient flexibility to meet competitive challenges, foreign and domestic? Second, *adaptability*. If we do not invest, can we adapt to unexpected conditions?

Resource Development.   Resources are more than a thing or a substance. They are the means of attaining given ends. They are instrumental in attaining economic wealth. Management is key to developing resources—human, natural, and technological. Managers who succeed must feel a strong need for achievement. This requires talent as well as education and experience (dimension 3). Managers must possess specific knowledge and skills related to both technologies and functions of management (dimension 2). Managers, finally, are dependent on the support they receive (dimension 1).

Job Creation. The cycle of products and services begins with research and ends at the marketplace. American management has been effective in developing new products and services based on high technology— but less so in their manufacturing and distribution for worldwide markets.

Technological progress and job creation are interrelated by the role of human capital. One way to improve the quality of labor is to invest in education and training. Hands-on experience in school, work, and play also helps. Other means of improving human capital is to promote health, flexible work hours, child care centers, and the like.

Summary

Entrepreneurship that primarily creates innovative centers is no longer enough to succeed in highly competitive world markets. Creative managers and innovative managers must develop products and services that companies can produce and sell more efficiently than competitors can. The ability to compete successfully requires a newer order of collaboration and cooperation among institutions that comprise our public-private infrastructure. Successful economic development usually takes longer and costs more than anticipated; and failures will occur along the way. Consequently, there needs to be creative management to start, innovation management to move forward, and creative and innovation management to finish. To build successful businesses, it takes all three.

68

Forging New Linkages: Business Incubators and University Relationships

Raymond W. Smilor

Executive Director, IC² Institute, The University of Texas at Austin

Michael D. Gill, Jr.

Associate, United Capital Ventures, Inc., and Research Fellow, IC² Institute

W. Arthur Porter

President and CEO, Houston Area Research Center

George P. Mitchell

Chairman, President, and CEO, Mitchell Energy & Development Corp.

Technology venturing is an emerging American response to changing economic conditions. It is an entrepreneurial process for commercializing science and technology by which for-profit corporations and businesses take and share risk with not-for-profit institutions, universities, and government. Technology venturing often links public sector initiatives with private sector investments through newer institutional arrangements. We examine two such arrangements: "business incubators" and "university-industry relationships."

Business Incubators

The primary driver of technology-based new business ventures is neither the availability of funds nor the advance of technology: It is the entrepreneur. New business incubators are a concept that provide the entrepreneur with services and support that complement natural talents and leverage potential. New venture development requires synergy among talent, technology, capital, and know-how. A new business incubator can be the integrating link that increases the chances for success. Incubators provide a framework for focusing and binding the critical elements of the entrepreneurial process. They can also telescope the learning curve of the business process, giving entrepreneurs more time to expand and more flexibility to learn from mistakes.

A variety of economic and social factors are today stimulating entrepreneurial activity. These factors include increasing interest in capital formation (through corporate joint ventures as well as venture capital investment), changing institutional relationships (such as universities and government laboratories seeking commercial collaboration), supportive federal and state incentives and programs, a reassessment of intellectual property assets by not-for-profit institutions, and new approaches to commercial innovation by academic institutions and government agencies.

How New Business Incubators Work

Incubator units are designed to assist technically oriented entrepreneurs in developing their business skills in an environment that simultaneously stimulates technical creativity. Although incubators vary in scope of assistance provided, there are some generic components. After screening potential entrepreneurs (a process that varies widely among incubators), an incubator provides low-cost office and/or laboratory space, administrative services (such as secretarial support and accounting services), access to library and computers, skilled consultants, and special contacts with bankers, venture capitalists, technologists, and government officials. In this environment, an aspiring entrepreneur is free to be creative since his or her energies can be exclusively devoted to product development rather than to managing the business organization. All the while the entrepreneur is associating with other entrepreneurs who are facing similar difficulties, thus energizing the drive for success and facilitating the solution of problems.

An incubator is not only an organization but also a physical unit. Incubators start as a single building or group of buildings in which entrepreneurs can work and interact. For university-related incubators, the advantages of being on or near a university campus are numerous: libraries, exposure to state-of-the-art technical thinking and equipment, undergraduates who form a pool of cheap but skilled labor, a creative environment, and potential employment as a lecturer. Companies within the incubator benefit from the best available consulting talent when they need it without having to carry a high-priced payroll. Science parks often accompany the incubator unit as an additional link between universities and industry. Located near universities, these parks have the objective of attracting both R&D and/or manufacturing facilities of established technology-based companies. Also called technology or research parks, they act as a lightning rod for growth companies and can be an area's lure for attracting new business.

Organizationally, incubators differ from one another by varying priorities. The key factor that has an impact on an incubator's organization is its source of support funding—whether federal, state, and local governments; communities; universities; foundations; private individuals; or corporations. Incubators can be associated with any of these funding sources and, therefore, have similar goals but different priorities. The general goals of incubators are to develop firms, often technically based, and to encourage entrepreneurship. Incubators may seek to develop jobs, create investment opportunities for college endowments, expand a tax base for local government, enhance the image of college technical programs, speed transfer of technological innovation from academic and research worlds to industry, fill a perceived gap in venture capital financing, provide corporations with windows on leading-edge technology, and act as a "farm system" for companies seeking diversification and expansion. A review of selected incubators by type provides insights on the structure, operation, and diversity of this innovative approach to business development.

University Related Incubators

The University City Science Center (UCSC) in Philadelphia has been a prototype university-related incubator-research center for 20 years. Organized as a non-profit corporation, UCSC has twenty-eight "shareholders," which are the major universities, colleges, and medical schools in the Philadelphia area plus the local community development organization. UCSC is composed of two groups, the Research Park Division and the Research Institutes Division. The Research Park Division is part incubator and part science park. Of the seventy-five companies currently housed in it, thirty-eight started operations there. The Research Park assists entrepreneurs with administrative support services, affordable space and facilities, development of business plans, evaluation of product ideas, financing, consulting, and seminars. Other tenants are more established businesses in technology-related areas. Plans call for a total capital investment in UCSC of $250 million. The envisioned Research Park would have 5 million square feet of space and employ over 20,000 persons. UCSC's Research Institutes Division has a professional staff of ninety who undertake contract research for tenant firms or other private and public sector clients. It has a definite advantage when competing for contracts because of its flexibility in acquiring expert research collaboration from member institutions. The Research Institute provides UCSC with invaluable visibility and prestige in academic, industry, and research circles and enhances its desirability as a location for start-up and existing firms. The UCSC is also the base for the Advanced Technology Center of Southeastern Pennsylvania under the state-sponsored Ben Franklin Partnership. These funds support cooperative R&D centers at UCSC, including centers for Advanced Sensor Technologies, Advanced Biomedical Technologies, and Technologies for the Handicapped. The synergy of research park, advanced technology center, research institute, and incubation unit amplifies entrepreneurial activity.

The Western Pennsylvania Advance Technology Center is Pittsburgh's counterpart to Philadelphia's UCSC. The objective of the Center is to create jobs. The integrated approach has three components: First, the Center sponsors joint industry-university R&D projects in robotics, biomedicine, high-tech materials, coal, and metals. Second, the Center offers assistance to entrepreneurs, small businesses, and regional industries; this function includes an incubator unit. Third, the Center helps education, training, and retraining programs meet regional labor needs. Since the Center is cosponsored by Carnegie-Mellon University, a critical-mass technology is available for business development.

Rensselaer Polytechnic Institute (RPI), in Troy, New York, started its incubator unit in 1980 and has nurtured in excess of thirty-five firms. RPI provides inexpensive space for operations and access to campus facilities and faculty. All transactions are on a cash basis, though RPI has accepted stock as payment for rent. The New York state legislature has established at RPI the New York State Center for Industrial Innovation. The state will spend $30 million building the center and lease the facilities to RPI for $600,000 per year. Private funds will provide $35 million of equipment. Center research focuses on the application of electronics and computers to manufacturing processes and productivity improvements, including robots and automated assembly. This combination of research facility and incubator unit makes RPI a premier location for job creation, technological innovation, and entrepreneurship.

The Georgia Advanced Technology Center (GATC) in Atlanta is a state-sponsored program that runs an integrated program of incubation and entrepreneurial stimulation and assistance. Started in 1980, the GATC has a consulting arm and incubation space and is funded on a line-item basis by the Georgia legislature. Its consulting division has a permanent staff of twelve, five of whom are "business types." GATC supports companies for no longer than 3 years, after which it helps them obtain other financing. GATC leverages outside financing as much as possible by sponsoring a venture capital conference at the Georgia Tech campus.

The Institute for Ventures in New Technology (INVENT) is a state-funded incubator headquartered at The Texas Engineering Experiment Station, which is part of the Texas A&M University System in College Station, Texas. INVENT provides companies with consulting in product development, business planning, market surveys, and equity funding availability. For its services, INVENT receives a share of a company's equity and acceptance fees from client firms. Consultants come from the university's faculty, and the Institute has about twelve full-time employees. INVENT has no physical facilities in which tenant companies could locate; in this sense it does not entirely qualify as an incubator. In accordance with its charter, INVENT must become self-supporting within 9 years of its inception.

Public-Private Incubators

The Utah Innovation Center (UIC), based in Salt Lake City, is a private incubation facility that began operations as a quasi-public organization affiliated with the University of Utah. Started in 1978 with a grant from the National Science Foundation, the UIC is privately funded by individuals. Dr. Wayne Brown, the founder and principal owner of UIC, is a former engineering dean at the University of Utah. He is a successful entrepreneur and the guiding force behind the incubator concept in Utah. UIC operations are funded from the Center's capitalization and from income from continuing operations. For cash flow, the Center consults with nonincubator firms, forms R&D partnerships to carry out research at the Center, leases office space in UIC buildings, and applies for government grants. Although it is not a venture capital firm, the UIC does take an equity position in firms located within its incubator and becomes a full business partner with the entrepreneur. In return, the UIC provides all services commonly associated with incubators. With a small, full-time staff, UIC contracts with consultants from both the University and industry to help incubator firms. As in other incubators, the UIC carefully screens prospective entrepreneurs, employing analytical methods used by venture capitalists—which generally means the Center invests more in people than ideas.

Los Alamos, New Mexico, has established a technology incubator as one way to promote technology transfer from Los Alamos National Laboratory to the community and state. This incubator provides opportunities for scientists and technicians in the massive government lab to commercialize their ideas and innovations. The incubator brings together financial resources, business talent, and professional support to speed the technology transfer process and thus contribute to economic development.

Private Sector Incubators

Conceptually, private sector incubators are similar to university-related incubators. Both provide appropriate facilities and services. Both want to develop new concepts into viable companies. However, private sector incubator units differ in two distinct areas: funding source and goals. Private sector incubators are founded and capitalized by individuals and companies; there is no direct government, industry, or community involvement. The primary motive is to make a profit and, in the case of company-sponsored incubators, to diversify and/or maintain windows on technology.

The investment strategy for private incubators is similar to that of most venture capital firms but with important differences. Incubators focus on preseed and seed-stage companies, whereas venture capital firms deal more with take-off growth stages. Private incubators place no boundaries on industries but prefer technology. Capital gains are emphasized over dividends, and the incubator's parent corporation distributes income to its investors on a variable basis. Further, an incubator is an ongoing concern and does not liquidate itself after its investments mature (like venture capital partnerships). Rather, it distributes income and/or reinvests proceeds in new companies within theincubator.

Companion venture capital pools are formed to invest in the private incubator's tenants or graduated companies. Incubators generally take a substantial portion of a company's equity in return for services offered. Few incubators, public or private, have sufficient capitalization to make the large follow-on investments required by small companies to continue growth. For this reason, most incubators look to venture capital to support successful tenant firms. For companies developed by publicly sponsored incubators, venture capital can be difficult to obtain. Venture capital firms may be wary of investing in a company that has a significant portion of its equity held by a passive investor.

The Technology Center, started in 1976 in Montgomeryville, Pennsylvania, was one of the nation's first incubators. It has since franchised its concept and operates six other centers nationwide. In addition to the usual support services, the Technology Center also offers a variety of consulting services. The "center champion" is the individual responsible for helping the tenant develop business plans, marketing strategies, and financing opportunities. As an experienced entrepreneur, the center champion acts as an expert with numerous personal contacts. Furthermore, the Technology Center networks its tenants through a newsletter and computer-based directory that includes a brief profile on each company and its product or service, providing access to hundreds of potential partners, suppliers, and customers.

Control Data Business and Technology Centers (CDBTC) is a franchise operation of a major computer company, Control Data Corporation (CDC). With twenty-two operating incubators and more than 7 years' experience, CDBTC seeks to provide a full range of support services for seed or start-up phase business. The goal of these centers is to reduce the failure rate of new businesses. Since the first center opened in 1979, CDC claims that more than 90 percent of the businesses have survived and are growing. CDC is unique in that it provides some services that other new business incubators cannot, such as sophisticated computers and access to CDC's PLATO computer-based education. There are over 700 daughter companies operating, using 2 million square feet of space and employing 6000 people.

University Relationships

The Houston Area Research Center (HARC) is a consortium of four of Texas' top institutions of higher learning: Rice University, Texas A&M University, the University of Houston, and the University of Texas at

Austin. It is a prime example of innovative interaction between industry and academia to commercialize state-of-the-art science and build the economy.

The impetus behind HARC came from the private sector. The creative spark, however, did not occur in a vacuum. Employing outside consultants, university personnel, and corporate staffs, a detailed look was taken at the three premier high-technology corridors in the United States: California's Silicon Valley, Boston's Route 128, and North Carolina's Research Triangle. Their growth patterns, histories, sources of funding, physical layout, and demographics were studied in order to learn perils and pitfalls as well as options and opportunities. HARC's master plan was derived from such research.

Cost-Benefit Analysis

A major issue in any formal university-corporate linkage, especially when more than one university or corporation is involved, is turf. Some key questions: Will my company's or university's autonomy be diminished, and if so, how much? Will the new organization cut into funding resources that otherwise might be available to my institution? Will proprietary information be compromised? Will academic freedom be stifled? Will my company staff or university faculty be committed to the newly formed relationship? Will real commercial value ever be realized? All legitimate issues must be discussed and resolved *before* linkages are formalized.

In HARC's case, support and encouragement of top corporate and academic (both faculty and administrative) leadership were obtained at an early stage. Any company or university contemplating a collaborative arrangement must obtain backing from all key players in all institutions involved. (The difficulty of securing such support increases as the *square* of the number of levels of cooperation that must be attained.)

What are the benefits of such a new institutional arrangement? One-sided relationships seldom last and almost never flourish. In business or any creative endeavor, collaboration necessarily embodies a certain degree of risk; as separate parties become closely aligned, each, to some degree, stakes part of its reputation on identifying with the other. When benefits outweigh costs, when rewards exceed risks, the relationship succeeds and synergism develops. Synergism requires that each party be committed to the other's purpose as well as its own. A successful cooperative venture must be flexible enough to meet each institution's changing needs.

How can university-industry linkages serve the purposes of both? The critical connection is educated, independent thinkers capable of making contributions in both environments. Talented people are what unify universities, industries, and governments. A viable, healthy economy depends upon having knowledgeable individuals who are productive in the competitive global marketplace. In this context, the ideal university-industry relationship is one that provides a learning environment in which creative thought is encouraged, knowledge of one or more subjects is demanded, and competitive productivity is measured. To that end, we examine HARC as a model for how such linkage can be created.

The Houston Area Research Center

HARC is dedicated to working on problems of importance to industry—problems that can best be addressed using the combined strength of member institutions' faculty and resources as well as HARC's own personnel. Research programs at HARC are generally large in scope and targeted at technology development and/or transfer. Research is conducted by scientists and engineers who work at the leading edge of their fields and who have demonstrated independent thinking in applying knowledge for the benefit of business and government. In addition to their HARC appointments, researchers typically hold faculty positions at one or more member universities, and thus graduate students can earn a degree while working at HARC. HARC provides faculty and students at each member institution with an opportunity not only to pursue independent thought in a particular discipline but also to apply their knowledge and skills in a competitive environment. In addition, HARC provides members with an off-campus location for conducting proprietary or classified research that may not otherwise be permitted in a university environment.

In a functional sense, HARC provides direction for those research projects that are most likely to strengthen the economic and industrial base of Texas and the nation. The initial focus is on projects that complement and support leading industries in Texas. Secondarily, the consortium concentrates on emerging industries and technologies. Playing to the strengths of Texas, particularly of the Houston area, HARC stresses the petroleum sciences. The Geotechnology Research Institute was established to bring together world-class geophysicists and petroleum engineers. Projects range from reservoir management and engineering to improved exploration and enhanced recovery techniques. A complementary area is hydrology, since water management is of growing importance. The Geotechnology Research Institute is HARC's best example of government-industry-university collaboration. The Institute is eligible to receive state money, but most of its funding comes from contract work for individual petroleum companies requiring proprietary research or from groups of such companies pooling resources to support a common R&D program.

With NASA's Johnson Space Center in Houston, space research is another appropriate activity for HARC. The Laser Applications Research Center (LARC) is working on directed energy in defense applications. HARC is also exploring the commercialization of space. Medicine is yet another of the state's existing strengths. With the large medical complex in Houston, there is opportunity to bring together physical scientists and engineers with medical scientists and physicians. HARC is closely associated with institutions of the Texas Medical Center, several of which plan to establish their own facilities adjacent to the HARC campus. The Baylor College of Medicine has opened facilities nearby; activities include a Magnetic Resonance Imaging Center for developing new generations of medical imaging and BCM Technologies, Inc., Baylor's technology transfer company. In addition to working with these institutions, HARC will conduct its own medical-related research program through LARC and other centers.

Most of HARC's research requires sophisticated computing capabilities. Therefore, a Computer Applications Center will operate its own large computer systems, and it will employ a resident corps of scientists and engineers to develop advanced software for technical applications and network communications. In keeping with HARC's strategy of integrating public, private, and academic sectors, cooperative ways of structuring this new center are being explored with major corporations.

HARC is designed to serve the mutual interests of business, government, and academia. It is governed by a board of directors that represents each of its participating universities and includes business and public leaders. The consortium seeks rapid response to research opportunities—whether identified by HARC, its member universities or corporate and community institutions. HARC is establishing itself by playing to existing economic and industrial strengths while pursuing areas with future importance. The creative aspects of HARC as an institution are reflected in its original master plan and current entrepreneurial spirit. For HARC, as for all university-industry relationships, the big payoff lies on the horizon.

Bibliography

Konecci, Eugene B. and Robert Lawrence Kuhn: *Technology Venturing: American Innovation and Risk-Taking,* Praeger, New York, 1985.

Kozmetsky, George, M. Gill, and R. Smilor: *Financing and Managing Fast Growth Companies: The Venture Capital Process,* Lexington Publishing Co., Lexington, MA, 1985.

Kuhn, Robert Lawrence: *Commercializing Defense-Related Technology,* Praeger, New York, 1985.

Smilor, Raymond W. and Michael D. Gill, Jr.: *The New Business Incubator,* Lexington Publishing Co., Lexington, MA, 1986.

69

Creative Directions for Business Education

Robert Lawrence Kuhn

*Investment Banker, Senior Research Fellow,
IC² Institute, The University of Texas at Austin and
Adjunct Professor, Graduate School of Business
Administration, New York University*

Business schools must reach out, not back. No longer is the loop between academic business and corporate business a pattern of fresh graduates going in one direction and fresh money going in the other. In a turbulent economic environment, with ambiguity and uncertainty more rule than exception, with specialization and technology attaining new levels of sophistication, only a "new partnership" between industry and university can insure mutual prosperity. Creative managers on both sides will take heed.

I believe that a primary American resource, a potent economic force largely untapped, is the faculties of business administration that are resident in our major universities. Here are experts in all disciplines and fields ofbusiness—marketing, accounting, finance, general management, production, management science, strategy and policy, organizational development, international management, management of technology, operations research, business law, business economics, computer science—the list is long. How we utilize this resource should be explored.

I am not advocating, of course, that theoreticians should become practitioners; that, say, finance professors should negotiate bankruptcy cases or marketing statisticians should become product managers. What I am saying is that we have an abundance of available skills, first-rate analytical capabilities, and extensive familiarity with a multitude of examples. Business schools are more than schools, more than academic arenas in which future gladiators of management are trained. Academic business departments must relate to the ongoing, real-time conduct of contemporary companies. Business by its very nature is distinct from other academic departments, which are passive, pedagogic, and reflective not active, contributory, and interventional. History departments, for example, do not affect current history; accounting departments, on the other hand, should affect current accounting.

Following are seven major issues for business schools, questions relevant for creative managers facing the final decade of the twentieth century.

Developing and Disseminating Business Schools' Research

How can we maximize support and use of faculty research, encouraging both fundamental and pragmatic work? The advancement of business knowledge is quite literally the growth of society. Business faculties occupy a unique position in the academic constellation. They have special opportunities to integrate and synthesize research from diverse areas. Work coming out of the physical, biological, and social sciences is all germane to business investigation and becomes the substrate of which new commercial concepts are fashioned. Similarly, the interaction between academic research and corporate R&D offers critical-mass potential for new products, processes, and systems. If economic development is dependent on the birth of new knowledge, gestation should take place in business schools.

Academic Business-Corporate Business Interaction

How can business faculties cross-fertilize with business executives, contributing their expertise without violating academic integrity? An easy answer is that universities should remain pure: advance knowledge and educate students but truncate any pecuniary involvement. Natural law, however, dictates otherwise. The pressure for higher dollars continues to drain away the best faculty to industry; it's ironic when graduating MBAs are hired by companies at higher salaries than their professors make at the university. For business schools to remain "pure," they may be forced to become poor. Too many good heads will leave. Better is to innovate. Put our best brains together and devise plans and programs to maximize the effectiveness of faculties. Develop systems in which academic business and corporate business can inter-mix, in which the free flow of ideas and intense force of implementation can occur without prejudice. Easily said, of course. But to effectuate, one must deal with dollars. Who gets what? Perhaps the university should take the initiative to structure such relationships. Rather than merely allowing faculty the traditional one-day-per-week for consulting, maybe a more proactive role can be taken. Could business schools form functional centers to work with corporations—state-of-the-art institutes with high expertise and operated as businesses? Could the university give faculty financial incentives for commercial successes? The issue of academic freedom is a real one but should not be a barrier to restrict the activities of some by those less able to compete in such new markets.

Corporate Business-Academic Business Interaction

How can business executives cross-fertilize with academic faculties, contributing their experiences in a meaningful and continuous manner? Business executives enjoy lecturing MBA students; it's a stimulating experience for a corporate manager to give an occasional seminar. But how can this interaction be augmented? How can executive input be elevated above altruism? Only by satisfying self-interest can we assure continued motivation. Creative corporate leaders must discover that participating within the business school environment enhances their career capabilities, broadening scope and expanding talents. Responsibility for designing programs to achieve such dynamism should lie with business school administrators and faculties.

Business Education for the Real World

How can business students be trained for the uncertainty, ambiguity, and discontinuity of the universe beyond the university? Graduate school in business is quite unlike graduate school in other disciplines; medicine, English, physics, and the like are cut from a different mold. In any of the normal content areas, knowledge and methodology are foundational to experience, and it would be nonsensical and contradictory to require prior work in the field as a prerequisite for study. Business is different; it just is. Of course, a basic background is desirable, but frankly it is neither sufficient nor necessary for success. On the other hand, the educational process in business becomes exceedingly rich when it can play against the experiences of real life. Accounting problems leap out of the text, organizational development theories become sources of salvation, operations research techniques are viewed as new tools for problem solution. An experienced manager hungers for further knowledge. Innovative educational programs, such as executive MBA programs for full-time managers, should be encouraged.

New Methodologies of Business Research

How can academics and executives integrate quantitative techniques of analysis with qualitative insights of intuition to produce the full range of managerial capabilities? The scientific method is the core paradigm of modern man. Scientific content is the foundation of many contemporary industries. Business executives must be literate in both (methodology as well as knowledge), and it is the duty of business schools to so educate them. Arguments abound regarding the effectiveness of numerical methods in managerial decision making. The computer unequivocally augments executive power to gather, collate, process, and sort information. But can such preformed patterns of thinking, programmed in advance, inadvertently inhibit the art of taking creative leaps? Computer-determined solutions are most effective on operational levels of business, becoming progressively less useful when moving into strategic strata. Yet even in the devising of long-range corporate strategies, computers can aid the creative process, not delimit it. Developing managers who can use computers as conceptual tools—for expanding horizons of vision and originality of thinking, for moving and manipulating data and ideas—is a major task for business schools.

New Technologies and Business Education and Information

How can business schools maximize the potential of telecommunications for education, instruction, and professional development? The electronic revolution, taught and analyzed in the business schools, ought to be developed and utilized there as well. Teleconferencing, computer transfer of information, interactive cable television, video cassettes and discs, direct broadcast from satellites—all are new tools for the communication of information ready-made for modern business information. I believe that joint ventures should be established combining the intellectual resources of business schools and the technical expertise of telecommunications corporations (together, perhaps, with the commercial experience of entertainment companies). A business information-education network should become, if intelligently conceived and properly managed, both vital and profitable. Business schools must seize the initiative so that control resides with the center of content not the channels of communications, with the "message" not the "medium." A "business information network" can become an international force within the next decade.

New Sector Development

How can business schools develop managers for the emerging areas of the economy: high technology, information, service, not-for-profit, government? A radical shift is occurring in the fundamental structure of the economy. Traditional manufacturing, however revitalized, must give ground to other sectors. Even high technology, although still a function of manufacturing, has a different cast to it. Employees have a new mentality, and the management of technology becomes an important area for organizational study and innovation. Information-based businesses are perhaps the greatest growth area as we approach the year 2000. Both the means of communication and the databases themselves are novel elements not long in existence. Future managers must be trained to be fully facile with issues and problems unique and germane to these uncharted regions. The increasing importance of not-for-profit (or quasi-profit-making) institutions—hospitals, schools, universities, museums, foundations, churches—requires area-specific managerial training, not just the assumed applicability of manufacturing-oriented business education. Future leaders of such institutions must be as sophisticated in first-rate management know-how as they are dedicated to their organization's laudatory goals. Government, as well, must benefit from expertise derived from competitive demands of the profit-making sector. Building bridges between government and industry creates two-way flows of benefits: It enables public servants to learn management techniques and systems from private executives, and it allows government to better serve the interests of business through more efficient regulatory procedures.

Business schools must assume a prominent role in the economy, indeed in society—locally, regionally, nationally. Traditional thinking in management must give way to the interdisciplinary, the strategic, the creative and innovative. Business schools must become pioneers, expanders and integrators of new business ideas. Creative managers must make them so.

70

Creative Management for Creative Culture

Robert Lawrence Kuhn

Investment Banker, Senior Research Fellow,
IC² Institute, University of Texas at Austin and
Adjunct Professor, Graduate School of Business
Administration, New York University

"To exist is to change. To exist a long time is to change often." So said the English churchman and writer John Henry Cardinal Newman 120 years ago, and it is more apt today than it was then. Change is perhaps the dominant characteristic of contemporary companies. Change, of course, can be either beneficial or detrimental, and it is often well into the process before you can even tell one from the other. There are only two things sure about change: it must occur, and its outcome is uncertain.

How to make change beneficial? David Ogilvy, founder of one of the world's largest advertising agencies, stated that businesses need "massive infusions of *talent*." But it is useless to be a creative, original thinker, he warned, "unless you can also *sell* what you create. Management cannot be expected to recognize a good idea unless it is presented to them by a good salesman."

Creativity and innovation are the engines of constructive change. Creativity has been heralded as the procedure for transforming problem into opportunity, for energizing the development of novel ideas and fresh approaches. Innovation has been called a mechanism for dealing with uncertainty, for asserting control over volatile events. Creativity is the input to innovation, the raw material of revolution. The issue before us, therefore, becomes one of *leveraging* creativity, of maximizing its appearances and applications. We need means of generating families of fresh ideas, clusters of original alternatives, so that in the analytical-evaluation phase best choices can be made. Creative and innovative management is the key to competitive position. But it too must be "sold." Such sales prowess is the purpose of this Handbook.

A New Discipline of Management

The emergence of a new discipline in management, like the eruption of a supernova in astronomy, is an event of remarkable impact, bold and beautiful in form, stark and stunning in content. In the 1950s it was management science, the application of quantitative methods to solve business problems. In the 1960s it was behavioral science, the recruitment of psychological theory for organizational understanding. In the 1970s it was long-range planning, the use of formal methods for forecasting futures and simulating corporate response. In the 1980s and 1990s it is creative and innovative management, the generation of original solutions for complex problems.

Human civilization is founded on social groupings, the gatherings of individuals in organizations and institutions of all kinds. The running of these transpersonal clusters, the capacity to develop and maintain cohesive order, is what "management" is all about. Throughout history, managers have made groups go. "Good" management was always defined operationally by "success," whatever success meant for each particular group. Managers were chosen by instinct and survival, and information was transferred by observation and osmosis. The system worked for generations, for millennia (though even Moses was advised to "delegate" by his father-in-law Jethro).

The world today is very different. As much as we have gained in technology and sophistication we have lost in robustness and stability. While we have progressed in collective power, we have retrogressed in individual control. One manager just cannot assimilate the incessant barrage of high-density data that are the nervous impulses of modern organizations. Internal triggers and external shocks overwhelm analytical capacity. Frameworks are needed to simplify and reduce, trading off precision for accessibility and accuracy for comprehension.

Management concepts and administrative systems have traditionally developed more by necessity than design. Always, it seems, what comes about is what is already essential; there is no time to savor the developing process. Management in this century—from Taylor's scientific management to functionalization to operations research to organizational structure and strategy—is the story of theory striving to keep pace with practice, of academics trying to formalize for executives what the best ones were already doing by gut feel. Once more we are at an impasse. Even strategic planning, having promised to forecast and guide, has often extrapolated the past and missed the future. What will happen is no longer governed by what has happened. Problems exist today that are difficult to factor into component parts, much less solve. Decision support systems and the like notwithstanding, what we need now is more than a new form of management; we need a new form of thinking!

"Nonroutine" pursuits and "nonprogrammable" activities are the focal point of creative management. Strategic management, of itself, falls short. Coordinating myriad quantas of data is beyond anyone's capacity to analyze fully, but decisions can be made with confidence when data reduction is combined with directed insight. Creative management, almost by definition, defies upfront quantification and early verification. You just can't judge originality too quickly. And the newer the concept, the harder the judgment and the longer the time. Creative solutions are often suboptimal when measured by conventional yardsticks. Yet such suboptimal initiatives can often overwhelm reason and blow out logic. These startling mental processes are performed constantly, often without awareness, by first-rate corporate executives. How we focus and direct such brilliance is a major thrust of the new field.

Creative Management versus Industrial Policy

"Industrial policy," we are told, is the national economic panacea for international competitive sickness. "IP," to those on the in, would plan and control from Washington the strategy and structure of American industry. IPers believe that the free market system is no longer efficient and that the government must intervene to support business and prop up jobs. Coined by intellectuals and caught by politicians, IP is a symptom of economic illness and political fever.

One cannot deny the appeal to industries suffering decline and workers without work. Nor can one negate the fact that in a tightly wired world foreign governments can shift the commercial balance of power by giving home-grown companies unfair advantage. Thus IP sparks the hope that federal funds might aid out-priced and outmoded companies regain former glory. But numerous industries will vie for the golden tap. Which to promote and which to protect? Which to ignore and which to forget? When the government picks "winners," it must, by that same decision, also pick "losers." To sustain one, we must shun another. An increase of jobs here must result in a decrease of jobs there. If automobiles are chosen, why should textiles be condemned? Who is to decide that midwest employment should go up while southwest employment should go down? One conjures up tortuous visions of procedural miasma, politicking and lobbying of unprecedented magnitude. Resources, we have come to learn, are not unlimited; available subsidy is only finite. (What, by the way, happens to IP when favorite industries do not make the Federal Hit Parade?)

Socialism, it is said, is a wonderful concept; the dream of economic equality and financial fairness is utopian. The only problem, of course, is that it just doesn't work. Theoretical idealism breaks up quickly against the rocks of pragmatic realism. Human beings function best when they are controlled least, when they prosper in proportion to personal initiative and self-driven intensity.

American business is still burdened by archaic regulations codified two generations ago. There were right and rigorous reasons then. We were fast becoming, in those heady days, the world's premier industrial power; our growth was unimpeded, domestic markets were burgeoning and foreign markets beckoning, Industries and industrialists became intoxicated with new-found powers, and consumers and workers, at the mercy of mammoths, needed protection. Yet times shift and paths twist. What worked then won't work now. Is passivity the answer? Should the status quo be bronzed? By no means. What American industry needs is simple: Not more control by government but more confidence in management. Not centralized planning by bureaucrats but aggressive leadership from businessmen. Not industrial policy but creative management. More micro and less macro.

American industry must be freed from constraints, not encumbered with more. American business must be invigorated, not suffocated. The mold for forging the future? Independent leadership not centralized command. But to critique is always easier than to construct. Industrial policy will not work. What will? It is one thing to describe the illness, quite another to prescribe the remedy. Alternatives proffered usually stress macroeconomic manipulation, such as looser money, tighter budgets, and the like. Yet something is missing. We've heard all this before.

One might believe by reading erudite arguments that industrial prosperity is linked to some "new economic policy," whether monetarist and supply side on the one hand or increased taxes and government spending on the other. A cardinal mistake here—and it permeates contemporary thought—is the notion that economic solutions to industrial problems will yield competitive advantage and business success. Macroeconomics surely has its place but not the whole place. Macroeconomics is vital in defining and modulating the pace and proportions of the economy, but it is deficient in securing and prospering individual firms. It's like trying to coach a basketball team by determining the theoretically proper mix of heights, weights, and talents of players without ever teaching any of them how to dribble, pass, or shoot.

Economists dominate economic thinking. Seem logical? Well, economists, when one thinks about them, don't run companies. They don't manage budgets and don't direct staffs. They never formulate corporate strategies and have no experience with corporate structures. "P&L," "personnel," "product positioning" are terms they do not use. Meeting payrolls is something they do not do. Making enterprises work is responsibility they do not have. Yet enterprises—for-profit businesses and not-for-profit institutions—are the components of the economy. Like cells in a body, they *are* the economy, and to treat the economy only by macroeconomics is to treat an epidemic only by epidemiology. Building businesses in the former, like curing people in the latter, must be addressed. To leave the economy solely in the hands of economists is to leave the sick solely in the hands of statisticians.

We must listen to the gross national product. We must hear the rhythms of small businesspeople, middle managers, corporate executives. We must feel the beat of individual firms. The world works because some have vision and brilliance with the tenacity and temerity to produce and provide.

Creative and innovative management is what industry needs, and government policy should be directed toward building it. But this is not a topic of macroeconomics; one does not study it in doctoral programs; there is little research, no Nobel Prizes, and minor media coverage. It is local not global, micro not macro. Yet the stakes are big not small: Creative and innovative management is the economic pulse of American health. It is the life blood for sustaining the strength of the economy, for improving the quality of management, for securing the robustness of business. It is the fulcrum for the final decade of the twentieth century.

Creative and innovative management concerns both collective policy and structure—macro and micro. But flourishing will not happen by accident. It is a way of thinking new and hard. No one risks for little reward. How will management make the right moves and take the right risks? This climate has two parallel elements: (1) an economic environment responsive to creativity and innovation and (2) a corporate culture conducive to novel and imaginative management.

Building a Creative Economic Environment

1. *Encourage risk by strengthening reward.*   Proprietary ownership is a powerful human motivator; it is capitalism's great advantage over communism and we must pound it without pause. We should strengthen patent laws, to include new forms of invention in the information and knowledge-based sciences. Government contracts should be structured to encourage recipients to reach and to risk—whether defense companies, university science departments, or national laboratories. Both institutions and individuals must benefit from their toil. Federal R&D funds, perhaps America's chief asset in building comprehensive national security, should embed economic as well as military forces, deriving maximally efficient value from each. Government contracts, for example, might be awarded to firms that generate original ideas or products or firms adept at commercializing defense-related technology, whether the firms be large or small. Differentiation by size may be missing the mark.

2. *Facilitate information transfer.*   Creativity and innovation are resources that increase with use: The more you use it, says Dr. George Kozmetsky, the more you have it. To enhance applications, we must publicize and promote. Although creativity and innovation are private processes, they can be fostered by information sharing and situation setting. Centers for innovation and invention should be established, funded by state and federal government (and perhaps administered by colleges and universities). National data banks can enable active researchers and potential entrepreneurs to access ideas and information.

3. *Focus government fiscal and tax policy.*   Many words are spoken in Washington; millions every year are written into record and law. None are heard more clearly, none read more carefully, than those dealing with taxes. By tax law the government directs public policy. A clear message for developing creative and innovative management will be given only when tax policy is the medium. We should reward creative and innovative companies through lower taxes rather than penalize their profits with higher taxes. Tax credits for incremental R&D is a

first, albeit halting step in the right direction. We might consider, say, tax credits for new patents, for new products, for R&D expenditures above industry norms.

4. *Understand the creative process.* Public policy should support research and education in creative and innovative management. Studying the process should become a national goal—not a curiosity, a necessity. Researchers should be funded and interdisciplinary work encouraged—from organizational psychology and decision science to artificial intelligence and neuroscience. The arts, too, should not be neglected. In concert with research, we must stimulate creative and innovative education. Principles can be taught at every age, from early education through high school and college. Schools of business should take the lead, instilling motivation to shift and change rather than drilling techniques to trend and continue. One danger of making business more rational, more analytical and computer-based, is the subtle pressure to stifle the new and inhibit the fresh. Businesspeople must be prepared to make nonrational (not *irr*ational) decisions, gambling on instinct and perception. Combining the art with the science is vital.

5. *Promote interaction among sectors.* Creative and innovative management is not sector specific. It occupies a unique place at the union of industry, government, and academia. Each sector must make special contributions, and critical mass can be generated only when all focus their force on the interface. Intersector interaction is not just a current fad, it is the white-hot core—and government policy should catalyze the reaction. The Department of Defense policy of rewarding companies with university ties higher scores for independent R&D funds is an excellent prototype. State government, too, must participate; they may, for example, offer matching incentives for state-based R&D, increasing operational leverage and financial appeal.

Building a Creative Corporate Culture

1. *Encourage risk by strengthening reward.* Most companies give mixed signals about risk. They praise new ventures with lofty works and reward failure with career wipeout. One such derailment incinerates the whole house of corporate cards. We must shift this risk-return tradeoff by decreasing the risk and increasing the reward. Incentives for originality and invention must be internalized and believed by the company underground. The organizational structure must support them; the informal networks must promote them; the grapevines must

confirm them. Participating in new ventures—not just making them successful—must be the pinnacle of corporate achievement. "Have the Guts to Fail" is the motto of one innovative company. Creativity and innovation have expression, one should note, in all areas of corporate life—not just high technology and new products. Managers who look beyond the traditional, who see the unusual, who dare to be different—upon these does posterity rely.

2. *Facilitate creative types.*   Egalitarianism, the belief that all are equal, is a fundamental American value. While wholly appropriate in politics and society, it is counterproductive in economics and business. People differ in every respect, with the capacity for creativity at the top of the list. A company must respect its creative types. They are a breed apart, absorbed in their quest, dedicated to intensity, oblivious to others. Creatives are often difficult to control. They work strange hours in strange places. They don't want supervision and demand personal satisfaction for personal achievement. Proprietary participation—peer recognition, career advancement, financial reward—is an essential motivation. How to find them? Don't look in the wrong place. Creative and innovative types may not be the smartest or brightest; they may not be aggressive or assertive or even realize their own gift. The best firms will treasure them.

3. *Focus corporate fiscal policy.*   Companies that talk innovation and invest elsewhere dig credibility gaps. Promoting creativity is no mean task. A firm must evidence its commitment, putting cash on the line. Nothing energizes more than the movement of money. Cough up the cash: You can't talk creativity and fund tradition. The resource allocation process must encourage creativity and innovation; new procedures must skew dollars to more risky ventures. Most critical, results cannot be expected quickly. Corporate executives must see beyond the horizon, beyond the quarterly reports, beyond the Street called Wall.

4. *Understand the creative process.*   Creativity appears with infinite variety. In a high-tech firm, for example, a person with a new method to speed receivable collections may not think herself creative—yet the benefit to the company may exceed most technical R&D. One good idea covers much ground. Creativity and innovation can happen by themselves, but not all the time. Since innovators are often not the brightest or most aggressive, the firm must find them or, more accurately, help them find themselves. One cannot train people to be inventive, but one can develop educational programs to facilitate the process. There are many proven creative techniques (see Part 2); not all will always work for any manager, but one or more will probably help every manager. But beware hucksters hawking their hidden wares: So-called "creativity

experts," with their special systems and private secrets (and phony degrees), seem to have a mystical call on corporate kitties. Make no mistake. *Real* creativity consultants can rejuvenate companies, energizing them with new fire and great ideas. Creativity stimulation really works. The best in the business are worth high multiples of their high fees. Just be sure you've got the right folks.

5. *Promote interaction among divisions and departments.* Scientific advance depends on constant communication among diverse disciplines. Likewise for top firms. When problems are attacked by divergent approaches and disparate facts, a wider range of solutions emerges. Task forces composed of different departments are not unusual in corporate life, but these are often established for coordinating current programs rather than creating new ones. Interdepartmental cooperation in companies, like interdisciplinary work in academics, is fraught with suspicion and worry about territoriality and dominance (the sociobiology of ant hills and wolf packs do not encourage creativity). A firm's new products division doesn't want manufacturing sticking its nose in; manufacturing says it's ridiculous to invent products that can't be made; marketing says so what if you invent them and make them, they can't be sold. Mechanisms must be found to break these barriers. The catalyst is often the person to whom the departments report; the boss must become actively and aggressively involved. But if he or she "recommends" the interaction without personal participation it will surely fail.

The opportunity is here, the time is now. Economists and executives must work together in building both a macro-economic environment and a micro-corporate culture. In the new realities approaching the year 2000, to achieve domestic vitality and world leadership, the trick is creative and innovative management.

Index